GARDNER'S
ART
THROUGH THE
AGES

GARDNER'S
ART
THROUGH THE
AGES

BOOK D: RENAISSANCE AND BAROQUE

FIFTEENTH EDITION

FRED S. KLEINER

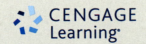

Australia • Brazil • Mexico • Singapore • United Kingdom • United States

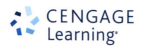

Gardner's Art through the Ages, Fifteenth Edition, Book D: Renaissance and Baroque
Fred S. Kleiner

Product Director: Monica Eckman

Product Manager: Sharon Adams Poore

Content Developer: Rachel Harbour

Associate Content Developer: Erika Hayden

Product Assistant: Rachael Bailey

Media Developer: Chad Kirchner

Marketing Manager: Jillian Borden

Senior Content Project Manager: Lianne Ames

Senior Art Director: Cate Rickard Barr

Manufacturing Planner: Sandee Milewski

IP Analyst: Jessica Elias

IP Project Manager: Farah Fard

Production Service and Layout: Dovetail
   Publishing Services

Compositor: Cenveo® Publisher Services

Text Designer: Frances Baca

Cover Designer: Mark Fox, Design is Play

Cover Image: Kunsthistorisches Museum,
   Vienna

For product information and technology assistance, contact us at
Cengage Learning Customer & Sales Support, 1-800-354-9706

For permission to use material from this text or product,
submit all requests online at **www.cengage.com/permissions.**
Further permissions questions can be emailed to
permissionrequest@cengage.com.

Library of Congress Control Number: 2014943688

Student Edition (Book D):
ISBN: 978-1-285-83801-4

Loose-leaf Edition (Book D):
ISBN: 978-1-305-85981-4

Cengage Learning
20 Channel Center Street
Boston, MA 02210
USA

Cengage Learning is a leading provider of customized learning solutions with office locations around the globe, including Singapore, the United Kingdom, Australia, Mexico, Brazil, and Japan. Locate your local office at **www.cengage.com/global.**

Cengage Learning products are represented in Canada by Nelson Education, Ltd.

To learn more about Cengage Learning Solutions, visit **www.cengage.com.**

Purchase any of our products at your local college store or at our preferred online store **www.cengagebrain.com.**

Printed in the United States of America
Print Number: 02   Print Year: 2015

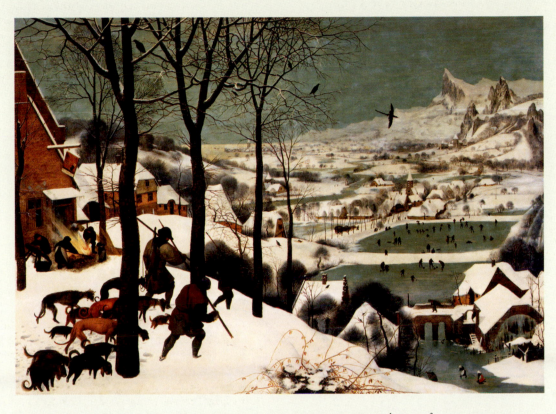

PIETER BRUEGEL THE ELDER, *Hunters in the Snow*, 1565. Oil on wood, 3' 10$\frac{1}{8}$" × 5' 3$\frac{3}{4}$". Kunsthistorisches Museum, Vienna.

The first painters, who covered the walls and ceilings of the caves of France and Spain beginning around 30,000 years ago, chose animals and occasionally humans as their exclusive subjects. The first landscapes appeared many thousands of years later, but soon became staples of most, but by no means all, artistic cultures worldwide.

Pieter Bruegel the Elder (ca. 1528–1569) was the greatest Netherlandish painter of the mid-16th century Renaissance in northern Europe. Like many of his contemporaries, Bruegel produced landscape paintings, and *Hunters in the Snow* is his finest. It is one of a series of six paintings that Bruegel produced for the home of Nicolaes Jongelinck, a wealthy Antwerp merchant. The paintings illustrate seasonal changes, with each of the panels representing a pair of months. This one is the December/January panel and shows the Netherlands locked in the particularly severe cold of the winter of 1565. The weary hunters return with their hounds, women build fires, skaters skim the frozen pond, and the town and its church huddle in their mantle of snow.

That we know Bruegel's name and the details of his career is not surprising, because it was during the Renaissance that the modern notion of individual artistic genius took root. But in many periods of the history of art, artists toiled in anonymity to fulfill the wishes of their patrons, whether Egyptian pharaohs, Roman emperors, or medieval monks. *Art through the Ages* surveys the art of all periods from prehistory to the present, and worldwide, and examines how artworks of all kinds have always reflected the historical contexts in which they were created.

Brief Contents

Contents

22 Renaissance and Mannerism in Cinquecento Italy 622

23 High Renaissance and Mannerism in Northern Europe and Spain 674

24 The Baroque in Italy and Spain 700

25 The Baroque in Northern Europe 730

Preface

I take great pleasure in introducing the extensively revised and expanded 15th edition of *Gardner's Art through the Ages: A Global History,* which, like the 14th edition, is a hybrid art history textbook—the first, and still the only, introductory survey of the history of art of its kind. This innovative new kind of "Gardner" retains all of the best features of traditional books on paper while harnessing 21st-century technology to significantly increase the number of works examined—without substantially increasing the size of the text or abbreviating the discussion of each work.

When Helen Gardner published the first edition of *Art through the Ages* in 1926, she could not have imagined that nearly a century later, instructors all over the world would still be using her textbook (available even in Mandarin Chinese) in their classrooms. Indeed, if she were alive today, she would not recognize the book that, even in its traditional form, long ago became—and remains—the world's most widely read introduction to the history of art and architecture. I hope that instructors and students alike will agree that this new edition lives up to the venerable Gardner tradition and even exceeds their high expectations.

The 15th edition follows the 14th in incorporating an innovative new online component that includes, in addition to a host of other features (enumerated below), *bonus essays* and *bonus images* (with zoom capability) of more than 300 additional important works of all eras, from prehistory to the present and worldwide. The printed and online components of the hybrid 15th edition are very closely integrated. For example, every one of the more than 300 bonus essays is cited in the text of the traditional book, and a thumbnail image of each work, with abbreviated caption, is inset into the text column where the work is mentioned. The integration extends also to the maps, index, glossary, and chapter summaries, which seamlessly merge the printed and online information.

KEY FEATURES OF THE 15TH EDITION

In this new edition, in addition to revising the text of every chapter to incorporate the latest research and methodological developments, I have added several important features while retaining the basic format and scope of the previous edition. Once again, the hybrid Gardner boasts roughly 1,700 photographs, plans, and drawings, nearly all in color and reproduced according to the highest standards of clarity and color fidelity. Included in this count are updated and revised maps along with hundreds of new images, among them a new series of superb photos taken by Jonathan Poore exclusively for *Art through the Ages* during three photographic campaigns in Germany and Rome in 2012–2014 (following similar forays into France and Tuscany in 2011–2013). The online component also includes custom videos made at architectural sites. This extraordinary new archive of visual material ranges from ancient temples in Rome; to medieval, Renaissance, and Baroque churches in France, Germany, and

Italy; to such modernist masterpieces as the Notre-Dame-du-Haut in Ronchamp, France, and the Guggenheim Museum in New York. The 15th edition also features an expanded number of the highly acclaimed architectural drawings of John Burge. Together, these exclusive photographs, videos, and drawings provide readers with a visual feast unavailable anywhere else.

Once again, a scale accompanies the photograph of every painting, statue, or other artwork discussed—another unique feature of the Gardner text. The scales provide students with a quick and effective way to visualize how big or small a given artwork is and its relative size compared with other objects in the same chapter and throughout the book—especially important given that the illustrated works vary in size from tiny to colossal.

Also retained in this edition are the Quick-Review Captions (brief synopses of the most significant aspects of each artwork or building illustrated) that students have found invaluable when preparing for examinations. These extended captions accompany not only every image in the printed book but also all the digital images in the online supplement. Each chapter also again ends with the highly popular full-page feature called *The Big Picture,* which sets forth in bullet-point format the most important characteristics of each period or artistic movement discussed in the chapter. Also retained from the 14th edition are the timeline summarizing the major artistic and architectural developments during the era treated (again in bullet-point format for easy review) and a chapter-opening essay called *Framing the Era,* which discusses a characteristic painting, sculpture, or building and is illustrated by four photographs.

Another pedagogical tool not found in any other introductory art history textbook is the *Before 1300* section that appears at the beginning of the second volume of the paperbound version of the book and at the beginning of Book D of the backpack edition. Because many students taking the second half of a survey course will not have access to Volume I or to Books A, B, and C, I have provided a special (expanded) set of concise primers on architectural terminology and construction methods in the ancient and medieval worlds, and on mythology and religion—information that is essential for understanding the history of art after 1300, both in the West and the East. The subjects of these special boxes are Greco-Roman Temple Design and the Classical Orders; Arches and Vaults; Basilican Churches; Central-Plan Churches; the Gods and Goddesses of Mount Olympus; the Life of Jesus in Art; Early Christian Saints and Their Attributes; Buddhism and Buddhist Iconography; and Hinduism and Hindu Iconography.

Boxed essays once again appear throughout the book as well. These essays fall under six broad categories, two of which are new to the 15th edition:

Architectural Basics boxes provide students with a sound foundation for the understanding of architecture. These discussions are concise explanations, with drawings and diagrams, of the major aspects of design and construction. The information included is essential to an understanding of architectural technology and terminology.

Materials and Techniques essays explain the various media that artists employed from prehistoric to modern times. Because materials and techniques often influence the character of artworks, these discussions contain essential information on why many monuments appear as they do.

Religion and Mythology boxes introduce students to the principal elements of the world's great religions, past and present, and to the representation of religious and mythological themes in painting and sculpture of all periods and places. These discussions of belief systems and iconography give readers a richer understanding of some of the greatest artworks ever created.

Art and Society essays treat the historical, social, political, cultural, and religious context of art and architecture. In some instances, specific monuments are the basis for a discussion of broader themes.

Written Sources present and discuss key historical documents illuminating important monuments of art and architecture throughout the world. The passages quoted permit voices from the past to speak directly to the reader, providing vivid and unique insights into the creation of artworks in all media.

In the *Artists on Art* boxes, artists and architects throughout history discuss both their theories and individual works.

New to the 15th edition are *The Patron's Voice* boxes. These essays underscore the important roles played by the individuals and groups who paid for the artworks and buildings in determining the character of those monuments. Also new are boxes designed to make students think critically about the decisions that went into the making of every painting, sculpture, and building from the Old Stone Age to the present. Called *Problems and Solutions* boxes, these essays address questions of how and why various forms developed, the problems painters, sculptors, and architects confronted, and the solutions they devised to resolve them.

Other noteworthy features retained from the 14th edition are the extensive (updated) bibliography of books in English; a glossary containing definitions of and page references for italicized terms introduced in both the printed and online texts; and a complete museum index, now housed online only, listing all illustrated artworks by their present location. The host of state-of-the-art online resources accompanying the 15th edition are enumerated on page xix).

ACKNOWLEDGMENTS

A work as extensive as a global history of art could not be undertaken or completed without the counsel of experts in all areas of world art. As with previous editions, Cengage Learning has enlisted more than a hundred art historians to review every chapter of *Art through the Ages* in order to ensure that the text lives up to the Gardner reputation for accuracy as well as readability. I take great pleasure in acknowledging here the important contributions to the 15th edition made by the following: Patricia Albers, San Jose State University; Kirk Ambrose, University of Colorado Boulder; Jenny Kirsten Ataoguz, Indiana University–Purdue University Fort Wayne; Paul Bahn, Hull; Denise Amy Baxter, University of North Texas; Nicole Bensoussan, University of Michigan-Dearborn; Amy R. Bloch, University at Albany, State University of New York; Susan H. Caldwell, The University of Oklahoma; David C. Cateforis, The University of Kansas; Thomas B. F. Cummins, Harvard University; Joyce De Vries, Auburn University; Verena Drake, Hotchkiss School; Jerome Feldman, Hawai'i Pacific University; Maria Gindhart, Georgia State University; Annabeth Headrick, University of Denver;

Shannen Hill, University of Maryland; Angela K. Ho, George Mason University; Julie Hochstrasser, The University of Iowa; Hiroko Johnson, San Diego State University; Julie Johnson, The University of Texas at San Antonio; Paul H.D. Kaplan, Purchase College, State University of New York; Rob Leith, Buckingham Browne & Nichols School; Brenda Longfellow, The University of Iowa; Susan McCombs, Michigan State University; Jennifer Ann McLerran, Northern Arizona University; Patrick R. McNaughton, Indiana University Bloomington; Mary Miller, Yale University; Erin Morris, Estrella Mountain Community College; Nicolas Morrissey, The University of Georgia; Basil Moutsatsos, St. Petersburg College–Seminole; Johanna D. Movassat, San Jose State University; Micheline Nilsen, Indiana University South Bend; Catherine Pagani, The University of Alabama; Allison Lee Palmer, The University of Oklahoma; William H. Peck, University of Michigan–Dearborn; Lauren Peterson, University of Delaware; Holly Pittman, University of Pennsylvania; Romita Ray, Syracuse University; Wendy Wassyng Roworth, The University of Rhode Island; Andrea Rusnock, Indiana University South Bend; Bridget Sandhoff, University of Nebraska Omaha; James M. Saslow, Queens College, City University of New York; Anne Rudolph Stanton, University of Missouri; Achim Timmermann, University of Michigan; David Turley, Weber State University; Lee Ann Turner, Boise State University; Marjorie S. Venit, University of Maryland; Shirley Tokash Verrico, Genesee Community College; Louis A. Waldman, The University of Texas at Austin; Ying Wang, University of Wisconsin-Milwaukee; Gregory H. Williams, Boston University; and Benjamin C. Withers, University of Kentucky.

I am especially indebted to the following for creating the instructor and student materials for the 15th edition: Ivy Cooper, Southern Illinois University Edwardsville; Patricia D. Cosper (retired), The University of Alabama at Birmingham; Anne McClanan, Portland State University; Amy M. Morris, The University of Nebraska Omaha; Erika Schneider, Framingham State University; and Camille Serchuk, Southern Connecticut State University. I also thank the more than 150 instructors and students who participated in surveys, focus groups, design sprints, and advisory boards to help us better understand readers' needs in our print and digital products.

I am also happy to have this opportunity to express my gratitude to the extraordinary group of people at Cengage Learning involved with the editing, production, and distribution of *Art through the Ages*. Some of them I have now worked with on various projects for nearly two decades and feel privileged to count among my friends. The success of the Gardner series in all of its various permutations depends in no small part on the expertise and unflagging commitment of these dedicated professionals, especially Sharon Adams Poore, product manager (as well as videographer extraordinaire); Rachel Harbour, content developer; Lianne Ames, senior content project manager; Chad Kirchner, media developer; Erika Hayden, associate content developer; Elizabeth Newell, associate media developer; Rachael Bailey, senior product assistant; Cate Barr, senior art director; Jillian Borden, marketing manager; and the incomparable group of local sales representatives who have passed on to me the welcome advice offered by the hundreds of instructors they speak to daily during their visits to college campuses throughout North America.

I am also deeply grateful to the following out-of-house contributors to the 15th edition: the incomparable quarterback of the entire production process, Joan Keyes, Dovetail Publishing Services; Helen Triller-Yambert, developmental editor; Michele Jones, copy editor; Susan Gall, proofreader; Mark Fox, Design is Play, cover designer; Frances Baca, text designer; PreMediaGlobal, photo researchers; Cenveo Publisher Services; Jay and John Crowley, Jay's Publishing Services;

Mary Ann Lidrbauch, art log preparer; and, of course, Jonathan Poore and John Burge, for their superb photos and architectural drawings.

I also owe thanks to two individuals not currently associated with this book but who loomed large in my life for many years: Clark Baxter, who retired in 2013 at the end of a long and distinguished career, from whom I learned much about textbook publishing and whose continuing friendship I value highly; and former coauthor and long-time friend and colleague, Christin J. Mamiya of the University of Nebraska–Lincoln, with whom I have had innumerable conversations not only about *Art through the Ages* but the history of art in general. Her thinking continues to influence my own, especially with regard to the later chapters on the history of Western art. I conclude this long (but no doubt incomplete) list of acknowledgments with an expression of gratitude to my colleagues at Boston University and to the thousands of students and the scores of teaching fellows in my art history courses since I began teaching in 1975, especially my research assistant, Angelica Bradley. From them I have learned much that has helped determine the form and content of *Art through the Ages* and made it a much better book than it otherwise might have been.

Fred S. Kleiner

CHAPTER-BY-CHAPTER CHANGES IN THE 15TH EDITION

The 15th edition is extensively revised and expanded, as detailed below. Each chapter contains a revised Big Picture feature, and all maps in the text are new to this edition. Instructors will find a very helpful figure number transition guide in the online instructor companion site.

Introduction: What Is Art History? Added 18th-century Benin Altar to the Hand and details of Claude Lorrain's *Embarkation of the Queen of Sheba.*

14: Late Medieval Italy. Expanded discussions of Nicola and Giovanni Pisano, Pietro Cavallini, and Orvieto Cathedral. Addition of Pisa Cathedral pulpit. New photographs of Giovanni Pisano's *Nativity*, Pietro Cavallini's *Last Judgment*, Giotto's *Entry into Jerusalem*, and the Doge's Palace in Venice.

20: Late Medieval and Early Renaissance Northern Europe. New Framing the Era essay "Rogier van der Weyden and Saint Luke." New Problems and Solutions box "How to Illustrate Printed Books." Revised Materials and Techniques box "Engraving and Etching." New in-text discussion of the *Hours of Mary of Burgundy.* New photograph of Riemenschneider's *Creglingen Altarpiece.*

21: The Renaissance in Quattrocento Italy. New Framing the Era essay "The Medici, Botticelli, and Classical Antiquity." New

Problems and Solutions box "Linear Perspective." New Artists on Art boxes "The *Commentarii* of Lorenzo Ghiberti" and "Leon Battista Alberti's *On the Art of Building.*" New section on Venice, with discussions of the Ca d'Oro, Giovanni Bellini's early work, and a new Written Sources box "The Tomb of Doge Pietro Mocenigo." New photographs of Donatello's *Gattamelata*, Brunelleschi's dome of Florence Cathedral, the Ca d'Oro and the tomb of Pietro Mocenigo in Venice, and the restored *Saint James Led to Martyrdom* by Mantegna.

22: Renaissance and Mannerism in Cinquecento Italy. Revised discussion of Mannerism. New Written Sources box "Giorgio Vasari's *Lives.*" New Problems and Solutions boxes "How to Impress a Pope" and "Rethinking the Basilican Church." New Patron's Voice box "Federigo Gonzaga, Giulio Romano, and the Palazzo del Tè." New photographs of Bramante's Tempietto, the Palazzo Farnese, and the exterior and interior of Il Gesù in Rome, and of the interior of San Giorgio Maggiore in Venice.

23: High Renaissance and Mannerism in Northern Europe and Spain. Major reorganization of the material discussed, with a new sequence of regions and also of individual artists. New Framing the Era essay "Albrecht Dürer, Melancholic Genius." New Art and Society box "Witchcraft, Disease, Plague, and Death." New Patron's Voice box "Francis I, Royal Art Patron and Collector." New photographs of Holbein's *French Ambassadors,* Bosch's *Garden of Earthly Delights,* and the Colegio de San Gregorio in Valladolid, Spain.

24: The Baroque in Italy and Spain. New Problems and Solutions boxes "Completing Saint Peter's," "Rethinking the Church Facade," and "How to Make a Ceiling Disappear." New Patron's Voice box "Velázquez and Philip IV." New in-text discussion of Caravaggio's *Musicians* and brief discussion of Elisabetta Sirani. Reorganized and expanded treatment of Spanish Baroque art and architecture, including colonial Latin America, with the addition of Metropolitan Cathedral in Mexico City and the Church of the Society of Jesus in Cuzco, Peru. New photographs of Bernini's Four Rivers Fountain; the facade of Santa Susanna; Saint Peter's (facade and aerial view); the exterior and interior of Borromini's San Carlo alle Quattro Fontane and the facade and dome of Sant'Ivo alla Sapienza; Gaulli's *Triumph in the Name of Jesus;* and Pozzo's *Glorification of Saint Ignatius.*

25: The Baroque in Northern Europe. New Framing the Era essay "The Art of Painting in a Dutch Home." New Problems and Solutions box "Frans Hals's Group Portraits." New Materials and Techniques box "Rembrandt's Use of Light and Shade." New Art and Society box "The Sun King's Palace at Versailles." New photographs of Girardon's *Apollo Attended by the Nymphs of Thetis* and the Baths of Apollo at Versailles (with new bonus essay).

ABOUT THE AUTHOR
Fred S. Kleiner

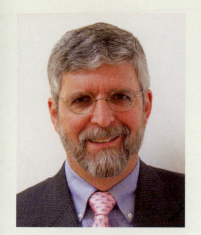

FRED S. KLEINER (Ph.D., Columbia University) has been the author or coauthor of *Gardner's Art through the Ages* beginning with the 10th edition in 1995. He has also published more than a hundred books, articles, and reviews on Greek and Roman art and architecture, including *A History of Roman Art,* also published by Cengage Learning. Both *Art through the Ages* and the book on Roman art have been awarded Texty prizes as the outstanding college textbook of the year in the humanities and social sciences, in 2001 and 2007, respectively. Professor Kleiner has taught the art history survey course since 1975, first at the University of Virginia and, since 1978, at Boston University, where he is currently professor of the history of art and architecture and classical archaeology and has served as department chair for five terms, most recently from 2005 to 2014. From 1985 to 1998, he was editor-in-chief of the *American Journal of Archaeology.*

Long acclaimed for his inspiring lectures and devotion to students, Professor Kleiner won Boston University's Metcalf Award for Excellence in Teaching as well as the College Prize for Undergraduate Advising in the Humanities in 2002, and he is a two-time winner of the Distinguished Teaching Prize in the College of Arts & Sciences Honors Program. In 2007, he was elected a Fellow of the Society of Antiquaries of London, and, in 2009, in recognition of lifetime achievement in publication and teaching, a Fellow of the Text and Academic Authors Association.

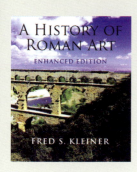

Also by Fred Kleiner: *A History of Roman Art, Enhanced Edition* (Wadsworth/Cengage Learning 2010; ISBN 9780495909873), winner of the 2007 Texty Prize for a new college textbook in the humanities and social sciences. In this authoritative and lavishly illustrated volume, Professor Kleiner traces the development of Roman art and architecture from Romulus's foundation of Rome in the eighth century BCE to the death of Constantine in the fourth century CE, with special chapters devoted to Pompeii and Herculaneum, Ostia, funerary and provincial art and architecture, and the earliest Christian art. The enhanced edition also includes a new introductory chapter on the art and architecture of the Etruscans and of the Greeks of South Italy and Sicily.

Resources

FOR FACULTY

Instructor Companion Site

Access the Instructor Companion Site to find resources to help you teach your course and engage your students. Here you will find the Instructor's Manual; Cognero computerized testing; and Microsoft PowerPoint slides with lecture outlines and images that can be used as offered or customized by importing personal lecture slides or other material.

Digital Image Library

Display digital images in the classroom with this powerful tool. This one-stop lecture and class presentation resource makes it easy to assemble, edit, and present customized lectures for your course. Available on Flashdrive, the Digital Image Library provides high-resolutions images (maps, diagrams, and the fine art images from the text) for lecture presentations and allows you to easily add your own images to supplement those provided. A zoom feature allows you to magnify selected portions of an image for more detailed display in class, or you can display images side-by-side for comparison.

Google Earth™

Take your students on a virtual tour of art through the ages! Resources for the 15th edition include Google Earth™ coordinates for all works, monuments, and sites discussed in the text, encouraging students to make geographical connections between places and sites. Use these coordinates to start your lectures with a virtual journey to locations all over the globe, or take aerial screenshots of important sites to incorporate in your lecture materials.

FOR STUDENTS

MindTap for *Art through the Ages*

MindTap for *Gardner's Art through the Ages: A Global History*, 15th edition, helps you engage with your course content and achieve greater comprehension. Highly personalized and fully online, the MindTap learning platform presents authoritative Cengage Learning content, assignments, and services offering you a tailored presentation of course curriculum created by your instructor.

MindTap guides you through the course curriculum via an innovative Learning Path Navigator where you will complete reading assignments, annotate your readings, complete homework, and engage with quizzes and assessments. Concepts are brought to life with: zoomable versions of close to 1,500 images; videos to reinforce concepts and expand knowledge of particular works or art trends; numerous study tools, including image flashcards; a glossary complete with an audio pronunciation guide; Google Earth™ coordinate links for all works, monuments, and sites discussed in the text; and much more! Additional features, such as the ability to synchronize your eBook notes with your personal EverNote account, provide added convenience to help you take your learning further, faster.

Slide Guides

The Slide Guide is a lecture companion that allows you to take notes alongside representations of the art images shown in class. This handy resource includes reproductions of the images from the book, with full captions and space for note-taking.

Before 1300

Students enrolled in the second semester of a yearlong introductory survey of the history of art may not have access to paperback Volume I (or backpack Books A, B, and C). Therefore, Volume II and Book D of *Art through the Ages: A Global History* open with a special set of concise primers on Greco-Roman and medieval architectural terminology and construction methods and on Greco-Roman, Christian, Buddhist, and Hindu iconography—information that is essential for understanding the history of art and architecture after 1300 both in the West and the East.

Contents

ARCHITECTURAL BASICS

Greco-Roman Temple Design and the Classical Orders

The gable-roofed columnar stone temples of the Greeks and Romans have had more influence on the later history of architecture in the Western world than any other building type ever devised. Many of the elements of classical temple architecture are present in buildings from the Renaissance to the present day.

The basic design principles of Greek and Roman temples and the most important components of the classical orders can be summarized as follows.

■ *Temple design* The core of a Greco-Roman temple was the *cella,* a room with no windows that usually housed the statue of the god or goddess to whom the shrine was dedicated. Generally, only the priests, priestesses, and chosen few would enter the cella. Worshipers gathered in front of the building, where sacrifices occurred at open-air altars. In most Greek temples, for example, the temple erected in honor of Hera or Apollo at Paestum, a *colonnade* was erected all around the cella to form a *peristyle.*

In contrast, Roman temples, for example, the Temple of Portunus in Rome, usually have freestanding columns only in a porch at the front of the building. Sometimes, as in the Portunus temple, *engaged* (attached) half-columns adorn three sides of the cella to give the building the appearance of a *peripteral* temple. Architectural historians call this a *pseudoperipteral* design. The Greeks and Romans also built round temples (called *tholos* temples), a building type that also had a long afterlife in Western architecture.

■ *Classical orders* The Greeks developed two basic architectural orders, or design systems: the *Doric* and the *Ionic.* The forms of the columns and *entablature* (superstructure) generally differentiate the orders. Classical columns have two or three parts, depending on the order: the shaft, which is usually marked with vertical channels (*flutes*); the *capital*; and, in the Ionic order, the *base.* The Doric capital consists of a round *echinus* beneath a square abacus block. Spiral *volutes* constitute the distinctive feature of the Ionic capital. Classical entablatures have three parts: the *architrave,* the *frieze,* and the triangular *pediment* of the gabled roof, framed by the *cornice.* In the Doric order, the frieze is subdivided into *triglyphs* and *metopes,* whereas in the Ionic, the frieze is left open.

The *Corinthian capital,* a later Greek invention very popular in Roman times, is more ornate than either the Doric or Ionic. It consists of a double row of acanthus leaves, from which tendrils and flowers emerge. Although this capital often is cited as the distinguishing element of the Corinthian order, in strict terms no Corinthian order exists. Architects simply substituted the new capital type for the volute capital in the Ionic order, as in the Roman temple probably dedicated to Vesta at Tivoli.

Sculpture played a major role on the exterior of classical temples, partly to embellish the deity's shrine and partly to tell something about the deity to those gathered outside. Sculptural ornament was concentrated on the upper part of the building, in the pediment and frieze.

DORIC ORDER

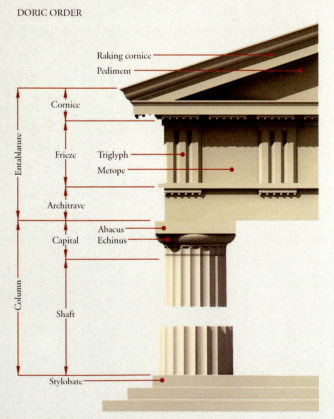

IONIC ORDER

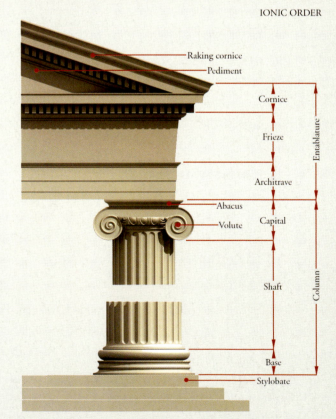

Doric and Ionic orders

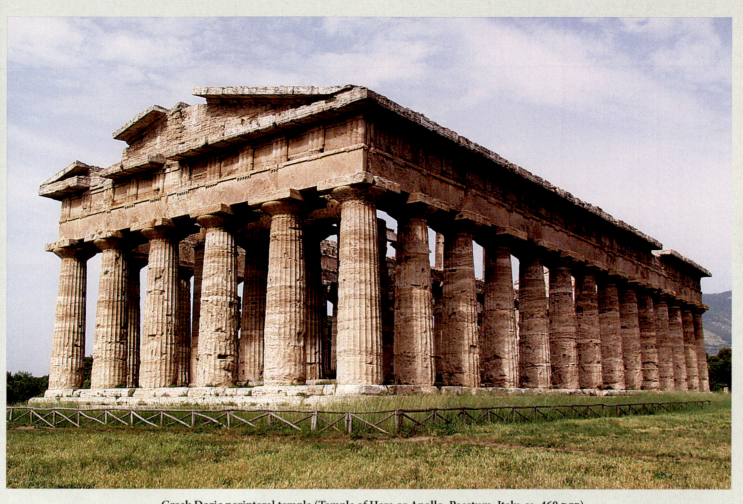

Greek Doric peripteral temple (Temple of Hera or Apollo, Paestum, Italy, ca. 460 BCE)

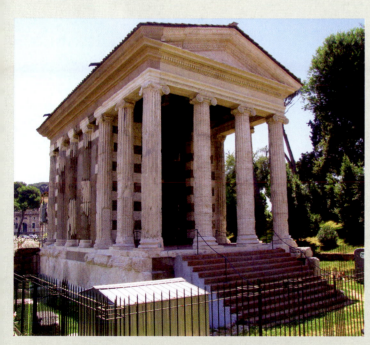

Roman Ionic pseudoperipteral temple
(Temple of Portunus, Rome, Italy, ca. 75 BCE)

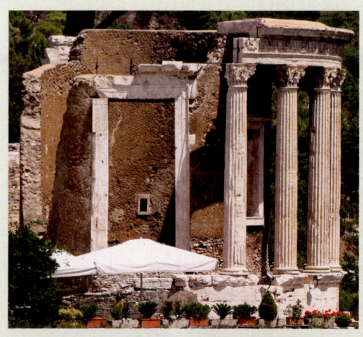

Roman Corinthian tholos temple
(Temple of Vesta, Tivoli, Italy, early first century BCE)

ARCHITECTURAL BASICS
Arches and Vaults

Although earlier architects used both arches and vaults, the Romans employed them more extensively and effectively than any other ancient civilization. The Roman forms became staples of architectural design from the Middle Ages until today.

- **Arch** The arch is one of several ways of spanning a passageway. The Romans preferred it to the *post-and-lintel* (column-and-architrave) system used in the Greek orders. Builders construct arches using wedge-shaped stone blocks called *voussoirs*. The central voussoir is the arch's *keystone*.
- **Barrel vault** Also called the *tunnel vault,* the barrel vault is an extension of a simple arch, creating a semicylindrical ceiling over parallel walls.
- **Groin vault** The groin vault, or *cross vault,* is formed by the intersection at right angles of two barrel vaults of equal size. When a series of groin vaults covers an interior hall, the open lateral arches of the vaults function as windows admitting light to the building.
- **Dome** The hemispherical dome may be described as a round arch rotated around the full circumference of a circle, usually resting on a cylindrical *drum*. The Romans normally constructed domes using *concrete,* a mix of lime mortar, volcanic sand, water, and small stones, instead of with large stone blocks. Concrete dries to form a solid mass of great strength, which enabled the Romans to puncture the apex of a concrete dome with an *oculus* (eye), so that much-needed light could reach the interior of the building.

Barrel vaults, as noted, resemble tunnels, and groin vaults are usually found in a series covering a similar *longitudinally* oriented interior space. Domes, in contrast, crown *centrally* planned buildings, so named because the structure's parts are of equal or almost equal dimensions around the center.

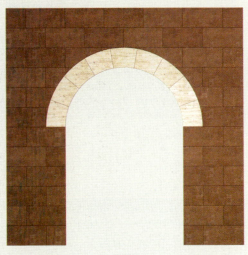

Arch

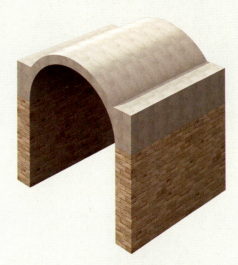

Barrel vault

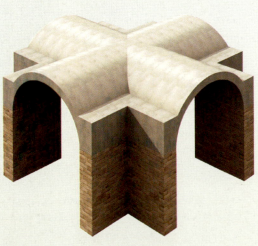

Groin vault

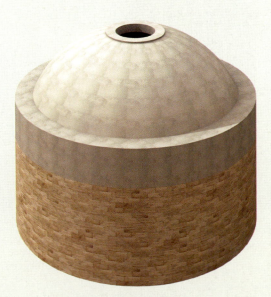

Hemispherical dome with oculus

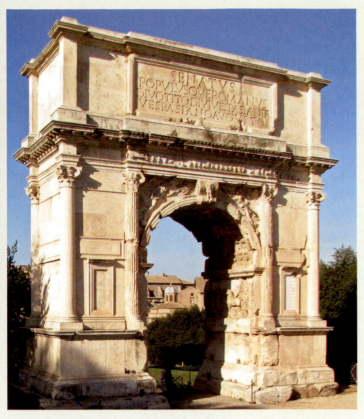

Roman arch (Arch of Titus, Rome, Italy, ca. 81)

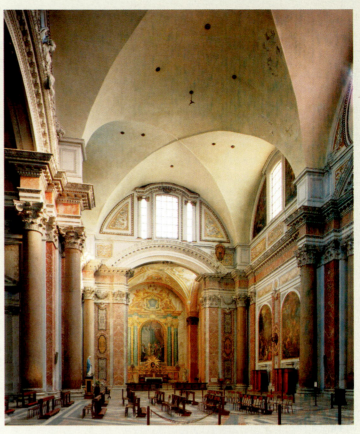

Roman hall with groin vaults (Baths of Diocletian, now
Santa Maria degli Angeli, Rome, Italy, ca. 298–306)

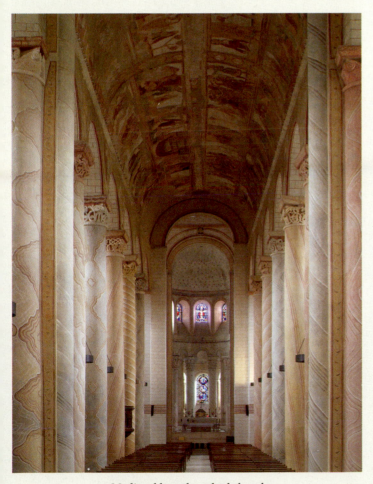

Medieval barrel-vaulted church
(Saint-Savin, Saint-Savin-sur-Gartempe, France, ca. 1100)

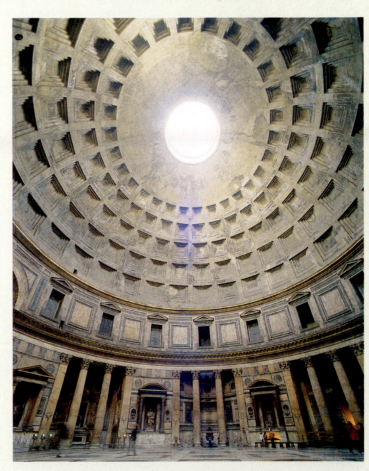

Roman dome with oculus (Pantheon, Rome, Italy, 118–125)

ARCHITECTURAL BASICS

Basilican Churches

Church design during the Middle Ages set the stage for ecclesiastical architecture from the Renaissance to the present. Both the longitudinal- and central-plan building types of antiquity had a long postclassical history.

In Western Christendom, the typical medieval church had a *basilican* plan, which evolved from the Roman columnar hall, or *basilica*. The great European *cathedrals* of the Gothic age, which were the immediate predecessors of the churches of the Renaissance and Baroque eras, shared many elements with the earliest basilican churches constructed during the fourth century, including a wide central *nave* flanked by *aisles* and ending in an *apse*. Some basilican churches also have a *transept,* an area perpendicular to the nave. The nave and transept intersect at the *crossing*. Gothic churches, however, have many additional features. The key components of Gothic design are labeled in the drawing of a typical French Gothic cathedral, which can be compared to the interior view of Amiens Cathedral and the plan of Chartres Cathedral.

Gothic architects frequently extended the aisles around the apse to form an *ambulatory,* onto which opened *radiating chapels* housing sacred relics. Groin vaults formed the ceiling of the nave, aisles, ambulatory, and transept alike, replacing the timber roof of the typical Early Christian basilica. These vaults rested on *diagonal* and *transverse ribs* in the form of *pointed arches*. On the exterior, *flying buttresses* held the nave vaults in place. These masonry struts transferred the thrust of the nave vaults across the roofs of the aisles to tall *piers* frequently capped by pointed ornamental *pinnacles*. This structural system made it possible to open up the walls above the *nave arcade* with huge *stained-glass* windows in the nave *clerestory*.

In the later Middle Ages, especially in the great cathedrals of the Gothic age, church *facades* featured extensive sculptural ornamentation, primarily in the portals beneath the stained-glass *rose windows* (circular windows with *tracery* resembling floral petals). The major sculpted areas were the *tympanum* above the doorway (akin to a Greco-Roman temple pediment), the *trumeau* (central post), and the *jambs*.

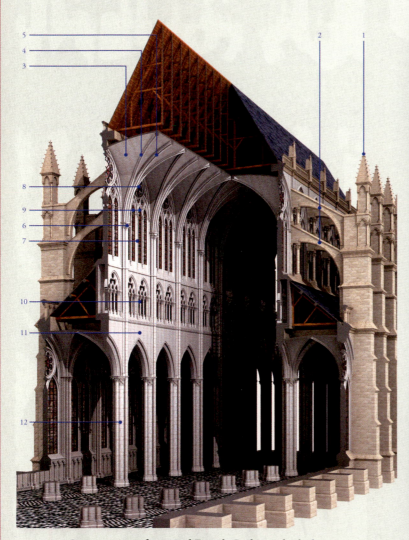

Cutaway view of a typical French Gothic cathedral
(1) pinnacle, (2) flying buttress, (3) vaulting web, (4) diagonal rib,
(5) transverse rib, (6) springing, (7) clerestory, (8) oculus, (9) lancet,
(10) triforium, (11) nave arcade, (12) compound pier with responds

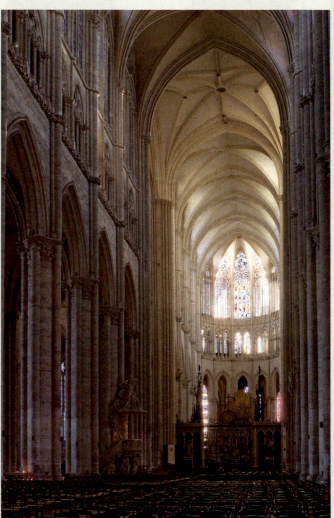

Nave of Amiens Cathedral, France, begun 1220

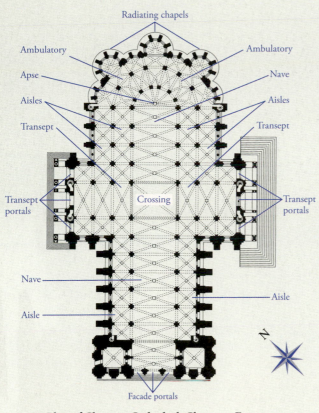

Plan of Chartres Cathedral, Chartres, France,
rebuilt after 1194

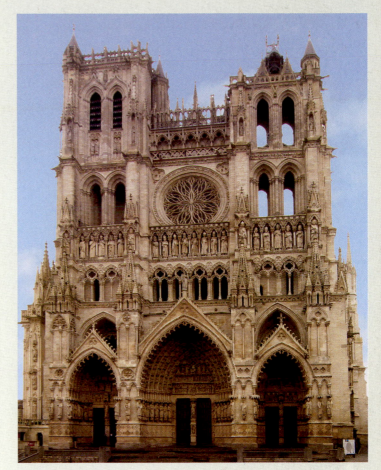

West facade of Amiens Cathedral, Amiens, France, begun 1220

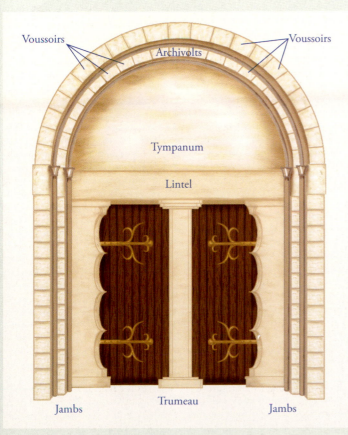

Diagram of medieval portal sculpture

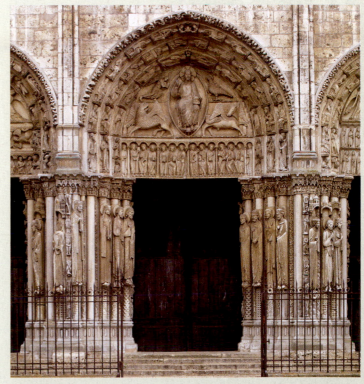

Central portal, west facade, Chartres Cathedral, ca. 1145–1155

ARCHITECTURAL BASICS
Central-Plan Churches

The domed central plan of classical antiquity dominated the architecture of the Byzantine Empire but with important modifications. Because the dome covered the crossing of a Byzantine church, architects had to find a way to erect domes on square bases instead of on the circular bases (cylindrical drums) of Roman buildings. The solution was *pendentive* construction in which the dome rests on what is in effect a second, larger dome. The top portion and four segments around the rim of the larger dome are omitted, creating four curved triangles, or pendentives. The pendentives join to form a ring and four arches whose planes bound a square. The first use of pendentives on a grand scale occurred in the sixth-century church of Hagia Sophia (Holy Wisdom) in Constantinople.

The interiors of Byzantine churches differed from those of basilican churches in the West not only in plan and the use of domes but also in the manner in which they were adorned. The original *mosaic* decoration of Hagia Sophia is lost, but at Saint Mark's in Venice, some 40,000 square feet of mosaics cover all the walls, arches, vaults, and domes.

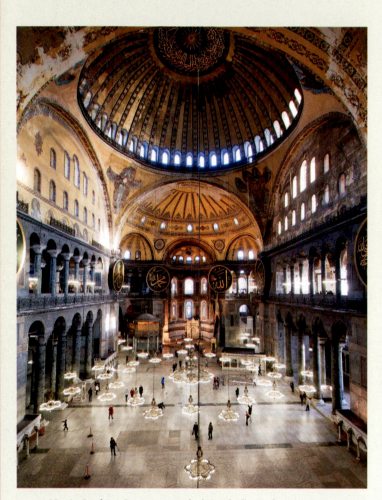

Hagia Sophia, Constantinople (Istanbul), Turkey, 532–537

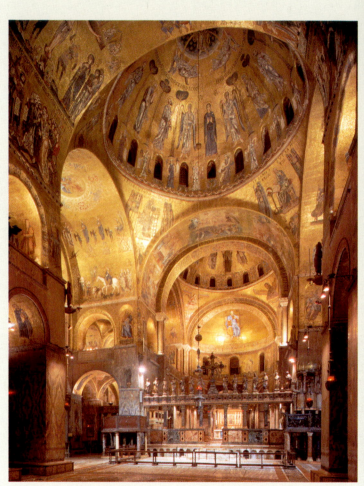

Saint Mark's, Venice, Italy, begun 1063

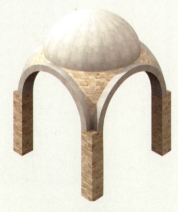

Dome on pendentives

RELIGION AND MYTHOLOGY
The Gods and Goddesses of Mount Olympus

The chief deities of the Greeks ruled the world from their home on Mount Olympus, Greece's highest peak. They figure prominently not only in Greek, Etruscan, and Roman art but also in art from the Renaissance to the present.

The 12 Olympian gods (and their Roman equivalents) were:

- **Zeus (Jupiter)** King of the gods, Zeus ruled the sky and allotted the sea to his brother Poseidon and the Underworld to his other brother, Hades. His weapon was the thunderbolt. Jupiter was also the chief god of the Romans.

- **Hera (Juno)** Wife and sister of Zeus, Hera was the goddess of marriage.

- **Poseidon (Neptune)** Poseidon was lord of the sea. He controlled waves, storms, and earthquakes with his three-pronged pitchfork (*trident*).

- **Hestia (Vesta)** Sister of Zeus, Poseidon, and Hera, Hestia was goddess of the hearth.

- **Demeter (Ceres)** Third sister of Zeus, Demeter was the goddess of grain and agriculture.

- **Ares (Mars)** God of war, Ares was the son of Zeus and Hera and the lover of Aphrodite. His Roman counterpart, Mars, was the father of the twin founders of Rome, Romulus and Remus.

- **Athena (Minerva)** Goddess of wisdom and warfare, Athena was a virgin born from the head of her father, Zeus.

- **Hephaistos (Vulcan)** God of fire and of metalworking, Hephaistos was the son of Zeus and Hera. Born lame and, uncharacteristically for a god, ugly, he married Aphrodite, who was unfaithful to him.

- **Apollo (Apollo)** God of light and music and son of Zeus, the young, beautiful Apollo was an expert archer, sometimes identified with the sun (**Helios/Sol**).

- **Artemis (Diana)** Sister of Apollo, Artemis was goddess of the hunt. She was occasionally equated with the moon (**Selene/Luna**).

- **Aphrodite (Venus)** Daughter of Zeus and a *nymph* (goddess of springs and woods), Aphrodite was the goddess of love and beauty.

- **Hermes (Mercury)** Son of Zeus and another nymph, Hermes was the fleet-footed messenger of the gods and possessed winged sandals. He carried the *caduceus*, a magical herald's rod.

Other important Greek gods and goddesses were:

- **Hades (Pluto)** Lord of the Underworld and god of the dead. Although the brother of Zeus and Poseidon, Hades never resided on Mount Olympus.

- **Dionysos (Bacchus)** God of wine, another of Zeus's sons.

- **Eros (Amor or Cupid)** The winged child-god of love, son of Aphrodite and Ares.

- **Asklepios (Aesculapius)** God of healing, son of Apollo. His serpent-entwined staff is the emblem of modern medicine.

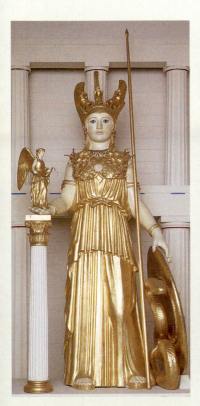

Athena, by Phidias, ca. 438 BCE

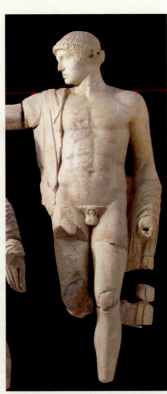

Apollo, from Olympia, ca. 470–456 BCE

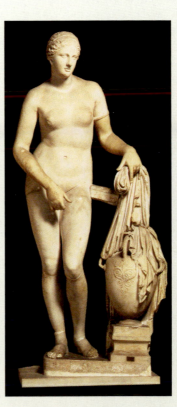

Aphrodite, by Praxiteles, ca. 350–340 BCE

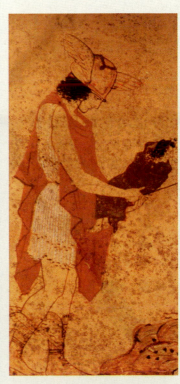

Hermes and infant Dionysos, by the Phiale Painter, ca. 440–435 BCE

RELIGION AND MYTHOLOGY
The Life of Jesus in Art

Christians believe that Jesus of Nazareth is the son of God, the *Messiah* (Savior, Christ) of the Jews prophesied in Hebrew scripture. His life—his miraculous birth from the womb of a virgin mother, his preaching and miracle working, his execution by the Romans and subsequent ascent to Heaven—has been the subject of countless artworks from Roman times through the present day.

INCARNATION AND CHILDHOOD

The first "cycle" of the life of Jesus consists of the events of his conception (incarnation), birth, infancy, and childhood.

- **Annunciation to Mary** The archangel Gabriel announces to the Virgin Mary that she will miraculously conceive and give birth to God's son, Jesus.
- **Visitation** The pregnant Mary visits her cousin Elizabeth, who is pregnant with John the Baptist. Elizabeth is the first to recognize that the baby Mary is bearing is the Son of God.
- **Nativity**, **Annunciation to the Shepherds**, and **Adoration of the Shepherds** Jesus is born at night in Bethlehem and placed in a basket. Mary and her husband, Joseph, marvel at the newborn, while an angel announces the birth of the Savior to shepherds in the field, who rush to adore the infant Jesus.
- **Adoration of the Magi** A bright star alerts three wise men (*magi*) in the East that the King of the Jews has been born. They travel 12 days to present precious gifts to the infant Jesus.
- **Presentation in the Temple** In accordance with Jewish tradition, Mary and Joseph bring their firstborn son to the temple in Jerusalem, where the aged Simeon recognizes Jesus as the prophesied savior of humankind.

- **Massacre of the Innocents** and **Flight into Egypt** King Herod, fearful that a rival king has been born, orders the massacre of all infants, but the holy family escapes to Egypt.
- **Dispute in the Temple** Joseph and Mary travel to Jerusalem for the feast of Passover. Jesus, only a boy, debates the astonished Jewish scholars in the temple, foretelling his ministry.

PUBLIC MINISTRY

The public-ministry cycle comprises the teachings of Jesus and the miracles he performed.

- **Baptism** Jesus's public ministry begins with his baptism at age 30 by John the Baptist in the Jordan River. God's voice is heard proclaiming Jesus as his son.
- **Calling of Matthew** Jesus summons Matthew, a tax collector, to follow him, and Matthew becomes one of his 12 disciples, or *apostles* (from the Greek for "messenger").
- **Miracles** Jesus performs many miracles, revealing his divine nature. These include acts of healing and raising the dead, turning water into wine, walking on water and calming storms, and creating wondrous quantities of food.
- **Delivery of the Keys to Peter** Jesus chooses the fisherman Peter (whose name means "rock") as his successor. He declares that Peter is the rock on which his church will be built and symbolically delivers to Peter the keys to the kingdom of Heaven.
- **Transfiguration** Jesus scales a mountain and, in the presence of Peter and two other disciples, is transformed into radiant light. God, speaking from a cloud, discloses that Jesus is his son.
- **Cleansing of the Temple** Jesus returns to Jerusalem, where he finds money changers and merchants conducting business in the temple. He rebukes them and drives them out.

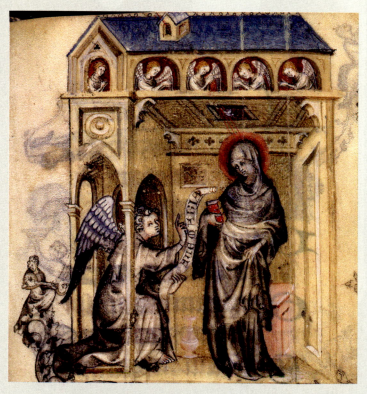

Annunciation, by Jean Pucelle, ca. 1325–1328

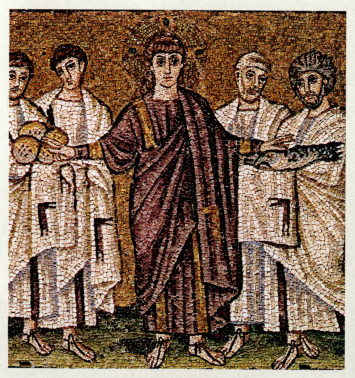

Miracle of Loaves and Fishes, Sant'Apollinare Nuovo, Ravenna, Italy, ca. 504

PASSION

The passion (Latin *passio*, "suffering") cycle includes the events leading to Jesus's trial, death, resurrection, and ascent to Heaven.

- **Entry into Jerusalem** On the Sunday before his crucifixion (Palm Sunday), Jesus rides into Jerusalem on a donkey.

- **Last Supper** In Jerusalem, Jesus celebrates Passover with his disciples. During this last supper, Jesus foretells his imminent betrayal, arrest, and death and invites the disciples to remember him when they eat bread (symbol of his body) and drink wine (his blood). This ritual became the celebration of *Mass* (*Eucharist*).

- **Agony in the Garden** Jesus goes to the Mount of Olives in the Garden of Gethsemane, where he struggles to overcome his human fear of death by praying for divine strength.

- **Betrayal** and **Arrest** The disciple Judas Iscariot betrays Jesus to the Jewish authorities for 30 pieces of silver. Judas identifies Jesus to the soldiers by kissing him, and Jesus is arrested.

- **Trials of Jesus** The soldiers bring Jesus before Caiaphas, the Jewish high priest, who interrogates Jesus about his claim to be the Messiah. Jesus is then brought before the Roman governor of Judaea, Pontius Pilate, on the charge of treason because he had proclaimed himself king of the Jews. Pilate asks the crowd to choose between freeing Jesus or Barabbas, a murderer. The people choose Barabbas, and the judge condemns Jesus to death.

- **Flagellation** The Roman soldiers who hold Jesus captive whip (flagellate) him and mock him by dressing him as king of the Jews and placing a crown of thorns on his head.

- **Carrying of the Cross, Raising of the Cross**, and **Crucifixion** The Romans force Jesus to carry the cross on which he will be crucified from Jerusalem to Mount Calvary. Soldiers erect the cross and nail Jesus's hands and feet to it. Jesus's mother, John the Evangelist, and Mary Magdalene mourn at the foot of the cross, while the soldiers torment Jesus. One of them stabs Jesus in the side with a spear. After suffering great pain, Jesus dies on Good Friday.

- **Deposition**, **Lamentation**, and **Entombment** Two disciples, Joseph of Arimathea and Nicodemus, remove Jesus's body from the cross (deposition) and take him to his tomb. Joseph, Nicodemus, the Virgin Mary, John the Evangelist, and Mary Magdalene mourn over the dead Jesus (lamentation). (When in art the isolated figure of the Virgin Mary cradles her dead son in her lap, it is called a *Pietà*—Italian for "pity.") Then his followers lower Jesus into a sarcophagus in the tomb (entombment).

- **Resurrection** and **Three Marys at the Tomb** On the third day (Easter Sunday), Christ rises from the dead and leaves the tomb. The Virgin Mary, Mary Magdalene, and Mary, the mother of James, visit the tomb but find it empty. An angel informs them that Jesus has been resurrected.

- **Noli Me Tangere**, **Supper at Emmaus**, and **Doubting of Thomas** During the 40 days between Christ's resurrection and his ascent to Heaven, he appears on several occasions to his followers. Christ warns Mary Magdalene, weeping at his tomb, with the words "Don't touch me" (*Noli me tangere* in Latin). At Emmaus he eats supper with two astonished disciples. Later, Christ invites Thomas, who cannot believe Christ has risen, to touch the wound in his side inflicted at his crucifixion.

- **Ascension** On the 40th day, on the Mount of Olives, with his mother and apostles as witnesses, Christ gloriously ascends to Heaven in a cloud.

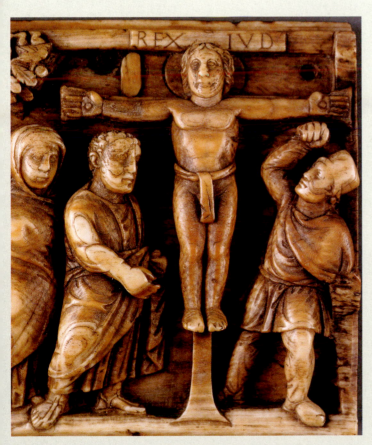

Crucifixion, ivory plaque, Italy, early fifth century

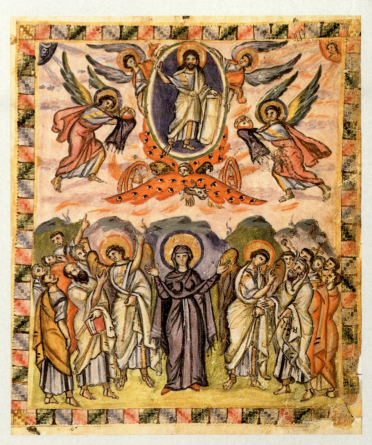

Ascension of Christ, Rabbula Gospels, 586

RELIGION AND MYTHOLOGY
Early Christian Saints and Their Attributes

A distinctive feature of Christianity is the veneration accorded to *saints* (from the Latin word for "holy"—*sanctus*), a practice dating to the second century. Most of the earliest Christian saints were *martyrs* who died for their faith at the hands of the Roman authorities, often after suffering cruel torture. During the first millennium of the Church, the designation of sainthood, or *canonization*, was an informal process, but in the late 12th century, Pope Alexander III (r. 1159–1181) ruled that only the papacy could designate individuals as saints, and only after a protracted review of the life, character, deeds, and miracles of the person under consideration. A preliminary stage is *beatification*, the official determination that a deceased individual is a *beatus* (blessed person).

In Christian art, saints almost always have *halos* around their heads. To distinguish individual saints, artists commonly depicted them with one or more characteristic *attributes*—often the means of their martyrdom, although saintly attributes take a wide variety of forms.

The most important saints during the early centuries of Christianity were contemporaries of Jesus. They may be classified in three general categories.

FAMILY OF JESUS AND MARY

■ **Anne** The parents of the Virgin Mary were Anne and Joachim, a childless couple after 20 years of marriage. Angels separately announced to them that Anne would give birth.

■ **Elizabeth** A cousin of Anne, Elizabeth was also an elderly barren woman. The angel Gabriel announced to her husband, the priest Zacharias, that she would give birth to a son named John. Six months later, Gabriel informed Mary that she would become the mother of the son of God (*Annunciation*), whereupon Mary visited Elizabeth (*Visitation*), and in Elizabeth's womb the future John the Baptist leaped for joy at the approach of the Mother of God.

■ **Joseph** Although a modest craftsman, Joseph was a descendant of King David. An elderly widower, he was chosen among several suitors to wed the much younger Mary when his staff miraculously blossomed. Joseph's principal attributes are the flowering staff and carpentry tools.

■ **John the Baptist** Elizabeth's son, John, became a preacher who promoted baptism as a means of cleansing Jews of their sins in preparation for the Messiah. John most often appears in art as a bearded hermit baptizing a much younger Jesus in the Jordan River, even though John was only six months older. His attribute is a lamb.

APOSTLES

During the course of his ministry, Jesus called 12 men to be his *apostles*, or messengers, to spread the news of the coming of the son of God. All 12 apostles were present at the *Last Supper*. After Judas's betrayal and suicide, the remaining 11 witnessed Jesus's *Ascension* and chose

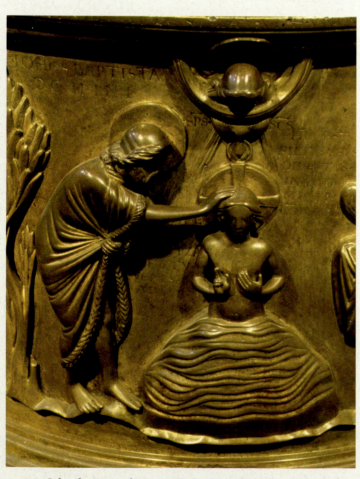

John the Baptist baptizing Jesus, Liège, Belgium, 1118

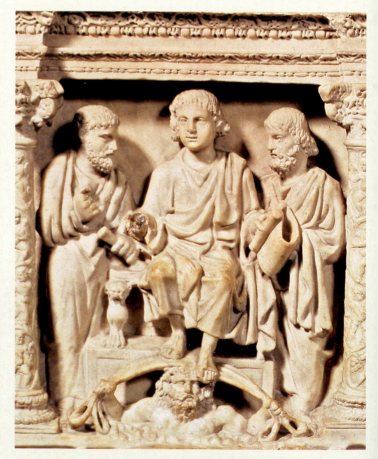

Christ between Saints Peter and Paul,
Sarcophagus of Junius Bassus, ca. 359

another follower of Jesus to replace Judas. At the *Pentecost*, the Holy Spirit assigned the 12 apostles the mission of spreading the Gospel throughout the world. All but John the Evangelist eventually suffered martyrdom. Four of the apostles figure prominently in the history of art.

- **Peter** The "prince of apostles," Peter was a fisherman whom Jesus designated as the rock on which he would found his Church. The Savior presented the apostle with the keys to the kingdom of Heaven. Peter was the first bishop of Rome and the head of the long line of popes. He was crucified upside down because he insisted that he was unworthy to die as Jesus did. Peter's chief attributes are the keys.

- **John the Evangelist** Another fisherman, John was the youngest apostle and "the disciple whom Jesus loved." He was one of two apostles who became *evangelists*—those who recorded Jesus's life in the Gospels. John also wrote the Book of Revelation. His attribute is an eagle.

- **Matthew** The second evangelist among the apostles, Matthew was a Jewish tax collector. Different accounts say that he was either stabbed to death or beheaded while saying Mass. Matthew appears most frequently in art as a seated robed figure writing his Gospel. His attribute is a winged man.

- **James** The brother of John the Evangelist and also a fisherman, James was the first apostle to be martyred—by beheading. According to tradition, before his martyrdom he preached the Gospel in Spain. James's attribute is a scallop shell, the emblem of pilgrims to his shrine at Santiago de Compostela.

OTHER EARLY SAINTS

Several other saints who died before Constantine ended the persecution of Christians have also frequently been the subjects of artworks:

- **Paul** Born a Jew named Saul, Paul fervently opposed Christian teaching until Christ spoke to him in a blinding burst of light. Paul became the "Apostle to the Gentiles," preaching the Gospel to non-Jews as well as Jews. His *Epistles* are the foundation of Christian theology. In Early Christian art, he holds a scroll and often appears with Peter flanking Christ, although, unlike the original apostles, Paul never met Jesus. In later representations he may hold the sword of his martyrdom.

- **Mark** One of the two evangelists who were not apostles, Mark accompanied Paul on his earliest missionary journey and became the first bishop of Alexandria, where he was martyred by being dragged with a rope around his neck. The Venetians acquired Mark's remains in 828. The saint's attribute—a lion—is the emblem of Venice to this day.

- **Luke** A Gentile physician in addition to being a Gospel author, Luke painted a portrait of Mary and the infant Jesus, and consequently became the patron saint of artists as well as doctors. His attribute is an ox.

- **Mary Magdalene** Born in Magdala on the Sea of Galilee, Mary Magdalene washed Jesus's feet with her tears and dried them with her hair. She was the first to discover Christ's empty tomb and to encounter the resurrected Savior. Mary's major attribute is her long hair.

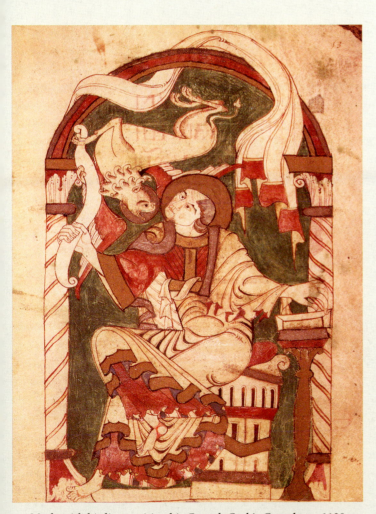

Mark, with his lion, writing his Gospel, *Corbie Gospels,* ca. 1120

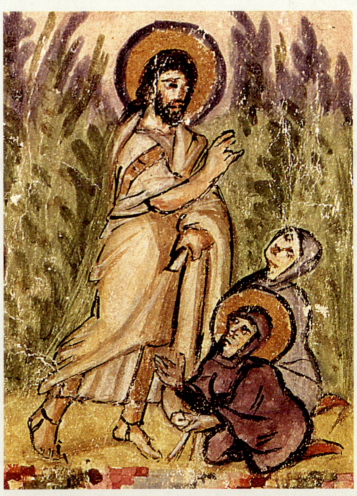

Mary Magdalene and the resurrected Christ, *Rabbula Gospels,* 586

RELIGION AND MYTHOLOGY
Buddhism and Buddhist Iconography

The Buddha (Enlightened One) was born around 563 BCE as Prince Siddhartha Gautama. When he was 29, he renounced his opulent life and became a wandering ascetic searching for knowledge through meditation. Six years later, he achieved complete enlightenment, or buddhahood, while meditating beneath a pipal tree (the Bodhi tree) at Bodh Gaya (place of enlightenment) in eastern India. The Buddha preached his first sermon in the Deer Park at Sarnath. There he set into motion the Wheel (*chakra*) of the Law (*dharma*) and expounded the Four Noble Truths: (1) life is suffering; (2) the cause of suffering is desire; (3) one can overcome and extinguish desire; (4) the way to conquer desire and end suffering is to follow the Buddha's Eightfold Path of right understanding, right thought, right speech, right action, right livelihood, right effort, right mindfulness, and right concentration. The Buddha's path leads to *nirvana,* the cessation of the endless cycle of painful life, death, and rebirth. The Buddha continued to preach until his death at age 80 at Kushinagara.

The earliest form of Buddhism is called Theravada (Path of the Elders) Buddhism. The second major school of Buddhist thought, Mahayana (Great Path) Buddhism, emerged around the beginning of the Christian era. Mahayana Buddhists refer to Theravada Buddhism as Hinayana (Lesser Path) Buddhism and believe in a larger goal than nirvana for an individual—namely, buddhahood for all. Mahayana Buddhists also revere *bodhisattvas* (Buddhas-to-be), exemplars of compassion who restrain themselves at the threshold of nirvana to aid others in earning merit and achieving buddhahood. A third important Buddhist sect, especially popular in East Asia, venerates the Amitabha Buddha (Amida in Japanese), the Buddha of Infinite Light and Life. The devotees of this Buddha hope to be reborn in the Pure Land Paradise of the West, where the Amitabha resides and can grant them salvation.

The earliest (first century CE) known depictions of the Buddha in human form show him as a robed monk. Artists distinguished the Enlightened One from monks and bodhisattvas by *lakshanas,* body attributes indicating the Buddha's suprahuman nature. These distinguishing marks include an *urna,* or curl of hair between the eyebrows; an *ushnisha,* or cranial bump; and, less frequently, palms of hands and soles of feet imprinted with a wheel. The Buddha is also recognizable by his elongated ears, the result of wearing heavy royal jewelry in his youth.

Representations of the Buddha also feature a repertory of mudras, or hand gestures. These include the *dhyana* (meditation) mudra, with the right hand over the left, palms upward; the *bhumisparsha* (earth-touching) mudra, right hand down reaching to the ground, calling the earth to witness the Buddha's enlightenment; the *dharmachakra* (Wheel of the Law, or teaching) mudra, a two-handed gesture with right thumb and index finger forming a circle; and the *abhaya* (do not fear) mudra, right hand up, palm outward, a gesture of protection or blessing.

Episodes from the Buddha's life are among the most popular subjects in all Buddhist artistic traditions. Four of the most important events are his birth at Lumbini from the side of his mother; his achievement of buddhahood while meditating beneath the Bodhi tree; his first sermon at Sarnath; and his attainment of nirvana when he died (*parinirvana*) at Kushinagara.

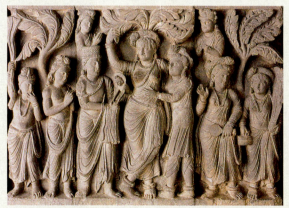

a

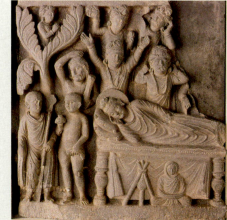

b

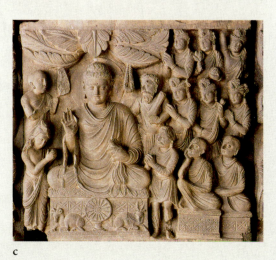

c

d

Life and death of the Buddha, from Gandhara, second century. (a) Birth at Lumbini, (b) enlightenment at Bodh Gaya, (c) first sermon at Sarnath, (d) death at Kushinagara (parinirvana)

RELIGION AND MYTHOLOGY
Hinduism and Hindu Iconography

Unlike Buddhism (and Christianity, Islam, and other religions), Hinduism recognizes no founder or great prophet. Hindism also has no simple definition, but means "the religion of the Indians." The practices and beliefs of Hindus vary tremendously, but ritual sacrifice is central to Hinduism. The goal of sacrifice is to please a deity in order to achieve release (*moksha,* liberation) from the endless cycle of birth, death, and rebirth (*samsara*) and become one with the universal spirit.

Not only is Hinduism a religion of many gods, but the Hindu deities also have various natures and take many forms. This multiplicity suggests the all-pervasive nature of the Hindu gods. The three most important deities are the gods Shiva and Vishnu and the goddess Devi. Each of the three major sects of Hinduism today considers one of these three to be supreme—Shiva in Shaivism, Vishnu in Vaishnavism, and Devi in Shaktism. (*Shakti* is the female creative force.)

- **Shiva** is the Destroyer, but, consistent with the multiplicity of Hindu belief, he is also a regenerative force and, in the latter role, can be represented in the form of a *linga* (a phallus or cosmic pillar). When Shiva appears in human form in Hindu art, he frequently has multiple limbs and heads, signs of his suprahuman nature, and matted locks piled atop his head, crowned by a crescent moon. Sometimes he wears a serpent scarf and has a third eye on his forehead (the emblem of his all-seeing nature). Shiva rides the bull **Nandi** and often carries a trident.

- **Vishnu** is the Preserver of the Universe. Artists frequently portray him with four arms holding various attributes, including a conchshell trumpet and discus, sometimes sleeping on the serpent Ananta floating on the waters of the cosmic sea as he dreams the universe into reality. When the evil forces in the world become too strong, he descends to earth to restore balance and assumes different forms (*avatars,* or incarnations), including a boar, fish, and tortoise, as well as **Krishna**, the divine lover, and even the Buddha himself.

- **Devi** is the Great Goddess who takes many forms and has many names. Hindus worship her alone or as a consort of male gods (**Parvati** or **Uma**, wife of Shiva; **Lakshmi**, wife of Vishnu), as well as **Radha**, lover of Krishna. She has both benign and horrific forms. She creates and destroys. In one manifestation, she is **Durga**, a multiarmed goddess who often rides a lion. Her son is the elephant-headed **Ganesha**.

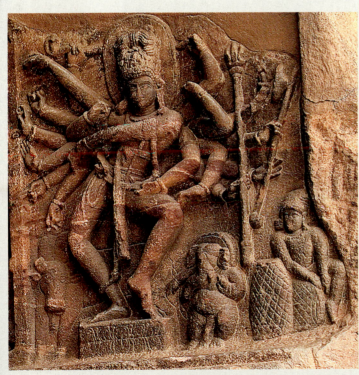

Dancing Shiva with Ganesha, Badami, India,
late sixth century

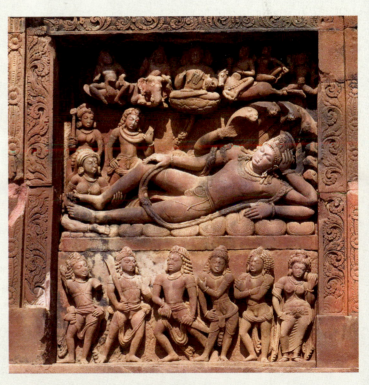

Vishnu Asleep on the Serpent Ananta, Deogarh, India,
early sixth century

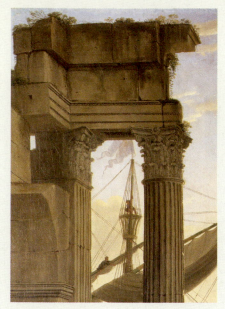

▲ **I-1a** Among the questions art historians ask is why artists chose the subjects they represented. Why would a 17th-century French painter set a biblical story in a contemporary harbor with a Roman ruin?

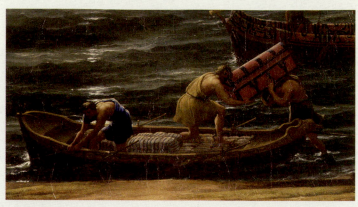

▲ **I-1b** Why is the small boat in the foreground much larger than the sailing ship in the distance? What devices did Western artists develop to produce the illusion of deep space in a two-dimensional painting?

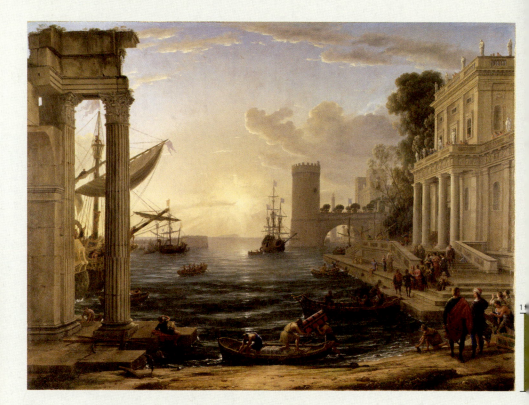

| I-1 | CLAUDE LORRAIN, *Embarkation of the Queen of Sheba*, 1648. Oil on canvas, 4' 10" × 6' 4". National Gallery, London. |

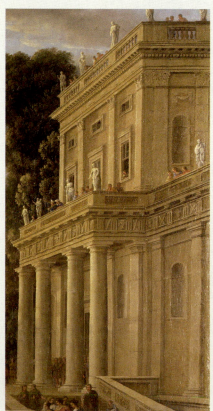

◀ **I-1c** Why does the large port building at the right edge of this painting seem normal to the eye when the top and bottom of the structure are not parallel horizontal lines, as they are in a real building?

What Is Art History?

What is art history? Except when referring to the modern academic discipline, people do not often juxtapose the words *art* and *history*. They tend to think of history as the record and interpretation of past human events, particularly social and political events. In contrast, most think of art, quite correctly, as part of the present—as something people can see and touch. Of course, people cannot see or touch history's vanished human events, but a visible, tangible artwork is a kind of persisting event. One or more artists made it at a certain time and in a specific place, even if no one now knows who, when, where, or why. Although created in the past, an artwork continues to exist in the present, long surviving its times. The first painters and sculptors died 30,000 years ago, but their works remain, some of them exhibited in glass cases in museums built only a few years ago.

Modern museum visitors can admire these objects from the remote past and countless others produced over the millennia—whether a large painting on canvas by a 17th-century French artist (FIG. I-1), a wood portrait from an ancient Egyptian tomb (FIG. I-14), an illustrated book by a medieval German monk (FIG. I-8), or an 18th-century bronze altar glorifying an African king (FIG. I-15)—without any knowledge of the circumstances leading to the creation of those works. The beauty or sheer size of an object can impress people, the artist's virtuosity in the handling of ordinary or costly materials can dazzle them, or the subject depicted can move them emotionally. Viewers can react to what they see, interpret the work in the light of their own experience, and judge it a success or a failure. These are all valid responses to a work of art. But the enjoyment and appreciation of artworks in museum settings are relatively recent phenomena, as is the creation of artworks solely for museum-going audiences to view.

Today, it is common for artists to work in private studios and to create paintings, sculptures, and other objects to be offered for sale by commercial art galleries. This is what American artist CLYFFORD STILL (1904–1980) did when he created his series of paintings (FIG. I-2) of pure color titled simply with the year of their creation. Usually, someone the artist has never met will purchase the artwork and display it in a setting that the artist has never seen. This practice is not a new phenomenon in the history of art—an ancient potter decorating a vase for sale at a village market stall probably did not know who would buy the pot or where it would be housed—but it is not at all typical. In fact, it is exceptional. Throughout history, most artists created paintings, sculptures, and other objects for specific patrons and settings and to fulfill a specific purpose, even if today no one knows the original contexts of those artworks. Museum visitors can appreciate the visual and tactile qualities of these objects, but they cannot understand why they were made or why they appear as they do without knowing the circumstances of their creation. Art *appreciation* does not require knowledge of the historical context of an artwork (or a building). Art *history* does.

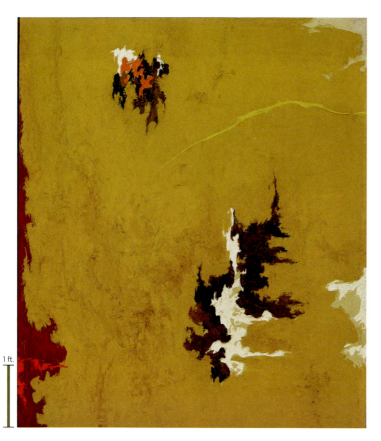

1 ft.

I-2 CLYFFORD STILL, *1948-C*, 1948. Oil on canvas, 6' 8⅞" × 5' 8¾". Hirshhorn Museum and Sculpture Garden, Smithsonian Institution, Washington, D.C. (purchased with funds of Joseph H. Hirshhorn, 1992).

Clyfford Still painted this abstract composition without knowing who would purchase it or where it would be displayed, but throughout history, most artists created works for specific patrons and settings.

Thus a central aim of art history is to determine the original context of artworks. Art historians seek to achieve a full understanding not only of why these "persisting events" of human history look the way they do but also of why the artistic events happened at all. What unique set of circumstances gave rise to the construction of a particular building or led an individual patron to commission a certain artist to fashion a singular artwork for a specific place? The study of history is therefore vital to art history. And art history is often indispensable for a thorough understanding of history. In ways that other historical documents may not, art objects and buildings can shed light on the peoples who made them and on the times of their creation. Furthermore, artists and architects can affect history by reinforcing or challenging cultural values and practices through the objects they create and the structures they build. Although the two disciplines are not the same, the history of art and architecture is inseparable from the study of history.

The following pages introduce some of the distinctive subjects that art historians address and the kinds of questions they ask, and explain some of the basic terminology they use when answering these questions. Readers armed with this arsenal of questions and terms will be ready to explore the multifaceted world of art through the ages.

ART HISTORY IN THE 21ST CENTURY

Art historians study the visual and tangible objects that humans make and the structures that they build. Scholars traditionally have classified these works as architecture, sculpture, the pictorial arts (painting, drawing, printmaking, and photography), and the craft arts, or arts of design. The craft arts comprise utilitarian objects, such as ceramics, metalwork, textiles, jewelry, and similar accessories of ordinary living—but the fact that these objects were used does not mean that they are not works of art. In fact, in some times and places, these so-called minor arts were the most prestigious artworks of all. Artists of every age have blurred the boundaries among these categories, but this is especially true today, when multimedia works abound.

Beginning with the earliest Greco-Roman art critics, scholars have studied objects that their makers consciously manufactured as "art" and to which the artists assigned formal titles. But today's art historians also study a multitude of objects that their creators and owners almost certainly did not consider to be "works of art." Few ancient Romans, for example, would have regarded a coin bearing their emperor's portrait as anything but money. Today, an art museum may exhibit that coin in a locked case in a climate-controlled room, and scholars may subject it to the same kind of art historical analysis as a portrait by an acclaimed Renaissance or modern sculptor or painter.

The range of objects that art historians study is constantly expanding and now includes, for example, computer-generated images, whereas in the past almost anything produced using a machine would not have been regarded as art. Most people still consider the performing arts—music, drama, and dance—as outside art history's realm because these arts are fleeting, impermanent media. But during the past few decades, even this distinction between "fine art" and "performance art" has become blurred. Art historians, however, generally ask the same kinds of questions about what they study, whether they employ a restrictive or expansive definition of art.

The Questions Art Historians Ask

HOW OLD IS IT? Before art historians can write a history of art, they must be sure they know the date of each work they study. Thus an indispensable subject of art historical inquiry is *chronology,* the dating of art objects and buildings. If researchers cannot determine a monument's age, they cannot place the work in its historical context. Art historians have developed many ways to establish, or at least approximate, the date of an artwork.

Physical evidence often reliably indicates an object's age. The material used for a statue or painting—bronze, plastic, or oil-based pigment, to name only a few—may not have been invented before a certain time, indicating the earliest possible date (the *terminus post quem*: Latin, "point after which") someone could have fashioned the work. Or artists may have ceased using certain materials—such as specific kinds of inks and papers for drawings—at a known time, providing the latest possible date (the *terminus ante quem*: Latin, "point before which") for objects made of those materials. Sometimes the material (or the manufacturing technique) of an object or a building can establish a very precise date of production or construction. The study of tree rings, for instance, usually can determine within a narrow range the date of a wood statue or a timber roof beam.

Documentary evidence can help pinpoint the date of an object or building when a dated written document mentions the work. For example, official records may note when church officials commissioned a new altarpiece—and how much they paid to which artist.

Internal evidence can play a significant role in dating an artwork. A painter might have depicted an identifiable person or a kind of hairstyle, clothing, or furniture fashionable only at a certain time. If so, the art historian can assign a more accurate date to that painting.

Stylistic evidence is also very important. The analysis of *style*—an artist's distinctive manner of producing an object—is the art historian's special sphere. Unfortunately, because it is a subjective assessment, an artwork's style is by far the most unreliable chronological criterion. Still, art historians find stylistic evidence a very useful tool for establishing chronology.

WHAT IS ITS STYLE? Defining artistic style is one of the key elements of art historical inquiry, although the analysis of artworks solely in terms of style no longer dominates the field the way it once did. Art historians speak of several different kinds of artistic styles.

Period style refers to the characteristic artistic manner of a specific era or span of years, usually within a distinct culture, such as "Archaic Greek" or "High Renaissance." But many periods do not

display any stylistic unity at all. How would someone define the artistic style of the second decade of the new millennium in North America? Far too many crosscurrents exist in contemporary art for anyone to describe a period style of the early 21st century—even in a single city such as New York.

Regional style is the term that art historians use to describe variations in style tied to geography. Like an object's date, its *provenance,* or place of origin, can significantly determine its character. Very often two artworks from the same place made centuries apart are more similar than contemporaneous works from two different regions. To cite one example, usually only an expert can distinguish between an Egyptian statue carved in 2500 BCE and one made in 500 BCE. But no one would mistake an Egyptian statue of 500 BCE for one of the same date made in Greece or Mexico.

Considerable variations in a given area's style are possible, however, even during a single historical period. In late medieval Europe, French architecture differed significantly from Italian architecture. The interiors of Beauvais Cathedral (FIG. I-3) and the church of Santa Croce (Holy Cross, FIG. I-4) in Florence typify the architectural styles of France and Italy, respectively, at the end of the 13th century. The rebuilding of the east end of Beauvais Cathedral began in 1284. Construction commenced on Santa Croce only 10 years later. Both structures employ the *pointed arch* characteristic of this era, yet the two churches differ strikingly. The French church has towering stone ceilings and large expanses of colored-glass windows, whereas the Italian building has a low timber roof and small,

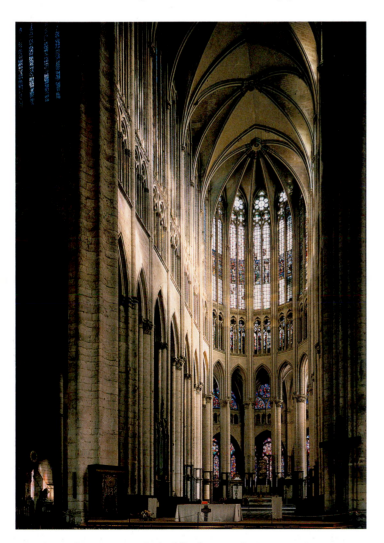

I-3 Choir of Beauvais Cathedral (looking east), Beauvais, France, rebuilt after 1284.

The style of an object or building often varies from region to region. This cathedral has towering stone vaults and large stained-glass windows typical of 13th-century French architecture.

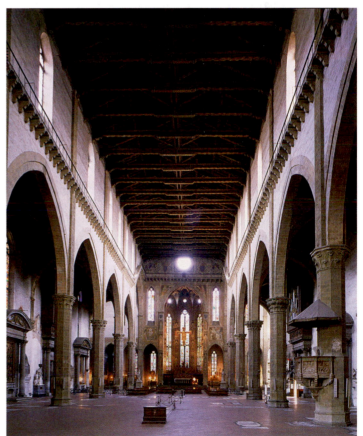

I-4 Interior of Santa Croce (looking east), Florence, Italy, begun 1294.

In contrast to Beauvais Cathedral (FIG. I-3), this contemporaneous Florentine church conforms to the quite different regional style of Italy. The building has a low timber roof and small windows.

Art History in the 21st Century   **3**

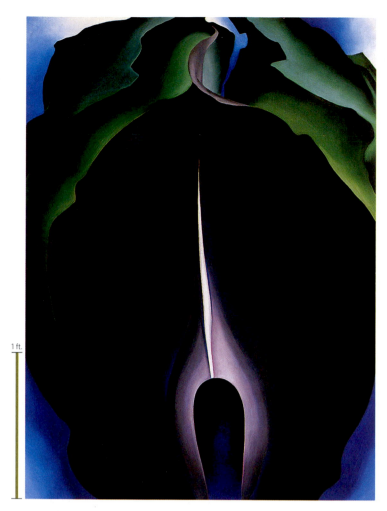

I-5 GEORGIA O'KEEFFE, *Jack-in-the-Pulpit No. 4,* 1930. Oil on canvas, 3' 4" × 2' 6". National Gallery of Art, Washington, D.C. (Alfred Stieglitz Collection, bequest of Georgia O'Keeffe).

O'Keeffe's paintings feature close-up views of petals and leaves in which the organic forms become powerful abstract compositions. This approach to painting typifies the artist's distinctive personal style.

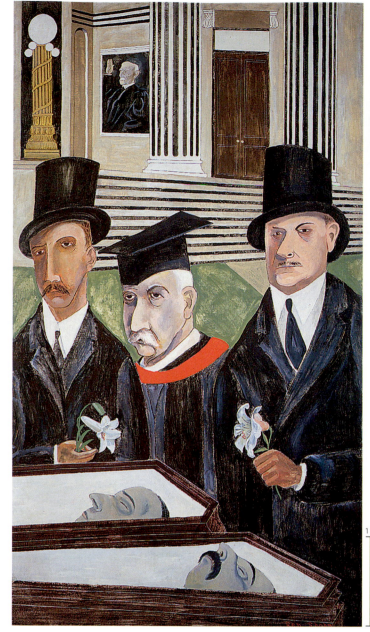

I-6 BEN SHAHN, *The Passion of Sacco and Vanzetti,* 1931–1932. Tempera on canvas, 7' $\frac{1}{2}$" × 4'. Whitney Museum of American Art, New York (gift of Edith and Milton Lowenthal in memory of Juliana Force).

O'Keeffe's contemporary, Shahn developed a style markedly different from hers. His paintings are often social commentaries on recent events and incorporate readily identifiable people.

widely separated clear windows. Because the two contemporaneous churches served similar purposes, regional style mainly explains their differing appearance.

Personal style, the distinctive manner of individual artists or architects, often decisively explains stylistic discrepancies among paintings, sculptures, and buildings of the same time and place. For example, in 1930, the American painter GEORGIA O'KEEFFE (1887–1986) produced a series of paintings of flowering plants. One of them—*Jack-in-the-Pulpit No. 4* (FIG. I-5)—is a sharply focused close-up view of petals and leaves. O'Keeffe captured the growing plant's slow, controlled motion while converting the plant into a powerful abstract composition of lines, forms, and colors (see the discussion of art historical vocabulary in the next section). Only a year later, another American artist, BEN SHAHN (1898–1969), painted *The Passion of Sacco and Vanzetti* (FIG. I-6), a stinging commentary on social injustice inspired by the trial and execution of two Italian anarchists, Nicola Sacco and Bartolomeo Vanzetti. Many people believed that Sacco and Vanzetti had been unjustly convicted of killing two men in a robbery in 1920. Shahn's painting compresses time in a symbolic representation of the trial and its aftermath. The two executed men lie in their coffins. Presiding over them are the three members of the commission (headed by a college president wearing

academic cap and gown) who declared that the original trial was fair and cleared the way for the executions. Behind, on the wall of a stately government building, hangs the framed portrait of the judge who pronounced the initial sentence. Personal style, not period or regional style, sets Shahn's canvas apart from O'Keeffe's. The contrast is extreme here because of the very different subjects that the artists chose. But even when two artists depict the same subject, the results can vary widely. The *way* O'Keeffe painted flowers and the *way* Shahn painted faces are distinctive and unlike the styles of their contemporaries. (See the "Who Made It?" discussion on page 6.)

The different kinds of artistic styles are not mutually exclusive. For example, an artist's personal style may change dramatically during a long career. Art historians then must distinguish among

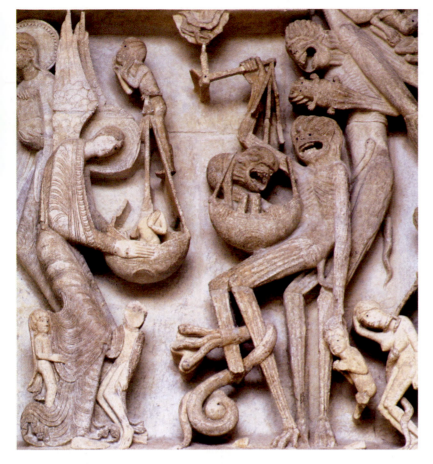

I-7 Gislebertus, weighing of souls, detail of *Last Judgment* (FIG. 12-15), west tympanum of Saint-Lazare, Autun, France, ca. 1120–1135.

In this high relief portraying the weighing of souls on judgment day, Gislebertus used disproportion and distortion to dehumanize the devilish figure yanking on the scales of justice.

the different period styles of a particular artist, such as the "Rose Period" and the "Cubist Period" of the prolific 20th-century artist Pablo Picasso.

WHAT IS ITS SUBJECT? Another major concern of art historians is, of course, subject matter, encompassing the story, or narrative; the scene presented; the action's time and place; the persons involved; and the environment and its details. Some artworks, such as modern abstract paintings (FIG. I-2), have no subject, not even a setting. The "subject" is the artwork itself—its colors, textures, composition, and size. But when artists represent people, places, or actions, viewers must identify these features to achieve complete understanding of the work. Art historians traditionally separate pictorial subjects into various categories, such as religious, historical, mythological, *genre* (daily life), portraiture, *landscape* (a depiction of a place), *still life* (an arrangement of inanimate objects), and their numerous subdivisions and combinations.

Iconography—literally, the "writing of images"—refers both to the content, or subject, of an artwork, and to the study of content in art. By extension, it also includes the study of *symbols,* images that stand for other images or encapsulate ideas. In Christian art, two intersecting lines of unequal length or a simple geometric cross can serve as an emblem of the religion as a whole, symbolizing the cross of Jesus Christ's crucifixion. A symbol also can be a familiar object that an artist has imbued with greater meaning. A balance or scale, for example, may symbolize justice or the weighing of souls on judgment day (FIG. I-7).

Artists may depict figures with unique *attributes* identifying them. In Christian art, for example, each of the authors of the biblical gospel books, the four evangelists (FIG. I-8), has a distinctive attribute. People can recognize Saint Matthew by the winged man associated with him, John by his eagle, Mark by his lion, and Luke by his ox.

Throughout the history of art, artists have used *personifications*—abstract ideas codified in human form. Because of the fame of the colossal statue set up in New York City's harbor in 1886, people everywhere visualize Liberty as a robed woman wearing a rayed crown and holding a torch. Four different personifications appear in *The Four Horsemen*

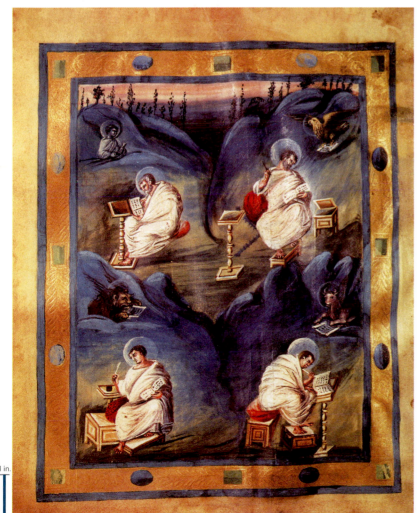

I-8 The four evangelists, folio 14 verso of the *Aachen Gospels,* ca. 810. Ink and tempera on vellum, $1' \times 9\frac{1}{2}''$. Domschatz-kammer, Aachen.

Artists depict figures with attributes in order to identify them for viewers. The authors of the four gospels have distinctive attributes—winged man (Matthew), eagle (John), lion (Mark), and ox (Luke).

Art History in the 21st Century **5**

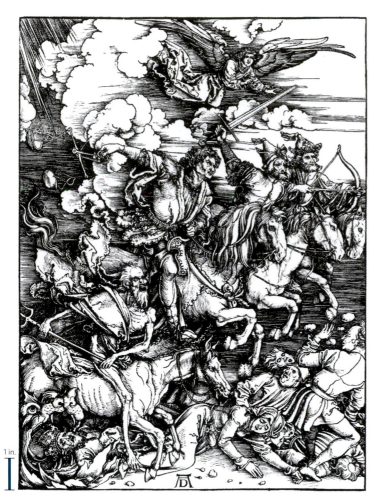

I-9 ALBRECHT DÜRER, *The Four Horsemen of the Apocalypse*, ca. 1498. Woodcut, 1' 3$\frac{1}{4}$" × 11". Metropolitan Museum of Art, New York (gift of Junius S. Morgan, 1919).

Personifications are abstract ideas codified in human form. Here, Albrecht Dürer represented Death, Famine, War, and Pestilence as four men on charging horses, each one carrying an identifying attribute.

of the Apocalypse (FIG. I-9) by German artist ALBRECHT DÜRER (1471–1528). The late-15th-century print is a terrifying depiction of the fateful day at the end of time when, according to the Bible's last book, Death, Famine, War, and Pestilence will annihilate the human race. Dürer personified Death as an emaciated old man with a pitchfork. Famine swings the scales for weighing human souls (compare FIG. I-7). War wields a sword, and Pestilence draws a bow.

Even without considering style and without knowing a work's maker, informed viewers can determine much about the work's period and provenance by iconographical and subject analysis alone. In *The Passion of Sacco and Vanzetti* (FIG. I-6), for example, the two coffins, the trio headed by an academic, and the robed judge in the background are all pictorial clues revealing the painting's subject. The work's date must be after the trial and execution, probably while the event was still newsworthy. And because the two men's deaths caused the greatest outrage in the United States, the painter–social critic was probably an American.

WHO MADE IT? If Ben Shahn had not signed his painting of Sacco and Vanzetti, an art historian could still assign, or *attribute* (make an *attribution* of), the work to him based on knowledge of the

artist's personal style. Although signing (and dating) works is quite common (but by no means universal) today, in the history of art, countless works exist whose artists remain unknown. Because personal style can play a major role in determining the character of an artwork, art historians often try to attribute anonymous works to known artists. Sometimes they assemble a group of works all thought to be by the same person, even though none of the objects in the group is the known work of an artist with a recorded name. Art historians thus reconstruct the careers of artists such as "the Achilles Painter," the anonymous ancient Greek artist whose masterwork is a depiction of the hero Achilles. Scholars base their attributions on internal evidence, such as the distinctive way an artist draws or carves drapery folds, earlobes, or flowers. It requires a keen, highly trained eye and long experience to become a *connoisseur*, an expert in assigning artworks to "the hand" of one artist rather than another. Attribution is subjective, of course, and ever open to doubt. For example, scholars continue to debate attributions to the famous 17th-century Dutch painter Rembrandt van Rijn.

Sometimes a group of artists works in the same style at the same time and place. Art historians designate such a group as a *school*. "School" does not mean an educational institution or art academy. The term connotes only shared chronology, style, and geography. Art historians speak, for example, of the Dutch school of the 17th century and, within it, of subschools such as those of the cities of Haarlem, Utrecht, and Leyden.

WHO PAID FOR IT? The interest that many art historians show in attribution reflects their conviction that the identity of an artwork's maker is the major reason the object looks the way it does. For them, personal style is of paramount importance. But in many times and places, artists had little to say about what form their work would take. They toiled in obscurity, doing the bidding of their *patrons*, those who paid them to make individual works or employed them on a continuing basis. The role of patrons in dictating the content and shaping the form of artworks is also an important subject of art historical inquiry, more so today than at any time in the past.

In the art of portraiture, to name only one category of painting and sculpture, the patron has often played a dominant role in deciding how the artist represented the subject, whether that person was the patron or another individual, such as a spouse, son, or mother. Many Egyptian pharaohs and some Roman emperors, for example, insisted that artists depict them with unlined faces and perfect youthful bodies no matter how old they were when portrayed. In these cases, the state employed the sculptors and painters, and the artists had no choice but to portray their patrons in the officially approved manner. This is why Augustus, who lived to age 76, looks so young in his portraits (FIG. I-10). Although Roman emperor for more than 40 years, Augustus demanded that artists always represent him as a young, godlike head of state.

All modes of artistic production reveal the impact of patronage. Learned monks provided the themes for the sculptural decoration of medieval church portals (FIG. I-7). Renaissance princes and popes dictated the subject, size, and materials of artworks destined for display in buildings also constructed according to their specifications. An art historian could make a very long list of commissioned works, and it would indicate that patrons have had diverse tastes and needs throughout history and consequently have demanded different kinds of art. Whenever a patron contracts with an artist or architect to paint, sculpt, or build in a prescribed manner, personal style often becomes a very minor factor in the ultimate

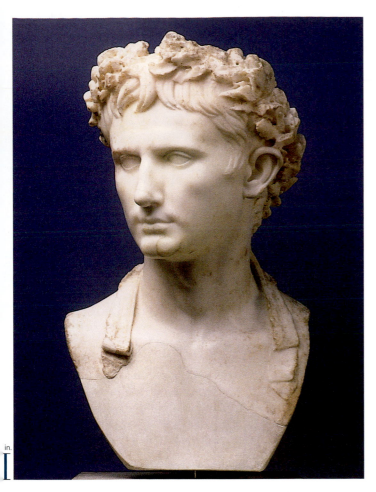

I-10 Bust of Augustus wearing the corona civica, early first century CE. Marble, 1' 5" high. Glyptothek, Munich.

Patrons frequently dictate the form that their portraits will take. Emperor Augustus demanded that he always be portrayed as a young, godlike head of state even though he lived to age 76.

their color, texture, and other qualities. *Composition* refers to how an artist *composes* (organizes) forms in an artwork, either by placing shapes on a flat surface or by arranging forms in space.

MATERIAL AND TECHNIQUE To create art forms, artists shape materials (pigment, clay, marble, gold, and many more) with tools (pens, brushes, chisels, and so forth). Each of the materials and tools available has its own potentialities and limitations. Part of all artists' creative activity is to select the *medium* and instrument most suitable to the purpose—or to develop new media and tools, such as bronze and concrete in antiquity and cameras and computers in modern times. The processes that artists employ, such as applying paint to canvas with a brush, and the distinctive, personal ways that they handle materials constitute their *technique*. Form, material, and technique interrelate and are central to analyzing any work of art.

LINE Among the most important elements defining an artwork's shape or form is *line*. A line can be understood as the path of a point moving in space, an invisible line of sight. More commonly, however, artists and architects make a line visible by drawing (or chiseling) it on a *plane,* a flat surface. A line may be very thin, wirelike, and delicate. It may be thick and heavy. Or it may alternate quickly from broad to narrow, the strokes jagged or the outline broken. When a continuous line defines an object's outer shape, art historians call it a *contour line*. All of these line qualities are present in Dürer's *Four Horsemen of the Apocalypse* (FIG. I-9). Contour lines define the basic shapes of clouds, human and animal limbs, and weapons. Within the forms, series of short broken lines create shadows and textures. An overall pattern of long parallel strokes suggests the dark sky on the frightening day when the world is about to end.

COLOR Light reveals all colors. Light in the world of the painter and other artists differs from natural light. Natural light, or sunlight, is whole or *additive light*. As the sum of all the wavelengths composing the visible *spectrum,* it may be disassembled or fragmented into the individual colors of the spectral band. The painter's light in art—the light reflected from pigments and objects—is *subtractive light*. Paint pigments produce their individual colors by reflecting a segment of the spectrum while absorbing all the rest. Green pigment, for example, subtracts or absorbs all the light in the spectrum except that seen as green.

Hue is the property giving a color its name. Although the spectrum colors merge into each other, artists usually conceive of their hues as distinct from one another. Color has two basic variables—the apparent amount of light reflected and the apparent purity. A change in one must produce a change in the other. Some terms for these variables are *value* or *tonality* (the degree of lightness or darkness) and *intensity* or *saturation* (the purity of a color, its brightness or dullness).

Artists call the three basic colors—red, yellow, and blue—the *primary colors*. The *secondary colors* result from mixing pairs of primaries: orange (red and yellow), purple (red and blue), and green (yellow and blue). *Complementary colors* represent the pairing of a primary color and the secondary color created from mixing the two other primary colors—red and green, yellow and purple, and blue and orange. They "complement," or complete, each other, one absorbing the colors that the other reflects.

Artists can manipulate the appearance of colors, however. One artist who made a systematic investigation of the formal aspects of art, especially color, was JOSEPH ALBERS (1888–1976), a German-born

appearance of the painting, statue, or building. In these cases, the identity of the patron reveals more to art historians than does the identity of the artist or school. The portrait of Augustus illustrated here (FIG. I-10)—showing the emperor wearing a *corona civica,* or civic crown—was the work of a virtuoso sculptor, a master wielder of hammer and chisel. But scores of similar portraits of this Roman emperor also exist today. They differ in quality but not in kind from this one. The patron, not the artist, determined the character of these artworks. Augustus's public image never varied.

The Words Art Historians Use

As in all fields of study, art history has its own specialized vocabulary consisting of hundreds of words, but certain basic terms are indispensable for describing artworks and buildings of any time and place. They make up the essential vocabulary of *formal analysis,* the visual analysis of artistic form. Definitions and discussions of the most important art historical terms follow.

FORM AND COMPOSITION *Form* refers to an object's shape and structure, either in two dimensions (for example, a figure painted on a wood panel) or in three dimensions (such as a statue carved from a marble block). Two forms may take the same shape but differ in

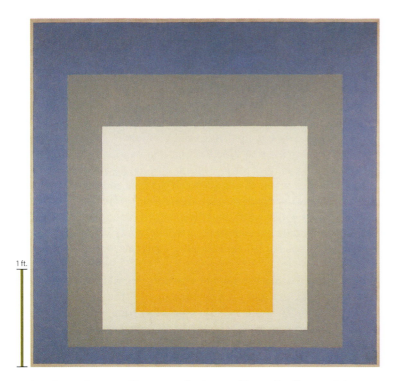

1 ft.

I-11 JOSEF ALBERS, *Homage to the Square: "Ascending,"* 1953. Oil on composition board, 3' 7$\frac{1}{2}$" × 3' 7$\frac{1}{2}$". Whitney Museum of American Art, New York.

Albers created hundreds of paintings using the same composition but employing variations in hue, saturation, and value in order to reveal the relativity and instability of color perception.

artist who emigrated to the United States in 1933. In connection with his studies, Albers created the series *Homage to the Square*—hundreds of paintings, most of which are color variations on the same composition of concentric squares, as in the illustrated example (FIG. I-11). The series reflected Albers's belief that art originates in "the discrepancy between physical fact and psychic effect."[1] Because the composition in most of these paintings remains constant, the works succeed in revealing the relativity and instability of color perception. Albers varied the hue, saturation, and value of each square in the paintings in this series. As a result, the sizes of the squares from painting to painting appear to vary (although they remain the same), and the sensations emanating from the paintings range from clashing dissonance to delicate serenity. Albers explained his motivation for focusing on color juxtapositions:

> They [the colors] are juxtaposed for various and changing visual effects. . . . Such action, reaction, interaction . . . is sought in order to make obvious how colors influence and change each other; that the same color, for instance—with different grounds or neighbors—looks different. . . . Such color deceptions prove that we see colors almost never unrelated to each other.[2]

TEXTURE The term *texture* refers to the quality of a surface, such as rough or shiny. Art historians distinguish between true texture—that is, the tactile quality of the surface—and represented texture, as when painters depict an object as having a certain texture even though the pigment is the true texture. Sometimes artists combine different materials of different textures on a single surface, juxtaposing paint with pieces of wood, newspaper, fabric, and so forth. Art historians refer to this mixed-media technique as *collage*. Texture

is, of course, a key determinant of any sculpture's character. People's first impulse is usually to handle a work of sculpture—even though museum signs often warn "Do not touch!" Sculptors plan for this natural human response, using surfaces varying in texture from rugged coarseness to polished smoothness. Textures are often intrinsic to a material, influencing the type of stone, wood, plastic, clay, or metal that a sculptor selects.

SPACE, MASS, AND VOLUME *Space* is the bounded or boundless "container" of objects. For art historians, space can be the real three-dimensional space occupied by a statue or a vase or contained within a room or courtyard. Or space can be *illusionistic,* as when painters depict an image (or illusion) of the three-dimensional spatial world on a two-dimensional surface.

Mass and *volume* describe three-dimensional objects and space. In both architecture and sculpture, mass is the bulk, density, and weight of matter in space. Yet the mass need not be solid. It can be the exterior form of enclosed space. Mass can apply to a solid Egyptian pyramid or stone statue; to a church, synagogue, or mosque (architectural shells enclosing sometimes vast spaces); and to a hollow metal statue or baked clay pot. Volume is the space that mass organizes, divides, or encloses. It may be a building's interior spaces, the intervals between a structure's masses, or the amount of space occupied by a three-dimensional object such as a statue, pot, or chair. Volume and mass describe both the exterior and interior forms of a work of art—the forms of the matter of which it is composed and the spaces immediately around the work and interacting with it.

PERSPECTIVE AND FORESHORTENING *Perspective* is one of the most important pictorial devices for organizing forms in space. Throughout history, artists have used various types of perspective to create an illusion of depth or space on a two-dimensional surface. The French painter CLAUDE LORRAIN (1600–1682) employed several perspective devices in *Embarkation of the Queen of Sheba* (FIG. I-1), a painting of a biblical episode set in a 17th-century European harbor with an ancient Roman ruin in the left foreground—an irrationally anachronistic combination that the art historian can explain only in the context of the cultural values of the artist's time and place. In Claude's painting, the figures and boats on the shoreline are much larger than those in the distance, because decreasing the size of an object makes it appear farther away. The top and bottom of the port building at the painting's right side are not parallel horizontal lines, as they are in a real building. Instead, the lines converge beyond the structure, leading the viewer's eye toward the hazy, indistinct sun on the horizon. These three perspective devices—the reduction of figure size, the convergence of diagonal lines, and the blurring of distant forms—have been familiar features of Western art since they were first employed by the ancient Greeks. It is important to state, however, that all kinds of perspective are only pictorial conventions, even when one or more types of perspective may be so common in a given culture that people accept them as "natural" or as "true" means of representing the natural world.

These perspective conventions are by no means universal. In *Waves at Matsushima* (FIG. I-12), a Japanese seascape painting on a six-part folding screen, OGATA KORIN (1658–1716) ignored these Western "tricks" for representing deep space on a flat surface. A Western viewer might interpret the left half of Korin's composition as depicting the distant horizon, as in the French painting, but the sky is an unnatural gold, and the clouds that fill that unnaturally colored sky are almost indistinguishable from the waves below.

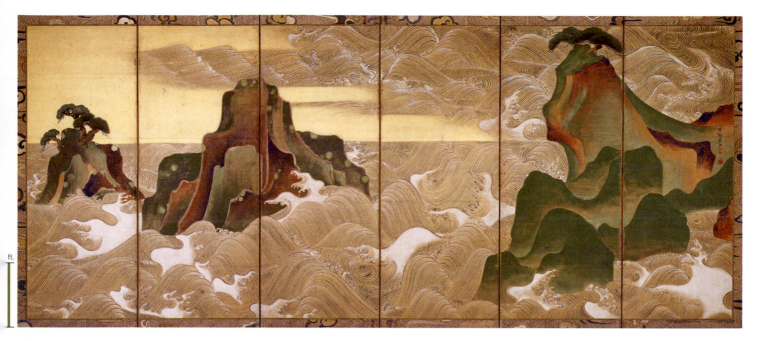

I-12 OGATA KORIN, *Waves at Matsushima,* Edo period, ca. 1700–1716. Six-panel folding screen, ink, color, and gold leaf on paper, 4' 11$\frac{1}{8}$" × 12' $\frac{7}{8}$". Museum of Fine Arts, Boston (Fenollosa-Weld Collection).

Asian artists rarely employed Western perspective (FIG. I-1). Korin was more concerned with creating an intriguing composition of shapes on a surface than with locating boulders, waves, and clouds in space.

The rocky outcroppings decrease in size with distance, but all are in sharp focus, and there are no shadows. The Japanese artist was less concerned with locating the boulders and waves and clouds in space than with composing shapes on a surface, playing the swelling curves of waves and clouds against the jagged contours of the rocks. Neither the French nor the Japanese painting can be said to project "correctly" what viewers "in fact" see. One painting is not a "better" picture of the world than the other. The European and Asian artists simply approached the problem of picture making differently.

Artists also represent single figures in space in varying ways. When Flemish artist PETER PAUL RUBENS (1577–1640) painted *Lion Hunt* (FIG. I-13), he used *foreshortening* for all the hunters and animals—that is, he represented their bodies at angles to the picture plane. When in life one views a figure at an angle, the body appears to contract as it extends back in space. Foreshortening is a kind of perspective. It produces the illusion that one part of the body is farther away than another, even though all the painted forms are on the same plane. Especially noteworthy in *Lion Hunt* are the gray horse at the left, seen from behind with the bottom of its left rear hoof facing viewers and most of its head hidden by its rider's shield, and the fallen hunter at the painting's lower right corner, whose barely visible legs and feet recede into the distance.

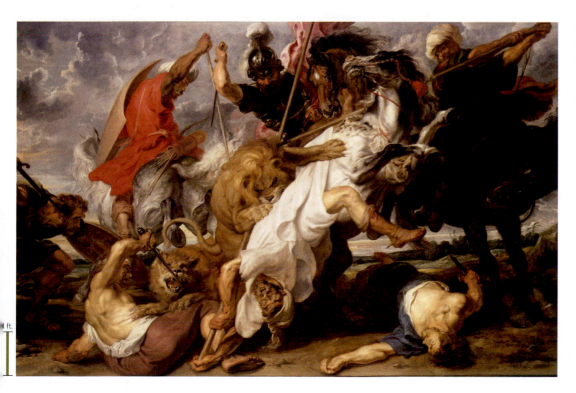

I-13 PETER PAUL RUBENS, *Lion Hunt,* 1617–1618. Oil on canvas, 8' 2" × 12' 5". Alte Pinakothek, Munich.

Foreshortening—the representation of a figure or object at an angle to the picture plane—is a common device in Western art for creating the illusion of depth. Foreshortening is a type of perspective.

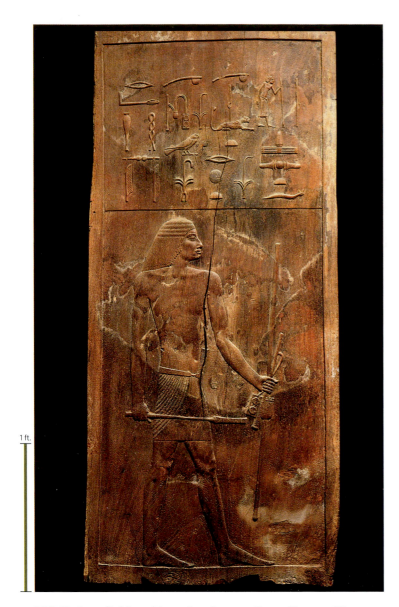

1 ft.

I-14 Hesire, relief from his tomb at Saqqara, Egypt, Dynasty III, ca. 2650 BCE. Wood, 3' 9" high. Egyptian Museum, Cairo.

Egyptian artists combined frontal and profile views to give a precise picture of the parts of the human body, as opposed to depicting how an individual body appears from a specific viewpoint.

The artist who carved the portrait of the ancient Egyptian official Hesire (FIG. **I-14**) for display in Hesire's tomb did not employ foreshortening. That artist's purpose was to present the various human body parts as clearly as possible, without overlapping. The lower part of Hesire's body is in profile to give the most complete view of the legs, with both the heel and toes of each foot visible. The frontal torso, however, allows viewers to see its full shape, including both shoulders, equal in size, as in nature. (Compare the shoulders of the hunter on the gray horse or those of the fallen hunter in *Lion Hunt*'s left foreground.) The result—an "unnatural" 90-degree twist at the waist—provides a precise picture of human body parts, if not an accurate picture of how a standing human figure really looks. Rubens and the Egyptian sculptor used very different means of depicting forms in space. Once again, neither is the "correct" manner.

PROPORTION AND SCALE *Proportion* concerns the relationships (in terms of size) of the parts of persons, buildings, or objects. People can judge "correct proportions" intuitively ("that statue's head

seems the right size for the body"). Or proportion can be a mathematical relationship between the size of one part of an artwork or building and the other parts within the work. Proportion in art implies using a *module,* or basic unit of measure. When an artist or architect uses a formal system of proportions, all parts of a building, body, or other entity will be fractions or multiples of the module. A module might be the diameter of a *column,* the height of a human head, or any other component whose dimensions can be multiplied or divided to determine the size of the work's other parts.

In certain times and places, artists have devised *canons,* or systems, of "correct" or "ideal" proportions for representing human figures, constituent parts of buildings, and so forth. In ancient Greece, many sculptors formulated canons of proportions so strict and all-encompassing that they calculated the size of every body part in advance, even the fingers and toes, according to mathematical ratios.

Proportional systems can differ sharply from period to period, culture to culture, and artist to artist. Part of the task that art history students face is to perceive and adjust to these differences. In fact, many artists have used disproportion and distortion deliberately for expressive effect. In the medieval French depiction of the weighing of souls on judgment day (FIG. I-7), the devilish figure yanking down on the scale has distorted facial features and stretched, lined limbs with animal-like paws for feet. Disproportion and distortion make him appear "inhuman," precisely as the sculptor intended.

In other cases, artists have used disproportion to focus attention on one body part (often the head) or to single out a group

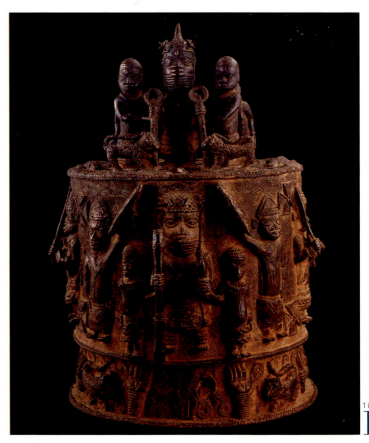

1 in

I-15 Altar to the Hand (ikegobo), from Benin, Nigeria, ca. 1735–1750. Bronze, 1' 5½" high. British Museum, London (gift of Sir William Ingram).

One of the Benin king's praise names is Great Head, and on this cast-bronze royal altar, the artist represented him larger than all other figures and with a disproportionately large head.

member (usually the leader). These intentional "unnatural" discrepancies in proportion constitute what art historians call *hierarchy of scale,* the enlarging of elements considered the most important. On the bronze altar from Benin, Nigeria, illustrated here (FIG. I-15), the sculptor varied the size of each figure according to the person's social status. Largest, and therefore most important, is the Benin king, depicted twice, each time flanked by two smaller attendant figures and shown wearing a multistrand coral necklace emblematic of his high office. The king's head is also disproportionately large compared to his body, consistent with one of the Benin ruler's praise names: Great Head.

One problem that students of art history—and professional art historians too—confront when studying illustrations in art history books is that although the relative sizes of figures and objects in a painting or sculpture are easy to discern, it is impossible to determine the absolute size of the work reproduced because they all are printed at approximately the same size on the page. Readers of *Art through the Ages* can learn the exact size of all artworks from the dimensions given in the captions and, more intuitively, from the scales positioned at the lower left or right corner of each illustration.

CARVING AND CASTING Sculptural technique falls into two basic categories, *subtractive* and *additive*. *Carving* is a subtractive technique. The final form is a reduction of the original mass of a block of stone, a piece of wood, or another material. Wood statues were once

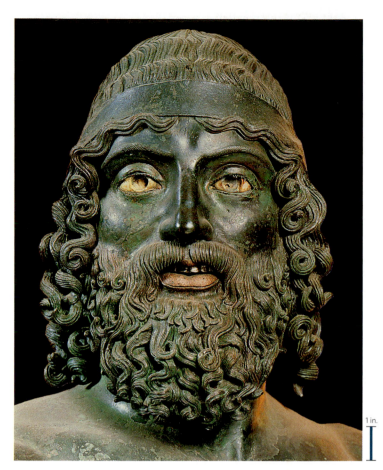

I-17 Head of a warrior, detail of a statue (FIG. 5-36) from the sea off Riace, Italy, ca. 460–450 BCE. Bronze, full statue 6' 6" high. Museo Archeologico Nazionale, Reggio Calabria.

The sculptor of this life-size statue of a bearded Greek warrior cast the head, limbs, torso, hands, and feet in separate molds, then welded the pieces together and added the eyes in a different material.

tree trunks, and stone statues began as blocks pried from mountains. The unfinished marble statue illustrated here (FIG. I-16) by renowned Italian artist MICHELANGELO BUONARROTI (1475–1564) clearly reveals the original shape of the stone block. Michelangelo thought of sculpture as a process of "liberating" the statue within the block. All sculptors of stone or wood cut away (subtract) "excess material." When they finish, they "leave behind" the statue—in this example, a twisting nude male form whose head Michelangelo never freed from the stone block.

In additive sculpture, the artist builds up the forms, usually in clay around a framework, or *armature*. Or a sculptor may fashion a *mold,* a hollow form for shaping, or *casting,* a fluid substance such as bronze or plaster. The ancient Greek sculptor who made the bronze statue of a warrior found in the sea near Riace, Italy, cast the head (FIG. I-17) as well as the limbs, torso, hands, and feet (FIG. 5-36) in separate molds and then *welded* them together (joined them by heating). Finally, the artist added features, such as the pupils of the eyes (now missing), in other materials. The warrior's teeth are silver, and his lower lip is copper.

RELIEF SCULPTURE *Statues* and *busts* (head, shoulders, and chest) that exist independent of any architectural frame or setting and that viewers can walk around are *freestanding sculptures,* or *sculptures in the round,* whether the artist produced the piece by carving (FIG. I-10) or casting (FIG. I-17). In *relief sculpture,* the subjects

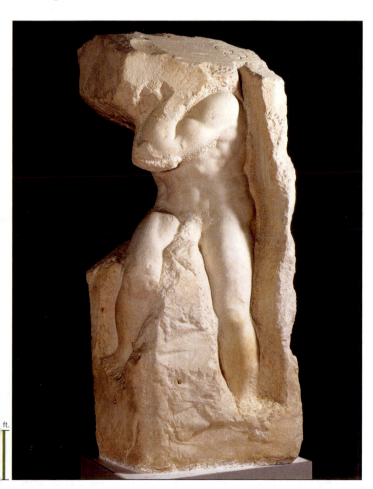

I-16 MICHELANGELO BUONARROTI, unfinished statue, 1527–1528. Marble, 8' 7½" high. Galleria dell'Accademia, Florence.

Carving a freestanding figure from stone or wood is a subtractive process. Michelangelo thought of sculpture as a process of "liberating" the statue contained within the block of marble.

project from the background but remain part of it. In *high-relief* sculpture, the images project boldly. In some cases, such as the medieval weighing-of-souls scene (FIG. I-7), the *relief* is so high that not only do the forms cast shadows on the background, but some parts are even in the round, which explains why some pieces—for example, the arms of the scales—broke off centuries ago. In *low-relief,* or *bas-relief,* sculpture, such as the portrait of Hesire (FIG. I-14), the projection is slight. Artists can produce relief sculptures, as they do sculptures in the round, either by carving or casting. The altar from Benin (FIG. I-15) is an example of bronze-casting in high relief (for the figures on the cylindrical altar) as well as in the round (for the king and his two attendants on the top).

ARCHITECTURAL DRAWINGS Buildings are groupings of enclosed spaces and enclosing masses. People experience architecture both visually and by moving through and around it, so they perceive architectural space and mass together. These spaces and masses can be represented graphically in several ways, including as plans, sections, elevations, and cutaway drawings.

A *plan,* essentially a map of a floor, shows the placement of a structure's masses and, therefore, the spaces they circumscribe and enclose. A *section,* a kind of vertical plan, depicts the placement of the masses as if someone cut through the building along a plane. Drawings showing a theoretical slice across a structure's width are *lateral sections.* Those cutting through a building's length are *longitudinal sections.* Illustrated here are the plan and lateral section of Beauvais Cathedral (FIG. **I-18**), which readers can compare with the photograph of the church's *choir* (FIG. I-3). The plan shows the choir's shape and the location of the *piers* dividing the *aisles* and supporting the *vaults* above, as well as the pattern of the crisscrossing vault *ribs.* The lateral section shows not only the interior of the choir with its vaults and tall *stained-glass* windows but also the structure of the roof and the form of the exterior *flying buttresses* holding the vaults in place.

Other types of architectural drawings appear throughout this book. An *elevation* drawing is a head-on view of an external or internal wall. A *cutaway* combines in a single drawing an exterior view with an interior view of part of a building.

This overview of the art historian's vocabulary is not exhaustive, nor have artists used only painting, drawing, sculpture, and architecture as media over the millennia. Ceramics, jewelry, textiles, photography, and computer graphics are just some of the numerous other arts. All of them involve highly specialized techniques described in distinct vocabularies. As in this introductory chapter, new terms are in *italics* when they first appear. The comprehensive Glossary at the end of the book contains definitions of all italicized terms.

Art History and Other Disciplines

By its very nature, the work of art historians intersects with the work of others in many fields of knowledge, not only in the humanities but also in the social and natural sciences. Today, art historians must go beyond the boundaries of what the public and even professional art historians of previous generations traditionally considered the specialized discipline of art history. In short, art historical research in the 21st century is typically interdisciplinary in nature. To cite one example, in an effort to unlock the secrets of a particular statue, an art historian might conduct archival research hoping to uncover new documents shedding light on who paid for the work and why, who made it and when, where it originally stood, how people of the time viewed it, and a host of other questions. Realizing, however, that the authors of the written documents often were not objective recorders of fact but observers with their own biases and agendas, the art historian may also use methodologies developed in such fields as literary criticism, philosophy, sociology, and gender studies to weigh the evidence that the documents provide.

At other times, rather than attempting to master many disciplines at once, art historians band together with other specialists in multidisciplinary inquiries. Art historians might call in chemists to date an artwork based on the composition of the materials used, or might

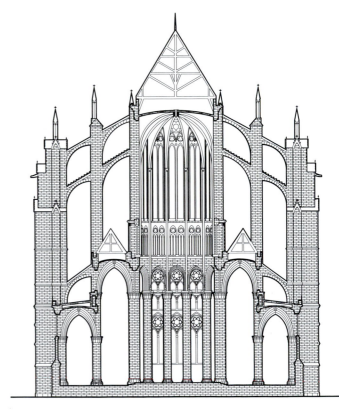

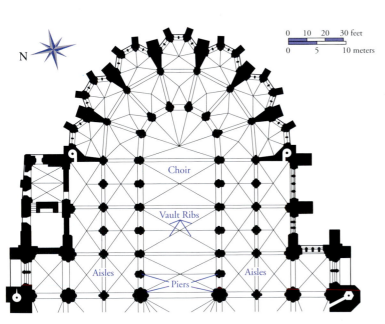

I-18 Plan (*left*) and lateral section (*right*) of Beauvais Cathedral, Beauvais, France, rebuilt after 1284.

Architectural drawings are indispensable aids for the analysis of buildings. Plans are maps of floors, recording the structure's masses. Sections are vertical "slices" across a building's width or length.

ask geologists to determine which quarry furnished the stone for a particular statue. X-ray technicians might be enlisted in an attempt to establish whether a painting is a forgery. Of course, art historians often reciprocate by contributing their expertise to the solution of problems in other disciplines. A historian, for example, might ask an art historian to determine—based on style, material, iconography, and other criteria—if any of the portraits of a certain king date after his death. Such information would help establish the ruler's continuing prestige during the reigns of his successors. Some portraits of Augustus (FIG. I-10), the founder of the Roman Empire, postdate his death by decades, even centuries, as do the portraits of several deceased U.S. presidents on coins and paper currency produced today.

DIFFERENT WAYS OF SEEING

The history of art can be a history of artists and their works, of styles and stylistic change, of materials and techniques, of images and themes and their meanings, and of contexts and cultures and patrons. The best art historians analyze artworks from many viewpoints. But no art historian (or scholar in any other field), no matter how broad-minded in approach and no matter how experienced, can be truly objective. Like the artists who made the works illustrated and discussed in this book, art historians are members of a society, participants in its culture. How can scholars (and museum visitors and travelers to foreign locales) comprehend cultures unlike their own? They can try to reconstruct the original cultural contexts of artworks, but they are limited by their distance from the thought patterns of the cultures they study and by the obstructions to understanding—the assumptions, presuppositions, and prejudices peculiar to their own culture—that their own thought patterns raise. Art historians may reconstruct a distorted picture of the past because of culture-bound blindness.

A single instance underscores how differently people of diverse cultures view the world and how various ways of seeing can result in sharp differences in how artists depict the world. Illustrated here are two contemporaneous portraits of a 19th-century Maori chieftain (FIG. I-19)—one by an Englishman, JOHN SYLVESTER (active early 19th century), and the other by the New Zealand chieftain himself, TE PEHI KUPE (d. 1829). Both reproduce the chieftain's facial *tattoo*. The European artist (FIG. I-19, *left*) included the head and shoulders and downplayed the tattooing. The tattoo pattern is one aspect of the likeness among many, no more or less important than the chieftain's European attire. Sylvester also recorded his subject's momentary glance toward the right and the play of light on his hair, fleeting aspects having nothing to do with the figure's identity.

In contrast, Te Pehi Kupe's self-portrait (FIG. I-19, *right*)—made during a trip to Liverpool, England, to obtain European arms to take back to New Zealand—is not a picture of a man situated in space and bathed in light. Rather, it is the chieftain's statement of the supreme importance of the tattoo design announcing his rank among his people. Remarkably, Te Pehi Kupe created the tattoo patterns from memory, without the aid of a mirror. The splendidly composed insignia, presented as a flat design separated from the body and even from the head, is Te Pehi Kupe's image of himself. Only by understanding the cultural context of each portrait can art historians hope to understand why either representation appears as it does.

As noted at the outset, the study of the context of artworks and buildings is one of the central concerns of art historians. *Art through the Ages* seeks to present a history of art and architecture that will help readers understand not only the subjects, styles, and techniques of paintings, sculptures, buildings, and other art forms created in all parts of the world during 30 millennia but also their cultural and historical contexts. That story now begins.

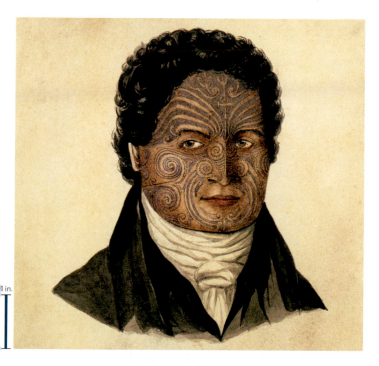
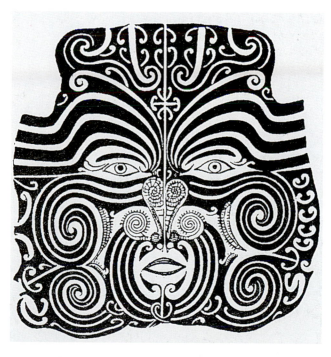

I-19 *Left:* **JOHN HENRY SYLVESTER**, *Portrait of Te Pehi Kupe*, 1826. Watercolor, $8\frac{1}{4}'' \times 6\frac{1}{4}''$. National Library of Australia, Canberra (Rex Nan Kivell Collection). *Right:* **TE PEHI KUPE**, *Self-Portrait*, 1826. From Leo Frobenius, *The Childhood of Man: A Popular Account of the Lives, Customs and Thoughts of the Primitive Races* (Philadelphia: J. B. Lippincott, 1909), 35, fig. 28.

These strikingly different portraits of the same Maori chief reveal the different ways of seeing by a European artist and an Oceanic one. Understanding the cultural context of artworks is vital to art history.

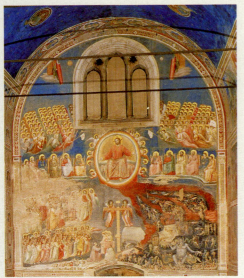

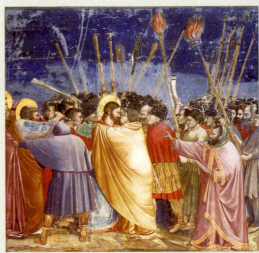

▶ **14-1b** Giotto's biblical frescoes in the Arena Chapel consist of 38 framed panels depicting the lives of the Virgin, her parents, and Jesus. The dramatic *Betrayal of Jesus* is one episode of the passion cycle.

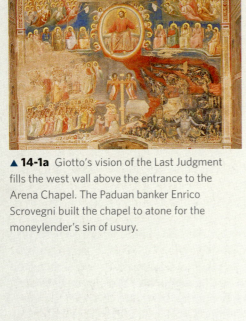

▲ **14-1a** Giotto's vision of the Last Judgment fills the west wall above the entrance to the Arena Chapel. The Paduan banker Enrico Scrovegni built the chapel to atone for the moneylender's sin of usury.

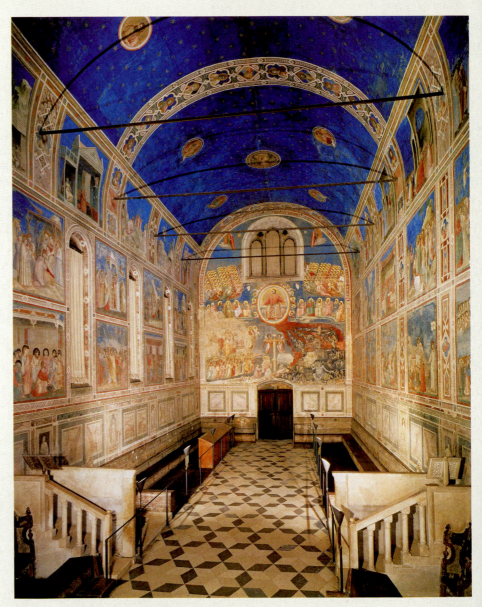

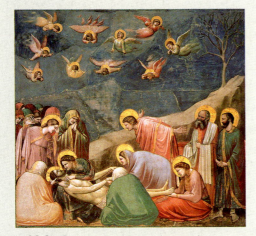

▲ **14-1c** Giotto was a pioneer in pursuing a naturalistic approach to representing figures in space. In *Lamentation,* set in a landscape, he revived the classical tradition of depicting some figures from the rear.

14-1   **GIOTTO DI BONDONE, interior of the Arena Chapel (Cappella Scrovegni; looking west), Padua, Italy, 1305–1306.**

Late Medieval Italy

LATE MEDIEVAL OR PROTO-RENAISSANCE?

Art historians debate whether the art of Italy between 1200 and 1400 is the last phase of medieval art or the beginning of the rebirth, or *Renaissance*, of Greco-Roman *naturalism*. All agree, however, that these two centuries mark a major turning point in the history of Western art and that the pivotal figure of this age was the Florentine painter GIOTTO DI BONDONE (ca. 1266–1337). Giotto's masterwork is the fresco cycle of the Arena Chapel (FIG. 14-1) in Padua, which takes its name from an adjacent ancient Roman arena (*amphitheater*). A banker, Enrico Scrovegni, built the chapel on a site adjacent to his palace and consecrated it in 1305, in the hope that the chapel would atone for the moneylender's sin of usury.

In 38 framed panels, Giotto presented, in the top level, the lives of the Virgin and her parents, Joachim and Anna; in the middle zone, the life and mission of Jesus; and, in the lowest level, the Savior's passion and resurrection. The climactic *Last Judgment* covers most of the west wall, where Scrovegni appears among the saved, kneeling as he presents his chapel to the Virgin.

The *Entry into Jerusalem*, *Betrayal of Jesus*, and *Lamentation* panels reveal the essentials of Giotto's style. In contrast to the common practice of his day, Giotto set his goal as emulating the appearance of the natural world—the approach championed by the ancient Greeks and Romans but largely abandoned in the Middle Ages in favor of representing spiritual rather than physical reality. Subtly scaled to the chapel's space, Giotto's stately and slow-moving half-life-size figures act out the religious dramas convincingly and with great restraint. The biblical actors are sculpturesque, simple, and weighty, often *foreshortened* (seen from an angle) and modeled with light and shading in the ancient manner. They convey individual emotions through their postures and gestures. Giotto's naturalism displaced the *Byzantine* style (see Chapter 9) in Italy, inaugurating an age some scholars call "early scientific." By stressing the preeminence of sight for gaining knowledge of the world, Giotto and his successors contributed to the foundation of empirical science. Praised in his own and later times for his fidelity to nature, Giotto was more than a mere imitator of it. He showed his generation a new way of seeing. With Giotto, European painters turned away from representing the spiritual world—the focus of medieval artists both in the Latin West and Byzantium—and once again made recording the visible world a central, if not the sole, aim of their art.

DUECENTO (13TH CENTURY)

When the Italian humanists of the 16th century condemned the art of the late Middle Ages in northern Europe as "Gothic" (see page 374), they did so by comparing it with the contemporaneous art of Italy (MAP 14-1), which consciously revived the *classical** art of antiquity. Italian artists and scholars regarded medieval artworks as distortions of the noble art of the Greeks and Romans. Interest in the art of classical antiquity was not entirely absent during the medieval period, however, even in France, the origin and center of the Gothic style. For example, on the west front of Reims Cathedral, the 13th-century statues of Christian *saints* and angels (FIG. 13-24) reveal the unmistakable influence of ancient Roman art on French sculptors. However, the classical revival that took root in Italy during the 13th and 14th centuries was much more pervasive and longer lasting.

Sculpture

Italian admiration for classical art surfaced early on at the court of Frederick II, King of Sicily (r. 1197–1250) and Holy Roman Emperor (r. 1220–1250). Frederick's nostalgia for Rome's past grandeur fostered a revival of classical sculpture in Sicily and southern Italy during the 13th century (the *Duecento,* the 1200s) not unlike the classical *renovatio* (renewal) that Charlemagne encouraged in Germany and France four centuries earlier (see page 322).

NICOLA PISANO The sculptor Nicola d'Apulia (Nicholas of Apulia), better known as NICOLA PISANO (active ca. 1258–1278) after his adopted city (see "Italian Artists' Names," page 413), received his early training in southern Italy during Frederick's rule. In 1250, Nicola traveled northward and eventually settled in Pisa. Then at the height of its political and economic power, the maritime city was a magnet for artists seeking lucrative commissions. Nicola specialized in carving marble reliefs and may have been the inventor of a new kind of church furniture—the monumental stone *pulpit*

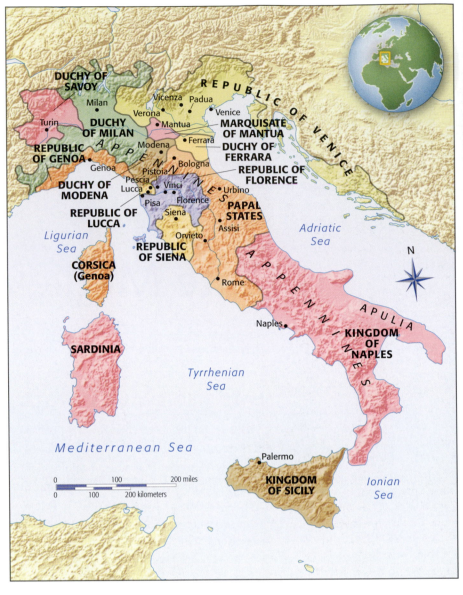

MAP 14-1 Italy around 1400.

(raised platform from which priests delivered sermons) with supports in the form of freestanding statues and wraparound narrative reliefs depicting biblical themes.

Nicola fashioned the first such pulpit (FIG. **14-2**) in 1260 for Pisa's century-old baptistery (FIG. 12-29, *left*). Some elements of the pulpit's design carried on medieval traditions—for example, the *trefoil* (triple-curved) *arches* and the lions supporting some of the *columns*—but Nicola also incorporated classical elements. The large *capitals* with two rows of thick overlapping leaves crowning the columns are a Gothic variation of the *Corinthian capital*

---

* In *Art through the Ages*, the adjective "Classical," with uppercase *C,* refers specifically to the Classical period of ancient Greece, 480–323 BCE. Lowercase "classical" refers to Greco-Roman antiquity in general—that is, the period treated in Chapters 5, 6, and 7.

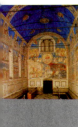

LATE MEDIEVAL ITALY

1200–1300
Duecento

- Bonaventura Berlinghieri and Cimabue are the leading painters working in the Italo-Byzantine style, or *maniera greca*
- Nicola and Giovanni Pisano, father and son, represent two contrasting sculptural styles, the classical and the Gothic respectively
- Pietro Cavallini's fresco cycles in Rome and those in San Francesco at Assisi foreshadow the revolutionary art of Giotto

1300–1400
Trecento

- In Florence, Giotto, considered the first Renaissance artist, pioneers a naturalistic approach to painting
- In Siena, Duccio softens the maniera greca and humanizes religious subject matter
- Secular themes emerge as important subjects in civic commissions, as in the frescoes of Siena's Palazzo Pubblico
- Florence, Siena, and Orvieto build new cathedrals that are stylistically closer to Early Christian basilicas than to French Gothic cathedrals

Italian Artists' Names

In contemporary societies, people have become accustomed to a standardized method of identifying individuals, in part because of the proliferation of official documents such as driver's licenses, passports, and student identification cards. Modern names consist of given names (names selected by the parents) and family names, although the order of the two (or more) names varies from country to country. In China, for example, the family name precedes the given name.

This kind of regularity in names was not, however, the norm in premodern Italy. Many individuals were known by their place of birth or adopted hometown. Nicola Pisano (FIGS. 14-2 and 14-3) was "Nicholas the Pisan," Giulio Romano was "Julius the Roman," and Domenico Veneziano was "Dominic the Venetian." Leonardo da Vinci ("Leonard from Vinci") hailed from the small town of Vinci, near Florence (MAP 14-1). Art historians therefore refer to these artists by their given names, not the names of their towns. (The title of Dan Brown's best-selling novel should have been *The Leonardo Code,* not *The Da Vinci Code.*)

Nicknames were also common. Giorgione was "Big George." People usually referred to Tommaso di Cristoforo Fini as Masolino ("Little Thomas") to distinguish him from his more famous pupil Masaccio ("Brutish Thomas"). Guido di Pietro was called Fra Angelico ("Angelic Friar"). Cenni di Pepo is remembered as Cimabue (FIG. 14-6), which means "bull's head."

The format of names was also impermanent and could be changed at will. This flexibility has resulted in significant challenges for historians, who often must deal with archival documents and other records referring to the same artist by different names.

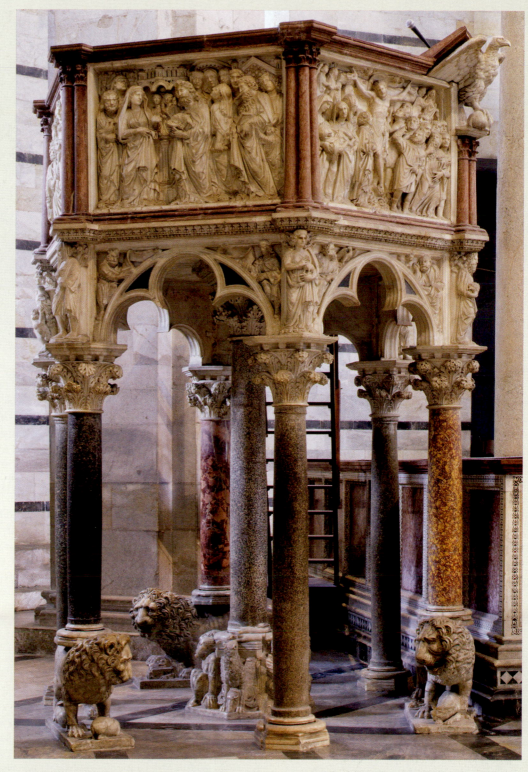

14-2 NICOLA PISANO, **pulpit of the baptistery, Pisa, Italy, 1259–1260. Marble, 15' high.**

The Pisa baptistery pulpit by Nicola Pisano (Nicholas of Pisa) retains many medieval features—for example, trefoil arches—but many of the figures derive from ancient Roman relief sculptures.

(FIG. 5-73). The arches are round, as in Roman architecture, rather than pointed (*ogival*), as in Gothic buildings. Also, each of the large rectangular relief panels resembles the sculptured front of a Roman *sarcophagus* (coffin; for example, FIG. 7-68).

The densely packed large-scale figures of the individual panels also seem to derive from the compositions found on Roman sarcophagi. One of the six panels of the baptistery pulpit depicts scenes from the infancy cycle of Christ (see "The Life of Jesus in Art,"

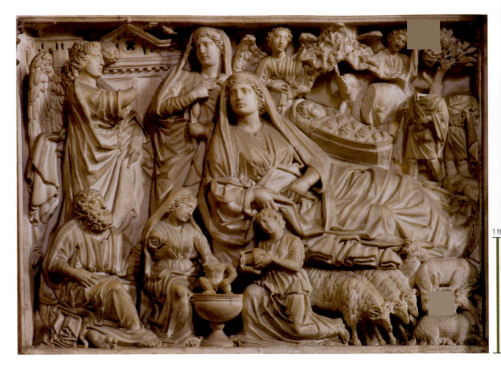

14-3 Nicola Pisano, *Annunciation, Nativity, and Adoration of the Shepherds,* relief panel on the pulpit of the baptistery, Pisa, Italy, 1259–1260. Marble, 2' 10" × 3' 9".

Classical sculptures inspired the faces, beards, coiffures, and draperies, as well as the bulk and weight of Nicola's figures. The *Nativity* Madonna resembles lid figures on Roman sarcophagi.

pages 240–241), including *Annunciation* (FIG. **14-3**, top left), *Nativity* (center and lower half), and *Adoration of the Shepherds* (top right). Mary appears twice, and her size varies. The focus of the composition is the reclining Virgin of the *Nativity* episode, whose posture and drapery are reminiscent of those of the lid figures on Etruscan (FIG. 6-6) and Roman (FIG. 7-59) sarcophagi. The face types, beards, and coiffures, as well as the bulk and weight of Nicola's figures, also reveal the influence of classical relief sculpture. Art historians have even been able to pinpoint the models of some of the pulpit figures, including the reclining Mary, in Roman sculptures in Pisa.

GIOVANNI PISANO Nicola's son, GIOVANNI PISANO (ca. 1250–1320), likewise became a sought-after sculptor of church pulpits. His career extended into the early 14th century, when he carved (singlehandedly, according to an inscription) the marble pulpit in Pisa's cathedral (FIG. 12-29, center). The pulpit is the largest known example of the type. It boasts nine curved narrative panels, including, in addition to the subjects Giovanni's father represented, scenes from the life of John the Baptist. The panel of the *Nativity* and related scenes (FIG. **14-4**) offers a striking contrast to Nicola's quiet, dignified presentation of the religious narrative. The younger sculptor arranged the figures loosely and dynamically. They twist and bend in excited animation, and the deep spaces between them suggest their motion. In *Annunciation* (top left), the Virgin shrinks from the angel's sudden appearance in a posture of alarm touched with humility. The same spasm of apprehension contracts her supple body as she reclines in *Nativity* (left center). The drama's principals share in a peculiar nervous agitation, as if spiritual passion suddenly moves all of them. Only the shepherds and the sheep (right) do not yet share in the miraculous event. The swiftly turning, slender and sinuous figures and the general emotionalism

of the scene are features not found in Nicola Pisano's interpretation. The father worked in the classical tradition, the son in a style derived from French Gothic. These styles were two of the three most important ingredients in the formation of the distinctive and original art of 14th-century Italy.

Painting and Architecture

The third major stylistic element in late medieval Italian art was the Byzantine tradition (see Chapter 9). Throughout the Middle Ages, the Byzantine style dominated Italian painting, but its influence was especially strong after the fall of Constantinople in 1204, which precipitated a migration of Byzantine artists to Italy.

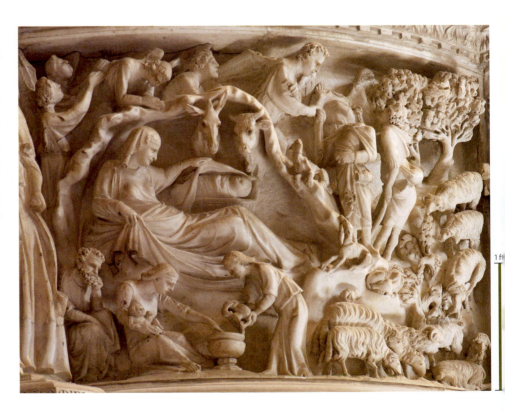

14-4 GIOVANNI PISANO, *Annunciation, Nativity, and Adoration of the Shepherds,* relief panel on the pulpit of the cathedral, Pisa, Italy, 1302–1310. Marble, 2' 10$\frac{3}{8}$" × 3' 7".

The French Gothic style had a greater influence on Giovanni Pisano, Nicola's son. Giovanni arranged his figures loosely and dynamically. They display a nervous agitation, as if moved by spiritual passion.

RELIGION AND MYTHOLOGY
The Great Schism, Mendicant Orders, and Confraternities

In 1305, the College of Cardinals (the collective body of all cardinals) elected a French pope, Clement V (r. 1305–1314), who settled in Avignon. Subsequent French popes remained in Avignon, despite their announced intentions to return to Rome. Understandably, the Italians, who saw Rome as the rightful capital of the universal Church, resented the Avignon papacy. The conflict between the French and the Italians resulted in the election in 1378 of two popes—Clement VII, who resided in Avignon (and who does not appear in the Catholic Church's official list of popes), and Urban VI (r. 1378–1389), who remained in Rome. Thus began what became known as the Great Schism. After 40 years, Holy Roman Emperor Sigismund (r. 1410–1437) convened a council that resolved this crisis by electing a new Roman pope, Martin V (r. 1417–1431), who was acceptable to all.

The pope's absence from Italy during much of the 14th century contributed to an increase in prominence of *monastic orders*. The Augustinians, Carmelites, and Servites became very active, ensuring a constant religious presence in the daily life of Italians, but the largest and most influential monastic orders were the *mendicants* (begging friars)—the Franciscans, founded by Francis of Assisi (ca. 1181–1226; FIGS. 14-5 and 14-5A), and the Dominicans, founded by the Spaniard Dominic de Guzman (ca. 1170–1221). As did other monks, the mendicant friars renounced all worldly goods and committed themselves to spreading God's word, performing good deeds, and ministering to the sick and dying. But unlike the many monks who resided in rural and often isolated monasteries, the mendicants lived in the heart of cities and preached to large urban crowds. The Dominicans, in particular, contributed significantly to establishing urban educational institutions. The Franciscans and Dominicans became very popular in Italy because of their concern for the poor and the personal relationship with God that they encouraged common people to cultivate.

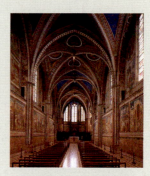

🔗 **14-5A** San Francesco, Assisi, 1228–1253.

Although both mendicant orders worked for the glory of God, a degree of rivalry nevertheless existed between the two. For example, in Florence they established their churches on opposite sides of the city—Santa Croce (FIG. I-4), the Franciscan church, on the eastern side, and the Dominicans' Santa Maria Novella (FIG. 14-5B) on the western (MAP 21-1).

Confraternities, organizations consisting of laypersons who dedicated themselves to strict religious observance, also grew in popularity during the 14th and 15th centuries. The mission of confraternities included tending the sick, burying the dead, singing hymns, and performing other good works. The confraternities as well as the mendicant orders continued to play an important role in Italian religious life through the 16th century. The numerous artworks and monastic churches they commissioned have ensured their enduring legacy.

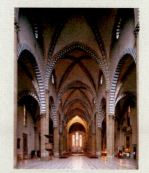

🔗 **14-5B** Santa Maria Novella, Florence, begun ca. 1246.

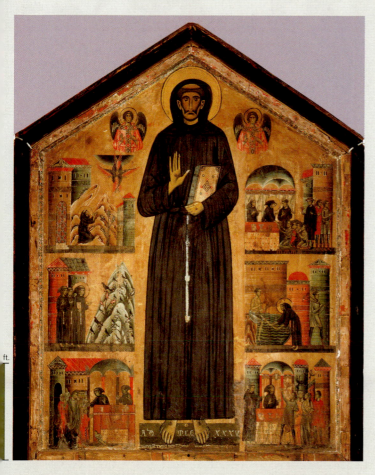

14-5 BONAVENTURA BERLINGHIERI, *Saint Francis Altarpiece*, San Francesco, Pescia, Italy, 1235. Tempera on wood, 5' × 3'.

Berlinghieri painted this altarpiece in the Italo-Byzantine style, or *maniera greca*, for the mendicant (begging) order of Franciscans. It is the earliest securely dated portrayal of Saint Francis of Assisi.

BONAVENTURA BERLINGHIERI One of the leading painters working in the Italo-Byzantine style, or *maniera greca* (Greek style), was BONAVENTURA BERLINGHIERI (active ca. 1235–1244) of Lucca. His most famous work is the *Saint Francis Altarpiece* (FIG. 14-5) in the church of San Francesco (Saint Francis) in Pescia. Painted in 1235 using *tempera* on wood panel (see "Tempera and Oil Painting," page 559), the *altarpiece* honors Saint Francis of Assisi, whose most important shrine (FIG. 14-5A) was at Assisi itself. The Pescia altarpiece highlights the increasingly prominent role of religious orders in late medieval Italy (see "The Great Schism, Mendicant Orders, and Confraternities," above). Saint Francis's Franciscan order worked diligently to impress on the public the saint's valuable example and to demonstrate the order's commitment to teaching and to alleviating suffering. Berlinghieri's altarpiece, painted only nine years after Francis's death, is the earliest securely dated representation of the saint.

Berlinghieri depicted Francis wearing the costume later adopted by all Franciscan monks: a coarse clerical robe tied at the waist with a rope. The saint displays the *stigmata*—marks resembling Christ's wounds—that miraculously appeared on his hands and feet. Flanking Francis are two angels, whose frontal poses, prominent *halos*, and lack of modeling reveal the Byzantine roots of Berlinghieri's style. So, too, does the use of *gold leaf* (gold beaten into tissue-paper-thin sheets, then applied to surfaces), which emphasizes the image's flatness and otherworldly, spiritual nature. Appropriately, Berlinghieri's panel focuses on the aspects of the saint's life that the Franciscans wanted to promote, thereby making visible (and thus more credible) the legendary life of this holy man. Saint Francis believed that he could get closer to God by rejecting worldly goods, and to achieve this he stripped himself bare in a public square and committed himself to a strict life of fasting, prayer, and meditation. His followers considered the appearance of stigmata on Francis's hands and feet (clearly visible in the saint's frontal image, which resembles a Byzantine *icon*; compare FIG. 9-16) as God's blessing, and viewed Francis as a second Christ. Fittingly, four of the six narrative scenes along the sides of the panel depict miraculous healings, connecting Saint Francis even more emphatically to Christ. The narrative scenes provide an active contrast to the stiff formality of the large central image of Francis. At the upper left, taking pride of place at the saint's right, Francis receives the stigmata. Directly below, the saint preaches to the birds, a subject that also figures prominently in the fresco program (FIG. **14-5C**) of San Francesco at Assisi, the work of a painter art historians call the SAINT FRANCIS MASTER. These and the scenes depicting Francis's

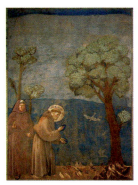

⊿14-5C ST. FRANCIS MASTER, *Francis Preaching to the Birds*, ca. 1290–1300.

miracle cures strongly suggest that Berlinghieri's source was one or more Byzantine *illuminated manuscripts* (compare FIGS. 9-17B, 9-18, and 9-18A) with biblical narrative scenes.

CIMABUE One of the first artists to break from the Italo-Byzantine style that dominated 13th-century Italian painting was Cenni di Pepo, better known as CIMABUE (ca. 1240–1302). Cimabue challenged some of the major conventions of late medieval art in pursuit of a closer approximation of the appearance of the natural world—the core of the classical naturalistic tradition. He painted *Madonna Enthroned with Angels and Prophets* (FIG. **14-6**) for Santa Trinità (Holy Trinity) in Florence, the Benedictine church near the Arno River built between 1258 and 1280. The composition and the gold background reveal the painter's reliance on Byzantine models (compare FIG. 9-19). Cimabue also used the gold embellishments common to Byzantine art for the folds of the Madonna's robe, but they are no longer merely decorative patterns. In his panel, they enhance the three-dimensionality of the drapery. Furthermore, Cimabue constructed a deeper space for the Madonna and the surrounding figures to inhabit than was common in Byzantine art. The Virgin's throne, for example, is a massive structure that Cimabue convincingly depicted as receding into space. The overlapping bodies of the angels on each side of the throne and the half-length prophets who look outward or upward from beneath it reinforce the sense of depth.

PIETRO CAVALLINI The authors of the most important Renaissance commentaries on Italian art of the 13th and 14th centuries

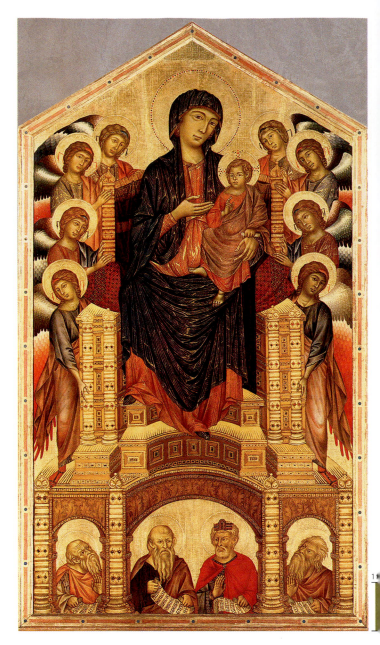

14-6 CIMABUE, *Madonna Enthroned with Angels and Prophets*, from Santa Trinità, Florence, ca. 1280–1290. Tempera and gold leaf on wood, 12' 7" × 7' 4". Galleria degli Uffizi, Florence.

Cimabue was one of the first artists to break away from the maniera greca. Although he relied on Byzantine models, Cimabue depicted the Madonna's massive throne as receding into space.

were all Florentines, and civic pride doubtless played a role in attributing the reorientation of the art of painting to Florentine artists, especially Giotto (FIG. 14-1). Giorgio Vasari (1511–1574), the "father of art history" (see "Vasari's *Lives*," page 636), lauded Giotto as the first to make a definitive break from the maniera greca of late medieval painting and to return to the naturalism of the ancients. But the stylistic revolution that Giotto represents was not solely his creation. Other artists paved the way for the Florentine master in the mural program (FIGS. 14-5A and 14-5C) of San Francesco at Assisi and in the churches of Rome.

The leading Roman painter at the end of the 13th century was Pietro dei Cerroni, known as PIETRO CAVALLINI (ca. 1240–ca. 1340), or "Little Horse" (see "Italian Artists' Names," page 413),

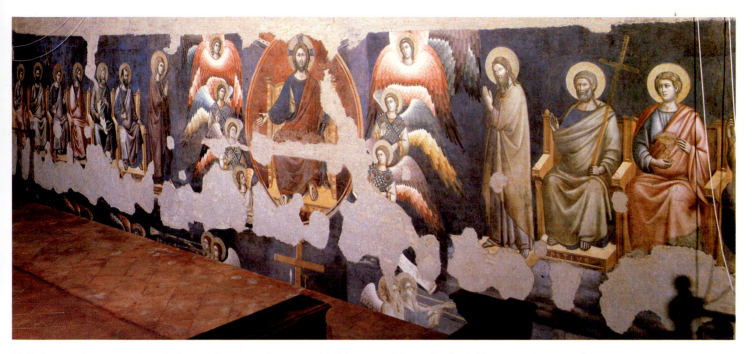

14-7 PIETRO CAVALLINI, *Last Judgment,* fresco on the west wall of the nave of Santa Cecilia in Trastevere, Rome, Italy, ca. 1290–1295.

A pioneer in the representation of fully modeled figures seen in perspective with light illuminating their faces and garments, Pietro Cavallini of Rome may have influenced Giotto di Bondone (FIG. 14-1).

who his son said lived to age 100. Cavallini enjoyed the patronage of Pope Nicholas III (r. 1277–1280), who commissioned him to restore the Early Christian frescoes in San Paolo fuori le mura (Saint Paul's Outside the Walls) in Rome. Cavallini's careful study and emulation of those Late Antique paintings must have profoundly influenced his later work, which unfortunately survives only in fragments.

Around 1290, Cavallini received two important commissions for churches in Trastevere, on the western bank of the Tiber near the Vatican. He produced mosaics depicting the life of the Virgin for Santa Maria in Trastevere, and painted a fresco cycle of Old and New Testament scenes in Santa Cecilia in Trastevere, of which only part of his *Last Judgment* (FIG. 14-7) survives, but what remains confirms his stature as an innovative artist of the highest order. Christ appears at the center with the Virgin Mary to his right, John the Baptist to his left, and six enthroned *apostles* to each side (see "Early Christian Saints," pages 236–237). Below the Savior is an altar with the instruments of his martyrdom (cross, nails, Longinus's spear, and so on). At each side of the altar, angels (at the left, the Savior's right side) present to Christ those about to be saved, while the agents of the Devil (on his left) claim the damned. The theme is familiar from Romanesque portal sculpture (FIG. 12-15), but here it appears inside the church on the entrance (west) wall as the culmination of the biblical cycle painted on the nave walls. Cavallini's apostles sit on deep thrones seen in *perspective* (the illusionistic depiction on a two-dimensional surface of three-dimensional objects in space). Both the disciples and their thrones face inward toward Christ, uniting both sides of the composition with the central figure. The apostles' garments have deep folds that catch the light. Light also illuminates the figures' faces. Cavallini used light effectively to create volume and mass, a radical departure from the maniera greca, but the light does not come from a uniform source, and the apostles appear against a neutral dark background.

Cavallini has not received the recognition he deserves because his extant works are few and poorly preserved and because of the enduring influence of Vasari's artist biographies, but he was a pioneering figure in the creation of the Renaissance style in Italy.

TRECENTO (14TH CENTURY)

In the 14th century (the *Trecento,* or 1300s), Italy consisted of numerous independent *city-states,* each corresponding to a geographic region centered on a major city (MAP 14-1). Most of the city-states, such as Venice, Florence, Lucca, and Siena, were republics—constitutional oligarchies governed by executive bodies, advisory councils, and special commissions. Other powerful 14th-century states included the Papal States, the Kingdom of Naples, and the duchies of Milan, Modena, Ferrara, and Savoy. As their names indicate, these states were politically distinct from the republics, but all the states shared in the prosperity of the period. The sources of wealth varied from state to state. Italy's port cities expanded maritime trade, whereas the economies of other cities depended on banking or the manufacture of arms or textiles.

The outbreak of the Black Death (bubonic plague) in the late 1340s threatened this prosperity, however. Originating in China, the Black Death swept across Europe. The most devastating natural disaster in European history, the Black Death eliminated between 25 and 50 percent of the Continent's population in about five years. The plague devastated Italy's inhabitants. In large Italian cities, where people lived in relatively close proximity, the death tolls climbed as high as 50 to 60 percent of the population. The Black Death also had a significant effect on art. It stimulated religious bequests and encouraged the commissioning of devotional images. The focus on sickness and death also led to a burgeoning in hospital construction.

Another significant development in 14th-century Italy was the blossoming of a vernacular literature (written in the commonly spoken language instead of Latin), which dramatically affected Italy's intellectual and cultural life. Latin remained the official language of Church liturgy and state documents. However, the creation of an Italian vernacular literature (based on the Tuscan dialect common in Florence) expanded the audience for philosophical and intellectual concepts because of its greater accessibility. Dante Alighieri (1265–1321, author of *The Divine Comedy*), the poet and scholar Francesco Petrarch (1304–1374), and Giovanni Boccaccio (1313–1375, author of *Decameron*) were most responsible for establishing this vernacular literature.

RENAISSANCE HUMANISM The development of easily accessible literature was one important sign that the essentially religious view that had dominated Europe during the Middle Ages was about to change dramatically in what historians call the *Renaissance*. Although religion continued to occupy a primary position in the lives of Europeans, a growing concern with the natural world, the individual, and humanity's worldly existence characterized the Renaissance period—the 14th through 16th centuries. The word *renaissance* in French and English (*rinascità* in Italian) refers to a "rebirth" of art and culture. A revived interest in classical cultures—indeed, the veneration of classical antiquity as a model—was central to this rebirth. The notion that the Renaissance represented the restoration of the glorious past of Greece and Rome gave rise to the concept of the "Middle Ages" as the era falling between antiquity and the Renaissance. The transition from the medieval to the Renaissance, though dramatic, did not come about abruptly, however. In fact, much that is medieval persisted in the Renaissance and in later periods.

Fundamental to the development of the Italian Renaissance was *humanism,* which emerged during the 14th century and became a central component of Italian art and culture in the 15th and 16th centuries. Humanism was more a code of civil conduct, a theory of education, and a scholarly discipline than a philosophical system. The chief concerns of Italian humanists, as their name suggests, were human values and interests as distinct from—but not opposed to—religion's otherworldly values. Humanists pointed to classical cultures as particularly praiseworthy. This enthusiasm for antiquity involved study of Latin literature, especially the elegant Latin of Cicero (106–43 BCE) and the Augustan age (27 BCE–14 CE), and a conscious emulation of what proponents believed were the Roman civic virtues. These included self-sacrificing service to the state, participation in government, defense of state institutions (especially the administration of justice), and stoic indifference to personal misfortune in the performance of duty. With the help of a new interest in and knowledge of Greek, the humanists of the late 14th and 15th centuries recovered a large part of Greek as well as Roman literature and philosophy that had been lost, left unnoticed, or cast aside in the Middle Ages. Indeed, classical cultures provided humanists with a model for living in this world, a model primarily of human focus derived not from an authoritative and traditional religious dogma but from reason.

Ideally, humanists sought no material reward for services rendered. The sole reward for heroes of civic virtue was fame, just as the reward for leaders of the holy life was sainthood. For the educated, the lives of heroes and heroines of the past became models of conduct as important as the lives of the saints. Petrarch wrote a book on illustrious men, and his colleague Boccaccio complemented it with 106 biographies of famous women—from Eve to Joanna, queen of Naples (r. 1343–1382). Both Petrarch and Boccaccio were renowned in their own day as poets, scholars, and men of letters—their achievements equivalent in honor to those of the heroes of civic virtue. In 1341 in Rome, Petrarch received the laurel wreath crown, the ancient symbol of victory and merit (compare FIGS. I-10, 7-69, and 7-79, *left*). The humanist cult of fame emphasized the importance of creative individuals and their role in contributing to the renown of the city-state and of all Italy.

Giotto

Celebrated in his own day as the first Renaissance painter, Giotto di Bondone (FIG. 14-1) is a towering figure in the history of art. Scholars still debate the sources of the Florentine painter's style, but one formative influence must have been Cimabue, whom Vasari identified as Giotto's teacher, while noting that the pupil eclipsed his master by abandoning the "crude *maniera greca*" (see "Vasari's *Lives*," page 636). The 13th-century *murals* of San Francesco at Assisi (FIGS. 14-5A and 14-5C) and those of Pietro Cavallini in Rome (FIG. 14-7) may also have influenced Giotto—although some scholars believe that the young Giotto himself was one of the leading painters of the Assisi church. French Gothic sculpture (which Giotto may have seen but which was certainly familiar to him from the work of Giovanni Pisano, who had spent time in Paris) and ancient Roman art probably also contributed to Giotto's artistic education. Yet no mere synthesis of these varied influences could have produced the significant shift in artistic approach that has led some scholars to describe Giotto as the father of Western pictorial art.

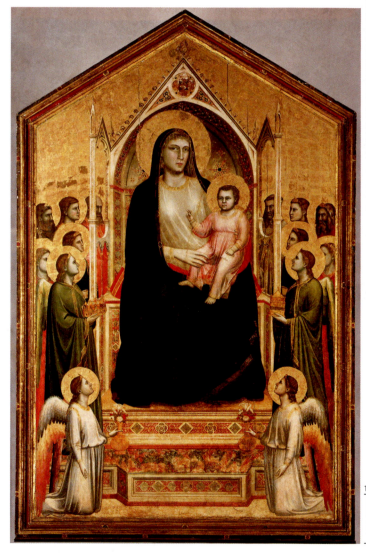

14-8 Giotto di Bondone, *Madonna Enthroned (Ognissanti Madonna)*, from the Chiesa di Ognissanti (All Saints' Church), Florence, ca. 1310. Tempera and gold leaf on wood, 10' 8" × 6' 8". Galleria degli Uffizi, Florence.

Giotto displaced the Byzantine style in Italian painting and revived classical naturalism. His figures have substance, dimensionality, and bulk, and create the illusion that they could throw shadows.

MATERIALS AND TECHNIQUES
Fresco Painting

Fresco painting has a long history, particularly in the Mediterranean region, where the Minoans (FIGS. 4-7 to 4-10) used it as early as the 17th century BCE. *Fresco* (Italian for "fresh") is a mural-painting technique involving the application of permanent limeproof pigments, diluted in water, on freshly laid lime plaster. Because the surface of the wall absorbs the pigments as the plaster dries, fresco is one of the most durable painting techniques. The stable condition of the ancient Minoan frescoes, as well as those found at Pompeii and other Roman sites (FIGS. 7-17 to 7-26), in San Francesco (FIGS. 14-5A and 14-5C) at Assisi, and in the Arena Chapel (FIGS. 14-1 and 14-9, 14-9A, and 14-9B) at Padua, testify to the longevity of this painting method. The colors have remained vivid (although dirt and soot have necessitated cleaning—most famously in the Vatican's Sistine Chapel; FIG. 22-18B) because of the chemically inert pigments the artists used.

This *buon fresco* ("true" fresco) process is time-consuming and demanding and requires several layers of plaster. Although buon fresco methods vary, generally the artist (or, more precisely, an apprentice in the master's workshop) prepares the wall with a rough layer of lime plaster called the *arriccio* (brown coat). The artist then transfers the composition to the wall, usually by drawing directly on the arriccio with a burnt-orange pigment called *sinopia* (most popular during the 14th century), or by transferring a *cartoon* (a full-size preparatory drawing). Cartoons increased in usage in the 15th and 16th centuries, largely replacing sinopia underdrawings. Finally, the painter lays the *intonaco* (painting coat) smoothly over the drawing in sections (called *giornate*—Italian for "days") only as large as the artist expects to complete in that session. (It is easy to distinguish the various giornate in Giotto's *Lamentation* [FIG. 14-9].) The buon fresco painter must apply the colors quickly, because once the plaster is dry, it will no longer absorb the pigment. Any unpainted areas of the intonaco after a session must be cut away so that fresh plaster can be applied for the next giornata.

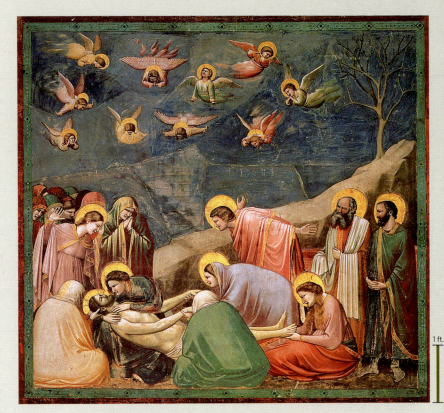

14-9 GIOTTO DI BONDONE, *Lamentation*, Arena Chapel (Cappella Scrovegni; FIG. 14-1), Padua, Italy, ca. 1305. Fresco, 6' 6¾" × 6' 6¾".

Giotto painted *Lamentation* in several sections, each corresponding to one painting session, or giornata. Artists employing the buon fresco technique must complete each section before the plaster dries.

In addition to the buon fresco technique, artists used *fresco secco* (dry fresco). Fresco secco involves painting on dried lime plaster, the method the ancient Egyptians employed (FIGS. 3-28 and 3-29). Although the finished product visually approximates buon fresco, the plaster wall does not absorb the pigments, which simply adhere to the surface, so fresco secco is not as permanent as buon fresco.

In areas of high humidity, such as Venice, fresco was less appropriate because moisture is an obstacle to the drying process. Over the centuries, fresco became less popular, although it did experience a revival in the 1930s with the Mexican muralists (FIGS. 29-74 and 29-75).

MADONNA ENTHRONED On nearly the same great scale as Cimabue's enthroned Madonna (FIG. 14-6) is Giotto's panel (FIG. **14-8**) depicting the same subject, painted for the high altar of Florence's Church of the Ognissanti (All Saints). Although still portrayed against the traditional gold background, Giotto's Madonna sits on her Gothic throne with the unshakable stability of an ancient marble goddess (compare FIG. 7-30). Giotto replaced Cimabue's slender Virgin, fragile beneath the thin ripplings of her drapery, with a weighty, queenly mother. In Giotto's painting, the Madonna's body is not lost—indeed, it is asserted. Giotto even showed Mary's breasts pressing through the thin fabric of her white undergarment. Gold highlights have disappeared from her heavy robe. Giotto aimed instead to construct a figure with substance, dimensionality, and bulk—qualities suppressed in favor of a spiritual immateriality in Byzantine and Italo-Byzantine art. The different approaches of teacher and pupil can also be seen in the angels flanking the Madon-

na's throne. Cimabue stacked his angels to fill the full height of the panel. Giotto's angels stand on a common level, leaving a large blank area above the heads of the background figures. Works painted in the new style portray statuesque figures projecting into the light and creating the illusion that they could throw shadows. Giotto's *Madonna Enthroned* marks the end of medieval painting in Italy and the beginning of a new naturalistic approach to art.

ARENA CHAPEL Projecting on a flat surface the illusion of solid bodies moving through space presents a double challenge. Constructing the illusion of a weighty, three-dimensional body also requires constructing the illusion of a space sufficiently ample to contain that body. In his *fresco* cycles (see "Fresco Painting," above), Giotto constantly strove to reconcile these two aspects of *illusionistic* painting. His murals in Enrico Scrovegni's Arena Chapel (FIGS. 14-1 and **14-9**) at Padua show his art at its finest. (Some

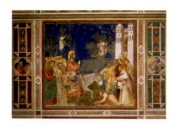

▲ **14-9A** Giotto, *Entry into Jerusalem*, ca. 1305.

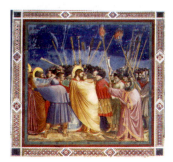

▲ **14-9B** Giotto, *Betrayal of Jesus*, ca. 1305.

scholars have suggested that Giotto may also have been the chapel's architect, because its design so perfectly suits its interior decoration. The rectangular hall has only six windows, all in the south wall, which provide ample illumination for the frescoes that fill the almost unbroken surfaces of the other walls.) In 38 framed scenes (FIGS. 14-9, **14-9A,** and **14-9B**), Giotto presented one of the most impressive and complete Christian pictorial cycles ever rendered. The narrative unfolds on the north and south walls in three zones, reading from top to bottom. Below, imitation marble veneer—reminiscent of ancient Roman *revetment* (FIG. 7-51), which Giotto may have seen—alternates with personified Virtues and Vices painted in *grisaille* (monochrome grays, often used for modeling in paintings) to resemble sculpture. On the west wall above the chapel's entrance is Giotto's dramatic *Last Judgment,* the culminating scene also of Cavallini's late-13th-century fresco cycle (FIG. 14-7) in Santa Cecilia in Trastevere in Rome. In fact, Giotto's enthroned apostles are strikingly similar to Cavallini's. The chapel's vaulted ceiling is blue, an azure sky dotted with golden stars symbolic of Heaven. Medallions bearing images of Christ, Mary, and various prophets also appear on the vault. Giotto painted the same blue in the backgrounds of the narrative panels on the walls below. The color thereby functions as a unifying agent for the entire decorative scheme.

LAMENTATION The panel in the lowest zone of the north wall, *Lamentation* (FIG. 14-9), illustrates particularly well the revolutionary nature of Giotto's style. In the presence of boldly foreshortened angels, seen head-on with their bodies receding into the background and darting about in hysterical grief, a congregation mourns over the dead Savior just before his entombment. Mary cradles her son's body. Mary Magdalene looks solemnly at the wounds in Christ's feet. Saint John the Evangelist throws his arms back dramatically. Giotto arranged a shallow stage for the figures, bounded by a thick diagonal rock incline defining a horizontal ledge in the foreground. Though narrow, the ledge provides firm visual support for the figures. The rocky setting recalls the landscape of a 12th-century Byzantine mural (FIG. 9-30) at Nerezi in Macedonia. Here, the steep slope leads the viewer's eye toward the picture's dramatic focal point at the lower left.

The postures and gestures of Giotto's figures convey a broad spectrum of grief. They range from Mary's almost fierce despair to the passionate outbursts of Mary Magdalene and John to the philosophical resignation of the two disciples at the right and the mute sorrow of the two hooded mourners in the foreground. In *Lamentation,* a single event provokes a host of individual responses in figures that are convincing presences both physically and psychologically. Painters before Giotto rarely attempted, let alone achieved, this combination of naturalistic representation, compositional complexity, and emotional resonance.

The formal design of the *Lamentation* fresco—the way Giotto grouped the figures within the constructed space—is worth close study. Each group has its own definition, and each contributes to the rhythmic order of the composition. The strong diagonal of the rocky ledge, with its single dead tree (the tree of knowledge of good and evil, which withered after Adam and Eve's original sin), concentrates the viewer's attention on the heads of Christ and his mother, which Giotto positioned dynamically off center. The massive bulk of the seated mourner in the painting's left corner arrests and contains all movement beyond Mary and her dead son. The seated mourner to the right establishes a relation with the center figures, who, by gazes and gestures, draw the viewer's attention back to Christ's head. Figures seen from the back, which are frequent in Giotto's compositions (compare FIG. 14-9B), represent an innovation in the movement away from the Italo-Byzantine style. These figures emphasize the foreground, aiding the visual placement of the intermediate figures farther back in space. This device, the very contradiction of Byzantine frontality, in effect puts viewers behind the "observer figures," who, facing the action as spectators, reinforce the sense of stagecraft as a model for painting. Also markedly different from the maniera greca is Giotto's habit of painting incomplete figures cut off by the composition's frame, a feature also of his Ognissanti Madonna (FIG. 14-8).

Giotto's new devices for depicting spatial depth and body mass could not, of course, have been possible without his management of light and shade. He shaded his figures to indicate both the direction of the light illuminating their bodies and the shadows (the diminished light), thereby giving the figures volume. In *Lamentation,* light falls upon the upper surfaces of the figures (especially the two central bending figures) and passes down to dark in their garments, separating the volumes one from the other and pushing one to the fore, the other to the rear. The graded continuum of light and shade, directed by an even, neutral light from a single steady source—not shown in the picture—was the first step toward the development of *chiaroscuro* (the use of contrasts of dark and light to produce modeling) in later Renaissance painting (see page 627).

The stagelike settings (FIGS. 14-9A and 14-9B) made possible by Giotto's innovations in perspective and lighting suited perfectly the dramatic narrative that the Franciscans emphasized then as a principal method for educating the faithful in their religion. In this new age of humanism, the old stylized presentations of the holy mysteries had evolved into *mystery plays.* Actors extended the drama of the Mass into one- and two-act tableaus and scenes and then into simple narratives offered at church portals and in city squares. (Eventually, confraternities also presented more elaborate religious dramas called *sacre rappresentazioni*—holy representations.) The great increase in popular sermons to huge city audiences prompted a public taste for narrative, recited as dramatically as possible. The arts of illusionistic painting, of drama, and of sermon rhetoric with all their theatrical flourishes developed simultaneously and were mutually influential. Giotto's art masterfully synthesized dramatic narrative, holy lesson, and truth to human experience in a visual idiom of his own invention, accessible to all. Not surprisingly, Giotto's frescoes served as textbooks for generations of Renaissance painters.

Siena

Among 14th-century Italian city-states, the Republics of Siena and Florence were the most powerful. Both were urban centers of bankers and merchants with widespread international contacts and large sums available for the commissioning of artworks (see "Artists' Guilds, Artistic Commissions, and Artists' Contracts," page 422).

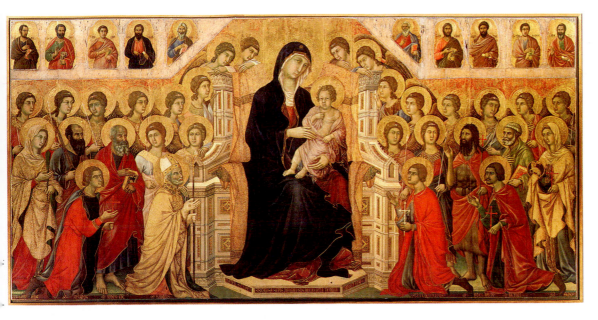

14-10 Duccio di Buoninsegna, *Virgin and Child Enthroned with Saints*, principal panel of the front of the *Maestà* altarpiece, from Siena Cathedral, Siena, Italy, 1308–1311. Tempera and gold leaf on wood, 7' × 13'. Museo dell'Opera del Duomo, Siena.

Duccio derived the formality and symmetry of his composition from Byzantine painting, but relaxed the rigidity and frontality of the figures, softened the drapery, and individualized the faces.

DUCCIO The works of Duccio di Buoninsegna (active ca. 1278–1318) are the supreme examples of 14th-century Sienese art. His most famous commission, the immense altarpiece called the *Maestà* (*Virgin Enthroned in Majesty;* FIG. 14-10), replaced a much smaller painting of the Virgin Mary on the high altar of Siena Cathedral (FIG. 14-13A). The Sienese believed that the Virgin had brought them victory over the Florentines at the battle of Monteperti in 1260, and she was the focus of the religious life of the republic. Duccio and his assistants began work on the prestigious commission in 1308 and completed the altarpiece in 1311, causing the entire city to celebrate. Shops closed, and the bishop led a great procession of priests, civic officials, and the populace at large in carrying the altarpiece from Duccio's studio outside the city gate

through the *Campo* (literally "field"—Siena's main *piazza*, or plaza), past the town hall (FIG. 14-16), and up to its home on Siena's highest hill. So great was Duccio's stature that the church's officials permitted him to include his name in the dedicatory inscription on the front of the altarpiece on the Virgin's footstool: "Holy Mother of God, be the cause of peace for Siena and of life for Duccio, because he painted you thus."

As originally executed, Duccio's *Maestà* consisted of the seven-foot-high central panel (FIG. 14-10) with the dedicatory inscription, surmounted by seven *pinnacles* above, and a *predella*, or raised shelf, of panels at the base, altogether some 13 feet high. Painted in tempera front and back (FIG. 14-11), the work unfortunately can no longer be seen in its entirety, because of its dismantling in

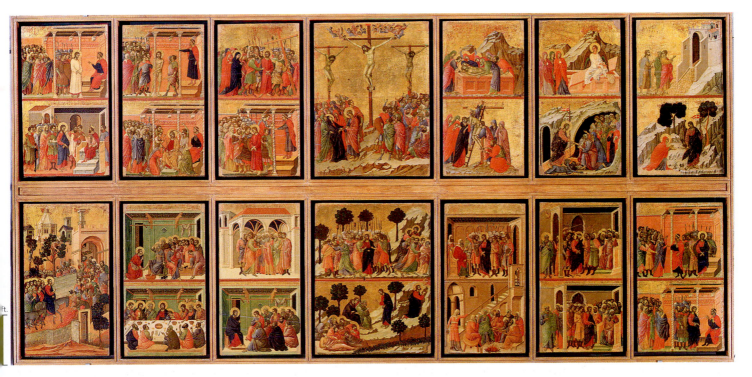

14-11 Duccio di Buoninsegna, *Life of Jesus*, 14 panels from the back of the *Maestà* altarpiece (FIG. 14-10), from Siena Cathedral, Siena, Italy, 1308–1311. Tempera and gold leaf on wood, 7' × 13'. Museo dell'Opera del Duomo, Siena.

On the back of the *Maestà* altarpiece, Duccio painted Jesus's passion in 24 scenes on 14 panels, beginning with *Entry into Jerusalem* (FIG. 14-11A), at the lower left, through *Noli me tangere*, at top right.

THE PATRON'S VOICE
Artists' Guilds, Artistic Commissions, and Artists' Contracts

The structured organization of economic activity during the 14th century, when Italy had established a thriving international trade and held a commanding position in the Mediterranean world, extended to many trades and professions. *Guilds* (associations of master craftspeople, apprentices, and tradespeople), which had emerged during the 12th century, became prominent. These associations not only protected members' common economic interests against external pressures, such as taxation, but also provided them with the means to regulate their internal operations (for example, training apprentices and assuring high-quality work).

Because of today's international open art market, the notion of an "artists' union" may seem strange. The general public tends to think of art as the creative expression of an individual artist. However, artists did not always enjoy this degree of freedom. Historically, they rarely undertook projects without receiving a specific commission. The patron contracting for the artist's services could be a civic group, religious institution, private individual, or even the artists' guild itself. Guilds, although primarily business organizations, also contributed to their city's religious and artistic life by subsidizing the building and decoration of numerous churches and hospitals. For example, the wool manufacturers' guild oversaw the start of Florence Cathedral (FIGS. 14-19 and 14-19A) in 1296, and the wool merchants' guild supervised the completion of its dome (FIG. 21-29A). The guild of silk manufacturers and goldsmiths provided the funds to build Florence's foundling hospital, the Ospedale degli Innocenti (FIG. 21-30).

Monastic orders, confraternities, and the Vatican were also major art patrons. In addition, wealthy families and individuals—for example, the Paduan banker Enrico Scrovegni (FIG. 14-1)—commissioned artworks for a wide variety of reasons. Besides the aesthetic pleasure these patrons derived from art, the images often also served as testaments to the patron's piety, wealth, and stature. (In Scrovegni's case, he hoped that building the Arena Chapel and decorating it with biblical frescoes would outweigh his sins as a moneylender and earn him a place in Heaven.) Because artworks during this period were the product of service contracts, a patron's needs or wishes played a crucial role in the final form of any painting, sculpture, or building.

Some early contracts between patrons and artists still exist. Patrons normally asked artists to submit drawings or models for approval, and they expected the artists they hired to adhere closely to the approved designs. The contracts usually stipulated certain conditions, such as the insistence on the artist's own hand in the production of the work, the quality of pigment and amount of gold or other costly materials to be used, completion date, payment terms, and penalties for failure to meet the contract's terms.

A few extant 13th- and 14th-century painting contracts are especially illuminating. Although they may specify the subject to be represented, these binding legal documents always focus on the financial aspects of the commission and the responsibilities of the painter to the patron (and vice versa). In a contract dated November 1, 1301, between Cimabue (FIG. 14-6) and another artist and the Hospital of Santa Chiara in Pisa, the artists agree to supply an altarpiece

> with colonnettes, tabernacles, and predella, painted with histories of the divine majesty of the Blessed Virgin Mary, of the apostles, of the angels, and with other figures and pictures, as shall be seen fit and shall please the said master of or other legitimate persons for the hospital.*

Other terms of the Santa Chiara contract specify the size of the panel and require the artists to use gold and silver gilding for parts of the altarpiece.

The contract for an altarpiece's frame was usually a separate document, because it necessitated employing the services of a master carpenter. For example, on April 15, 1285, the leading painter of Siena, Duccio di Buoninsegna (FIGS. 14-10, 14-11, 14-11A, and 14-12), signed a contract with the rectors of the Confraternity of the Laudesi, the lay group associated with the Dominican church of Santa Maria Novella (FIG. 14-5B) in Florence. The contract specified only that Duccio was to provide the painting, not its frame—and it imposed conditions that the painter had to meet if he was to be paid.

> [The rectors] promise . . . to pay the same Duccio . . . as the payment and price of the painting of the said panel that is to be painted and done by him in the way described below . . . 150 lire of the small florins. . . . [Duccio, in turn, promises] to paint and embellish the panel with the image of the blessed Virgin Mary and of her omnipotent Son and other figures, according to the wishes and pleasure of the lessors, and to gild [the panel] and do everything that will enhance the beauty of the panel, his being all the expenses and the costs. . . . If the said panel is not beautifully painted and it is not embellished according to the wishes and desires of the same lessors, they are in no way bound to pay him the price or any part of it.†

Sometimes patrons furnished the materials and paid artists by the day instead of a fixed amount. That was the arrangement Duccio made on October 9, 1308, when he agreed to paint the *Maestà* (FIG. 14-10) for the high altar of Siena Cathedral.

> Duccio has promised to paint and make the said panel as well as he can and knows how, and he further agreed not to accept or receive any other work until the said panel is done and completed. . . . [The church officials promise] to pay the said Duccio sixteen solidi of the Sienese denari as his salary for the said work and labor for each day that the said Duccio works with his own hands on the said panel . . . [and] to provide and give everything that will be necessary for working on the said panel so that the said Duccio need contribute nothing to the work save his person and his effort.§

In all cases, the artists worked for their patrons and could count on being compensated for their talents and efforts only if the work they delivered met the standards of those who ordered it.

*Translated by John White, *Duccio: Tuscan Art and the Medieval Workshop* (London: Thames & Hudson, 1979), 34.
†Translated by James H. Stubblebine, *Duccio di Buoninsegna and His School* (Princeton, N.J.: Princeton University Press, 1979), 1: 192.
§Stubblebine, *Duccio*, 1: 201.

subsequent centuries. Many of Duccio's panels are on display today as single masterpieces, scattered among the world's museums.

The main panel on the front of the altarpiece represents the Virgin enthroned as queen of Heaven amid choruses of angels and saints. Duccio derived the composition's formality and symmetry, along with the figures and facial types of the principal angels and saints, from Byzantine tradition. But the artist relaxed the strict frontality and rigidity of the figures. They turn to each other in quiet conversation. Further, Duccio individualized the faces of the four patron saints of Siena (Ansanus, Savinus, Crescentius, and Victor) kneeling in the foreground, who perform their ceremonial gestures without stiffness. Similarly, he softened the usual Byzantine hard body outlines and drapery patterning. The folds of the garments, particularly those of the female saints at both ends of the panel, fall and curve loosely. This is a feature familiar in French Gothic works (FIG. 13-37) and is a mark of the artistic dialogue between Italy and northern Europe in the 14th century.

Despite these changes revealing Duccio's interest in the new naturalism, he respected the age-old requirement that as an altarpiece, his *Maestà* would be the focus of worship in Siena's largest and most important church, its *cathedral,* the seat of the bishop of Siena. Duccio knew that the altarpiece should be an object holy in itself—a work of splendor to the eyes, precious in its message and its materials—and recognized how the function of the artwork limited experimentation in depicting narrative action and producing illusionistic effects (such as Giotto's) by modeling forms and adjusting their placement in pictorial space.

Instead, the queen of Heaven panel is a miracle of color composition and texture manipulation, unfortunately not fully revealed in photographs. Close inspection of the original reveals what the Sienese artist learned from other sources. In the 13th and 14th centuries, Italy was the distribution center for the great silk trade from China and the Middle East (see "Silk and the Silk Road," page 467). After processing the silk in city-states such as Lucca and Florence, the Italians exported the precious fabric throughout Europe to satisfy an immense market for elegant dress. (Dante, Petrarch, and many other humanists decried the appetite for luxury in costume,

which to them represented a decline in civic and moral virtue.) People throughout Europe (Duccio and other artists among them) prized fabrics from China, Persia, Byzantium, and the Islamic world. In his depiction of the enthroned Virgin among saints, Duccio created the glistening and shimmering effects of textiles, adapting the motifs and design patterns of exotic materials. Complementing the sumptuous fabrics and the (lost) gilded wood frame are the halos of the holy figures, which feature tooled decorative designs in gold leaf (*punchwork*). But, as did Giotto in his *Ognissanti Madonna* (FIG. 14-8), Duccio eliminated almost all the gold patterning of the figures' garments in favor of creating three-dimensional volume. Traces remain only in the Virgin's red dress.

In contrast to the main panel, the predella and the back (FIG. 14-11) of the *Maestà* present an extensive series of narrative panels of different sizes and shapes, beginning with the annunciation of Jesus's birth to Mary and culminating with the Savior's resurrection and other episodes following his crucifixion (see "The Life of Jesus in Art," pages 240–241). The section reproduced here, consisting of 24 scenes in 14 panels, relates the events of Christ's passion. The largest scene, at top center, is the *Crucifixion*—highly appropriate for an altarpiece where the Sienese bishop celebrated Mass, the ritual reenactment of the Savior's sacrifice. Duccio drew the details of his scenes from the accounts in all four Gospels. The viewer reads the pictorial story in zigzag fashion, beginning with *Entry into Jerusalem* (FIG. 14-11A) at the lower left. The narrative ends with Christ's appearance to Mary Magdalene (*Noli me tangere*) at the top right. Duccio consistently dressed Jesus in blue robes in most of the panels, but beginning with *Transfiguration*, the Savior's garment is gilded.

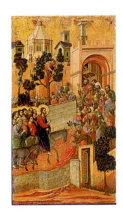

🔾 **14-11A** Duccio, *Entry into Jerusalem*, 1308–1311.

On the front panel, Duccio showed himself as the great master of the traditional altarpiece. However, in the small accompanying panels, front and back, he allowed himself greater latitude for experimentation. (Worshipers could always view both sides of the *Maestà* because the high altar stood at the center of the sanctuary.) The New Testament scenes on the back of the altarpiece reveal Duccio's powers as a narrative painter. In *Betrayal of Jesus* (FIG. 14-12; compare FIG. 14-9B), for example, the artist

14-12 DUCCIO DI BUONINSEGNA, *Betrayal of Jesus*, panel on the back (FIG. 14-11) of the *Maestà* altarpiece (FIG. 14-10), from Siena Cathedral, Siena, Italy, 1308–1311. Tempera and gold leaf on wood, 1' 10$\frac{1}{2}$" × 3' 4". Museo dell'Opera del Duomo, Siena.

In this dramatic depiction of Judas's betrayal of Jesus, the actors display a variety of individual emotions. Duccio here took a decisive step toward the humanization of religious subject matter.

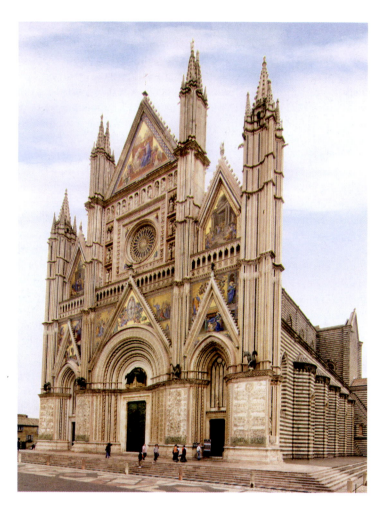

14-13 LORENZO MAITANI, Orvieto Cathedral (looking northeast), Orvieto, Italy, begun 1310.

The pointed gables over the doorways, the rose window, and the large pinnacles derive from French Gothic architecture, but the facade of Orvieto Cathedral masks a traditional timber-roofed basilica.

represented several episodes of the event—the betrayal of Jesus by Judas's false kiss, the disciples fleeing in terror, and Peter cutting off the ear of the high priest's servant. Although the background, with its golden sky and rock formations, remains traditional, the style of the figures before it has changed radically. The bodies are not the flat frontal shapes of Italo-Byzantine art. Duccio imbued them with mass, modeled them with a range of tonalities from light to dark, and arranged their draperies around them convincingly. Even more novel and striking is the way the figures seem to react to the central event. Through posture, gesture, and even facial expression, they display a variety of emotions. Duccio carefully differentiated among the anger of Peter, the malice of Judas (echoed in the faces of the throng about Jesus), and the apprehension and timidity of the fleeing disciples. These figures are actors in a religious drama that the artist interpreted in terms of thoroughly human actions and reactions. In this and the other narrative panels—for example, *Entry into Jerusalem* (FIG. 14-11A), a theme treated also by Giotto in the Arena Chapel (FIG. 14-9A)—Duccio took a decisive step toward the humanization of religious subject matter.

ORVIETO CATHEDRAL While Duccio was working on the *Maestà* altarpiece for Siena's most important church, a Sienese architect, LORENZO MAITANI, received the commission to design Orvieto's

Cathedral (FIG. 14-13). The Orvieto *facade,* like the earlier facade of Siena Cathedral (FIG. 14-13A), begun by Giovanni Pisano (FIG. 14-4), highlights the appeal of the vocabulary of French Gothic art and architecture in Italy at the end of the 13th and beginning of the 14th century. Characteristically French are the pointed gables over Orvieto Cathedral's three

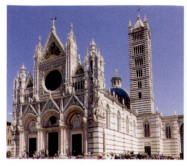

14-13A Siena Cathedral, begun ca. 1226.

doorways, the *rose window* and statues in niches in the *kings' gallery* of the upper zone, and the four large *pinnacles* dividing the facade into three *bays* (see "Building a High Gothic Cathedral," page 381, for the architectural terminology). The outer pinnacles serve as miniature substitutes for the tall northern European west-front towers. Adorning the four piers flanking the three portals are elaborate reliefs representing, from left to right, Old Testament scenes, the Tree of Jesse, New Testament scenes, and the Last Judgment. The individual episodes of the stories fill the spaces between tree branches. Both compositionally and iconographically, the Orvieto reliefs derive from the French Late Gothic tradition.

Maitani's facade, however, is a Gothic overlay masking a marble-revetted *basilican* structure in the Tuscan *Romanesque* tradition, as the three-quarter view of the cathedral in FIG. 14-13 reveals. Few Italian architects fully embraced the Gothic style. The Orvieto facade resembles a great altar screen. Its single plane may be covered with carefully placed Gothic carved and painted decoration, but in principle, Orvieto Cathedral belongs with Pisa Cathedral (FIG. 12-29) and other earlier Italian buildings, rather than with the French cathedrals at Amiens (FIG. 13-22) and Reims (FIG. 13-1). Inside, the Orvieto church has a timber-roofed *nave* with a two-story *elevation* (columnar *arcade* and *clerestory*) in the Early Christian manner. Both the *chancel arch* framing the *apse* and the nave arcade's arches are round as opposed to pointed.

SIMONE MARTINI Duccio's successors in the Sienese school also produced innovative works. SIMONE MARTINI (ca. 1285–1344) was a pupil of Duccio's and may have assisted him in painting the *Maestà* altarpiece. Martini was a close friend of Petrarch's, and the poet praised him highly for his portrait of "Laura" (the woman to whom Petrarch dedicated his sonnets). Martini worked for the French kings in Naples and Sicily and, in his last years, produced paintings for the papal court at Avignon, where he came in contact with French painters. By adapting the elegant and luxuriant patterns of the Gothic style to Sienese art and, in turn, by acquainting painters north of the Alps with the Sienese style, Martini was instrumental in creating the so-called *International Gothic* style. This new style swept Europe during the late 14th and early 15th centuries because it appealed to the aristocratic taste for brilliant colors, lavish costumes, intricate ornamentation, and themes involving splendid processions (compare FIG. 21-17).

The Saint Ansanus altarpiece (FIG. 14-14) Martini created for Siena Cathedral (FIG. 14-13A) features radiant colors, fluttering lines, and weightless elongated figures in a spaceless setting—all hallmarks of the artist's style. The complex etiquette of the European chivalric courts probably inspired Martini's presentation of the annunciation. The angel Gabriel has just alighted, the breeze of his passage lifting his mantle, his iridescent wings still beating.

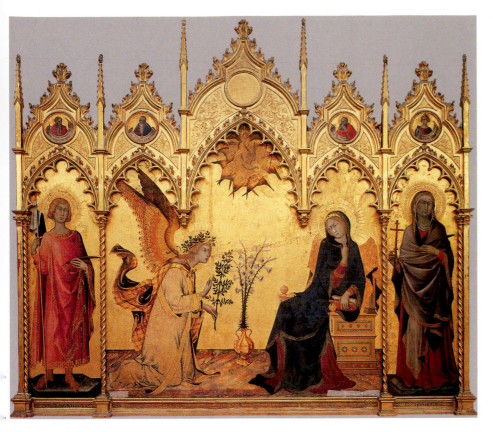

14-14 SIMONE MARTINI and LIPPO MEMMI, *Annunciation*, from the altar of Saint Ansanus, Siena Cathedral, Siena, Italy, 1333 (frame reconstructed in the 19th century). Tempera and gold leaf on wood, center panel 10' 1" × 8' 8¾". Galleria degli Uffizi, Florence.

A pupil of Duccio's, Simone Martini was instrumental in the creation of the International Gothic style. Its hallmarks are radiant colors, flowing lines, and weightless figures in golden, spaceless settings.

of the Virgin's purity. Despite Mary's modesty and diffidence and the tremendous import of the angel's message, the scene subordinates drama to court ritual, and structural experimentation to surface splendor. The intricate *tracery* of the richly tooled (reconstructed) French Gothic–inspired frame and the elaborate punchwork halos (by then a characteristic feature of Sienese panel painting) enhance the tactile magnificence of the altarpiece.

Simone Martini and his student and assistant, LIPPO MEMMI (active ca. 1317–1350), signed the *Annunciation* panel and dated it (1333). The latter's contribution to the altarpiece is still a matter of debate, but most art historians believe that he painted the two lateral saints (Ansanus at left, Margaret at right). These figures, which are reminiscent of the jamb statues of Gothic church portals, have greater solidity and lack the linear elegance of Martini's central pair. Given the nature of medieval and Renaissance workshop practices, it is often difficult to distinguish the master's hand from those of assistants, especially if the master corrected or redid part of the pupil's work (see "Artistic Training in Renaissance Italy," page 426).

The gold of his sumptuous gown signals that he has descended from Heaven to deliver his message. The Virgin, putting down her book of devotions, shrinks demurely from Gabriel's reverent bow—an appropriate act in the presence of royalty. Mary draws about her the deep-blue, golden-hemmed mantle, colors befitting the queen of Heaven. Between the two figures is a vase of white lilies, symbolic

PIETRO LORENZETTI Another of Duccio's students, PIETRO LORENZETTI (ca. 1280–1348), contributed significantly to the general experiments in pictorial realism taking place in 14th-century Italy. Surpassing even his renowned master, Lorenzetti achieved a remarkable degree of spatial illusionism in his *Birth of the Virgin* (FIG. 14-15), a large *triptych* (three-part panel painting) created for the altar of Saint Savinus in Siena Cathedral (FIG. 14-13A). Lorenzetti painted the timber architectural members dividing the altarpiece into three sections as though they extended back into the painted space. Viewers seem to look through the frame (added later) into a boxlike stage, where the event takes place. That one of the vertical members cuts across a figure, blocking part of it from view, strengthens the illusion. In subsequent centuries, artists exploited this use of

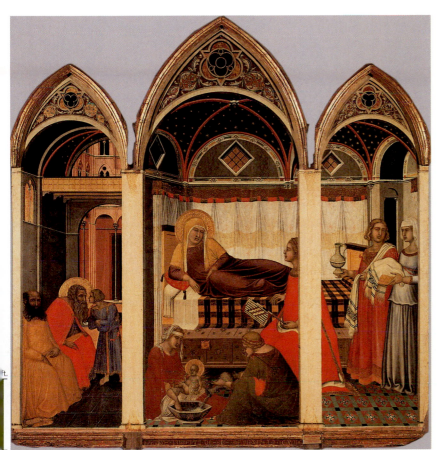

14-15 PIETRO LORENZETTI, *Birth of the Virgin*, from the altar of Saint Savinus, Siena Cathedral, Siena, Italy, 1342. Tempera on wood, 6' 1" × 5' 11". Museo dell'Opera del Duomo, Siena.

In this triptych, Pietro Lorenzetti revived the pictorial illusionism of ancient Roman murals and painted the architectural members dividing the panel as if they extended back into the painted space.

ART AND SOCIETY

Artistic Training in Renaissance Italy

In Italy during the 14th through 16th centuries, training to become a professional artist capable of earning membership in the appropriate guild was a laborious and lengthy process. Aspiring artists started their training at an early age, anytime from 7 to 15 years old. Their fathers would negotiate an arrangement with a master artist whereby each youth lived with that master for a specified number of years, usually five or six. During that time, the boys served as apprentices to the master of the workshop, learning the trade. (This living arrangement served as a major obstacle for women who wished to become professional artists, because it was inappropriate for young girls to live in a male master's household.) The guilds supervised this rigorous training. They wanted not only to ensure their professional reputations by admitting only the most talented members but also to control the number of artists (and thereby limit competition). Toward this end, they frequently tried to regulate the number of apprentices working under a single master.

The skills that apprentices learned varied with the type of studio they joined. Those apprenticed to painters learned to grind pigments, draw, prepare wood panels for painting, gild, and lay plaster for fresco. Sculptors in training learned to manipulate different materials—wood, stone, *terracotta* (baked clay), or bronze—although many sculpture workshops specialized in only one or two of these materials. For stone carving, apprentices learned their craft by blocking out the master's designs for statues. As their skills developed, apprentices took on increasingly difficult tasks.

Cennino Cennini (ca. 1370–1440) explained the value of this apprenticeship system and, in particular, the advantages for young artists in studying and copying the works of older masters, in an influential book he published in 1400, *Il libro dell'arte* (*The Handbook of Art*):

> Having first practiced drawing for a while, . . . take pains and pleasure in constantly copying the best things which you can find done by the hand of great masters. And if you are in a place where many good masters have been, so much the better for you. But I give you this advice: take care to select the best one every time, and the one who has the greatest reputation. And, as you go on from day to day, it will be against nature if you do not get some grasp of his style and of his spirit. For if you undertake to copy after one master today and after another one tomorrow, you will not

acquire the style of either one or the other, and you will inevitably, through enthusiasm, become capricious, because each style will be distracting your mind. You will try to work in this man's way today, and in the other's tomorrow, and so you will not get either of them right. If you follow the course of one man through constant practice, your intelligence would have to be crude indeed for you not to get some nourishment from it. Then you will find, if nature has granted you any imagination at all, that you will eventually acquire a style individual to yourself, and it cannot help being good; because your hand and your mind, being always accustomed to gather flowers, would ill know how to pluck thorns.*

After completing their apprenticeships, artists entered the appropriate guilds. For example, painters, who ground pigments, joined the guild of apothecaries. Sculptors were members of the guild of stoneworkers, and goldsmiths entered the silk guild, because metalworkers often stretched gold into threads wound around silk for weaving. Guild membership served as certification of the artists' competence, but did not mean that they were ready to open their own studios. New guild-certified artists usually served as assistants to master artists, because until they established their reputations, they could not expect to receive many commissions, and the cost of establishing their own workshops was high. In any case, this arrangement was not permanent, and workshops were not necessarily static enterprises. Although well-established and respected studios existed, workshops could be organized around individual masters (with no set studio locations) or organized for a specific project, especially an extensive decoration program.

Generally, assistants to painters were responsible for gilding frames and backgrounds, completing decorative work, and, occasionally, rendering architectural settings. Artists regarded figures, especially those central to the represented subject, as the most important and difficult parts of a painting, and the master reserved these for himself. Sometimes assistants painted secondary or marginal figures but only under the master's close supervision. That was probably the case with Simone Martini's *Annunciation* altarpiece (FIG. 14-14), in which the master painted the Virgin and angel, and the flanking saints are probably the work of his assistant, Lippo Memmi.

---

*Translated by Daniel V. Thompson Jr., *Cennino Cennini, The Craftsman's Handbook (Il Libro dell'Arte)* (New York: Dover Publications, 1960; reprint of 1933 ed.), 14–15.

---

architectural elements to enhance the illusion of painted figures acting out a drama a mere few feet away. This kind of pictorial illusionism characterized ancient Roman mural painting (FIGS. 7-18 and 7-19, *right*), but had not been practiced in Italy for a thousand years.

The setting for *Birth of the Virgin* also represented a marked step in the advance of worldly realism. Unlike in other altarpieces of this era, the figures in Lorenzetti's painting are not seen against an otherworldly gold background. Instead, the Sienese master painted a detailed interior of an upper-class Italian home of the period, complete with floor tiles and fabrics whose receding lines enhance the sense of depth. Lorenzetti removed the front walls of the house to enable the viewer to peer inside, where Saint Anne (see "Early Christian Saints," page 236) props herself up wearily as the midwives wash the newborn Virgin and the women bring gifts. Anne, like Nicola Pisano's *Nativity* Virgin (FIG. 14-3), resembles a reclining figure on the lid of a Roman

sarcophagus (FIG. 7-59). At the left, in a side chamber, Joachim eagerly awaits news of the delivery. Lorenzetti's altarpiece is as noteworthy for the painter's careful inspection and recording of details of the everyday world as for his innovations in spatial illusionism.

PALAZZO PUBBLICO Not all Sienese painting of the early 14th century was religious in character. One of the most important fresco cycles of the period (discussed next) was a civic commission for Siena's *Palazzo Pubblico* ("public palace" or city hall; FIG. 14-16). Siena was a proud commercial and political rival of Florence. The secular center of the community, the civic meeting hall in the main square (the Campo), was almost as great an object of civic pride as the city's cathedral (FIG. 14-13A). The Palazzo Pubblico has a slightly concave facade (to conform to the irregular shape of the Campo) and a gigantic tower visible from miles around (compare FIGS. 13-29 and

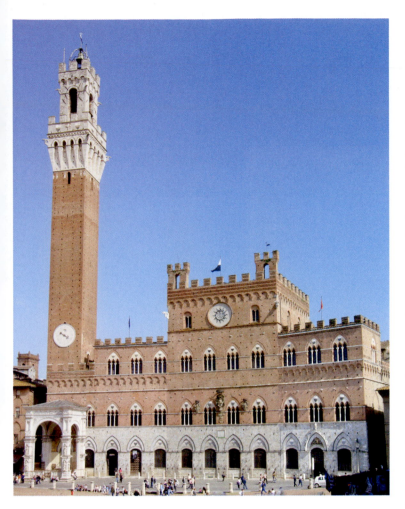

14-16 Palazzo Pubblico (looking east), Siena, Italy, 1288–1309.

Siena's Palazzo Pubblico has a concave facade and a gigantic tower visible for miles around. The tower served as both a defensive lookout over the countryside and a symbol of the city-state's power.

14-19B). The imposing building and tower must have earned the admiration of Siena's citizens as well as of visitors to the city, inspiring in them respect for the republic's power and success. The tower served as a lookout over the city and the countryside around it and as a bell tower (*campanile*) for ringing signals of all kinds to the populace. Siena, like other Italian city-states, had to defend itself against neighboring cities and often against kings and emperors. In addition, it had to secure itself against internal upheavals common in the history of the Italian city-republics. Class struggle, feuds among rich and powerful families, and even uprisings of the whole populace against the city governors (known as "the Nine" in Siena) were constant threats in medieval Italy. The heavy walls and *battlements* (fortified *parapets*) of the Sienese town hall eloquently express how frequently the city governors needed to defend themselves against their own citizens. The Palazzo Pubblico tower, out of reach of most missiles, incorporates *machicolated galleries* (galleries with holes in their floors to enable defenders to dump stones or hot liquids on attackers below) built out on *corbels* (projecting supporting architectural members) for defense of the tower's base.

AMBROGIO LORENZETTI The painter entrusted with the major fresco program in the Palazzo Pubblico was Pietro Lorenzetti's younger brother, Ambrogio Lorenzetti (ca. 1290–1348). In the frescoes Ambrogio produced for the Sala della Pace (Hall of Peace; FIG. **14-16A**), he elaborated his brother's advances in illusionistic representation in spectacular fashion while giving visual form to Sienese

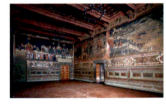

⬀**14-16A** Sala della Pace, Siena, 1338–1339.

civic concerns in a series of allegorical paintings: *Allegory of Good Government, Bad Government and the Effects of Bad*

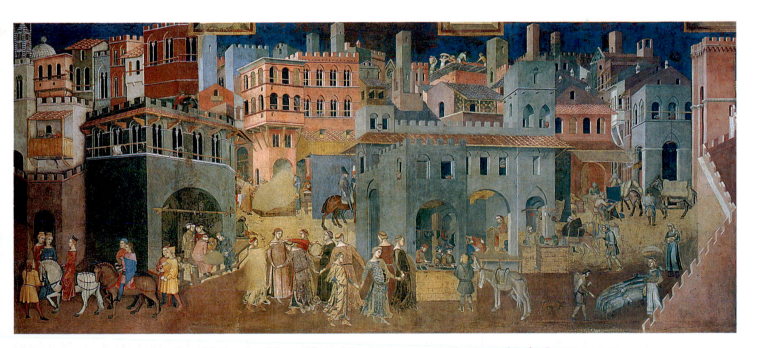

14-17 AMBROGIO LORENZETTI, *Peaceful City,* detail from *Effects of Good Government in the City and in the Country,* east wall of the Sala della Pace (FIG. 14-16A) in the Palazzo Pubblico (FIG. 14-16), Siena, Italy, 1338–1339. Fresco.

In the Hall of Peace of Siena's city hall, Ambrogio Lorenzetti painted an illusionistic panorama of a bustling 14th-century city. The fresco is an allegory of good government in the Sienese republic.

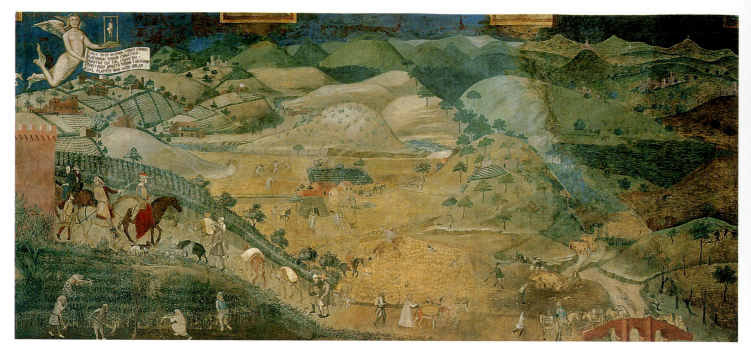

14-18 AMBROGIO LORENZETTI, *Peaceful Country*, detail from *Effects of Good Government in the City and in the Country*, east wall of the Sala della Pace (FIG. 14-16A) in the Palazzo Pubblico (FIG. 14-16), Siena, Italy, 1338–1339. Fresco.

This sweeping view of the countryside is one of the first instances of pure landscape painting in Western art since antiquity. The winged figure of Security promises safety to all who live under Sienese law.

Government in the City and *Effects of Good Government in the City and in the Country*. The turbulent politics of the Italian cities—the violent party struggles, the overthrow and reinstatement of governments—called for solemn reminders of fair and just administration, and the city hall was just the place to display murals contrasting good and bad government. Indeed, the Sienese leaders who commissioned this fresco series had undertaken the "ordering and reformation of the whole city and countryside of Siena."

In *Effects of Good Government in the City and in the Country*, Ambrogio depicted the urban and rural effects of good government. *Peaceful City* (FIG. 14-17) is a panoramic view of Siena, with its clustering palaces, markets, towers, churches, streets, and walls, reminiscent of the townscapes of ancient Roman murals (FIG. 7-19, *left*). The city's traffic moves peacefully, guild members ply their trades and crafts, and radiant maidens, clustered hand in hand, perform a graceful circling dance. Dances were regular features of festive springtime rituals. Here, dancing also serves as a metaphor for a peaceful commonwealth. The artist fondly observed the life of his city, and its architecture gave him an opportunity to apply Sienese artists' rapidly growing knowledge of perspective.

In *Peaceful Country* (FIG. 14-18), Ambrogio's representation of the countryside beyond Siena's walls, the painter presented a bird's-eye view of the undulating Tuscan terrain—its villas, castles, plowed farmlands, and peasants going about their occupations at different seasons of the year. Although it is an allegory, not a snapshot of the Tuscan countryside on a specific day, Lorenzetti's *Peaceful Country*, like his *Good Government in the City*, has the character of a portrait of a specific place and environment. *Peaceful Country* is one of the first examples of a pure *landscape* in Western art since antiquity (FIG. 7-20).

A *personification* of Security hovers above the hills and fields, unfurling a scroll promising safety to all who live under the rule of law—that is, the law administered by the Nine, who met in this room to oversee Sienese affairs. The Nine had the power to enforce their laws by imposing penalties, including even capital punishment. As a warning to those who might defy the Nine, Security carries a model of a gallows with a hanged criminal.

The Nine, however, could not protect Siena's citizens from the plague sweeping through Europe in the mid-14th century. The Black Death (see page 417) killed thousands of Sienese and may have ended the careers of the Lorenzetti brothers. They disappear from historical records in 1348.

Florence

Like Siena, the Republic of Florence was a dominant city-state during the 14th century. The historian Giovanni Villani (ca. 1270–1348), for example, described Florence as "the daughter and the creature of Rome," suggesting a preeminence inherited from the Roman Empire. Florentines were fiercely proud of what they perceived as their economic and cultural superiority. Florence controlled the textile industry in Italy, and the republic's gold *florin* was the standard coin of exchange everywhere in Europe.

SANTA MARIA DEL FIORE Florentines translated their pride in their predominance into such landmark buildings as Santa Maria del Fiore (Saint Mary of the Flower; FIGS. 14-19 and 14-19A), Florence's cathedral, the site of the most important religious observances in the city. ARNOLFO DI CAMBIO (ca. 1245–1302) began work on the cathedral (*Duomo* in Italian) in

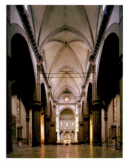

⬈ **14-19A** Florence Cathedral, begun 1296.

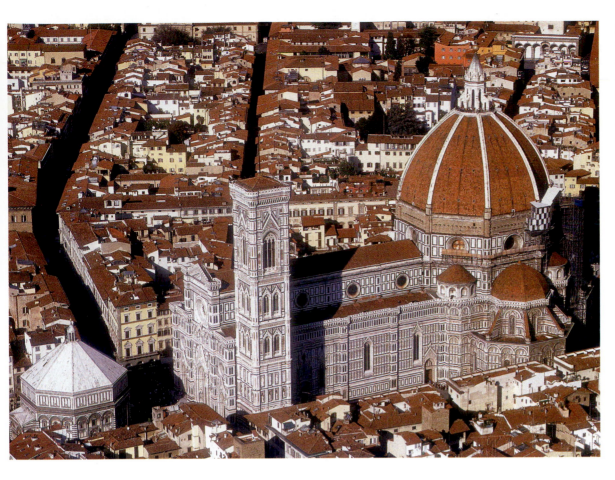

14-19 ARNOLFO DI CAMBIO and others, aerial view of Santa Maria del Fiore (and the Baptistery of San Giovanni; looking northeast), Florence, Italy, begun 1296. Campanile designed by GIOTTO DI BONDONE, 1334.

The Florentine Duomo's marble revetment carries on the Tuscan Romanesque architectural tradition, linking this basilican church more closely to Early Christian Italy than to Gothic France.

1296, three years before he received the commission to build the city's town hall, the Palazzo della Signoria (FIG. **14-19B**). Intended as the "most beautiful and honorable church in Tuscany," the cathedral reveals the competitiveness Florentines felt with cities such as Siena (FIG. 14-13A) and Pisa (FIG. 12-29). Church authorities planned for the Duomo to hold the city's entire population, and although its capacity is only about 30,000 (Florence's population at the time was slightly less than 100,000), the building seemed so large that even the noted architect Leon Battista Alberti (see page 608) com-

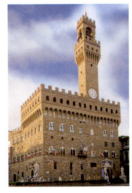

14-19B Palazzo della Signoria, Florence, 1299–1310.

mented that it seemed to cover "all of Tuscany with its shade." The builders ornamented the cathedral's surfaces, in the old Tuscan fashion, with marble geometric designs, matching the revetment to that of the facing 11th-century Romanesque baptistery of San Giovanni (FIGS. 12-30 and 14-19, *left*).

The vast gulf separating Santa Maria del Fiore from its northern European counterparts becomes evident in a comparison between the Florentine church and the High Gothic cathedrals of Amiens (FIG. 13-22), Reims (FIG. 13-1), and Cologne (FIG. 13-51A). Gothic architects' emphatic stress on the vertical produced an awe-inspiring upward rush of unmatched vigor and intensity. The French and German buildings express organic growth shooting heavenward, as the pierced, translucent stone tracery of the spires merges with the atmosphere. Florence Cathedral, in contrast, clings to the ground and has no aspirations to flight. All emphasis is on

the horizontal elements of the design, and the building rests firmly and massively on the ground. The clearly defined simple geometric volumes of the cathedral show no tendency to merge either into each other or into the sky.

Giotto di Bondone designed the Duomo's campanile in 1334. In keeping with Italian tradition (FIGS. 12-23A, 12-29, and 12-29A), it stands apart from the church. In fact, it is essentially self-sufficient and could stand anywhere else in the city without looking out of place. The same cannot be said of the bell towers of Amiens, Reims, and Cologne cathedrals. They are essential elements of the structures behind them, and it would be unthinkable to detach one of them and place it somewhere else. No individual element of Gothic churches seems capable of an independent existence. One form merges into the next in a series of rising movements pulling the eye upward and never permitting it to rest until it reaches the sky. The Florentine campanile is entirely different. Neatly subdivided into cubic sections, Giotto's tower is the sum of its component parts. Not only could this tower be removed from the building without adverse effects, but also each of the parts—cleanly separated from each other by continuous moldings—seems capable of existing independently as an object of considerable aesthetic appeal. This compartmentalization is reminiscent of the Romanesque style, but it also forecasts the ideals of Renaissance architecture. Artists hoped to express structure in the clear, logical relationships of the component parts and to produce self-sufficient works that could exist in complete independence. Compared with northern European towers, Giotto's campanile has a cool and rational quality more appealing to the intellect than to the emotions.

The facade of Florence Cathedral was not completed until the 19th century, and then in a form much altered from its original

14-20 ANDREA PISANO, south doors of the Baptistery of San Giovanni (FIG. 12-30), Florence, Italy, 1330–1336. Gilded bronze, doors 16′ × 9′ 2″; individual panels 1′ 7$\frac{1}{4}$″ × 1′ 5″.

Andrea Pisano's bronze doors have 28 panels with figural reliefs in French Gothic quatrefoil frames. The lower eight depict Christian virtues. The rest represent the life of John the Baptist.

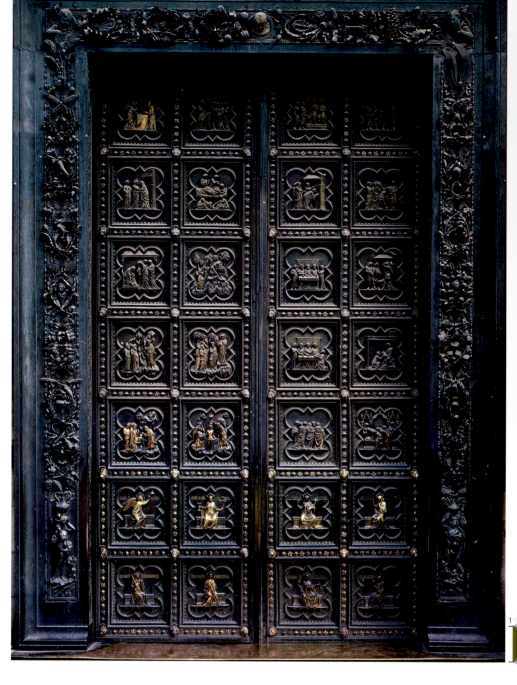

design. In fact, until the 17th century, Italian builders exhibited little concern for the facades of their churches, and dozens remain unfinished to this day. One reason for this may be that Italian architects did not conceive the facades as integral parts of the structures but rather, as in the case of Orvieto Cathedral (FIG. 14-13), as screens that could be added to the church exterior at any time.

ANDREA PISANO A generation after work began on Santa Maria del Fiore, the Florentines decided also to beautify their 11th-century baptistery (FIGS. 12-30 and 14-19, *left*) with a set of bronze doors (FIG. **14-20**) for the south entrance to the building. The sponsors were the members of Florence's guild of wool importers, who competed for business and prestige with the wool manufacturers' association, an important sponsor of the cathedral building campaign. The wool importers' guild hired ANDREA PISANO (ca. 1290–1348), a native of Pontedera in the territory of Pisa—unrelated to Nicola and Giovanni Pisano (see "Italian Artists' Names," page 413)—to create the doors. Andrea designed 28 bronze panels for the doors, each cast separately, of which 20 depict episodes from the life of John the Baptist, to whom the baptistery was dedicated. Eight panels (at the bottom) represent personified Christian virtues. The *quatrefoil* (four-lobed, cloverlike) frames are of the type used earlier for reliefs flanking the doorways of Amiens Cathedral (FIG. 13-22), suggesting that French Gothic sculpture was one source of Andrea's style. The gilded figures stand on projecting ledges in each quatrefoil. Their proportions and flowing robes also reveal a debt to French sculpture, but the compositions, both in general conception (small groups of figures in stagelike settings)

and in some details, owe a great deal to Giotto, for whom Andrea had earlier executed reliefs for the cathedral's campanile, perhaps according to Giotto's designs.

The wool importers' patronage of the baptistery did not end with this project. In the following century, the guild paid for the even more prestigious east doors (FIG. 21-10), directly across from the cathedral's west facade, and also for a statue of John the Baptist on the facade of Or San Michele. The latter was a multipurpose building housing a 14th-century tabernacle (FIG. **14-20A**) by ANDREA ORCAGNA (active ca. 1343–1368) featuring the painting *Madonna and Child Enthroned with Saints* by BERNARDO DADDI (active ca. 1312–1348).

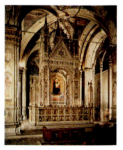

↗14-20A ORCAGNA, Or San Michele tabernacle, 1355–1359.

Pisa

Siena and Florence were inland centers of commerce. Pisa was one of Italy's port cities, which, with Genoa and Venice, controlled the rapidly growing maritime avenues connecting western Europe with the lands of Islam, with Byzantium and Russia, and with China. As prosperous as Pisa was as a major shipping power, however, it was not immune from the disruption that the Black Death wreaked across all of Italy and Europe in the late 1340s. Concern with death, a significant theme in art even before the onset of the plague, became more prominent in the years after midcentury.

CAMPOSANTO *Triumph of Death* (FIGS. 14-21 and 14-22) is a tour de force of death imagery. The creator of this large-scale fresco measuring more than 18 by 49 feet remains disputed. Some art historians attribute the work to FRANCESCO TRAINI (active ca. 1321–1363), while others argue for BUONAMICO BUFFALMACCO (active ca. 1315–1336). Painted on one wall of the Camposanto (Holy Field), the enclosed burial ground adjacent to Pisa's cathedral (FIG. 12-29), the immense fresco captures the horrors of death and forces viewers to confront their mortality. The painter rendered each scene with naturalism and emotive power. In the left foreground (FIG. **14-21**), stylish young aristocrats mounted on fine horses encounter three coffin-encased corpses in differing stages of decomposition. As the horror of the confrontation with death strikes them, the ladies turn away with delicate disgust, while a gentleman holds his nose. (The animals, horses and dogs, sniff excitedly.) At the far left, Marcarius, an early hermit saint, unrolls a scroll bearing an inscription commenting on the folly of pleasure and the inevitability of death. On the far right (FIG. **14-22**), ladies and gentlemen ignore dreadful realities, occupying themselves in an orange grove with music and amusements while all around them angels and demons reminiscent of the grieving angels of Giotto's *Lamentation* (FIG. 14-9) struggle for the souls of the corpses heaped in the foreground.

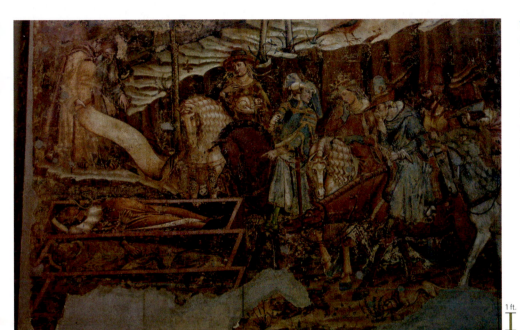

14-21 FRANCESCO TRAINI or BUONAMICO BUFFALMACCO, riders discover three corpses, detail of *Triumph of Death,* Camposanto, Pisa, Italy, 1330s. Full fresco, 18' 6" × 49' 2".

Befitting its location on a wall in Pisa's Camposanto, the enclosed burial ground adjacent to the cathedral, this fresco captures the horrors of death and forces viewers to confront their mortality.

1 ft.

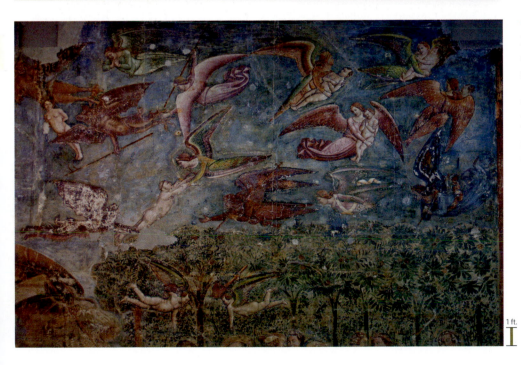

14-22 FRANCESCO TRAINI or BUONAMICO BUFFALMACCO, angels and demons vie for souls, detail of *Triumph of Death,* Camposanto, Pisa, Italy, 1330s. Full fresco, 18' 6" × 49' 2".

Above a scene of the good life of music and feasting in an orange grove, angels and demons struggle for the souls of the corpses in this dramatic vision of the triumph of death in Pisa's major cemetery.

1 ft.

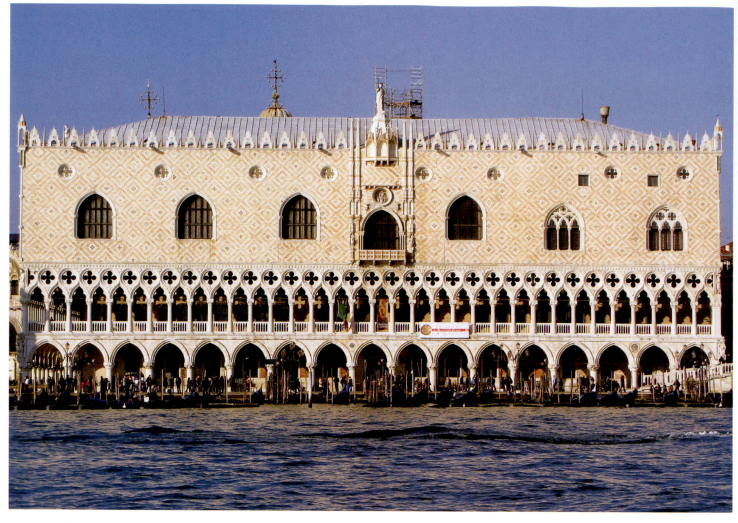

14-23 Doge's Palace (looking north), Venice, Italy, begun ca. 1340–1345; expanded and remodeled, 1424–1438.

The delicate patterning in cream- and rose-colored marbles, the pointed and ogee arches, and the quatrefoil medallions of the Doge's Palace constitute a Venetian variation of northern Gothic architecture.

In addition to these direct and straightforward scenes, the mural contains details conveying more subtle messages. For example, the painter depicted those who appear unprepared for death—and thus unlikely to achieve salvation—as wealthy and reveling in luxury. Given that the Dominicans—an order committed to a life of poverty (see "Mendicant Orders," page 415)—played a role in designing this fresco program, this imagery surely was a warning against greed and lust.

Venice

One of the wealthiest cities of late medieval Italy—and of Europe—was Venice, renowned for its streets of water. Situated on a lagoon on the northeastern coast of Italy, Venice was secure from land attack and could rely on a powerful navy for protection against invasion from the sea. Internally, Venice was a tight corporation of ruling families that, for centuries, provided stable rule and fostered economic growth.

DOGE'S PALACE The Venetian republic's seat of government was the Doge's (Duke's) Palace (FIG. **14-23**), situated on the Grand Canal adjacent to Venice's most important church, San Marco (Saint Mark's; FIG. 9-27). Begun around 1340 to 1345 and significantly remodeled after 1424, Venice's ducal palace was the most ornate public building in medieval Italy. In a stately march, the first level's short and heavy columns support rather severe *pointed arches* that look strong enough to carry the weight of the upper structure. Their rhythm doubles in the upper arcades, where more slender columns carry *ogee arches* (made up of double-curving lines), which terminate in flamelike tips between medallions pierced with quatrefoils. Each story is taller than the one beneath it, the topmost as high as the two lower arcades combined. Yet the building does not look top-heavy. This is due in part to the complete absence of articulation in the top story and in part to the walls' delicate patterning, in cream- and rose-colored marbles, which makes them appear paper thin. The palace in which Venice's *doges* conducted state business represents a delightful and charming variant of Late Gothic architecture. Colorful, decorative, light and airy in appearance, their Venetian palace is ideally suited to the unique Italian city that floats between water and air.

LATE MEDIEVAL ITALY

Duecento (13th Century)

- Diversity of style characterizes the art of 13th-century Italy, with some artists working in the *maniera greca,* or Italo-Byzantine style, some in the mode of Gothic France, and others in the newly revived classical naturalistic tradition.

- The leading painters working in the Italo-Byzantine style were Bonaventura Berlinghieri and Cimabue, whose most famous pupil was Giotto di Bondone. Both drew inspiration from Byzantine icons and illuminated manuscripts. Berlinghieri's *Saint Francis Altarpiece* is the earliest dated portrayal of Saint Francis of Assisi, who died in 1226.

- Trained in southern Italy in the court style of Frederick II (r. 1197–1250), Nicola Pisano was a master sculptor who settled in Pisa and carved pulpits incorporating marble panels that, both stylistically and in individual motifs, derive from ancient Roman sculptures. Nicola's son, Giovanni Pisano, whose career extended into the 14th century, also was a sculptor of church pulpits, but his work more closely reflects French Gothic sculpture.

- At the end of the 13th century, in Rome and Assisi, Pietro Cavallini and other fresco painters created mural programs foreshadowing the revolutionary art of Giotto.

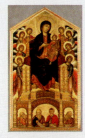

Cimabue, *Madonna Enthroned,* ca. 1280–1290

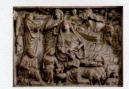

Nicola Pisano, Pisa Baptistery pulpit, 1259–1260

Trecento (14th Century)

- During the 14th century, Italy suffered the most devastating natural disaster in European history— the Black Death—but it was also the time when Renaissance humanism took root. Although religion continued to occupy a primary position in Italian life, scholars and artists became increasingly concerned with the natural world.

- Art historians from Giorgio Vasari in the 16th century to today regard Giotto di Bondone of Florence as the first Renaissance painter. His masterpiece is the extensive series of frescoes adorning the interior of the Arena Chapel in Padua, where he established himself as a pioneer in pursuing a naturalistic approach to representation, which was at the core of the classical tradition in art. The Renaissance marked the rebirth of classical values in art and society.

- The greatest master of the Sienese school of painting was Duccio di Buoninsegna, whose *Maestà* retains many elements of the maniera greca. However, Duccio relaxed the frontality and rigidity of his figures, and in the *Maestà*'s narrative scenes took a decisive step toward humanizing religious subject matter by depicting actors displaying individual emotions.

- Secular themes also came to the fore in 14th-century Italy, most notably in Ambrogio Lorenzetti's frescoes for Siena's Palazzo Pubblico. His representations of the city and its surrounding countryside are among the first landscapes in Western art since antiquity.

- The prosperity of the 14th century led to many major building campaigns, both religious and secular, including new cathedrals in Florence, Siena, and Orvieto, and new administrative palaces in Florence, Siena, and Venice.

- The 14th-century architecture of Italy underscores the regional character of late medieval art. Orvieto Cathedral's facade, for example, incorporates many elements of the French Gothic vocabulary, but it is a screen masking a timber-roofed structure in the Early Christian tradition with round arches in the nave arcade.

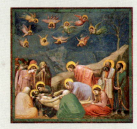

Giotto, *Lamentation,* ca. 1305

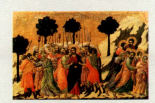

Duccio, *Betrayal of Jesus,* 1308–1311

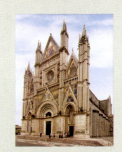

Orvieto Cathedral, begun 1310

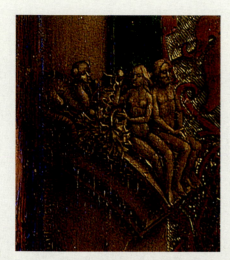

◀ **20-1a** Many details have symbolic meaning. The armrest depicting Adam, Eve, and the serpent reminded viewers that Mary is the new Eve and Christ the new Adam who will redeem humanity from original sin.

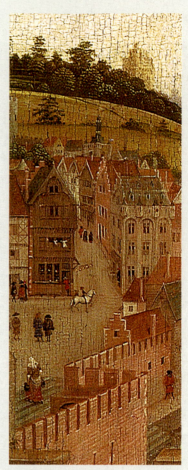

▲ **20-1b** The Virgin Mary has invited Saint Luke to paint her portrait in her elegant home—the type that wealthy 15th-century Flemish merchants owned. In the background is a view of a typical Flemish town.

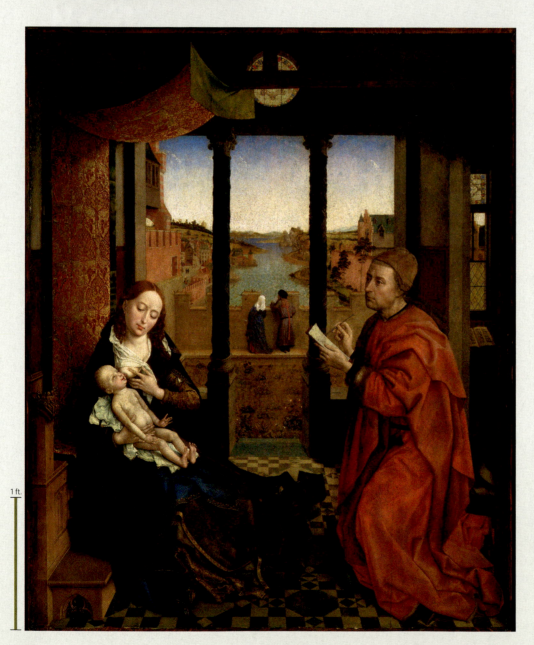

1 ft.

20-1 ROGIER VAN DER WEYDEN, *Saint Luke Drawing the Virgin*, ca. 1435–1440. Oil and tempera on wood, 4' 6 1/8" × 3' 7 5/8". Museum of Fine Arts, Boston (gift of Mr. and Mrs. Henry Lee Higginson).

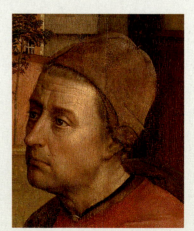

▲ **20-1c** Probably commissioned by the painters' guild in Brussels, *Saint Luke* honors the first Christian artist and the profession of painting. Saint Luke may be a self-portrait of Rogier van der Weyden.

Late Medieval and Early Renaissance Northern Europe

ROGIER VAN DER WEYDEN AND SAINT LUKE

In the 15th-century, Flanders—a region corresponding to what is today Belgium, the Netherlands, Luxembourg, and part of northern France (MAP 20-1)—enjoyed widespread prosperity. Successful merchants and craft guilds joined the clergy and royalty in commissioning artists to produce works for both public and private venues. Especially popular were paintings prepared using the recently perfected medium of oil-based pigments, which soon became the favored painting medium throughout Europe (see "Tempera and Oil Painting," page 559).

One of the early masters of oil painting was ROGIER VAN DER WEYDEN (ca. 1400–1464) of Tournai in present-day Belgium. Rogier made Brussels his home in 1435 and soon thereafter painted *Saint Luke Drawing the Virgin* (FIG. 20-1), probably for the city's artists' *guild,* the Guild of Saint Luke. Luke was the patron saint of artists because legend said that he had painted a portrait of the Virgin Mary (see "Early Christian Saints," page 237). Rogier's subject was therefore perfectly suited for the headquarters of a painters' guild. It shows Luke (his identifying attribute, the ox, is at the right; see "The Four Evangelists," page 318) at work in the kind of private residence that wealthy Flemish merchants of this era owned. Mary has miraculously appeared before Luke and invited him to paint her portrait as she nurses her son. The saint begins the process by making a preliminary drawing using a *silverpoint* (a sharp *stylus* that creates a fine line), the same instrument Rogier himself would have used when he began this commission. The painting thus not only honors Luke but also pays tribute to the profession of painting in Flanders (see "The Artist's Profession in Flanders," page 566) by documenting the preparatory work required before artists can begin painting the figures and setting.

The subject also draws attention to the venerable history of portrait painting. A rare genre during the Middle Ages, portraiture became a major source of income for Flemish artists, and Rogier was one of the best portrait painters (FIG. 20-8A) in Flanders. In fact, many scholars believe that Rogier's Saint Luke is a self-portrait, identifying the painter with the first Christian artist and underscoring the holy nature of painting. *Saint Luke Drawing the Virgin* is also emblematic of 15th-century Flemish painting in aiming to record every detail of a scene with loving fidelity to optical appearance, seen here in the rich fabrics, the patterned floor, and the landscape visible through the window. Also characteristic of Flemish art is the imbuing of many of the painting's details with symbolic significance. For example, the carved armrest of the Virgin's bench depicts Adam, Eve, and the serpent, reminding the viewer that Mary is the new Eve and Christ the new Adam who will redeem humanity from Adam and Eve's original sin.

NORTHERN EUROPE IN THE 15TH CENTURY

As the 15th century opened, Rome and Avignon were still the official seats of two competing popes (see "The Great Schism," page 415), and the Hundred Years' War (1337–1453) between France and England still raged. The general European movement toward centralized royal governments, begun in the 12th century, continued apace, but the corresponding waning of *feudalism* brought social turmoil. Nonetheless, despite widespread conflict and unrest, a new economic system emerged—the early stage of European capitalism. In response to the financial requirements of trade, new credit and exchange systems created an economic network of enterprising European cities. Trade in money accompanied trade in commodities, and the former financed industry. Both were in the hands of international banking companies, such as those of Jacques Coeur in Bourges (see page 393) and the Medici in Florence (see page 581). In 1460, Flemish entrepreneurs established the first international commercial stock exchange in Antwerp. In fact, the French word for stock market (*bourse*) comes from the name of the van der Beurse family of Bruges, the wealthiest city in 15th-century Flanders.

Art also thrived in northern Europe during this time, under royal, ducal, church, and private patronage. Two developments in particular were of special significance: the adoption by Rogier van der Weyden (FIG. 20-1) and his contemporaries of oil-based pigment as the preferred medium for painting, and the blossoming of printmaking as a major art form, which followed the invention of moveable type. These new media had a dramatic influence on artistic production both north and south of the Alps.

BURGUNDY AND FLANDERS

In the 15th century, Flanders was not an independent state but a region under the control of the duke of Burgundy, the ruler of the fertile east-central region of France still famous for its wines (MAP 20-1). Duke Philip the Bold (r. 1363–1404) was one of four sons of King John II (r. 1350–1364) of France. In 1369, Philip married Margaret de Mâle, the daughter of the count of Flanders, and

MAP 20-1 France, the duchy of Burgundy, and the Holy Roman Empire in 1477.

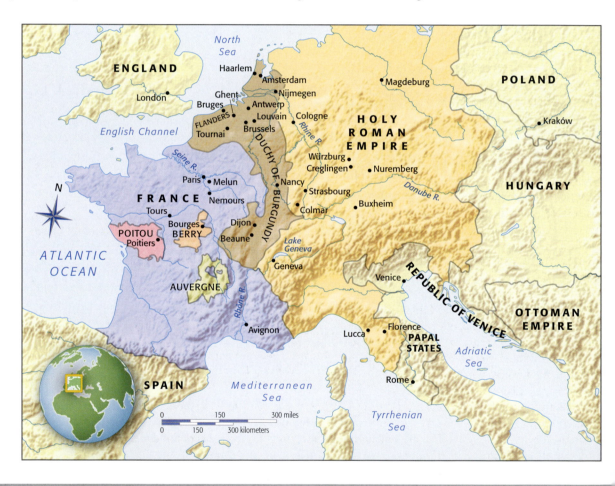

LATE MEDIEVAL AND EARLY RENAISSANCE NORTHERN EUROPE

1395–1425
- Claus Sluter carves life-size statues of biblical figures with portraitlike features for Philip the Bold, duke of Burgundy
- The Limbourg brothers expand the illusionistic capabilities of manuscript illumination for Jean, duke of Berry

1425–1450
- In Flanders, Robert Campin, Jan van Eyck, and Rogier van der Weyden use oil paints to record the exact surface appearance of objects, fabrics, and faces
- Flemish painters establish portraiture as a major art form
- German graphic artists pioneer woodcut printing, making art affordable to the masses

1450–1475
- The second generation of Flemish master painters—Petrus Christus, Dieric Bouts, and Hugo van der Goes—continues to use oil paints for altarpieces featuring naturalistic representations of religious themes
- In Germany, Johannes Gutenberg invents moveable type and prints the first Bibles on a letterpress

1475–1500
- In Flanders, Hans Memling specializes in paintings of the Madonna and Child and portraits of wealthy merchants
- The Late Gothic style lingers in Germany in the large wood altarpieces carved by Veit Stoss and Tilman Riemenschneider
- Martin Schongauer becomes the first northern European master of metal engraving

acquired territory in the Netherlands. Thereafter, the major source of Burgundian wealth was Bruges, the city that made Burgundy a powerful rival of France, which then, as in the Gothic age, was a much smaller kingdom geographically than the modern nation-state. Bruges initially derived its wealth from the wool trade, but soon expanded into banking, becoming the financial clearinghouse for all of northern Europe. Indeed, Bruges so dominated Flanders that the duke of Burgundy eventually chose to make the city his capital and moved his court there from Dijon.

Due to the expanded territory and the prosperity of the duchy of Burgundy, Philip the Bold and his successors were probably the most powerful northern European rulers during the first three quarters of the 15th century. Although members of the French royal family, they usually supported England during the Hundred Years' War because they relied on English raw materials for their wool industry. At times, the dukes of Burgundy controlled much of northern France, including Paris, the seat of the French monarchy. At the height of Burgundian power, the ducal lands stretched from the Rhône River to the North Sea.

Chartreuse de Champmol

The great wealth that the dukes of Burgundy acquired enabled them to become major patrons of the arts. The dukes fully appreciated that artworks could support their dynastic and political goals as well as adorn their castles and townhouses. Philip the Bold's grandest artistic enterprise was the Chartreuse de Champmol, near Dijon. A *chartreuse* ("charter house" in English) is a Carthusian monastery. The Carthusian order, founded by Saint Bruno (ca. 1030–1101) in the late 11th century at Chartreuse, near Grenoble in southeastern France, consisted of monks who devoted their lives to solitary living and prayer. Unlike monastic orders that earned income from farming and other work, the Carthusians generated no revenues. Philip's generous endowment at Champmol was therefore the sole funding for an ambitious artistic program inspired by the French royal abbey at Saint-Denis (FIGS. 13-1A and 13-2), the burial site of the French kings. The duke's choice for architect was DROUET DE DAMMARTIN, who had worked for his brother, King Charles V (r. 1364–1380), on the Louvre (FIG. 20-16), the French royal palace in Paris. In 1372, Philip appointed as chief sculptor the Netherlandish master Jean de Marville (d. 1389), who had also worked for Charles V, but at Rouen Cathedral. Philip intended the Dijon chartreuse to become a ducal *mausoleum* and

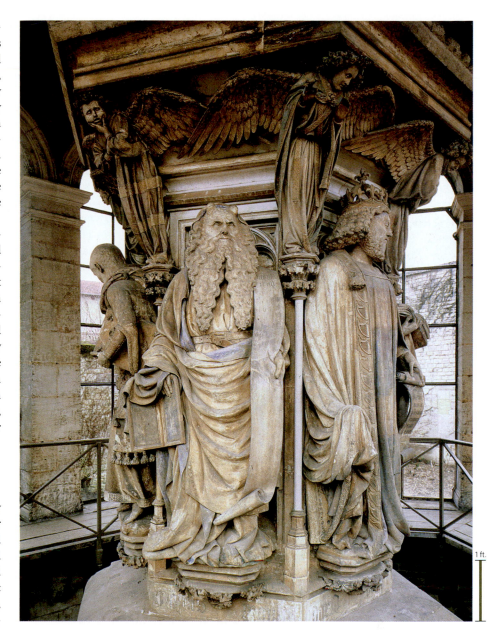

20-2 CLAUS SLUTER, *Well of Moses*, Chartreuse de Champmol, Dijon, France, 1396–1406. Asnières limestone, painted and gilded by JEAN MALOUEL, Moses 6' high.

The *Well of Moses*, a symbolic fountain of life made for the duke of Burgundy, originally supported a crucifixion group. Sluter's figures recall French Gothic jamb statues but are far more realistic.

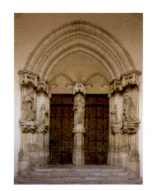

20-2A SLUTER, Chartreuse de Champmol portal, 1390–1393.

serve both as a means of securing salvation in perpetuity for the Burgundian dukes (the monks prayed continuously for the souls of the ducal family) and as a dynastic symbol of Burgundian power.

CLAUS SLUTER In 1389, following the death of Jean de Marville, Philip the Bold placed the Netherlandish sculptor CLAUS SLUTER (ca. 1360–1406) of Haarlem in charge of the sculptural program (FIGS. **20-2** and **20-2A**). Sluter had joined the Chartreuse de Champmol sculpture workshop as Jean's assistant in 1385. For the portal (FIG. **20-2A**) of the monastery's chapel, Sluter's workshop produced statues of the duke and his wife kneeling before the Virgin and Child. For the cloister, Sluter designed a large sculptural fountain located in a well (FIG. 20-2). The well served as a water source for the monastery, but water probably did not spout from the fountain because the Carthusian commitment to silence and prayer would have precluded anything producing sound.

Sluter's *Well of Moses* features statues of Moses and five other prophets (David, Daniel, Isaiah, Jeremiah, and Zachariah) ringing a base that once supported a 25-foot-tall group of Christ on the cross, the Virgin Mary, John the Evangelist, and Mary Magdalene. The Carthusians called the *Well of Moses* a *fons vitae,* a fountain of everlasting life. The blood of the crucified Christ symbolically flowed down over the grieving angels and Old Testament prophets, spilling into the well below, washing over Christ's prophetic predecessors and redeeming anyone who would drink water from the well. Whereas the models for the Dijon chapel statues were the sculptured portals of French Gothic cathedrals, the inspiration for the *Well of Moses* may have come in part from contemporaneous *mystery plays* in which actors portraying prophets frequently delivered commentaries on events in Christ's life.

The six prophets have almost portraitlike features and distinct individual personalities and costumes. For example, David is an elegantly garbed Gothic king and Moses an elderly horned prophet (compare FIG. 12-38) with a waist-length beard. Sluter intensely studied the natural appearance of faces and fabrics in order to sculpt the biblical figures in minute detail. Heavy draperies with voluminous folds swathe the life-size statues. Sluter succeeded in making their difficult, complex surfaces seem remarkably naturalistic. He enhanced this effect by skillfully differentiating textures, from coarse drapery to smooth flesh and silky hair. Originally, paint, much of which has flaked off, further augmented the naturalism of the figures. (The painter was JEAN MALOUEL [ca. 1365–1415], another Netherlandish master.) This fascination with the specific and tangible in the visible world became one of the chief characteristics of 15th-century Flemish art.

MELCHIOR BROEDERLAM Philip the Bold also commissioned a major altarpiece for the main altar in the chapel of the Chartreuse. A collaborative project between two Flemish artists, this altarpiece consisted of a large sculptured shrine by Jacques de Baerze (active ca. 1384–1399) and a pair of painted exterior panels (FIG. **20-3**) by MELCHIOR BROEDERLAM (active ca. 1387–1409).

Altarpieces were a major art form north of the Alps in the late 14th and 15th centuries. From their position behind the altar, they served as backdrops for the *Mass.* The Mass represents a ritual celebration of the Holy *Eucharist.* At the last supper, Christ commanded his apostles to repeat in memory of him the communion credo that he is tendering them his body to eat and his blood to drink, as reenacted in the Eucharist (see "The Life of Jesus in Art," page 241). This act serves as the nucleus of the Mass, which involves this reenactment as well as prayer and contemplation of the word of God. Because the Mass involves not only a memorial rite but Christian doctrine as well, art has traditionally played an important role in giving visual form to complex theological concepts for the faithful. Like the narrative reliefs in medieval church portals, these altarpieces had an important teaching function, especially for the illiterate. By reinforcing Church doctrines, they also stimulated devotion.

Given their placement in churches as backdrops to the Mass, it is not surprising that many altarpieces depict scenes directly related to Christ's sacrifice. The Champmol altarpiece, or *retable,* for example, features sculpted passion scenes on the interior. These altarpieces most often took the form of *polyptychs*—hinged multipaneled paintings or multiple carved relief panels. The hinges enabled the clergy to close the polyptych's side wings over the central panel(s). Artists decorated both the exterior and interior of the altarpieces. This multi-image format provided the opportunity to construct narratives through a sequence of images, somewhat as in manuscript illustration.

Although concrete information is lacking about when the clergy opened and closed the altarpieces, the wings probably normally remained closed but were opened on Sundays and feast days. On this schedule, viewers could have seen both the interior and exterior—diverse imagery at various times according to the liturgical calendar.

On the painted wings (FIG. 20-3) of the *Retable de Champmol* are *Annunciation* and *Visitation* (on the left panel) and *Presentation in the Temple* and *Flight into Egypt* (on the right; see "The Life of Jesus in Art," page 240). Dealing with Christ's birth and infancy, Broederlam's painted images on the altarpiece's exterior set the stage for de Baerze's interior sculpted passion scenes (not illustrated). The exterior panels are an unusual combination of different styles, locales, and religious symbolism. The two paintings include both landscape and interior scenes. Broederlam depicted the buildings in both *Romanesque* and *Gothic* styles. Scholars have suggested that the juxtaposition of different architectural styles in the left panel is symbolic. The *rotunda* (round building, usually with a dome, a common antique type) refers to the Old Testament, whereas the "modern" Gothic porch with its *lancet* windows and *tracery* relates to the New Testament. In the right panel, a statue of a Greco-Roman god falls from the top of a column as the holy family approaches. These and other details symbolically announce the coming of the new order under Christ.

Stylistically, Broederlam's panels are a mixture of three-dimensional rendition of the landscape and buildings with a solid gold background and flat golden halos for the holy figures, regardless of the positions of their heads. Despite these lingering medieval pictorial conventions, the altarpiece is an early example of many of the artistic developments that preoccupied European artists throughout the 15th century, especially the illusionistic depiction of three-dimensional objects and the naturalistic representation of landscape.

OIL PAINTING The *Retable de Champmol* also foreshadowed another significant development in 15th-century art—the widespread adoption of *oil paints,* which Broederlam mixed with *tempera* in this early example (see "Tempera and Oil Painting," page 559). Oil paints facilitated the exactitude in rendering details so characteristic of northern European painting. Although the Italian biographer Giorgio Vasari (see "Giorgio Vasari's *Lives,*" page 636) and other 16th-century commentators credited the Flemish master Jan van Eyck (FIGS. 20-5 to 20-8) with the invention of oil painting, recent evidence has revealed that oil paints had been known for some time, well before Melchior Broederlam liberally used oils for Philip the Bold's Dijon altarpiece. Flemish painters built up their pictures by superimposing translucent paint layers on a layer of underpainting, which in turn had been built up from a carefully planned drawing (compare Saint Luke at work in FIG. 20-1) made on a panel prepared with a white ground. With the oil medium, artists could create richer colors than previously possible, giving their paintings an intense tonality, the illusion of glowing light, and glistening surfaces. These traits differed significantly from the high-keyed color, sharp light, and rather *matte* (dull) surface of tempera. The brilliant and versatile oil medium suited perfectly the formal intentions of the generation of Flemish painters after Broederlam, who aimed for sharply focused clarity of detail in their representation of objects ranging in scale from large to almost invisible.

Master of Flémalle

One of the greatest Flemish painters of the generation after Melchior Broederlam was the man known as the MASTER OF FLÉMALLE, whom most art historians identify as ROBERT CAMPIN

MATERIALS AND TECHNIQUES
Tempera and Oil Painting

The generic words *paint* and *pigment* encompass a wide range of substances that artists have used through the ages. Fresco aside (see "Fresco Painting," page 419), during the 14th century, egg *tempera* was the material of choice for most painters, both in Italy and northern Europe. Tempera consists of egg combined with a wet paste of ground pigment. In his influential 1437 guidebook *Il libro dell'arte* (*The Handbook of Art*; see page 426), Cennino Cennini (ca. 1370–ca. 1440) noted that artists mixed only the egg yolk with the ground pigment, but analyses of paintings from this period have revealed that some artists chose to use the entire egg. Images painted with tempera have a velvety sheen. Artists usually applied tempera to the painting surface with a light touch because thick application of the pigment mixture would result in premature cracking and flaking.

Some artists used oil paints (powdered pigments mixed with linseed oil) as far back as the eighth century, but not until the early 1400s did oil painting become widespread. Melchior Broederlam (FIG. 20-3) and other Flemish artists were among the first to employ oils extensively (often mixing them with tempera, as Broederlam did), and Italian painters quickly followed suit. The discovery of better drying components in the early 15th century enhanced the setting capabilities of oils. Rather than apply these oils in the light, flecked brushstrokes that the tempera technique encouraged, artists laid down the oils in transparent layers, or *glazes,* over opaque or semiopaque underlayers. In this manner, painters could build up deep tones through repeated *glazing.* Unlike works in tempera, whose surface dries quickly due to water evaporation, oils dry more uniformly and slowly, giving the artist time to rework areas. This flexibility must have been particularly appealing to artists who worked very deliberately, such as Rogier van der Weyden (FIGS. 20-1, 20-9, and 20-9A), Robert Campin (FIG. 20-4), Jan van Eyck (FIGS. 20-5 to 20-8), and the other Flemish masters discussed in this chapter, as well as the Italian Leonardo da Vinci (FIGS. 22-2 and 22-5). Leonardo also preferred oil paint because its gradual drying process and consistency enabled him to blend the pigments, thereby creating the impressive *sfumato* (smoky) effect that contributed to his fame. Moreover, while drying, oil paints smooth out, erasing any trace of the brush that applied the paint. Oil paints also reflect natural light, giving the surface a glow and creating a rich visual effect unlike the duller sheen of the more light-absorbent tempera medium.

Both tempera and oils can be applied to various surfaces. Through the early 16th century, wood panels served as the foundation for most paintings. Italians painted on poplar. Northern European artists used oak, lime, beech, chestnut, cherry, pine, and silver fir. Local availability of these timbers determined the choice of wood. Linen canvas became increasingly popular in the late 16th century. Although evidence suggests that artists did not intend permanency for their early images on canvas, the material proved particularly useful in areas such as Venice where high humidity warped wood panels and made fresco unfeasible. Furthermore, until artists began to use wood bars to stretch the canvas to form a taut surface, canvas paintings could be rolled and were lighter and more compact and therefore more easily portable than wood panels.

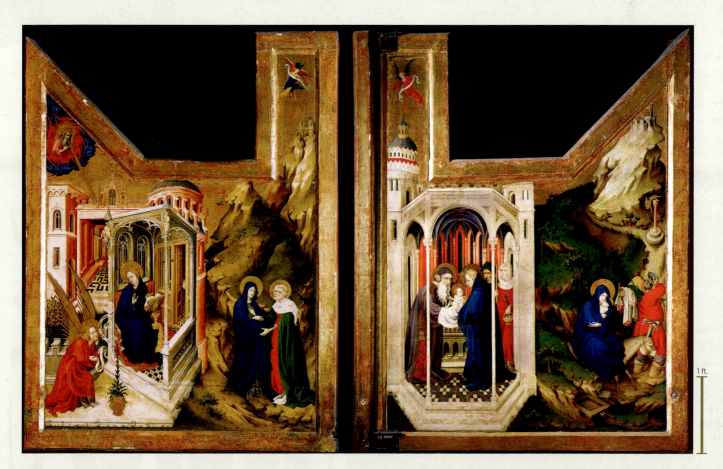

20-3 MELCHIOR BROEDERLAM, *Retable de Champmol,* from the chapel of the Chartreuse de Champmol, Dijon, France, installed 1399. Oil and tempera on wood, each wing 5' 5¾" × 4' 1¼". Musée des Beaux-Arts, Dijon.

This early example of oil painting attempts to represent the three-dimensional world on a two-dimensional surface, but the gold background and flat halos recall medieval pictorial conventions.

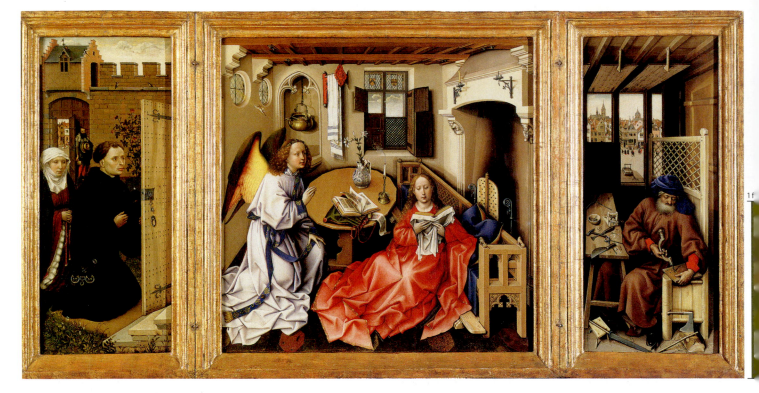

20-4 ROBERT CAMPIN (MASTER OF FLÉMALLE), *Mérode Altarpiece* (open), ca. 1425–1428. Oil on wood, center panel 2' 1⅜" × 2' ⅞", each wing 2' 1⅜" × 10⅞". Metropolitan Museum of Art, New York (The Cloisters Collection, 1956).

Campin was the leading painter of Tournai and an early master of oil painting. In the *Mérode Altarpiece,* he set the Annunciation in a Flemish merchant's home in which many objects have symbolic significance.

(ca. 1375–1444), the leading painter of Tournai. His most famous work is the *Mérode Altarpiece* (FIG. **20-4**), one of the many small altarpieces of this period produced for private patrons and intended for household prayer. Perhaps the most striking feature of these private devotional images is the integration of religious and secular concerns. For example, artists often presented biblical scenes as taking place in a house (compare FIG. 20-1). Religion was such an integral part of Flemish life that separating the sacred from the secular was almost impossible—and undesirable. Furthermore, the presentation in religious art of familiar settings and objects no doubt strengthened the direct bond that the patron or viewer felt with biblical figures.

Annunciation, the popular theme prophesied in Isaiah 7:14, occupies the Mérode triptych's central panel. Unseen by the Virgin, a tiny figure of Christ carrying the cross of his martyrdom and of human salvation enters the room on a ray of light, a potent symbol of the incarnation and a foreshadowing of what lies ahead for the future Mother of God and her son. The archangel Gabriel approaches Mary, who sits reading inside a well-kept Flemish home. Through the window in the background of the right wing, the viewer sees a local cityscape, as in Rogier van der Weyden's *Saint Luke* (FIG. 20-1). The depicted accessories, furniture, and utensils confirm the locale as Flanders. However, the objects represented are not merely decorative. They also function as religious symbols.

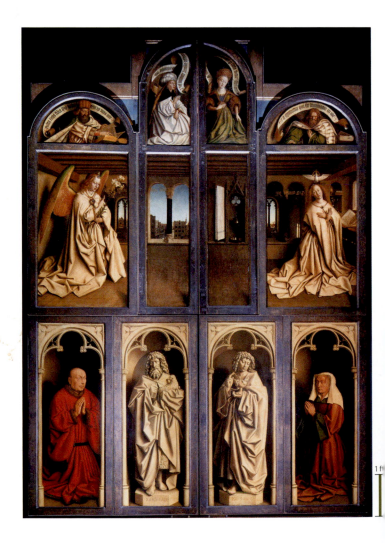

20-5 HUBERT and JAN VAN EYCK, *Ghent Altarpiece* (closed), Saint Bavo Cathedral, Ghent, Belgium, ca. 1423–1432. Oil on wood, 11' 5" × 7' 6".

Monumental painted altarpieces were popular in Flemish churches. Artists decorated both the interiors and exteriors of these polyptychs, which often, as here, included donor portraits.

The book, extinguished candle, and lilies on the table; the copper basin in the corner niche; the towels, fire screen, and bench all symbolize, in different ways, the Virgin's purity and her divine mission.

In the right panel, Joseph, apparently unaware of the angel's arrival, has constructed two mousetraps, symbolic of the theological concept that Christ is bait set in the trap of the world to catch the Devil. The ax, saw, and rod that Campin painted in the foreground of Joseph's workshop not only are tools of the carpenter's trade but also are mentioned in Isaiah 10:15. In the left panel, the closed garden is symbolic of Mary's purity, and the flowers Campin included relate to Mary's virtues, especially humility.

The altarpiece's donor, Peter Inghelbrecht, a wealthy merchant, and his wife, Margarete Scrynmakers, kneel in the garden and witness the momentous event through an open door. *Donor portraits*—portraits of the individual(s) who commissioned (or "donated") the work—became very popular in the 15th century. In this instance, in addition to asking to be represented in their altarpiece, the Inghelbrechts probably specified the subject. Inghelbrecht

means "angel bringer," descriptive of the Annunciation theme of the central panel. Scrynmakers means "cabinet- or shrine-makers," and probably inspired the workshop scene in the right panel.

Jan van Eyck

The first Netherlandish painter to achieve international fame was JAN VAN EYCK (ca. 1395–1441), who in 1425 became the court painter of Philip the Good, duke of Burgundy (r. 1419–1467). In 1431, he moved his studio to Bruges, where the duke maintained his official residence.

GHENT ALTARPIECE The year Jan arrived in Bruges, he set out to complete the *Ghent Altarpiece* (FIGS. **20-5** and **20-6**), which, according to the dedicatory inscription, his older brother HUBERT VAN EYCK (ca. 1385–1426) had begun. Given Jan's stature today, it is noteworthy that the inscription describes Hubert as an artist "than whom there was no greater" and Jan as "his brother, second in art." The nearly 12-foot-tall Ghent retable is one of the largest of the 15th century. Jodocus Vyd (d. 1439), diplomat-retainer of Philip the Good, and his wife, Elisabeth Borluut (d. 1443), commissioned the polyptych as the centerpiece of the chapel that Vyd built in the Ghent church originally dedicated to Saint John the Baptist (since 1540, Saint Bavo Cathedral). Vyd's largesse and the political and social connections that the *Ghent Altarpiece* revealed to its audience contributed to Vyd's appointment as the city's *burgomeister* (chief

20-6 HUBERT and JAN VAN EYCK, *Ghent Altarpiece* (open), Saint Bavo Cathedral, Ghent, Belgium, ca. 1423–1432. Oil on wood, 11′ 5″ × 15′ 1″.

In this sumptuous painting of salvation from the original sin of Adam and Eve, God the Father presides in majesty. The van Eyck brothers used oil paints to render every detail with loving fidelity to appearance.

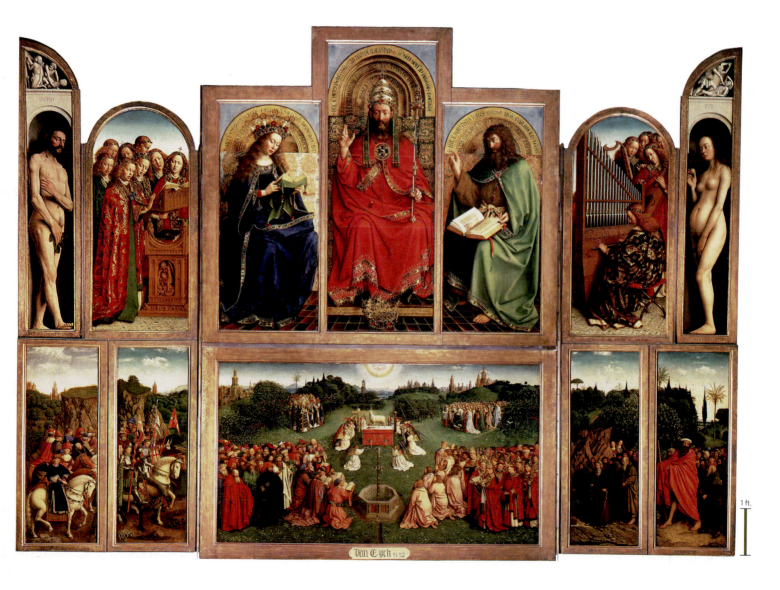

magistrate; mayor) shortly after the unveiling of the work. Two of the exterior panels (FIG. 20-5) depict the donors. The husband and wife, in paired niches with Gothic tracery, kneel with their hands clasped in prayer. They gaze piously at two illusionistically rendered stone statues that reflect the innovative style of Claus Sluter (FIGS. 20-2 and 20-2A). The sculptures represent Ghent's patron saints, John the Baptist and John the Evangelist (who was probably also Vyd's patron saint). The Annunciation appears on the upper register, with a careful representation of a Flemish town outside the painted window of the center panel (compare FIGS. 20-1 and 20-4). In the uppermost arched panels, Jan depicted the Old Testament prophets Zachariah and Micah, along with *sibyls,* Greco-Roman mythological female prophets whose writings the Church interpreted as prophecies of Christ.

When open (FIG. 20-6), the altarpiece reveals a sumptuous, superbly colored painting of human redemption through Christ. In the upper register, God the Father—wearing the pope's triple tiara, with a worldly crown at his feet and resplendent in a deep-scarlet mantle—presides in majesty. To God's right is the Virgin, represented, as in the Gothic age and in a small Jan van Eyck *diptych* (two-paneled painting; FIG. **20-6A**), as the queen of Heaven, with a crown of 12 stars upon her head. John the Baptist sits to God's left. To either side is a choir of angels, with an angel playing an organ on the right. Adam and Eve appear in the far panels. The inscriptions in the arches above Mary and Saint John extol the Virgin's virtue and purity and Saint John's greatness as the forerunner of Christ (see "Early Christian Saints," page 236). The inscription above the Lord's head translates as "This is God, all-powerful in his divine majesty; of all the best, by the gentleness of his goodness; the most liberal giver, because of his infinite generosity." The step behind the crown at the Lord's feet bears the inscription, "On his head, life without death. On his brow, youth without age. On his right, joy without sadness. On his left, security without fear." The entire altarpiece amplifies the central theme of salvation. Even though humans, personified by Adam and Eve, are sinful, they will be saved because God, in his infinite love, will sacrifice his own son for their sake.

The panels of the lower register extend the symbolism of the upper. In the center panel, saints arrive from the four corners of the earth through an opulent, flower-spangled landscape. They proceed toward the altar of the lamb and the octagonal fountain of life (compare FIG. 20-2). The book of Revelation passage that recounts the adoration of the Lamb is the main reading on All Saints' Day (November 1). The Lamb symbolizes the sacrificed son of God, whose heart bleeds into a chalice, while into the fountain spills the "pure river of water of life, clear as crystal, proceeding out of the throne of God and of the Lamb" (Rev. 22:1). On the right, the 12 apostles and a group of martyrs in red robes advance. On the left appear prophets. In the right background come the virgin martyrs, and in the left background the holy confessors approach. On the lower wings, hermits, pilgrims, knights, and judges enter from left and right. They symbolize the four cardinal virtues: Temperance, Prudence, Fortitude, and Justice, respectively. The altarpiece celebrates the whole

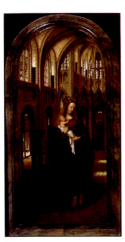

20-6A VAN EYCK, *Madonna in a Church,* ca. 1430–1440.

Christian cycle from the fall of man to the redemption, presenting the Church triumphant in heavenly Jerusalem.

Jan used oil paints to render the entire altarpiece in a shimmering splendor of color that defies reproduction. No small detail escaped the painter. With pristine specificity, he revealed the beauty of the most insignificant object. He depicted the soft texture of hair, the glitter of gold in the heavy brocades, the luster of pearls, and the flashing of gems, all with loving fidelity to appearance. This kind of meticulous attention to recording the exact surface appearance of humans, animals, objects, and landscapes, already evident in the *Mérode Altarpiece* (FIG. 20-4), became a hallmark of Flemish panel painting in the 15th century.

GIOVANNI ARNOLFINI Emerging capitalism led to prosperity in Europe's booming urban centers and fueled in turn the growing bourgeois market for art objects, particularly in Bruges, Antwerp, and, later, Amsterdam. The increased wealth of the merchant class contributed to an expanded market for secular art in addition to religious artworks. It is noteworthy, for example, that both the *Mérode Altarpiece* and the *Ghent Altarpiece*—certainly to be categorized as "religious art"—include painted portraits of their donors. These paintings marked a significant revival of portraiture, a genre that had languished since antiquity. Private commissions for portraits as independent artworks began to multiply as both artists and patrons became interested in the reality (both physical and psychological) that portraits could reveal.

In the 15th century, Flemish patrons eagerly embraced the opportunity to have their likenesses painted. The elite wanted to memorialize themselves in their dynastic lines and to establish their identities, ranks, and stations with images far more concrete than heraldic coats of arms. Portraits also served to represent state officials at events that they could not attend. Sometimes, royalty, nobility, and the very rich would send artists to paint the likeness of a prospective bride or groom. For example, when young King Charles VI (r. 1380–1422) of France sought a bride, he dispatched a painter to three different royal courts to make portraits of the candidates. But prosperous merchants also commissioned portraits for their homes.

An early example of secular portraiture is Jan van Eyck's oil painting *Giovanni Arnolfini and His Wife* (FIG. **20-7**). Jan depicted the Lucca financier (who had established himself in Bruges as an agent of the Medici family) in his home. Arnolfini holds the hand of his second wife, whose name is not known. That much is certain, but the purpose and meaning of the double portrait remain the subject of considerable debate. According to the traditional interpretation of the painting, Jan recorded the couple taking their marriage vows. As in the *Mérode Altarpiece* (FIG. 20-4), almost every object portrayed carries meaning. For example, the little dog symbolizes fidelity (the common canine name *Fido* originated from the Latin *fidere,* "to trust"). The *finial* (crowning ornament) of the marriage bed at the right is a tiny statue of Saint Margaret, patron saint of childbirth. (The bride is not yet pregnant, although the fashionable costume she wears makes her appear so.) From the finial hangs a whisk broom, symbolic of domestic care. Indeed, even the placement of the two figures in the room is meaningful. The woman stands near the bed and well into the room, whereas the man stands near the open window, symbolic of the outside world.

Many art historians, however, dispute this interpretation because, among other things, the room in which Arnolfini and his wife stand is a public reception area, not a bedchamber. One scholar

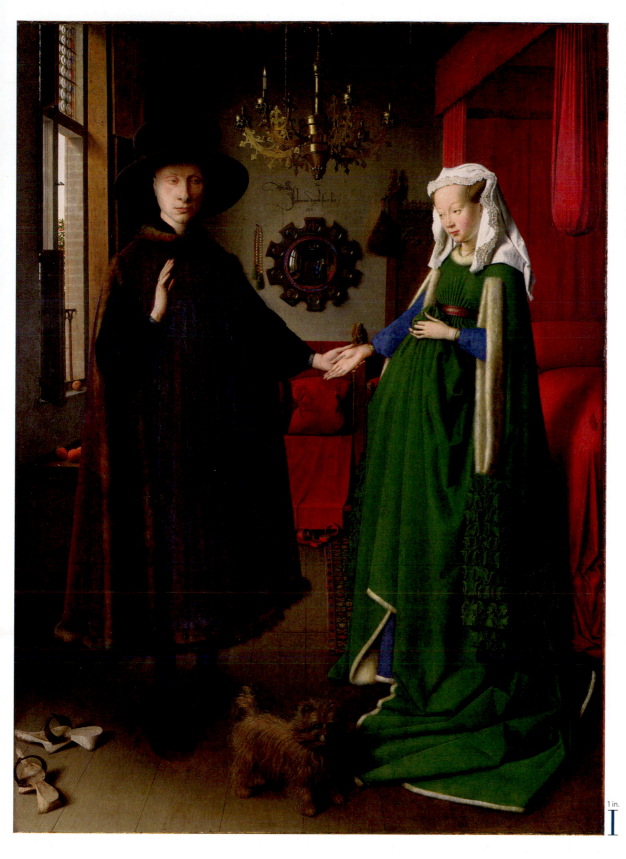

20-7 JAN VAN EYCK, *Giovanni Arnolfini and His Wife,* 1434. Oil on wood, 2' 9" × 1' 10½". National Gallery, London.

Jan van Eyck played a major role in establishing portraiture as an important Flemish art form. In this portrait of an Italian financier and his wife, he also portrayed himself in the mirror.

1 in.

has suggested that Arnolfini is conferring legal privileges on his wife to conduct business in his absence. In either case, an important aspect of the painting is that the artist functions as a witness to whatever event is taking place. In the background, between the two figures, is a convex mirror (complete with its spatial distortion, brilliantly recorded), in which Jan depicted not only the principals, Arnolfini and his wife, but also two persons who look into the room

through the door. (Arnolfini's raised right hand may be a gesture of greeting to the two men.) One of these must be the artist himself, as the elegant inscription above the mirror, *Johannes de Eyck fuit hic* ("Jan van Eyck was here"), announces that he was present. The self-portrait also underscores the painter's self-consciousness as a professional artist whose role deserves to be recorded and remembered.

MATERIALS AND TECHNIQUES
Framed Paintings

Until the mid-20th century, when painters began simply to affix canvas to wood *stretcher bars* to provide a taut painting surface devoid of ornamentation, artists considered the frame an integral part of the painting. Frames served a number of functions, some visual, others conceptual. For paintings such as large-scale altarpieces that were part of a larger environment, frames often served to integrate the painting with its surroundings. Frames could also be used to reinforce the illusionistic nature of the painted image. For example, the Italian painter Giovanni Bellini, in his *San Zaccaria Altarpiece* (FIG. 22-32), duplicated the carved *pilasters* of the architectural frame in the painting itself, thereby enhancing the illusion of space and giving the painted figures an enhanced physical presence. In the *Ghent Altarpiece,* the frame seems to cast shadows on the floor between the angel and Mary in the *Annunciation* (FIG. 20-5, *top*). More commonly, artists used frames specifically to distance the viewer from the (often otherworldly) scene by calling attention to the separation of the image from the viewer's space.

Most 15th- and 16th-century paintings included elaborate frames that the artists themselves helped design and construct. Extant contracts reveal that the frame could account for as much as half of the cost of an altarpiece. Frequently, the commissions called for painted or gilded frames, adding to the expense. For small works, artists sometimes affixed the frames to the panels before painting, so that the frame was a point of reference as they worked. Occasionally, a single piece of wood served as both panel and frame, and the artist (or, in practice, an assistant) carved the painting surface from the wood, leaving the edges as a frame. Larger images with elaborate frames, such as altarpieces, required the services of a professional woodcarver or stonemason. The painter worked closely with the individual constructing the frame to ensure its appropriateness for the image(s) produced.

Unfortunately, over time, many frames have been removed from their paintings. For instance, in 1566 church officials dismantled the *Ghent Altarpiece* and detached its elaborately carved frame in order to protect the sacred work from Protestant *iconoclasts* (see page 682). As ill luck would have it, when the panels were reinstalled in 1587, no one could find the frame. Sadly, the absence of many of the original frames of old paintings deprives viewers today of the painter's complete artistic vision. Conversely, when the original frames

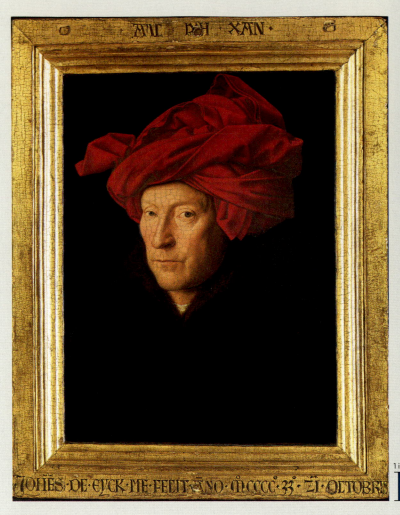

20-8 JAN VAN EYCK, *Man in a Red Turban,* 1433. Oil on wood, 1' $1\frac{1}{8}$" × $10\frac{1}{4}$". National Gallery, London.

Man in a Red Turban is the first known Western painted portrait in a thousand years in which the sitter looks directly at the viewer. The inscribed frame suggests that it is a self-portrait of Jan van Eyck.

exist, they sometimes provide essential information, such as the subject, name of the painter, and date. For example, the inscriptions on the frame of Jan van Eyck's *Man in a Red Turban* (FIG. 20-8) state that he painted it on October 21, 1433, and the inclusion of "As I can" and omission of the sitter's name suggest that the painting is a self-portrait.

MAN IN A RED TURBAN Whatever the intended meaning of *Giovanni Arnolfini and His Wife,* the painting is representative of the emergence of secular portraiture in 15th-century Flanders. In *Man in a Red Turban* (FIG. **20-8**), the man Jan van Eyck portrayed looks directly at the viewer. This is the first known Western painted portrait in a thousand years where the sitter does so. The level, composed gaze, directed from a true three-quarter head pose, must have impressed observers deeply. The painter created the illusion that from whatever angle a viewer observes the face, the eyes return that gaze. Jan, with his considerable observational skill and controlled painting style, injected a heightened sense of specificity into this portrait by including beard stubble, veins in the bloodshot left eye, and weathered, aged skin. Although a definitive identification of the sitter has yet to be made, most art historians consider *Man in a Red Turban* a self-portrait, which Jan painted by looking at his image in a mirror (as he depicted himself in the mirror in the Arnolfinis' home; FIG. 20-7). The inscriptions on the frame (see "Framed Paintings," above) reinforce this identification. Across the top, Jan wrote "As I can" in Flemish using Greek letters. One suggestion is that this portrait was a demonstration piece intended for prospective clients, who could compare the painting with the painter and judge what he "could do" in terms of recording a faithful likeness. Across the bottom appear the date and a statement in Latin: "Jan van Eyck made me." The use of both Greek and Latin suggests that the artist viewed himself as both a learned man and a worthy successor to the fabled painters of antiquity.

Rogier van der Weyden

When Jan van Eyck received the commission for the *Ghent Altarpiece*, Rogier van der Weyden (FIG. 20-1) was an assistant in the workshop of Robert Campin (FIG. 20-4), but the younger Tournai painter's fame eventually rivaled Jan's. Rogier quickly became renowned for his portraits (FIG. **20-8A**) and his dynamic compositions stressing human action and drama. He concentrated on Christian themes, especially those episodes in the life of Jesus that elicited powerful emotions—for example, the crucifixion and *Pietà* (the Virgin Mary cradling the dead body of her son)—moving observers deeply by vividly portraying the sufferings of Christ.

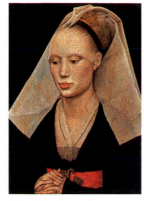

⬈ **20-8A** VAN DER WEYDEN, *Portrait of a Lady*, ca. 1460.

DEPOSITION One of Rogier's early masterworks is *Deposition* (FIG. 20-9), the center panel of a triptych commissioned by the archers' guild of Louvain for the church of Notre-Dame hors-les-murs (Church of Our Lady—the Virgin—outside the [town] walls). Rogier acknowledged the patrons of this large painting by incorporating the crossbow (the guild's symbol) into the decorative tracery in the corners. Instead of creating a deep landscape setting, as Jan van Eyck might have, Rogier compressed the figures and action onto a shallow stage with a golden back wall, imitating the large sculptured shrines so popular in the 15th century, especially in the Holy Roman Empire (FIGS. 20-20 and 20-21). The device admirably served his purpose of expressing maximum action within a limited space, but the setting of the crucifixion in a box is unrealistic, as is the size of the cross, the arms of which are not wide enough for Jesus's hands to have been nailed to them. The painting, with the artist's crisp drawing and precise modeling of forms, resembles a stratified relief carving, and the viewer may wonder if this is a painting of the biblical event or a painting of a shrine representing the event. In

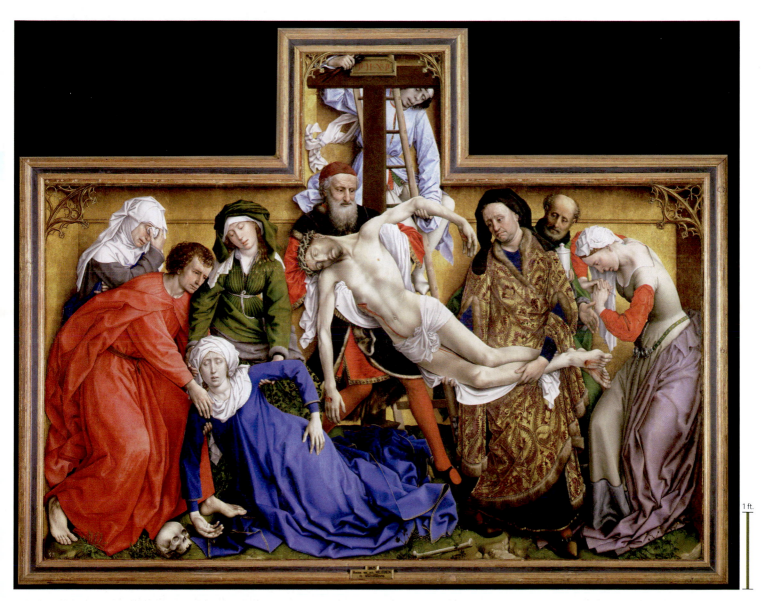

20-9 ROGIER VAN DER WEYDEN, *Deposition,* center panel of a triptych from Notre-Dame hors-les-murs, Louvain, Belgium, ca. 1435–1442. Oil on wood, 7' 2⅝" × 8' 7⅛". Museo del Prado, Madrid.

Deposition resembles a relief carving in which the biblical figures act out a drama of passionate sorrow as if on a shallow theatrical stage. The painting makes an unforgettable emotional impression.

any case, a series of lateral undulating movements gives the group a compositional unity, a formal cohesion that Rogier strengthened by depicting the sorrowful anguish many of the figures share. Present are the Virgin, several of her half-sisters, Joseph of Arimathea, Nicodemus, Saint John the Evangelist, and Mary Magdalene. The similar poses of Christ and his mother further unify the composition and reflect the belief that Mary suffered the same pain at the crucifixion as her son. Their echoing postures also resemble the shape of a crossbow.

Rogier's extraordinary ability to represent flesh and fabric rivaled the skill of Jan van Eyck, and few painters, not even Jan, have equaled the Tournai master in rendering passionate sorrow as it vibrates through a figure or distorts a tearstained face. Rogier's

depictions of the agony of loss in *Deposition* and of the terror of the damned in *Last Judgment* (FIG. 20-9A) are among the most moving and unforgettable images in religious art. It was probably Rogier whom Michelangelo had in mind when, according to the Portuguese painter Francisco de Hollanda (1517–1584), the Italian master observed, "Flemish painting [will] please the devout better than any painting of Italy, which will never cause him to shed a tear, whereas that of Flanders will cause him to shed many."[1]

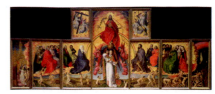

⊙ **20-9A** VAN DER WEYDEN, *Last Judgment Altarpiece*, ca. 1443–1451.

ART AND SOCIETY
The Artist's Profession in Flanders

As in Italy (see "Artistic Training," page 426), guilds controlled artistic production in Flanders. To pursue a craft, individuals had to belong to the guild controlling that craft. Painters, for example, sought admission to the Guild of Saint Luke, the patron saint of painters because Luke made a portrait of the Virgin Mary (FIG. 20-1). The patron saint of the metalworkers' guild was Saint Eligius (FIG. 20-10), who was a goldsmith before devoting himself to the Church and eventually becoming bishop of Tournai.

The path to eventual membership in the guild began, for men, at an early age, when the father apprenticed his son in boyhood to a master, with whom the young aspiring painter lived. The master taught the fundamentals of his craft—how to make implements, prepare panels with *gesso* (plaster mixed with a binding material), and mix colors, oils, and varnishes. Once the youth mastered these procedures and learned to work in the master's traditional manner, he usually spent several years working as a journeyman in various cities, observing and absorbing ideas from other masters. He then was eligible to become a master and could apply for admission to the guild. Fees could be very high, especially if an artist was not a citizen of the same city. Sometimes, an artist seeking admission to a guild would marry the widow of a member. (A woman could inherit her husband's workshop but could not run it.) Guild membership was essential for establishing an artist's reputation and for obtaining commissions. The guild inspected paintings to evaluate workmanship and ensure that its members used quality materials. It also secured adequate payment for its artists' labor.

Women had many fewer opportunities than men to train as artists, in large part because of social and moral constraints that forbade women to reside as apprentices in the homes of male masters. Moreover, from the 16th century, when academic training courses supplemented and then replaced guild training, until the 20th century, women would not as a rule expect or be permitted instruction in figure painting, because it involved dissection of cadavers and study of the nude male model. Flemish women interested in pursuing art as a career—for example, Caterina van Hemessen (FIG. 23-16)—most often received tutoring from fathers and husbands who were professionals and whom the women assisted in all the technical

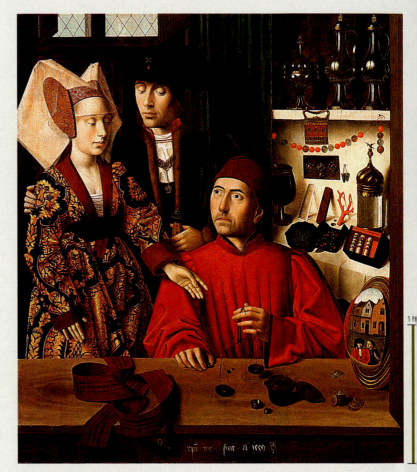

20-10 PETRUS CHRISTUS, *A Goldsmith in His Shop*, 1449. Oil on wood, 3′ 3″ × 2′ 10″. Metropolitan Museum of Art, New York (Robert Lehman Collection, 1975).

Once thought to depict Eligius, the patron saint of goldsmiths, Christus's painting, made for the Bruges goldsmiths' guild, is more likely a genre scene of a couple shopping for a wedding ring.

procedures of the craft. Despite these obstacles, membership records of the art guilds of Bruges and other cities reveal that a substantial number of Flemish women were able to establish themselves as artists during the 15th century. That they succeeded in negotiating the difficult path to acceptance as professionals is a testament to both their tenacity and their artistic skill.

Later Flemish Painters

Robert Campin, Jan van Eyck, and Rogier van der Weyden were the leading figures of the first generation of "Northern Renaissance" painters. (Art historians usually transfer to northern Europe, with less validity than in its original usage, the term "Renaissance," coined to describe the conscious revival of classical art in Italy.) The second generation of Flemish masters, active during the latter half of the 15th century, had much in common with their illustrious predecessors, especially a preference for using oil paints to create naturalistic representations, often, although not always, of traditional Christian subjects for installation in churches.

PETRUS CHRISTUS One work of uncertain Christian content is *A Goldsmith in His Shop* (FIG. **20-10**) by PETRUS CHRISTUS (ca. 1410–1472), who settled in Bruges in 1444. According to the traditional interpretation, *A Goldsmith in His Shop* portrays Saint Eligius (who was initially a master goldsmith before committing his life to God) sitting in his stall, showing an elegantly attired couple a selection of rings. The bride's betrothal girdle lies on the table as a symbol of chastity, and the woman reaches for the ring the goldsmith weighs. The artist's inclusion of a crystal container for Eucharistic wafers (on the lower shelf to the right of Saint Eligius) and the scales (a reference to the Last Judgment) supports a religious interpretation of this painting and continues the Flemish tradition of imbuing everyday objects with symbolic significance. A halo once encircled the goldsmith's head, seemingly confirming the religious nature of

this scene. Scientists have determined, however, that the halo was a later addition by another artist, and restorers have removed it.

Most scholars now think that the painting, although not devoid of religious content, should be seen as a vocational painting of the type often produced for installation in Flemish guild chapels. Although the couple's presence suggests a marriage portrait, the patrons were probably not the couple portrayed but rather the goldsmiths' guild in Bruges. Saint Eligius was the patron saint of gold- and silversmiths, blacksmiths, and metalworkers, all of whom shared a chapel in a building adjacent to their meetinghouse. The reconsecration of this chapel took place in 1449, the same date as the Christus painting. Therefore, it seems probable that the artist painted *A Goldsmith in His Shop*, which illustrates an economic transaction and focuses on the goldsmith's profession, specifically for the guild chapel. A guild chapel is also the likely setting of Rogier van der Weyden's *Saint Luke Drawing the Virgin* (FIG. 20-1). As noted, in the 15th century, in addition to their primary function as "trade unions," guilds played an increasingly important role in community life and often became major patrons of art in their cities (see "The Artist's Profession in Flanders," page 566).

Christus went to great lengths to produce a historically credible image. For example, the variety of objects depicted in the painting serves as advertisement for the goldsmiths' guild. Included are the goldsmiths' raw materials (precious stones, beads, crystal, coral, and seed pearls) scattered among finished products (rings, buckles, and brooches). The pewter vessels on the upper shelves are donation pitchers, which town leaders gave to distinguished guests. All these meticulously painted objects not only attest to the centrality and importance of goldsmiths to both the secular and sacred communities but also enhance the naturalism of the painting. The convex mirror in the foreground showing another couple and a street with houses serves to extend the painting's space into the viewer's space, further creating the illusion of reality, as in Jan van Eyck's Arnolfini portrait (FIG. 20-7).

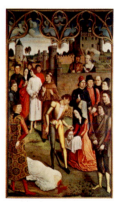

20-11A BOUTS, *Beheading of the Count*, ca. 1473–1481.

DIERIC BOUTS In *Last Supper* (FIG. **20-11**), DIERIC BOUTS (ca. 1415–1475) of Haarlem chose a different means of suggesting spatial recession. The painting is the central panel of the *Altarpiece of the Holy Sacrament*, which the Confraternity of the Holy Sacrament in Louvain commissioned in 1464. Four years later, Bouts became the city's official painter and was asked to produce a series of panels—including *Wrongful Beheading of the Count* (FIG. **20-11A**) and *Justice of Otto III* (FIG. **20-11B**)—for Louvain's town hall. Bouts's *Last Supper* is one of the earliest Northern Renaissance paintings to employ *linear perspective* and a *vanishing point* to create the illusion of depth. All of the central room's *orthogonals* (converging diagonal lines imagined to be behind and perpendicular to the picture plane) lead to the vanishing point in the center of the mantelpiece above Jesus's head. The small side room, however, has its own vanishing point, and neither it nor the vanishing point of the main room falls on the horizon of the landscape (the *horizon*

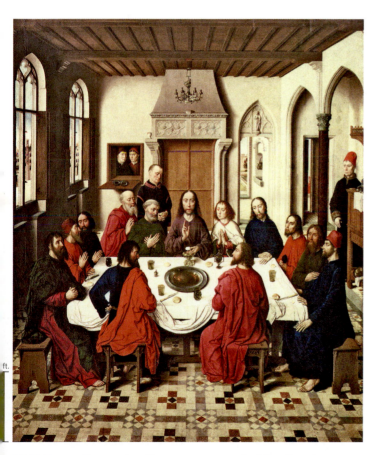

20-11 DIERIC BOUTS, *Last Supper*, center panel of the *Altarpiece of the Holy Sacrament*, Saint Peter's, Louvain, Belgium, 1464–1468. Oil on wood, 6' × 5'.

One of the earliest Northern Renaissance paintings to employ Italian linear perspective, this *Last Supper* includes four servants in Flemish attire—portraits of the altarpiece's patrons.

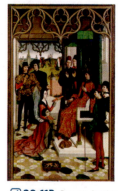

20-11B BOUTS, *Justice of Otto III*, ca. 1470–1473.

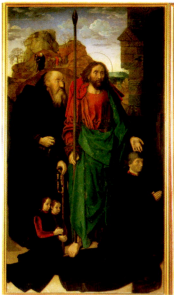
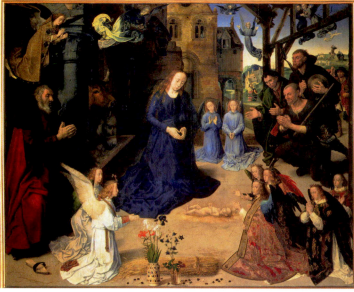
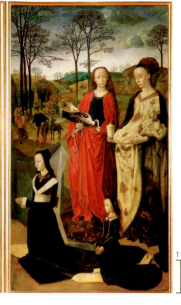

20-12 Hugo van der Goes, *Adoration of the Shepherds* (*Portinari Altarpiece,* open), from Sant'Egidio, Florence, Italy, ca. 1473–1478. Tempera and oil on wood, center panel 8' 3½" × 10', each wing 8' 3½" × 4' 7½". Galleria degli Uffizi, Florence.

This altarpiece is a rare instance of the awarding of a major commission in Italy to a Flemish painter. The Florentines admired Hugo's realistic details and brilliant portrayal of human character.

line) seen through the windows, as in Italian Renaissance paintings composed according to the strict rules of linear perspective (see "Linear Perspective," page 587).

In *Last Supper,* Bouts did not depict the biblical narrative itself but instead presented Jesus in the role of a priest performing the liturgical ritual of the consecration of the Eucharistic wafer. By divid-

ing the apostles into two asymmetrical groups with no one sitting at the middle of the near side of the table, Bouts focused attention on the Savior and the food platter and wine chalice at the table's center. Bouts's *Last Supper* contrasts strongly with other depictions of the same subject, which often represented Jesus's prediction of Judas's betrayal or his comforting of John. The Confraternity of the

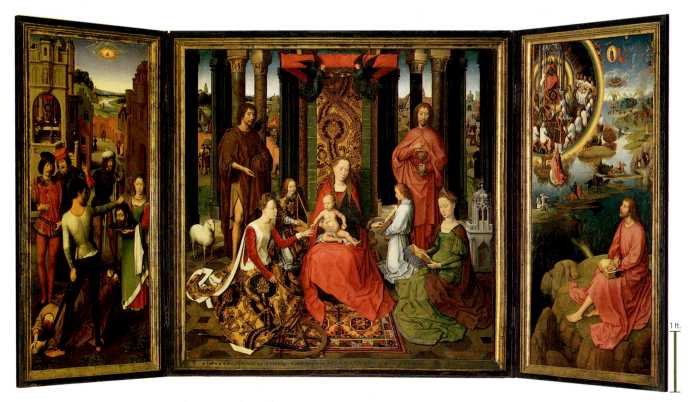

20-13 Hans Memling, *Virgin with Saints and Angels,* center panel of the *Saint John Altarpiece,* Hospitaal Sint Jan, Bruges, Belgium, 1479. Oil on wood, center panel 5' 7¾" × 5' 7¾", each wing 5' 7¾" × 2' 7⅛".

Memling specialized in images of the Madonna. His *Saint John Altarpiece* exudes an opulence that results from the sparkling and luminous colors and the realistic depiction of rich tapestries and brocades.

Holy Sacrament dedicated itself to the worship of the Eucharist, and the smaller panels on the altarpiece's wings depict Old Testament *prefigurations* of the Eucharist. Bouts also added four servants (two looking through the windowlike opening in the rear wall and two standing) not mentioned in the biblical account, all dressed in Flemish attire. These are portraits of the four members of the confraternity who contracted Bouts to paint the altarpiece, continuing the Flemish tradition of inserting into representations of biblical events portraits of the painting's patrons, first noted in the *Mérode Altarpiece* (FIG. 20-4).

HUGO VAN DER GOES By the mid-15th century, Flemish art had achieved renown throughout Europe. The *Portinari Altarpiece* (FIG. 20-12), for example, is a large-scale Flemish work in a family chapel in Florence, Italy. The artist who received the commission was HUGO VAN DER GOES (ca. 1440–1482), who joined the painters' guild of Ghent as a master in 1467 and served as the guild's dean from 1473 to 1475. Hugo painted the triptych in Flanders for Tommaso Portinari, an Italian shipowner and agent in Bruges for the powerful Medici bank of Florence. The altarpiece was Portinari's gift to the church of Sant'Egidio, and he appears on the wings with his family and their patron saints. The main panel, *Adoration of the Shepherds*, depicts a subject based on the 14th-century vision of a Swedish saint in which Mary, instead of cradling her newborn son, kneels solemnly to join Joseph, the angels, and the shepherds in adoring the infant Savior, who lies on the ground and glows with divine light. In order to situate the main actors at the center of the panel, Hugo tilted the ground, a compositional device he may have derived from the tilted stage floors of 15th-century mystery plays. Three shepherds enter from the right rear. Hugo represented them in attitudes of wonder, piety, and gaping curiosity. Their lined faces, work-worn hands, and uncouth dress and manner seem immediately familiar.

The architecture and a continuous wintry northern European landscape unify the three panels. Symbols surface throughout the altarpiece. Iris and columbine flowers are emblems of the sorrows of the Virgin. The angels represent the 15 joys of Mary. A sheaf of wheat stands for Bethlehem (the "house of bread" in Hebrew), a reference to the Eucharist. The harp of David, emblazoned over the building's portal in the middle distance (just to the right of the Virgin's head), signifies the ancestry of Christ. To stress the meaning and significance of the illustrated event, Hugo revived medieval pictorial devices. Small scenes shown in the background of the altarpiece represent (from left to right) the journey of Mary and Joseph to Bethlehem, the annunciation to the shepherds, and the arrival of the magi. Hugo's variation in the scale of his figures to differentiate them by their importance to the central event also reflects older traditions. Still, he put a vigorous, penetrating realism to work in a new direction, characterizing human beings according to their social level while showing their common humanity.

After Portinari placed the altarpiece in his family's chapel in the Florentine church of Sant'Egidio, it created a considerable stir among Italian artists. Although the painting may have seemed unstructured to them, Hugo's masterful technique and what the Florentines deemed incredible realism in representing drapery, flowers, animals, and, above all, human character and emotion made a deep impression on them. At least one Florentine artist, Domenico Ghirlandaio (FIGS. 21-26 and 21-27), paid tribute to the Flemish master by using Hugo's most striking motif, the adoring shepherds, in one of his own *Nativity* paintings.

HANS MEMLING Hugo's contemporary, HANS MEMLING (ca. 1430–1494), may have trained as a painter in Rogier van der Weyden's studio. He became a citizen of Bruges in 1465 and received numerous commissions from the city's wealthy merchants, Flemish and foreign alike. He specialized in portraits of his patrons (one of whom was Tommaso Portinari; FIG. 20-14A) and images of the Madonna. Memling's many paintings of the Virgin portray young, slight, pretty princesses, each holding a doll-like infant Jesus. The center panel of the *Saint John Altarpiece* is *Virgin with Saints and Angels* (FIG. 20-13). The patrons of this altarpiece—two brothers and two sisters of the order of the Hospital of Saint John in Bruges—appear on the exterior side panels (not illustrated). In the main panel, two angels, one playing a musical instrument and the other holding a book, flank the Virgin. To the sides of Mary's throne stand Saints John the Baptist on the left and John the Evangelist on the right. Seated in the foreground are Saints Catherine and Barbara. This gathering celebrates the *mystic marriage* of Saint Catherine of Alexandria, one of many virgin saints believed to have entered into a spiritual marriage with Christ. As one of the most revered virgins of Christ, Saint Catherine provided a model of devotion that resonated with women viewers (especially nuns). The altarpiece exudes an opulence that results from the rich colors, the meticulously depicted tapestries and brocades, and the serenity of the figures. The composition is balanced and serene, the color sparkling and luminous, and the execution of the highest technical quality.

Memling combined portraiture and Madonna imagery again in a much less ambitious—and more typical—work (FIG. 20-14) he painted for Martin van Nieuwenhove (1464–1500). The smaller scale of the private commission and its

20-14 HANS MEMLING, *Diptych of Martin van Nieuwenhove*, 1487. Oil on wood, each panel 1' 5$\frac{3}{8}$" × 1' 1". Memlingmuseum, Bruges.

In this diptych, the Virgin and Child pay a visit to the home of 23-year-old Martin van Nieuwenhove. A round convex mirror reflects the three figures and unites the two halves of the diptych spatially.

much more intimate character underscore the different approaches the same painter regularly took when producing artworks for different kinds of patrons and for public versus private settings. Martin van Nieuwenhove was the scion of an important Bruges family that held various posts in the civic government. He himself served as burgomeister of Bruges in 1497. The painting takes the form of a diptych, with the patron portrayed on the right wing praying to the Madonna and Child on the left wing. According to inscriptions on the frames, van Nieuwenhove commissioned the work in 1487 when he was 23 years old. He died only 13 years later, 3 years after becoming mayor.

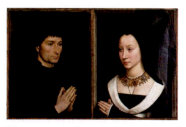

20-14A MEMLING, *Tommaso Portinari and Maria Baroncelli*, ca. 1470.

The format of the van Nieuwenhove diptych follows the pattern that Memling used earlier for his wedding triptych *Tommaso Portinari and Maria Baroncelli* (FIG. 20-14A) but with only a single (male) portrait. (The lost central section of the Portinari triptych probably closely resembled the van Nieuwenhove Madonna and Child.) Memling's portrayals of Mary and Jesus consistently feature a tender characterization of the young Virgin and her nude infant son. Here, however, Memling set both the Madonna and her patron in the interior of a well-appointed Flemish home featuring stained-glass windows. The window to the left of the Virgin's head bears van Nieuwenhove's coat of arms. The window behind the donor depicts his patron saint, Martin of Tours. These precisely recorded details identify the home as van Nieuwenhove's (the Minnewater Bridge in Bruges is visible through the open window), and the Madonna and Child have honored him by coming to his private residence. Even Saint Luke had to go to the Virgin's home to paint her portrait (FIG. 20-1), but the conceit is a familiar one in Flemish painting. An early example is the Annunciation taking place in the home of Peter Inghelbrecht in Robert Campin's *Mérode Altarpiece* (FIG. 20-4). In the Memling portrait diptych, the Christ Child sits on the same ledge as the donor's open prayer book. Also uniting the two wings of the diptych is the round convex mirror behind the Virgin's right shoulder in which the viewer sees the reflection of the Virgin and van Nieuwenhove as well as the rest of the room (compare FIGS. 20-7 and 20-10).

FRANCE

In contrast to the prosperity and peace that Flanders enjoyed during the 15th century, in France the Hundred Years' War crippled economic enterprise and prevented political stability. The anarchy of war and the weakness of the kings gave rise to a group of duchies, each with significant power and the resources to commission major artworks. The strongest and wealthiest of these has already been examined—the duchy of Burgundy, which controlled Flanders. But the dukes of Berry, Bourbon, and Nemours as well as members of the French royal court were also important art patrons.

Manuscript Painting

During the 15th century, French artists built on the achievements of Gothic painters (see page 395) and produced exquisitely refined illuminated manuscripts. Among the most significant developments in French manuscript painting was a new conception and presentation of space. Paintings in manuscripts took on more pronounced char-

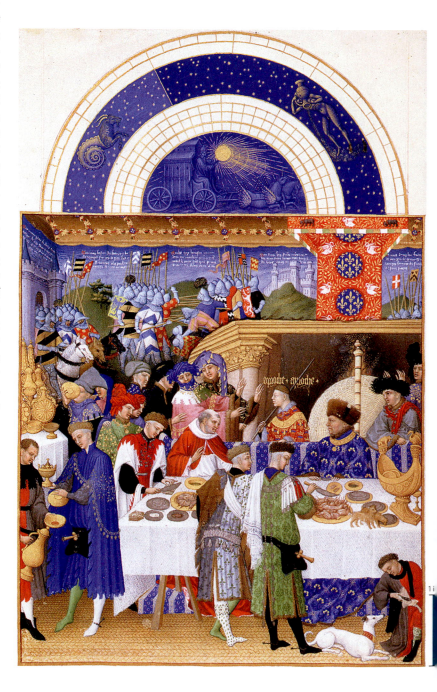

20-15 LIMBOURG BROTHERS (POL, HERMAN, JEAN), *January*, from *Les Très Riches Heures du Duc de Berry*, 1413–1416. Colors and ink on vellum, $8\frac{7}{8}$" × $5\frac{3}{8}$". Musée Condé, Chantilly.

The sumptuous pictures in *Les Très Riches Heures* depict characteristic activities of each month. The prominence of genre subjects reflects the increasing integration of religious and secular art.

acteristics as illusionistic scenes. Increased contact with Italy, where Renaissance artists had revived the pictorial principles of classical antiquity, may have influenced French painters' interest in illusionism.

LIMBOURG BROTHERS The most innovative early-15th-century manuscript illuminators were the three Limbourg brothers—Pol, Herman, and Jean—from Nijmegen in the Netherlands. They were nephews of Jean Malouel, the court artist of Philip the Bold (see page 558). Following in the footsteps of earlier illustrators such as Jean Pucelle (FIGS. 13-35 and 13-35A), the Limbourg brothers expanded the illusionistic capabilities of illumination. Trained in the Netherlands, the brothers moved to Paris no later than 1402, and between 1405 and their death in 1416, probably from the plague, they worked in Paris and Bourges for Jean, duke of Berry (r. 1360–1416) and brother of Philip the Bold of Burgundy and King Charles V (r. 1364–1380) of France.

Jean ruled the western French regions of Berry, Poitou, and Auvergne (MAP 20-1). The duke was an avid art patron and focused on collecting manuscripts, jewels, and rare artifacts. Among the more than 300 manuscripts he owned were Pucelle's *Belleville Breviary* (FIG. 13-35) and the *Hours of Jeanne d'Évreux* (FIG. 13-35A) as well as *Les Très Riches Heures du Duc de Berry* (*The Very Sumptuous Hours of the Duke of Berry;* FIGS. 20-15 and 20-16), which he commissioned the Limbourg brothers to produce. A *Book of Hours,* like a *breviary,* was a book used for reciting prayers (see "Medieval Books," page 316). As prayer books, they replaced the traditional *psalters* (books of psalms), which were the only liturgical books in private hands until the mid-13th century. The centerpiece of a Book of Hours was the "Office [prayer] of the Blessed Virgin," which contained liturgical passages to be read privately at set times during the day, from *matins* (dawn prayers) to *compline* (the last of the prayers recited daily). An illustrated calendar containing local religious feast days usually preceded the Office of the Blessed Virgin. Penitential psalms, devotional prayers, litanies to the saints, and other prayers, including those of the Holy Cross and for the dead, followed the centerpiece. Books of Hours became favorite possessions of the northern European aristocracy during the 14th and 15th centuries. These costly books eventually became available to affluent merchants and contributed to the decentralization of religious practice that was one factor in the Protestant Reformation in the early 16th century (see page 680).

The full-page calendar pictures of *Les Très Riches Heures* are the most famous in the history of manuscript illumination. They represent the 12 months in terms of the associated seasonal tasks, alternating scenes of nobility and peasantry, and featuring the duke's relationship with his courtiers and peasants. Above each picture is a *lunette* in which the Limbourgs depicted the zodiac signs and the chariot of the sun as it makes its yearly cycle through the heavens. Beyond its function as a religious book, *Les Très Riches Heures* also furnishes a picture of life in the territory the duke ruled—a picture designed to flatter the Limbourgs' patron. For example, the colorful calendar picture for January (FIG. **20-15**) portrays a New Year's reception at court. The duke appears as magnanimous host, his head circled by the fire screen, almost halolike, behind him. His chamberlain stands next to him, urging the guests forward with the words "*aproche, aproche.*" The lavish spread of food on the table and the large tapestry on the back wall augment the richness and extravagance of the setting and the occasion.

In contrast, the illustration for October (FIG. **20-16**) focuses on the peasantry. Here, the Limbourg brothers depicted a sower, a man plowing on horseback, and washerwomen, along with city dwellers, who promenade in front of the Louvre (the French king's residence at the time, now one of the world's great art museums). The peasants do not appear

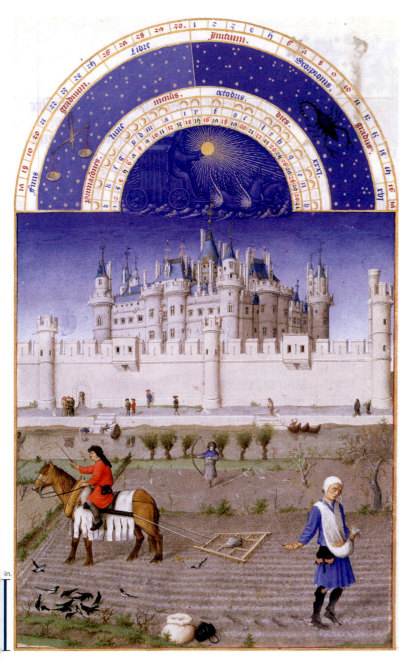

in.

20-16 Limbourg brothers (Pol, Herman, Jean), *October,* from *Les Très Riches Heures du Duc de Berry,* 1413–1416. Colors and ink on vellum, 8⅞" × 5⅜". Musée Condé, Chantilly.

The Limbourg brothers expanded the illusionistic capabilities of manuscript painting with their care in rendering architectural details and their convincing depiction of cast shadows.

discontented as they go about their various tasks. Surely, this imagery flattered the duke's sense of himself as a compassionate master. The growing artistic interest in naturalism is evident here in the careful way the painter recorded the architectural details of the Louvre and in the convincing shadows of the people and objects (such as the archer scarecrow and the horse) in the scene.

As a whole, *Les Très Riches Heures* reinforced the image of the duke of Berry as a devout man, cultured *bibliophile* (lover of books), sophisticated art patron, and powerful and magnanimous leader. Further, the expanded range of subject matter, especially the prominence of *genre* subjects in a religious book, reflected the increasing integration of religious and secular concerns in both art and life at the time. Although all three Limbourg brothers worked on *Les Très Riches Heures,* art historians have never been able to ascertain definitively which brother painted which images. (One scholar has suggested that because the book was left unfinished at the time the brothers died, some of the details are the work of a fourth artist, who completed the illustrations around the middle of the century.) Given the common practice of collaboration on artistic projects at this time, however, the determination of specific authorship is not very important. Together, the *Très Riches Heures* illuminators reoriented the art of manuscript illumination to approximate more closely the art of panel painting, treating the pages of books as if they were windows onto the world of 15th-century northern Europe.

MARY OF BURGUNDY The Limbourgs' most accomplished successor at the end of the century was an anonymous illuminator known as the MASTER OF MARY OF BURGUNDY. Some scholars identify him as ALEXANDER BENING (ca. 1444–1519) of Ghent, a painter in the circle of Hugo van der Goes (FIG. 20-12). The two facing pages illustrated here (FIG. 20-17) are the opening full-page illumination and one of the daily prayers in the private devotional Book of Hours that belonged to Mary, the last duchess of Burgundy (r. 1477–1482) and daughter of Charles the Bold. She is the elegantly dressed woman sitting in a private chapel with her pet dog on her lap, reading from a prayer book of the same size and format as the one in which her portrait appears. On a ledge to her left are her rosary beads and a tall vase with purple irises, flowers associated with the Virgin Mary. The masterful representation of rich fabrics, of Mary's transparent veil, and of the still life of flowers all attest to this painter's skill and powers of observation.

Even more remarkable is the illuminator's meticulously detailed depiction—at only half the size of Jan van Eyck's *Madonna in a Church* (FIG. 20-6A)—of the Gothic church seen through the window of Mary's chapel. The scene presented to the viewer through the chapel window within the page's "window onto the world"— a brilliant conception in itself—is the realization of Mary's prayers. The duchess has been granted a private audience with the Virgin without any interceding priest. She, accompanied by her ladies-in-

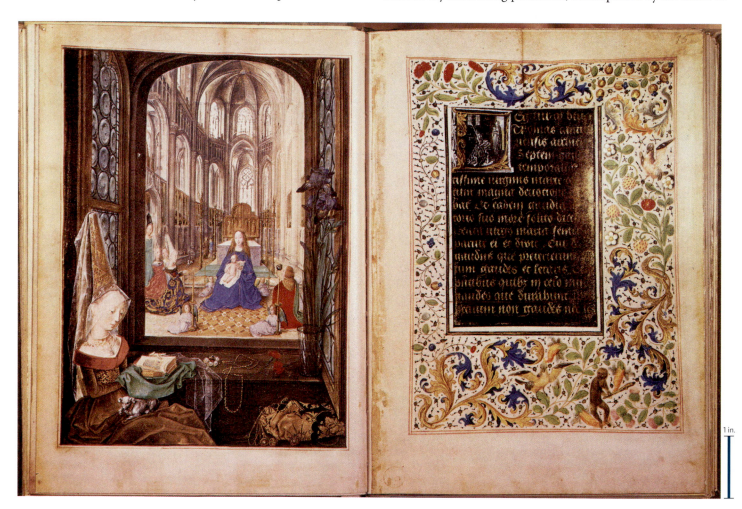

20-17 MASTER OF MARY OF BURGUNDY, *Mary of Burgundy at Prayer,* folios 14 verso and 15 recto of the *Hours of Mary of Burgundy,* ca. 1477. Colors and ink on parchment, illumination on left page 7 3/8" × 5 1/8". Österreichische Nationalbibliothek, Vienna.

In this Book of Hours, the page became literally a window onto the world. Mary of Burgundy prays in a private chapel. Seen through a window is the answer to her prayers—an audience with the Virgin.

waiting, kneels before the Virgin, who sits before the church altar, attended by angels and holding the Christ Child in her lap. Both holy figures turn their heads to look at the duchess. The illumination has few peers in the history of art as an image of pious devotion.

Panel Painting

In addition to illustrated books, independent paintings were popular in France, as in Flanders, for private devotional use. The preferred medium was oil paint on wood panels.

JEAN FOUQUET Among the French artists whose paintings were in high demand was JEAN FOUQUET (ca. 1425–1478). Fouquet's workshop was in Tours, and he received important commissions from King Charles VII (r. 1422–1461, the patron and client of Jacques Coeur; FIG. 13-30) and from the duke of Nemours and other elite members of the French aristocracy. Fouquet painted a diptych (FIG. 20-18) for Étienne Chevalier, who, despite his lowly birth as the son of one of Charles VII's secretaries, rose to become royal treasurer in 1452. In the left panel of the *Melun Diptych* (named for its original location in Melun Cathedral), Chevalier appears with his patron saint, Saint Stephen (Étienne in French). Appropriately, Fouquet's donor portrait of Chevalier depicts his prominent patron as devout—kneeling, with hands clasped in prayer. The representation of the pious donor with his standing saint recalls Flemish art, as do the three-quarter stances and the realism of Chevalier's portrait.

The artist portrayed Saint Stephen, whose head also has a portrait-like quality, holding the stone symbolizing his martyrdom (death by stoning) atop a volume of the holy scriptures, thereby ensuring that viewers can properly identify the saint. Fouquet rendered the entire image in meticulous detail and included a highly ornamented architectural setting.

In its original diptych form (the two panels are now in different museums), the viewer would follow the gaze of Chevalier and Saint Stephen over to the right panel, which depicts the Virgin Mary and Christ Child in a most unusual way—with marblelike flesh, surrounded by red and blue *cherubs* (chubby winged child angels). The juxtaposition of these two images enabled the patron to bear witness to the sacred. The integration of sacred and secular (especially the political or personal), prevalent in other Northern Renaissance artworks, also emerges here, which complicates the reading of this diptych. Agnès Sorel (1421–1450), the mistress of King Charles VII (see page 393), was Fouquet's model for the Virgin Mary, whose left breast is exposed, presumably to nurse the infant Jesus, but she does not look at her son or the viewer. (Mary as nursing mother is a rare although not unique way of representing the Virgin in northern Europe; compare FIG. 20-1.) Chevalier commissioned this painting after Sorel's death, probably by poisoning while pregnant with the king's child. Thus, in addition to the religious interpretation of this diptych, there is surely a personal and political narrative here as well, made all the more complex given that Sorel gave birth to three of the king's daughters, but never a son.

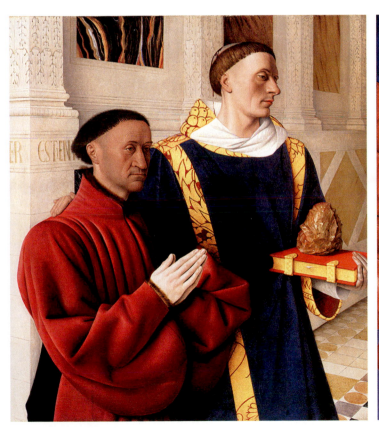 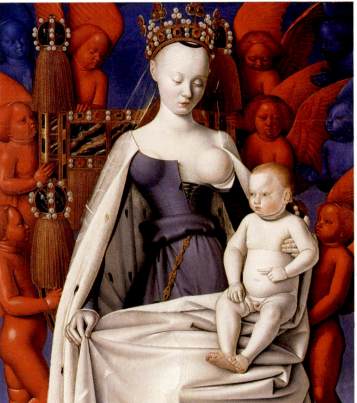

20-18 JEAN FOUQUET, *Melun Diptych*, ca. 1452. Left wing: *Étienne Chevalier and Saint Stephen*. Oil on wood, $3'\frac{1}{2}'' \times 2'9\frac{1}{2}''$. Gemäldegalerie, Staatliche Museen zu Berlin, Berlin. Right wing: *Virgin and Child*. Oil on wood, $3'1\frac{1}{4}'' \times 2'9\frac{1}{2}''$. Koninklijk Museum voor Schone Kunsten, Antwerp.

Fouquet's meticulous representation of a pious kneeling donor with a standing patron saint recalls Flemish painting, as do the three-quarter stances and the realism of the donor's portrait head.

20-19 KONRAD WITZ, *Miraculous Draft of Fish,* exterior wing of *Altarpiece of Saint Peter,* from the Chapel of Notre-Dame des Maccabées, Cathedral of Saint Peter, Geneva, Switzerland, 1444. Oil on wood, 4' 3" × 5' 1". Musée d'Art et d'Histoire, Geneva.

Konrad Witz set this biblical story on Lake Geneva. The painting is one of the first 15th-century works depicting a specific locale and is noteworthy for the painter's skill in rendering water effects.

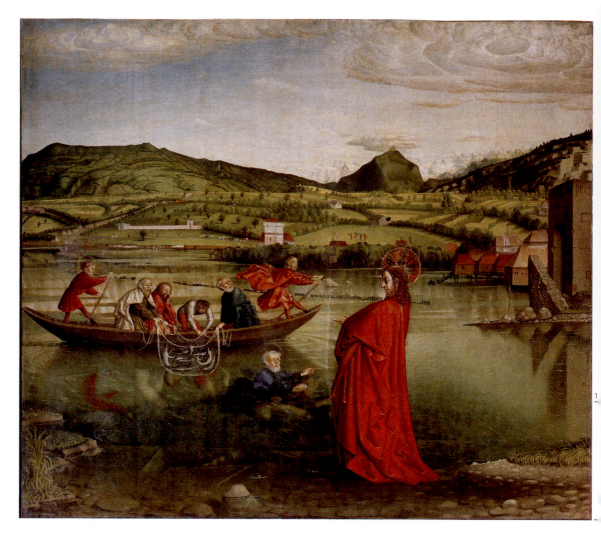

HOLY ROMAN EMPIRE

Because the Holy Roman Empire (whose core was Germany) did not participate in the drawn-out saga of the Hundred Years' War, its economy remained stable and prosperous. Without a dominant court to commission artworks, wealthy merchants and clergy became the primary German art patrons during the 15th century.

Panel Painting

The art of the early Northern Renaissance in the Holy Roman Empire displays a pronounced stylistic diversity. Some artists followed developments in Flemish painting, and large-scale altarpieces featuring naturalistically painted biblical themes were familiar sights in the Holy Roman Empire.

KONRAD WITZ Among the most notable 15th-century German altarpieces is the *Altarpiece of Saint Peter,* painted by KONRAD WITZ (ca. 1400–1446) for the chapel of Notre-Dame des Maccabées in the Cathedral of Saint Peter in Geneva, Switzerland. Signed by "Magister Conradus of Basel" and dated 1444, the altarpiece is a triptych featuring Witz's paintings on both the exterior and interior. *Miraculous Draft of Fish* (FIG. **20-19**) appears on one of the exterior wings. The other (not illustrated) depicts the release of Saint Peter from prison. The central panel is lost. On the interior wings, Witz painted scenes of the adoration of the magi and of

Saint Peter's presentation of the donor (Bishop François de Mies) to the Virgin and Child. *Miraculous Draft of Fish* shows Peter, the first pope, unsuccessfully trying to emulate Christ walking on water. The choice of this episode from among others in Peter's life (see "Early Christian Saints," page 236) may be a commentary on the part of Witz's patron, the Swiss cardinal, on the limited power of the pope in Rome.

The painting is particularly significant because of the landscape's prominence. Witz showed precocious skill in the study of water effects—the shimmering sky on the slowly moving lake surface, the mirrored reflections of the figures in the boat, and the transparency of the shallow water in the foreground. He observed and represented the landscape so carefully that art historians have been able to determine the exact location shown. Witz presented a view of the shores of Lake Geneva, with the town of Geneva on the right and Le Môle Mountain in the distance behind Christ's head. This painting is one of the first 15th-century works depicting a specific, identifiable site. The work of other leading German painters of the mid-15th century—for example, STEFAN LOCHNER (ca. 1400–1451)—retained medieval features to a much greater degree, as is immediately evident in a comparison between Witz's landscape and Lochner's *Madonna in the Rose Garden* (FIG. **20-19A**).

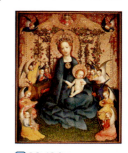

20-19A LOCHNER, *Madonna in the Rose Garden,* ca. 1435–1440.

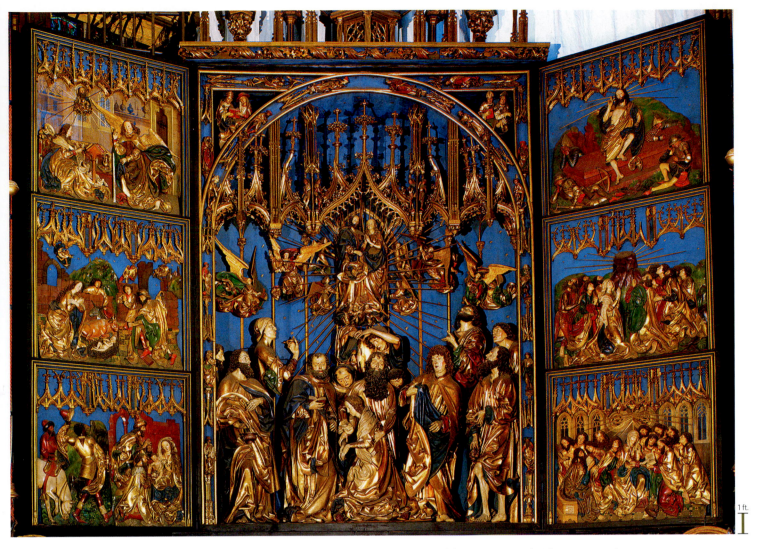

20-20 VEIT STOSS, *Death and Assumption of the Virgin*, center panel of the *Altarpiece of the Virgin Mary* (with wings open), Church of Saint Mary, Kraków, Poland, 1477–1489. Painted and gilded lime-wood, central panel 23' 9" high.

In this huge painted and gilded sculptured wood altarpiece, Stoss used every figural and ornamental element from the vocabulary of Gothic art to heighten the emotion and glorify the sacred event.

Sculpture

In contrast to Flanders, where painted altarpieces were the norm, in the Holy Roman Empire many of the leading 15th-century artists specialized in carving large wood retables. These grandiose sculpted altarpieces reveal the lingering power of the Late Gothic style.

VEIT STOSS The sculptor VEIT STOSS (ca. 1447–1533) trained in the Upper Rhine region, possibly in Strasbourg, but settled in Kraków (in present-day Poland) in 1477. In that year, he began work on a monumental altarpiece for the church of Saint Mary in Kraków, paid for by the city's citizens. In the central boxlike shrine is *Death and Assumption of the Virgin* (FIG. **20-20**), peopled by huge carved, painted, and gilded figures, some 9 feet high. (An altarpiece of this kind may have inspired Rogier van der Weyden's *Deposition* [FIG. 20-9].) On both the outer and inner faces of the wings, Stoss portrayed scenes from the lives of Christ and Mary. The altar forcefully expresses the intense piety of Gothic culture in its late phase, when artists used every figural and ornamental motif in the repertoire of Gothic art to heighten the emotion and to glorify sacred

events. In the center panel of the Kraków altarpiece, Christ's disciples congregate around the Virgin, who collapses, dying. One of them supports her, while another wrings his hands in grief. Above, Mary rises to Heaven with the resurrected Christ. Stoss posed others in attitudes of woe and psychic shock, striving for realism in every minute detail. He engulfed the figures in restless, twisting, and curving swaths of drapery whose broken and writhing lines unite the whole tableau in a vision of agitated emotion. The artist's massing of sharp, broken, and pierced forms that dart flamelike through the composition—at once unifying and animating it—recalls the design principles of Late Gothic architecture (FIG. 13-27). Indeed, in the Kraków altarpiece, Stoss merged sculpture and architecture, enhancing their union with paint and gilding.

The Kraków altarpiece gives modern viewers the opportunity to appreciate the polychromy that was standard in ancient and medieval sculpture in both wood and stone. Examples such as this one are unfortunately rare. The vast majority of preserved statues and reliefs from antiquity and the Middle Ages give a false impression of their original appearance (compare FIGS. 3-13A and 5-63A) because the paint has disappeared.

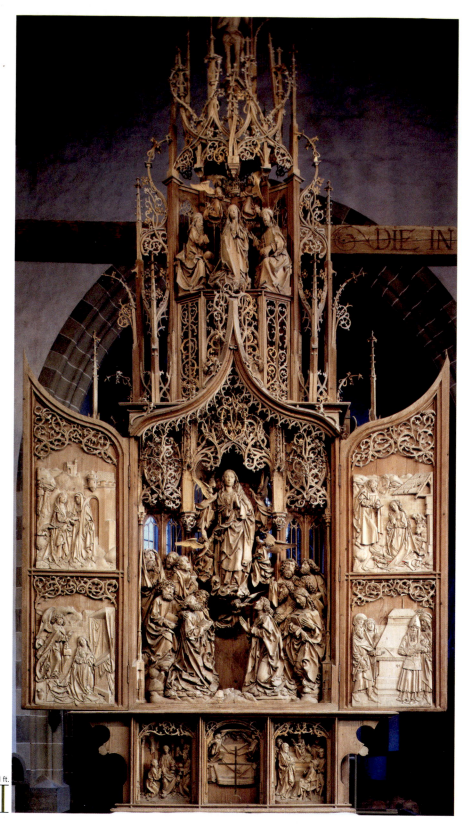

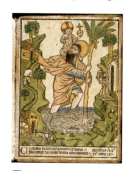

intricate Gothic forms, especially in the altarpiece's elaborate canopy, but unlike Stoss, he did not paint the figures or the background. By employing an endless and restless line running through the garments of the figures, the Würzburg master succeeded in setting the whole design into fluid motion, and no individual element functions without the rest. The draperies float and flow around bodies lost within them, serving not as descriptions but as design elements that tie the figures to one another and to the framework. A look of psychic strain, a facial expression common in Riemenschneider's work, heightens the spirituality of the figures, immaterial and weightless as they appear.

Graphic Arts

A new age blossomed in the 15th century with a sudden technological advance that had widespread effects—the invention by Johannes Gutenberg (ca. 1400–1468) of moveable type around 1450 and the development of the printing press. Printing had been known in China centuries before, but had never fostered, as it did in 15th-century Europe, a revolution in written communication and in the generation and management of information. Printing provided new and challenging media for artists, and the earliest form was the *woodcut*. Artists produced inexpensive woodcuts such as the *Buxheim Saint Christopher* (FIG. 20-21A) before the development of moveable-type printing. But when a rise in literacy and the improved economy necessitated the production of illustrated books on a grand scale, artists met the challenge of bringing the woodcut picture onto the same letterpress text pages (see "How to Illustrate Printed Books," page 577).

🔼 **20-21A** *Buxheim Saint Christopher*, 1423(?).

MARTIN SCHONGAUER The woodcut medium hardly had matured when printmakers introduced the technique of *engraving* (see "Engraving and Etching," page 578). Begun in the 1430s and well developed by 1450, engraving proved much more flexible than woodcut. Predictably, in the second half of the century, engraving began to replace the woodcut process for making both book illustrations and widely popular single prints. Not surprisingly, many of the earliest engravers were professional goldsmiths, who easily applied their training to the new art form.

MARTIN SCHONGAUER (ca. 1430–1491) of Colmar, a painter and the son of a goldsmith, was the most skilled and subtle northern

20-21 TILMAN RIEMENSCHNEIDER, *Assumption of the Virgin* (*Creglingen Altarpiece*), Herrgottskirche, Creglingen, Germany, ca. 1495–1505. Lime-wood, 30' 2" high.

Riemenschneider specialized in carving large wood retables. His works feature intricate Gothic tracery and religious figures whose bodies are almost lost within their swirling garments.

TILMAN RIEMENSCHNEIDER *Assumption of the Virgin* is also the center panel of the *Creglingen Altarpiece* (FIG. 20-21), carved by TILMAN RIEMENSCHNEIDER (ca. 1460–1531) of Würzburg for a parish church in Creglingen, Germany. Riemenschneider incorporated

PROBLEMS AND SOLUTIONS
How to Illustrate Printed Books

With the invention of moveable type in the 15th century and the new widespread availability of paper from commercial mills, the art of print-making developed rapidly in Europe. A *print* is an artwork on paper, usually produced in multiple impressions. The set of prints an artist creates from a single print surface is called an *edition.* Like the manufac-turing of books on a press, the printmaking process involves the transfer of ink from a printing surface to paper. This can be accomplished in several ways. The oldest and simplest is the *relief* method—carving the design into a surface, usually a soft wood, such as pear. Relief printing requires artists to conceptualize their images in reverse—that is, they must draw mirror images of the intended design on the wood block. They then remove the surface areas around the drawn lines using a gouging instrument. Thus, when the printmaker inks the ridges that correspond to the original (reversed) drawing, the hollow areas remain dry, and a correctly oriented image results when the artist presses the printing block against paper. Because artists produce *woodcuts* through a subtractive process (removing parts of the material), it is difficult to create very thin, fluid, and closely spaced lines. Moreover, if the ridges are too thin, they will break during printing. As a result, woodcut prints (for example, FIGS. I-9, 20-21A, and 20-22) tend to exhibit stark con-trasts between the dark lines and the blank background.

During the later 15th century, publishers realized that the wood-cut was the ideal medium for solving the problem of illustrating their new printed books. The new technology quickly led to the demise of the manuscript illuminator as well as the scribe, both of whom had been essential for the production of illustrated books through the late Middle Ages, whether they were monks working in monastic *scriptoria* or lay professionals employed in the for-profit workshops of Paris and other cities.

The most ambitious early effort to produce low-cost mass-pro-duced printed books was the so-called *Nuremberg Chronicle,* a history of the world produced in Nuremberg by ANTON KOBERGER (ca. 1445–1513), with more than 650 illustrations furnished by the workshop of MICHAEL WOLGEMUT (1434–1519). The hand-colored page illustrated here (FIG. 20-22) represents *Madeburga* (modern Magdeburg, Germany). The blunt, simple lines of the woodcut technique give a detailed per-spective of Magdeburg, its harbor and shipping, its walls and towers, its churches and municipal buildings, and a statue-topped columnar monument. Despite the numerous architectural structures, this illus-tration is not an accurate depiction of the city but the product of the artist's fanciful imagination. Wolgemut often used the same image to illustrate different cities, even those with very little in common—for example, Verona, Italy, and Damascus, Syria. This depiction of Magde-burg is a generic view of a late medieval German town, not a portrait of a specific place. Regardless, the *Nuremberg Chronicle* is a monument to a new craft, which expanded in concert with the art of the printed book.

20-22 MICHAEL WOLGEMUT and workshop, *Madeburga*, page from the *Nuremberg Chronicle*, 1493. Woodcut, 1' 6$\frac{1}{8}$" × 2' 1$\frac{5}{8}$". Printed by ANTON KOBERGER.

The *Nuremberg Chronicle* is an early example of woodcut illustrations in printed books. The more than 650 pictures include detailed views of towns, but they are generic rather than specific portrayals.

MATERIALS AND TECHNIQUES
Engraving and Etching

In contrast to the production of relief prints, in the *intaglio* method of printmaking, the artist *incises* (cuts) the lines on a metal plate, often copper, rather than cuts away the area around the lines, as the relief printer does. The image can be created on the plate manually (*engraving* or *drypoint*; for example, FIG. 20-23) using a tool (a *burin* or *stylus*) or chemically (*etching*; for example, FIG. 25-16). In the etching process, an acid bath eats into the exposed parts of the plate where the artist has drawn through an acid-resistant coating. When the artist inks the surface of the intaglio plate and wipes it clean, the ink is forced into the incisions. Then the artist runs the plate and paper through a roller press, and the paper absorbs the remaining ink, creating the print. Because the artist "draws" the image onto the plate, intaglio prints differ in character from relief prints, such as woodcuts. Engravings, drypoints, and etchings generally present a wider variety of linear effects, as is immediately evident in a comparison of the roughly contemporaneous woodcut (FIG. 20-22) by Michael Wolgemut and an engraving (FIG. 20-23) by Martin Schongauer. Intaglio prints also often reveal to a greater extent evidence of the artist's touch, the result of the hand's changing pressure and shifting directions.

The paper and inks that artists use also affect the finished look of the printed image. During the 15th and 16th centuries, European printmakers used papers produced from cotton and linen rags that papermakers mashed with water into a pulp. The papermakers then applied a thin layer of this pulp to a wire screen and allowed it to dry to create the paper. As contact with Asia increased, printmakers made greater use of what was called Japan paper (of mulberry fibers) and China paper. Artists, then as now, could select from a wide variety of inks. The type and proportion of the ink ingredients affect the consistency, color, and oiliness of inks, which various papers absorb differently.

Paper is lightweight, and the portability of prints has been an important factor in their appeal to artists. The opportunity to produce numerous impressions from the same print surface also made printmaking attractive to 15th- and 16th-century artists. In addition, prints can be sold at much lower prices than paintings or sculptures. Consequently, prints reached a far wider audience than did one-of-a-kind artworks. The number and quality of existing 15th- and 16th-century European prints attest to the importance of the new print medium.

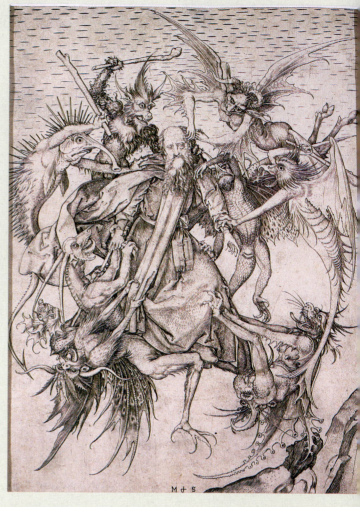

20-23 MARTIN SCHONGAUER, *Saint Anthony Tormented by Demons*, ca. 1480. Engraving, 1' $\frac{1}{4}$" × 9". Fondazione Magnani Rocca, Corte di Mamiano.

Schongauer was the most skilled of the early masters of metal engraving. By using a burin to incise lines in a copper plate, he was able to create a marvelous variety of tonal values and textures.

European master of metal engraving. His *Saint Anthony Tormented by Demons* (FIG. **20-23**) shows both the versatility of the medium and the artist's mastery of it. The stoic saint is caught in a revolving thornbush of spiky demons, who claw and tear at him furiously. With unsurpassed skill and subtlety, Schongauer incised lines of varying thickness and density into a metal plate and created marvelous distinctions of tonal values and textures—from smooth skin to rough cloth, from the furry and feathery to the hairy and scaly. The use of *cross-hatching* (sets of engraved lines at right angles) to describe forms, which Schongauer probably developed, became standard among German graphic artists. The Italians preferred *parallel hatching* (FIG. 21-29) and rarely adopted cross-hatching, which, in keeping with the general Northern Renaissance approach to art, tends to describe the surfaces of things rather than their underlying structures.

Schongauer probably engraved *Saint Anthony* around the year 1480. By then, the political geography of Europe had changed dramatically. Charles the Bold, who had assumed the title of duke of Burgundy in 1467, died in 1477, bringing to an end the Burgundian dream of forming a strong middle kingdom between France and the Holy Roman Empire. After Charles's death at the battle of Nancy, the French monarchy reabsorbed the southern Burgundian lands, and the Netherlands passed to the Holy Roman Empire by virtue of the dynastic marriage of Charles's daughter, Mary of Burgundy (FIG. 20-17), to Maximilian of Habsburg, inaugurating a new political and artistic era in northern Europe (see page 676). The next two chapters, however, explore Italian developments in painting, sculpture, and architecture during the 15th and 16th centuries.

LATE MEDIEVAL AND EARLY RENAISSANCE NORTHERN EUROPE

Burgundy and Flanders

- The most powerful rulers north of the Alps during the first three quarters of the 15th century were the dukes of Burgundy. They controlled Flanders, which derived its wealth from wool and banking, and were great art patrons. Duke Philip the Bold (r. 1363–1404) endowed the Carthusian monastery at Champmol, near Dijon, which became a ducal mausoleum. The head of Philip's sculptural workshop was Claus Sluter, whose *Well of Moses* features innovative statues of prophets with portraitlike features and realistic costumes.

- Flemish artists popularized the use of oil paints on wood panels. By superimposing translucent glazes, painters could create richer colors than possible using tempera or fresco. One of the earliest examples of oil painting is Melchior Broederlam's *Retable de Champmol* (1339), painted for Philip the Bold.

- A major art form in churches and private homes alike was the altarpiece with folding wings. In Robert Campin's *Mérode Altarpiece,* the Annunciation takes place in a Flemish home. The work's donors, depicted on the left wing, are anachronistically present as witnesses to the sacred event. As is typical of "Northern Renaissance" art, the everyday objects in the triptych often have symbolic significance.

- Jan van Eyck, Rogier van der Weyden, and others established portraiture as an important art form in 15th-century Flanders. Their subjects were successful businessmen, both Flemish and foreign, and occasionally themselves. Jan portrayed himself wearing a red turban, and Rogier represented himself in the guise of Saint Luke drawing the Virgin.

- Among the other major Flemish painters were Petrus Christus and Hans Memling of Bruges, Dieric Bouts of Louvain, and Hugo van der Goes of Ghent, all of whom produced both altarpieces for churches and portraits for the homes of wealthy merchants.

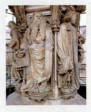

Sluter, *Well of Moses,*
1396–1406

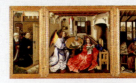

Campin, *Mérode Altarpiece,*
ca. 1425–1428

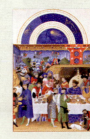

Van Eyck, *Man in a Red Turban,* 1433

France

- During the 15th century, the Hundred Years' War crippled the French economy, but dukes and members of the royal court still commissioned some notable artworks.

- The Limbourg brothers expanded the illusionistic capabilities of manuscript illumination in the Book of Hours they produced for Jean, duke of Berry (r. 1360–1416) and brother of King Charles V (r. 1364–1380). Their full-page calendar pictures alternately represent the nobility and the peasantry, always in seasonal, naturalistic settings with realistically painted figures.

- French court art—for example, Jean Fouquet's *Melun Diptych*—owes a large debt to Flemish painting in style and technique as well as in the integration of sacred and secular themes.

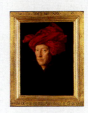

Limbourg brothers, *Les Très Riches Heures du Duc de Berry,* 1413–1416

Holy Roman Empire

- The Late Gothic style remained popular in 15th-century Germany for large carved wood retables featuring highly emotive figures amid Gothic tracery. The leading sculptors were Veit Stoss and Tilman Riemenschneider.

- The major German innovation of the 15th century was the development of the printing press, which publishers soon used to produce books with woodcut illustrations. Woodcuts are relief prints in which the artist carves out the areas around the lines to be printed.

- German artists, such as Martin Schongauer, were also the earliest masters of engraving. The intaglio technique allows for a wider variety of linear effects because the artist incises the image directly onto a metal plate.

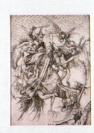

Schongauer, *Saint Anthony,*
ca. 1480

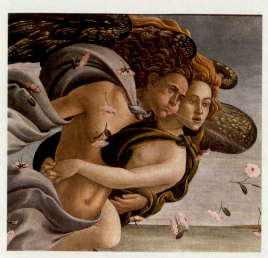

◄ **21-1a** Inspired by a poem by Angelo Poliziano, Botticelli painted *Birth of Venus* for the Medici between 1484 and 1486. At the left, Zephyrus, carrying Chloris, blows Venus on a cockleshell to Cyprus.

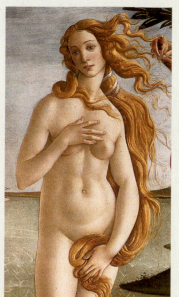

◄ **21-1b** Botticelli's revival of the theme of the female nude, largely absent from medieval art, was consistent with the Neo-Platonic view that beholding physical beauty prompts the contemplation of spiritual beauty.

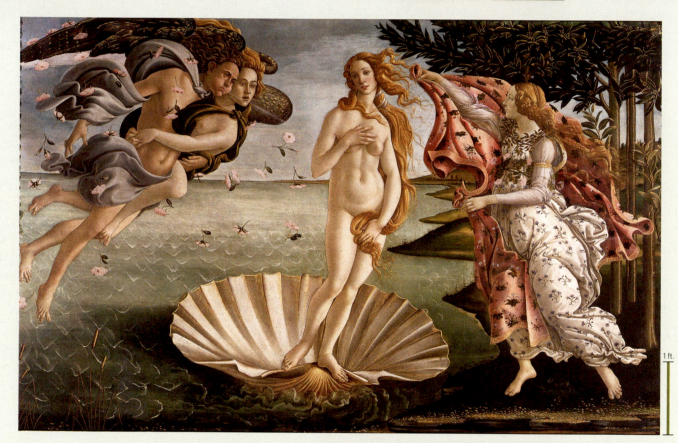

1 ft.

■ **21-1** **SANDRO BOTTICELLI**, *Birth of Venus*, ca. 1484–1486. Tempera on canvas, 5' 9" × 9' 2". Galleria degli Uffizi, Florence.

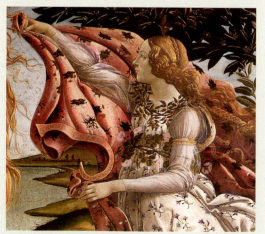

◄ **21-1c** Awaiting the newborn goddess of love on her sacred island is the nymph Pomona, who runs to meet Venus with a brocaded mantle. Her draperies undulate loosely in the gentle gusts of wind.

The Renaissance in Quattrocento Italy

THE MEDICI, BOTTICELLI, AND CLASSICAL ANTIQUITY

The name of one family—the Medici of Florence—has become synonymous with the extraordinary cultural phenomenon called the Italian Renaissance. By early in the 15th century (the 1400s, or *Quattrocento* in Italian), the banker Giovanni di Bicci de' Medici (ca. 1360–1429) had established the family fortune. His son Cosimo (1389–1464) became a great patron of art and of learning in the broadest sense. Cosimo's grandson Lorenzo (1449–1492), called *Il Magnifico* (the Magnificent), gathered about him a galaxy of artists and gifted men in all fields as a member of the Platonic Academy of Philosophy. Lorenzo spent lavishly on buildings, paintings, and sculptures. Indeed, scarcely a single great Quattrocento architect, painter, sculptor, philosopher, or humanist scholar failed to enjoy Medici patronage.

Of all the Florentine masters the Medici employed, perhaps the most famous today is SANDRO BOTTICELLI (1444–1510). His work is a testament to the intense interest that Quattrocento humanist scholars and the Medici had in the art, literature, and mythology of the Greco-Roman world—often interpreted in terms of Christianity according to the philosophical tenets of *Neo-Platonism.*

Botticelli painted *Birth of Venus* (FIG. 21-1) for the Medici based on a poem by Angelo Poliziano (1454–1494), a leading humanist of the day. In Botticelli's representation of Poliziano's version of the Greek myth, Venus (the Roman equivalent of the Greek goddess Aphrodite), born of the sea foam (*aphros*), stands on a floating cockleshell at the center of the painting. Zephyrus, the west wind, carrying the *nymph* Chloris, blows Venus to her sacred island, Cyprus. There, the nymph Pomona runs to meet her with a brocaded mantle. Zephyrus's breath moves all the figures without effort. Draperies undulate easily in the gentle gusts, perfumed by rose petals that fall on the whitecaps.

The most remarkable aspect of *Birth of Venus* is that Botticelli used as a model for his Venus an ancient statue similar to the *Aphrodite of Knidos* (FIG. 5-62) by the famed Greek sculptor Praxiteles. The nude, especially the female nude, was exceedingly rare during the Middle Ages. The artist's depiction of Venus unclothed (especially on such a large scale—roughly life-size) could have drawn harsh criticism. But in the more accommodating Renaissance culture and under the protection of the powerful Medici, Botticelli's nude Venus went unchallenged, in part because his painting was susceptible to a Neo-Platonic reading. Marsilio Ficino (1433–1499), for example, made the case in his treatise *On Love* (1469) that those who embrace the contemplative life of reason—including, of course, the humanists in the Medici circle—will immediately contemplate spiritual and divine beauty whenever they behold physical beauty. In this manner, Italian Renaissance patrons made classical learning and Christian faith compatible.

RENAISSANCE HUMANISM

The humanism that Petrarch and Boccaccio promoted during the 14th century (see page 418) fully blossomed in the 15th century. Increasingly, Italians in elite circles embraced the tenets underlying humanism—an emphasis on education and on expanding knowledge (especially of classical antiquity), the exploration of individual potential and a desire to excel, and a commitment to civic responsibility and moral duty. Quattrocento Italy also enjoyed an abundance of artistic talent. The fortunate coming together of artistic genius, the spread of humanism, and economic prosperity nourished the Renaissance, forever changing the direction and perception of art in the Western world.

For the Italian humanists, the quest for knowledge began with the legacy of the Greeks and Romans—the writings of Plato, Aristotle, Ovid, and others. The development of a vernacular literature based on the commonly spoken Tuscan dialect expanded the audience for humanist writings. Further, the invention of moveable metal type in Germany around 1445 (see page 576) facilitated the printing and wide distribution of books. Italians greeted this new printing process enthusiastically. By 1464, Subiaco (near Rome) boasted a press, and by 1469, Venice had established one as well. Among the first books printed in Italy using this new technology was Dante's *Divine Comedy,* his epic about Heaven, Purgatory, and Hell. The production of editions in Foligno (1472), Mantua (1472), Venice (1472), Naples (1477 and 1478–1479), and Milan (1478) testifies to the widespread popularity of Dante's work.

The humanists also avidly acquired information in a wide range of fields, including botany, geology, geography, optics, medicine, and engineering. Leonardo da Vinci's phenomenal expertise in many fields—from art and architecture to geology, aerodynamics, hydraulics, botany, and military science, among many others (see page 624)—still defines the modern notion of the "Renaissance man." Humanism also fostered a belief in individual potential and encouraged personal achievement, as well as civic responsibility. Whereas people in medieval society accorded great power to divine will in determining the events that affected lives, those in Renaissance Italy adopted a more secular stance. Humanists not only encouraged individual improvement but also rewarded excellence with fame and honor. Achieving and excelling through hard work became moral imperatives.

Quattrocento Italy witnessed constant fluctuations in its political and economic spheres, including shifting power relations among the numerous city-states and the rise of princely courts (see "Art in the Princely Courts of Renaissance Italy," page 613). *Condottieri* (military leaders) with large numbers of mercenary troops at their disposal played a major role in the ongoing struggle for power. At Urbino, Mantua, and elsewhere, courts headed by dukes and condottieri emerged as cultural and artistic centers alongside the great civic art centers of the 14th century, especially the Republic of Florence. The association of humanism with education and culture appealed to accomplished individuals of high status, and humanism had its greatest impact among the elite and powerful—the most influential art patrons—whether in the republics or the princely courts. As a result, humanist ideas came to permeate Italian Renaissance art. The intersection of art with humanist doctrines during the Renaissance is evident in the popularity of subjects selected from classical history or mythology (for example, FIG. 21-1), in the increased concern with developing perspective systems and depicting anatomy accurately, in the revival of portraiture and other self-promoting forms of patronage, and in citizens' extensive commissions of civic and religious art.

FLORENCE

Because high-level patronage required significant accumulated wealth, those individuals, whether princes or merchants, who had managed to prosper came to the fore in artistic circles. The best-known Italian Renaissance art patrons were the Medici, the leading bankers of the Republic of Florence (see "The Medici," page 581), yet the earliest important artistic commission in 15th-century Florence (MAP 21-1, page 603) was not a Medici project but rather a competition held by the Cathedral of Santa Maria del Fiore and sponsored by the city's guild of wool merchants.

Sculpture

In 1401, at a time when Florence was threatened from without, the cathedral's art directors held a competition to make bronze doors for the east portal of the Baptistery of San Giovanni (Saint John the Baptist; FIG. 12-30). In the late 1390s, Giangaleazzo Visconti, the first duke of Milan (r. 1378–1395), had begun a military campaign to take over the Italian peninsula. By 1401, when the cathedral's art directors initiated the baptistery doors competition, Visconti's troops had surrounded Florence, and its independence was in serious jeopardy. Despite dwindling water and food supplies, Florentine officials exhorted the public to defend the city's freedom. For example, the humanist chancellor Coluccio Salutati (1331–1406) urged his fellow citizens to adopt the republican ideal of civil and political liberty associated with ancient Rome and to identify themselves with its spirit. To be a citizen of the Florentine Republic was to be Roman. Freedom was the distinguishing virtue of both societies. The decision to beautify the city's baptistery in the face of Visconti's threat was an expression of Florentine freedom and defiance—and an opportunity for the wool merchants to assert their preeminence among Florentine guilds. In 1402, when Visconti died suddenly, Florence retained its independence, and the wool guild proceeded with the baptistery doors.

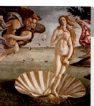

THE RENAISSANCE IN QUATTROCENTO ITALY

1400–1425
- Ghiberti wins the competition to design new doors for Florence's baptistery
- Nanni di Banco, Donatello, and others create statues for Or San Michele
- Masaccio carries Giotto's naturalism further in the Brancacci chapel
- Brunelleschi develops linear perspective and designs the Ospedale degli Innocenti, the first Renaissance building

1425–1450
- Ghiberti installs the *Gates of Paradise* facing Florence Cathedral
- Donatello revives freestanding nude male statuary
- Michelozzo builds the new Medici palace in Florence
- Alberti publishes his treatise on painting
- Marino Contarini builds his "House of Gold" in Venice

1450–1475
- Federico da Montefeltro brings Piero della Francesca to the Urbino court
- Alberti applies the principles of his *On the Art of Building* to architectural projects in Florence and Mantua
- Mantegna creates illusionistic paintings for the Camera Picta in Mantua
- Pietro Lombardo and his sons carve tombs for the doges of Venice

1475–1500
- Botticelli paints Neo-Platonic mythological allegories for the Medici
- Savonarola condemns humanism, and the Medici flee Florence
- Pope Sixtus IV employs leading painters to decorate the Sistine Chapel
- Bellini founds the Venetian High Renaissance school of painting

SACRIFICE OF ISAAC The Florentines considered the baptistery doors commission singularly prestigious because the east entrance to the baptistery faced the cathedral (FIG. 14-19). The competition is historically important not only for the quality of the work submitted by those seeking the commission but also because it showcased several key elements associated with mature Renaissance art: personal or, in this case, guild patronage as both a civic duty and a form of self-promotion; the esteem accorded to individual artists; and the development of a new pictorial illusionism.

Between 1330 and 1335, Andrea Pisano had designed the south doors (FIG. 14-20) of the baptistery with reliefs framed by Gothic quatrefoils. The jurors of the 1401 competition for the second set of doors required each entrant to submit a similarly framed relief panel depicting the sacrifice of Isaac. This episode from the book of Genesis (22:2–13) centers on God's order to Abraham to sacrifice his son Isaac as a demonstration of Abraham's devotion (see "Jewish Subjects in Christian Art," page 238). As Abraham was about to comply, an angel intervened and stopped him from plunging the knife into his son's throat. Because of the parallel between Abraham's willingness to sacrifice Isaac and God's sacrifice of his son, Jesus, to redeem humankind, Christians viewed the sacrifice of Isaac as a *prefiguration* (prophetic forerunner) of Jesus's crucifixion.

BRUNELLESCHI AND GHIBERTI The jury selected seven semifinalists from among the many artists who entered the widely advertised competition. Only the panels of the two finalists, FILIPPO BRUNELLESCHI (1377–1446) and LORENZO GHIBERTI (1378–1455),

have survived. At 24 and 23 years old respectively, they were also the two youngest entrants in the competition. As instructed, both artists used the same French-style frames and depicted the same moment of the narrative—the angel's interruption of the action. Brunelleschi's entry (FIG. 21-2) is a vigorous interpretation of the theme and recalls the emotional agitation of Giovanni Pisano's relief sculptures (FIG. 14-4). Abraham seems suddenly to have summoned the dreadful courage needed to murder his son at God's command. He lunges forward, robes flying, and exposes the terrified Isaac's throat to the knife. Matching Abraham's energy, the saving angel flies in from the left, grabbing Abraham's arm to stop the killing. Brunelleschi's figures demonstrate his ability to represent faithfully and dramatically all the elements in the biblical narrative.

Whereas Brunelleschi imbued his image with violent movement and high emotion, Ghiberti emphasized grace and smoothness. In Ghiberti's panel (FIG. 21-3), Abraham appears in a typically Gothic pose with outthrust hip (compare FIG. 13-26) and seems to contemplate the act he is about to perform, even as he draws back his arm to strike. The figure of Isaac, beautifully posed and rendered, recalls Greco-Roman statuary, and many art historians cite it as the first classical nude since antiquity. (Compare, for example, the torsion of Isaac's body and the dramatic turn of his head with the posture of the ancient statue of a Gaul plunging a sword into his own chest, FIG. 5-81.) Unlike his medieval predecessors, Ghiberti revealed a genuine appreciation of the nude male form and a deep interest in how the muscular system and skeletal structure move the human body. Even the altar on which Isaac kneels displays Ghiberti's

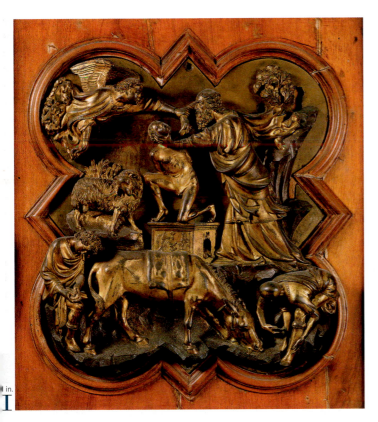

21-2 FILIPPO BRUNELLESCHI, *Sacrifice of Isaac*, competition panel for the east doors of the Baptistery of San Giovanni, Florence, Italy, 1401–1402. Gilded bronze, 1' 9" × 1' 5½". Museo Nazionale del Bargello, Florence.

Brunelleschi's entry in the competition to create new bronze doors for the Florentine baptistery shows a frantic angel about to halt an emotional, lunging Abraham clothed in swirling Gothic robes.

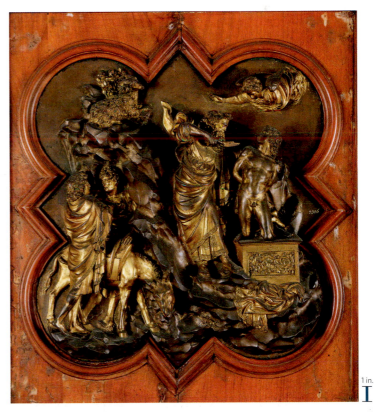

21-3 LORENZO GHIBERTI, *Sacrifice of Isaac*, competition panel for the east doors of the Baptistery of San Giovanni, Florence, Italy, 1401–1402. Gilded bronze, 1' 9" × 1' 5½". Museo Nazionale del Bargello, Florence.

In contrast to Brunelleschi's panel (FIG. 21-2), Ghiberti's entry in the baptistery competition features gracefully posed figures that recall classical statuary. Isaac's altar has a Roman acanthus frieze.

The *Commentarii* of Lorenzo Ghiberti

In addition to his many achievements as an artist, Lorenzo Ghiberti was also the first Renaissance art historian. His *Commentarii* in three books opens with an admiring account of the naturalistic art of classical antiquity that is heavily dependent on Pliny the Elder (see page 129) and Vitruvius (see "Vitruvius's *Ten Books on Architecture*," page 199). Book 2 deals with the art of his own time and the previous century and notably includes the earliest preserved autobiography of an artist. The third book enumerates the disciplines that a successful sculptor must master, including anatomy and optics.

Ghiberti's account of Early Renaissance art in his second *Commentary*, like Vasari's later biographies (see page 636), centers on individual artists. It opens with the author's lament that Constantine's embrace of Christianity brought an end to the glorious art of classical antiquity chronicled in the first *Commentary*. In Ghiberti's view, art "began to rise again" only when Cimabue, who painted "in the Greek [that is, Byzantine] manner" discovered Giotto drawing in a field and took him into his workshop. Ghiberti describes Giotto as having "brought about the new art; he left behind the coarseness of the Greeks" and was "the inventor and discoverer of so much knowledge which had been buried for around six hundred years" (2.3). Among the other 13th- and 14th-century masters whom Ghiberti singled out for praise were Pietro Cavallini, Andrea Orcagna, Ambrogio Lorenzetti, Simone Martini, and Duccio, although Ghiberti tempers his praise of Duccio by noting that he, like Cimabue, "adhered to the Greek manner" (2.15). The sculptors whom Ghiberti admired included Giovanni and Andrea Pisano (FIGS. 14-4 and 14-20).

In the spirit of Quattrocento humanism, Ghiberti frequently quotes from classical literature and dates the artists he discusses according to Olympiads, reviving the ancient Greek practice of dating events to four-year periods corresponding to the Olympic Games, which had not been held since 390 (see page 250). Ghiberti inserts himself into the history of art beginning in the year 1400 and describes how he

> tried to investigate how nature manifests itself and, in order to approximate nature, how appearances reach the eye and how the visual faculties work and how visual things function and in what way the theory of statuary art and of painting should be put into practice (2.18).

Then follows Ghiberti's account of the Florentine baptistery doors competition, culminating in his boast about the outcome, which also reveals the fame and glory increasingly accorded to individual achievement in 15th-century Italy:

> The palm of the victory was granted to me by all the skilled men and by all those who had competed with me. The glory was universally conceded to me without any exception. To all it appeared that I had surpassed the others at that time without any exception, after very great deliberation and examination by learned men. . . . There were thirty-four judges from the city and the other surrounding regions; by all the confirmation of victory was given in my favor (2.19).*

*All translations by Christie Knapp Fengler, *Lorenzo Ghiberti's* Second Commentary: *The Translation and Interpretation of a Fundamental Renaissance Treatise on Art* (Diss. University of Wisconsin, 1974), 16–19, 45, 54, 57–58.

---

emulation of antique models. Decorating it are acanthus scrolls of a type that commonly adorned Roman temple friezes in Italy and throughout the former Roman Empire (for example, FIG. 7-32). These classical references reflect the influence of humanism in Quattrocento Italy. Ghiberti's entry in the baptistery competition is also noteworthy for the artist's interest in spatial illusion. The rocky landscape seems to emerge from the blank panel toward the viewer, as does the strongly foreshortened angel. Brunelleschi's image, in contrast, emphasizes the planar orientation of the surface.

Ghiberti's training included both painting and metalwork. His careful treatment of the gilded bronze surfaces, with their sharply and accurately incised detail, proves his skill as a goldsmith. That Ghiberti cast his panel in only two pieces (thereby reducing the amount of bronze needed) no doubt also impressed the selection committee. Brunelleschi's panel consists of several cast pieces. Thus, not only would Ghiberti's doors, as proposed, be lighter. They also represented a significant cost savings. The younger artist's submission clearly had much to recommend it, both stylistically and technically, and the judges awarded the commission to him—an achievement that he noted with exceptional pride in his *Commentaries* (see "The *Commentarii* of Lorenzo Ghiberti," above).

OR SAN MICHELE A second major Florentine sculptural project of the early 1400s was the placement of statues on the exterior of Or San Michele (FIG. 14-20A), an early-14th-century building prominently located on the main street connecting the Palazzo della Signoria (FIG. 14-19B; seat of Florence's governing council) and the Duomo (cathedral; FIG. 14-19; see MAP 21-1, page 603). At various

times, Or San Michele housed a church, a granary, and the headquarters of Florence's guilds. City officials had assigned the niches on the building's four sides to specific guilds, instructing each guild to place a statue of its patron saint in its niche.

Nearly a century after completion of Or San Michele, however, the guilds had filled only 5 of the 14 niches. In 1406, the Signoria ordered the guilds to comply with the original plan to embellish their assigned niches. A few years later, Florence was once again under siege, this time by King Ladislaus (r. 1399–1414) of Naples. Ladislaus had marched north, occupied Rome and the Papal States (MAP 14-1) by 1409, and threatened to overrun Florence. As they had done when Visconti was at the city's doorstep, Florentine officials urged citizens to stand firm and defend the republic from tyranny. Once again, Florence escaped unscathed. Ladislaus, on the verge of military success in 1414, fortuitously died. The guilds may well have viewed this new threat as an opportunity to perform their civic duty by rallying their fellow Florentines while also promoting their own importance and position in Florentine society. By 1423, statues by Ghiberti and other leading Florentine artists were on display in the nine remaining niches of Or San Michele.

NANNI DI BANCO Among the niches filled during the Neapolitan king's siege was the one assigned to the Florentine guild of stone- and woodworkers. They chose a guild member, the sculptor NANNI DI BANCO (ca. 1384–1421), to create four life-size marble statues of the guild's martyred patron saints. (Below the statues is a relief depicting guild members at work.) These four Early Christian sculptors had defied an order from Diocletian (r. 284–305; see page 223)

postures and gestures, the Quattrocento sculptor arrived at a unified spatial composition. A remarkable psychological unity also connects these unyielding figures, whose bearing expresses the discipline and integrity necessary to face adversity. As the figure on the right speaks, pointing to his right, the two men opposite listen, and the one next to him (carved from the same block of marble) looks out into space, pondering the meaning of the words and reinforcing the formal cohesion of the figural group with psychological cross-references.

Four Crowned Saints, consistent with the renewed interest in ancient statues, also reveals Nanni's close study of Roman portraits. The emotional intensity of the faces of the two inner saints owes much to the extraordinarily moving portrayals in stone of third-century Roman emperors (FIGS. 7-66 and 7-66A), and the bearded heads of the outer saints make evident Nanni's familiarity with second-century imperial portraiture (FIGS. 7-57 and 7-57A). Renaissance artists seeking to portray individual personalities often turned to ancient Roman models for inspiration, but they did not simply copy them. Rather, they strove to interpret or offer commentary on their classical models in the manner of humanist scholars dealing with classical texts.

DONATELLO Another sculptor who carved statues for Or San Michele's niches was Donato di Niccolo Bardi, called DONATELLO (ca. 1386–1466), a former apprentice in Ghiberti's workshop, who incorporated Greco-Roman sculptural principles in his *Saint Mark* (FIG. 21-5), executed for the guild of linen makers and

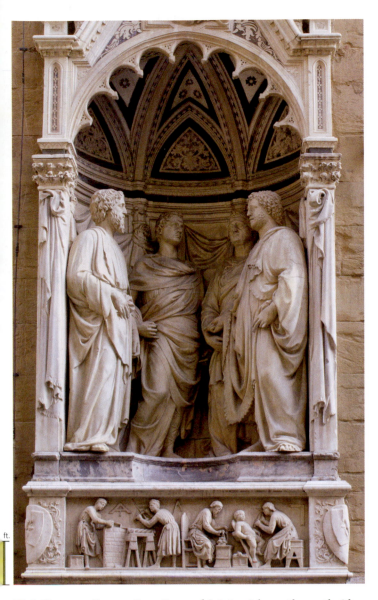

21-4 NANNI DI BANCO, *Four Crowned Saints,* niche on the north side of Or San Michele, Florence, Italy, ca. 1410–1414. Marble, figures 6' high. Modern copy; original sculpture in museum on second floor of Or San Michele, Florence.

Nanni's group representing the four martyred patron saints of Florence's sculptors' guild is an early example of Renaissance artists' attempt to liberate statuary from its architectural setting.

to carve a statue of a Roman deity. In response, the emperor ordered them put to death. Because they placed their faith above all else, these saints, in addition to representing the sponsoring guild, were perfect role models for the 15th-century Florentines whom city leaders exhorted to stand fast in the face of Ladislaus's armies.

Nanni's sculptural group, *Four Crowned Saints* (FIG. 21-4), is an early Renaissance attempt to solve the problem of integrating figures and architecture on a monumental scale. The artist's positioning of the figures, which stand in a niche that is *in* but confers some separation *from* the wall, furthered the gradual emergence of sculpture from its architectural setting. This process began with works such as the 13th-century statues (FIG. 13-24) on the jambs of the west facade portals of Reims Cathedral. At Or San Michele, the niche's spatial recess presented Nanni di Banco with a dramatic new possibility for the interrelationship of the figures. By placing them in a semicircle within their deep niche and relating them to one another by their

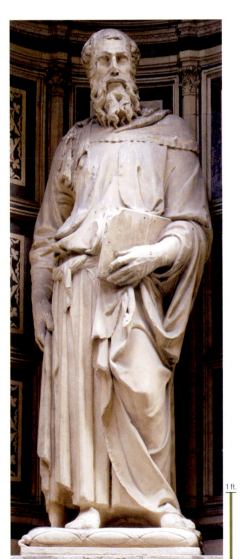

21-5 DONATELLO, *Saint Mark,* niche on the south side of Or San Michele, Florence, Italy, ca. 1411–1413. Marble, figure 7' 9" high. Modern copy; original sculpture in museum on second floor of Or San Michele, Florence.

In this statue carved for the guild of linen makers and tailors, Donatello introduced classical contrapposto into Quattrocento sculpture. The drapery falls naturally and moves with the body.

21-6 Donatello, *Saint George*, niche on the north side of Or San Michele, Florence, Italy, ca. 1415–1418. Marble, figure 6' 10" high. Modern copy; original in Museo Nazionale del Bargello, Florence.

Donatello's statue for the armorers' guild once had a bronze sword and helmet. The warrior saint stands defiantly, ready to spring from his niche to defend Florence, his sword pointed at the spectator.

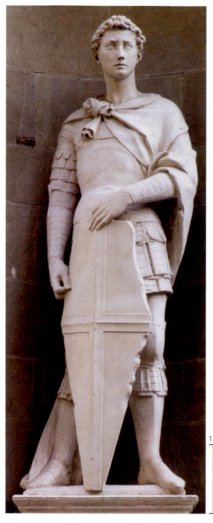

tailors. (The saint stands on one of the guild's pillows. Below him [not visible in FIG. 21-5] is his symbol, the lion; see "The Four Evangelists," page 318.) In this sculpture, Donatello took a fundamental step toward depicting motion in the human figure by recognizing the principle of weight shift, or *contrapposto*. Greek sculptors of the fifth century BCE were the first to grasp that the act of standing requires balancing the position and weight of the different parts of the human body, as they demonstrated in works such as *Kritios Boy* (FIG. 5-35) and *Doryphoros* (FIG. 5-41). In contrast to earlier sculptors, Greek artists recognized that the human body is not a rigid mass but a flexible structure that moves by continuously shifting its weight from one supporting leg to the other. Donatello reintroduced this concept into Renaissance statuary. As the saint's body "moves," his garment "moves" with it, hanging and folding naturally from and around different body parts so that the viewer senses the figure as a nude human wearing clothing, not as a stone statue with arbitrarily composed drapery folds. Donatello's *Saint Mark* is

the first Renaissance statue whose voluminous robe (the pride of the Florentine guild that paid for the statue) does not conceal but accentuates the movement of the arms, legs, shoulders, and hips. This development further contributed to the sculpted figure's independence from its architectural setting. Saint Mark's stirring limbs, shifting weight, and mobile drapery suggest impending movement out of the niche.

SAINT GEORGE For the Or San Michele niche assigned to the guild of armorers and sword makers, Donatello created *Saint George* (FIG. 21-6). The saintly knight stands proudly with his shield in front of him. He once held a bronze sword in his right hand and wore a bronze helmet on his head, both fashioned by the sponsoring guild. The statue continues the Gothic tradition of depicting warrior saints on church facades, as seen in the statue of Saint Theodore (FIG. 13-19) on the westernmost jamb of the south *transept* portal of Chartres Cathedral, but here it has a civic role to play. Saint George stands in a defiant manner—ready to spring from his niche to defend Florence against attack from another Visconti or Ladislaus, his sword jutting out threateningly at all passersby. The saint's body is taut, and Donatello gave him a face filled with nervous energy.

Directly below the statue's base is Donatello's marble relief (FIG. 21-7) representing Saint George slaying a dragon to rescue a princess (see "Early Christian Saints," page 237). The relief marks a turning point in Renaissance sculpture. Even the landscapes in the baptistery competition reliefs (FIGS. 21-2 and 21-3) are modeled forms seen against a blank background. In *Saint George and the Dragon*, Donatello created an atmospheric effect by using incised lines. It is impossible to talk about a background plane in this work. The landscape recedes into distant space, and the depth of that space cannot be measured. The sculptor conceived the relief as a window onto an infinite vista. To create that effect, Donatello used a pictorial device already known to the ancients—*atmospheric perspective* (see page 191). Artists (painters more frequently than sculptors) using atmospheric perspective (sometimes called *aerial perspective*) exploit the principle that the farther back an object is in space, the blurrier and less detailed it appears. In Donatello's *Saint George and the Dragon*, the foreground figures are much sharper than the landscape elements in the background.

FEAST OF HEROD Donatello's mastery of perspective in relief sculpture is also evident in *Feast of Herod* (FIG. 21-8), a bronze relief on the baptismal font in Siena Cathedral's baptistery. Appropriately, the subject of the relief is an episode in the life of John the Baptist. Salome, a figure based on a popular classical motif, dances before

21-7 Donatello, *Saint George and the Dragon*, relief below the statue of Saint George (FIG. 21-6), Or San Michele, Florence, Italy, ca. 1417–1420. Marble, 1' 3¼" × 3' 11¼". Modern copy; original relief in Museo Nazionale del Bargello, Florence.

Donatello's relief marks a turning point in Renaissance sculpture. He took a painterly approach, creating an atmospheric effect by using incised lines. The depth of the background cannot be measured.

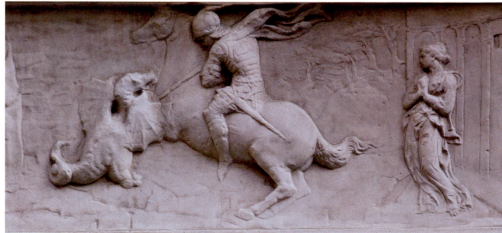

PROBLEMS AND SOLUTIONS
Linear Perspective

In the 14th century, Italian artists, such as Giotto, Duccio, and the Lorenzetti brothers (see Chapter 14), had used several devices to indicate distance, but with the development of *linear perspective,* Quattrocento artists acquired a way to make the illusion of distance certain and consistent. To solve the problem of representing depth in a two-dimensional painting or relief, Renaissance artists conceived the picture plane as a transparent window through which the observer looks to see the constructed pictorial world. (The literal meaning of *perspective* is "to see through.") This discovery was enormously important, for it made possible what has been called the "rationalization of sight." It brought all random and infinitely various visual sensations under a simple rule that could be expressed mathematically. Indeed, Renaissance artists' interest in linear perspective reflects the emergence at this time of modern science itself. Of course, 15th-century artists were not primarily scientists. They simply found perspective an effective way to order and clarify their compositions. Nonetheless, there can be little doubt that linear perspective, with its new mathematical certitude, conferred a kind of aesthetic legitimacy on painting and relief sculpture by making the picture measurable and exact. The projection of measurable objects on flat surfaces not only influenced the character of Renaissance paintings and reliefs but also made possible scale drawings, maps, charts, graphs, and diagrams—means of exact representation that laid the foundation for modern science and technology.

Renaissance artists were not the first to focus on depicting illusionistic space. Both the Greeks and the Romans were well versed in perspective rendering. Many of the frescoes that adorn the walls of Roman houses represent buildings and colonnades (for example, FIG. 7-19, *right*) using a Renaissance-like system of converging lines. However, the Renaissance rediscovery of and interest in perspective contrasted sharply with the portrayal of space during the Middle Ages, when spiritual concerns superseded the desire to depict objects illusionistically.

Developed by Filippo Brunelleschi, linear perspective enables artists to determine mathematically the relative size of rendered objects to correlate them with the visual recession into space. The artist first must identify a horizontal line that marks, in the image, the horizon in the distance (hence the term *horizon line*). The artist then selects a *vanishing point* on that horizon line (often located at the exact center of the line). By drawing *orthogonals* (diagonal lines) from the edges of the picture to the vanishing point, the artist creates a structural grid that organizes the image and determines the size of objects within the image's illusionistic space. Among the Quattrocento works that provide clear examples of linear perspective are Donatello's *Feast of Herod* (FIG. 21-8), Ghiberti's *Isaac and His Sons* (FIG. **21-9**), Masaccio's *Holy Trinity* (FIG. 21-20), and Perugino's *Christ Delivering the Keys of the Kingdom to Saint Peter* (FIG. 21-41).

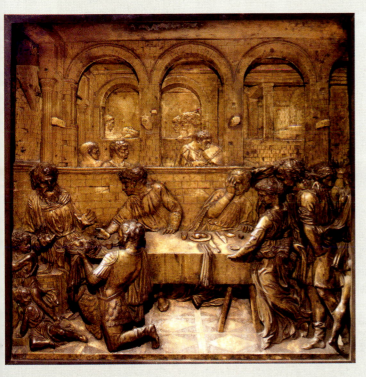

21-8 DONATELLO, *Feast of Herod,* panel on the baptismal font of the baptistery, Siena Cathedral, Siena, Italy, 1423–1427. Gilded bronze, 1' 11½" × 1' 11½".

Donatello's *Feast of Herod* marked the introduction of rationalized perspective space in Renaissance relief sculpture. Two arched courtyards of diminishing size open the space of the action into the distance.

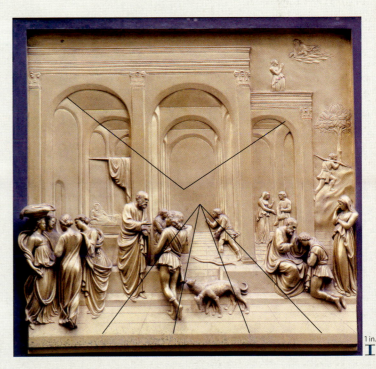

21-9 LORENZO GHIBERTI, *Isaac and His Sons* (detail of FIG. 21-10, with overlay of perspective orthogonals), east doors (*Gates of Paradise*) of the Baptistery of San Giovanni, Florence, Italy, 1425–1452. Gilded bronze, 2' 7½" × 2' 7½". Museo dell'Opera del Duomo, Florence.

All the orthogonals of the floor tiles in this early example of linear perspective converge on a vanishing point on the central axis of the composition, but the orthogonals of the architecture do not.

King Herod. At the left, Salome's wish granted, the kneeling executioner delivers John's severed head to the king. The other figures recoil in horror in two groups. At the right, one man covers his face with his hand. At the left, Herod and two terrified children shrink back in dismay. The psychic explosion drives the human elements apart, leaving a gap across which the emotional electricity crackles.

Forming the backdrop for this dramatic staging of the biblical story are two successive arched courtyards in Herod's palace. Donatello's rendition of the architectural setting in the *Feast of Herod* marks the introduction of rationalized perspective in Renaissance art. As in *Saint George and the Dragon* (FIG. 21-7), Donatello opened the space of the action well into the distance. But, instead of atmospheric perspective, he employed the new mathematically based science of *linear perspective,* in which the size of the piers and arches and even the bricks in the walls as well as the figures in the courtyards decrease in size systematically with increasing distance from the viewer (see "Linear Perspective," page 587).

The inventor (or rediscoverer) of linear perspective was Filippo Brunelleschi. In his biography of the Florentine artist, written around 1480, Antonio Manetti (1423–1497) described Brunelleschi's perspective system as a new "science":

[Filippo Brunelleschi] propounded and realized what painters today call perspective, since it forms part of that science which, in effect, consists of setting down properly and rationally the reductions and enlargements of near and distant objects as perceived by the eye of man: buildings, plains, mountains, places of every sort and location, with figures and objects in correct proportion to the distance in which they are shown. He originated the rule that is essential to whatever has been accomplished since his time in that area. We do not know whether centuries ago the ancient painters . . . knew about perspective or employed it rationally. If indeed they employed it by rule (I did not previously call it a science without reason) as he did later, . . . [no] records about it have been discovered. . . . Through industry and intelligence [Brunelleschi] either rediscovered or invented it.[1]

GATES OF PARADISE Lorenzo Ghiberti, Brunelleschi's chief rival in the baptistery competition, was, with Donatello, among the first artists to embrace Brunelleschi's scientific system for representing space. Ghiberti's enthusiasm for perspective illusion is on display in the new east doors (FIG. **21-10**) for Florence's baptistery (FIG. 12-30), which the cathedral officials commissioned him to make in 1425. Ghiberti's patrons moved his first pair of doors to the north entrance to make room for the new

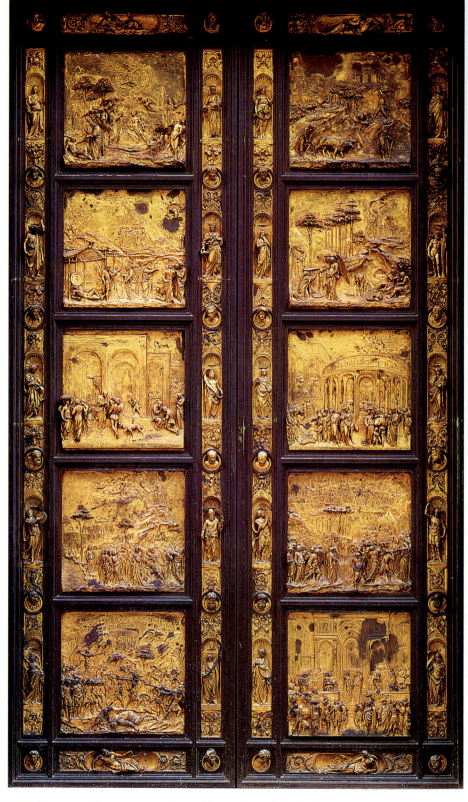

21-10 LORENZO GHIBERTI, east doors (*Gates of Paradise*) of the Baptistery of San Giovanni, Florence, Italy, 1425–1452. Gilded bronze, 17' high. Modern replica, 1990. Original panels in Museo dell'Opera del Duomo, Florence.

In Ghiberti's later doors for the Florentine baptistery, the sculptor abandoned Gothic quatrefoil frames for the biblical scenes (compare FIG. 21-3) and employed painterly illusionistic devices.

ones that they commissioned him to make for the prestigious east side. Michelangelo later declared Ghiberti's second doors as "so beautiful that they would do well for the gates of Paradise."[2] In the *Gates of Paradise,* as the doors have been called since then, Ghiberti abandoned the quatrefoil frames of Andrea Pisano's south doors (FIG. 14-20) and his own earlier doors and reduced the number of panels from 28 to 10. Each panel contains a relief set in plain molding and depicts an episode from the Old Testament. The complete gilding of the reliefs creates an effect of great splendor and elegance.

The individual panels, such as *Isaac and His Sons* (FIG. 21-9), clearly recall painting techniques in their depiction of space as well as in their treatment of the narrative. Some exemplify more fully than painting many of the principles that the architect and theorist Leon Battista Alberti formulated in his 1435 treatise, *On Painting*. In his relief, Ghiberti created the illusion of space partly through the use of linear perspective and partly by sculptural means. He represented the pavement on which the figures stand according to a painter's vanishing-point perspective construction (note the overlay of orthogonal lines in FIG. 21-9), but the figures themselves appear almost fully in the round. In fact, some of their heads stand completely free. As the eye progresses upward, the relief increasingly flattens, concluding with the architecture in the background, which Ghiberti depicted using barely raised lines. As Donatello did in *Feast of Herod* (FIG. 21-8), Ghiberti here employed atmospheric perspective, making the forms appear less distinct the deeper they are in space. Regardless of the height of the reliefs, however, the size of each figure decreases in exact correspondence to its distance from the foreground, just as do the dimensions of the floor tiles, as specified in Alberti's treatise.

Ghiberti described his employment of perspective in the baptistery's east doors as follows:

> I strove to imitate nature as closely as I could, and with all the perspective I could produce [to have] excellent compositions rich with many figures. In some scenes I placed about a hundred figures, in some less, and in some more. . . . There were ten stories, all in frames because the eye from a distance measures and interprets the scenes in such a way that they appear round. The scenes are in the lowest relief and the figures are seen in the planes; those that are near appear large, those in the distance small, as they do in reality. I executed this entire work with these principles.[3]

In the reliefs of the *Gates of Paradise,* Ghiberti achieved a greater sense of depth than had previously seemed possible in sculpture. His principal figures do not occupy the architectural space he created for them. Rather, the artist arranged them along a parallel plane in front of the grandiose architecture. (According to Alberti, the grandeur of the architecture reflects the dignity of the events shown in the foreground.)

Ghiberti's figure style mixes a Gothic patterning of rhythmic line, classical poses and motifs, and a new realism in characterization, movement, and surface detail. But the Florentine sculptor retained the medieval narrative method of presenting several episodes within a single frame. In *Isaac and His Sons,* the women in the left foreground attend the birth of Esau and Jacob in the left background. In the central foreground, Isaac sends Esau and his dogs to hunt game. In the right foreground, Isaac blesses the kneeling Jacob as Rebecca looks on. Yet viewers experience little confusion because of Ghiberti's careful and subtle placement of each scene. The figures, in varying degrees of projection, gracefully twist and turn, appearing to occupy and move through a convincing stage space, which Ghiberti deepened by showing some figures from behind.

Ghiberti's classicism derived from his close study of ancient art. The artist admired and collected classical sculpture, bronzes, and coins. Their influence appears throughout the *Isaac and His Sons*

panel, particularly in the figure of Rebecca, which Ghiberti based on a popular Greco-Roman statuary type. The emerging practice of collecting classical art in the 15th century had much to do with the incorporation of classical motifs and the emulation of classical style in Renaissance art (compare Botticelli's Venus [FIG. 21-1], based on an ancient statue).

DONATELLO, *DAVID* The use of perspective systems in relief sculpture and painting represents only one aspect of the Renaissance revival of classical principles and values in the arts. Another was the revival of the freestanding nude statue. The first Renaissance sculptor to portray the nude male figure in statuary was Donatello. He probably cast his bronze *David* (FIG. 21-11) sometime between 1440 and 1460 for display in the courtyard (FIG. 21-36) of the Medici palace in Florence. In the Middle Ages, the clergy regarded nude statues as both indecent and idolatrous, and, as noted in the opening discussion of *Birth of Venus* (page 581), nudity in general appeared only rarely in medieval art—and then only in biblical or moralizing contexts, such as the story of Adam and Eve or depictions of sinners in Hell. With *David,* Donatello reinvented the classical nude. His subject, however, was not a Greco-Roman god, hero, or athlete but the youthful biblical slayer of Goliath who had become the symbol of the Florentine Republic—and therefore an ideal choice of subject for the residence of the most powerful family in Florence. The Medici were aware of Donatello's earlier *David* in Florence's town

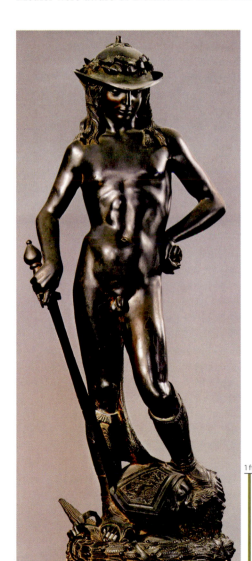

21-11 DONATELLO, *David,* from the Palazzo Medici, Florence, Italy, ca. 1440–1460. Bronze, 5' 2¼" high. Museo Nazionale del Bargello, Florence.

Donatello's *David* possesses both the relaxed contrapposto and the sensuous beauty of nude Greek gods (FIG. 5-63). The revival of classical statuary style appealed to the sculptor's patrons, the Medici.

1 ft.

hall (FIG. 14-19B), which the artist had produced during the threat of invasion by King Ladislaus. Their selection of the same subject suggests that the Medici identified themselves with Florence or, at the very least, shared Florence's ideals and the Florentine desire for freedom and independence. To underscore that association, the Medici added an inscription to the base of the *David* statue:

> The victor is whoever defends the fatherland. God crushes the wrath of an enormous foe. Behold! A boy overcame a great tyrant. Conquer, O citizens![4]

The invoking of classical poses and formats also appealed to the Medici as humanists. Donatello's *David* possesses both the relaxed classical contrapposto stance and the proportions and sensuous beauty of the gods that Praxiteles portrayed in his statues (FIG. 5-63). These qualities were, not surprisingly, absent from medieval figures—and they are also lacking, for different reasons, in Donatello's depiction of the aged Mary Magdalene. The contrast between the sculptor's *David* and his *Penitent Mary Magdalene* (FIG. **21-11A**) demonstrates the extraordinary versatility of this Florentine master.

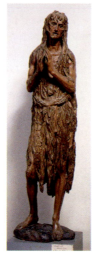

21-11A
DONATELLO, *Penitent Mary Magdalene*, ca. 1455.

VERROCCHIO Another *David* (FIG. **21-12**), by ANDREA DEL VERROCCHIO (1435–1488), one of the most important sculptors during the second half of the 15th century, reaffirms the Medici family's identification with the heroic biblical king and with Florence. A painter as well as a sculptor, Verrocchio directed a flourishing *bottega* (workshop) in Florence that attracted many students, among them Leonardo da Vinci. Verrocchio's *David* contrasts strongly in its narrative realism with the quiet classicism of Donatello's *David*. Verrocchio's hero is a sturdy, wiry youth clad in a leather doublet who stands with a jaunty pride. As in Donatello's version, Goliath's head lies at David's feet. He poses like a hunter with his kill. The easy balance of the weight and the lithe, still thinly adolescent musculature, with prominent veins, show how closely Verrocchio read the biblical text and how clearly he knew the psychology of brash young men. The Medici eventually sold Verrocchio's bronze *David* to the Florentine Republic for placement in the Palazzo della Signoria. After the expulsion of the Medici from Florence, civic officials appropriated Donatello's *David* for civic use and moved it to the city hall as well.

POLLAIUOLO The Renaissance interest in classical culture naturally also led to the revival of Greco-Roman mythological themes in art. The Medici were Florence's leading patrons in this sphere as well, and Botticelli (FIGS. 21-1 and 21-28) was only one of the artists they hired to produce artworks with classical myths for subjects. Around 1470, ANTONIO DEL POLLAIUOLO (ca. 1431–1498), who was also an important painter and engraver (FIG. 21-29), received a Medici commission to produce a small-scale sculpture, *Hercules and Antaeus* (FIG. **21-13**). The mythological subject matter and the emphasis on human anatomy reflect the Medici preference for humanist imagery. Even more specifically, the Florentine seal had featured Hercules since the end of the 13th century. As commissions such as the two *David* sculptures demonstrate, the Medici clearly embraced every opportunity to associate themselves with the glory of the Florentine Republic and claimed much of the credit for its preeminence.

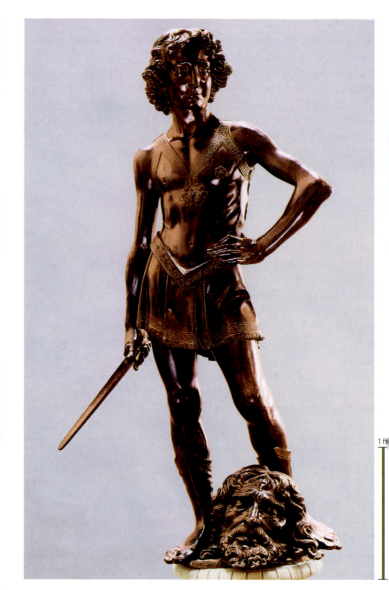

1 ft

21-12 ANDREA DEL VERROCCHIO, *David,* from the Palazzo della Signoria, Florence, Italy, ca. 1465–1470. Bronze, 4' 1½" high. Museo Nazionale del Bargello, Florence.

Verrocchio's *David*, also made for the Medici, displays a brash confidence. The statue's narrative realism contrasts strongly with the quiet classicism of Donatello's *David* (FIG. 21-11).

In contrast to the quiet stance of Donatello's *David* (FIG. 21-11), Pollaiuolo's bronze statuette exhibits the stress and strain of the human figure in violent action. The 18-inch-tall *Hercules and Antaeus* departs dramatically from the convention of frontality that had dominated statuary during the Middle Ages and the Early Renaissance. Indeed, by placing the two wrestling figures on an unusual triangular pedestal, Pollaiuolo established three possible "fronts" for the statuette, encouraging the viewer to look at it from different angles. The group illustrates the wrestling match between Antaeus (Antaios), a giant and son of the goddess Earth, and Hercules (Herakles), a theme the Greek painter Euphronios had represented on an ancient Greek vase (FIG. 5-23) 2,000 years before. The subject embodies the ferocity and vitality of elemental physical conflict. According to the Greek myth, each time Hercules threw him down, Antaeus sprang up again, his strength renewed by contact with the earth. Finally, Hercules held him aloft—so that Antaeus could not touch the ground—and strangled him around the waist.

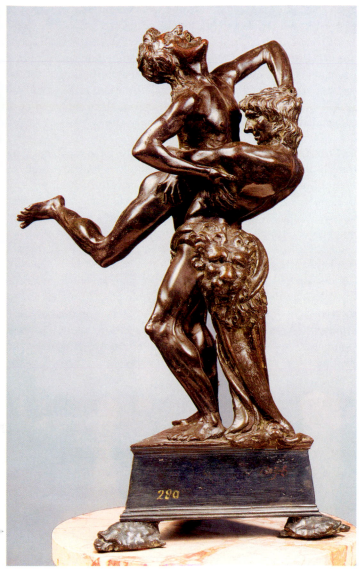

21-13 ANTONIO DEL POLLAIUOLO, *Hercules and Antaeus,* from the Palazzo Medici, Florence, Italy, ca. 1470–1475. Bronze, 1' 6" high with base. Museo Nazionale del Bargello, Florence.

The Renaissance interest in classical culture led to the revival of Greco-Roman mythological themes in art. *Hercules and Antaeus* exhibits the stress and strain of the human figure in violent action.

Pollaiuolo strove to convey the final excruciating moments of the struggle—the strained sinews of the combatants, the clenched teeth of Hercules, and the kicking and screaming of Antaeus. The figures intertwine and interlock as they fight, and the flickering reflections of light on the dark gouged bronze surface contribute to a fluid play of planes and the effect of agitated movement.

TOMB OF LEONARDO BRUNI Given the increased emphasis on individual achievement and recognition that humanism fostered, it is not surprising that portraiture enjoyed a revival in the 15th century. In addition to likenesses of elite individuals made during their lifetime, commemorative portraits of the deceased were common in Quattrocento Italy, as in ancient Rome. Leonardo Bruni (1369–1444) of Arezzo was one of the leading Early Renaissance humanist scholars. Around 1403, he wrote a *laudatio* (essay of praise) in honor of Florence, celebrating the city as the heir of the ancient Roman Republic. His most ambitious work, published

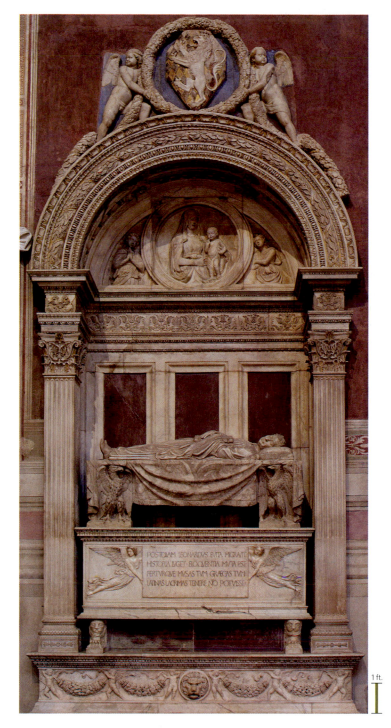

1 ft.

21-14 BERNARDO ROSSELLINO, tomb of Leonardo Bruni, Santa Croce, Florence, Italy, ca. 1444–1450. Marble, 23' 3½" high.

Rossellino's tomb in honor of the humanist scholar and chancellor Leonardo Bruni combines ancient Roman and Christian motifs. It established the pattern for Renaissance wall tombs (FIG. 21-39).

in 1429 when he served as Florence's chancellor (1427–1444), was a history of the Florentine Republic. When Bruni died on March 9, 1444, the Signoria ordered a state funeral "according to ancient custom," during which the eminent humanist Giannozzo Manetti (1396–1459) delivered the eulogy and placed a laurel wreath on the head of Bruni's toga-clad corpse. The Florentine government also commissioned BERNARDO ROSSELLINO (1409–1464) to carve a monumental tomb (FIG. 21-14) for the right wall of the nave of Santa Croce (FIG. I-4) honoring the late chancellor. Rossellino was the most prominent member of a family of stonecutters from Settignano, a town near Florence noted for its quarries.

Rossellino's monument in honor of Leonardo Bruni established the wall tomb as a major genre of Italian Renaissance sculpture. Later examples include Pietro Lombardo's tomb of Pietro Mocenigo (FIG. 21-39) in Venice and Michelangelo's tombs of the Medici (FIG. 22-16) in Florence and of Pope Julius II (FIGS. 22-14 and 22-15) in Rome. Bruni's tomb is rich in color—white, black, and red marbles with selective gilding. Rossellino based his effigy of Bruni on ancient Roman sarcophagi (FIG. 7-59). The chancellor lies on a funerary bier supported by Roman eagles atop a sarcophagus resting on the foreparts of lions. Bruni, dressed in a toga and crowned with a laurel wreath, as during his state funeral, holds one of his books, probably his history of Florence. The realism of Bruni's head has led many scholars to postulate that Rossellino based his portrait on a wax death mask following ancient Roman practice (see "Roman Ancestor Portraits," page 183). Two winged Victories hold aloft a plaque with a Latin inscription stating that History mourns the death of Leonardus, Eloquence is now silenced, and the Greek and Latin muses cannot hold back their tears. Framing the effigy is a round-arched niche with Corinthian *pilasters*. The base of the tomb is a frieze of *putti* (cupids) carrying garlands, a standard motif on Roman sarcophagi, which also commonly have lions as supports (FIG. 7-68). The classically inspired

tomb stands in sharp contrast to the Gothic tomb (FIG. 13-42A) of King Edward II in Gloucester Cathedral. But the Renaissance tomb is a creative variation of classical models, not a copy, and the motifs are a mix of classical and Christian themes. In the lunette beneath the arch is a *tondo* of the Madonna and Child between praying angels. Above the arch, two putti hold up a wreath circling the lion of the Florentine Republic. A lion's head is also the central motif in the putto-and-garland frieze below the deceased's coffin.

GATTAMELATA The grandest and most costly Quattrocento portraits in the Roman tradition were over-life-size bronze equestrian statues. The supremely versatile Donatello also excelled in this genre. In 1443, he left Florence for northern Italy to accept a lucrative commission from the Republic of Venice to create a commemorative monument (FIG. 21-15) in honor of the recently deceased Venetian condottiere Erasmo da Narni (1370–1443), nicknamed Gattamelata ("honeyed cat," a wordplay on his mother's name, Melania Gattelli). Condottieri played a major role in the power politics of Quattrocento Italy. Because Florence, Venice, and other republics barred their citizens from bearing arms, those states hired mercenary armies to fight on their behalf. They often owed the condottieri who commanded those armies a debt of gratitude as well as payment for their services. Although Gattamelata's family bore the cost of the

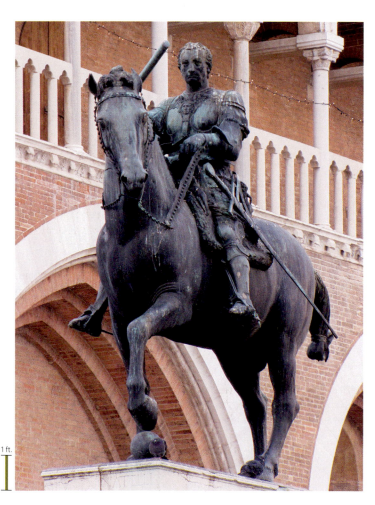

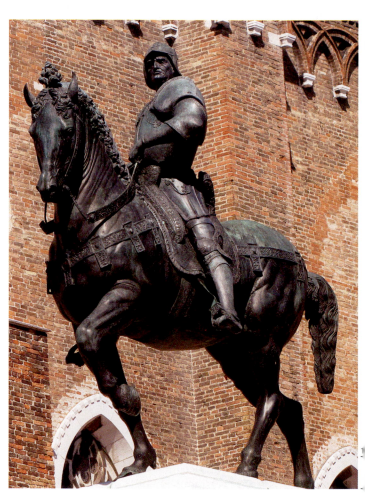

1 ft.

21-15 DONATELLO, *Gattamelata* (equestrian statue of Erasmo da Narni), Piazza del Santo, Padua, Italy, ca. 1445–1453. Bronze, 12′ 2″ high.

Donatello based his gigantic portrait of a Venetian general on equestrian statues of ancient Roman emperors (FIG. 7-57). Together, man and horse convey an overwhelming image of irresistible strength.

21-16 ANDREA DEL VERROCCHIO, *Bartolommeo Colleoni* (equestrian statue), Campo dei Santi Giovanni e Paolo, Venice, Italy, ca. 1481–1495. Bronze, 13′ high.

Eager to compete with Donatello's *Gattamelata* (FIG. 21-15), Bartolommeo Colleoni provided the funds in his will for his own equestrian statue, which stands on a pedestal even taller than *Gattamelata*'s.

general's equestrian portrait, the Venetian senate had to authorize its placement in the square in front of the church of Sant'Antonio in Padua, the condottiere's birthplace. Equestrian statues occasionally had been set up in Italy in the late Middle Ages, but Donatello's *Gattamelata* was the first since antiquity to rival the grandeur of Roman imperial mounted portraits, such as that of Marcus Aurelius (FIG. 7-57), which the artist must have seen in Rome. Donatello's contemporaries, one of whom described Gattamelata as sitting on his horse "with great magnificence like a triumphant Caesar,"[5] recognized this reference to antiquity. The statue stands on a lofty elliptical base, set apart from its surroundings, celebrating the Renaissance liberation of sculpture from architecture. Massive and majestic, the great horse bears the armored general easily, for, unlike the sculptor of the Marcus Aurelius statue, Donatello did not represent the Venetian commander as superhuman and disproportionately larger than his horse. Gattamelata dominates his mighty steed by force of character rather than sheer size. The Italian rider, his face set in a mask of dauntless resolution and unshakable will, is the very portrait of the Renaissance individualist. Such a man—intelligent, courageous, ambitious, and frequently of humble origin—could, by his own resourcefulness and on his own merits, rise to a commanding position in the world, even become a head of state (see page 612). Together, man and horse convey an overwhelming image of irresistible strength and unlimited power—an impression Donatello reinforced visually by placing the left forefoot of the horse on an orb, reviving a venerable ancient symbol for domination of the world (compare FIG. 11-13). The imperial imagery is all the more remarkable because Erasmo da Narni was not an emperor, king, or duke.

BARTOLOMMEO COLLEONI Verrocchio also received a commission to fashion an equestrian statue of a Venetian condottiere, Bartolommeo Colleoni (1400–1475). His portrait (FIG. 21-16) provides a counterpoint to Donatello's statue. Eager to garner the same fame that the *Gattamelata* portrait achieved, Colleoni provided funds in his will for his own statue. Because both Donatello and Verrocchio executed their statues after the deaths of their subjects, neither artist knew personally the individual he portrayed. The result is a fascinating difference of interpretation (like that between their two *Davids*) as to the demeanor of a professional captain of armies. Verrocchio placed the statue of the bold equestrian general on a pedestal even taller than the one Donatello used for *Gattamelata,* elevating it so that viewers could see the dominating, aggressive figure from all approaches to the piazza (the Campo dei Santi Giovanni e Paolo). In contrast with the near repose of *Gattamelata,* the *Colleoni* horse moves in a prancing stride, arching and curving its powerful neck, while the commander seems suddenly to shift his whole weight to the stirrups and rise from the saddle with a violent twist of his body. The artist depicted both horse and rider with an exaggerated tautness—the animal's bulging muscles and the man's fiercely erect and rigid body together convey brute strength. In *Gattamelata,* Donatello created a portrait of a grim commander. Verrocchio's *Bartolommeo Colleoni* is a portrait of merciless might.

Painting

In Quattrocento Italy, humanism and the celebration of classical artistic values also largely determined the character of panel and mural painting. The new Renaissance style did not, however, immediately displace all vestiges of the Late Gothic style. In particular, the *International Gothic* style, the dominant mode in painting around 1400 (see page 424), persisted well into the 15th century.

GENTILE DA FABRIANO The leading Quattrocento master of the International Gothic style was GENTILE DA FABRIANO (ca. 1370–1427), who in 1420 moved his workshop from Brescia in northern Italy to Florence, where he hoped to share in the opportunities to work for the city's many wealthy patrons. Three years later, Gentile painted *Adoration of the Magi* (FIG. 21-17) as the altarpiece for the family

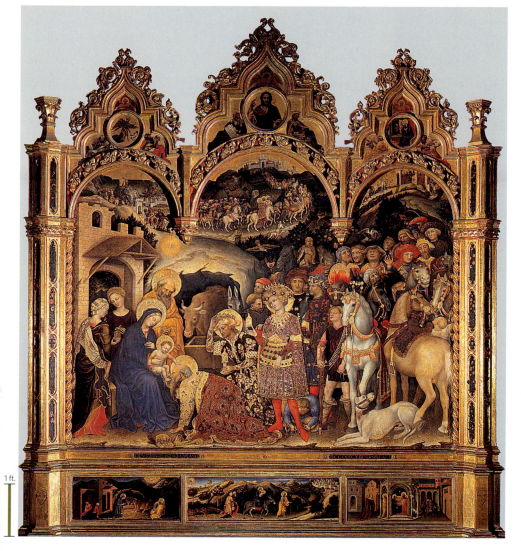

21-17 GENTILE DA FABRIANO, *Adoration of the Magi,* altarpiece from the Strozzi chapel, Santa Trinità, Florence, Italy, 1423. Tempera on wood, 9' 11" × 9' 3". Galleria degli Uffizi, Florence.

Gentile was the leading Florentine painter working in the International Gothic style. He successfully blended naturalistic details with late medieval splendor in color, costume, and framing ornamentation.

1 ft.

ART AND SOCIETY

Imitation and Emulation in Renaissance Art

Although many of the values championed by Renaissance humanists endure to the present day, the premium that modern Western society places on artistic originality is a fairly recent phenomenon. In contrast, imitation and emulation were among the concepts that Renaissance artists most valued. Many 15th- and 16th-century artists, of course, developed unique, recognizable styles, but convention, in terms of both subject matter and representational practices, predominated. In Italian Renaissance art, certain themes, motifs, and compositions appear with great regularity, fostered by training practices that emphasized the importance of tradition for aspiring Renaissance artists.

- **Imitation** The starting point in a young artist's training (see "Artistic Training in Renaissance Italy," page 426) was imitation. Italian Renaissance artists believed that the best way to learn was to copy the works of masters. Accordingly, much of an apprentice's training consisted of copying exemplary artworks.

For example, even a supreme master such as Leonardo da Vinci filled his sketchbooks with drawings of well-known sculptures and frescoes, and the boldly original Michelangelo spent days sketching artworks in churches around Florence and Rome.

- **Emulation** The next step was emulation, which involved modeling one's art after that of another artist. Although imitation provided the foundation for this practice, an artist used features of another's art only as a springboard for improvements or innovations. Thus, developing artists went beyond previous artists and attempted to prove their own competence and skill by improving on the work of established and recognized masters. Comparison and a degree of competition were integral to emulation. To evaluate the "improved" artwork, viewers had to be familiar with the original "model."

Renaissance artists believed that young artists would ultimately develop their own distinctive, if related, style through this process of imitation and emulation. But the boldest of them would quickly break away from their masters' influence, and some, like Massaccio (FIGS. 21-18 to 21-20), would redirect the history of art through brilliant innovation.

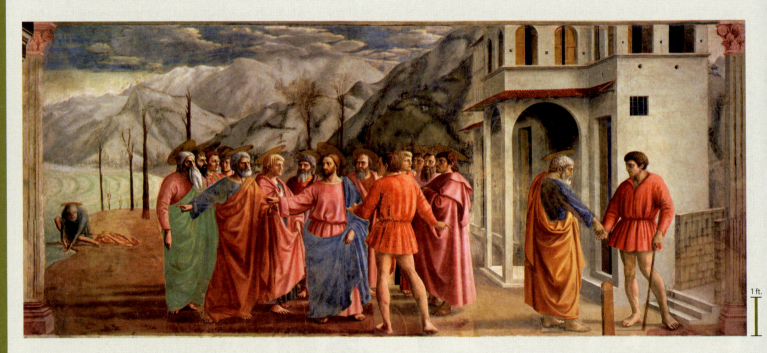

21-18 MASACCIO, *Tribute Money,* Brancacci chapel, Santa Maria del Carmine, Florence, Italy, ca. 1424–1427. Fresco, 8' 4⅛" × 19' 7⅛".

Masaccio's figures recall Giotto's in their simple grandeur, but they convey a greater psychological and physical credibility. He modeled his figures with light coming from a source outside the picture.

chapel of Palla Strozzi (1372–1462) in the church of Santa Trinità in Florence. At the beginning of the 15th century, the Strozzi family was the richest in the city. The altarpiece, with its elaborate gilded Gothic frame, is testimony to the patron's lavish tastes. So too is the painting itself, with its gorgeous surface and sumptuously costumed kings, courtiers, captains, and retainers (among whom, according to some sources, are portraits of Palla Strozzi and his father). Accompanying the kings and their entourage is a menagerie of exotic animals. Gentile portrayed all these elements in a rainbow of color with extensive use of gold. The painting presents all the pomp and ceremony of chivalric etiquette in a religious scene centered on the Madonna and Child.

Although the style is fundamentally International Gothic, Gentile inserted striking naturalistic details. For example, the artist depicted animals from a variety of angles and foreshortened the forms convincingly, most notably the horse at the far right seen in a three-quarter rear view. Gentile did the same with human figures, such as the kneeling man removing the spurs from the standing *magus* in the center foreground. In the left panel of the predella, Gentile painted what may have been the first nighttime nativity scene with the central light source—the radiant Christ Child—introduced into the picture itself. Although predominantly conservative, Gentile demonstrated that he was not oblivious to Quattrocento experimental trends and could blend naturalistic and inventive elements skillfully and subtly into a traditional composition without sacrificing Late Gothic splendor in color, costume, and framing ornamentation.

MASACCIO The artist who personifies the innovative spirit of early-15th-century Florentine painting was Tommaso di ser Giovanni di Mone Cassai, known as MASACCIO (1401–1428). Although his presumed teacher, Masolino da Panicale (see "Italian Artists' Names," page 413), had worked in the International Gothic style, Masaccio broke sharply from the normal practice of imitating his master's style (see "Imitation and Emulation in Renaissance Art," page 594). He moved suddenly, within the short span of six years, into unexplored territory. Most art historians recognize no other painter in history to have contributed so much to the development of a new style as quickly as Masaccio, whose untimely death at age 27 cut short his brilliant career. Masaccio was the artistic descendant of Giotto (see page 418), whose calm, monumental style he carried further by introducing a whole new repertoire of representational devices that generations of Renaissance painters later studied and developed.

BRANCACCI CHAPEL The frescoes Masaccio painted in the family chapel that Felice Brancacci (1382–1447) sponsored in Santa Maria del Carmine in Florence provide excellent examples of his innovations. In *Tribute Money* (FIG. 21-18), painted shortly before his death, Masaccio depicted an episode from the Gospel of Matthew (17:24–27). As the tax collector confronts Jesus at the entrance to the Roman town of Capernaum, Jesus directs Saint Peter to the shore of Lake Galilee. There, as Jesus foresaw, Peter finds the tribute coin in the mouth of a fish and returns to pay the tax. Masaccio divided the story into three parts within the fresco. In the center, Jesus, surrounded by his disciples, tells Peter to retrieve the coin from the fish, while the tax collector stands in the foreground, his back to spectators and hand extended, awaiting payment. At the left, in the middle distance, Peter extracts the coin from the fish's mouth, and, at the right, he thrusts the coin into the tax collector's hand.

Masaccio's figures recall Giotto's in their simple grandeur, but they convey a greater psychological and physical credibility. Masaccio created the figures' bulk through modeling not with a flat, neutral light lacking an identifiable source but with a light coming from a specific source outside the picture. The light comes from the right (as if through a real window in the chapel wall) and strikes the figures at an angle, illuminating the parts of the solids obstructing its path and leaving the rest in shadow, producing the illusion of deep sculptural relief. Between the extremes of light and dark, the light appears as a constantly active but fluctuating force highlighting the scene in varying degrees. In his frescoes, Giotto used light only to model the masses. In Masaccio's works, light has its own nature, and the masses are visible only because of its direction and intensity. The viewer can imagine the light as playing over forms—revealing some and concealing others, as the artist directs it. The individual figures in *Tribute Money* are solemn and weighty, but they also move freely and reveal body structure, as do Donatello's statues. Masaccio's representations adeptly suggest bones, muscles, and the pressures and tensions of joints. Each figure conveys a maximum of contained energy. *Tribute Money* provides support for Giorgio Vasari's assessment of Masaccio's place in the history of art: "[T]he works made before his [Masaccio's] day can be said to be painted, while his are living, real, and natural."[6]

Masaccio's arrangement of the figures is equally inventive. They do not stand in a line in the foreground. Instead, the artist, probably inspired by Nanni di Banco's *Four Crowned Saints* (FIG. 21-4), grouped them in circular depth around Jesus, and he placed the whole group in a spacious landscape, rather than in the confined stage space of earlier frescoes. The group itself generates the foreground space, and the architecture on the right amplifies it. Masaccio depicted the building in perspective, locating the vanishing point, where all the orthogonals converge, at Jesus's head. He also diminished the brightness of the colors as the distance increases, an aspect of atmospheric perspective understood and applied only by the most skilled painters. Although ancient Roman painters used aerial perspective (FIG. 7-20), medieval artists had abandoned it. Thus it virtually disappeared from art until Masaccio and his contemporaries rediscovered it. They came to realize that the light and air interposed between viewers and what they see are two parts of the visual experience called "distance."

In an awkwardly narrow space at the entrance to the Brancacci chapel, to the left of *Tribute Money*, Masaccio painted *Expulsion of Adam and Eve from Eden* (FIG. 21-19), a fresco that also displays the representational innovations seen in *Tribute Money*. For example, the sharply slanted light from an outside source creates deep relief, with lights placed alongside darks, and acts as a strong unifying agent. Masaccio also presented the figures with convincing structural accuracy, thereby suggesting substantial body weight. Further,

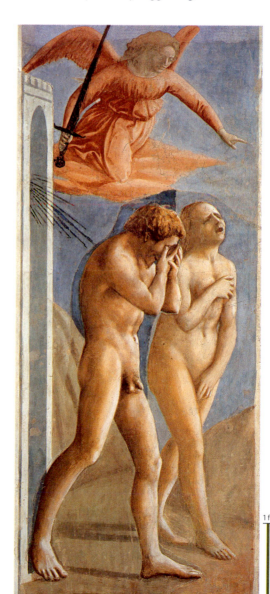

21-19 MASACCIO, *Expulsion of Adam and Eve from Eden*, Brancacci chapel, Santa Maria del Carmine, Florence, Italy, ca. 1424–1427. Fresco, 7' × 2' 11".

Adam and Eve, expelled from Eden, stumble on blindly, driven by the angel's will and their own despair. The hazy background specifies no locale but suggests a space around and beyond the figures.

the hazy background specifies no locale but suggests a space around and beyond the figures. Adam's feet, clearly in contact with the ground, mark the human presence on earth, and the cry issuing from Eve's mouth voices her anguish. The angel does not force them physically from Eden. Rather, they stumble on blindly, the angel's will and their own despair driving them. The composition is starkly simple, its message incomparably eloquent.

HOLY TRINITY Masaccio's *Holy Trinity* (FIG. 21-20) in Santa Maria Novella, another of the young artist's masterworks, is the premier early-15th-century example of the application of mathematics to the depiction of space. In this fresco, Masaccio painted the composition on two levels of unequal height. Above, in a barrel-vaulted chapel reminiscent of a Roman *triumphal arch* (FIGS. 7-40 and 7-44A; compare FIG. 21-49A), the Virgin Mary and Saint John appear on either side of the crucified Christ. (Mary, unlike in almost all other representations of the crucifixion, appears as an older woman, her true age at the time of her adult son's death.) God the Father emerges from behind Christ, supporting the arms of the cross and presenting his son to the worshiper as a devotional object. Christ's blood runs down the cross onto the painted ledge below—a reference to the symbolic blood of the wine of the Eucharist on the church's altar. The dove of the Holy Spirit hovers between God's head and Christ's head. Masaccio also included portraits of the donors of the painting, Lorenzo Lenzi and his wife, who kneel just in front of the pilasters framing the chapel's entrance. Below, the artist painted a tomb containing a skeleton. An inscription in Italian above the skeleton reminds the spectator, "I was once what you are, and what I am you will become."

The illusionism of *Holy Trinity* is breathtaking, a brilliant demonstration of the principles and potential of Brunelleschi's new science of perspective. Indeed, some art historians have suggested that Brunelleschi may have collaborated with Masaccio on this commission. The vanishing point of the composition is at the foot of the cross. With this point at eye level, spectators look up at the Trinity and down at the tomb. About 5 feet above the floor level, the vanishing point pulls the two views together, creating the illusion of a real structure transecting the wall's vertical plane. Whereas the tomb seems to project forward into the church, the chapel recedes visually behind the wall and appears as an extension of the spectator's space. This adjustment of the picture's space to the viewer's position was an important innovation in illusionistic painting that other artists of the Renaissance and the later Baroque period would develop further. Masaccio was so exact in his metrical proportions that it is possible to calculate the dimensions of the chapel (for example, the span of the painted vault is 7 feet, and the depth of the chapel is 9 feet). Thus he achieved not only a successful illusion but also a rational measured coherence that is responsible for the unity and harmony of the fresco.

Holy Trinity is, however, much more than a highly successful application of Brunelleschi's perspective system or a showpiece for the painter's ability to represent fully modeled figures bathed in light. In this painting, Masaccio also powerfully conveyed one of the central tenets of Christian faith. The ascending pyramid of figures leads viewers from the despair of death to the hope of resurrection and eternal life through Christ's crucifixion. Masaccio's *Holy Trinity* clearly reveals that humanism and religion were not mutually exclusive.

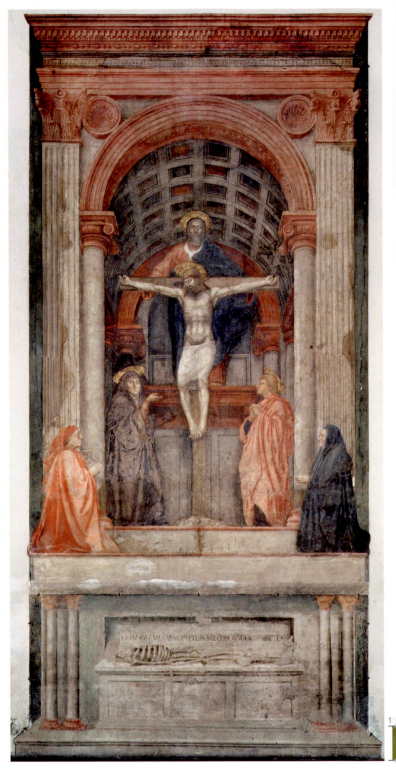

21-20 MASACCIO, *Holy Trinity,* Santa Maria Novella, Florence, Italy, ca. 1424–1427. Fresco, 21' 10$\frac{5}{8}$" × 10' 4$\frac{3}{4}$".

Masaccio's pioneering *Holy Trinity* is the premier early-15th-century example of the application of mathematics to the depiction of space according to Filippo Brunelleschi's system of perspective.

FRA ANGELICO For many other Quattrocento Italian artists, humanist concerns were not a primary consideration, however. The art of FRA ANGELICO (ca. 1400–1455) focused on serving the Roman Catholic Church. In the late 1430s, the abbot of the Dominican monastery of San Marco (Saint Mark) in Florence asked Fra Angelico to produce a series of frescoes for the order's Florentine compound. The Dominicans (see "Mendicant Orders," page 415) of

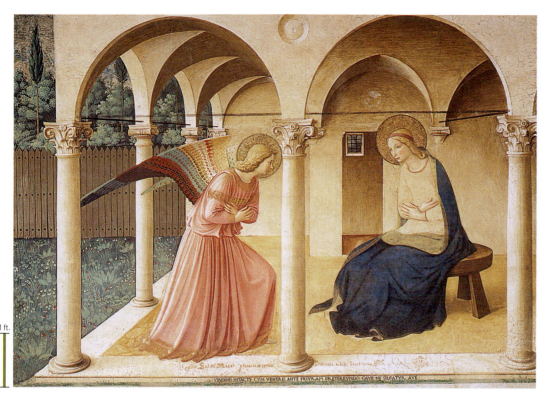

1 ft.

21-21 FRA ANGELICO, *Annunciation,* San Marco, Florence, Italy, ca. 1438–1447. Fresco, 7' 1" × 10' 6".

Painted for the Dominican monks of San Marco, Fra Angelico's fresco is simple and direct. Its figures and architecture have a pristine clarity befitting the fresco's function as a devotional image.

San Marco had dedicated themselves to lives of prayer and work, and their monastery was mostly spare and austere to encourage the monks to immerse themselves in their devotional lives. Fra Angelico's *Annunciation* (FIG. 21-21) appears at the top of the stairs leading to the friars' sleeping cells. Appropriately, Fra Angelico presented the scene of the Virgin Mary and the Archangel Gabriel with simplicity and serenity. The two figures appear in a plain *loggia* resembling the *portico* of San Marco's *cloister,* and the artist painted all the fresco elements with a pristine clarity. The figures do not cast shadows, however. Although Fra Angelico constructed the loggia according to the rules of Renaissance perspective (but with too few columns to support the vaults), the unnatural lighting removes the sacred event from the everyday world. Underscoring the devotional function of the image, Fra Angelico included a small inscription at the base of the fresco admonishing the friars: "As you venerate, while passing before it, this figure of the intact Virgin, beware lest you omit to say a Hail Mary." Like most of Fra Angelico's paintings, *Annunciation,* with its simplicity and directness, still has an almost universal appeal and fully reflects the artist's simple, humble character.

ANDREA DEL CASTAGNO Fra Angelico's younger contemporary ANDREA DEL CASTAGNO (ca. 1421–1457) also accepted a commission to produce a series of frescoes for a religious establishment. Castagno's *Last Supper* (FIG. 21-22) in the *refectory* (dining hall) of Sant'Apollonia in Florence, a convent for Benedictine nuns, faithfully follows the biblical narrative, although the lavishly appointed, marble-revetted room that Jesus and his 12 disciples occupy has no basis in the Gospels. The setting Castagno chose reflected his

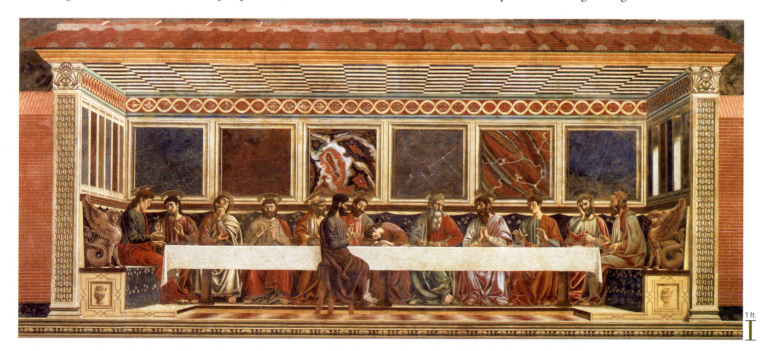

1 ft.

21-22 ANDREA DEL CASTAGNO, *Last Supper,* refectory of the convent of Sant'Apollonia, Florence, Italy, 1447. Fresco, 15' 5" × 32'.

In this *Last Supper* on the wall of a nuns' dining room, Judas sits isolated. Castagno's depiction of the setting for the apostles' meal reflects his preoccupation with the new science of perspective.

21-23 PAOLO
UCCELLO, *Battle of
San Romano,* from
the Palazzo Medici,
Florence, Italy, ca.
1435 or ca. 1455.
Tempera on wood,
6' × 10' 5". National
Gallery, London.

In this panel once in
Lorenzo de' Medici's
bedchamber, Niccolò
da Tolentino leads the
charge against the
Sienese. The foreshort-
ened spears and figures
reveal Uccello's fascina-
tion with perspective.

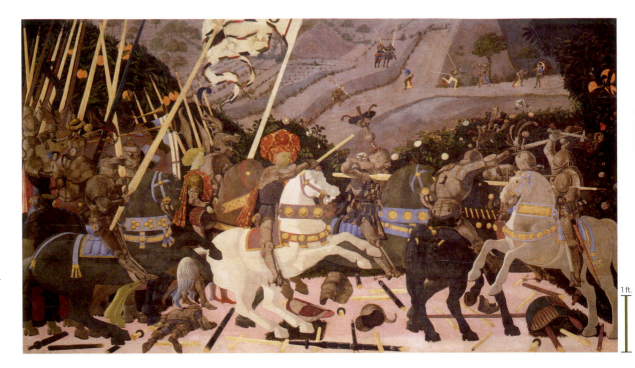

interest in employing linear perspective to create the illusion of
three-dimensional space, but close scrutiny reveals inconsistencies
in his application of Brunelleschian principles. For example, in the
Florentine perspective system, it is impossible to see both the ceiling
from inside and the roof from outside, as Castagno depicted. The
two side walls also do not appear parallel.

In placing the figures inside the biblical dining room, Castagno chose a conventional compositional format, with Jesus and the
apostles seated at a horizontally placed table. The painter derived
the apparent self-absorption of most of the disciples and the men-
acing features of Judas (who sits alone on the outside of the table)
from the Gospel of Saint John, rather than the more familiar version
of the Last Supper recounted in the Gospel of Saint Luke. Castagno's
dramatic and spatially convincing depiction of the event no doubt
was a powerful presence for the nuns during their daily meals.

PAOLO UCCELLO A much rarer genre of Quattrocento Florentine
art was history painting. A masterpiece of this secular side of Renaissance art is *Battle of San Romano* (FIG. 21-23) by PAOLO UCCELLO
(1397–1475), who trained in the International Gothic style. The
large panel painting is one of three that Lorenzo de' Medici acquired
for his bedchamber in the palatial Medici residence (FIGS. 21-35 and
21-36) in Florence. There is some controversy about the date of the
painting because documents have been discovered suggesting that
Lorenzo may have purchased at least two of the paintings from a
previous owner instead of commissioning the full series himself.
The scenes commemorate the Florentine victory over the Sienese
in 1432 and must have been painted no earlier than the mid-1430s.
The traditional date assigned to the commission is 1455, but a date
around 1435 is more likely. In the panel illustrated here, Niccolò da
Tolentino (ca. 1350–1435), a friend and supporter of Cosimo de'
Medici, leads the charge against the Sienese. Mounted on a white
horse and wearing an elegant red hat in place of a more practical
helmet, Niccolò cuts a dashing figure.

In *Battle of San Romano,* Uccello created a composition that
recalls the processional splendor of Gentile da Fabriano's International Gothic–style *Adoration of the Magi* (FIG. 21-17) yet also

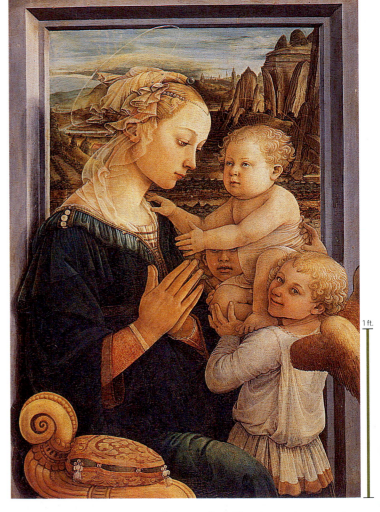

21-24 FRA FILIPPO LIPPI, *Madonna and Child with Angels,* ca. 1460–
1465. Tempera on wood, 2' 11½" × 2' 1". Galleria degli Uffizi, Florence.

Fra Filippo, a monk guilty of many misdemeanors, represented the Madonna
and Christ Child in a distinctly worldly manner, carrying the humanization of
the holy family further than any artist before him.

21-25 PIERO DELLA FRANCESCA, *Resurrection*, Palazzo Comunale, Borgo San Sepolcro, Italy, ca. 1463–1465. Fresco, 7' 4⅝" × 6' 6¼".

Christ miraculously rises from his tomb while the Roman guards sleep. The viewer sees the framing portico and the soldiers from below, but has a head-on view of the seminude muscular figure of Christ.

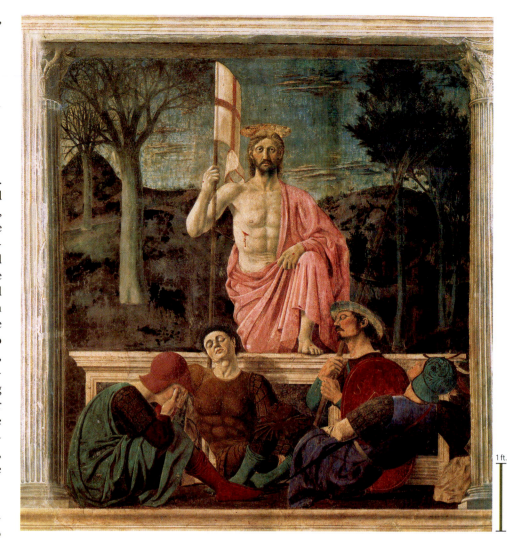

reflects Uccello's obsession with perspective. In contrast with Gentile, who emphasized surface decoration, Uccello painted life-size, classically inspired figures arranged in the foreground and, in the background, a receding landscape resembling the low cultivated hillsides between Florence and Lucca. He foreshortened broken spears, lances, and a fallen soldier and carefully placed them along the converging orthogonals of the perspective system (compare FIG. 21-9) to create a base plane akin to a checkerboard, on which he then placed the larger volumes in measured intervals. The rendering of three-dimensional form, used by other painters for representational or expressive purposes, became for Uccello a preoccupation. For him, it had a magic of its own, which he exploited to satisfy his inventive and original imagination.

FRA FILIPPO LIPPI Another younger contemporary of Fra Angelico, FRA FILIPPO LIPPI (ca. 1406–1469), was also a friar—but there all resemblance ends. Fra Filippo was unsuited for monastic life. He indulged in misdemeanors ranging from forgery and embezzlement to the abduction of a pretty nun, Lucretia, who became his mistress and the mother of his son, the painter Filippino Lippi (1457–1504). Only the intervention of the Medici on his behalf at the papal court preserved Fra Filippo from severe punishment and total disgrace. An orphan, Fra Filippo spent his youth in a monastery adjacent to the church of Santa Maria del Carmine, and when he was still in his teens, he must have met Masaccio there and witnessed the decoration of the Brancacci chapel. Fra Filippo's early work survives only in fragments, but these show that he tried to work with Masaccio's massive forms. Later, probably under the influence of Ghiberti's and Donatello's relief sculptures, he developed a linear style that emphasized the contours of his figures and enabled him to suggest movement through flying and swirling draperies.

In a painting from Fra Filippo's later years, *Madonna and Child with Angels* (FIG. 21-24), the Virgin sits in prayer at a slight angle to the viewer. Her body casts a shadow on the window frame behind her. But the painter's primary interest was not in space but in line, which unifies the composition and contributes to the precise and smooth delineation of forms. The Carmelite brother interpreted his subject in a surprisingly worldly manner. The Madonna is a beautiful young mother, albeit with a transparent halo, in an elegantly furnished Florentine home, and neither she nor the Christ Child, whom two angels hold up, has a solemn expression. One of the angels, in fact, sports the mischievous, puckish grin of a boy refusing to behave for the pious occasion. Significantly, all of the figures reflect the use of live models (perhaps Lucretia for the Madonna). Fra Filippo plainly relished the charm of youth and beauty as he found it in this world. He preferred the real in landscape also. The background, seen through the window, incorporates recognizable features of the Arno valley. Compared with the earlier Madonnas by Giotto (FIG. 14-8) and Duccio (FIG. 14-10), this work shows how far artists had carried the humanization of this traditional religious theme. Whatever the ideals of spiritual perfection may have meant to artists in past centuries, Renaissance artists realized those ideals in terms of the sensuous beauty of this world.

PIERO DELLA FRANCESCA One of the most renowned painters in 15th-century Italy was PIERO DELLA FRANCESCA (ca. 1420–1492), a native of Borgo San Sepolcro in southeastern Tuscany, who worked for diverse patrons, including the Medici in Florence and Federico de Montefeltro in Urbino (see page 614). In Tuscany, his commissions included the frescoes *Resurrection* (FIG. 21-25) for the town hall of his birthplace and *Legend of the True Cross* (FIG. 21-25A) for the church of San Francesco at Arezzo. He painted

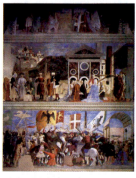

21-25A PIERO DELLA FRANCESCA, *Legend of the True Cross*, ca. 1450–1455.

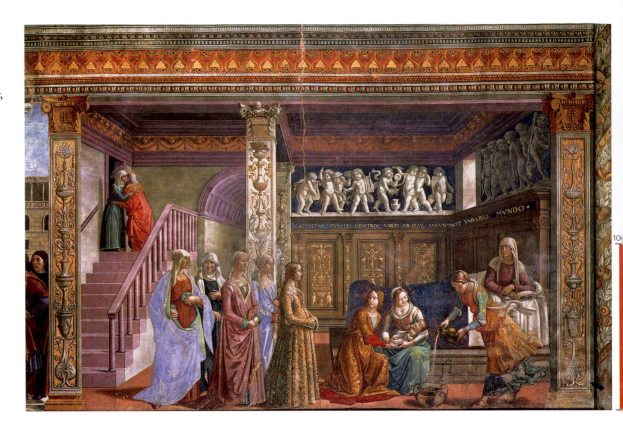

21-26 DOMENICO GHIRLANDAIO, *Birth of the Virgin,* Cappella Maggiore, Santa Maria Novella, Florence, Italy, ca. 1485–1490. Fresco, 24' 4" × 14' 9".

Ludovica Tornabuoni holds as prominent a place in Ghirlandaio's fresco as she must have held in Florentine society—evidence of the secularization of sacred themes in 15th-century Italian painting.

Resurrection on the wall facing the entrance to Borgo San Sepolcro's newly remodeled Palazzo Comunale at the request of the civic council. Normally, the subjects chosen for city halls were scenes of battles, townscapes, or allegories of enlightened governance, as in Siena's Palazzo Pubblico (FIGS. 14-16A, 14-17, and 14-18). But the San Sepolcro council chose a religious subject instead. The town's name—Holy Sepulcher—derived from the legend that two 10th-century saints, Arcanus and Egidius, brought a fragment of Christ's tomb to the town from the Holy Land. (Christ's resurrection was also the subject of the central panel of the altarpiece painted between 1346 and 1348 by the Sienese painter Niccolò di Segna for the cathedral of San Sepolcro.)

In Piero's *Resurrection,* the viewer witnesses the miracle of the risen Christ through the *Corinthian columns* of a classical portico (preserved only in part because the painting was trimmed during its installation in a new location). Piero chose a viewpoint corresponding to the viewer's position and depicted the architectural frame at a sharp angle from below. The Roman soldiers who have fallen asleep when they should be guarding the tomb are also seen from below in a variety of foreshortened poses. (The bareheaded guard second from the left with his head resting on Christ's sarcophagus may be a self-portrait of the artist.) The soldiers form the base of a compositional triangle culminating at Christ's head. For Christ, Piero violated the perspective of the rest of the fresco and used a head-on view of the resurrected savior, imbuing the figure with an iconic quality. Christ's muscular body has the proportions of Greco-Roman nude statues. His pastel cloak stands out prominently from the darker colors of the soldiers' costumes. Christ holds the banner of his victory over death and displays his wounds. His face has portraitlike features. The tired eyes and somber expression are the only indications of his suffering on the cross.

DOMENICO GHIRLANDAIO Although projects undertaken with church, civic, and Medici patronage were significant sources of income for Florentine artists, other wealthy families also offered attractive commissions. Toward the end of the 15th century, DOMENICO

GHIRLANDAIO (1449–1494) received the contract for an important project for Giovanni Tornabuoni, one of the wealthiest Florentines of his day. Tornabuoni asked Ghirlandaio to paint a cycle of frescoes depicting scenes from the lives of the Virgin and Saint John the Baptist for the choir of Santa Maria Novella (FIG. 14-5B), the Dominican church where Masaccio had earlier painted his revolutionary *Holy Trinity* (FIG. 21-20). In *Birth of the Virgin* (FIG. **21-26**), Mary's mother, Saint Anne (see "Early Christian Saints," page 236), reclines in a palatial Renaissance room embellished with fine wood inlay and sculpture, while midwives prepare the infant's bath. From the left comes a solemn procession of women led by a young Tornabuoni family member, probably Ludovica, Giovanni's only daughter. Ghirlandaio's composition effectively summarizes the goals of Quattrocento Florentine painting: clear spatial representation, statuesque figures, and rational order and logical relations among all figures and objects. If any remnant of earlier traits remains here, it is the arrangement of the figures, which still cling somewhat rigidly to layers parallel to the picture plane. New, however, and in striking contrast to the dignity and austerity of Fra Angelico's frescoes (FIG. 21-21) for the Dominican monastery of San Marco, is the dominating presence of the donor's family in the religious tableau. Ludovica holds as prominent a place in the composition (close to the central axis) as she must have held in Florentine society. Her appearance in the painting (a different female member of the house appears in each fresco) is conspicuous evidence of the secularization of sacred themes—and of the importance of women in Florence's elite families. Artists depicted living women and men of high rank not only as present at biblical dramas (as Masaccio did in *Holy Trinity*) but also even stealing the show from the saints—as here, where the Tornabuoni women upstage the Virgin and Child. The display of patrician elegance tempers the biblical narrative and subordinates the fresco's devotional nature.

Ghirlandaio also painted individual portraits of wealthy Florentines. His 1488 panel painting (FIG. **21-27**) of an aristocratic young woman is probably a portrait of Giovanna Tornabuoni, a member of the powerful Albizzi family and wife of Lorenzo Tornabuoni, one

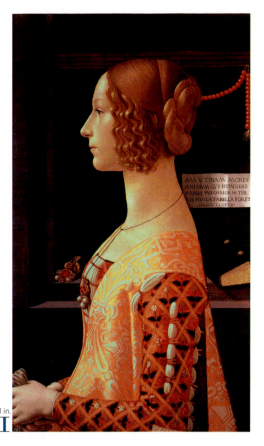

21-27 DOMENICO GHIRLANDAIO, *Giovanna Tornabuoni(?)*, 1488. Oil and tempera on wood, 2' 6" × 1' 8". Museo Thyssen-Bornemisza, Madrid.

Renaissance artists revived the ancient art of portraiture. This portrait reveals the wealth, courtly manners, and humanistic interest in classical literature that lie behind much 15th-century Florentine art.

of Lorenzo de' Medici's cousins. Although artists at this time were beginning to employ three-quarter and full-face views for portraits (FIG. 21-28A) in place of the more traditional profile pose, Ghirlandaio used the older format. This did not prevent him from conveying a character reading of the sitter. His portrait reveals the proud bearing of a sensitive and beautiful young woman. It also tells viewers much about the advanced state of culture in Florence, the value and careful cultivation of beauty in life and art, the breeding of courtly manners, and the great wealth behind it all. In addition, the painting shows the powerful attraction that classical literature held for Italian humanists. In the background, an epitaph (Giovanna Tornabuoni died in childbirth in 1488 at age 20) quotes the ancient Roman poet Martial:

> If art could depict character and soul,
> No painting on earth would be more beautiful.[7]

BOTTICELLI, *PRIMAVERA* The appeal of Greek and Latin literature to the elite families of Quattrocento Florence is most evident, however, in the paintings produced by Sandro Botticelli for members of the Medici family in the 1480s (see "The Medici, Botticelli, and Classical Antiquity," page 581). Botticelli painted *Primavera* (FIG. **21-28**) for Lorenzo di Pierfrancesco de' Medici (1463–1503), one of Lorenzo the Magnificent's cousins, probably a couple of years before *Birth of Venus* (FIG. 21-1). The artist made reference to his patron by setting the scene in a grove of orange fruit—*mela medica* (Italian, "medicinal apples"). Because the name Medici means "doctors," this fruit was a fitting symbol of the family.

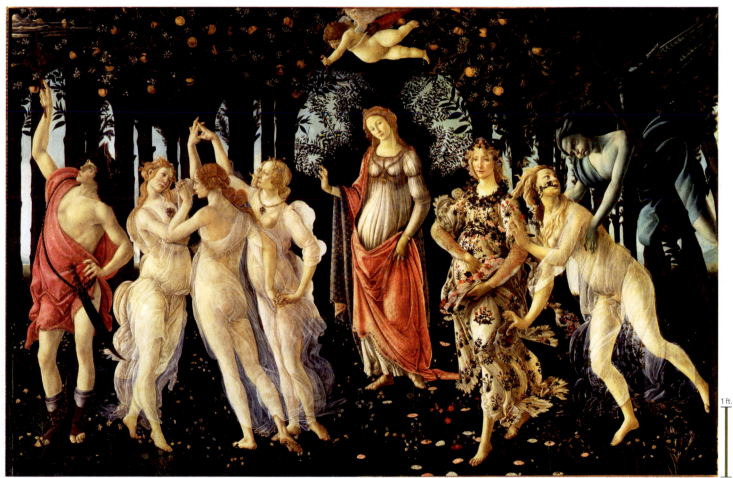

21-28 SANDRO BOTTICELLI, *Primavera*, ca. 1482. Tempera on wood, 6' 8" × 10' 4". Galleria degli Uffizi, Florence.

In Botticelli's lyrical painting celebrating love in springtime, the blue, ice-cold Zephyrus, the west wind, carries off and marries the nymph Chloris, whom he transforms into Flora, goddess of spring.

Venus stands just to the right of center with her son Cupid hovering above her head. Botticelli drew attention to the goddess of love by opening the landscape behind her to reveal a portion of sky that forms a kind of halo around Venus's head. To her right (the viewer's left) are the dancing Three Graces, who seem to be the target of Cupid's arrow. Botticelli's Graces are based closely on ancient prototypes, but they are clothed, albeit in thin, transparent garments. At the right are two of the key figures in *Birth of Venus*. The blue ice-cold Zephyrus is about to carry off and marry Chloris, whom he transforms into Flora, goddess of spring, appropriately shown wearing a rich floral gown. At the far left, Mercury turns away from all the others and reaches up with his distinctive staff, the *caduceus*, perhaps to dispel storm clouds. The sensuality of the representation, the appearance of Venus in springtime, and the abduction and marriage of Chloris all suggest that the occasion for the painting was young Lorenzo's wedding to Semiramide d'Appiani in May 1482. But the painting also sums up the Neo-Platonists' view that earthly love is compatible with Christian theology. In their reinterpretation of classical mythology, Venus as the source of love provokes desire through Cupid. Desire can lead either to lust and violence (Zephyrus) or, through reason and faith (Mercury), to the love of God. *Primavera*, read from right to left, served to urge the newlyweds to seek God through love.

Botticelli's paintings stand apart from those of the many other Quattrocento artists who sought to comprehend humanity and the natural world through a rational, empirical order. Indeed, Botticelli's elegant and beautiful linear style (he was a pupil of Fra Filippo Lippi, FIG. 21-24) seems removed from all the scientific knowledge 15th-century artists had gained in the areas of perspective and anatomy. For example, the seascape in *Birth of Venus* (FIG. 21-1) is a flat backdrop devoid of atmospheric perspective. Botticelli's style paralleled the Florentine allegorical pageants that were chivalric tournaments structured around allusions to classical mythology. The same trend is evident in the poetry of the 1470s and 1480s. Artists and poets at this time did not directly imitate classical antiquity but used the myths, with delicate perception of their charm, in a way still tinged with medieval romance. Ultimately, Botticelli created a style of visual poetry parallel to the love poetry of Lorenzo de' Medici. His paintings possess a lyricism and courtliness that appealed to cultured Florentine patrons, whether the Medici themselves or associates of the family (FIG. **21-28A**).

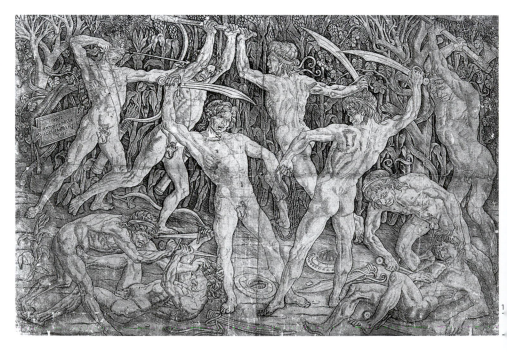

⤴ **21-28A** BOTTICELLI, *Young Man Holding a Medal*, ca. 1474–1475.

ENGRAVING Although the most prestigious commissions in 15th-century Florence were for large-scale panel paintings and frescoes and for monumental statues and reliefs, some artists also produced important small-scale works, such as Pollaiuolo's *Hercules and Antaeus* (FIG. 21-13). Pollaiuolo also experimented with the new medium of engraving, which northern European artists had pioneered around the middle of the century. But whereas German graphic artists, such as Martin Schongauer (FIG. 20-23), described their forms with hatching that followed the forms, Italian engravers, such as Pollaiuolo, preferred parallel hatching. The former method was in keeping with the general Northern Renaissance approach to art, which tended to describe surfaces of forms rather than their underlying structures, whereas the latter better suited the anatomical studies that preoccupied Pollaiuolo and his Italian contemporaries.

Battle of Ten Nudes (FIG. **21-29**), like Pollaiuolo's *Hercules and Antaeus* (FIG. 21-13), reveals the artist's interest in the realistic presentation of human figures in action. Earlier artists, such as Donatello (FIG. 21-11) and Masaccio (FIG. 21-19), had dealt effectively with the problem of rendering human anatomy, but they usually depicted their figures at rest or in restrained motion. As is evident in his engraving as well as in his sculpture, Pollaiuolo took delight in showing violent action. He conceived the body as a powerful machine and liked to display its mechanisms, such as knotted muscles and taut sinews that activate the skeleton as ropes pull levers. To show this to best effect, Pollaiuolo developed a figure so lean and muscular that it appears as if it has no skin. Pollaiuolo's figures also have strongly accentuated delineations at the wrists, elbows, shoulders, and knees. *Battle of Ten Nudes*—which has no identifiable subject or protagonists—shows this figure type in a variety of poses and from numerous viewpoints, enabling Pollaiuolo to demonstrate his prowess in rendering the nude male figure. In this, he was a kindred spirit of late-sixth-century Greek vase painters, such as Euthymides (FIG. 5-24), whose experiments with foreshortening also took precedence over narrative content. Even though the figures in *Ten Nudes* hack and slash at each other without mercy, they nevertheless seem somewhat stiff and frozen because Pollaiuolo depicted *all* the muscle groups at maximum tension. Not until several decades later did an even greater anatomist, Leonardo da Vinci (see page 629), observe that only some of the body's muscle groups participate in any one action, while the others remain relaxed.

21-29 ANTONIO DEL POLLAIUOLO, *Battle of Ten Nudes*, ca. 1465. Engraving, 1' 3$\frac{1}{8}$" × 1' 11$\frac{1}{4}$". Metropolitan Museum of Art, New York (bequest of Joseph Pulitzer, 1917).

Pollaiuolo was fascinated by how muscles and sinews activate the human skeleton. He delighted in showing nude figures in violent action and from numerous foreshortened viewpoints.

Architecture

Filippo Brunelleschi's ability to codify a system of linear perspective derived in part from his skill as an architect. Although according to his biographer, Antonio Manetti, Brunelleschi turned to architecture out of disappointment over the loss to Lorenzo Ghiberti of the commission for the baptistery doors (FIGS. 21-2 and 21-3), he continued to work as a sculptor for several years and received commissions for sculpture as late as 1416. It is true, however, that as the 15th century progressed, Brunelleschi's interest turned increasingly toward architecture—a field that he would reorient. Several trips to Rome (the first in 1402, probably with his friend Donatello), where the ruins of ancient Rome captivated him, heightened his fascination with buildings. His close study of Roman monuments and his effort to make an accurate record of what he saw may have been the catalyst that led Brunelleschi to develop his revolutionary system of linear perspective.

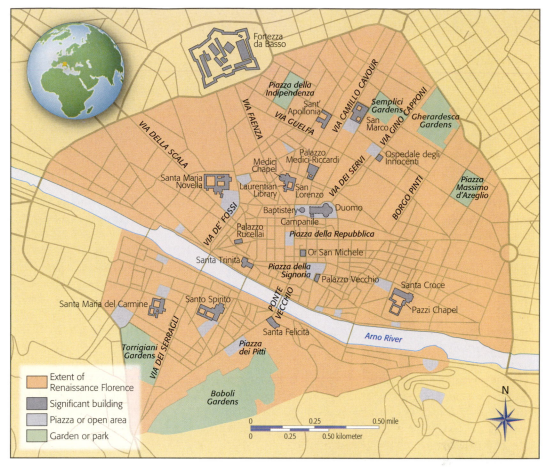

MAP 21-1
Renaissance Florence.

OSPEDALE DEGLI INNOCENTI At the end of the second decade of the 15th century, Brunelleschi received two important architectural commissions in Florence (MAP 21-1)—to construct a dome (FIGS. 21-29A and 21-29B) for the city's late medieval cathedral (FIG. 14-19) and to design the Ospedale degli Innocenti (Hospital of the Innocents, FIG. 21-30), a home for Florentine orphans and foundlings. The orphanage commission came from Florence's guild of silk manufacturers and goldsmiths, of which Brunelleschi, a goldsmith, was a member. The site chosen, adjacent to the church of the Santissima Annunziata (Most Holy Annunciation), was appropriate. The church housed a miracle-working *Annunciation* that attracted large numbers of pilgrims. With the construction of the new foundling hospital, the Madonna would now watch over

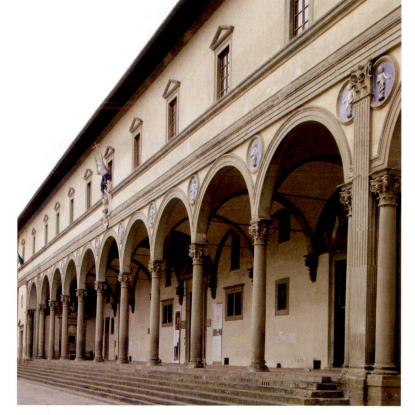

21-30 FILIPPO BRUNELLESCHI, loggia of the Ospedale degli Innocenti (Foundling Hospital; looking northeast), Florence, Italy, begun 1419.

Often called the first Renaissance building, the loggia of the orphanage sponsored by Florence's silk and goldsmith guild features a classically austere design based on a module of 10 braccia.

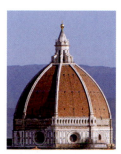

⬈**21-29A** BRUNELLESCHI, Florence Cathedral dome, 1420–1436.

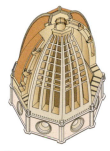

⬈**21-29B** BRUNELLESCHI, Florence Cathedral dome, cutaway.

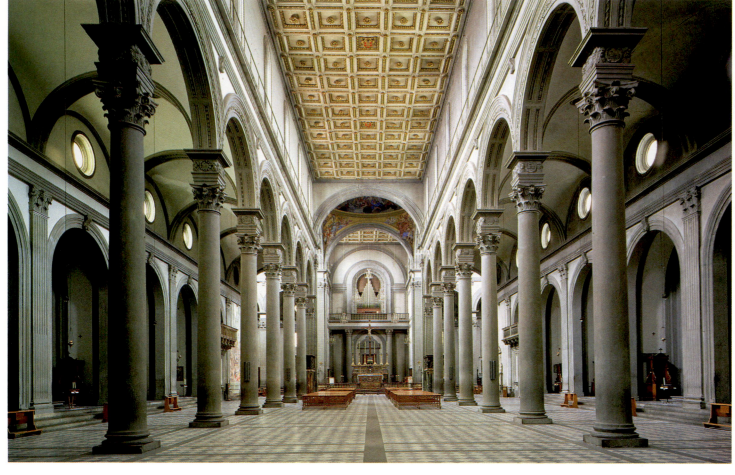

21-31 FILIPPO BRUNELLESCHI, interior of San Lorenzo (looking east), Florence, Italy, ca. 1421–1469.

The mathematical clarity and austerity of the decor of San Lorenzo are key elements of Brunelleschi's classically inspired architectural style, which contrasts sharply with the soaring drama of Gothic churches.

infants as well, assisted by the guild, which supported the orphanage with additional charitable donations.

Most scholars regard Brunelleschi's Ospedale degli Innocenti as the first building to embody the new Renaissance architectural style. As in earlier similar buildings, the facade of the Florentine orphanage is a loggia opening onto the street, a sheltered portico where, in this case, parents could anonymously deliver unwanted children to the care of the foundling hospital. Brunelleschi's arcade consists of a series of round arches on slender Corinthian columns. Each bay is a domed compartment with a *pediment*-capped window above. Both plan and elevation conform to a *module* that embodies the rationality of classical architecture. Each column is 10 *braccia* (approximately 20 feet; 1 braccia, or arm, equals 23 inches) tall. The distance between the columns of the facade and the distance between the columns and the wall are also 10 braccia. Thus each of the bays is a cubical unit 10 braccia wide, deep, and high. The height of the columns also equals the diameter of the arches (except in the two outermost bays, which are slightly wider and serve as framing elements in the overall design). The color scheme, which would become a Brunelleschi hallmark, is austere: white stucco walls with gray pietra serena ("serene stone") columns and moldings.

SAN LORENZO In 1418, the year before Brunelleschi began work on the Ospedale degli Innocenti, Giovanni de' Medici became the official banker of the Vatican, a position that enabled him and his heirs to amass both wealth and power (see "The Medici," page 581).

Giovanni became the leader of a group of Florentine citizens that financed the rebuilding of the church of San Lorenzo (Saint Lawrence; FIG. **21-31**). The church, one of the largest in the city, had a venerable history. The original church was dedicated in 393, but an 11th-century Romanesque church that replaced the Early Christian *basilica* still stood on the site in the early 15th century. In 1421, the commission for the new church went to Brunelleschi, who did not live to see his design executed in full. In fact, at the time of his death in 1446, not a single column of the nave was yet in place.

San Lorenzo is one of two basilican churches in Florence designed by Brunelleschi, and its plan and elevation closely resemble those of Santo Spirito (FIGS. **21-31A** and **21-31B**), begun about a decade later on the opposite side of the Arno River (MAP 21-1). Both churches embody the new Renaissance spirit of the Florentine orphanage loggia in their austerity and rationality. As in the

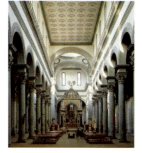

21-31A BRUNELLESCHI, Santo Spirito interior, begun 1446.

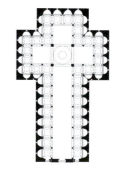

21-31B BRUNELLESCHI, Santo Spirito plan, begun 1446.

Italian Renaissance Family Chapel Endowments

During the 14th through 16th centuries in Italy, wealthy families regularly endowed chapels in or adjacent to major churches. These family chapels were usually situated on either side of the choir near the altar at the church's east end. Very wealthy families sponsored chapels in the form of separate buildings constructed adjacent to churches. For example, the Medici Chapel (Old Sacristy) abuts San Lorenzo in Florence. The Pazzi family commissioned a chapel (FIGS. 21-32 to 21-34) adjacent to Santa Croce. Other powerful banking families—the Baroncelli, Bardi, and Peruzzi—each sponsored chapels inside the church. The Brancacci family paid for the decorative program (FIGS. 21-18 and 21-19) of their chapel in Santa Maria del Carmine, and the Strozzi for their family chapel in Santa Trinità (FIG. 21-17).

These families and many others, not only in Florence but throughout Italy, endowed chapels to ensure the well-being of the souls of individual family members and ancestors. The chapels served as burial sites and as spaces for liturgical celebrations and commemorative services. Chapel owners sponsored Masses for the dead, praying to the Virgin Mary and the saints for intercession on behalf of their deceased loved ones.

Changes in Christian doctrine prompted these concerted efforts to enhance donors' chances for eternal salvation. Until the 13th century, most Christians believed that after death, souls went either to Heaven or to Hell. In the late 1100s and early 1200s, the concept of Purgatory—a way station between Heaven and Hell where souls could atone for sins before judgment day—increasingly won favor. Pope Innocent III (1198–1216) officially recognized the existence of such a place in 1215. Because Purgatory represented a chance for the faithful to improve the likelihood of eventually gaining admission to Heaven, Christians eagerly embraced this opportunity.

When the Church extended to the living the concept of earning salvation in Purgatory, charitable work, good deeds, and devotional practices proliferated. Family chapels provided the space necessary for the performance of devotional rituals. Most chapels included altars, as well as chalices, vestments, candlesticks, and other objects used in the

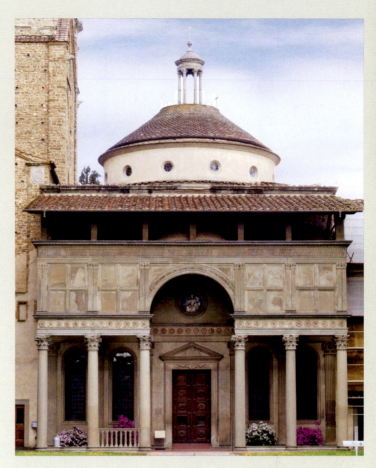

21-32 FILIPPO BRUNELLESCHI, west facade of the Pazzi Chapel, Santa Croce, Florence, Italy, begun 1433.

The Pazzi family erected this chapel as a gift to the Franciscan church of Santa Croce. It served as the monks' chapter house and is one of the first independent Renaissance central-plan buildings.

Mass. In consultation with the relevant church officials, most patrons also commissioned decorations, such as painted altarpieces, frescoes on the walls, and sculptural objects. The chapels were therefore not only expressions of piety and devotion but also opportunities for donors to enhance their stature in the larger community.

earlier building, Brunelleschi adopted an all-encompassing modular design for the church that extended even to the diameter of the shafts of the nave columns and the dimensions of their Corinthian capitals. The nave has a simple two-story elevation (nave arcade and clerestory) with a flat, coffered timber roof. The columns support *impost blocks* from which round arches spring. Ample light enters through the arcuated clerestory windows and through *oculi* in the aisle walls, one over each chapel opening onto the domed aisle bays. The restrained color scheme of white stucco wall surfaces and moldings in gray pietra serena became standard in Florentine churches for 500 years.

The calculated logic of the design echoes that of ancient Roman buildings, but contrasts sharply with the soaring drama and spirituality of the nave arcades and vaults of Gothic churches (for example, FIGS. 13-20 and 13-21). San Lorenzo's rational interior even deviates from Florence Cathedral's nave (FIG. 14-19A), whose verticality is

restrained in comparison to its northern European counterparts. San Lorenzo fully expresses the new Renaissance spirit that placed its faith in reason rather than in the emotions.

PAZZI CHAPEL Shortly after Brunelleschi began work on San Lorenzo, the Pazzi family commissioned him to design the chapel (FIGS. 21-32 to 21-34) they intended to donate to the Franciscan church of Santa Croce in Florence (see "Italian Renaissance Family Chapel Endowments," above). The project was not completed, however, until the 1460s, long after Brunelleschi's death, and the exterior (FIG. 21-32) probably does not reflect his original design. The loggia, admirable as it is, likely was added as an afterthought, perhaps by the sculptor-architect Giuliano da Maiano (1432–1490). The Pazzi Chapel served as the *chapter house* (meeting hall) of the local chapter of Franciscan monks. Historians have suggested that the monks needed the expansion to accommodate more of their brethren.

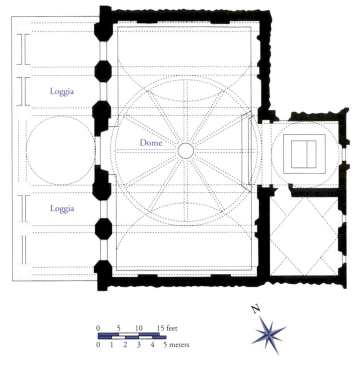

21-33 FILIPPO BRUNELLESCHI, plan of the Pazzi Chapel, Santa Croce, Florence, Italy, begun 1433.

Although the Pazzi Chapel is rectangular, rather than square or round, Brunelleschi created a central plan by placing all emphasis on the dome-covered space at the heart of the building.

Behind the loggia stands one of the first independent Renaissance buildings conceived basically as a *central-plan* structure (compare FIGS. 8-11 and 8-12), so called because the various aspects of the interior resemble one another, no matter where an observer stands, in contrast to the *longitudinal plan* of basilican churches. Although the Pazzi Chapel's plan (FIG. **21-33**) is rectangular, rather than square or round, Brunelleschi placed all emphasis on the central dome-covered space. The short *barrel-vaulted* sections bracing the dome on two sides appear to be incidental appendages. The interior trim (FIG. **21-34**) is Brunelleschi's favorite gray pietra serena, which stands out against the white stuccoed walls and crisply defines the modular relationships of plan and elevation. As he did in his design for the Ospedale degli Innocenti (FIG. 21-30) and later for Santo Lorenzo (FIG. 21-31), Brunelleschi used a basic unit that enabled him to construct a balanced, harmonious, and regularly proportioned space.

Circular medallions (tondi) in the dome's *pendentives* (see "Placing a Dome over a Square," page 264) consist of *terracotta* reliefs representing the four evangelists. The technique for manufacturing these baked clay reliefs was of recent invention. Around 1430, LUCA DELLA ROBBIA (1400–1482) perfected the application of vitrified (heat-fused) colored potters' *glazes* to sculpture (FIG. **21-34A**). Inexpensive, durable, and decorative, these ceramic sculptures became extremely popular and provided the basis for a lucrative family business. Luca's nephew Andrea della Robbia (1435–1525) produced *roundels* of babies in swaddling clothes for

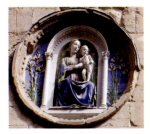

21-34A LUCA DELLA ROBBIA, *Madonna and Child*, ca. 1455–1460.

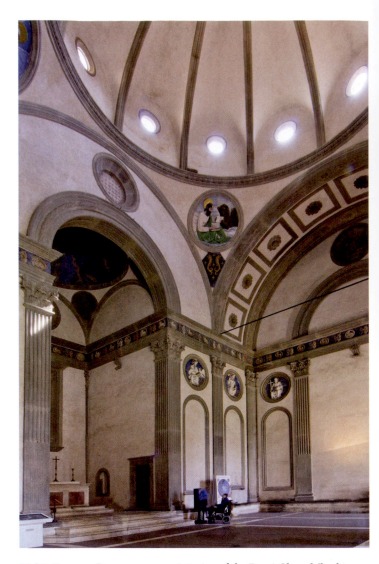

21-34 FILIPPO BRUNELLESCHI, interior of the Pazzi Chapel (looking southeast), Santa Croce, Florence, Italy, begun 1433.

The interior trim of the Pazzi Chapel is gray pietra serena, which stands out against the white stuccoed walls and crisply defines the modular relationships of Brunelleschi's plan and elevation.

Brunelleschi's loggia of the Ospedale degli Innocenti (FIG. 21-30) in 1487 (the only indication on the building's facade of its charitable function), and Andrea's sons, Giovanni della Robbia (1469–1529) and Girolamo della Robbia (1488–1566), carried on this tradition well into the 16th century. Most of the tondi in the Pazzi Chapel are the work of Luca della Robbia himself. Together with the images of the 12 apostles on the pilaster-framed wall panels, they add striking color accents to the tranquil interior.

PALAZZO MEDICI It seems curious that Brunelleschi, the most renowned architect of his time, did not participate in the upsurge of palace building that Florence experienced in the 1430s and 1440s. This proliferation of *palazzi* testified to the stability of the Florentine economy and to the affluence and confidence of the city's leading citizens. Brunelleschi, however, confined his efforts in this field to work on the Palazzo di Parte Guelfa (headquarters of Florence's then-ruling "party") and to a rejected model for a new palace that Cosimo de' Medici intended to build. When the Medici returned to Florence in 1434 after a brief exile imposed upon them by other elite families who resented the Medicis' consolidation of power, Cosimo,

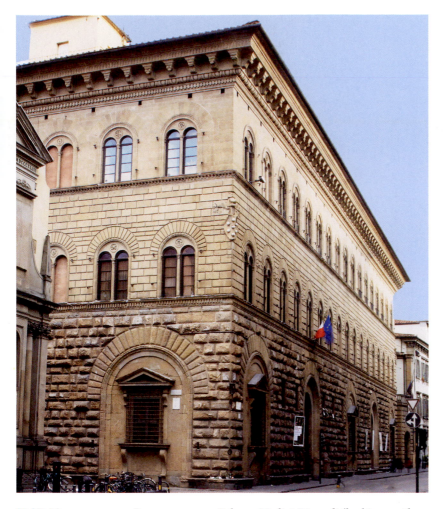

aware of the importance of public perception, attempted to maintain a lower profile and to wield his power from behind the scenes. In all probability, this attitude accounted for his rejection of Brunelleschi's design for the new Medici residence, which he evidently found too imposing and ostentatious to be politically wise. Cosimo eventually awarded the commission to MICHELOZZO DI BARTOLOMMEO (1396–1472), a young architect who had been Donatello's collaborator in several sculptural enterprises. Although Cosimo passed over Brunelleschi, the architect's style nevertheless deeply influenced Michelozzo. To a limited extent, the Palazzo Medici (FIG. 21-35) reflects Brunelleschian principles.

Later bought by the Riccardi family (hence the name Palazzo Medici-Riccardi), who almost doubled the facade's length in the 18th century, the palace, in both its original and its extended form, is a simple, massive structure. Heavy *rustication* (rough, unfinished masonry) on the ground floor accentuates its strength. Michelozzo divided the building block into stories of decreasing height by using long, unbroken *stringcourses* (horizontal bands), which give it coherence. *Dressed masonry* (smooth, finished) *ashlar* blocks on the second level and an even smoother surface on the top story modify the severity of the ground floor and make the building appear progressively lighter as the eye moves upward. The extremely heavy *cornice*, which Michelozzo related not to the top story but to the building as a whole, dramatically reverses this effect. Like the ancient Roman cornices that served as Michelozzo's models (compare FIGS. 7-32, 7-40, and 7-44A), the Palazzo Medici-Riccardi cornice is a very effective lid for the structure, clearly and emphatically defining its proportions. Michelozzo perhaps also was inspired by the many extant examples of Roman rusticated masonry, and Roman precedents even exist for the juxtaposition of rusticated and dressed

21-35 MICHELOZZO DI BARTOLOMMEO, Palazzo Medici-Riccardi (looking north-west), Florence, Italy, begun 1445.

The Medici palace, with its combination of dressed and rusticated masonry and classical moldings, draws heavily on ancient Roman architecture, but Michelozzo creatively reinterpreted his models.

21-36 MICHELOZZO DI BARTOLOMMEO, interior court of the Palazzo Medici-Riccardi (looking west), Florence, Italy, begun 1445.

The Medici palace's interior court surrounded by a round-arched colonnade was the first of its kind, but the austere design clearly reveals Michelozzo's debt to Brunelleschi (FIG. 21-30).

Leon Battista Alberti's *On the Art of Building*

Although he wrote treatises on painting and sculpture, Leon Battista Alberti's most ambitious work, modeled on Vitruvius's *Ten Books on Architecture* (see page 199) was *De re aedificatori libri X* (*On the Art of Building in Ten Books*), written about 1450 and published in 1486. Alberti was the first to study Vitruvius's treatise in detail, and his knowledge of it, combined with his own archaeological investigations, made him the first Renaissance architect to understand classical architecture in depth. His own buildings (FIGS. **21-36A, 21-37,** and **21-45 to 21-47**), however, are not ancient replicas but highly original designs.

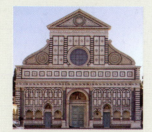

21-36A ALBERTI, Santa Maria Novella, Florence, 1456–1470.

Alberti's treatise, in addition to serving as a practical manual for architects, also celebrated and sought to ennoble the profession of architect. In his prologue, Alberti argued that

> The security, dignity, and honor of the republic depend greatly on the architect: it is he who is responsible for our delight, entertainment, and health while at leisure, and our profit and advantage while at work, and in short, that we live in a dignified manner, free from any danger. In view then of the delight and wonderful grace of his works, and of how indispensable they have proved, and in view of the benefit and convenience of his inventions, and their service to posterity, he should no doubt be accorded praise and respect, and be counted among those most deserving of mankind's honor and recognition.*

Alberti believed that architectural design should reflect the laws of nature and conform to mathematical formulas for beautiful proportions.

> The great experts of antiquity . . . have instructed us that a building is very like an animal, and that Nature must be imitated when we delineate it. . . . Beauty is a form of sympathy and consonance of the parts within a body, according to definite number, outline, and position, . . . the absolute and fundamental rule of Nature. This is the main object of the art of building, and the source of her dignity, charm, authority, and worth (IX.5).

Alberti shared this conviction with Brunelleschi, and this fundamental dependence on classically derived mathematics distinguished their architectural work from that of most of their medieval predecessors. They believed in the eternal and universal validity of numerical ratios as the source of beauty. In this respect, Alberti and Brunelleschi revived the true spirit of the High Classical age of ancient Greece, following the lead of the architect Iktinos and the sculptor Polykleitos, who produced canons of proportions for the perfect temple and the perfect statue (see "The Perfect Temple," page 103, and "Polykleitos's Prescription for the Perfect Statue," page 129).

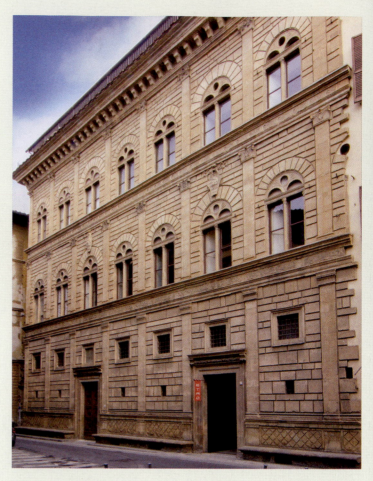

21-37 LEON BATTISTA ALBERTI and BERNARDO ROSSELLINO, Palazzo Rucellai (looking northwest), Florence, Italy, ca. 1452–1470.

Alberti was an ardent student of classical architecture. By adapting the Roman use of different orders for each story, he created the illusion that the Palazzo Rucellai becomes lighter toward its top.

Two of Alberti's prescriptions for good architectural design are of particular interest. In contrast to the long tradition of building basilican churches with nave arcades, Alberti believed that the central plan was the ideal form for churches and that arches should not rest on columns.

> It is obvious from all that is fashioned, produced, or created under her influence that Nature delights primarily in the circle. Need I mention the earth, the stars, the animals, their nests, and so on, all of which she has made circular. . . . The round plan is defined by the circle (VII.4).

> For arched colonnades quadrangular columns are required. The work would be defective with round columns (VII.131).

Many later architects took both suggestions to heart.

*All passages translated by Joseph Rykwert, Neil Leach, and Robert Tavernor, *Leon Battista Alberti: On the Art of Building in Ten Books* (Cambridge, Mass.: MIT Press, 1988), 5, 196, 236, 301, 303.

---

stone masonry on the same facade (FIG. 7-34). However, nothing in the ancient world precisely compares with Michelozzo's design. The Palazzo Medici exemplifies the simultaneous respect for and independence from the antique that characterizes the Early Renaissance in Italy.

The heart of the Palazzo Medici is an open colonnaded court (FIG. 21-36) that clearly shows Michelozzo's debt to Brunelleschi. The round-arched colonnade, although more massive in its proportions, closely resembles Brunelleschi's foundling-hospital loggia (FIG. 21-30) and the nave colonnades of San Lorenzo (FIG. 21-31) and Santo Spirito (FIG. 21-31A). As in Brunelleschi's loggia and the Pazzi Chapel (FIG. 21-34), roundels (here framing Medici coats-of-arms) are prominent motifs in the arcades, although in the Palazzo Medici they appear in the frieze above the arcade, alternating with garlands, a popular motif in ancient Roman architecture (for example, FIG. 7-4). The Palazzo Medici's internal court surrounded by an arcade was the first of its kind in Renaissance architecture and influenced a long line of descendants in Italian domestic architecture (for example, FIG. 22-27).

LEON BATTISTA ALBERTI Although he entered the profession of architecture rather late in life, LEON BATTISTA ALBERTI (1404–1472) made a major contribution to architectural design (see "Leon Battista Alberti's *On the Art of Building*," page 608). Alberti's architectural style represents a scholarly application of classical elements to contemporaneous buildings. Most architectural historians believe that he designed the Palazzo Rucellai (FIG. 21-37) in Florence, although his pupil and collaborator, Bernardo Rossellino (FIG. 21-14), constructed the building using Alberti's plans and sketches. The facade of the palace is much more severe than that of the Palazzo Medici-Riccardi (FIG. 21-35). Pilasters define each story, and a classical cornice crowns the whole. Between the smooth pilasters are subdued and uniform wall surfaces. Alberti created the sense that the structure becomes lighter in weight toward its top by adapting the ancient Roman manner of using different capitals for the pilasters of each story. He chose the severe capitals of ancient *Tuscan columns* (the Etruscan variant of the Greek *Doric order* [FIG. 5-13, *left*], used also by the Romans) for the ground floor, capitals of his own invention with acanthus leaves and *palmettes* (palm leaves) for the second story, and Corinthian capitals for the third floor. Alberti modeled his facade on the most imposing Roman ruin of all, the Colosseum (FIG. 7-37), but he was no slavish copyist. On the Colosseum's facade, the capitals employed are, from the bottom up, Tuscan, Ionic, and Corinthian. Moreover, Alberti adapted the Colosseum's varied surface to a flat facade, which does not allow the deep penetration of the building's mass that is so effective in the Roman structure. By converting his ancient model's *engaged columns* (half-round columns attached to a wall) into shallow pilasters that barely project from the wall, Alberti created a large-meshed linear net. Stretched tightly across the front of his building, it not only unifies the three levels but also emphasizes the wall's flat, two-dimensional qualities.

GIROLAMO SAVONAROLA In the 1490s, Florence underwent a political, cultural, and religious upheaval. Florentine artists and their fellow citizens responded then not only to humanist ideas but also to the incursion of French armies and especially to the preaching of the Dominican monk Girolamo Savonarola (1452–1498), the reformist priest-dictator who denounced the humanistic secularism of the Medici and their artists, philosophers, and poets. Savonarola exhorted the people of Florence to repent their sins, and when Lorenzo de' Medici died in 1492, the priest prophesied the downfall of the city and of Italy and assumed absolute control of the state. As did a large number of citizens, Savonarola believed that the Medici family's political, social, and religious power had corrupted Florence and invited the scourge of foreign invasion. In his sermons, Savonarola condemned the worldly and irreverent representation of holy figures—for example, Fra Filippo Lippi's *Madonna and Child with Angels* (FIG. 21-24)—and those families who spent their fortunes on chapels dedicated to perpetuating their memory instead of aiding the poor (see "Family Chapel Endowments," page 605).

He encouraged citizens to burn their classical texts, scientific treatises, and philosophical publications. The Medici fled in 1494.

Scholars still debate the significance of Savonarola's brief span of power. Apologists for the undoubtedly sincere monk deny that his actions played a role in the decline of Florentine culture at the end of the 15th century. But the puritanical spirit that moved Savonarola must have dampened considerably the enthusiasm for classical antiquity of the Florentine Early Renaissance. Certainly, Savanarola's condemnation of humanism as heretical nonsense, and his banishing of the Medici, Tornabuoni, and other wealthy families from Florence, deprived local artists of some of their major patrons, at least in the short term. There were, however, commissions aplenty for artists elsewhere in Italy—beginning long before Savonarola launched his attacks on Florentine humanism.

VENICE

At the dawn of the Renaissance, Venice was one of the richest states in Italy and the major commercial and cultural link to the Byzantine Empire. In the realm of architecture, it boasted one of the greatest churches in Europe, the five-domed mosaic-filled Saint Mark's (FIG. 9-27) dedicated to the city's patron saint, and one of the gems of late medieval secular architecture, the palace (FIG. 14-23) of the city's ruling *doges* (dukes). The design of the seat of Venetian power contrasts vividly with Florence's fortresslike Palazzo della Signoria (FIG. 14-19B) and reflects the fact that Venice, unlike Florence, was free of civil conflict.

CA D'ORO That happy state of affairs also dictated the design of private palaces. The most spectacular 15th-century Venetian palace (FIG. **21-38**) looks nothing like the Palazzo Medici (FIG. 21-35). It belonged to Marino Contarini, the scion of one of the city's wealthiest merchant families. Built between 1421 and 1437, the Palazzo Contarini has an asymmetrical three-story facade facing Venice's

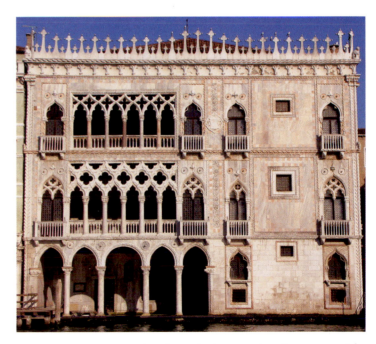

21-38 Palazzo Contarini (Ca d'Oro; looking northeast), Venice, Italy, 1421–1437.

In vivid contrast to the fortresslike Florentine Palazzo Medici (FIG. 21-35), Marino Contarini's "House of Gold" displays the Venetian's taste for flowery painted and gilded Gothic ornamentation.

The Tomb of Doge Pietro Mocenigo

Upon entering the basilican church in Venice dedicated to Saints John and Paul, visitors today are greeted by so many tombs of the city's former rulers that the church has been dubbed the "pantheon of the doges." The tombs impressed earlier tourists as well, including Felix Faber (ca. 1441–1502), a Dominican theologian who stopped in Venice in 1480 during a pilgrimage to Jerusalem and recorded what he saw in his diary. The doges' tombs in Santi Giovanni e Paolo made a profound impression on Faber, especially that of Pietro Mocenigo (FIG. 21-39), carved by Pietro Lombardo and his workshop. The focus of Mocenigo's tomb is his portrait in armor, framed by a triumphal arch. The statue rests on the doge's sarcophagus, held aloft by three warriors of different ages and decorated with reliefs commemorating major achievements of his short reign as duke. More statues of soldiers stand in superposed niches to the left and right. Below are reliefs depicting the Labors of Hercules. At the summit is the resurrected Christ above a relief representing the Three Marys at the Savior's empty tomb.

Faber took special interest in the combination of Christian iconography and classical mythology on Mocenigo's tomb—a distinctive feature of much Italian Renaissance art—and the ease with which those not schooled in Greco-Roman art and literature could confuse antique heroes with Old and New Testament figures.

> The Dominican church in Venice has the tombs of many doges. Never have I beheld tombs so full of beauty and pomp. Not even the tombs of the popes in Rome stand up by comparison. The tombs are embedded in the wall above the floor and are completely covered in various marbles and sculptures and decorated in gold and silver more than is proper. There are images of Christ, the Blessed Virgin, the Apostles, martyrs and other saints all according to the wish of the patrons. . . . To the right of the church entrance I saw the precious tomb of [Doge Pietro Mocenigo], upon which is carved the image of Hercules fighting. He is portrayed as usual but is wearing the skin of a lion he has killed rather than a cloak. Then there is another image of Hercules wrestling the hydra, a fearful monster which immediately grows seven new heads as soon as one of the old ones is chopped off. . . . Many of these pagan images alternate with those of our redemption, and thus it is that simple souls, believing they are saints, worship Hercules, mistaking him for Samson, and Venus, taking her for Mary Magdalene, and so on.*

*Quoted by Wolfgang Wolters in Giandomencio Romanelli, ed., *Venice: Art & Architecture* (Cologne: Könemann, 2005), 202–203.

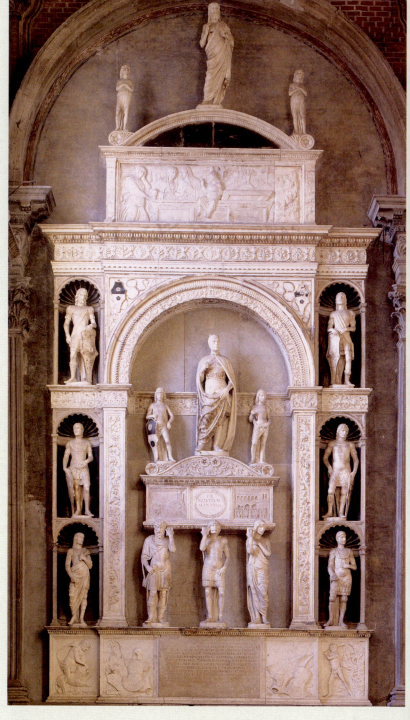

21-39 PIETRO LOMBARDO, tomb of Doge Pietro Mocenigo, Santi Giovanni e Paolo, Venice, 1476–1480.

This immense wall tomb by the leading Quattrocento Venetian sculptor and his sons presents Doge Pietro Mocenigo as a conquering warrior and incorporates both Christian and classical mythological themes.

primary waterway, the Grand Canal. The lowest floor—it cannot accurately be called the "ground" floor—has a simple loggia with wide bays for the unloading of goods from boats. Behind it is a corridor running the length of the house flanked by storerooms and a small courtyard and garden. (The palace was Contarini's warehouse as well as residence.) On the main (second) floor—the *piano nobile* ("noble floor")—were the public reception rooms behind a loggia of ornate Late Gothic multilobed arches. The family's private chambers were on the third floor.

Detailed building accounts show that Contarini spared no expense in making his home a showcase of his wealth. He instructed painters to decorate the facade in white and blue enamel and stonemasons to oil the red Veronese marble blocks to make them shine brightly. Most of the intricately carved architectural ornamentation was gilded—hence the palace's longstanding nickname: Ca d'Oro (House of Gold). To achieve the look and quality he sought, Contarini hired artists from far and wide, including Matteo Raverti, one of the sculptors who worked at Milan Cathedral, and the French painter known in Italy as Zuan di Franza. The Ca d'Oro is a testimonial not only to Contarini's financial success but also to the survival of flowery Gothic taste in Venice at the same time that Filippo Brunelleschi was designing classically austere buildings (FIGS. 21-30 to 21-34) in Florence.

PIETRO LOMBARDO The leading sculptural workshop of Renaissance Venice was established around 1467 by PIETRO LOMBARDO (ca. 1435–1515), whose sons, Tullio and Antonio, continued to win major commissions in the 16th century. The specialty of the family workshop was funerary sculpture, particularly the grandiose wall tomb (compare FIG. 21-14). The basilica of Santi Giovanni e Paolo in Venice (next to which Colleoni's equestrian statue [FIG. 21-16] stands on a towering pedestal) became a showcase for their work. The church housed the wall tombs of several doges, of which probably the most impressive is that of Pietro Mocenigo (r. 1474–1476; FIG. **21-39**), carved by Pietro, assisted by his sons and others, between 1476 and 1481 (see "The Tomb of Doge Pietro Mocenigo," page 610).

GIOVANNI BELLINI In the 16th century, Venice emerged as one of three great centers of Renaissance painting in Italy, along with Florence and Rome. The man credited with establishing the Venetian High Renaissance school of painting was GIOVANNI BELLINI (ca. 1430–1516). Trained in the International Gothic style by his father, Jacopo, a student of Gentile da Fabriano (FIG. 21-17), Giovanni worked in the family shop and did not develop his own style until after his father's death in 1470 (see "Imitation and Emulation in Renaissance Art," page 594). His early independent works show the dominant influence of his brother-in-law Andrea Mantegna (FIGS. 21-48 to 21-50). But in the late 1470s, he came into contact with the work of the Sicilian-born painter Antonello da Messina (ca. 1430–1479). Antonello received his early training in Naples, where he must have encountered Flemish painting and mastered using mixed oil (see "Tempera and Oil Painting," page 559). This more flexible medium is wider in coloristic range than either tempera or fresco. Antonello arrived in Venice in 1475 and during his two-year stay introduced his Venetian colleagues to the possibilities that the new oil technique offered.

In *Saint Francis in the Desert* (FIG. **21-40**), Bellini's most famous work of this period, the Venetian master depicted the founder of the Franciscan order as a hermit in the wilderness—although not

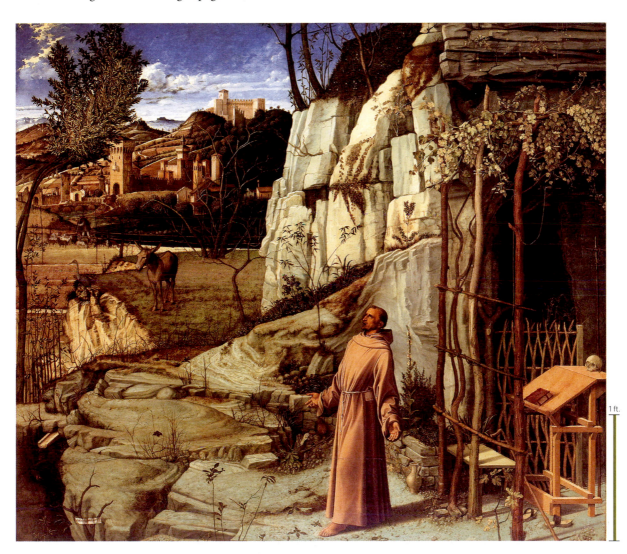

21-40 GIOVANNI BELLINI, *Saint Francis in the Desert,* ca. 1477–1479. Oil and tempera on wood, 4' 1" × 4' 7⅞". Frick Collection, New York (Henry Clay Frick Bequest).

Mixing tempera and oil, Bellini depicted Saint Francis communing with God in a landscape filled with references to the crucifixion and to Moses, whom the Franciscans identified with their founder.

too far removed from the medieval Italian town that Bellini placed in the background. Saint Francis has stepped out of his cave home, where he has set up beneath a grape bower a simple wooden desk with a skull on it (symbolic of the crucifixion and the blood of Christ). He spreads his arms, displaying his *stigmata*, the marks of his identification with Christ (see page 416), and gazes skyward at a burst of golden light (at the upper left corner of the panel) that signals God's presence.

Emulating Netherlandish masters, Bellini filled his painting of Saint Francis's ecstatic communion with God with symbols and allusions. The Franciscans viewed their founding saint as a new Moses, who had communed with God in the desert before the burning bush, perhaps alluded to by the windblown tree before the burst of light. Certainly, the water trickling from a spout in the rocks at the lower left beneath the quivering tree is a reference to the water that miraculously appeared when Moses struck the rock at Mount Horeb with his staff. Francis also stands barefoot (his sandals are beside his desk), just as Moses did in the desert when God commanded him to remove his shoes because he stood on sacred ground. The donkey, a traditional symbol of patience appropriate for a hermit saint, may also refer to Francis's description of his own body as Brother Ass.

Bellini painted *Saint Francis in the Desert* using a mixture of tempera and oil, following the lead of Antonello da Messina. He soon became a master of the new medium and developed a sensuous coloristic manner destined to characterize Venetian painting of the 16th century (see page 650).

THE PRINCELY COURTS

The governments, churches, guilds, and merchants of the republics of Florence and Venice were not the only sponsors of the "rebirth" of art in Quattrocento Italy. The "princely courts" in Rome, Urbino, Mantua, and elsewhere were also instrumental in nurturing Renaissance art, whether the "prince" was a duke, marquis, count, condottiere, or pope. In the 15th century, princely courts proliferated throughout the Italian peninsula (MAP 14-1), notably in Rome and the papal states (FIGS. 21-40A, 21-41, and 21-42), Milan, Naples, Ferrara, Savoy, Urbino (FIGS. 21-43, 21-44, and 21-44A), and Mantua (FIGS. 21-45 to 21-50).

The efficient functioning of a princely court required a sophisticated administrative structure. Each prince employed an extensive household staff, ranging from counts, nobles, cooks, waiters, stewards, footmen, stable hands, and ladies-in-waiting to dog handlers, leopard keepers, pages, and runners. The duke of Milan had more than 40 chamberlains to attend to his personal needs alone. Each prince also needed an elaborate bureaucracy to oversee political, economic, and military operations and to ensure his continued control. These officials included secretaries, lawyers, captains, ambassadors, and condottieri. Burgeoning international diplomacy and trade made each prince the center of an active and privileged sphere. Their domains extended to the realm of culture, for they saw themselves as more than political, military, and economic leaders (see "Art in the Princely Courts of Renaissance Italy," page 613).

Rome and the Papal States

Although not a secular ruler, the pope in Rome was the head of a court with enormous wealth at his disposal. With the election of a French pope in 1305 (see "The Great Schism," page 415), however, papal commissions in Rome had ceased, and for more than a century, the once-glorious city became an artistic backwater. Even with the succession of Martin V (r. 1417–1431) and the return of papal power to Rome from Avignon, significant papal patronage did not resume immediately. Upon his election in 1471, however, Pope Sixtus IV (r. 1471–1484) initiated a major building campaign in Rome that included the restoration of churches, bridges, streets, and aqueducts; the construction in 1475 of a new papal library in the Vatican; and a new chapel bearing his name (the Sistine Chapel; FIG. 22-1).

PERUGINO Between 1481 and 1483, Sixtus IV summoned a group of artists to Rome to decorate the walls of his new chapel. Among the artists the pope employed were Botticelli, Ghirlandaio, and Pietro Vannucci, known as PERUGINO (ca. 1450–1523) after his birthplace—Perugia, in Umbria. The project followed immediately the completion of the new Vatican library, which the pope also ordered decorated with frescoes by MELOZZO DA FORLÌ (1438–1494; FIG. 21-40A) and others. Perugino's contribution to the Sistine Chapel fresco cycle was *Christ Delivering the Keys of the Kingdom to Saint Peter* (FIG. 21-41). The papacy had, from the beginning, based its claim to infallible and total authority over the Roman Catholic Church on this biblical event, and therefore the subject was one of obvious appeal to Sixtus IV.

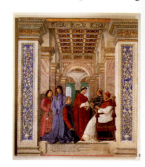

↗ **21-40A** MELOZZO DA FORLÌ, *Sixtus IV Confirming Platina*, ca. 1477–1481.

In Perugino's fresco, Christ hands the keys to Saint Peter, who stands amid an imaginary gathering of the 12 apostles and Renaissance contemporaries. These figures occupy the apron of a great stage space that extends into the distance to a point of convergence in the doorway of a central-plan temple. (Perugino used parallel and converging lines in the pavement to mark off the intervening space; compare FIG. 21-9.) The smaller figures in the middle distance enhance the sense of depth and also act out important New Testament stories—for example (at the left), the episode of Jesus, Peter, and the tribute money (compare FIG. 21-18).

At the corners of the great piazza, duplicate triumphal arches serve as the base angles of a distant compositional triangle whose apex is in the central building. Perugino modeled the arches closely on the Arch of Constantine (FIG. 7-73) in Rome. Although anachronisms in a painting depicting a scene from Jesus's life, the arches served to underscore the close ties between Saint Peter and Constantine, the first Christian emperor of Rome and builder of the great basilica (FIG. 8-9) over Saint Peter's tomb. In fact, the inscriptions on the arches compare Sixtus IV to Constantine. Christ and Peter flank the triangle's central axis, which runs through the temple's doorway, the vanishing point of Perugino's perspective scheme. Brunelleschi's new spatial science enabled the Umbrian artist to organize the action systematically. The composition interlocks both two-dimensional and three-dimensional space, and the placement of central actors emphasizes the axial center.

LUCA SIGNORELLI Another Umbrian painter whom Sixtus IV employed for the decoration of the Sistine Chapel was LUCA SIGNORELLI (ca. 1445–1523), in whose work the fiery passion of Savonarola's sermons found its pictorial equal. Signorelli further

ART AND SOCIETY

Art in the Princely Courts of Renaissance Italy

As the wealthiest individuals in their regions, Renaissance princes possessed the means to commission numerous artworks and buildings. In addition to being a source of visual pleasure, art functioned in several capacities in the princely courts—as evidence of princely sophistication and culture, as a form of prestige or commemoration, as a demonstration of wealth, and even as propaganda. For example, in the mural (FIG. 21-41) that Pope Sixtus IV commissioned Perugino to paint for the Sistine Chapel in the Vatican, the subject chosen glorified the papacy itself.

Princes and their advisers carefully researched the reputations and styles of the artists and architects they employed because the quality of the work reflected not solely on the artist but on the patron as well. Sometimes, princes bestowed on selected individuals the title of "court artist." Serving as a court artist had its benefits, among them a guaranteed salary (not always paid), living quarters in the palace, liberation from guild restrictions, and, on occasion, status as a member of the prince's inner circle, perhaps even a knighthood. For artists struggling to elevate their profession from the ranks of craftspeople, working for a prince presented an unparalleled opportunity. Until the 16th century, artists had limited status, and most people considered them in the same class as small shopkeepers and petty merchants. Indeed, at court dinners, artists usually sat with the other members of the salaried household: tailors, cobblers, barbers, and upholsterers. Thus the possibility of social advancement was a powerful and constant incentive in addition to the income received from princely commissions.

In return for the salaries and lofty titles they offered, princes demanded a great deal from court artists. Artists not only created the frescoes, portraits, and sculptures that have become their legacies but also designed tapestries, seat covers, costumes, masks, and decorations for various court festivities. Because princes constantly received ambassadors and dignitaries and needed to maintain a high profile to reinforce their authority, lavish social functions were the norm. Artists often created gifts for visiting nobles and potentates. Recipients judged these gifts on the quality of both the work and the materials. By using expensive materials—gold leaf, silver leaf, lapis lazuli (a rich azure-blue stone imported from Afghanistan), silk, and velvet brocade—and employing the best artists—princes could impress others with their wealth and good taste.

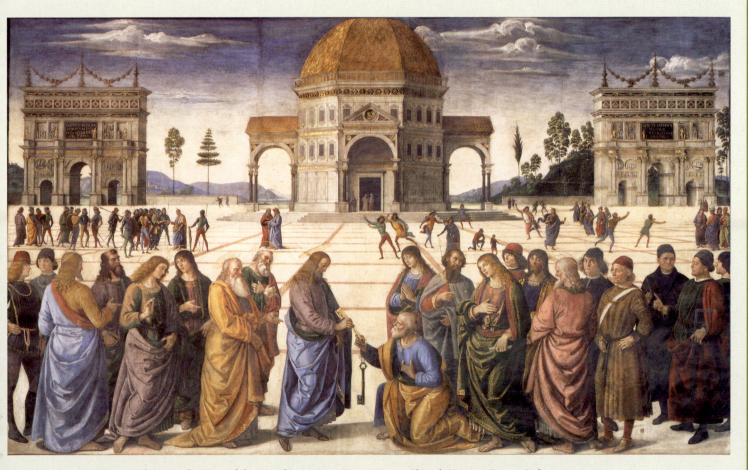

21-41 PERUGINO, *Christ Delivering the Keys of the Kingdom to Saint Peter*, Sistine Chapel, Vatican, Rome, Italy, 1481–1483. Fresco, 11' 5½" × 18' 8½".

Painted for the Vatican, this fresco depicts the event on which the papacy bases its authority. The converging lines of the pavement connect the action in the foreground with the background.

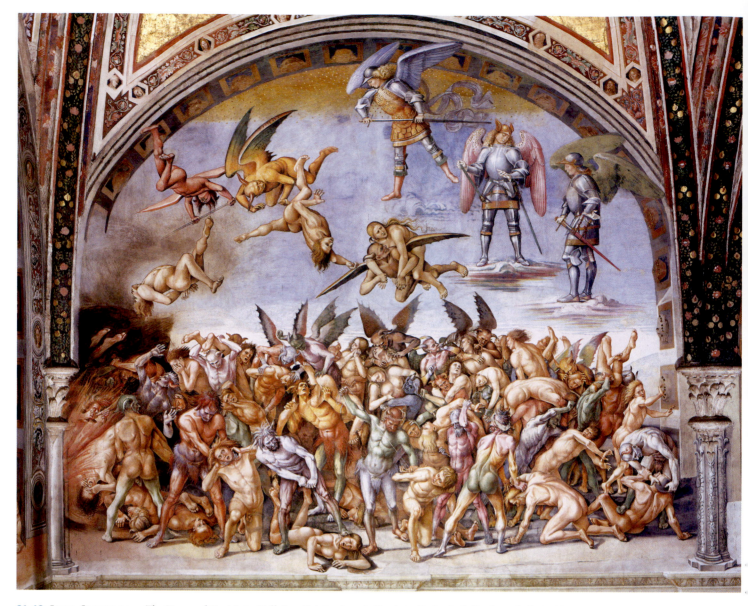

21-42 Luca Signorelli, *The Damned Cast into Hell,* San Brizio chapel, Orvieto Cathedral, Orvieto, Italy, 1499–1502. Fresco, 23' wide.

Few figure compositions of the 15th century match the psychic impact of Signorelli's fresco in Orvieto Cathedral showing writhing, foreshortened muscular bodies tortured by demons in Hell.

developed Pollaiuolo's interest in the depiction of muscular bodies in violent action in a wide variety of poses and foreshortenings. In the San Brizio chapel in the cathedral (FIG. 14-13) of the papal city of Orvieto (MAP 14-1), Signorelli painted for Pope Alexander VI (r. 1492–1503) scenes depicting the end of the world, including *The Damned Cast into Hell* (FIG. 21-42). Few Quattrocento figure compositions equal Signorelli's in psychic impact. Saint Michael and the hosts of Heaven hurl the damned into Hell, where, in a dense, writhing mass, they are vigorously tortured by demons, some winged. The horrible consequences of a sinful life had not been so graphically depicted since Gislebertus carved his vision of the Last Judgment (FIG. 12-15) in the west *tympanum* of Saint-Lazare at Autun around 1130. The figures—nude, lean, and muscular—assume every conceivable posture of anguish. Signorelli was a master both of foreshortening the human figure and depicting bodies in violent movement. Although each figure is clearly a study from a model, Signorelli incorporated the individual studies into a convincing and coherent narrative composition. Terror and rage pass like storms through the wrenched and twisted bodies. The fiends, their hair flaming and their bodies the color of putrefying flesh, lunge at their victims in ferocious frenzy.

Urbino

Under the patronage of the condottiere Duke Federico da Montefeltro (1422–1482), Urbino, southeast of Florence across the Apennines (MAP 14-1), became an important center of Renaissance art and culture. In fact, the humanist writer Paolo Cortese (1465–1540) described Federico as one of the two greatest artistic patrons of the 15th century (the other was Cosimo de' Medici). Federico was so renowned for his military expertise that he was in demand by popes and kings, and soldiers came from across Europe to study under his direction.

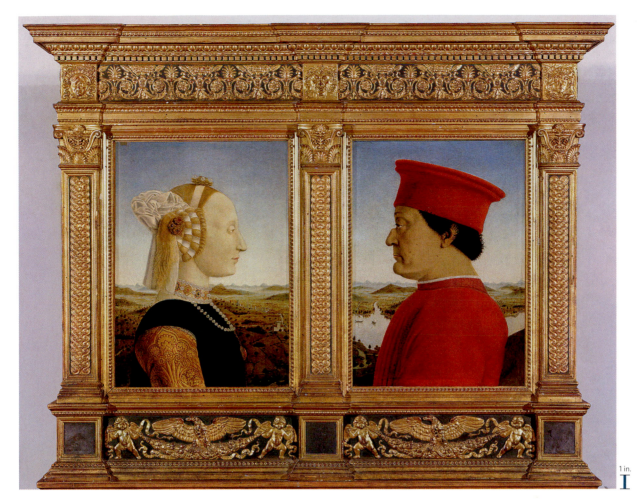

21-43 PIERO DELLA FRANCESCA, *Battista Sforza and Federico da Montefeltro,* ca. 1472–1474. Oil and tempera on wood in modern frame, each panel 1′ 6½″ × 1′ 1″. Galleria degli Uffizi, Florence.

Piero's portraits of Federico da Montefeltro and his recently deceased wife, Battista Sforza, combine the profile views on Roman coins with the landscape backgrounds of Flemish portraiture (FIG. 20-14).

PIERO DELLA FRANCESCA One of the artists who received several commissions from Federico was Piero della Francesca, who had already established a major reputation in his native Tuscany (FIGS. 21-25 and 21-25A). Among the works Piero produced for Federico is a double portrait (FIG. **21-43**) of the count and his second wife, Battista Sforza (1446–1472), whom he married in 1460 when she was 14 years old. The daughter of Alessandro Sforza (1409–1473), lord of Pesaro and brother of the duke of Milan (see page 620), Battista was a well-educated humanist who proved to be an excellent administrator of Federico's territories during his frequent military campaigns. She gave birth to eight daughters in 11 years and finally, on January 25, 1472, to the male heir for which the couple had prayed. When the countess died of pneumonia five months later at age 26, Federico went into mourning for virtually the rest of his life. He never remarried.

Federico commissioned Piero della Francesca to paint their double portrait shortly after Battista's death to pay tribute to her and to have a memento of their marriage. The present frame is a 19th-century addition. Originally, the two portraits formed a hinged diptych. The format—two bust-length portraits with a landscape background—followed Flemish models, such as the portraits by Hans Memling (FIGS. 20-14 and 20-14A), as did Piero's use of oil-based pigment (see "Tempera and Oil Painting," page 559). Piero would have been familiar with the latest artistic developments in northern Europe because Federico employed Flemish painters at his court. But Piero depicted the Urbino count and countess in profile, in part to emulate the profile portraits on Roman coins (FIGS. 7-10 and 7-79, *left*) that Renaissance humanists avidly collected, and in part to conceal the disfigured right side of Federico's face. (He lost his right eye and part of the bridge of his nose in a tournament in 1450.) That injury also explains why Federico is on the right in left profile (compare FIG. 21-44). Roman coins normally show the emperor in right profile, and Renaissance marriage portraits almost always place the husband at the viewer's left.

Piero probably based Battista's portrait on her death mask, and the pallor of her skin may be a reference to her death. Latin inscriptions on the reverse of the two portraits refer to Federico in the present tense and to Battista in the past tense, confirming the posthumous date of her portrait. The backs of the panels (not illustrated) also bear paintings. They represent Federico and Battista in triumphal chariots accompanied by personifications of their respective virtues, including Justice, Prudence, and Fortitude (Federico) and Faith, Charity, and Chastity (Battista). The placement of scenes of triumph on the reverse of profile portraits also emulates ancient Roman coinage.

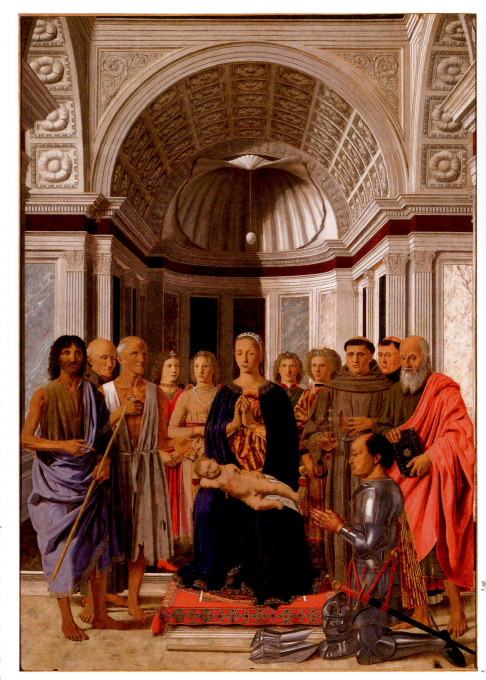

21-44 Piero della Francesca, *Enthroned Madonna and Saints Adored by Federico da Montefeltro* (*Brera Altarpiece*), ca. 1472–1474. Oil on wood, 8' 2" × 5' 7". Pinacoteca di Brera, Milan.

The illusionism of Piero's *Brera Altarpiece* is so convincing that the viewer is compelled to believe in Federico da Montefeltro's presence before the Virgin Mary, Christ Child, and saints.

BRERA ALTARPIECE Federico also appears in left profile in Piero's altarpiece (FIG. 21-44) now in the collection of the Brera Pinacoteca (picture gallery) in Milan. The condottiere, clad in armor, kneels piously at the feet of the enthroned Madonna. Directly behind him stands Saint John the Evangelist, his patron saint. Where the viewer would expect to see Federico's wife (on the lower left, kneeling and facing her husband), no figure is present. Battista had died shortly before Federico commissioned Piero to paint the *Brera Altarpiece.* Thus her absence clearly announced his loss. Piero further called attention to it by depicting Saint John the Baptist, Battista's patron saint, at the far left. The ostrich egg suspended from a shell over Mary's head was common over altars dedicated to the Virgin. The figures appear in the space below the intersection of illusionistically painted coffered barrel vaults, perhaps corresponding to part of the interior of the church of San Bernadino degli Zoccolanti near Urbino, the painting's intended location. If so, the viewer would be compelled to believe in Federico's presence in the church before the Virgin, Christ Child, and saints.

The *Brera Altarpiece* reveals Piero's deep interest in the properties of light and color. In his effort to make the clearest possible distinction among forms, he flooded his pictures with light, imparting a silver-blue tonality. To avoid heavy shadows, he illuminated the dark sides of his forms with reflected light. By moving the darkest tones of his modeling toward the centers of his volumes, he separated shapes from their backgrounds. Because of this technique, Piero's paintings lack some of Masaccio's relieflike qualities but gain in spatial clarity, as each shape forms an independent unit surrounded by an atmospheric envelope and moveable to any desired position, akin to a figure on a chessboard. The precise placement of figures in space also characterizes Piero's most difficult-to-interpret painting, *Flagellation* (FIG. 21-44A), which he may also have painted for Federico da Montefeltro.

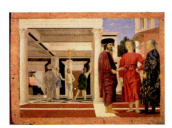

21-44A Piero della Francesca, *Flagellation*, ca. 1455–1465.

Mantua

Marquis Ludovico Gonzaga (1412–1478) ruled the court of Mantua in northeastern Italy (MAP 14-1) during the mid-15th century. A famed condottiere like Federico da Montefeltro, Gonzaga established his reputation as a fierce military leader while general of the Milanese armies. The visit of Pope Pius II (r. 1458–1464) to Mantua in 1459 stimulated the marquis's determination to transform his city into one that all Italy would envy.

SANT'ANDREA One of the major projects Gonzaga instituted was the redesign of the church of Sant'Andrea (FIGS. 21-45 to 21-47) to replace an 11th-century church. Gonzaga turned to the renowned architect Leon Battista Alberti (FIGS. 21-36A and 21-37) for this important commission. The facade (FIG. 21-45) that Alberti designed incorporated two major ancient Roman architectural motifs—the

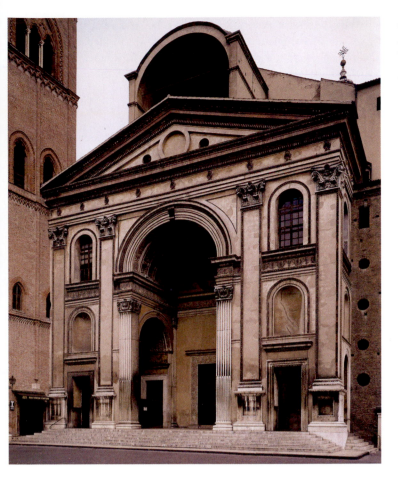

Alberti's design for Sant'Andrea reflects his study of ancient Roman architecture. Employing a colossal order, the architect combined a triumphal arch and a Roman temple front with pediment.

temple front and the triumphal arch. The combination was already a familiar feature of Roman buildings still standing in Italy. For example, many triumphal arches, including a late-first-century BCE arch at Rimini on Italy's northeast coast, feature a pediment over the arcuated passageway and engaged columns, but there is no close parallel in antiquity for Alberti's eclectic and ingenious design. The Renaissance architect's concern for proportion (see "Alberti's *On the Art of Building,*" page 608) led him to equalize the vertical and horizontal dimensions of the facade, which left it considerably shorter than the church behind it. Because of the primary importance of visual appeal, many Renaissance architects made this concession not only to the demands of a purely visual proportionality in the facade but also to the facade's relation to the small square in front of it, even at the expense of continuity with the body of the building. Yet structural correspondences to the building do exist in Sant'Andrea's facade. The pilasters are the same height as those on the nave's interior walls; and the large barrel vault over the central portal, with smaller barrel vaults branching off at right angles, introduces on a smaller scale the arrangement of the church's nave and chapels (FIGS. 21-46 and 21-47). The facade pilasters, as part of the wall, run uninterrupted

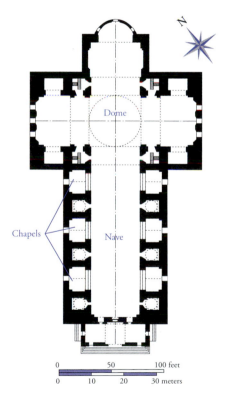

21-46 LEON BATTISTA ALBERTI, plan of Sant'Andrea, Mantua, Italy, designed 1470, begun 1472.

In *On the Art of Building,* Alberti criticized the traditional basilican plan as impractical. He designed Sant'Andrea as a single huge hall with independent chapels branching off at right angles.

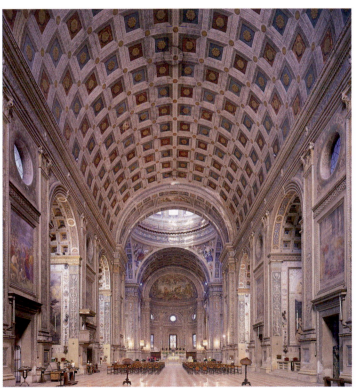

21-47 LEON BATTISTA ALBERTI, interior of Sant'Andrea (looking east), Mantua, Italy, designed 1470, begun 1472.

For the nave of Sant'Andrea, Alberti abandoned the traditional columnar arcade. The tremendous vaults suggest that Constantine's Basilica Nova (FIG. 7-76) in Rome may have served as a prototype.

through three stories in an early application of the *colossal* or *giant order* (pilasters that extend through more than one level) that became a favorite motif of Michelangelo (FIG. 22-25).

The tremendous vaults in the interior of Sant'Andrea suggest that Alberti's model may have been Constantine's Basilica Nova (FIG. 7-76) in Rome—erroneously thought in the Middle Ages and Renaissance to be a Roman temple. Consistent with his belief that arches should not be used with freestanding columns (see page 608), Alberti abandoned the medieval columnar arcade that Brunelleschi still used in San Lorenzo (FIG. 21-31) and Santo Spirito (FIG. 21-31A). Thick walls alternating with vaulted chapels, interrupted by a massive dome over the crossing, support the huge coffered barrel vault. Because FILIPPO JUVARA (1678–1736) added the present dome in the 18th century, the effect may be somewhat different from what Alberti planned. Regardless, the vault calls to mind the vast interior spaces and dense enclosing masses of Roman architecture. In *On the Art of Building*, Alberti criticized the traditional basilican plan (with continuous aisles flanking the central nave) as impractical because the colonnades conceal the ceremonies from the faithful in the aisles. For this reason, he designed a single huge hall (FIG. 21-47) with independent chapels branching off at right angles (FIG. 21-46). This break with a Christian building tradition that had endured for a thousand years was extremely influential in later Renaissance and Baroque church planning.

ANDREA MANTEGNA Like other princes, Ludovico Gonzaga believed that it was important to surround himself with humanist scholars and talented artists, and he made Mantua one of Europe's leading cultural centers. The marquis also knew that an impressive palace was an important visual expression of his authority. One of the most spectacular rooms in the Palazzo Ducale (Ducal Palace) is Ludovico's bedchamber and audience hall, the so-called Camera degli Sposi (Room of the Newlyweds), originally the Camera Picta (Painted Chamber; FIG. 21-48). ANDREA MANTEGNA (ca. 1431–1506) of Padua took almost nine years to complete the extensive fresco program in which he sought to glorify Ludovico Gonzaga and his family. The particulars of each scene are still a matter

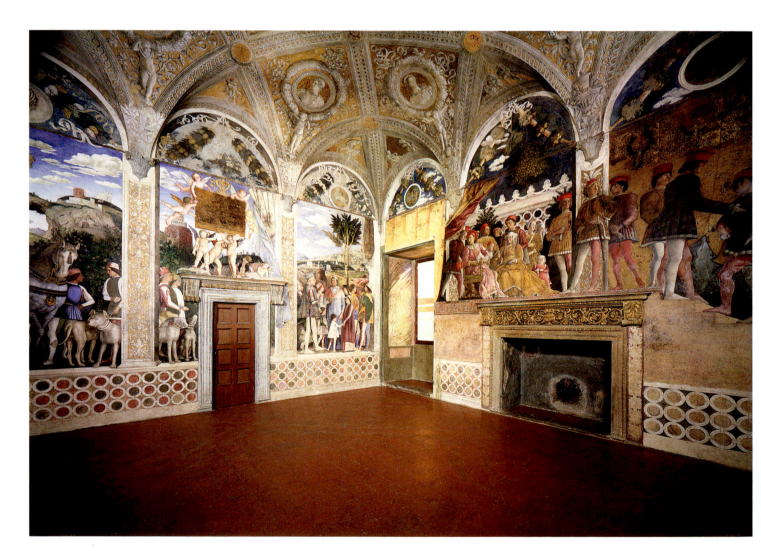

21-48 ANDREA MANTEGNA, interior of the Camera Picta (Painted Chamber), Palazzo Ducale, Mantua, Italy, 1465–1474. Fresco.

Working for Ludovico Gonzaga, who established Mantua as a great art city, Mantegna produced for the duke's palace the first completely consistent illusionistic decoration of an entire room.

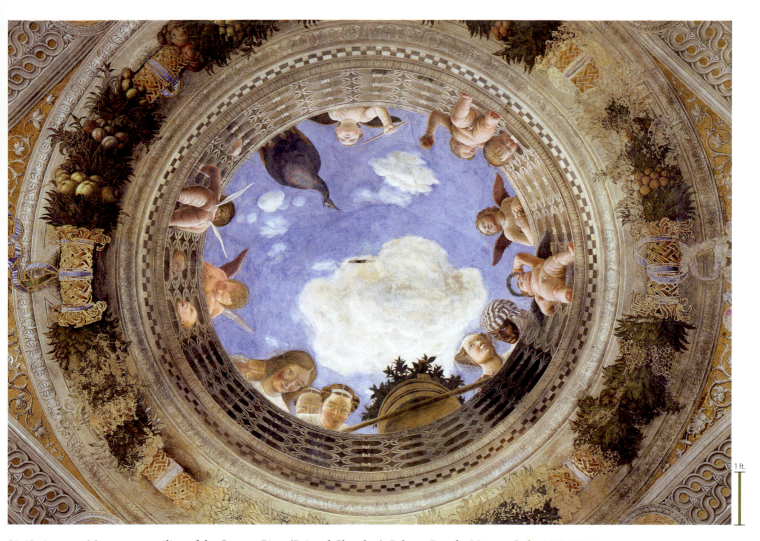

21-49 ANDREA MANTEGNA, ceiling of the Camera Picta (Painted Chamber), Palazzo Ducale, Mantua, Italy, 1465–1474. Fresco, 8′ 9″ in diameter.

Inside the Camera Picta, the viewer becomes the viewed as figures gaze into the room from a painted oculus opening onto a blue sky. This is the first perspective view of a ceiling from below.

of scholarly debate, but any viewer standing in the Camera Picta surrounded by the spectacle and majesty of courtly life cannot help but be thoroughly impressed by both the commanding presence and elevated status of the patron and the dazzling artistic skills of Mantegna.

In the Camera Picta, Mantegna performed a triumphant feat by producing the first completely consistent illusionistic decoration of an entire room. By integrating real and painted architectural elements, Mantegna illusionistically dissolved the room's walls in a manner foretelling 17th-century Baroque decoration (see page 720). The Camera Picta recalls the efforts more than 15 centuries earlier by Italian painters on the Bay of Naples to merge mural painting and architecture in frescoes of the so-called Second Style of Roman painting (FIGS. 7-18 and 7-19). Mantegna's *trompe l'oeil* (French, "deceives the eye") design, however, went far beyond anything preserved from ancient Italy. The Renaissance painter's daring experimentalism led him to complete the room's decoration with the first perspective of a ceiling (FIG. **21-49**) seen from below (called, in Italian, *di sotto in sù,* "from below upward"). Baroque ceiling decorators (FIGS. 24-22 to 24-24) later broadly developed this technique. Inside the Camera Picta, the viewer becomes the viewed as figures

look down into the room from the painted *oculus* ("eye"). Seen against the convincing illusion of a cloud-filled blue sky, several putti, strongly foreshortened, set the amorous mood of the Room of the Newlyweds, as the painted spectators (who are not identified and include an exotic black man wearing a turban) smile down on the scene. The prominent peacock, perched precariously as if ready to swoop down into the room, is an attribute of Juno, Jupiter's bride, who oversees lawful marriages. This brilliant feat of illusionism is the climax of decades of experimentation with perspective representation by numerous Quattrocento artists as well as by Mantegna himself—for example, in his frescoes (FIG. **21-49A**) in the Church of the Eremitani (Church of the Hermits) in Padua.

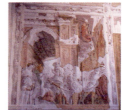

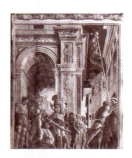

🔗 **21-49A** MANTEGNA, *Saint James Led to Martyrdom,* 1454-1457.

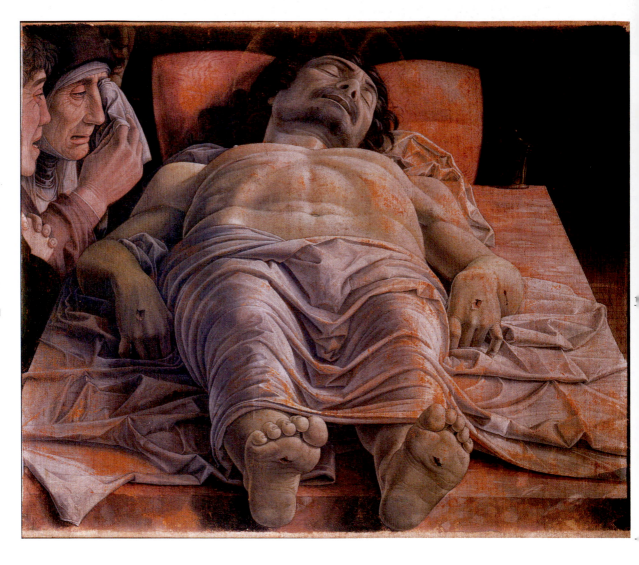

21-50 ANDREA MANTEGNA, *Foreshortened Christ (Lamentation over the Dead Christ)*, ca. 1500. Tempera on canvas, 2' 2¾" × 2' 7⅞". Pinacoteca di Brera, Milan.

In this work of overwhelming emotional power, Mantegna presented both a harrowing study of a strongly foreshortened cadaver and an intensely poignant depiction of a biblical tragedy.

FORESHORTENED CHRIST One of Mantegna's later paintings (FIG. 21-50) is another example of the artist's mastery of perspective. In fact, Mantegna seems to have set up for himself difficult problems in perspective simply for the joy he took in solving them. The painting often called *Lamentation over the Dead Christ* but recorded under the name *Foreshortened Christ* at the time of Mantegna's death is a work of overwhelming power. At first glance, as its 16th-century title implies, this painting seems to be a strikingly realistic study in foreshortening. Careful examination, however, reveals that Mantegna reduced the size of Christ's feet, which, as he surely knew, would cover much of the body if properly represented according to the rules of perspective, in which the closest objects, people, or body parts are the largest. Thus, tempering naturalism with artistic license, Mantegna presented both a harrowing study of a strongly foreshortened cadaver and an intensely poignant depiction of a biblical tragedy. Remarkably, in the supremely gifted

hands of Mantegna, all of Quattrocento science here served the purpose of devotion.

Milan

The leading city of northwestern Italy at this time was Milan (MAP 14-1), ruled by the powerful Sforza family, which also sought to lure the best artists to its court. In 1481, Ludovico Sforza (1451–1508) accepted a proposal from Leonardo da Vinci that the famed artist leave Florence for Milan to work for the Milanese court as military engineer, architect, sculptor, and painter. Several of Leonardo's early masterworks, including his world-famous *Last Supper* (FIG. 22-4), date to the closing years of the 15th century when he was in Milan. A discussion of those works opens the examination of the High Renaissance in Italy in Chapter 22.

THE RENAISSANCE IN QUATTROCENTO ITALY

Florence

- The fortunate coming together of artistic genius, the spread of humanism, and economic prosperity nourished the flowering of the new artistic culture that historians call the Renaissance—the rebirth of classical values in art and life. The greatest center of Renaissance art in the 15th century was Florence, home of the powerful Medici, who were among the most ambitious art patrons in history.

- Some of the earliest examples of the new Renaissance style in sculpture are the statues that Nanni di Banco and Donatello made for Or San Michele. Donatello's later *David,* which emulates classical contrapposto, was the first nude male statue since antiquity. Donatello was also a pioneer in relief sculpture, the first to incorporate the principles of linear and atmospheric perspective, devices also employed brilliantly by Lorenzo Ghiberti in his *Gates of Paradise.*

- The Renaissance interest in classical culture naturally also led to the revival of Greco-Roman mythological themes in art—for example, Antonio del Pollaiuolo's *Hercules and Antaeus*—and to the revival of equestrian portraits, such as Donatello's *Gattamelata* and Andrea del Verrocchio's *Bartolommeo Colleoni.*

- Although some painters continued to work in the late medieval International Gothic style, others broke fresh ground by exploring new modes of representation. Masaccio's figures recall Giotto's, but have a greater psychological and physical credibility, and the light shining on Masaccio's figures comes from a source outside the picture. His *Holy Trinity* owes its convincing illusionism to Filippo Brunelleschi's new science of linear perspective.

- The secular side of Quattrocento Italian painting is on display in historical works, such as Paolo Uccello's *Battle of San Romano,* and in portraiture—for example, Domenico Ghirlandaio's *Giovanna Tornabuoni.* The humanist love of classical themes comes to the fore in the works of Sandro Botticelli, whose lyrical *Primavera* and *Birth of Venus* were inspired by poetry and Neo-Platonic philosophy.

- Italian architects also revived the classical style. Brunelleschi's San Lorenzo conforms to a strict modular scheme and showcases the Roman-inspired rationality of 15th-century Florentine architecture. The treatise of the ancient Roman architect Vitruvius was the model for Leon Battista Alberti's *On the Art of Building.*

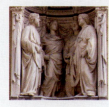

Nanni di Banco, *Four Crowned Saints,* ca. 1410–1414

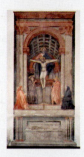

Masaccio, *Holy Trinity,* ca. 1424–1427

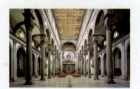

Brunelleschi, San Lorenzo, ca. 1421–1469

Venice and the Princely Courts

- Quattrocento architecture in Venice was still essentially Late Gothic, but at the end of the century, Giovanni Bellini founded the Venetian High Renaissance school of painting, which rivaled the schools of Florence and Rome.

- Among the important papal commissions of the Quattrocento was the decoration of the walls of the Sistine Chapel with frescoes, including Perugino's *Christ Delivering the Keys of the Kingdom to Saint Peter,* a prime example of the application of Renaissance linear perspective.

- Under the patronage of Federico da Montefeltro, Urbino became a major center of Renaissance art and culture. The leading painter in Federico's employ was Piero della Francesca, a master of color and light and the author of the first theoretical treatise on perspective.

- Mantua became an important art center under Marquis Ludovico Gonzaga, who commissioned Alberti to rebuild the church of Sant'Andrea. Alberti applied the principles that he had developed in his architectural treatise to the project and freely adapted forms from Roman religious and civic architecture. Gonzaga also hired Andrea Mantegna, who painted the Camera Picta of the ducal palace, producing the first completely consistent illusionistic decoration of an entire room.

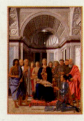

Piero della Francesca, *Brera Altarpiece,* ca. 1472–1474

Alberti, Sant'Andrea, Mantua, 1470

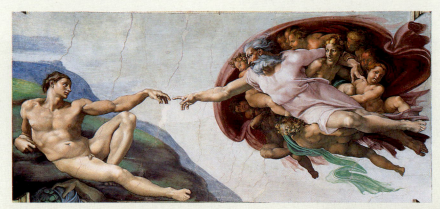

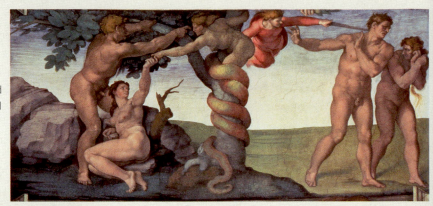

▶ **22-1a** Michelangelo, the Renaissance genius who was primarily a sculptor, reluctantly spent almost four years painting the ceiling of the Sistine Chapel under commission from Pope Julius II.

▼ **22-1b** The fresco cycle illustrates the creation and fall of humankind as related in Genesis. Michelangelo always painted with a sculptor's eye. His heroic figures resemble painted statues.

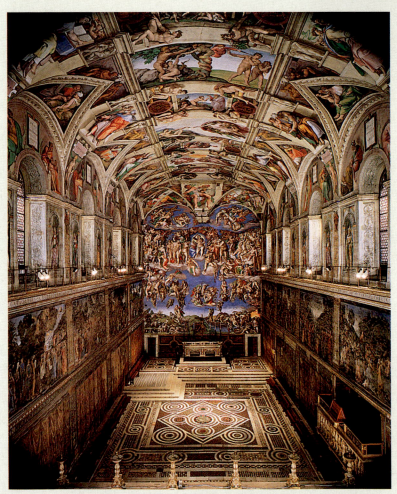

| 22-1 | Interior of the Sistine Chapel (looking west), Vatican City, Rome, Italy, built 1473; ceiling and altar wall frescoes by MICHELANGELO BUONARROTI, 1508–1512 and 1536–1541, respectively. |

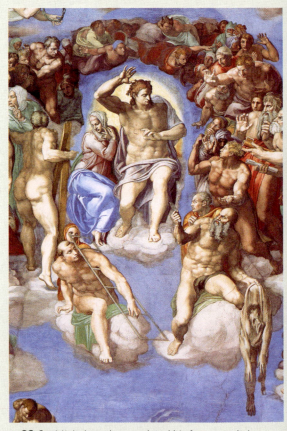

▲ **22-1c** Michelangelo completed his fresco cycle in the Sistine Chapel for another pope—Paul III—with this terrifying vision of the fate awaiting sinners. The *Last Judgment* includes his self-portrait.

Renaissance and Mannerism in Cinquecento Italy

MICHELANGELO IN THE SERVICE OF JULIUS II

The first artist in history whose exceptional talent and brooding personality matched today's image of the temperamental artistic genius was MICHELANGELO BUONARROTI (1475–1564). The Florentine artist's self-imposed isolation, creative furies, proud independence, and daring innovations led Italians of his era to speak of the charismatic personality of the man and the expressive character of his works in one word—*terribilità,* the sublime shadowed by the fearful. Yet, unlike most modern artists, who create works in their studios and offer them for sale later, Michelangelo and his contemporaries produced most of their paintings and sculptures under contract for wealthy patrons who dictated the content—and sometimes the form—of their artworks.

In Italy in the 1500s—the *Cinquecento*—the greatest art patron was the Catholic Church headed by the pope in Rome. Michelangelo's most famous work today—the ceiling of the Sistine Chapel (FIG. **22-1**) in the Vatican—was, in fact, a commission he did not want. His patron was Julius II (r. 1503–1513), an immensely ambitious man who sought to extend his spiritual authority into the temporal realm, as other medieval and Renaissance popes had done. Julius selected his name to associate himself with Julius Caesar and found inspiration in ancient Rome. His enthusiasm for engaging in battle earned Julius the designation "warrior-pope," but his ten-year papacy was most notable for his patronage of the arts. Julius fully appreciated the propagandistic value of visual imagery and, upon his election, immediately commissioned artworks that would present an authoritative image of his rule and reinforce the primacy of the Catholic Church.

When Julius asked Michelangelo to take on the challenge of providing frescoes for the ceiling of the Sistine Chapel, the artist insisted that painting was not his profession—a protest that rings hollow after the fact, but Michelangelo's major works until then had been in sculpture. The artist had no choice, however, but to accept the pope's assignment.

In the Sistine Chapel frescoes, as in his sculptures, Michelangelo relentlessly concentrated his expressive purpose on the human figure. To him, the body was beautiful not only in its natural form but also in its spiritual and philosophical significance. The body was the manifestation of the character of the soul. In the *Creation of Adam, Fall of Man,* and *Last Judgment* frescoes, Michelangelo represented the body in its most elemental aspect—in the nude or simply draped, with almost no background and no ornamental embellishment. He always painted with a sculptor's eye for how light and shadow reveal volume and surface. It is no coincidence that many of the figures in the Sistine Chapel seem to be painted statues.

HIGH AND LATE RENAISSANCE

The art and architecture of 16th-century Italy built on the foundation of the Early Renaissance of the 15th century, but no single artistic style characterized Italian 16th-century art, and regional differences abounded, especially between central Italy (Florence and Rome) and Venice. The period opened with the brief era that art historians call the High Renaissance—the quarter century between 1495 and the deaths of Leonardo da Vinci in 1519 and Raphael in 1520. The Renaissance style and the interest in classical culture, perspective, proportion, and human anatomy dominated the remainder of the 16th century (the Late Renaissance), but a new style, called *Mannerism,* challenged Renaissance naturalism almost as soon as Raphael had been laid to rest (inside the ancient Roman Pantheon, FIG. 7-51). The one constant in Cinquecento Italy is the astounding quality, both technical and aesthetic, of the art and architecture produced.

Indeed, the modern notion of the "fine arts" and the exaltation of the artist-genius originated in Renaissance Italy. Humanist scholars and art patrons alike eagerly adopted the ancient Greek philosopher Plato's view of the nature of poetry and of artistic creation in general: "All good poets . . . compose their beautiful poems not by art, but because they are inspired and possessed. . . . For not by art does the poet sing, but by power divine."[1] In Cinquecento Italy, the pictorial arts achieved the high status formerly held only by poetry, and painters and sculptors became international celebrities for the first time. None achieved greater fame than Leonardo da Vinci, Raphael, and Michelangelo, the three greatest masters of the High Renaissance, although even they could not create totally freely but had to satisfy the wishes of their patrons (see "Michelangelo in the Service of Julius II," page 623).

Leonardo da Vinci

Born in the small town of Vinci, near Florence, LEONARDO DA VINCI (1452–1519) trained in the studio of Andrea del Verrocchio (FIGS. 21-12 and 21-16). The quintessential "Renaissance man," Leonardo possessed unequaled talent and an unbridled imagination. Art was but one of his innumerable interests, the scope and depth of which were without precedent. His unquenchable curiosity is evident in the voluminous notes he interspersed with sketches in his notebooks dealing with botany, geology, geography, cartography, zoology, military engineering, animal lore, anatomy, and aspects of physical science, including hydraulics and mechanics. Leonardo stated repeatedly that his scientific investigations made him a better painter. That is undoubtedly the case. For example, Leonardo's in-depth exploration of optics provided him with a thorough understanding of perspective, light, and color. Leonardo was a true artist-scientist. Indeed, his scientific drawings (FIG. 22-6) are themselves artworks.

Leonardo's great ambition in his painting, as well as in his scientific endeavors, was to discover the laws underlying the processes and flux of nature. With this end in mind, he also studied the human body and contributed immeasurably to the fields of physiology and psychology. Leonardo believed that reality in an absolute sense is inaccessible and that humans can know it only through its changing images. He considered the eyes the most vital organs and sight the most essential function. Better to be deaf than blind, he argued, because through the eyes, individuals can grasp reality most directly and profoundly.

LEONARDO IN MILAN In 1482, Leonardo left Florence for Milan after offering his services to Ludovico Sforza (1451–1508). The political situation in Florence was uncertain, and Leonardo must have felt that his particular skills would be in greater demand in one of Italy's princely courts (see "Art in the Princely Courts of Renaissance Italy," page 613). He clearly believed that the Sforza court in Milan could provide him with increased financial security. The letter that Leonardo wrote to Ludovico seeking employment in Milan is preserved and is, at first sight, surprising. The Florentine artist devoted most of the letter to advertising his qualifications as a military engineer, mentioning only at the end his abilities as a painter and sculptor. The letter illustrates the breadth of Leonardo's competence and also underscores the decisive role that individual patrons played in the history of Renaissance art.

> And in short, according to the variety of cases, I can contrive various and endless means of offense and defense. . . . In time of peace I believe I can give perfect satisfaction and to the equal of any other in architecture and the composition of buildings, public and private; and in guiding water from one place to another. . . . I can carry out sculpture in marble, bronze, or clay, and also I can do in painting whatever may be done, as well as any other, be he whom he may.[2]

That Leonardo selected expertise in military engineering as his primary attraction for the Sforzas is an index of the period's instability. In any event, Ludovico accepted Leonardo's offer, although he did not give the Florentine artist a salaried position until several years later. Leonardo remained in Milan for the next 17 years, during which he created the masterpieces that are the basis for his lofty reputation then and now.

MADONNA OF THE ROCKS Shortly after settling in Milan, Leonardo painted *Madonna of the Rocks* (FIG. 22-2) as the central panel of an altarpiece for the chapel of the Confraternity of the Immaculate Conception in San Francesco Grande. Leonardo presented the Madonna, Christ Child, infant John the Baptist, and angel in a pyramidal grouping. The four figures pray, point, and bless, and these

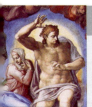

RENAISSANCE AND MANNERISM IN CINQUECENTO ITALY

1495–1520
- Leonardo da Vinci paints *Last Supper* in Milan and *Mona Lisa* in Florence
- High Renaissance art emerges in Rome under Pope Julius II
- Raphael paints *School of Athens* for the papal apartments
- Michelangelo carves *David* for the Palazzo della Signoria in Florence and paints the ceiling of the Sistine Chapel in Rome

1520–1550
- Paul III launches the Counter-Reformation
- Michelangelo paints *Last Judgment* in the Sistine Chapel
- In Venice, Titian uses rich colors and establishes oil on canvas as the preferred medium of Western painting
- Mannerism emerges as an alternative to High Renaissance style in the work of Pontormo, Parmigianino, Bronzino, and Giulio Romano

1550–1575
- The Council of Trent defends religious art
- Andrea Palladio becomes chief architect of the Venetian Republic
- Giorgio Vasari publishes his *Lives* of the leading Italian painters, sculptors, and architects, from Cimabue to Titian

1575–1600
- Tintoretto is the leading Venetian Mannerist painter
- Veronese creates a huge illusionistic ceiling painting for the Doge's Palace
- Giovanni da Bologna uses spiral compositions for Mannerist statuary groups
- The Jesuits construct Il Gesù in Rome

Leonardo and Michelangelo on Painting versus Sculpture

Both Leonardo da Vinci and Michelangelo produced work in a variety of artistic media, earning enviable reputations not just as painters and sculptors but also as architects. The two disagreed, however, on the relative merits of the different media. In particular, Leonardo, with his intellectual and analytical mind, preferred painting (FIGS. 22-2, 22-4, and 22-5) to sculpture, which he regarded as lowly manual labor. In contrast, Michelangelo, who worked in a more intuitive manner, saw himself primarily as a sculptor. Two excerpts from their writings reveal their positions on the relationship between the two media.

Leonardo da Vinci wrote the following in his so-called *Treatise on Painting*:

> Painting is a matter of greater mental analysis, of greater skill, and more marvelous than sculpture, since necessity compels the mind of the painter to transform itself into the very mind of nature, to become an interpreter between nature and art. Painting justifies by reference to nature the reasons of the pictures which follow its laws: in what ways the images of objects before the eye come together in the pupil of the eye; which, among objects equal in size, looks larger to the eye; which, among equal colors will look more or less dark or more or less bright; which, among things at the same depth, looks more or less low; which, among those objects placed at equal height, will look more or less high, and why, among objects placed at various distances, one will appear less clear than the other.
>
> This art comprises and includes within itself all visible things such as colors and their diminution, which the poverty of sculpture cannot include. Painting represents transparent objects but the sculptor will show you the shapes of natural objects without artifice. The painter will show you things at different distances with variation of color due to the air lying between the objects and the eye; he shows you mists through which visual images penetrate with difficulty; he shows you rain which discloses within it clouds with mountains and valleys; he shows the dust which discloses within it and beyond it the combatants who stirred it up; he shows streams of greater or lesser density; he shows fish playing between the surface of the water and its bottom; he shows the polished pebbles of various colors lying on the washed sand at the bottom of rivers, surrounded by green plants; he shows the stars at various heights above us, and thus he achieves innumerable effects which sculpture cannot attain.*

As if in response, although decades later, Michelangelo wrote these excerpts in a letter to Benedetto Varchi (1502–1565), a Florentine poet best known for his 16-volume history of Florence:

> I believe that painting is considered excellent in proportion as it approaches the effect of relief, while relief is considered bad in proportion as it approaches the effect of painting.
>
> I used to consider that sculpture was the lantern of painting and that between the two things there was the same difference as that between the sun and the moon. But . . . I now consider that painting and sculpture are one and the same thing.
>
> Suffice that, since one and the other (that is to say, both painting and sculpture) proceed from the same faculty, it would be an easy matter to establish harmony between them and to let such disputes alone, for they occupy more time than the execution of the figures themselves. As to that man [Leonardo] who wrote saying that painting was more noble than sculpture, if he had known as much about the other subjects on which he has written, why, my serving-maid would have written better!†

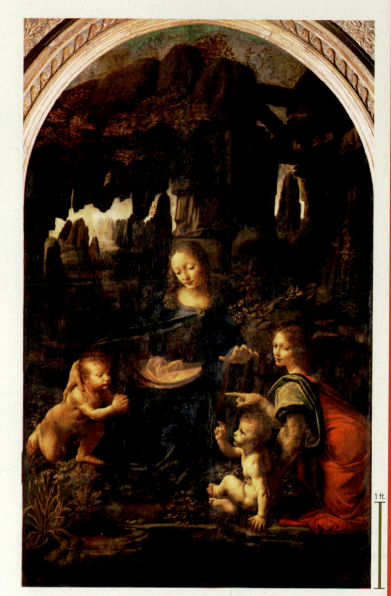

1 ft.

22-2 LEONARDO DA VINCI, *Madonna of the Rocks,* from San Francesco Grande, Milan, Italy, 1483–1490. Oil on wood (transferred to canvas), 6' 6½" × 4'. Musée du Louvre, Paris.

In this groundbreaking work, Leonardo demonstrated the oil painter's ability to represent all the figures sharing the same light-infused environment, something impossible to achieve in sculpture.

---

*Leonardo da Vinci, *Treatise on Painting,* 51. Robert Klein and Henri Zerner, *Italian Art 1500–1600: Sources and Documents* (Evanston, Ill.: Northwestern University Press, 1966), 7–8.
†Michelangelo to Benedetto Varchi, Rome, 1549. Klein and Zerner, 13–14.

22-3 LEONARDO DA VINCI, cartoon for *Madonna and Child with Saint Anne and the Infant Saint John*, ca. 1505–1507. Charcoal heightened with white on brown paper, 4' 6" × 3' 3". National Gallery, London.

In this cartoon for a painting of the Madonna and Child and two saints, Leonardo drew a scene of tranquil grandeur filled with monumental figures reminiscent of classical statues of goddesses.

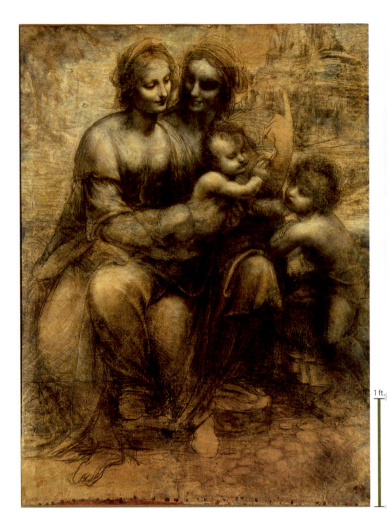

acts and gestures, although their meanings are uncertain, visually unite the individuals portrayed. The angel points to the infant John and, through his outward glance, involves the viewer in the tableau. John prays to the Christ Child, who blesses him in return. The Virgin herself completes the series of interlocking gestures, her left hand reaching toward the Christ Child and her right hand resting protectively on John's shoulder. The melting mood of tenderness, which the caressing light enhances, suffuses the entire composition. Indeed, Leonardo's most notable achievement in *Madonna of the Rocks* was to paint the figures as sharing the same environment. Leonardo built on Masaccio's understanding and usage of *chiaroscuro*, the subtle play of light and dark. The biblical figures emerge through nuances of light and shade from the half-light of the mysterious cavernous landscape. Light simultaneously veils and reveals the forms, immersing them in a layer of atmosphere. Leonardo's groundbreaking achievement—the unified representation of objects in an atmospheric setting—was a manifestation of his scientific curiosity about the invisible substance surrounding things. It was also in large part due to his mastery of the relatively new medium of oil painting, which had previously been used mostly by northern European painters (see "Tempera and Oil Painting," page 559). Oil-based pigments enabled Leonardo to realize the full potential of the painter's craft, which he considered superior to sculpture (see "Leonardo and Michelangelo on Painting versus Sculpture," page 625). By creating an emotionally compelling, visually unified, and spatially convincing image, Leonardo achieved what he believed to be the two chief goals of a good painter: "to paint man and the intention of his soul. The former is easy, the latter hard, for it must be expressed by gestures and the movement of the limbs."[3]

MADONNA AND CHILD CARTOON Leonardo's style fully emerges in *Madonna and Child with Saint Anne and the Infant Saint John* (FIG. 22-3), a preliminary drawing (*cartoon*) for a painting (see

22-4 LEONARDO DA VINCI, *Last Supper*, ca. 1495–1498. Oil and tempera on plaster, 13' 9" × 29' 10". Refectory, Santa Maria delle Grazie, Milan.

Jesus has just announced that one of his disciples will betray him, and each one reacts. He is both the psychological focus of Leonardo's fresco and the focal point of all the converging perspective lines.

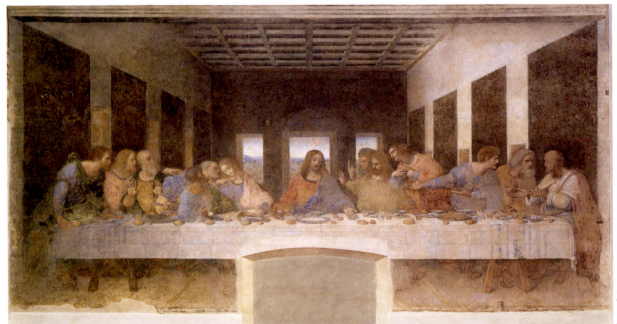

"Renaissance Drawings," page 628) he made in 1505 or shortly thereafter. Here, the glowing light falls gently on the majestic forms in a scene of tranquil grandeur and balance. Leonardo ordered every part of his cartoon with an intellectual pictorial logic that results in an appealing visual unity. The figures are robust and monumental, the stately grace of their movements reminiscent of the Greek statues of goddesses (FIG. 5-49) in the pediments of the Parthenon. However, Leonardo's infusion of the principles of classical art into his designs cannot be attributed to specific knowledge of Greek monuments. He and his contemporaries never visited Greece. Their acquaintance with classical art extended only to Etruscan and Roman monuments, Roman copies of Greek statues in Italy, and ancient texts describing Greek and Roman works of art and architecture.

LAST SUPPER For Ludovico Sforza, Leonardo painted *Last Supper* (FIG. **22-4**) in the refectory of the church of Santa Maria delle Grazie in Milan. Both formally and emotionally, *Last Supper* is Leonardo's most impressive work. It is also his largest. On the wall opposite a *Crucifixion* with portraits of Ludovico and his family, Leonardo painted Jesus and his 12 disciples sitting at a long table placed parallel to the picture plane in a simple, spacious room. The austere setting amplifies the painting's highly dramatic action. Jesus, with outstretched hands, has just said, "One of you is about to betray me" (Matt. 26:21). A wave of intense excitement passes through the group as each disciple asks himself and, in some cases, his neighbor, "Is it I?" (Matt. 26:22). Leonardo visualized a sophisticated coupling of the dramatic "One of you is about to betray me" with the initiation of the ancient liturgical ceremony of the Eucharist, when Jesus, blessing bread and wine, said, "This is my body, which is given for you. Do this for a commemoration of me. . . . This is the chalice, the new testament in my blood, which shall be shed for you" (Luke 22:19–20).

In the center, Jesus appears isolated from the disciples and in perfect repose, the calm eye of the swirling emotion around him. The central window at the back, whose curved pediment arches above his head, frames his figure. The pediment is the only curve in the architectural framework, and it serves here, along with the diffused light, as a halo. Jesus's head is the focal point of all converging perspective lines in the composition. Thus the still, psychological focus and cause of the action is also the perspective focus, as well as the center of the two-dimensional surface. In Leonardo's *Last Supper,* the two-dimensional, the three-dimensional, and the psychodimensional focuses are the same.

Leonardo presented the agitated disciples in four groups of three, united among and within themselves by the figures' gestures and postures. The artist sacrificed traditional iconography to pictorial and dramatic consistency by placing Judas on the same side of the table as Jesus and the other disciples (compare FIG. 21-22). Judas's face is in shadow (the light source in the painting corresponds to the windows in the Milanese refectory). He clutches a money bag in his right hand as he reaches his left forward to fulfill Jesus's declaration: "But yet behold, the hand of him that betrayeth me is with me on the table" (Luke 22:21). The two disciples at the table ends are quieter than the others, as if to bracket the energy of the composition, which is more intense closer to Jesus, whose serenity both halts and intensifies it. The disciples register a broad range of emotional responses, including fear, doubt, protestation, rage, and love. Leonardo's numerous preparatory studies—using live models—suggest that he thought of each figure as carrying a particular charge and type of emotion. Like a stage director, he read the Gospel story carefully, and scrupulously cast his actors as the Bible described their roles. In this work, as in his other religious paintings, Leonardo revealed his extraordinary ability to apply his voluminous knowledge about the observable world to the pictorial representation of a religious scene, resulting in a psychologically complex and compelling painting.

Leonardo's *Last Supper* is unfortunately in poor condition today, even after the completion in 1999 of a cleaning and restoration project lasting more than two decades. In a bold experiment in mural painting, instead of using fresco, which has a matte surface, Leonardo mixed oil and tempera, and applied much of it *a secco* (to dried, rather than wet, plaster) in order to create a surface appearance that more closely approximated oil painting on canvas or wood. But because the wall did not absorb the pigment as in the *buon fresco* technique, the paint quickly began to flake (see "Fresco Painting," page 419). The humidity of Milan further accelerated the deterioration. The restoration involved extensive scholarly, chemical, and computer analysis. Like similar projects elsewhere, however, most notably in the Sistine Chapel (FIGS. 22-1 and 22-18B), this one was not without controversy. One scholar has claimed that 80 percent of what is visible today is the work of the modern restorers, not Leonardo.

MONA LISA Leonardo's *Mona Lisa* (FIG. **22-5**) is probably the world's most famous portrait. In his biography of Leonardo, Vasari

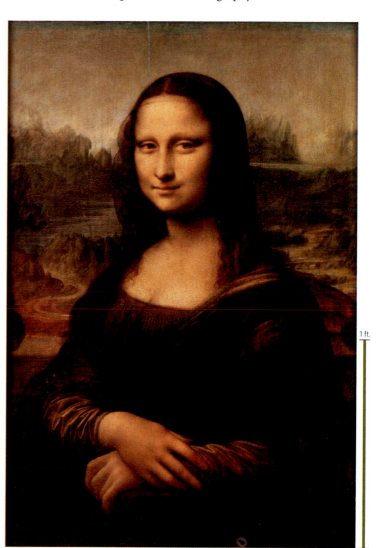

22-5 LEONARDO DA VINCI, *Mona Lisa,* ca. 1503–1505. Oil on wood, 2′ 6¼″ × 1′ 9″. Musée du Louvre, Paris.

Leonardo's skill with chiaroscuro and atmospheric perspective is on display in this new kind of portrait depicting the sitter as an individual personality who engages the viewer psychologically.

High and Late Renaissance **627**

MATERIALS AND TECHNIQUES
Renaissance Drawings

In Cinquecento Italy, drawing assumed a position of greater artistic prominence than ever before. Until the late 15th century, the expense of drawing surfaces and their lack of availability limited the production of preparatory sketches. Most artists drew on *parchment* (prepared from the skins of calves, sheep, and goats) or on *vellum* (made from the skins of young animals; FIG. 13-36). Because of the high cost of these materials, drawings in the 14th and 15th centuries tended to be extremely detailed and meticulously executed. Artists often drew using a silverpoint stylus (FIG. 20-1) because of the fine line it produced and the sharp point it maintained. The introduction in the late 15th century of less expensive paper made of fibrous pulp produced for the developing printing industry (see "Printed Books," page 577) enabled artists to experiment more and to draw with greater freedom. As a result, sketches proliferated. Artists executed these drawings in pen and ink (FIGS. **22-5A** and **22-6**), chalk, charcoal (FIG. 22-3), brush, and graphite or lead.

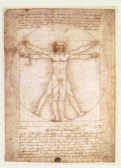

22-5A LEONARDO, *Vitruvian Man,* ca. 1485–1490.

During the Renaissance, the importance of drawing transcended the mechanical or technical possibilities that it afforded artists. The Italian term for drawing—*disegno*—refers also to design, an integral component of good art. Design was the foundation of art, and drawing was the fundamental element of design. In his 1607 treatise *L'idea de' pittori, scultori ed architetti*, Federico Zuccari (1542–1609), director of the Accademia di San Luca (Academy of Saint Luke), the Roman painting academy, summed up this philosophy when he stated that drawing is the external physical manifestation (*disegno esterno*) of an internal intellectual idea or design (*disegno interno*).

The design dimension of art production became increasingly important as artists cultivated their own styles. The early stages of artistic training largely focused on imitation and emulation (see "Imitation and Emulation," page 594), but to achieve widespread recognition, artists had to develop their own styles. Although the artistic community and public at large acknowledged technical skill, the conceptualization of the artwork—its theoretical and formal development—was paramount. Disegno, or design in this case, represented an artist's conceptualization and intention. In the Italian literature of the period, the terms often invoked to praise esteemed artists included *invenzione* (invention), *ingegno* (innate talent), *fantasia* (imagination), and *capriccio* (originality).

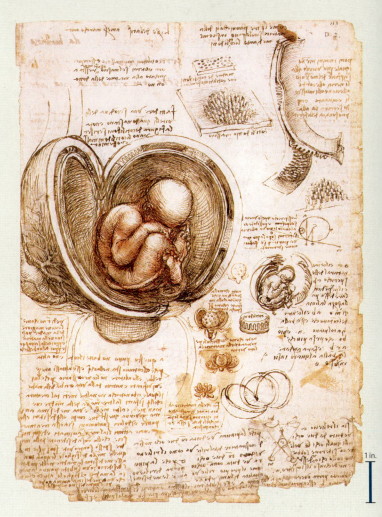

22-6 LEONARDO DA VINCI, *The Fetus and Lining of the Uterus,* ca. 1511–1513. Pen and ink with wash over red chalk and traces of black chalk on paper, $1' \times 8\frac{5}{8}''$. Royal Library, Windsor Castle.

The introduction of less expensive paper in the late 15th century enabled artists to draw more frequently. Leonardo's analytical anatomical studies exemplify the scientific spirit of the Renaissance.

(see "Giorgio Vasari's *Lives*," page 636) identified the woman portrayed as Lisa di Antonio Maria Gherardini, the wife of Francesco del Giocondo, a wealthy Florentine—hence, "Mona (an Italian contraction of *ma donna,* "my lady") Lisa." Unlike earlier portraits, Leonardo's representation of Gherardini, who was about 25 years old when she posed for Leonardo, does not serve solely as an icon of status. Indeed, Gherardini wears no jewelry and holds no attribute associated with wealth. Leonardo's concern was rather to paint a convincing representation of a specific individual, both in terms of appearance and personality. Mona Lisa sits quietly, her hands folded, her mouth forming a gentle smile, and her gaze directed at the viewer. Renaissance etiquette dictated that a woman should not look directly into a man's eyes. Leonardo's portrayal of this self-assured young woman without the trappings of power but engaging the audience psychologically is unprecedented and accounts in large part for the painting's unparalleled reputation today.

The enduring appeal of *Mona Lisa* also derives from Leonardo's decision to set his subject against the backdrop of a mysterious uninhabited landscape. This setting, with roads and bridges seemingly leading nowhere, recalls that of his *Madonna of the Rocks* (FIG. 22-2). The composition also resembles Fra Filippo Lippi's *Madonna and Child with Angels* (FIG. 21-24) with figures seated in front of a window through which the viewer glimpses a distant landscape. Originally, the artist represented Gherardini in a loggia. A later owner trimmed the painting, eliminating the columns, but partial column bases remain to the left and right of Mona Lisa's shoulders.

The painting is darker today than 500 years ago, and the colors are less vivid, but *Mona Lisa* still reveals Leonardo's fascination and skill with chiaroscuro and atmospheric perspective. The portrait is a prime example of the artist's famous smoky *sfumato* (misty haziness)—his subtle adjustment of light and blurring of precise planes.

ANATOMICAL STUDIES *Mona Lisa* is also exceptional because Leonardo completed very few paintings. His perfectionism, relentless experimentation, and far-ranging curiosity diffused his efforts. However, the drawings (see "Renaissance Drawings," page 628) in his notebooks preserve an extensive record of his ideas. His interests focused increasingly on science in his later years, and he embraced knowledge of all facets of the natural world. His investigations in anatomy, based in part on dissection, yielded drawings of great precision and beauty of execution. *The Fetus and Lining of the Uterus* (FIG. 22-6), although it does not meet 21st-century standards for accuracy (for example, Leonardo regularized the uterus's shape to a sphere, and his characterization of the lining is incorrect), was an astounding achievement in its day. Leonardo's analytical anatomical studies exemplify the scientific spirit of the Renaissance, establishing that era as a prelude to the modern world and setting it in sharp contrast to the preceding Middle Ages. Although Leonardo may not have been the first scientist of the modern world (at least not in today's sense of the term), he did originate the modern method of scientific illustration incorporating *cutaway* views. Scholars have long recognized the importance of his drawings for the development of anatomy as a science, especially in an age predating photographic methods such as X-rays.

ARCHITECTURE AND SCULPTURE Leonardo also won renown in his time as both architect and sculptor, although no extant buildings or sculptures can be definitively attributed to him. Like many of his contemporaries, he studied the ancient Roman architectural treatise by Vitruvius (see "Vitruvius's *Ten Books on Architecture*," page 199, and FIG. 22-5A). From his many drawings of central-plan structures (FIG. 22-6A), it is evident that he shared the interest of other Renaissance architects in this building type. As for Leonardo's sculptures, numerous drawings of monumental equestrian statues survive, and he made a full-scale model for a monument to Francesco Sforza (1401–1466), Ludovico's father. The French used the statue as a target and shot it to pieces when they occupied Milan in 1499. The defacement of ruler portraits, documented at least as far back

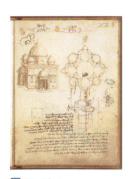

22-6A LEONARDO, central-plan church, ca. 1487–1490.

as the third millennium BCE (FIG. 2-12), is eloquent testimony to the power of images in public life.

Leonardo left Milan when the French captured the city. He served for a while as a military engineer for Cesare Borgia (1476–1507), who, with the support of his father, Pope Alexander VI (r. 1492–1503), tried to conquer the cities of the Romagna region in north-central Italy and create a Borgia duchy. Leonardo eventually returned to Milan in the service of the French. At the invitation of King Francis I (see "Francis I, Royal Art Patron and Collector," page 693), he then went to France, where he died at the château of Cloux in 1519.

Raphael

Alexander VI's successor was Julius II. Among the many projects that the ambitious new pope sponsored were a design for a modern Saint Peter's (FIGS. 22-22 and 22-23) to replace the timber-roofed fourth-century basilica (FIG. 8-9), the decoration of the papal apartments

(FIG. 22-9), and the construction of his tomb (FIGS. 22-14 and 22-15), in addition to commissioning Michelangelo to paint the Sistine Chapel ceiling (see "Michelangelo in the Service of Julius II," page 623, and FIG. 22-1).

In 1508, Julius II called Raffaello Santi (or Sanzio), known as RAPHAEL (1483–1520) in English, to the papal court in Rome, which would soon displace Florence, Urbino, and Mantua as the leading Italian patron of art and architecture (see "Art in the Princely Courts of Renaissance Italy," page 613). Born in a small town in Umbria near Urbino, Raphael probably learned the rudiments of his art from his father, Giovanni Santi (d. 1494), a painter connected with the ducal court of Federico da Montefeltro (see page 614), before entering the studio of Perugino (FIG. 21-41) in Perugia. Although strongly influenced by Perugino, Leonardo, and others, Raphael developed an individual style that embodied the ideals of High Renaissance art. Although he died at an early age, Raphael completed a large body of work, and several of his assistants became leaders of the next generation of Italian artists, extending his influence well into the century.

MARRIAGE OF THE VIRGIN Among Raphael's early works is *Marriage of the Virgin* (FIG. 22-7), which he painted for the chapel of Saint Joseph in the church of San Francesco in Città di Castello,

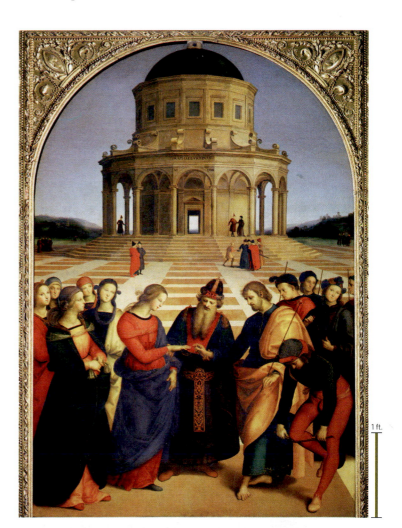

22-7 RAPHAEL, *Marriage of the Virgin*, from the Albizzini chapel, San Francesco, Città di Castello, Italy, 1504. Oil on wood, 5' 7" × 3' 10½". Pinacoteca di Brera, Milan.

In this early work depicting the marriage of the Virgin to Saint Joseph, Raphael demonstrated his mastery of foreshortening and of the perspective system he learned from Perugino (FIG. 21-41).

southeast of Florence. The subject was a fitting one for Saint Joseph (see "Early Christian Saints," page 236). According to the *Golden Legend* (a 13th-century collection of stories about the lives of the saints), Joseph competed with other suitors for Mary's hand. The high priest was to give the Virgin to whichever suitor presented to him a rod that had miraculously bloomed. Raphael depicted Joseph with his flowering rod in his left hand. In his right hand, Joseph holds the wedding ring he is about to place on Mary's finger. Other virgins congregate at the left, and the unsuccessful suitors stand on the right. One of them breaks his rod in half over his knee in frustration, giving Raphael an opportunity to demonstrate his mastery of foreshortening. The perspective system he used is the one he learned from Perugino (compare FIG. 21-41). The temple in the background is Raphael's version of a centrally planned building, featuring Brunelleschian arcades (FIG. 21-30).

MADONNA IN THE MEADOW Raphael spent the four years from 1504 to 1508 in Florence. There, still in his early 20s, he discovered that the painting style he had learned so painstakingly from Perugino was already outmoded (as was Brunelleschi's Early Renaissance architectural style). Florentine crowds flocked to the church of Santissima Annunziata to see Leonardo's recently unveiled cartoon of the Virgin, Christ Child, Saint Anne, and Saint John (probably an earlier version of FIG. 22-3). Under Leonardo's influence, Raphael began to modify the Madonna compositions he had employed in Umbria. In *Madonna in the Meadow* (FIG. **22-8**) of 1505–1506, Raphael adopted Leonardo's pyramidal composition and modeling of faces and figures in subtle chiaroscuro. Yet the Umbrian artist placed the large, substantial figures in a Peruginesque landscape, with his former master's typical feathery trees in the middle ground. Although Raphael experimented with Leonardo's dusky modeling, he tended to return to Perugino's lighter tonalities and blue skies. Raphael preferred clarity to obscurity, not fascinated, as Leonardo was, with mystery. Raphael quickly achieved fame for his Madonnas, which depict Mary as a beautiful young mother tenderly interacting with her young son. In *Madonna of the Meadow*, Mary almost wistfully watches Jesus play with John the Baptist's cross-shaped staff, as if she has a premonition of how her son will die. Raphael's work, as well as Leonardo's, deeply influenced the slightly younger ANDREA DEL SARTO (1486–1530), whose most famous painting is *Madonna of the Harpies* (FIG. **22-8A**).

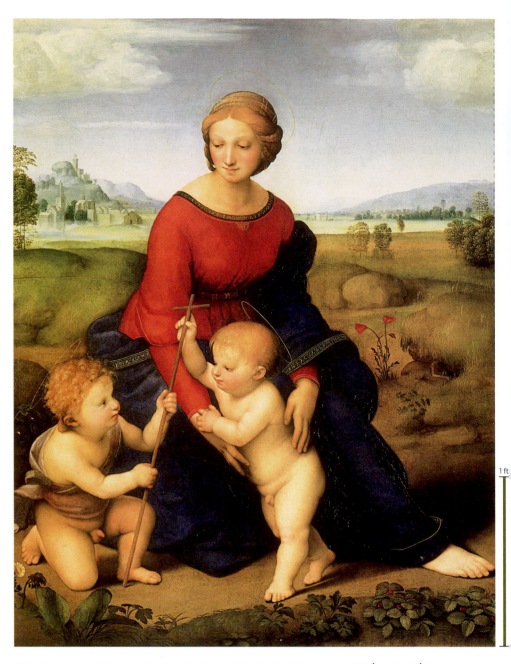

22-8 RAPHAEL, *Madonna in the Meadow*, 1505–1506. Oil on wood, 3' 8½" × 2' 10¼". Kunsthistorisches Museum, Vienna.

Emulating Leonardo's pyramidal composition (FIG. 22-2) but rejecting his dusky modeling and mystery, Raphael set his Madonna in a well-lit landscape and imbued her with grace, dignity, and beauty.

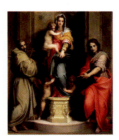

⏎ 22-8A ANDREA DEL SARTO, *Madonna of the Harpies*, 1517.

SCHOOL OF ATHENS Three years after completing *Madonna in the Meadow*, Raphael received one of the most important painting commissions that Julius II awarded—the decoration of the papal apartments in the Apostolic Palace of the Vatican (MAPS 22-1 and 24-1). Of the suite's several rooms (*stanze*), Raphael painted the room that came to be called the Stanza della Segnatura (Room of the Signature—Julius's papal library, where later popes signed official documents) and the Stanza d'Eliodoro (Room of Heliodorus—the pope's private audience room, named for one of the paintings there). His pupils completed the others following his sketches. On the four walls of the Stanza della Segnatura, Raphael presented images symbolizing the four branches of human knowledge and wisdom under the headings *Theology, Law (Justice), Poetry,* and *Philosophy*—the learning required of a Renaissance pope. Given Julius II's desire for recognition as both a spiritual and temporal leader, the *Theology*

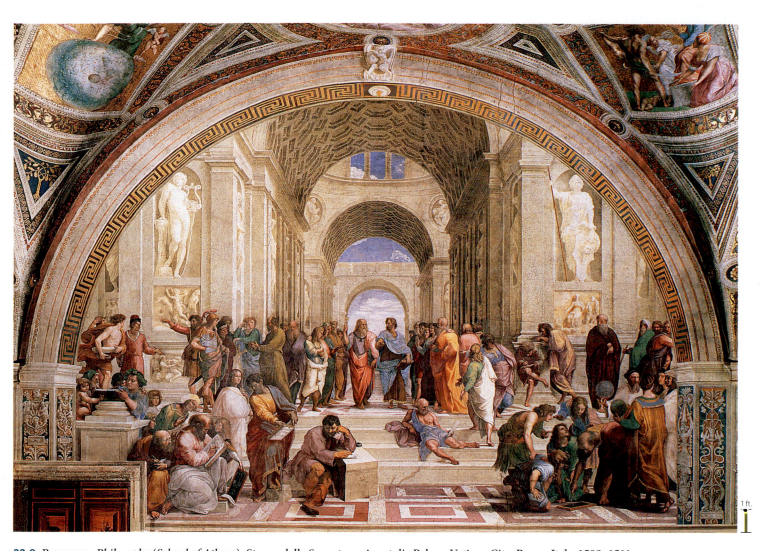

22-9 RAPHAEL, *Philosophy* (*School of Athens*), Stanza della Segnatura, Apostolic Palace, Vatican City, Rome, Italy, 1509–1511. Fresco, 19' × 27'.

Raphael included himself in this gathering of great philosophers and scientists whose self-assurance conveys calm reason. The setting recalls the massive vaults of the ancient Basilica Nova (FIG. 7-76).

and *Philosophy* frescoes face each other. The two images present a balanced picture of the pope—as a cultured, knowledgeable individual and as a wise, divinely ordained religious authority.

In Raphael's *Philosophy* mural (commonly called *School of Athens,* FIG. 22-9), the setting is not a "school" but a congregation of the great philosophers and scientists of the ancient world. Raphael depicted these luminaries, revered by Renaissance humanists, conversing and explaining their various theories and ideas. The setting is a vast hall covered by massive vaults that recall ancient Roman architecture, especially the much-admired coffered barrel vaults of the Basilica Nova (FIG. 7-76). Colossal statues of Apollo and Athena, patron deities of the arts and of wisdom, oversee the interactions. Plato and Aristotle are the central figures around whom Raphael carefully arranged the others. Plato holds his book *Timaeus* and points to Heaven, the source of his inspiration, while Aristotle carries his book *Nichomachean Ethics* and gestures toward the earth, from which his observations of reality sprang. Appropriately, ancient philosophers, men concerned with the ultimate mysteries that transcend this world, stand on Plato's side. On Aristotle's side are the philosophers and scientists concerned with practical matters, such as mathematics. At the lower left, Pythagoras writes as a servant holds up the harmonic scale. In the foreground, Heraclitus (probably a portrait of Michelangelo) broods alone. Diogenes sprawls on the steps. At the right, students surround Euclid, who demonstrates a theorem. Euclid may be a portrait of the architect Bramante, whom Julius II had recently commissioned to design the new church (FIGS. 22-22 and 22-23) to replace Constantine's 1,200-year-old Saint Peter's (FIG. 8-9). (*School of Athens* probably reflects Bramante's 1505 design for the interior of Saint Peter's; compare FIG. 24-5. According to Vasari, Bramante advised Raphael about the architectural setting.) At the extreme right, just to the right of the astronomers Zoroaster and Ptolemy, both holding globes, is a young man wearing a black hat—Raphael's self-portrait.

The groups appear to move easily and clearly, with eloquent poses and gestures that symbolize their doctrines and present an engaging variety of figural positions. The self-assurance and natural dignity of the figures convey calm reason, balance, and measure—those qualities that Renaissance thinkers admired as the heart of philosophy. Significantly, Raphael placed himself among the mathematicians and scientists in *School of Athens*. Certainly, the evolution of pictorial science approached perfection in this fresco in which Raphael convincingly depicted a vast space on a two-dimensional surface.

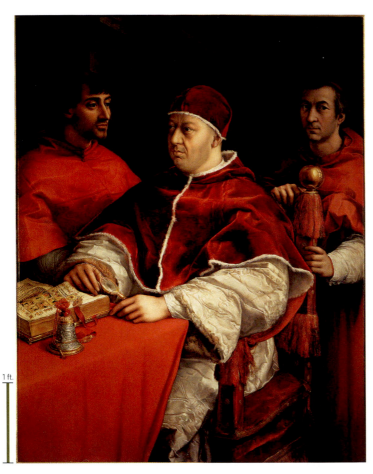

22-10 RAPHAEL, *Pope Leo X with Cardinals Giulio de' Medici and Luigi de' Rossi*, ca. 1517. Oil on wood, 5' $\frac{5}{8}$" × 3' 10 $\frac{7}{8}$". Galleria degli Uffizi, Florence.

In this dynastic portrait of the Medici pope and two Medici cardinals, Raphael depicted Leo X as an art collector and man of learning. The meticulous details reveal a debt to Netherlandish painting.

School of Athens also reveals Raphael's matured psychological insight. As in Leonardo's *Last Supper* (FIG. 22-4), all the characters communicate moods that reflect their beliefs, and the artist's placement of each figure tied these moods together. From the center, where Plato and Aristotle stand, Raphael arranged the groups of figures in an ellipse with a wide opening in the foreground. Moving along the floor's perspective pattern, the viewer's eye penetrates the assembly of philosophers and continues, by way of the reclining Diogenes, up to the here-reconciled leaders of the two great opposing camps of Renaissance philosophy. The vanishing point falls on Plato's left hand, drawing attention to *Timaeus*. In the Stanza della Segnatura, Raphael reconciled and harmonized not only the Platonists and Aristotelians but also classical humanism and Christianity, surely a major factor in the fresco's appeal to Julius II.

LEO X Succeeding Julius II as Raphael's patron was Pope Leo X (r. 1513–1521). By this time, Raphael had achieved renown throughout Italy and moved in the highest circles of the papal court. The new pope entrusted the Umbrian artist with so many projects in Rome, including overseeing construction of Saint Peter's, that Raphael became a wealthy man at a young age. Leo himself (Giovanni de' Medici) was a scion of Italy's most famous family. The second son of Lorenzo the Magnificent, he received a princely humanistic education. His election as pope came only a year after the return of the

Medici to Florence following nearly two decades of exile (see page 606), and Leo used his position to advance the family's interests. The portrait (FIG. 22-10) that he commissioned Raphael to paint in 1517—a few years after the artist portrayed the famed courtier Baldassare Castiglione (FIG. 22-10A)—is, in essence, a dynastic portrait. Appropriately, the pope dominates the composition, seated in his study before a table with an illuminated 14th-century manuscript, the magnifying glass he required because of his impaired eyesight, and a bell engraved with classical decorative motifs. Raphael portrayed Leo as he doubtless wished to be represented—as a man of learning and a collector of beautiful objects rather than as a head of state. To the

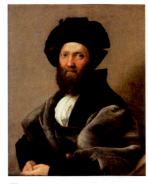

22-10A RAPHAEL, *Baldassare Castiglione*, ca. 1514.

pope's right is his cousin Cardinal Giulio de' Medici, who became Pope Clement VII (r. 1523–1534). Behind Leo's chair is Luigi de' Rossi (1474–1519), his cousin on his mother's side, whom the pope appointed cardinal. The three men look neither at one another nor at the painter or spectator, but are absorbed in their own thoughts.

Raphael's mastery of the oil technique is evident in every detail. His depiction of the rich satin, wool, velvet, and fur garments skillfully conveys their varied textures. His reproduction of the book on the pope's desk is so meticulous that scholars have been able to identify it as the *Hamilton Bible* in the Berlin Staatsbibliothek, open to folio 400 verso, the beginning of the Gospel of Saint John with illustrations of Christ's passion. The light illuminating the scene comes from the right—from a window reflected in the spherical brass finial of the pope's chair, in which the viewer can also see the indistinct form of the painter. In details such as these, Raphael revealed his knowledge and admiration of Netherlandish painting, especially the works of Jan van Eyck (compare the mirror in FIG. 20-7).

GALATEA As a star at the papal court, Raphael also enjoyed the patronage of other prominent figures in Rome. Agostino Chigi (1465–1520), an immensely wealthy banker who managed the Vatican's financial affairs, commissioned Raphael to decorate his palace on the Tiber River with scenes from classical mythology. Outstanding among the frescoes Raphael painted in the small but splendid Villa Farnesina is *Galatea* (FIG. 22-11), which he based on *Stanzas for the Joust of Giuliano de' Medici* by Angelo Poliziano, whose poetry had earlier inspired Botticelli to paint *Birth of Venus* (FIG. 21-1). In Raphael's fresco, Galatea flees on a shell drawn by leaping dolphins to escape her uncouth lover, the cyclops Polyphemus (painted on another wall by a different artist). Sea creatures and playful cupids surround her. The painting is an exultant song in praise of human beauty and zestful love. Compositionally, Raphael enhanced the liveliness of the image by placing the sturdy figures around Galatea in bounding and dashing movements that always return to her as the energetic center. The cupids, skillfully foreshortened, repeat the circling motion. Raphael conceived his figures sculpturally, and Galatea's body—supple, strong, and vigorously in motion—contrasts with Botticelli's delicate, hovering, almost dematerialized Venus while suggesting the spiraling compositions of Hellenistic statuary (FIG. 5-81). In *Galatea*, classical myth presented in monumental form, in vivacious movement, and in a spirit of passionate delight resurrects the naturalistic art and poetry of the Greco-Roman world.

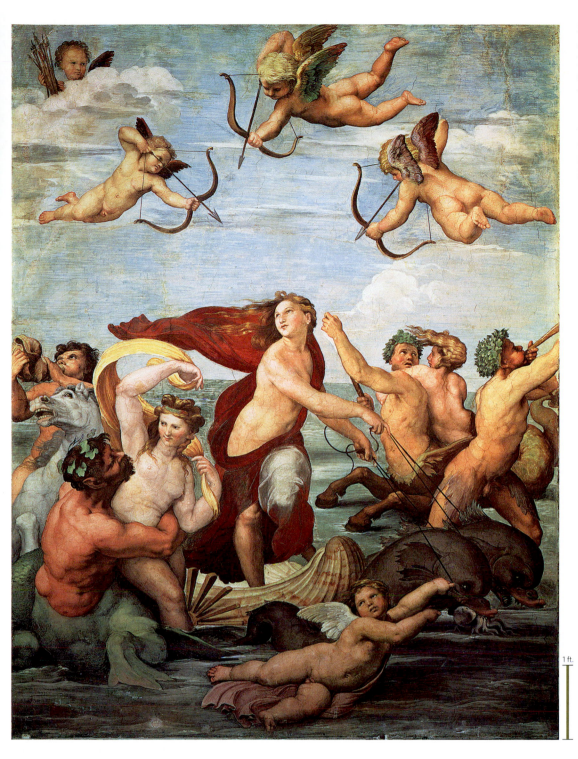

22-11 RAPHAEL, *Galatea*, Sala di Galatea, Villa Farnesina, Rome, Italy, ca. 1513. Fresco, 9' 8" × 7' 5".

Based on a poem by Poliziano, Raphael's fresco depicts Galatea fleeing Polyphemus. The painting, made for the palace of Vatican banker Agostino Chigi, celebrates human beauty and zestful love.

Michelangelo

Although Michelangelo is most famous today as the painter of the Sistine Chapel frescoes (FIG. 22-1), he was also an architect, poet, engineer, and, first and foremost, sculptor. Michelangelo considered sculpture superior to painting because the sculptor shares in the divine power to "make man" (see "Leonardo and Michelangelo on Painting versus Sculpture," page 625). Drawing a conceptual parallel to Plato's ideas, Michelangelo believed that the image which the artist's hand produces must come from the idea in the artist's mind. The idea, then, is the reality that the artist's genius has to bring forth. But artists are not the creators of the ideas they conceive. Rather, they find their ideas in the natural world, reflecting the absolute idea, which, for the artist, is beauty. One of Michelangelo's best-known observations about sculpture is that the artist must proceed by finding the idea—the image—locked in the stone. By removing the excess stone, the sculptor extricates the idea from the block (FIG. I-16), bringing forth the living form. The artist, Michelangelo felt, works for many years to discover this unceasing process of revelation and "arrives late at novel and lofty things."[4]

Michelangelo did indeed arrive "at novel and lofty things," for he broke sharply from the lessons of his predecessors and contemporaries in one important respect: he mistrusted the application of mathematical methods as guarantees of beauty in proportion. Measure and proportion, he believed, should be "kept in the eyes." Vasari quoted Michelangelo as declaring that "it was necessary to have the compasses in the eyes and not in the hand, because the hands work and the eye judges."[5] Thus Michelangelo set aside Vitruvius,

Alberti, Leonardo, and others who tirelessly sought the perfect measure, and insisted that the artist's inspired judgment could identify other pleasing proportions. In addition, Michelangelo argued that the artist must not be bound, except by the demands made by realizing the idea. This assertion of the artist's authority was typical of Michelangelo and anticipated the modern concept of the right to a self-expression of talent limited only by the artist's own judgment. The artistic license to aspire far beyond the "rules" was, in part, a manifestation of the pursuit of fame and success that humanism fostered. In this context, Michelangelo created works in architecture, sculpture, and painting that departed from High Renaissance regularity. He put in its stead a style of vast, expressive strength conveyed through complex, eccentric, and often titanic forms that loom before the viewer in tragic grandeur.

As a youth, Michelangelo was an apprentice in the studio of the painter Domenico Ghirlandaio (FIGS. 21-26 and 21-27), but he left before completing his training. Although Michelangelo later claimed that he owed nothing artistically to anyone, he made detailed drawings based on the work of the great Florentines Giotto and Masaccio. Early on, he came to the attention of Lorenzo the Magnificent and studied sculpture under one of Lorenzo's favorite artists, Bertoldo di Giovanni (ca. 1420–1491), a former collaborator of Donatello's. When Lorenzo died in 1492 and the Medici fell two years later, Michelangelo left Florence for Venice and then Bologna, where the sculptures of the Sienese artist Jacopo della Quercia (1367–1438) impressed him.

PIETÀ Michelangelo made his first trip to Rome in the summer of 1496, and two years later, still in his early 20s, he produced his first masterpiece there: a *Pietà* (FIG. 22-12) for Jean de Bilhères Lagraulas (1439–1499), Cardinal of Saint-Denis and the French king's envoy to the Vatican. The cardinal commissioned the statue to be placed in the rotunda attached to the south transept of Old Saint Peter's (not shown in FIG. 8-9) in which he was to be buried beside other French churchmen. (The work is now on view in the new church [FIG. 24-4] that replaced the fourth-century basilica.) The theme—Mary cradling the dead body of Christ in her lap—was a staple in the repertoire of French and German artists, and Michelangelo's French patron doubtless chose the subject. The Italian sculptor, however, rendered the northern European theme in an unforgettable manner. Michelangelo transformed marble into flesh, hair, and fabric with a sensitivity for texture almost without parallel. The best photographs can capture something of the luminosity of the marble surface, but the exquisite nature of Michelangelo's carving and polishing can be fully appreciated only in the presence of the original. Also breathtaking is the tender sadness of the beautiful and youthful Mary as she mourns the death of her son. In fact, her age—seemingly less than that of Christ—was a subject of controversy from the moment the statue was unveiled. Michelangelo explained Mary's ageless beauty as an integral part of her purity and virginity. Beautiful, too, is the son whom she holds. (In fact, Michelangelo's figure of the adult Christ is too small in relation to the size of Mary. This may be an intentional allusion to the imagery of the Madonna and Child subject of innumerable artworks.) Christ seems less to have died a martyr's crucifixion than to have drifted off into peaceful sleep in Mary's maternal arms. His wounds are barely visible. It is hard to imagine a starker contrast in conception and style than that between the *Röttgen Pietà* (FIG. 13-50) and Michelangelo's.

DAVID Michelangelo returned to Florence in 1501. In 1495, during the Medici exile, the Florentine Republic had ordered the transfer of Donatello's *David* (FIG. 21-11) from the Medici residence to the Palazzo della Signoria to join Verrocchio's *David* (FIG. 21-12) there. The importance of David as a civic symbol led the Florence Cathedral building committee to invite Michelangelo to work a great block of marble left over from an earlier aborted commission into still another *David* for the Signoria. The colossal statue (FIG. 22-13)—Florentines referred to it as "the Giant"—that Michelangelo created from that block forever assured his reputation as an extraordinary talent. Vasari, a great admirer of Michelangelo's (see "Giorgio Vasari's *Lives*," page 636), extolled the work, claiming:

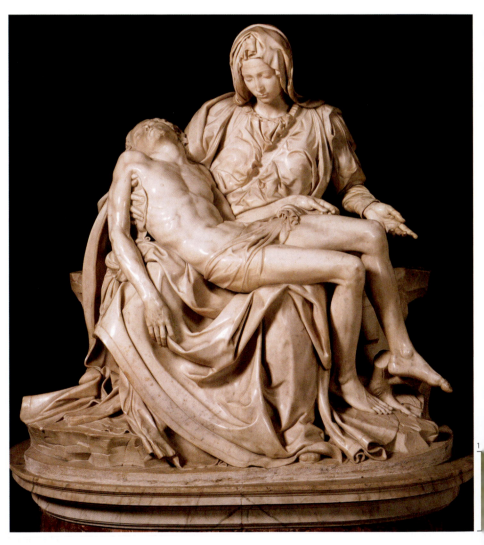

22-12 MICHELANGELO, *Pietà*, ca. 1498–1500. Marble, 5' 8½" high. Saint Peter's, Vatican City, Rome.

Michelangelo's representation of Mary cradling Christ's corpse captures the sadness and beauty of the young Virgin but was controversial because the Madonna seems younger than her son.

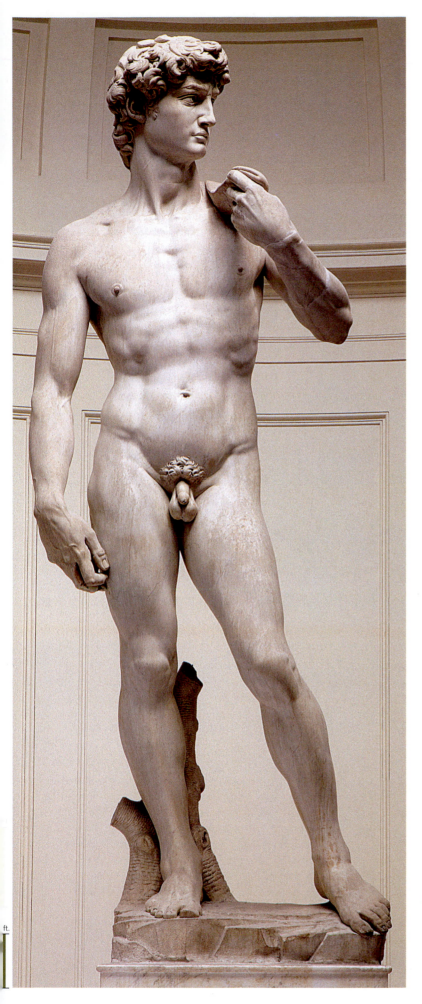

without any doubt [Michelangelo's *David*] has put in the shade every other statue, ancient or modern, Greek or Roman . . . [The statue] was intended as a symbol of liberty [in front of Florence's city hall], signifying that just as David had protected his people and governed them justly, so whoever ruled Florence should vigorously defend the city and govern it with justice.[6]

Despite the traditional association of David with heroic triumph over a fearsome adversary, Michelangelo chose to represent the young biblical warrior not after his victory, with Goliath's head at his feet (as Donatello and Verrocchio had done), but before the encounter, with David sternly watching his approaching foe. *David* exhibits the characteristic representation of energy in reserve that imbues Michelangelo's later figures with the tension of a coiled spring. The anatomy of David's body plays an important part in this prelude to action. His rugged torso, sturdy limbs, and large hands and feet alert viewers to the triumph to come. Each swelling vein and tightening sinew amplifies the psychological energy of David's pose.

Michelangelo doubtless had the classical nude in mind when he conceived his *David*. Like many of his colleagues, he greatly admired Greco-Roman statues, in particular the skillful and precise rendering of heroic physique. Without strictly imitating the antique style, which he studied firsthand in Rome, the Renaissance sculptor captured in his portrayal of the biblical hero the tension that is a key ingredient of the athletes (FIG. 5-65) of the Late Classical sculptor Lysippos, and the psychological insight and emotionalism of Hellenistic statuary (FIGS. 5-81, 5-82, and 5-90). His *David* differs from Donatello's and Verrocchio's creations in much the same way that later Hellenistic statues departed from their Classical predecessors (see Chapter 5). Michelangelo abandoned the self-contained compositions of the 15th-century *David*s by abruptly turning the hero's head toward his gigantic adversary. This *David* is compositionally and emotionally connected to an unseen presence beyond the statue, a feature also of Hellenistic sculpture (FIG. 5-86). As early as 1501, then, Michelangelo invested his efforts in presenting towering, pent-up emotion rather than calm, ideal beauty. He transferred his own doubts, frustrations, and passions into the great figures he created or planned.

TOMB OF JULIUS II The formal references to classical antiquity in Michelangelo's *David* surely appealed to Julius II, who associated himself with the humanists and with Roman emperors. Thus this sculpture and the fame that accrued to Michelangelo on its completion called the artist to the pope's attention, leading shortly thereafter to major papal commissions (see "Michelangelo in the Service of Julius II," page 623). The first project that Julius II commissioned from Michelangelo was the pontiff's tomb, to be placed in

22-13 MICHELANGELO BUONARROTI, *David,* from Piazza della Signoria, Florence, Italy, 1501–1504. Marble, 17' high. Galleria dell'Accademia, Florence.

In this colossal statue for the Florentine Signoria, Michelangelo represented David in heroic classical nudity, capturing the tension of Lysippos's athletes and the emotionalism of Hellenistic statuary.

High and Late Renaissance **635**

WRITTEN SOURCES

Giorgio Vasari's *Lives*

Giorgio Vasari (1511–1574) of Arezzo was an architect and painter who trained in Michelangelo's Florentine workshop. He enjoyed considerable success, especially as an architect, and received several major commissions, most notably to design the complex of offices next to the Palazzo della Signoria in Florence—the Uffizi—that now houses the world's greatest collection of Italian Renaissance art. Vasari's most significant achievement, however, was as a biographer and art historian. Sometimes called "the father of art history," Vasari published *Lives of the Most Excellent Painters, Sculptors, and Architects* in 1530. A second, definitive edition appeared in 1568. Vasari's *Lives* is far more than a compendium of facts and anecdotes about Italian artists. Vasari virtually created the discipline of art history, and the story of Renaissance art that art historians tell today remains rooted in Vasari's account.

Indeed, art historians, and the general public as well, owe the very concept of the "Renaissance" to Vasari. In his preface, Vasari placed all the biographies to follow in the context of his view that the history of art had three major periods: the glorious Greco-Roman age; the Middle Ages, when only inferior art was produced; and the Renaissance, when, beginning in the 14th century, classical art was reborn (see pages 374 and 416).

> What was the most infinitely harmful and damaging to those professions [painting, sculpture, and architecture] . . . was the fervent zeal of the new Christian religion . . . [which] cast to the ground all the marvelous statues, sculptures, paintings, mosaics, and ornaments of the false pagan gods, but it also . . .
> destroy[ed] the most honored temples of the pagan idols. . . .
> Once [today's artists] have seen how art reached the summit of perfection . . . and how it had fallen into complete ruin . . . [and how the arts], like human bodies, are born, grow up, become old, and die, they will now be able to recognize more easily the progress of art's rebirth and the state of perfection to which it has again ascended in our own times.*

Vasari also divided the Renaissance into three ages—the era of Cimabue and Giotto, when artists broke away from the *maniera greca* (see page 415); the Quattrocento, when artists began to employ linear perspective and produced works exhibiting greater naturalism (the ultimate goal of art, according to Vasari); and the Cinquecento, when Leonardo, Raphael, and especially Michelangelo achieved perfection.

Consistent with his view that the excellence of Renaissance art was due to the inspired genius and limitless talent of individual artists—a celebratory biographical approach to the history of art that persists even today—Vasari's *Lives* is often unrestrained in its flattery of the artists he admired most (Florentine artists above all others). Some brief excerpts:

Leonardo da Vinci: Truly wondrous and divine was Leonardo. . . . [W]ith his birth, Florence truly received the greatest of all gifts, and at his death, the loss was incalculable. To the art of painting, he added a kind of shadowing to the method of coloring with oils which has enabled the moderns to endow their figures with great energy and relief.[†]

Raphael: [A]lthough other paintings may be called paintings, those of Raphael are living things: for the flesh in his figures seems palpable, they breathe, their pulses beat. . . . [B]ecause of Raphael, the arts of painting, coloring, and invention were harmoniously brought to a stage of completion and perfection that could hardly be hoped for.[‡]

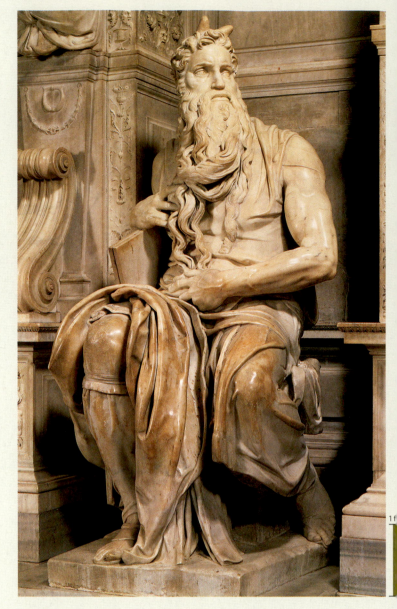

22-14 **Michelangelo Buonarroti**, *Moses*, from the tomb of Pope Julius II, Rome, Italy, ca. 1513–1515. Marble, 7' 8½" high. San Pietro in Vincoli, Rome.

Not since Hellenistic times had a sculptor captured as much emotional and physical energy in a seated statue as Michelangelo did in *Moses*. Vasari believed that God bequeathed Michelangelo to Florence.

Michelangelo: [T]he most benevolent Ruler of Heaven . . . decided . . . to send to earth a spirit who, working alone, was able to demonstrate in every art and every profession the meaning of perfection in the art of design . . . and because He saw that in the practice of . . . painting, sculpture, and architecture, Tuscan minds were always among the greatest, . . . He wanted to bequeath [Michelangelo] to . . . Florence, the most worthy among all the other cities, so that the perfection Florence justly achieved with all her talents might finally reach its culmination in one of her own citizens.[§]

*Translated by Julia Conaway Bondanella and Peter Bondanella, *Giorgio Vasari: The Lives of the Artists* (New York: Oxford University Press, 1991), 5–6.
[†]Ibid., 284, 298.
[‡]Ibid., 325, 332.
[§]Ibid., 415–416.

Old Saint Peter's. The sculptor's original 1505 design called for a freestanding, two-story structure with more than 40 statues. The proposed monument, of unprecedented size and complexity, would have given Michelangelo the latitude to sculpt numerous human figures while providing Julius II with a grandiose memorial that would associate the Cinquecento pope with the first pope, Peter himself. Shortly after Michelangelo began work on this project, however, the pope interrupted the commission, possibly because funds had to be diverted to the rebuilding of Saint Peter's. After Julius II's death in 1513, Michelangelo reluctantly reduced the scale of the project step-by-step until, in 1542, a final contract specified a simple wall tomb (compare FIGS. 21-14 and 21-39) with fewer than one-third of the originally planned figures. Michelangelo completed the tomb in 1545 and saw it placed in San Pietro in Vincoli (MAP 22-1), where Julius II had served as cardinal before his accession to the papacy. Given Julius's ambitions, it is safe to say that had he seen the final design of his tomb or known where it would eventually be located, he would have been bitterly disappointed.

The spirit of the tomb may be summed up in *Moses* (FIG. **22-14**), which Michelangelo carved between 1513 and 1515 during one of his sporadic resumptions of work on the project. Meant to be seen from below and to be balanced with seven other massive forms related to it in spirit, *Moses* in its final comparatively paltry setting does not convey the impact originally intended. Michelangelo depicted the Old Testament prophet seated, the Tablets of the Law under one arm and his hands gathering his voluminous beard. The horns on Moses's head were a convention in Christian art (based on a mistranslation of the Hebrew word for "rays") and helped Renaissance viewers identify the prophet (compare FIGS. 12-38 and 20-2). Here, as in his *David,* Michelangelo used the device of the turned head, in this case to concentrate the expression of awful wrath stirring in the prophet's mighty frame and eyes. Moses's muscles bulge, his veins swell, and his great legs seem to begin slowly to move. Not since Hellenistic times (FIGS. 5-85 and 5-86) had a sculptor imbued a seated figure with so much torsion and emotionalism.

Michelangelo also intended to incorporate in the pope's tomb some 20 statues of captives, popularly known as slaves, in various attitudes of revolt and exhaustion. Art historians have traditionally believed that *Bound Slave,* or *Rebellious Prisoner* (FIG. **22-15**), and the unfinished statue shown in FIG. I-16 to be two of those destined for Julius's tomb. Some scholars now doubt this attribution, and some even reject the identification of the statues as "slaves" or "captives." Whatever their identity, these statues, like Michelangelo's *David* and *Moses,* testify to the sculptor's ability to create figures embodying powerful emotional states. In *Bound Slave,* the defiant figure's violent contrapposto is the image of frantic but impotent struggle. Michelangelo based his whole art on his conviction that whatever can be said greatly through sculpture and painting must be said through the human figure.

TOMB OF GIULIANO DE' MEDICI Following the death of Julius II, Michelangelo, like Raphael, went into the service of Leo X and his successor, Clement VII. These Medici popes chose not to spend their resources on their predecessor's unfinished tomb. Instead, immediately following the death in May 1519 of Lorenzo de' Medici (1492–1519), duke of Urbino, they (Pope Leo X and the then-cardinal Giulio de' Medici; FIG. 22-10) commissioned Michelangelo to design a funerary chapel, the New Sacristy, attached to Brunelleschi's San Lorenzo (FIG. 21-31) in Florence, to house twin tombs of Lorenzo and Giuliano de' Medici (1478–1516), duke of Nemours (south of Paris), who had died three years before.

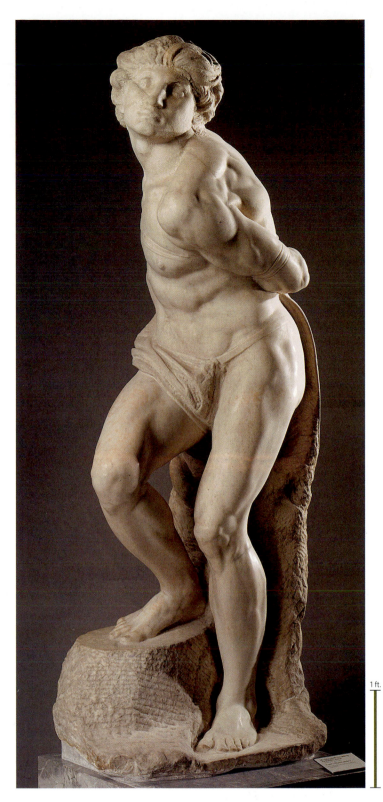

1 ft.

22-15 MICHELANGELO BUONARROTI, *Bound Slave* (*Rebellious Prisoner*), from the tomb of Pope Julius II, Rome, Italy, ca. 1513–1516. Marble, 7' $\frac{5}{8}$" high. Musée du Louvre, Paris.

For Pope Julius II's grandiose tomb, Michelangelo planned a series of statues of captives or slaves in various attitudes of revolt and exhaustion. This defiant figure exhibits violent contrapposto.

The chapel was also to contain the tombs of the dukes' namesakes, Lorenzo the Magnificent and his murdered brother, Giuliano, and was intended as a dynastic mausoleum for Florence's leading family. Michelangelo finished neither tomb. Today, the tombs of Lorenzo

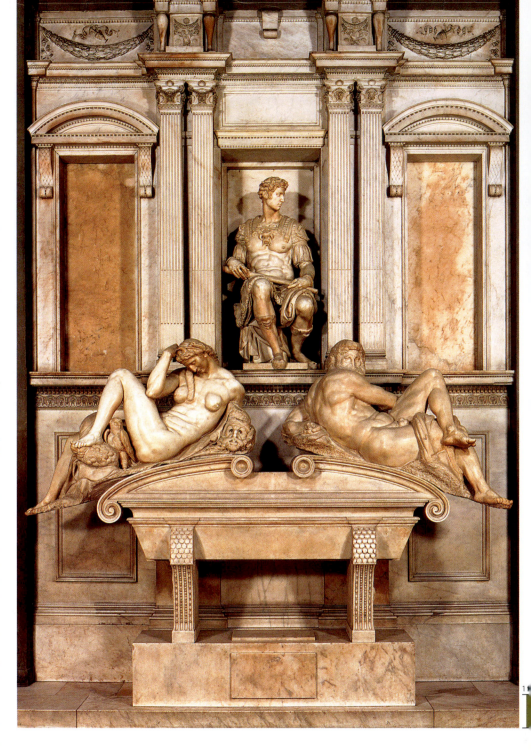

22-16 Michelangelo Buonarroti, tomb of Giuliano de' Medici, New Sacristy (Medici Chapel), San Lorenzo, Florence, Italy, 1519–1534. Marble, central figure 5' 11" high.

Michelangelo depicted the deceased Giuliano de' Medici in Roman armor, the model of the active and decisive man. Below him are the anguished, twisting figures of Night and Day.

and Giuliano (FIG. 22-16), as completed by the master's pupils, face each other on opposite walls of the New Sacristy. Scholars believe that Michelangelo intended to place pairs of recumbent river gods at the bottom of the sarcophagi, balancing the pairs of figures resting on the sloping sides, but his grand design for the tombs remains a puzzle.

According to the traditional interpretation, the arrangement Michelangelo planned mirrors the soul's ascent through the levels of the Neo-Platonic universe. Neo-Platonism, the school of thought based on Plato's idealistic, spiritualistic philosophy, embraced in the 15th century by the humanists in the Medici circle, experienced a renewed popularity in the 16th century. The lowest level of the tomb, which the river gods represent, would have signified the Underworld of brute matter, the source of evil. The two statues on the sarcophagi would symbolize the realm of time—the specifically human world of the cycles of dawn, day, evening, and night. Humanity's state in this world of time was one of pain and anxiety, of frustration and exhaustion. At left, the muscular female Night—Michelangelo used male models even for his female figures—and, at right, the male Day appear to be chained into never-relaxing tensions. Both exhibit the anguished twisting of the body's masses in contrary directions seen also in Michelangelo's *Bound Slave* (FIG. 22-15; compare FIG. I-16) and in his Sistine Chapel paintings (FIGS. 22-18 and 22-18A). This contortion is a staple of Michelangelo's figural art. Day, with a body the thickness of a great tree and the anatomy of Hercules (or of a reclining Greco-Roman river god that may have inspired Michelangelo's statue), strains his huge limbs against each other, his unfinished visage rising menacingly above his shoulder. Night, the symbol of rest, twists as if in troubled sleep, her posture wrenched and feverish. The artist surrounded her with an owl, poppies, and a hideous mask symbolic of nightmares. Some scholars argue, however, that the Night and Day personifications allude not to humanity's pain but to the life cycle and the passage of time leading ultimately to death.

On their respective tombs, seated statues of Lorenzo and Giuliano appear in niches at the apex of the structures. Transcending worldly existence, they represent the two ideal human types—the contemplative man (Lorenzo) and the active man (Giuliano; FIG. 22-16). The latter wears the armor of a Roman general and holds a commander's baton, his head turned alertly as if in council (he looks toward the statue of the Virgin at one end of the chapel). Across the room, Lorenzo appears deep in thought, his face in shadow. Together, they symbolize the two ways that human beings might achieve union with God—through meditation or through the active life fashioned after that of Christ. In this sense, they are not individual portraits. Indeed, Michelangelo declined to

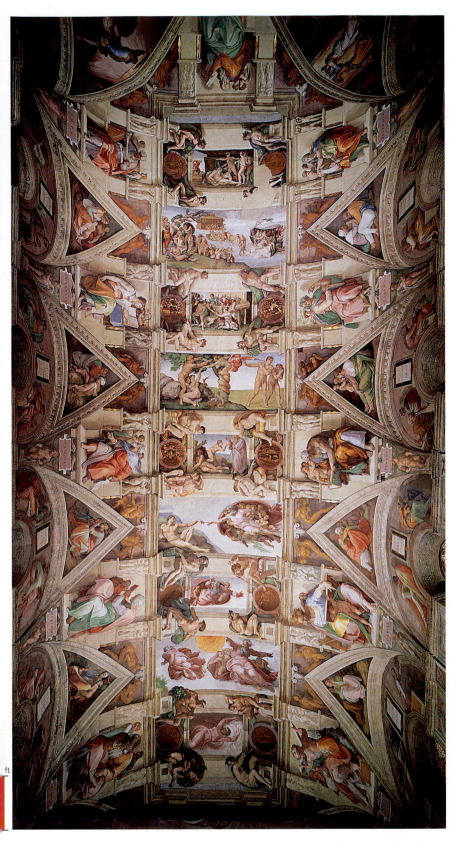

22-17 Michelangelo Buonarroti, ceiling of the Sistine Chapel, Vatican City, Rome, Italy, 1508–1512. Fresco, 128' × 45'.

Michelangelo labored almost four years for Pope Julius II on the frescoes for the ceiling of the Sistine Chapel (FIG. 22-1). He painted more than 300 figures illustrating the creation and fall of humankind.

SISTINE CHAPEL CEILING When Julius II suspended work on his tomb, the pope offered the bitter Michelangelo the commission to paint the ceiling (FIG. 22-17) of the Sistine Chapel (FIG. 22-1) in 1508. The chapel, built by Sixtus IV in 1479 to 1481 between the Vatican's apostolic palace and Saint Peter's (see page 644 and MAPS 22-1 and 24-1), served as the private chapel of the pope and the papal court. It was also the place where the College of Cardinals gathered after the death of a pope to select his successor. Some of the leading Quattrocento painters had provided frescoes (FIG. 21-41) for its walls, but the commission for the ceiling dwarfed the earlier mural projects in both size and complexity. Michelangelo faced enormous difficulties: the ceiling's dimensions (some 5,800 square feet), its height above the pavement (almost 70 feet), and the complicated perspective problems that the vault's height and curve presented—in addition to his inexperience in the fresco technique. (Michelangelo had to redo the first section he completed because of faulty preparation of the intonaco; see "Fresco Painting," page 419.) Yet, in less than four years, the Florentine sculptor produced an extraordinary series of frescoes incorporating his patron's agenda, Church doctrine, and his own interests. In depicting the most august and solemn themes of all, the creation, fall, and redemption of humankind—subjects most likely selected by Julius II with input from Michelangelo and Cardinal Marco Vigerio della Rovere (1446–1516)—Michelangelo spread a colossal compositional scheme across the vast surface. He succeeded in weaving together more than 300 figures in an ultimate grand drama of the human race.

Nine narrative panels describing the creation, as recorded in Genesis, run along the crown of the vault, from *God's Separation of Light and Darkness* (above the altar) to *Drunkenness of Noah* (nearest the entrance to the chapel). Thus as viewers enter the chapel, look up, and walk toward the altar, they review, in reverse order, the history of the fall of humankind. (When facing those assembled in the chapel, the presiding priest—the pope—sees the narrative scenes in the correct order, but upside down.) The Hebrew prophets and ancient *sibyls* (FIG. 22-18B) who foretold the coming of Christ appear seated in large thrones on both sides of the central row of scenes from Genesis, where the vault curves down. In the four corner pendentives, Michelangelo placed four Old Testament scenes with David, Judith, Haman, and Moses and the Brazen Serpent. Scores of lesser figures also appear. The ancestors of Christ fill the triangular compartments above the windows, nude youths punctuate the corners of the central panels, and small pairs of putti

sculpt likenesses of Lorenzo and Giuliano. Who, he asked, would care what they looked like in a thousand years? The rather generic visages of the two Medici captains of the Church are consistent with Michelangelo's lifelong approach to figural art, in painting as well as sculpture. Throughout his career, he demonstrated less concern for facial features and expressions than for the overall human form. Michelangelo's "portraits" are thus fundamentally different from those of Leonardo (FIG. 22-5) and Raphael (FIGS. 22-10 and 22-10A).

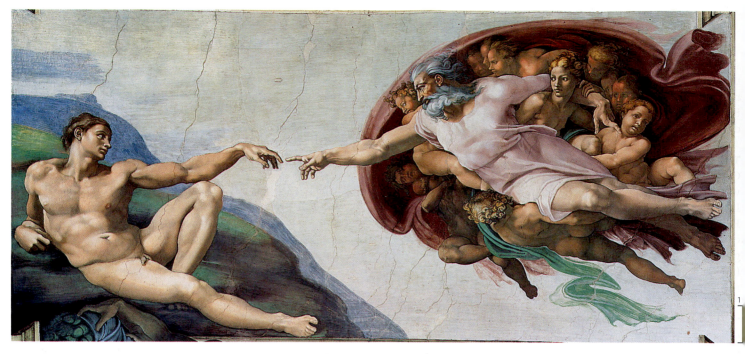

22-18 MICHELANGELO BUONARROTI, *Creation of Adam,* detail of the ceiling of the Sistine Chapel (FIG. 22-17), Vatican City, Rome, Italy, 1511–1512. Fresco, 9' 2" × 18' 8".

Life leaps to Adam like a spark from the extended hand of God in this fresco, which recalls the communication between gods and heroes in the classical myths that Renaissance humanists greatly admired.

in *grisaille* (to imitate sculpture) support the painted cornice surrounding the entire central corridor. The overall conceptualization of the ceiling's design and narrative structure not only presents a sweeping chronology of Christianity but also is in keeping with Renaissance ideas about Christian history. These ideas included interest in the conflict between good and evil and between the energy of youth and the wisdom of age. The conception of the entire ceiling was astounding in itself, and the articulation of it in its thousands of details was a superhuman achievement.

Unlike Andrea Mantegna's decoration of the ceiling of the Camera Picta (FIGS. 21-48 and 21-49) in Mantua, the strongly marked unifying architectural framework in the Sistine Chapel does not construct "picture windows" framing illusions within them. Rather, the viewer focuses on figure after figure, each sharply outlined against the neutral tone of the architectural setting or the plain background of the panels.

CREATION OF ADAM The two central panels of Michelangelo's ceiling are *Creation of Adam* (FIG. **22-18**) and *Fall of Man* (FIG. **22-18A**). In both cases, Michelangelo rejected traditional iconographical convention in favor of bold new interpretations of these momentous events. In *Creation of Adam,* God and Adam confront each other in a primordial unformed landscape of which Adam is still a

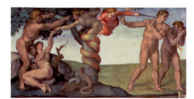

📐 **22-18A** MICHELANGELO, *Fall of Man,* ca. 1510.

material part, heavy as earth. The Lord transcends the earth, wrapped in a billowing cloud of drapery and borne up by his powers. Life leaps to Adam like a spark from the extended and mighty hand of God. The communication between gods and heroes, so familiar in classical myth, is here concrete. This blunt depiction of the Lord as ruler of Heaven in the classical, Olympian sense indicates how easily High

Renaissance thought joined classical and Christian traditions. Yet the classical trappings do not obscure the essential Christian message.

Beneath the Lord's sheltering left arm is a woman, apprehensively curious but as yet uncreated. Scholars traditionally believed that she is Eve, but many now think she is the Virgin Mary (with the Christ Child at her knee). If the second identification is correct, it suggests that Michelangelo incorporated into his fresco one of the essential tenets of Christian faith—the belief that Adam's original sin eventually led to the sacrifice of Christ, which in turn made possible the redemption of all humankind (see "Jewish Subjects in Christian Art," page 238).

As God reaches out to Adam, the viewer's eye follows the motion from right to left, but Adam's extended left arm leads the eye back to the right, along the Lord's right arm, shoulders, and left arm to his left forefinger, which points to the Christ Child's face. The focal point of this right-to-left-to-right movement—the fingertips of Adam and the Lord—is dramatically off-center. Michelangelo replaced the straight architectural axes found in Leonardo's compositions with curves and diagonals. For example, the bodies of the two great figures are complementary—the concave body of Adam fitting the convex body and billowing "cloak" of God. Thus motion directs not only the figures but also the whole composition. The reclining positions of the figures, the heavy musculature, and the twisting poses are all intrinsic parts of Michelangelo's style.

The photographs of the Sistine Chapel reproduced here record the appearance of Michelangelo's frescoes after the completion of a 12-year cleaning project (1977–1989). The painstaking restoration (FIG. **22-18B**) elicited considerable controversy because it revealed vivid colors that initially shocked art historians, producing accusations that

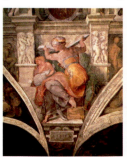

📐 **22-18B** Sistine Chapel restoration, 1977-1989.

the restorers were destroying Michelangelo's masterpieces. That reaction, however, was largely attributable to the fact that for centuries everyone had seen Michelangelo's frescoes only in their soot-and-grime-covered state. Today, all can see that Michelangelo's true palette—so different from Leonardo's (FIGS. 22-2 to 22-5)—resembles, not surprisingly, the colors favored by Quattrocento Florentine fresco painters such as Masaccio (FIG. 21-19) and Piero della Francesca (FIG. 21-25).

THE COUNTER-REFORMATION Paul III (r. 1534–1549) succeeded Clement VII as pope in 1534 at a time of widespread dissatisfaction with the leadership and policies of the Roman Catholic Church. Led by clerics such as Martin Luther and John Calvin in the Holy Roman Empire (see page 680), early-16th-century reformers directly challenged papal authority, especially regarding secular issues. Disgruntled Catholics voiced concerns about the sale of *indulgences* (pardons for sins, reducing the time a soul spent in purgatory), nepotism (the appointment of relatives to important positions; compare FIG. 22-10), and high Church officials pursuing personal wealth. This Reformation movement resulted in the establishment of Protestantism, with sects such as Lutheranism and Calvinism. Central to Protestantism was a belief in personal faith rather than

adherence to decreed Church practices and doctrines. Because the Protestants believed that the only true religious relationship was the personal relationship between an individual and God, they were, in essence, eliminating the need for Church intercession, which is central to Catholicism.

The Catholic Church, in response, mounted a full-fledged campaign to counteract the defection of its members to Protestantism. Led by Paul III, this response, the Counter-Reformation, consisted of numerous initiatives. The Council of Trent, which met intermittently from 1545 through 1563, was a major component of this effort (see "The Council of Trent," page 642). Composed of cardinals, archbishops, bishops, abbots, and theologians, the Council of Trent dealt with issues of Church doctrine, including many that the Protestants contested. Many papal art commissions during this period should be viewed as an integral part of the Counter-Reformation effort. Popes long had been aware of the power of visual imagery to construct and reinforce ideological claims, and 16th-century popes exploited this capability.

LAST JUDGMENT Among Paul III's first papal commissions was an enormous (48-foot-tall) fresco for the Sistine Chapel. Michelangelo agreed to paint *Last Judgment* (FIG. 22-19) on the chapel's altar (west) wall. Here, the artist depicted Christ as the stern judge of the world, but—in vivid contrast to both the Byzantine (FIG. 9-24) and European medieval (FIG. 12-15) traditions—as a twisting, almost nude, giant who raises his mighty right arm in a gesture of damnation so broad and universal as to suggest that he will destroy all creation. The choirs of Heaven surround the youthful judge and pulse with anxiety and awe. Crowded into the space below are trumpeting angels, the ascending figures of the saved, and the downward-hurtling figures of the damned. The Virgin is already in Heaven, on Christ's right side, the side of the blessed. On the opposite side, demons, whose gargoyle masks and burning eyes revive the demons of Romanesque tympana, torment the damned.

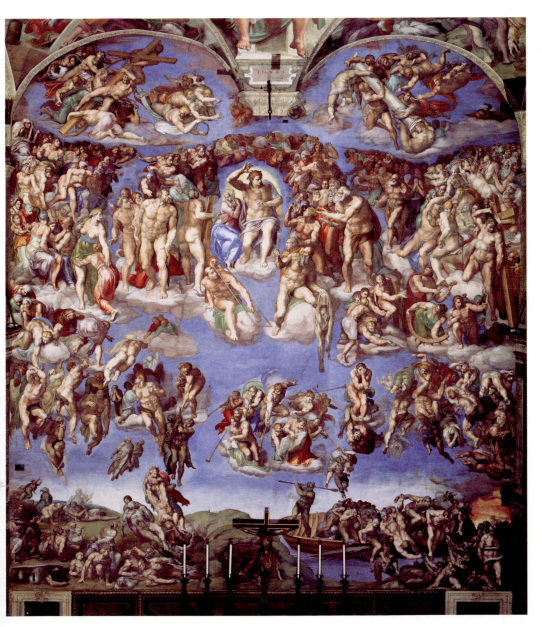

22-19 MICHELANGELO BUONARROTI, *Last Judgment*, altar wall of the Sistine Chapel, Vatican City, Rome, Italy, 1536–1541. Fresco, 48' × 44'.

Michelangelo completed his fresco cycle in the Sistine Chapel with this terrifying vision of the fate awaiting sinners. Near the center, he placed his own portrait on the flayed skin that Saint Bartholomew holds.

Both Catholics and Protestants took seriously the role of devotional imagery in religious life. However, their views differed dramatically. Catholics deemed art valuable for cultivating piety. Protestants believed that religious imagery encouraged idolatry and distracted the faithful from the goal of developing a personal relationship with God (see page 681). As part of the Counter-Reformation effort, Pope Paul III convened the Council of Trent in 1545 to review controversial Church doctrines. At its conclusion in 1563, the council issued the following edict regarding the Church's role as patron of paintings and sculptures:

> The holy council commands all bishops and others who hold the office of teaching and have charge of the *cura animarum* ["care of souls"—the responsibility of laboring for the salvation of souls], that in accordance with the usage of the Catholic and Apostolic Church, received from the primitive times of the Christian religion, and with the unanimous teaching of the holy Fathers and the decrees of sacred councils, they above all instruct the faithful diligently in matters relating to intercession and invocation of the saints, the veneration of relics, and the legitimate use of images. . . . Moreover, that the images of Christ, of the Virgin Mother of God, and of the other saints are to be placed and retained especially in the churches, and that due honor and veneration is to be given them; . . . because the honor which is shown them is referred to the prototypes which they represent, so that by means of the images which we kiss and before which we uncover the head and prostrate ourselves, we adore Christ and venerate the saints whose likeness they bear. That is what was defined by the decrees of the councils, especially of the Second Council of Nicaea, against the opponents of images.
>
> Moreover, let the bishops diligently teach that by means of the stories of the mysteries of our redemption portrayed in paintings and other representations the people are instructed and confirmed in the articles of faith, which ought to be borne in mind and constantly reflected upon; also that great profit is derived from all holy images, not only because the people are thereby reminded of the benefits and gifts bestowed on them by Christ, but also because through the saints the miracles of God and salutary examples are set before the eyes of the faithful, so that they may give God thanks for those things, may fashion their own life and conduct in imitation of the saints and be moved to adore and love God and cultivate piety. . . . That these things may be the more faithfully observed, the holy council decrees that no one is permitted to erect or cause to be erected in any place or church, howsoever exempt, any unusual image unless it has been approved by the bishop.*

In taking this position, the Catholic Church reaffirmed its role as the greatest art patron of the Cinquecento and assured that it would retain that status throughout the succeeding Baroque era, both in Europe and in Spain's vast territories in the New World.

Canons and Decrees of the Council of Trent, December 3–4, 1563. Robert Klein and Henri Zerner, *Italian Art 1500–1600: Sources and Documents* (Evanston, Ill.: Northwestern University Press, 1966), 120–121.

Michelangelo's terrifying vision of the fate awaiting sinners goes far beyond even Signorelli's gruesome images (FIG. 21-42). Martyrs who suffered especially agonizing deaths crouch below the judge. One of them, Saint Bartholomew, who was skinned alive, holds the flaying knife and the skin, its face a grotesque self-portrait of Michelangelo. The figures are huge and violently twisted, with small heads and contorted features. Yet while this frightening fresco impresses on viewers Christ's wrath on judgment day, it also holds out hope. A group of saved souls—the elect—crowd around Christ, and on the far right appears a figure with a cross, most likely the Good Thief (crucified with Christ) or a saint martyred by crucifixion, such as Saint Andrew.

UNFINISHED *PIETÀ* Six years after completing the *Last Judgment* fresco and nearly 50 years after carving the *Pietà* (FIG. 22-12) for the burial chapel of Cardinal Bilhères Lagraulas, Michelangelo, already in his 70s, began work on another *Pietà* (FIG. **22-20**), this one destined for his own tomb in Santa Maria Maggiore in Rome. For this *Pietà*, the aged master set for himself an unprecedented technical challenge—to surpass the sculptors of the ancient *Laocoön* (FIG. 5-89) and carve four life-size figures from a single marble block.

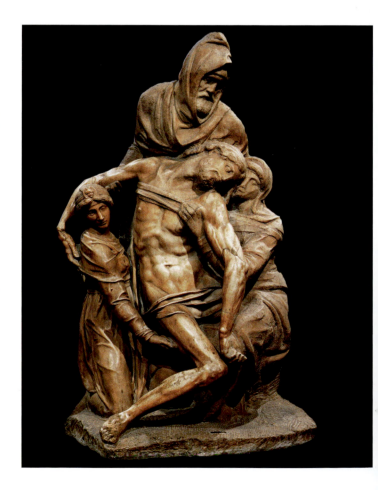

22-20 MICHELANGELO BUONARROTI, *Pietà*, ca. 1547–1555. Marble, 7' 8" high. Museo dell'Opera del Duomo, Florence.

Left unfinished, this *Pietà*, begun when Michelangelo was in his 70s and intended for his own tomb, includes a self-portrait of the sculptor as Nicodemus supporting the lifeless body of the Savior.

He did not succeed. Christ's now-missing left leg became detached, perhaps because of a flaw in the marble, and in 1555 Michelangelo abandoned the project and began to smash the statue. His assistants intervened, and he eventually permitted one of them, Tiberio Calcagni (1532–1565), to repair some of the damage and finish the work in part.

In composition and tone, the Santa Maria Maggiore *Pietà*—really a *Deposition* (see "The Life of Jesus in Art," page 241)—stands in stark contrast to the work of Michelangelo's youth. The composition is vertical, with three figures—the Virgin, Mary Magdalene, and Nicodemus—supporting the lifeless body of Christ. The Virgin is now a subsidiary figure, half hidden by her son, whose left leg originally rested on her left thigh. The undersized Mary Magdalene is in a kneeling position. Forming the apex of the composition is the hooded Nicodemus, a self-portrait of Michelangelo. This late work is therefore very personal in nature, not surprising when the artist was also the patron.

Architecture: Rome

Michelangelo was an accomplished architect as well as a sculptor and painter, and his Vatican commissions included work on a new church to replace the basilica that Constantine had erected over the site of Saint Peter's burial place (Old Saint Peter's, FIG. 8-9 and MAPS 22-1 and 24-1). By the 15th century, it was obvious that the ancient timber-roofed church was insufficient for the needs and aspirations of the Renaissance papacy. Rebuilding the fourth-century basilica would occupy several popes and some of the leading architects of Italy for more than a century.

BRAMANTE The first in the distinguished line of architects of the new Saint Peter's was DONATO D'ANGELO BRAMANTE (1444–1514). Born in Urbino and trained as a painter (perhaps by Piero della Francesca), Bramante went to Milan in 1481 and, as Leonardo did, stayed there until the French captured the city in 1499. In Milan, Bramante abandoned painting to become his generation's most renowned architect. Under the influence of Filippo Brunelleschi, Leon Battista Alberti, and perhaps Leonardo, all of whom strongly favored the art and architecture of classical antiquity, Bramante developed the High Renaissance form of the central-plan church.

The architectural style Bramante championed was, consistent with the humanistic values of the day, based on ancient Roman models. Bramante's first major work in the classical mode was the small architectural gem known as the Tempietto (FIG. 22-21) on the Janiculum hill overlooking the Vatican. The building received its name because, to contemporaries, it had the look of a small ancient temple. "Little Temple" is, in fact, a perfect nickname for the structure, because the round temples of Roman Italy, including two in Rome—one in the Roman Forum and another on the east bank of the Tiber—and a third at nearby Tivoli (FIG. 7-4), directly inspired Bramante's design. King Ferdinand (r. 1479–1516) and Queen Isabella of Spain commissioned the Tempietto to mark what they believed was the spot of Saint Peter's crucifixion. (The Vatican cemetery in which Peter was buried lies at the northern foot of the Janiculum.) Bramante undertook the project in 1502, but construction may not have begun until the end of the decade. Today, the Tempietto stands inside the rectangular cloister of the monastery of San Pietro in Montorio, but Bramante planned, although never executed, a circular colonnaded courtyard to frame the "temple." His intent was to coordinate the Tempietto and its surrounding portico by aligning the columns of the two structures.

The Tempietto's design is severely rational and features a stately circular *stylobate* (stepped temple platform) and austere *Tuscan col-*umns. Bramante achieved a wonderful balance and harmony in the relationship of the parts (dome, drum, and base) to one another and to the whole. Conceived as a tall domed cylinder projecting from the lower, wider cylinder of its colonnade, the "temple" is in some respects more a monument than a building. Bramante's sculptural eye is most evident in the rhythmic play of light and shadow around the columns and balustrade and across the deep-set rectangular windows alternating with shallow shell-capped niches in the *cella* (central room of a temple), walls, and drum. Although the Tempietto, superficially at least, may resemble a Greco-Roman *tholos* (a circular shrine; FIG. 5-72), and although antique models (for example, FIG. 7-4) provided the inspiration for all its details, the combination of parts and details was new and original. (Classical tholoi, for instance, were never two-story structures and had neither a drum nor a balustrade.)

One of the main differences between the Early and High Renaissance styles of architecture is the former's emphasis on adorning flat wall surfaces versus the latter's sculptural handling of architectural masses. Bramante's Tempietto initiated the High Renaissance era in architecture. Andrea Palladio, a brilliant theorist as well as a major later 16th-century architect (FIGS. 22-28 to 22-31), included the Tempietto in his survey of ancient temples because Bramante was "the first to bring back to light the good and beautiful architecture that from antiquity to that time had been hidden."[7] (Note the kinship with Ghiberti's and Vasari's views of the history of painting; see pages 584 and 636.) Round in plan and elevated on a base that isolates it from its surroundings, the Tempietto conforms to Alberti's and Palladio's strictest demands for an ideal church, although it is far too small to house a congregation.

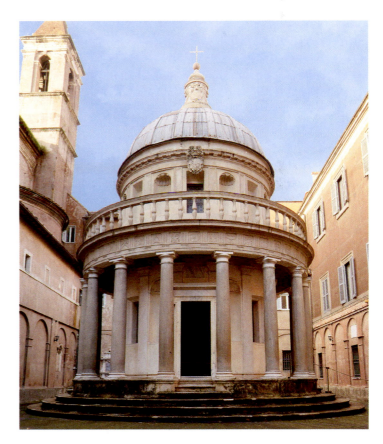

22-21 DONATO D'ANGELO BRAMANTE, Tempietto, San Pietro in Montorio, Rome, Italy, begun 1502.

Contemporaries celebrated Bramante as the first architect to revive the classical style. Roman temples (FIG. 7-4) inspired his "little temple," but Bramante combined the classical parts in new ways.

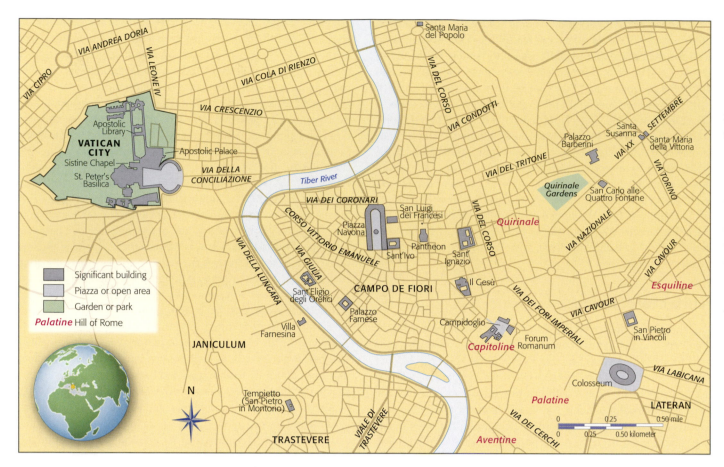

MAP 22-1 Rome with Renaissance and Baroque monuments.

SAINT PETER'S As noted, Bramante was the architect whom Julius II selected to design a replacement for the basilica of Old Saint Peter's (FIG. 8-9). The fourth-century building had fallen into considerable disrepair and, in any event, did not suit the ambitious pope's taste for the colossal. Many members of the papal *Curia* ("court") opposed tearing down the venerable shrine, but Julius could not be dissuaded. He dreamed of gaining control over all Italy and making the Rome of the popes the equal of (if not more

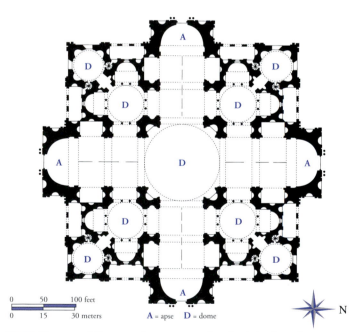

22-22 DONATO D'ANGELO BRAMANTE, plan for Saint Peter's, Vatican City, Rome, Italy, 1505.

Bramante proposed to replace the Constantinian basilica of Saint Peter's (FIG. 8-10) with a central-plan church featuring a cross with arms of equal length, each of which terminated in an apse.

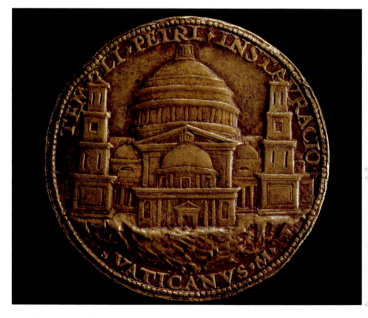

22-23 CRISTOFORO FOPPA CARADOSSO, reverse side of a medal showing Bramante's design for Saint Peter's, 1506. Bronze, $2\frac{1}{4}''$ diameter. British Museum, London.

Bramante's unexecuted 1506 design for Saint Peter's called for a large dome over the crossing, smaller domes over the subsidiary chapels, and a boldly sculptural treatment of the walls and piers.

splendid than) the Rome of the caesars (see "Julius II," page 623). A crumbling basilica did not serve his purposes. A magnificent new church did, especially one that revived the classical architectural vocabulary of imperial Rome. Like its predecessor, the new Saint Peter's was to serve as a *martyrium* to mark the apostle's grave, but Julius also intended to install his own tomb (FIGS. 22-14 and 22-15) in the church. Constantine's basilica was not large enough to house the mammoth tomb that the pope envisioned (see page 637).

Bramante's ambitious design (FIG. 22-22) for the new Saint Peter's consisted of a cross with arms of equal length, each terminating in an apse. A large dome would have covered the crossing, and smaller domes over subsidiary chapels would have capped the diagonal axes of the roughly square plan. Bramante's design also called for a boldly sculptural treatment of the walls and piers under the dome. The organization of the interior space was complex in the extreme: nine interlocking crosses, five of them supporting domes. The scale of Bramante's Saint Peter's was gigantic. The architect boasted that he would place the dome of the Pantheon (FIGS. 7-49 to 7-51) over the Basilica Nova (Basilica of Constantine; FIG. 7-76).

A commemorative medal (FIG. 22-23) by CRISTOFORO FOPPA CARADOSSO (ca. 1452–1526) shows how Bramante planned to accomplish that feat. As in the Pantheon, Saint Peter's dome would be hemispherical, but Bramante broke up the massive unity of the ancient temple by adding two towers and a medley of domes and porticos. In light of Julius II's interest in the Roman Empire, it is not surprising that the pope approved using the Pantheon as a model for the new church. That Bramante's design appeared on a commemorative medal is in itself noteworthy. Such medals proliferated in the 15th century (FIG. 21-28A), reviving the ancient Roman practice of placing images of important imperial building projects on the reverse side of coins. The fronts of those coins bore portraits of the emperors who commissioned the buildings. Predictably, a portrait of Julius II, not Bramante, appears on the front of the Caradosso medal.

MICHELANGELO, SAINT PETER'S During Bramante's lifetime, construction of Saint Peter's did not advance beyond the erection of the crossing piers and the lower choir walls. After his death, the work passed from one architect to another and, in 1546, to Michelangelo, whom Pope Paul III had already put in charge of the reorganization of the Capitoline Hill (FIG. 22-23A) in Rome. With the Church facing challenges to its supremacy, the pope surely felt a sense of urgency about the completion of this project. Michelangelo's work on Saint Peter's became a long-term show of dedication, thankless and without pay. Among Michelangelo's difficulties was his struggle to preserve and carry through Bramante's original plan (FIG. 22-22), which he praised and chose to retain as the basis for his own design (FIGS. 22-24 and 22-25). Michelangelo shared Braman-

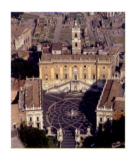

22-23A MICHELANGELO, Campidoglio, Rome, 1538–1564.

te's conviction that a central plan was the ideal form for a church. Always a sculptor at heart, Michelangelo carried his obsession with human form over to architecture and reasoned that buildings should follow the form of the human body. This meant organizing their units symmetrically around a central axis, as the arms relate to the body or the eyes to the nose. "For it is an established fact," he wrote, "that the members of architecture resemble the members of man. Whoever neither has been nor is a master at figures, and especially at anatomy, cannot really understand architecture."[8]

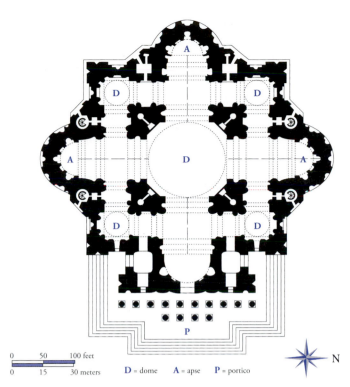

0   50   100 feet
0   15   30 meters   **D** = dome   **A** = apse   **P** = portico

N

22-24 MICHELANGELO BUONARROTI, plan for Saint Peter's, Vatican City, Rome, Italy, 1546.

Michelangelo admired Bramante's plan (FIG. 22-22) for Saint Peter's, but modified it. He replaced the core of interlocking crosses in Bramante's design with a compact domed Greek cross inscribed in a square.

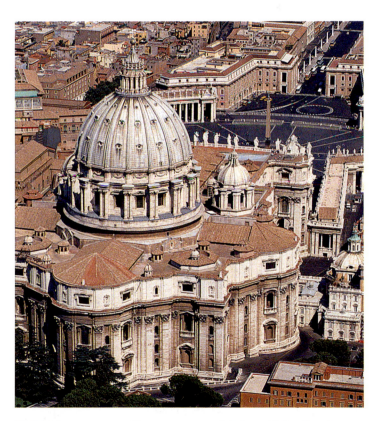

22-25 MICHELANGELO BUONARROTI, aerial view of Saint Peter's (looking northeast), Vatican City, Rome, Italy, 1546–1564. Dome completed by GIACOMO DELLA PORTA, 1590.

The west end of Saint Peter's offers the best view of Michelangelo's intentions. The giant pilasters of his colossal order march around the undulating wall surfaces of the central-plan building.

High and Late Renaissance   **645**

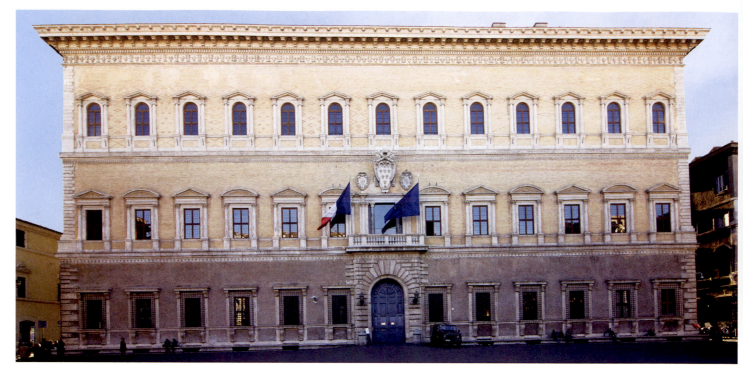

22-26 Antonio da Sangallo the Younger, *Palazzo Farnese* (looking southwest), Rome, Italy, 1517–1546; completed by Michelangelo Buonarroti, 1546–1550.

Pope Paul III commissioned this lavish palace when he was Cardinal Farnese. The facade features a rusticated central doorway and quoins and alternating triangular and segmental pediments.

In his modification of Bramante's plan, Michelangelo replaced the core of interlocking crosses in Bramante's design with a compact domed *Greek cross* inscribed in a square and fronted with a double-columned portico. Without destroying the centralizing features of Bramante's plan, Michelangelo, with a few strokes of the pen, converted its crystalline complexity into massive, cohesive unity. His treatment of the building's exterior further reveals his interest in creating a unified design. Because of later changes to the front of the church, the west (apse) end (FIG. 22-25) offers the best view of Michelangelo's style and intention. His design incorporated the colossal order, the two-story pilasters first seen in more reserved fashion in Alberti's Mantuan church of Sant'Andrea (FIG. 21-45). The giant pilasters seem to march around the undulating wall surfaces, confining the movement without interrupting it. The architectural sculpturing here extends up from the ground through the attic stories and into the drum and dome, unifying the whole building from base to summit.

The domed west end—as majestic as it is today and as influential as it has been on architecture throughout the centuries—is not quite as Michelangelo intended it. Originally, he had planned a dome with an ogival section, like the one Brunelleschi designed for Florence Cathedral (FIGS. 14-19, 21-29A, and 21-29B). But in his final version, he decided on a hemispherical dome to temper the verticality of the design of the lower stories and to establish a balance between dynamic and static elements. However, when Giacomo della Porta (FIG. 22-57) executed the dome (FIGS. 22-25 and 24-4) after Michelangelo's death, he restored the earlier high design, ignoring Michelangelo's later version. Giacomo's reasons were probably the same ones that had impelled Brunelleschi to use an ogival section for the Florentine dome—greater stability and ease of construction. The result is that the dome seems to rise from its base, rather than rest firmly on it—an effect Michelangelo might not have approved.

PALAZZO FARNESE Another architectural project Michelangelo took over at the request of Paul III was to complete the construction of the lavish palace (FIG. 22-26) the pope had commissioned when he was Cardinal Alessandro Farnese. The future pope had selected Antonio da Sangallo the Younger (1483–1546) as the architect. Antonio, the youngest of a family of architects, arrived in Rome around 1503 and became Bramante's draftsman and assistant. He is the perfect example of the professional architect. Indeed, his family constituted an architectural firm, often planning and drafting for other architects.

The broad, majestic front of the Palazzo Farnese asserts to the public the exalted station of a great family. It is significant that Paul chose to enlarge the original rather modest palace to its present grandiose form after his election as head of the Catholic Church in 1534—a reflection of his ambitions both for his family and for the papacy. Facing a spacious paved square, the facade is the very essence of princely dignity in architecture. The *quoins* (rusticated building corners) and cornice firmly anchor the rectangle of the smooth front, and lines of windows (the central row with alternating triangular and curved [*segmental*] pediments, in Bramante's fashion) mark a majestic march across it. The window frames are not flush with the wall, as in the Palazzo Medici-Riccardi (FIG. 21-35), but project from its surface, so instead of being a flat, thin plane, the facade is a spatially active three-dimensional mass. The rusticated doorway and second-story balcony, surmounted by the Farnese coat of arms, emphasize the central axis and bring the design's horizontal and vertical forces into harmony. Those centralizing features are absent from the palaces of Michelozzo (FIG. 21-35) and Alberti

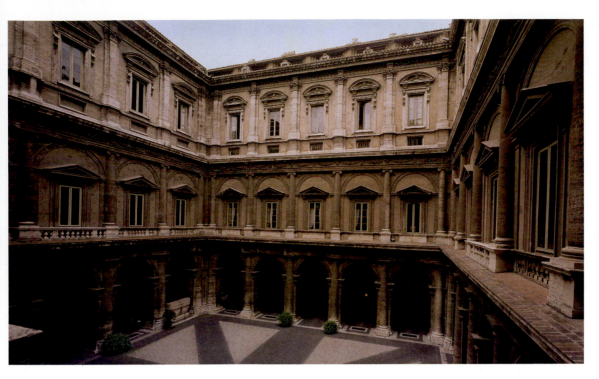

(FIG. 21-37). In the Palazzo Farnese, the portal is the external end of a central corridor axis running through the entire building and continuing in the garden beyond. Around this axis, Sangallo arranged the rooms with strict regularity.

The interior courtyard (FIG. **22-27**) displays stately column-framed arches on the first two levels, as in the Colosseum (FIG. 7-37). On the third level, Michelangelo, after Sangallo's death in 1546, incorporated his sophisticated variation on that theme (based in part on the Colosseum's fourth-story Corinthian pilasters), with overlapping pilasters replacing the weighty columns of Sangallo's design. The Palazzo Farnese set the standard for Italian Renaissance palaces and fully expresses the classical order, regularity, simplicity, and dignity of the High Renaissance architectural style.

Architecture: Venice

For centuries a major Mediterranean port, Venice served as the gateway to the Orient. After reaching the height of its commercial and political power during the 15th century, the city saw its fortunes decline in the 16th century. Even so, Venice and the Papal States were the only Italian sovereignties to retain their independence during the century of strife. Either France or Spain dominated all others. Although the discoveries in the New World and the economic shift from Italy to areas such as the Netherlands were largely responsible for the decline of Venice, even more immediate and pressing events drained its wealth and power. After their conquest of Constantinople (see page 258), the Turks began to vie with the Venetians for control of the eastern Mediterranean. The Ottoman Empire evolved into a constant threat to Venice. Early in the century, the European powers of the League of Cambrai also attacked the Italian port city. Formed and led by Pope Julius II, who coveted Venetian holdings on Italy's mainland, the league included Spain, France, and the Holy Roman Empire, in addition to the Papal States. Despite these challenges, Venice developed a flourishing, independent, and influential school of artists and architects.

ANDREA PALLADIO The chief architect of the Venetian Republic from 1570 until his death a decade later was Andrea di Pietro of Padua, known as ANDREA PALLADIO (1508–1580). (The surname derives from Pallas Athena, Greek goddess of wisdom, an appropriate reference for an architect schooled in the classical tradition of Alberti and Bramante.) Palladio began his career as a stonemason and decorative sculptor in Vicenza. At age 30, however, he turned to architecture, engineering, military science, and the ancient literature on architecture. In order to study the ancient buildings firsthand, Palladio made several trips to Rome. In 1556, he illustrated Daniele Barbaro's edition of Vitruvius's *De architectura* (see page 199) and later wrote his own treatise on architecture, *I quattro libri dell'architettura* (*The Four Books of Architecture*), originally published in 1570. That work had wide-ranging influence on succeeding generations of architects throughout Europe. Palladio's influence outside Italy, most significantly in England and in colonial America (see pages 787 and 789), was stronger and more lasting than any other architect's.

Palladio accrued his significant reputation from his many designs for *villas,* built on the Venetian mainland. Nineteen still stand, and they especially influenced later architects. The same spirit that prompted the ancient Romans to build villas in the countryside motivated a similar villa-building boom in 16th-century Venice, which, with its very limited space, was highly congested. But a longing for the countryside was not the only motive. Declining fortunes prompted the Venetians to develop their mainland possessions with new land investment and reclamation projects. Citizens who could afford to do so set themselves up as aristocratic farmers and developed swamps into productive agricultural land. The villas were thus the elegant residential centerpieces of income-producing farms surrounded by service outbuildings (like the much later American plantations, which emulated many aspects of Palladio's architectural style). Palladio generally arranged the outbuildings in long, low wings branching out from the main building and enclosing a large rectangular court area.

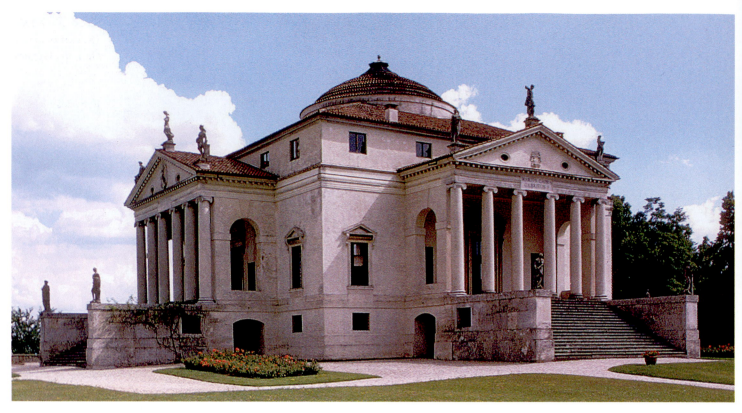

22-28 Andrea Palladio, Villa Rotonda (looking southwest), near Vicenza, Italy, ca. 1550–1570.

The Villa Rotonda has four identical facades, each one resembling a Roman temple with a columnar porch. In the center is a great dome-covered rotunda modeled on the Pantheon (FIG. 7-49).

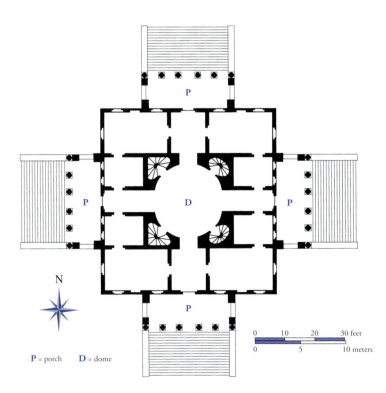

22-29 Andrea Palladio, plan of the Villa Rotonda, near Vicenza, Italy, ca. 1550–1570.

Andrea Palladio published an influential treatise on architecture in 1570. Consistent with his design theories, all parts of the Villa Rotonda relate to one another in terms of mathematical ratios.

VILLA ROTONDA Palladio's most famous villa, Villa Rotonda (FIG. 22-28), near Vicenza, is exceptional because the architect did not build it for an aspiring gentleman farmer but for a retired monsignor in the papal court in Rome, Paolo Almerico, who wanted a villa for social events. Palladio planned and designed Villa Rotonda, located on a hilltop, as a kind of *belvedere* (literally "beautiful view"; in architecture, a structure with a view of the countryside or the sea), without the usual wings of secondary buildings. It has a central plan (FIG. 22-29) featuring four identical facades with projecting porches, each of which resembles a Roman Ionic temple. In placing a traditional temple porch in front of a dome-covered unit, Palladio doubtless had the Pantheon (FIG. 7-49) in mind. (The villa's name "La Rotonda," proposed by Almerico, is a reference to Santa Maria Rotonda in Rome—the name of the Pantheon after its remodeling as a church with twin bell towers added to its ancient facade.) But, as Bramante did in his Tempietto (FIG. 22-21), Palladio transformed his model into a new design without parallel in antiquity, rotating the plan 45 degrees from the cardinal points in order for natural sunlight to illuminate every room. Each of the villa's four porches doubles as a columnar facade and a platform for enjoying a different view of the surrounding landscape. In this design, the central dome-covered rotunda logically functions as a circular reception area from which visitors may turn in any direction for the preferred view. The result is a building with functional parts systematically related to one another in terms of calculated mathematical relationships. Villa Rotonda embodies all the qualities of self-sufficiency and formal completeness that most Renaissance architects sought.

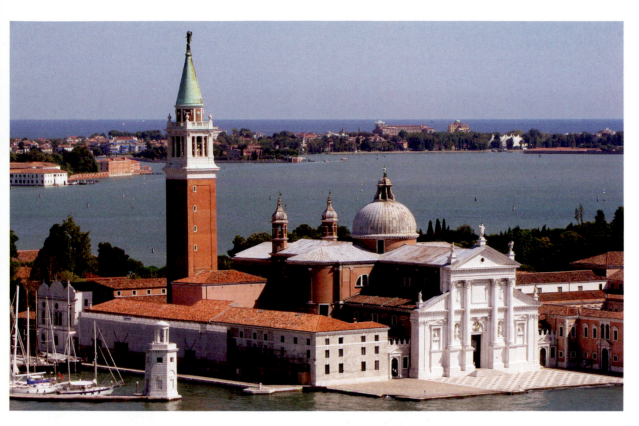

22-30 ANDREA PALLADIO, San Giorgio Maggiore (looking southeast), Venice, Italy, begun 1566.

Dissatisfied with earlier solutions to the problem of integrating a high central nave and lower aisles into a unified facade, Palladio superimposed a tall and narrow classical porch on a low broad one.

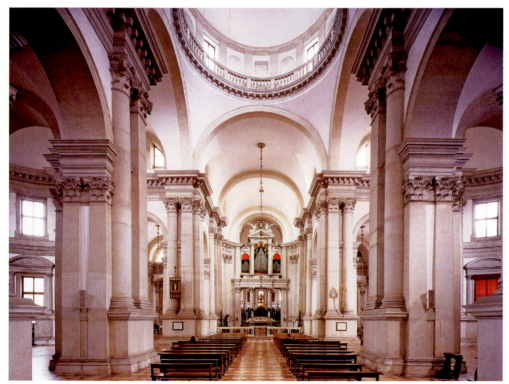

22-31 ANDREA PALLADIO, interior of San Giorgio Maggiore (looking east), Venice, Italy, begun 1566.

In contrast to the somewhat irrational intersection of two temple facades on the exterior of San Giorgio Maggiore, Palladio's interior is strictly logical, consistent with classical architectural theory.

SAN GIORGIO MAGGIORE One of the most dramatically placed buildings in Venice is San Giorgio Maggiore (FIGS. 22-30 and 22-31), directly across the Grand Canal from Piazza San Marco. Palladio began work on the church a few years before he succeeded JACOPO SANSOVINO (1486–1570; FIG. 22-31A) as Venice's official

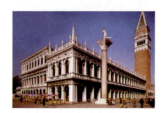

22-31A SANSOVINO, Mint and Library, Venice, begun 1536.

architect. Dissatisfied with earlier solutions to the problem of integrating a high central nave and lower aisles into a unified facade design, Palladio solved it by superimposing a tall and narrow classical porch on a low broad one. This solution reflects the building's interior arrangement (dome-covered nave and single-story aisles) and in that sense is strictly logical, but the intersection of two temple facades is irrational and ambiguous, consistent with contemporaneous developments in Mannerist architecture (see page 668). Palladio's design also created the illusion of three-dimensional depth, an effect intensified by the strong projection of the central columns and the shadows they cast. The play of shadow across the building's surfaces, its reflection in the water, and its gleaming white against sea and sky create a remarkably colorful effect. The interior of the church lacks the ambiguity of the facade and exhibits strong roots in High Renaissance architectural style. Light floods the interior and crisply defines the contours of the rich wall moldings with their archaeologically correct profiles, an exemplar of classical architectural theory.

Venetian Painting

The leading Venetian painter at the turn of the century was Giovanni Bellini (FIG. 21-40). Bellini developed a coloristic oil painting style that became the foundation of the distinctive High Renaissance style of the maritime republic, setting Cinquecento Venetian art apart from Florentine and Roman art.

SAN ZACCARIA ALTARPIECE Bellini earned great recognition for his many Madonnas, which he painted both in half-length (with or without accompanying saints) on small devotional panels and in full-length on monumental altarpieces representing a *sacra conversazione* (holy conversation). In the sacra conversazione, which became a popular theme for religious paintings from the middle of the 15th century on, saints from different epochs occupy the same space and seem to converse either with each other or with the audience. (Raphael employed much the same concept in his *School of Athens* [FIG. 22-9], where he gathered Greek philosophers of different eras.)

Bellini carried on the tradition in the *San Zaccaria Altarpiece* (FIG. **22-32**), which he painted in 1505, already in his 70s. (He died in his mid-80s in 1516. Bellini's long career explains in part his profound influence on the next generation of Venetian painters.) In an architectural setting that Bellini carefully coordinated with the church's real columns, pilasters, and arches, the Virgin Mary sits enthroned, holding the Christ Child, with saints flanking her. Attributes aid the identification of all the saints: Saint Lucy holds a tray with her plucked-out eyes displayed on it; Peter, his key and book; Catherine, the palm of martyrdom and a broken wheel; and Jerome, a book (representing his translation of the Bible into Latin). At the foot of the throne sits an angel playing a viol. The painting radiates a feeling of serenity and spiritual calm. Viewers derive this sense less from the figures (no interaction occurs among them) than from Bellini's harmonious and balanced presentation of color and light. Line is not the chief agent of form, as it generally is in paintings produced in Rome and Florence. Indeed, outlines dissolve in light and shadow. Glowing color produces a soft radiance that envelops the forms with an atmospheric haze and enhances their majestic serenity.

22-32 GIOVANNI BELLINI, *Madonna and Child with Saints* (*San Zaccaria Altarpiece*), 1505. Oil on wood transferred to canvas, 16' 5½" × 7' 9". San Zaccaria, Venice.

In this *sacra conversazione* uniting saints from different eras, Bellini created a feeling of serenity and spiritual calm through the harmonious and balanced presentation of color and light.

FEAST OF THE GODS Painted a decade later, *Feast of the Gods* (FIG. **22-33**) is one of Bellini's acknowledged masterpieces. By this time, the aged master was already looking to the work of some of his students for inspiration. *Feast of the Gods* draws upon the poetic "Arcadian" landscapes of Giorgione (FIG. 22-34). Derived from Arcadia, a region in southern Greece, the term *Arcadian* referred, by the time of the Renaissance, to an idyllic place of rustic peace and simplicity. After Giorgione's premature death, Bellini embraced his student's interests and, in *Feast of the Gods,* developed a new kind of mythological painting. The duke of Ferrara, Alfonso d'Este (r. 1505–1534), commissioned this work for the Camerino d'Alabastro (Alabaster Room), a private apartment in the Palazzo Ducale complex. Alfonso hired four painters—Bellini, Titian (Bellini's greatest student; FIGS. 22-35 to 22-41), Raphael, and Fra Bartolommeo (1472–1517) of Florence—to provide four paintings of related mythological subjects for the room, carefully selected for the duke by the humanist scholar Mario Equicola (1470–1515). Both Raphael and Fra Bartolommeo died before fulfilling the commission.

For his painting, Bellini drew some of the figures from the standard repertoire of Greco-Roman art—most notably, the nymph carrying a vase on her head and the sleeping nymph in the lower

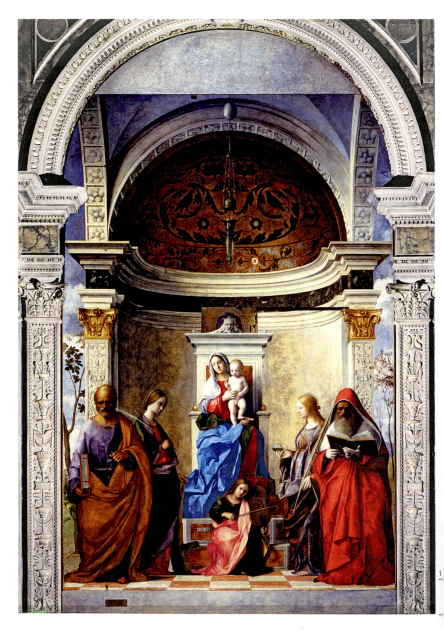

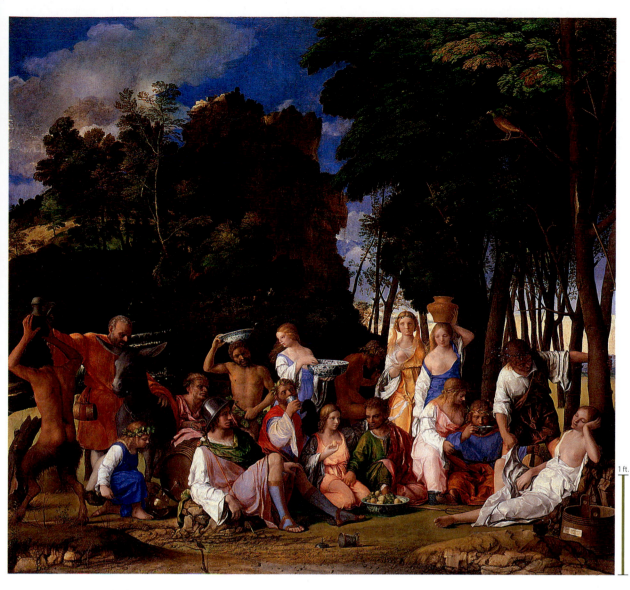

22-33 GIOVANNI BELLINI, *Feast of the Gods,* from the Camerino d'Alabastro, Palazzo Ducale, Ferrara, Italy, 1514; repainted in part by TITIAN, 1529. Oil on canvas, 5' 7" × 6' 2". National Gallery of Art, Washington (Widener Collection).

In *Feast of the Gods,* based on Ovid's *Fasti,* Bellini developed a new kind of mythological painting in which the Olympian deities appear as peasants enjoying a picnic in the soft afternoon light.

1 ft.

right corner. But Bellini's Olympian gods appear as peasants enjoying a picnic in a shady glade. The ancient literary source was the *Fasti* (1:391–440; 6:319–348) by the Roman poet Ovid, who described banquets of gods. In Bellini's painting, satyrs attend the gods, nymphs bring jugs of wine, and couples engage in love play. At the far right, Priapus lifts the dress of the sleeping nymph with exposed breast. (All four paintings in the Camerino centered on Venus or Bacchus, the Roman gods of love and wine.) The mellow light of a long afternoon glows softly around the gathering, caressing the surfaces of colorful fabrics, smooth flesh, and polished metal. Here, Bellini communicated the delight that the Venetian school took in the beauty of texture revealed by the full resources of gently and subtly harmonized color. Behind the warm, lush tones of the figures, a background of cool green tree-filled glades extends into the distance. At the right, a screen of trees—painted in 1529 by Titian—creates a verdant shelter. The atmosphere is idyllic, a lush countryside providing a setting for the never-ending pleasure of the immortal gods.

With Bellini, Venetian art became the great complement of the schools of Florence and Rome. The Venetians' instrument was color, that of the Florentines and Romans sculpturesque form. Scholars often distill the contrast between these two approaches down to *colorito* (colored or painted) versus *disegno* (drawing and design).

Whereas most central Italian artists emphasized careful design preparation based on preliminary drawing (see "Renaissance Drawings," page 628), Venetian artists focused on color and the process of paint application. Vasari, who held the artists of his native Florence in greater esteem than Venice's, disapprovingly drew attention to the different working methods of the Venetians and attributed them largely to Giorgione (FIG. 22-34):

> Giorgione of Castelfranco . . . made use of live and natural objects and copied them as best he knew how with colors, tinting them with the crude and soft colors that Nature displays, without making preliminary drawings since he was firmly convinced that painting alone with its colors, and without any other preliminary study of designs on paper, was the truest and best method of working.[9]

In addition, the general thematic focus of Venetian artists differed from those of Florence and Rome. The Venetians painted the poetry of the senses and delighted in nature's beauty and the pleasures of humanity. Florentine and Roman artists gravitated toward more intellectual themes—the epic of humanity, the masculine virtues, the grandeur of the ideal, and the lofty conceptions of religion involving the heroic and sublime. Much of the history of later Western art involves a dialogue between these two traditions.

22-34 Giorgione da Castelfranco, *The Tempest*, ca. 1509–1510. Oil on canvas, 2' 8$\frac{1}{4}$" × 2' 4$\frac{3}{4}$". Galleria dell'Accademia, Venice.

The subject of this painting featuring a nude woman in a lush landscape beneath a stormy sky is uncertain, contributing, perhaps intentionally, to the painting's intriguing air of mystery.

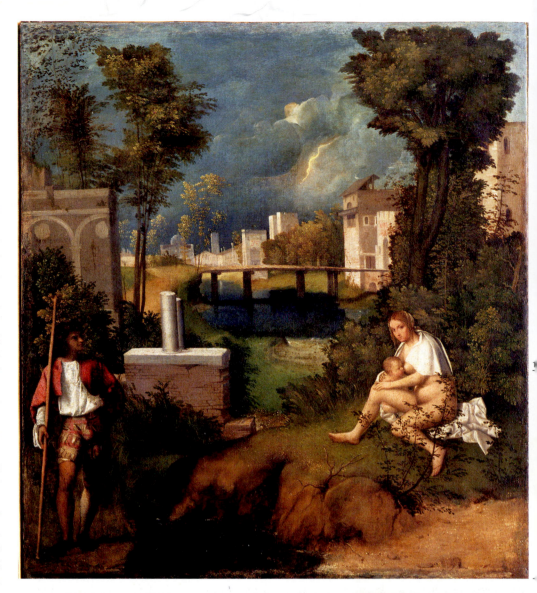

GIORGIONE Describing Venetian art as "poetic" is particularly appropriate, given the development of *poesia*, or painting meant to operate in a manner similar to poetry. Both classical and Renaissance poetry inspired Venetian artists, and their paintings focused on the lyrical and sensual. Thus, in many Venetian artworks, identifying specific subjects is impossible. That is certainly the case with *The Tempest* (FIG. **22-34**), a painting that continues to defy interpretation. It is the greatest work attributed to the short-lived Giorgione da Castelfranco (ca. 1477–1510), the Venetian artist who deserves much of the credit for developing the poetic manner of painting and whose lush landscapes served as an inspiration for his teacher, Bellini, in works such as *Feast of the Gods*. In Giorgione's *Tempest*, stormy skies and lightning in the middle background threaten the tranquility of the pastoral setting, however. And, in contrast to Bellini, Giorgione pushed off to both sides the few human figures depicted—a young woman nursing a baby in the right foreground and, on the left, a man with a staff.

Giorgione painted *The Tempest* for a wealthy private collector, Gabriele Vendramin, and much scholarly debate has centered on the painting's subject, fueled by X-rays of the canvas, which revealed that the Venetian master altered many of the details as

22-35 Titian, *Pastoral Symphony*, ca. 1508–1511. Oil on canvas, 3' 7$\frac{1}{4}$" × 4' 6$\frac{1}{4}$". Musée du Louvre, Paris.

Venetian art conjures poetry. In this painting, Titian so eloquently evoked the pastoral mood that the inability to decipher the picture's meaning is not distressing. The mood and rich color are enough.

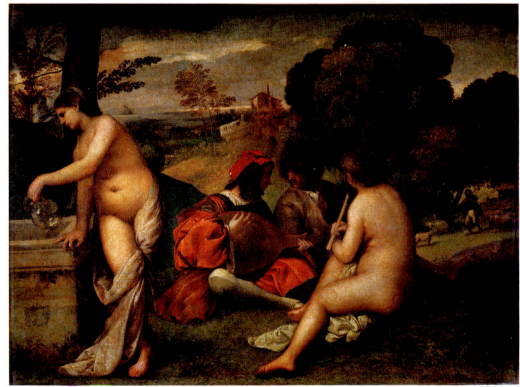

work progressed. Most notably, a seated nude woman originally occupied the position where Giorgione subsequently placed the standing man, whose elegant garb is out of place in this rustic setting. The changes the painter made have led many art historians to believe that Giorgione did not intend the painting to have a definitive narrative, which is appropriate for a Venetian poetic rendering. Other scholars have suggested various mythological and biblical narratives. The uncertainty about the subject contributes to the painting's intriguing air, however.

TITIAN Giorgione's masterful handling of light and color and his interest in landscape, poetry, and music—Vasari reported that he was an accomplished lutenist and singer—influenced not only his much older yet constantly inquisitive teacher, Bellini, but also his younger contemporary, Tiziano Vecelli, called TITIAN (ca. 1490–1576) in English. Indeed, a masterpiece long attributed to Giorgione—*Pastoral Symphony* (FIG. 22-35)—is now widely believed to be an early work of Titian. Out of dense shadow emerge the soft forms of figures and landscape. Titian, a supreme colorist and master of the oil medium, cast a mood of tranquil reverie and dreaminess over the entire scene, evoking the landscape of a lost but never forgotten paradise. As in Giorgione's *Tempest,* the theme is as enigmatic as the lighting. Two nude women occupy the foreground. The seated one resembles the woman in *The Tempest,* but seen from behind. Accompanying them are two clothed young men, the lute player wearing elegant city clothes, the other dressed like a shepherd. The four figures occupy a bountiful landscape. In the middle ground is a shepherd and his sheep. In the distance, a villa crowns a hill.

Titian so eloquently evoked the pastoral mood that the viewer does not find the uncertainty about the picture's precise meaning distressing. The mood is enough. The musician symbolizes the poet. The pipes and lute symbolize his poetry. The two women may be thought of as the young men's invisible inspiration, their muses. One turns to lift water from the sacred well of poetic inspiration. Smoky shadow softly models the voluptuous bodies of the women. The fullness of their figures became the standard in Venetian art and contributes to their effect as poetic personifications of nature's abundance. Venetian painters, unlike their counterparts in Florence and Rome, generally painted directly on the canvas without preparatory drawings. Their nudes are neither precise anatomical studies nor idealized forms based on mathematics and geometry.

ASSUMPTION OF THE VIRGIN On Bellini's death in 1516, the Republic of Venice appointed Titian as its official painter. Shortly thereafter, the prior of the Franciscan basilica of Santa Maria Gloriosa dei Frari commissioned Titian to paint a gigantic altarpiece (nearly 23 feet high) for the high altar of the church. In *Assumption of the Virgin* (FIG. 22-36), a fitting theme for the shrine of the "glorious Saint Mary," Titian's remarkable coloristic sense and his ability to convey light

through color are again on display. The subject is the ascent of the Virgin to Heaven on a great white cloud borne aloft by putti. Above, golden clouds, so luminous that they seem to glow and radiate light into the church, envelop the Virgin, whose head is on the vertical axis of the composition and is the center of a circle formed by the arched frame and the U-shaped band of clouds. God the Father appears above, slightly off-center, awaiting Mary with open arms. Below, closest to the viewer, over-life-size apostles gesticulate wildly as they witness the glorious event. Many have their backs to the worshipers, who join the apostles as observers looking up with them at the Virgin's miraculous ascent. Through his mastery of the oil medium—fresco was not a good choice for Venetian churches because of the dampness and salinity of this city with saltwater streets—Titian used vibrant color to infuse the image with intensity and amplify the drama.

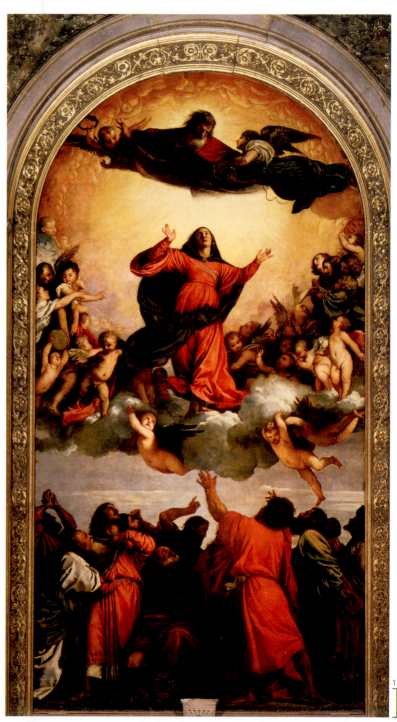

22-36 TITIAN, *Assumption of the Virgin,* 1515–1518. Oil on wood, 22' 7½" × 11' 10". Santa Maria Gloriosa dei Frari, Venice.

Titian won renown for his skill in conveying light through color. In this dramatic depiction of the Virgin Mary's ascent to Heaven, the golden clouds seem to glow and radiate light into the church.

1 ft.

PESARO *MADONNA* A year after installing *Assumption of the Virgin* in the main altar of the Venetian church of the Frari, Titian received a commission to paint *Madonna of the Pesaro Family* (FIG. **22-37**) for the same church. Jacopo Pesaro (d. 1547), bishop of Paphos in Cyprus and commander of the papal fleet, had led a successful expedition in 1502 against the Turks during the Venetian-Turkish war. He dedicated a family chapel in Santa Maria Gloriosa and donated Titian's altarpiece in gratitude. In a stately sunlit setting in what may be the Madonna's palace in Heaven, Mary receives the commander, who kneels dutifully at the foot of her throne. A soldier (Saint George?) behind the commander carries a banner with the *escutcheons* (shields with coats of arms) of the Borgia pope, Alexander VI, and of Pesaro. Behind him is a turbaned Turk, a prisoner of war of the Christian forces. Saint Peter appears on the steps of the throne, and Saint Francis introduces other Pesaro family members,

who kneel solemnly in the right foreground. (All of the kneeling figures are male. Italian depictions of donors in this era typically excluded women and children.) Thus Titian entwined the human and the heavenly, depicting the Madonna and saints honoring the achievements of a specific man. A quite worldly transaction takes place (albeit beneath a heavenly cloud bearing angels) between a queen and her court and loyal servants, consistent with Renaissance protocol and courtly splendor.

A prime characteristic of High Renaissance painting is the massing of monumental figures, singly and in groups, within a weighty and majestic architecture. But here Titian did not compose a horizontal and symmetrical arrangement, as did Leonardo in *Last Supper* (FIG. 22-4) and Raphael in *School of Athens* (FIG. 22-9). Rather, he placed the figures on a steep diagonal, positioning the Madonna, the focus of the composition, well off the central axis. Titian drew attention to her with the perspective lines, the inclination of the figures, and the directional lines of gaze and gesture. The banner that forms a diagonal accent at the left beautifully brings the design into equilibrium, balancing the rightward and upward tendencies of its main direction. This kind of composition is more dynamic than most High Renaissance examples and foreshadowed a new kind of pictorial design—one built on movement rather than rest. It also anticipated some of the most daring illusionistic mural and ceiling paintings of the Baroque era in taking the viewer's position into consideration (see page 720). The Pesaro *Madonna* is on the wall in the left aisle of the Frari church. Worshipers approach the painting from the left and look up at the Virgin in the same way Jacopo Pesaro does. Then, if they turn to the right and look at the apse, they see Titian's *Assumption of the Virgin* (FIG. 22-36).

BACCHUS AND ARIADNE After the deaths of Raphael and Fra Bartolommeo, Titian took over their commissions to paint *bacchanal* scenes for Alfonso d'Este's Camerino d'Alabastro, in addition to his own assignment. Titian also contributed the landscape background to Bellini's *Feast of the Gods* (FIG. 22-33). Completed in 1523, *Meeting of Bacchus and Ariadne* (FIG. **22-38**), based on an ancient Latin poem by Catullus, is a roughly 6-foot-square canvas in which Bacchus, accompanied by a boisterous group, arrives on the island of Naxos in a leopard-drawn chariot to save Ariadne, whom Theseus had abandoned there. Consistent with the mythological subject, Titian looked to classical art for models and derived one of the figures, the snake-entwined satyr, from the recently unearthed *Laocoön* (FIG. 5-89), a marble statue that also made an indelible impression on Michelangelo and many others. Titian's rich and luminous colors, especially his lavish use of ultramarine, the most expensive oil pigment, add greatly to the sensuous appeal of the painting, making it perfect for what Alfonso called his "pleasure chamber."

VENUS OF URBINO In 1538, at the height of his powers, Titian painted the so-called *Venus of Urbino* (FIG. **22-39**), probably for Guidobaldo II, who became the duke of Urbino the following year (r. 1539–1574). The title (given to the painting later) elevates to the status of classical mythology what is probably a representation of a sensual Italian woman in her bedchamber. Whether the nude woman is divine or mortal, Titian based his version on an earlier (and pioneering) painting of Venus (not illustrated) by Giorgione. Here, Titian established the compositional elements and the standard for paintings of the reclining female nude. This "Venus" reclines on the gentle slope of her luxurious pillowed couch. Her softly rounded body contrasts with the sharp vertical edge of the curtain behind her, which serves to direct the viewer's attention to her left hand

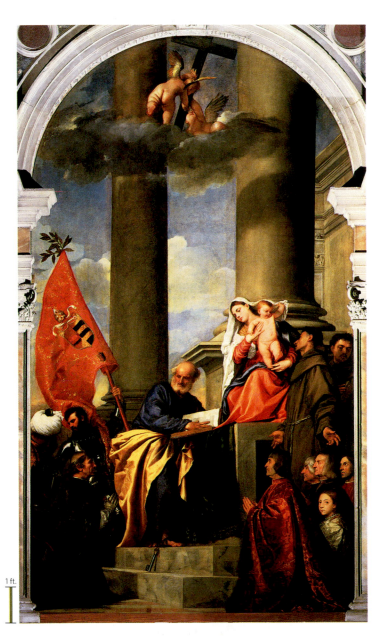

1 ft.

22-37 TITIAN, *Madonna of the Pesaro Family,* 1519–1526. Oil on canvas, 15' 11" × 8' 10". Pesaro Chapel, Santa Maria Gloriosa dei Frari, Venice.

In this dynamic composition foreshadowing a new kind of pictorial design, Titian placed the figures on a steep diagonal, positioning the Madonna, the focus of the composition, well off the central axis.

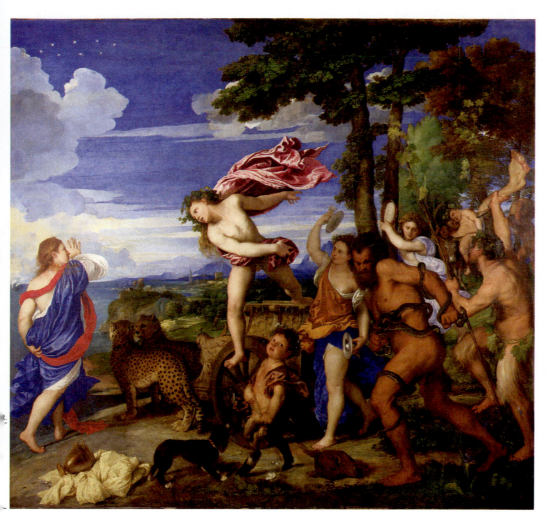

22-38 TITIAN, *Meeting of Bacchus and Ariadne,* from the Camerino d'Alabastro, Palazzo Ducale, Ferrara, Italy, 1522–1523. Oil on canvas, 5' 9" × 6' 3". National Gallery, London.

Titian's rich and luminous colors add greatly to the sensuous appeal of this mythological painting in which he based one of the figures on the recently unearthed *Laocoön* (FIG. 5-89).

a chest, apparently searching for garments (Renaissance households stored clothing in carved wood chests called *cassoni*) to clothe their reclining nude mistress. Beyond them, a smaller vista opens into a landscape. Titian masterfully constructed the view backward into the room and the division of the space into progressively smaller units.

As in other Venetian paintings, color plays a prominent role in *Venus of Urbino.* The red tones of the matron's skirt and the muted reds of the tapestries against the neutral whites of the matron's sleeves and the kneeling girl's gown echo the deep Venetian reds set off against the pale neutral whites of the linen and the warm ivory gold of the flesh. The viewer must study the picture carefully to realize the subtlety of color planning. For instance, the two deep reds (in the foreground cushions and in the background skirt) play a critical role in the composition as a gauge of distance and as indicators of an implied diagonal opposed to the real one of the reclining figure. Here, Titian used color not simply to record surface appearance but also to organize his placement of forms.

and pelvis as well as to divide the foreground from the background. At the woman's feet is a slumbering lapdog—where Cupid would be if this were Venus (compare FIG. 7-59). In the right background, near the window opening onto a landscape, two servants bend over

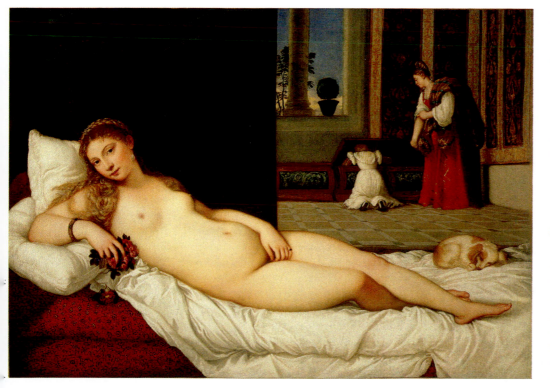

22-39 TITIAN, *Venus of Urbino,* 1536–1538. Oil on canvas, 3' 11" × 5' 5". Galleria degli Uffizi, Florence.

Titian established oil-based pigment on canvas as the preferred painting medium in Western art. Here, he also set the standard for representations of the reclining female nude, whether divine or mortal.

High and Late Renaissance **655**

ART AND SOCIETY

Women in the Renaissance Art World

The Renaissance art world was decidedly male-dominated. Few women could become professional artists because of the many obstacles they faced. In particular, training practices requiring residence in a master's house (see "Artists' Guilds," page 422) prevented women from gaining the necessary experience to establish their own studios and attract patrons. In addition, social proscriptions, such as those barring women from drawing from nude models, hampered an aspiring woman artist's advancement through the accepted avenues of artistic training in Renaissance Europe.

Still, some determined Renaissance women surmounted these barriers and produced not only considerable bodies of work but earned enviable reputations as well. One was Sofonisba Anguissola (FIG. 22-47), the first Italian woman to have ascended to the level of international art celebrity. Lavinia Fontana (1552–1614; FIG. 22-40A) also achieved notable success, and her paintings constitute the largest surviving body of work by any woman artist before 1700.

Perhaps more challenging for women than the road to becoming a professional painter was the mastery of sculpture, made more difficult by the physical demands of the medium. Yet Properzia de' Rossi (ca. 1490–1530)

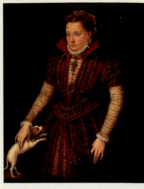

22-40A Fontana, *Portrait of a Noblewoman,* ca. 1580.

established herself as a professional sculptor and was the only woman artist that Vasari included in his *Lives.* Active in the early 16th century, she died of the plague in 1530, bringing her promising career to an early end.

Beyond the realm of art production, Renaissance women exerted significant influence as art patrons—and probably to a much greater degree than the available evidence suggests, because women often wielded their influence and decision-making power behind the scenes. Many of them attained their positions through marriage. Their power was thus indirect and provisional, based on their husbands' wealth and status. Thus documentation of the networks within which women patrons operated and of the processes they used to exert power in a society dominated by men is meager compared to what is known about male patrons.

Nonetheless, there can be no doubt that one of the most important Renaissance art patrons, male or female, was Isabella d'Este (1474–1539), the marquess of Mantua, one of the leading art centers of Renaissance Italy (see page 616). The daughter of Ercole d'Este, duke of Ferrara (r. 1471–1505), and brought up in the cultured princely court there, Isabella married Marquis Francesco Gonzaga of Mantua in 1490. The marriage gave Isabella access to the position and wealth necessary to become a major force in the Renaissance art world. An avid collector, she enlisted the aid of agents who scoured Italy for appealing artworks. Isabella did not limit her collection to painting and sculpture but included ceramics, glassware, gems, cameos, medals, classical texts, musical manuscripts, and musical instruments. She also commissioned several portraits of herself from the most esteemed artists of her day—Leonardo da Vinci, Andrea Mantegna, and Titian (FIG. 22-40). The detail and complexity of many of Isabella's contracts with artists reveal her insistence on control over the diverse series of works she paid for.

Other Renaissance women also positioned themselves as serious art patrons. One was Caterina Sforza (1462–1509), daughter of Galeazzo Maria Sforza (heir to the duchy of Milan), who married Girolamo Riario (1443–1488) in 1484. The death of her husband, lord of Imola and count of Forlì, gave Sforza, who survived him by two decades, access to power denied most women. Another female art patron was Lucrezia Tornabuoni (1425–1482), who married Piero di Cosimo de' Medici (1416–1469), one of many Medici, both men and women, who earned reputations as lavish art patrons.

Further archival investigation of women's roles in Renaissance Italy undoubtedly will produce more evidence of how women established themselves as patrons and artists and the extent to which they contributed to the careers of various artists and the development of Renaissance art in general.

22-40 Titian, *Isabella d'Este,* 1534–1536. Oil on canvas, 3' 4$\frac{1}{8}$" × 2' 1$\frac{3}{16}$". Kunsthistorisches Museum, Vienna.

Isabella d'Este, marquess of Mantua, was one of the most powerful women of the Renaissance era. When, at age 60, she hired Titian to paint her portrait, she insisted that the artist depict her in her 20s.

ARTISTS ON ART
Palma il Giovane on Titian

An important change occurring in the mid-16th century was the almost universal adoption of canvas, primed with a coat of white to furnish a smooth surface, in place of wood panels for paintings. The most famous painter of the time was Titian, and his works established oil-based pigment on canvas as the standard medium of the Western pictorial tradition thereafter. Palma il Giovane, one of Titian's students, who completed the *Pietà* (FIG. 22-41) that Titian intended for his tomb in Santa Maria Gloriosa dei Frari in Venice, wrote a valuable account of his teacher's working methods and of how Titian used the new medium to great advantage:

> Titian [employed] a great mass of colors, which served . . . as a base for the compositions. . . . I too have seen some of these, formed with bold strokes made with brushes laden with colors, sometimes of a pure red earth, which he used, so to speak, for a middle tone, and at other times of white lead; and with the same brush tinted with red, black and yellow he formed a highlight; and observing these principles he made the promise of an exceptional figure appear in four brushstrokes. . . . Having constructed these precious foundations he used to turn his pictures to the wall and leave them there without looking at them, sometimes for several months. When he wanted to apply his brush again he would examine them with the utmost rigor . . . to see if he could find any faults. . . . In this way, working on the figures and revising them, he brought them to the most perfect symmetry that the beauty of art and nature can reveal. . . . [T]hus he gradually covered those quintessential forms with living flesh, bringing them by many stages to a state in which they lacked only the breath of life. He never painted a figure all at once and . . . in the last stages he painted more with his fingers than his brushes.*

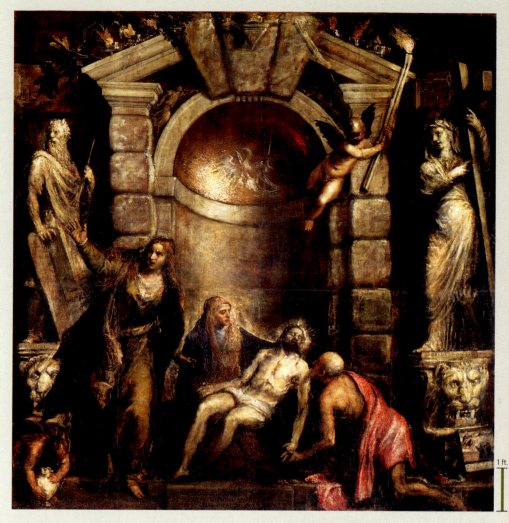

22-41 TITIAN and PALMA IL GIOVANE, *Pietà*, ca. 1570–1576. Oil on canvas, 11' 6" × 12' 9". Galleria dell'Accademia, Venice.

In this late work characterized by broad brushstrokes and a thick impasto, Titian portrayed himself as Saint Jerome kneeling before the dead Christ. Titian intended the work for his own tomb.

1 ft.

*Francesco Valcanover, *Titian: Prince of Painters* (Venice: Marsilio, 1990), 23–24.

ISABELLA D'ESTE Titian was also a highly esteemed portraitist. More than 50 portraits by his hand survive, reflecting the great demand for his services by wealthy patrons desirous of immortalizing themselves. One of Titian's best portraits is of Isabella d'Este (FIG. 22-40), one of the most prominent women of the Renaissance (see "Women in the Renaissance Art World," page 656). Isabella was the sister of Alfonso d'Este, for whom Titian painted three mythological scenes for the Ferrara ducal palace. At 16, she married Francesco Gonzaga, marquis of Mantua (1466–1519; see page 616), and through her patronage of art and music was instrumental in developing the Mantuan court into an important cultural center. Portraits by Titian generally emphasize his psychological reading of the subject's head and hands. Thus here Titian sharply highlighted Isabella's face, whereas her black dress fades into the undefined darkness of the background. The unseen light source also illuminates the sitter's hands, and Titian painted the sleeves of Isabella's elegant gown with incredible detail to further draw viewers' attention to her hands. This portrait reveals not only Titian's skill but the patron's wish too. Painted when Isabella was 60 years old, the portrait depicts her in her 20s—at her specific request. Titian used an earlier likeness of her as his guide, but his portrait is no copy. Rather, *Isabella d'Este* is a distinctive portrayal of the artist's poised and self-assured patron that owes little to its model.

PIETÀ As Michelangelo had done late in his life, Titian began to contemplate death and salvation, and around 1570 he decided to create a memorial for his tomb. Titian, too, chose *Pietà* (FIG. 22-41) as the theme, albeit for a painting, not a statuary group, as in Michelangelo's case (FIG. 22-20). Intended for the altar of his burial chapel in the right aisle of Santa Maria Gloriosa dei Frari in Venice, which housed two of his earlier altarpieces (FIGS. 22-36 and 22-37), Titian's *Pietà* remained unfinished when he died of the plague in 1576. His assistant, Jacopo Negretti, known as PALMA IL GIOVANE (1548–1628)—Palma the Younger—completed the painting.

Titian set the scene of grief over Christ's death in a rusticated niche reminiscent of the bays of Sansovino's Venetian Mint (FIG. 22-31A, *left*). The Virgin cradles her son's body, while Mary Magdalene runs forward with her right arm raised in a gesture of extreme distress. (Echoing her form, but in reverse, is the torch-carrying angel added by Palma.) The other penitent mourner is Saint Jerome, seen from behind kneeling at the Savior's side. His head has the features of the aged, balding Titian—another parallel with Michelangelo's *Pietà*. Both artists apparently wanted to portray themselves touching Christ's body, hoping for salvation.

For this huge (roughly 12-foot-square) canvas, Titian employed one of his favorite compositional devices (compare FIG. 22-37), creating a bold diagonal movement beginning at Jerome's feet and leading through Christ, the Virgin, and Mary Magdalene to the statue of Moses with the Ten Commandments at the left. (The other statue represents Faith. The votive painting leaning against its pedestal depicts Titian and his son Orazio, who also died of the plague in 1576, praying before another *Pietà*.) But unlike Titian's early and mature works, in which he used smooth and transparent oil glazes, this *Pietà* features broken brushstrokes and rough, uneven patches of pigment built up like paste (*impasto*) so that they catch the light, like his other late paintings. Many Baroque painters, especially Peter Paul Rubens (FIGS. 25-2 to 25-4) and Rembrandt van Rijn (FIGS. 25-12 to 25-15A), subsequently adopted Titian's innovative and highly expressive manner of applying thick paint to canvas (see "Palma il Giovane on Titian," page 657).

MANNERISM

The High Renaissance styles of Rome, Florence, and Venice dominated Italian painting, sculpture, and architecture for most of the 16th century, but as early as the 1520s, leading artists of the post-Leonardo, post-Raphael generation began to explore new modes of artistic expression. Art historians long ago dubbed the work of these artists *Mannerist,* a term derived from the Italian word *maniera,* meaning "style" or "manner," which in turn derives from *mano* ("hand"). In the field of art history, the term *style* usually refers to a characteristic or representative mode, especially of an artist or period (for example, Titian's style or Gothic style; see page 3). Style can also refer to an absolute quality of fashion (for example, someone "has style" or "is stylish"). The first art historians to adopt the term argued that Mannerism's style (or representative mode) was characterized by style (being stylish, cultured, elegant).

The term is unfortunate in many respects. First, when originally applied to the artworks examined in the next section, "Mannerism" had negative connotations, just as "Gothic" did when first used by Giorgio Vasari (see page 374). Mannerist works are not, however, of inferior quality compared to High Renaissance works, although they are unquestionably different. Second, Mannerism is not a unified style. It encompasses diverse contemporaneous personal styles, even if they all represent a break from High Renaissance norms. Nonetheless, "Mannerism," like "Gothic," is too firmly entrenched in art history to be discarded.

Painting

What specifically constitutes Mannerism in art? Among the features most closely associated with Mannerism is artifice. Of course, all art involves artifice, in the sense that art is not "natural." It is something fashioned by human hands. But many artists, including High Renaissance painters such as Leonardo and Raphael, chose to conceal that artifice by using devices such as perspective and shading to make their representations of the world look natural. In contrast, Mannerist painters consciously revealed the constructed nature of their art. In other words, Renaissance artists generally strove to create art that appeared natural, whereas Mannerist artists were less inclined to disguise the contrived nature of art production. This is why artifice is a central feature of discussions about Mannerism, and why Mannerist works can seem, appropriately, "mannered." The conscious display of artifice in Mannerism often reveals itself

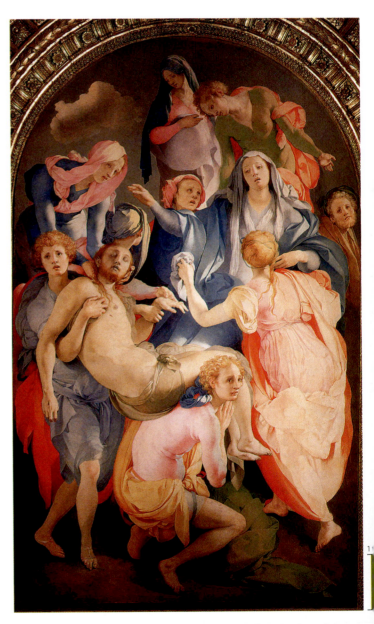

22-42 JACOPO DA PONTORMO, *Entombment of Christ,* Capponi chapel, Santa Felicità, Florence, Italy, 1525–1528. Oil on wood, 10' 3" × 6' 4".

Mannerist paintings such as this one represent a departure from the compositions of the earlier Renaissance. Instead of concentrating masses in the center of the painting, Pontormo left a void.

in imbalanced compositions and unusual complexities, both visual and conceptual. Ambiguous space, departures from expected conventions, and unusual presentations of traditional themes also surface frequently in Mannerist art.

PONTORMO *Entombment of Christ* (FIG. **22-42**) by the Florentine painter Jacopo Carucci, known as JACOPO DA PONTORMO (1494–1557) after his birthplace, exhibits almost all the stylistic features characteristic of Mannerism's early phase in painting—as does *Fall of the Rebel Angels* (FIG. **22-42A**) by Pontormo's older contemporary DOMENICO BECCAFUMI (1481–1551). Christ's descent from the cross and subsequent entombment had frequently been depicted in art, and Pontormo exploited the familiarity 16th-century viewers would have had by playing off their expectations. For example, he omitted from the painting both the cross and the tomb, and consequently scholars debate whether the artist meant to represent Christ's descent from the cross or his entombment. Also, instead of presenting the action

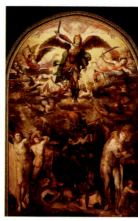

🔗 **22-42A** BECCAFUMI, *Fall of the Rebel Angels*, ca. 1524.

as taking place across the perpendicular picture plane, as Rogier van der Weyden did (FIG. 20-9; compare FIG. 14-9), Pontormo rotated the conventional figural groups along a vertical axis. Several of the figures seem to float in the air. Those that touch the ground do so on tiptoes, enhancing the sense of weightlessness. Unlike High Renaissance artists, who concentrated their masses in the center of the painting, Pontormo left a void. This emptiness accentuates the grouping of hands filling that hole, calling attention to the void—symbolic of loss and grief. The artist enhanced the painting's ambiguity with the curiously anxious glances that the figures cast in all directions. (The bearded young man at the upper right who looks out at the viewer is probably a self-portrait of Pontormo.) Many of the figures have elastically elongated limbs and undersized heads, and move unnaturally. For example, the torso of the foreground figure bends in an anatomically impossible way. The contrasting colors, primarily light blues and pinks, add to the dynamism and complexity of the work. The painting represents a pronounced departure from the balanced, harmoniously structured compositions of the High Renaissance.

PARMIGIANINO Nine years younger than Pontormo, Girolamo Francesco Maria Mazzola of Parma, known as PARMIGIANINO (1503–1540), achieved a reputation as a gifted painter while still in his teens, and at age 21, he made a deep impression on Pope Clement VII with an unconventional self-portrait (FIG. **22-43;** see "How to Impress a Pope," below). Parmigianino's best-known work,

PROBLEMS AND SOLUTIONS
How to Impress a Pope

Because Renaissance artists depended on commissions from churches, town councils, princes, and wealthy merchants, attracting the attention of a prominent patron early in one's career was essential if the artist was going to enjoy success. When he was 21, Parmigianino, who soon became a leading figure among the "Mannerists" who were exploring stylistic alternatives to the classical art of Raphael, devised an unusual way to impress Pope Clement VII with his skill. During a visit to a barber's shop, Parmigianino saw his reflection in a convex mirror, which inspired him to paint a self-portrait (FIG. 22-43) of unconventional format with the intention of presenting it to Pope Clement VII as a demonstration of his virtuosity.

To imitate the appearance of a convex mirror, Parmigianino had a carpenter prepare a section of a wood sphere of the same size and shape as a barber's mirror (about 10 inches in diameter) and used oil glazes to produce a surface luster that heightened the illusion of the viewer looking into a mirror and not at a painting. The viewer in this case is also the painter, whose handsome countenance Giorgio Vasari described as an angel's, not a man's. The pope remarked that Parmigianino's portrait of himself in his studio was "a marvel" and "astonishing" in its success in creating the appearance of someone gazing at his reflection. As in a real convex mirror, the artist's face—at the center of the reflective surface and some distance from it—is free of distortion, but his hand and sleeve are of exaggerated size. The emphasis on the hand no doubt is also a statement on Parmigianino's part about the supreme importance of the painter's hand in fashioning an artwork. That emphasis on artifice as the essence of painting is the core principle of Mannerism.

Parmigianino, whom Vasari described as possessing charm as well as good looks and precocious artistic talent, quickly became the favorite painter of the elite in Rome, the successor to Raphael, who had died just four years before Parmigianino's arrival at the papal court.

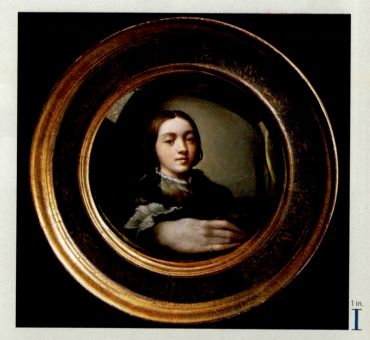

1 in.

22-43 PARMIGIANINO, *Self-Portrait in a Convex Mirror*, 1524. Oil on wood, 9⅝" diameter. Kunsthistorisches Museum, Vienna.

Painted to impress Pope Clement VII with his virtuosity, Parmigianino's self-portrait brilliantly reproduces the young Mannerist's distorted appearance as seen in a barber's convex mirror.

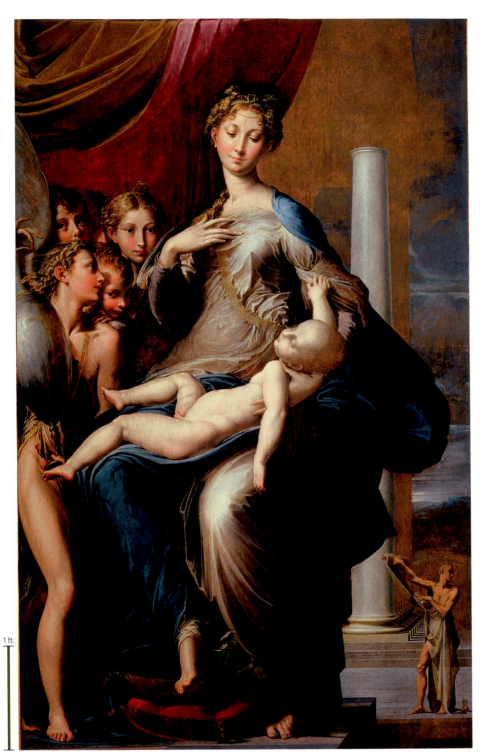

1 ft.

22-44 Parmigianino, *Madonna with the Long Neck,* from the Baiardi Chapel, Santa Maria dei Servi, Parma, Italy, 1534–1540. Oil on wood, 7' 1" × 4' 4". Galleria degli Uffizi, Florence.

Parmigianino's Madonna displays the stylish elegance that was a principal aim of Mannerism. Mary has a small oval head, a long and slender neck, attenuated hands, and a sinuous body.

and a mysterious figure with a scroll, perhaps Saint James, whose distance from the foreground is immeasurable and ambiguous—the antithesis of rational Renaissance perspective diminution of size with distance.

Although the elegance and sophisticated beauty of the painting are due in large part to the Madonna's attenuated neck and arms, that exaggeration is not solely decorative in purpose. *Madonna with the Long Neck* takes its subject from a simile in medieval hymns comparing the Virgin's neck with a great ivory tower or column, such as the one Parmigianino depicted to the right of the Madonna.

BRONZINO *Venus, Cupid, Folly, and Time* (FIG. **22-45**), by Agnolo di Cosimo, called Bronzino (1503–1572), also displays all the chief features of Mannerist painting. A pupil of Pontormo, Bronzino was a Florentine and painter to the first grand duke of Tuscany, Cosimo I de' Medici (r. 1537–1574). In this painting, which Cosimo commissioned as a gift for King Francis I of France (see "Francis I, Royal Art Patron and Collector," page 693), Bronzino demonstrated the Mannerists' fondness for learned allegories that often had lascivious undertones, a shift from the simple and monumental statements and forms of the High Renaissance. Bronzino depicted Cupid—here not an infant but an adolescent who has reached puberty—fondling his mother, Venus, while provocatively thrusting his buttocks at the viewer. Folly prepares to shower the "couple" with rose petals. Time, who appears in the upper right corner, draws back the curtain to reveal the playful incest in progress. Other figures in the painting represent other human qualities and emotions, including Envy. The masks, a favorite device of the Mannerists, symbolize deceit.

Bronzion's *Venus, Cupid, Folly, and Time* seems to suggest that love—accompanied by envy and plagued by inconstancy—is foolish and that lovers will discover its folly in time. But as in many Mannerist paintings, the meaning here is ambiguous, and interpretations of the painting vary. Compositionally, Bronzino placed the figures around the front plane, and they almost entirely block

however, is *Madonna with the Long Neck* (FIG. **22-44**), which exemplifies the elegant stylishness that was a principal aim of Mannerism. In Parmigianino's hands, this traditional, usually sedate, religious subject became a picture of exquisite grace and precious sweetness. The Madonna's small oval head, her long and slender neck, the otherworldly attenuation and delicacy of her hand, and the sinuous, swaying elongation of her frame—all are marks of the aristocratic, sumptuously courtly taste of Mannerist artists and patrons alike. Parmigianino amplified this elegance by expanding the Madonna's form as viewed from head to toe. On the left stands a bevy of angelic creatures, melting with emotions as soft and smooth as their limbs. On the right, the artist included a line of columns without capitals

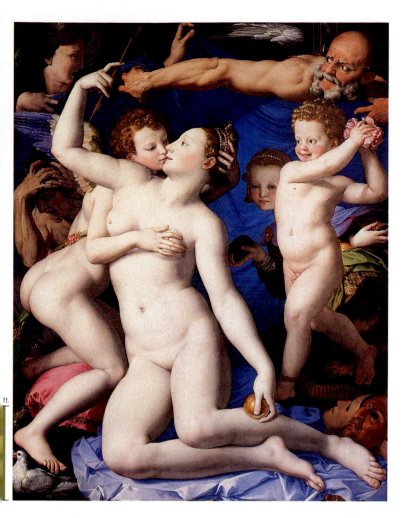

22-45 BRONZINO, *Venus, Cupid, Folly, and Time*, ca. 1546. Oil on wood, 5' 1" × 4' 8¼". National Gallery, London.

In this painting of Cupid fondling his mother, Venus, Bronzino demonstrated a fondness for learned allegories with lascivious undertones. As in many Mannerist works, the meaning is ambiguous.

the space. The contours are strong and sculptural, the surfaces of enamel smoothness. Of special interest are the heads, hands, and feet, for the Mannerists considered the extremities to be the carriers of grace, and the clever depiction of them evidence of artistic skill.

ELEANORA OF TOLEDO In 1540, Cosimo I de' Medici married Eleanora of Toledo (1519–1562), daughter of Charles V's viceroy in Naples, and thereby cemented an important alliance with the Spanish court. Several years later, Cosimo asked Bronzino to paint Eleanora and their second son, Giovanni (FIG. **22-46**), who then was about three years old. Bronzino painted dozens of portraits of members of the Medici family, but never portrayed Eleanora with any of her daughters (she and Cosimo had three daughters as well as eight sons). This painting therefore should be seen as a formal dynastic portrait intended to present the duke's wife as the mother of one of his heirs.

As in other Bronzino portraits (FIG. **22-46A**), the subjects appear aloof and emotionless. Bronzino idealized both Eleanora and Giovanni, giving both of them perfect features and blemishless skin that glows like alabaster. Eleanora's figure takes up most of the panel's surface, and Bronzino further underscored her primacy by lightening the blue background around her head, creating a halolike frame for her face and perhaps associating the mother and son with the Madonna and Christ Child.

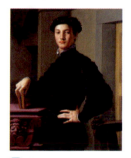

22-46A BRONZINO, *Portrait of a Young Man*, ca. 1530-1545.

Seated with one arm around Giovanni and the other resting on her lap, Eleanora looks out at the viewer with cool detachment. She is richly attired in a brocaded gown and wears a costly pearl necklace and a tiara. The painter reproduced the various textures of fabric, jewels, hair, and flesh with supreme skill. The boy stands stiffly, staring forward, suppressing all playful thoughts in order to behave as expected on this formal occasion. Bronzino's portrayal of Eleanora and Giovanni is in some ways less a portrait of a mother and child than of a royal audience.

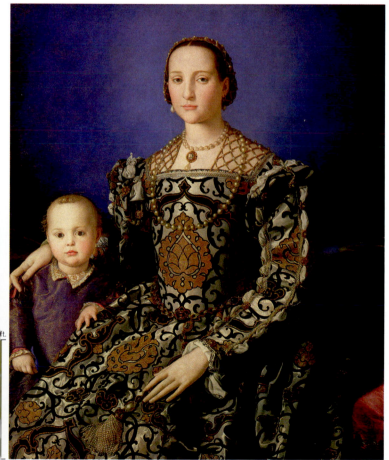

22-46 BRONZINO, *Eleanora of Toledo and Giovanni de' Medici*, ca. 1546. Oil on wood, 3' 9¼" × 3' 1¾". Galleria degli Uffizi, Florence.

Bronzino was the official portraitist of Grand Duke Cosimo de' Medici. His portrayal of Cosimo's Spanish wife and their second son features rich costumes and coolly detached personalities.

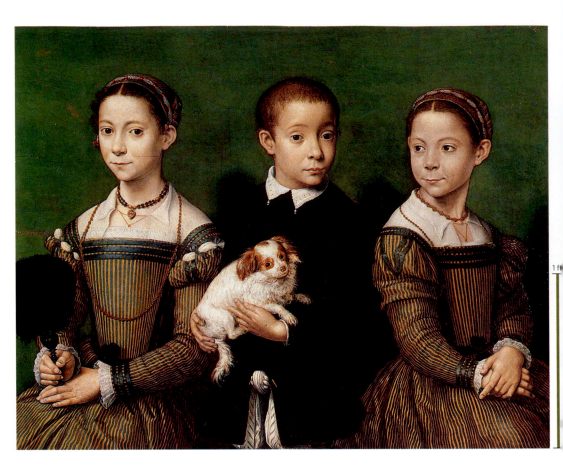

22-47 Sofonisba Anguissola, *Portrait of the Artist's Sisters and Brother*, ca. 1555. Oil on wood, 2' 5¼" × 3' 1½". Methuen Collection, Corsham Court, Wiltshire.

Anguissola was the leading woman artist of her time. Her contemporaries admired her use of relaxed poses and expressions in intimate and informal group portraits such as this one of her family.

SOFONISBA ANGUISSOLA The aloof formality of Bronzino's dynastic portrait is much relaxed in the portraiture of SOFONISBA ANGUISSOLA (ca. 1532–1625) of Cremona in northern Italy. Anguissola introduced a new kind of group portrait of irresistible charm, characterized by an informal intimacy and by subjects that are often moving, conversing, or engaged in activities. Like many of the other works she produced before settling in Spain in 1559, the portrait illustrated here (FIG. **22-47**) represents members of her family. Against a neutral ground, Anguissola placed her two sisters and brother in an affectionate pose meant not for official display but for private showing. The sisters, wearing matching striped gowns, flank their brother, who caresses a lapdog. The older sister (at the left) summons the dignity required for the occasion, while the boy looks quizzically at the portraitist with an expression of naive curiosity, and the other girl diverts her attention toward something or someone to the painter's left.

Anguissola's use of relaxed poses and expressions, her sympathetic personal presentation, and her graceful treatment of the forms brought her international acclaim (see "Women in the Renaissance Art World," page 656). She received praise from the aged Michelangelo, was court painter to Phillip II (r. 1556–1598) of Spain, and, at the end of her life, gave advice on art to a young admirer of her work, Anthony Van Dyck (FIG. 25-5), the great Flemish master.

TINTORETTO Venetian painting of the later 16th century built on established High Renaissance Venetian ideas, but incorporated many elements of the Mannerist style. Jacopo Robusti, known as TINTORETTO (1518–1594), claimed to be a student of Titian and aspired to combine Titian's color with Michelangelo's drawing, but art historians consider Tintoretto the outstanding Venetian representative of Mannerism. He adopted many Mannerist pictorial devices, which he employed to produce works imbued with dramatic power, depth of spiritual vision, and glowing Venetian color schemes.

Toward the end of Tintoretto's life, his art became spiritual, even visionary, as solid forms melted away into swirling clouds of dark shot through with fitful light. In Tintoretto's *Last Supper* (FIG. **22-48**), painted for the right wall next to the high altar in Andrea Palladio's church of San Giorgio Maggiore (FIG. 22-31), the figures appear in a dark interior illuminated by a single light in

the upper left of the image. The shimmering halos establish the biblical nature of the scene. The ability of this dramatic scene to engage viewers was fully in keeping with Counter-Reformation ideals (see "The Council of Trent," page 642) and the Catholic Church's belief in the didactic nature of religious art.

Tintoretto's *Last Supper* incorporates many Mannerist devices, including an imbalanced composition and visual complexity. In terms of design, the contrast with Leonardo's *Last Supper* (FIG. 22-4) is both extreme and instructive. Leonardo's composition, balanced and symmetrical, parallels the picture plane in a geometrically organized and closed space. The figure of Jesus is the tranquil center of the drama and the perspective focus. In Tintoretto's painting, Jesus is above and beyond the converging perspective lines racing diagonally away from the picture surface, creating disturbing effects of limitless depth and motion. The viewer locates Tintoretto's Jesus via the light flaring, beaconlike, out of darkness. The contrast of the two pictures reflects the direction Renaissance painting took in the 16th century, as it moved away from architectonic clarity of space and neutral lighting toward the dynamic perspectives and dramatic chiaroscuro of the coming Baroque.

VERONESE Among the great Venetian masters was Paolo Caliari of Verona, called PAOLO VERONESE (1528–1588). Whereas Tintoretto gloried in monumental drama and deep perspectives, Veronese specialized in splendid pageantry painted in superb color and set within majestic classical architecture. Like Tintoretto, Veronese painted on a huge scale, with canvases often as large as 20 by 30 feet or more. His usual subjects, painted for the refectories of wealthy monasteries, afforded him an opportunity to display magnificent companies at table.

Veronese painted *Christ in the House of Levi* (FIG. **22-49**), originally called *Last Supper*, for the dining hall of Santi Giovanni e Paolo

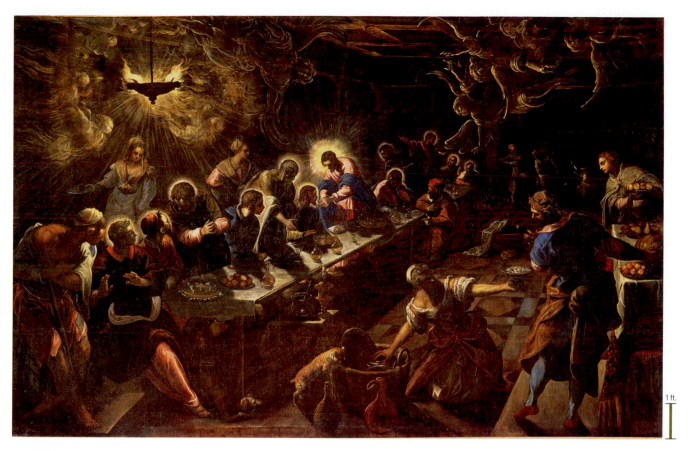

22-48 TINTORETTO, *Last Supper,* 1594. Oil on canvas, 12′ × 18′ 8″. San Giorgio Maggiore, Venice.

Tintoretto adopted many Mannerist pictorial devices to produce oil paintings imbued with emotional power, depth of spiritual vision, glowing Venetian color schemes, and dramatic lighting.

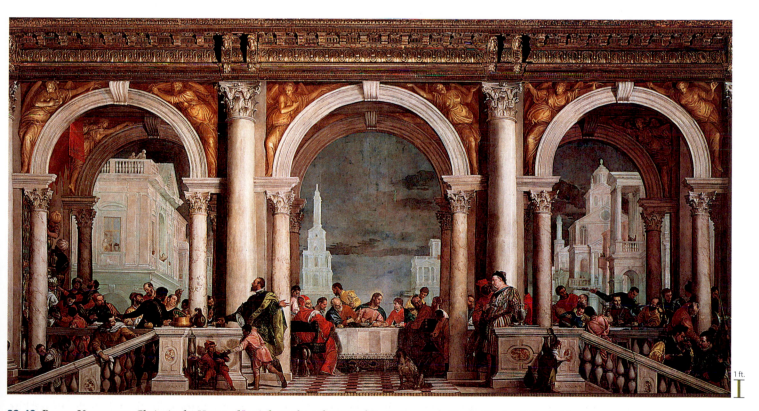

22-49 PAOLO VERONESE, *Christ in the House of Levi,* from the refectory of Santi Giovanni e Paolo, Venice, Italy, 1573. Oil on canvas, 18′ 3″ × 42′. Galleria dell'Accademia, Venice.

Veronese's paintings feature superb color and majestic classical settings. The Catholic Church accused him of impiety for including dogs and dwarfs near Christ in this work originally titled *Last Supper.*

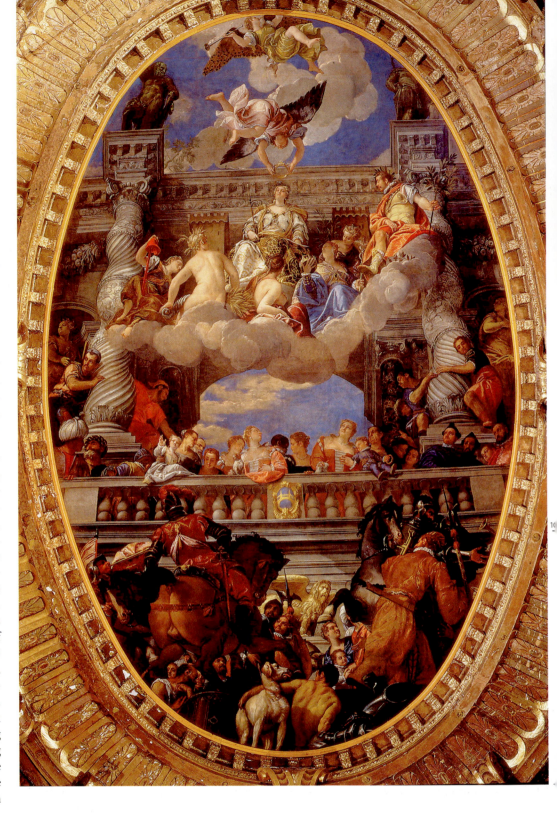

22-50 PAOLO VERONESE, *Triumph of Venice*, ca. 1585. Oil on canvas, 29' 8" × 19'. Hall of the Grand Council, Doge's Palace, Venice.

Veronese's immense oval ceiling painting presents a tableau of Venice crowned by Fame amid columns, clouds, and personifications. Baroque painters adopted this 45-degree view from the ground.

in Venice. As Palladio looked to the example of classically inspired High Renaissance architecture, so Veronese returned to High Renaissance composition, its symmetrical balance, and its ordered architectonics. His shimmering colors span the whole spectrum, although he avoided solid colors in favor of half shades (light blues, sea greens, lemon yellows, roses, and violets), creating veritable flowerbeds of tone. In a great open loggia framed by three monumental arches, Christ sits at the center of the splendidly garbed elite of Venice. In the foreground, with a courtly gesture, the very image of gracious grandeur, the chief steward welcomes guests. Robed lords, their colorful retainers, dogs, and dwarfs crowd into the spacious loggia. Also present are exotic figures wearing turbans, and others of African descent. Painted in 1573 during the Counter-Reformation, this depiction prompted criticism from the Catholic Church. The Holy Office of the Inquisition put the painter on trial, accusing Veronese of impiety for painting "lowly creatures" so close to the Lord and ordering him to make changes at his own expense within three months. Reluctant to do so, he simply changed the painting's title, converting the subject to a less solemn one. His patrons were quite amenable to this solution, for they found nothing objectionable in the painting. Magnificent feasts and carnivals were a source of pride for Venetians.

TRIUMPH OF VENICE Veronese, like Tintoretto, also received prestigious commissions from the Venetian Republic itself. Both artists were hired to decorate the grand chambers and council rooms of the Doge's Palace (FIG. 14-23). In *Triumph of Venice* (FIG. 22-50) in the grandiose Hall of the Grand Council, Veronese revealed himself a master of illusionistic ceiling compositions. Within an oval frame, he presented personified Venice, crowned by Fame, enthroned between two great twisted columns in a balustrade-capped loggia, garlanded with clouds, and attended by figures symbolic of the maritime republic's glories. Unlike Mantegna's *di sotto in sù* (FIG. 21-49) perspective, Veronese's is not a projection directly up from below,

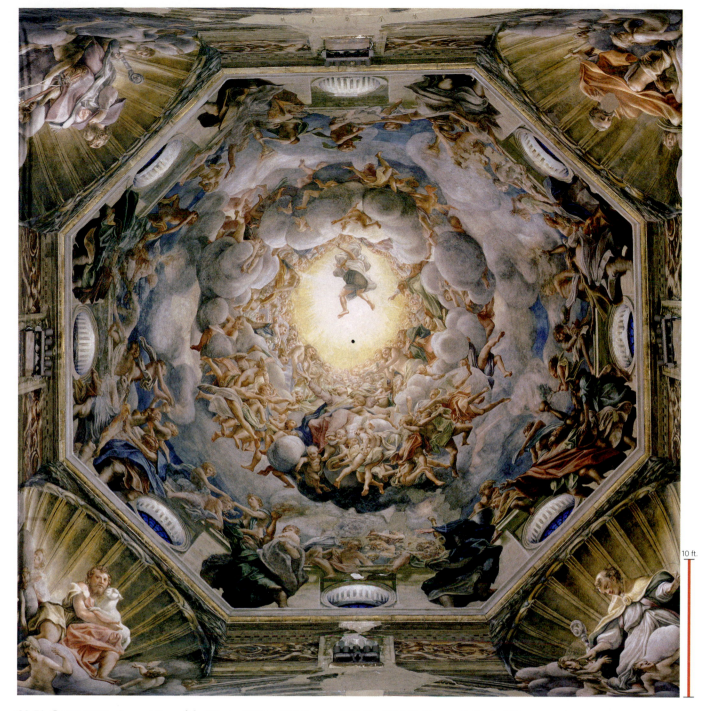

22-51 CORREGGIO, *Assumption of the Virgin*, 1526–1530. Fresco, 35' 10" × 37' 11". Parma Cathedral, Parma.

Working long before Veronese, Correggio, the teacher of Parmigianino, won little fame in his day, but his illusionistic ceiling designs, such as this one in Parma Cathedral, inspired many Baroque painters.

but at a 45-degree angle to spectators, a technique used by many later Baroque decorators (for example, FIGS. 24-22 to 24-24).

CORREGGIO One painter who developed a personal style almost impossible to classify was Antonio Allegri, known as CORREGGIO (ca. 1489–1534) from his birthplace near Parma. The teacher of Parmigianino, Correggio pulled together many stylistic trends, including those of Leonardo, Raphael, and the Venetians. His most enduring contribution was the further development of illusionistic ceiling perspective painting. In Parma Cathedral, he painted away the entire dome with his *Assumption of the Virgin* (FIG. 22-51; see

"How to Make a Ceiling Disappear," page 720). Opening up the *cupola*, the artist showed worshipers a view of the sky, with concentric rings of clouds where hundreds of soaring figures perform a wildly pirouetting dance in celebration of the Assumption. Versions of these angelic creatures became permanent tenants of numerous Baroque churches in later centuries. Correggio was also an influential painter of religious panels, anticipating in them many other Baroque compositional devices. Correggio's *Assumption of the Virgin* predates Veronese's *Triumph of Venice* by more than a half century, but contemporaries expressed little appreciation for his achievement. Later, during the 17th century, Baroque painters recognized him as a kindred spirit.

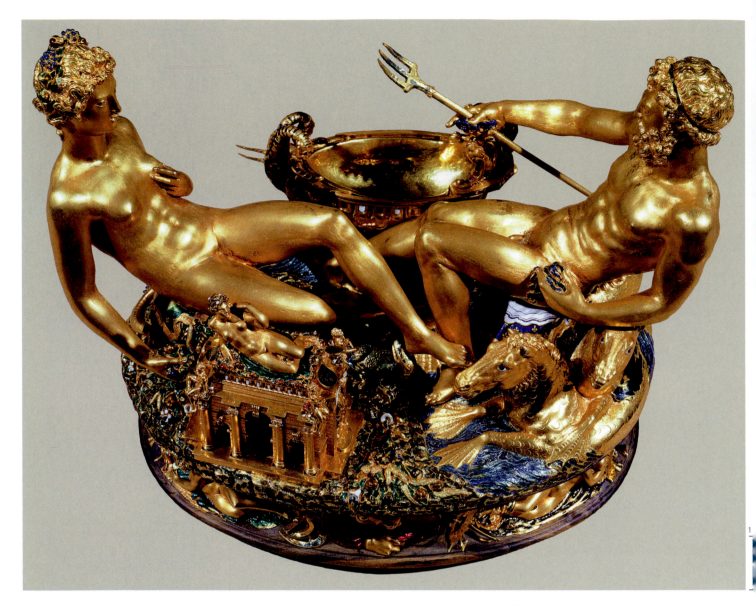

22-52 BENVENUTO CELLINI, *Saltcellar of Francis I*, 1540–1543. Gold, enamel, and ebony, $10\frac{1}{4}$" × 1' $1\frac{1}{8}$". Kunsthistorisches Museum, Vienna.

Famed as a master goldsmith, Cellini fashioned this costly saltcellar for the table of Francis I of France. The elongated proportions of the figures clearly reveal Cellini's Mannerist approach to form.

Sculpture

Mannerism extended beyond painting. Artists translated its principles into sculpture and architecture as well.

BENVENUTO CELLINI Among those who made their mark as Mannerist sculptors was BENVENUTO CELLINI (1500–1571), the author of a fascinating autobiography. It is difficult to imagine a medieval artist composing an autobiography. Only in the Renaissance, with the birth of the notion of individual artistic genius, could a work such as Cellini's (or Vasari's *Lives*) have been conceived and written. Cellini's literary self-portrait presents him not only as a highly accomplished artist but also as a statesman, soldier, and lover, among many other roles.

Cellini was, first of all, a goldsmith, but only one of his major works in that medium survives, the saltcellar (FIG. 22-52) he made for the royal table of Francis I (see "Francis I, Royal Art Patron and Collector," page 693). The king had hired Cellini with a retainer of an annual salary, supplemented by fees for the works he produced—for example, his *Genius of Fontainebleau* (FIG. 22-52A) for the royal hunting lodge outside Paris. The price Francis paid Cellini for the luxurious gold-and-*enamel* saltcellar illustrated here was almost 50 percent greater than the artist's salary for the year.

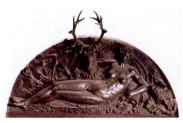

⬀ **22-52A** CELLINI, *Genius of Fontainebleau*, 1542–1543.

The two sculpted figures of Cellini's saltcellar are Neptune and Tellus (or, as the artist named them, Sea—the source of salt—and Land). They recline atop an ebony base decorated with relief figures of Dawn, Day, Twilight, Night, and the four winds—some based on Michelangelo's statues in the New Sacristy (FIG. 22-16) attached to

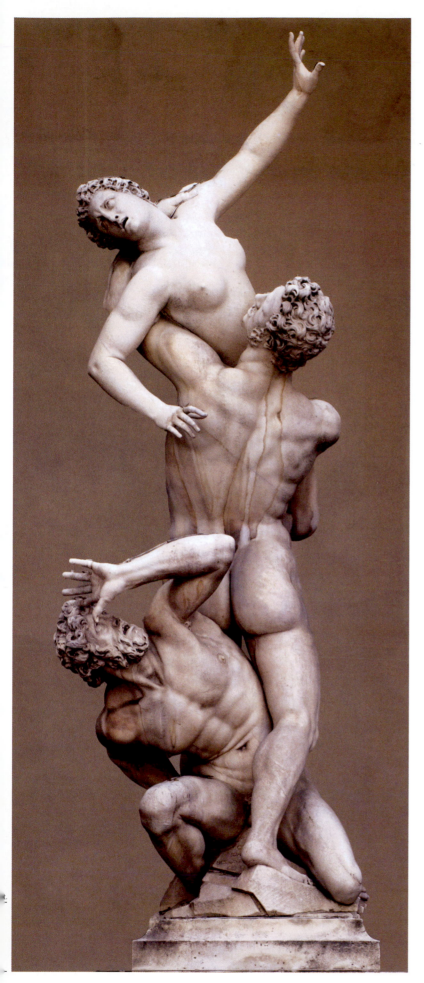

San Lorenzo. The boat next to Neptune's right leg is the salt container, and the triumphal arch (compare FIG. 7-73) next to the right leg of the earth goddess held the pepper. The elongated proportions of the figures, especially the slim, small-breasted figure of Tellus, whom ancient artists always represented as a matronly woman (FIG. 7-30), reveal Cellini's Mannerist approach to form.

GIOVANNI DA BOLOGNA The lure of Italy drew a brilliant young Flemish sculptor, Jean de Boulogne, to Italy, where he practiced his art under the equivalent Italian name of Giovanni da Bologna or, in its more common contracted form, GIAMBOLOGNA (1529–1608). His *Abduction of the Sabine Women* (FIG. **22-53**) exemplifies Mannerist principles of figure composition. Drawn from the legendary history of early Rome, the group of figures received its current title—relating how the Romans abducted wives for themselves from the neighboring Sabines—only after its exhibition. Earlier, it was *Paris Abducting Helen,* among other mythological titles. In fact, Giambologna did not intend to depict any particular subject. He created the group as a demonstration piece. His goal was to achieve a dynamic spiral figural composition involving an old man, a young man, and a woman, all nude in the tradition of ancient statues portraying deities and mythological figures.

Although Giambologna would have known Antonio Pollaiuolo's *Hercules and Antaeus* (FIG. 21-13), whose Greek hero lifts his opponent off the ground, he turned directly to ancient sculpture for inspiration, especially to the much-admired *Laocoön* (FIG. 5-89), discovered in Rome earlier in the century. *Abduction of the Sabine Women* includes references to that ancient statue in the crouching old man and in the woman's up-flung arm. The three bodies interlock on a vertical axis, creating an ascending spiral movement.

To appreciate *Abduction of the Sabine Women* fully, the viewer must walk around the statuary group, because the work changes radically according to the viewing point. One factor contributing to the shifting imagery is the prominence of open spaces passing through the masses (for example, the space between an arm and a body), which have as great an effect as the solids. This sculpture was the first large-scale group since classical antiquity designed to be seen from multiple viewpoints, although Giambologna's figures do not break out of the spiral vortex but remain as if contained within a cylinder.

22-53 GIAMBOLOGNA, *Abduction of the Sabine Women,* **Loggia dei Lanzi, Piazza della Signoria, Florence, Italy, 1579–1583. Marble, 13' 5½" high.**

This sculpture was the first large-scale group since classical antiquity designed to be seen from multiple viewpoints. The three bodies interlock to create a vertical spiral movement.

THE PATRON'S VOICE

Federigo Gonzaga, Giulio Romano, and the Palazzo del Tè

As during the Middle Ages, when the clergy were the primary source of artistic commissions, Renaissance patrons, whether popes, dukes, or bankers, had a powerful—often a controlling—voice in the content and even the form of the artworks they paid for (see "Art in the Princely Courts of Renaissance Italy," page 613, and "Michelangelo in the Service of Julius II," page 623). But there were also many instances of a give-and-take between artists and patrons. One well-documented example is the relationship between Federigo Gonzaga, duke of Mantua, and Giulio Romano, the painter and architect he lured to northern Italy in 1524. Giorgio Vasari describes in detail how Gonzaga showered Giulio with gifts and then accepted the artist's proposal to construct a grandiose palace when the duke had planned only to invest in a modest retreat:

> Giulio was celebrated as the best artist in Italy after the death of Raphael, and Count Baldassare Castiglione [FIG. 22-10A], in Rome at that time as the ambassador of Federigo Gonzaga, . . . was ordered to procure an architect . . . and the count worked at

this so diligently with entreaties and promises that Giulio declared he would go at any time provided it was by the leave of Pope Clement. Once this permission had been obtained, . . . Castiglione presented Giulio to [Federigo] who, after many acts of kindness, gave Giulio an honorably furnished home and provided a salary and food for him. . . . [and] sent Giulio several lengths of velvet and satin, as well as other kinds of cloth and fabric for his clothing. And afterwards, learning that Giulio had no horse, he had one of his own favorite horses, called Luggieri, brought out and gave it to Giulio, and when Giulio had mounted the horse, they went off . . . to where His Excellency had a place and some stables call the Tè in the middle of a meadow. . . . [Federigo declared] he would like to prepare a small place where he could go and take refuge on occasion to have lunch or amuse himself at dinner. . . . Giulio surveyed everything, took the ground-plan for the site, and set to work. . . . [Federigo] later decided, after such a humble beginning, to make the entire edifice into a grand palace [FIGS. 22-54 and 22-55], for Giulio executed a very beautiful model, its courtyard rusticated inside and out, which pleased that ruler so much that he ordered an ample provision of money.*

*Giorgio Vasari, "The Life of Giulio Romano, Painter," translated by Julia Conaway Bondanella and Peter Bondanella, *Giorgio Vasari: The Lives of the Artists* (New York: Oxford University Press, 1991), 366–367.

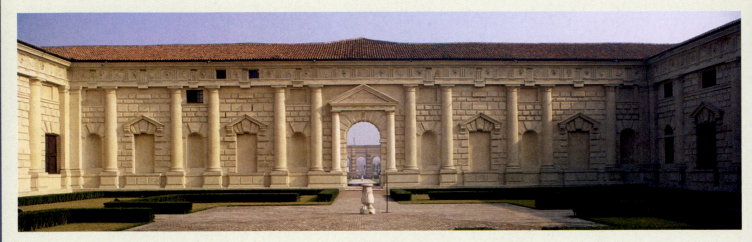

22-54 GIULIO ROMANO, courtyard of the Palazzo del Tè (looking southeast), Mantua, Italy, 1525–1535.

Federico Gonzaga was greatly pleased by Giulio's Mannerist divergences from architectural convention in the Palazzo del Tè. The design constitutes a parody of Bramante's classical style.

Architecture

Mannerist architects used classical architectural elements in a highly personal and unorthodox manner, rejecting the balance, order, and stability that were the hallmarks of the High Renaissance style, and aiming instead to reveal the contrived nature of architectural design.

GIULIO ROMANO Applying that unorthodox approach was the goal of GIULIO ROMANO (ca. 1499–1546) when he designed the Palazzo del Tè (FIG. 22-54) in Mantua and, with it, formulated almost the entire architectural vocabulary of Mannerism. Early in his career, Giulio was Raphael's chief assistant in decorating the Vatican stanze. After Raphael's premature death in 1520, Giulio became

his master's artistic executor, completing Raphael's unfinished frescoes and panel paintings. In 1524, Giulio went to Mantua (opening an opportunity at the papal court for Parmigianino), having been courted by Duke Federigo Gonzaga (r. 1530–1540), for whom he built and decorated the Palazzo del Tè between 1525 and 1535 (see "Federigo Gonzaga, Giulio Romano, and the Palazzo del Tè," above). Gonzaga intended the palace to serve as both suburban summer residence and stud farm for his famous stables. Originally planned as a relatively modest country villa, Giulio's building so pleased his patron that Gonzaga soon commissioned the architect to enlarge the structure. In a second building campaign, Giulio expanded the villa to a palatial scale by adding three wings, which he placed around a square central court. This once-paved court, which functions both as a passage and as the focal point of the design, has a nearly urban character. Its surrounding buildings form a self-enclosed unit with a large garden, flanked by a stable, attached to it on the east side.

Giulio's Mannerist style is on display in the facades facing the palace's courtyard (FIG. 22-54), where the divergences from architectural convention are pronounced. Indeed, the Palazzo del Tè constitutes an enormous parody of Bramante's classical style, a veritable Mannerist manifesto announcing the artifice of architectural design. In a building laden with structural surprises and contradictions, the courtyard is the most unconventional of all. The *keystones* (central *voussoirs*), for example, either have not fully settled or seem to be slipping from the arches—and, even more eccentrically, Giulio placed voussoirs in the pediments over the rectangular niches, where no arches exist. The massive Tuscan columns flanking these niches carry incongruously narrow *architraves*. That these architraves break midway between the columns stresses their apparent structural insufficiency, and they seem unable to support the weight of

the *triglyphs* of the *Doric frieze* above (see "Doric and Ionic Orders," page 114 and FIG. 5-13), which threaten to crash down on the head of anyone foolish enough to stand beneath them. To be sure, only a highly sophisticated observer can appreciate Giulio's witticism. Recognizing some quite subtle departures from the norm presupposes a thorough familiarity with the established rules of classical architecture. That the duke delighted in Giulio's mannered architectural inventiveness speaks to his cultivated taste.

SALA DEI GIGANTI Federigo also entrusted Giulio with the interior decoration of his suburban pleasure palace. In the Sala dei Giganti (Room of the Giants; FIG. 22-55), painted to serve as the reception hall for the second visit to Mantua of Charles V, frescoes cover every square inch of the walls and ceiling. At the top (almost entirely out of view in the photograph reproduced here) is an illusionistic oculus that pays tribute to, but is a Mannerist commentary on, Mantegna's earlier *tromple-l'oeil* ceiling in the Camera Picta (FIG. 21-49) of

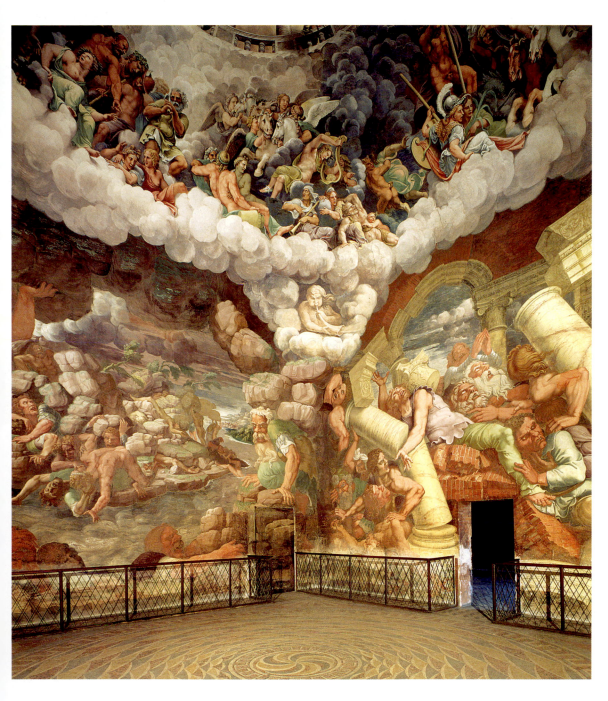

22-55 Giulio Romano, *Fall of the Giants from Mount Olympus,* fresco in the Sala dei Giganti, Palazzo del Tè, Mantua, Italy, 1530–1532.

Giulio Romano's dramatic ceiling fresco of giants battling the Greek gods of Mount Olympus continues the theme of collapsing architecture that he used on the Palazzo del Tè's exterior (FIG. 22-54).

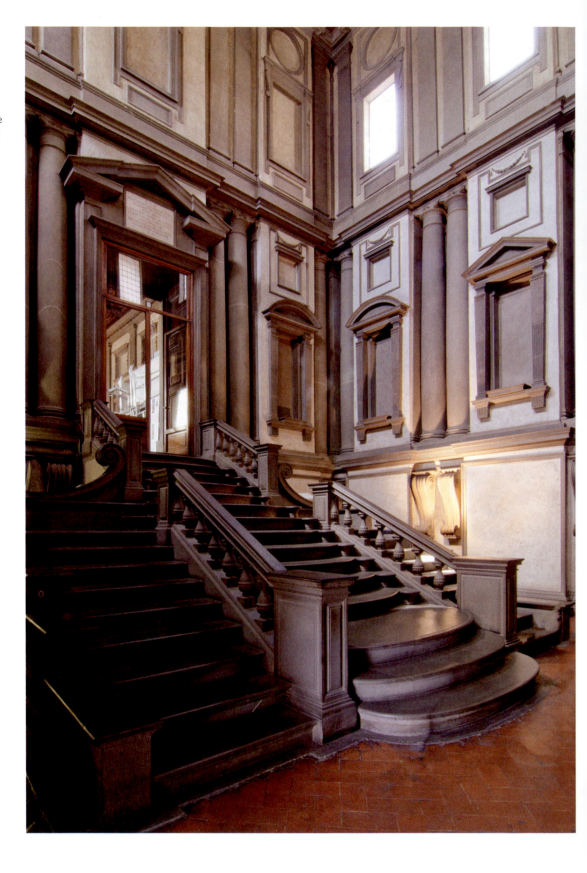

22-56 MICHELANGELO BUONARROTI, vestibule of the Laurentian Library, Florence, Italy, 1524–1534; staircase, 1558–1559.

With his customary independence of spirit, Michelangelo, working in a Mannerist mode in the Laurentian Library vestibule, disposed willfully of almost all the rules of classical architecture.

the ducal palace in Mantua. The *Fall of the Giants from Mount Olympus* revives the venerable classical theme of the *gigantomachy* (battle of gods and giants), which was popular in ancient Greece (FIGS. 5-18 and 5-80) because the defeat of the giants at the hands of the Olympian gods served as an allegory of the triumph of Greek civilization over barbarism. In Renaissance Mantua, Duke Federigo may have seen himself as a modern-day Zeus/Jupiter, who in Giulio's fresco hurls thunderbolts at the giants who have

stormed Mount Olympus, causing them to fall back to earth amid collapsing classical temples.

The gigantic fresco merits comparison with Michelangelo's dramatic vision in his *Last Judgment* (FIG. 22-19), painted later in the decade for the east wall of the Sistine Chapel in Rome. But despite the tumultuous details of Michelangelo's fresco of heroically nude cloud-borne figures, the composition retains classical balance and symmetry, whereas Giulio's fresco embodies the instability and asymmetry that Mannerist artists and patrons alike preferred. In the Palazzo del Tè, where the architect and the painter were the same man and had the full support of his ducal patron, Giulio carried his critical and whimsical commentary on classical architecture indoors. Visitors to the pleasure palace surely would have been reminded of the triglyphs about to crash down from the Doric frieze of the building's exterior (FIG. 22-54) when they encountered the collapsing entablatures and crumbling columns of the frescoes in the Sala dei Giganti.

LAURENTIAN LIBRARY Although for most people, Michelangelo personifies the High Renaissance artist, he, like Giulio Romano, also experimented with architectural designs that flouted most of the classical rules of order and stability. The restless nature of Michelangelo's genius is evident in the vestibule (FIG. 22-56) he designed for the Medici library adjoining the Florentine church of San Lorenzo. The Laurentian Library had two contrasting spaces that Michelangelo had to unite: the long horizontal of the library proper and the vertical of the vestibule. The need to place the vestibule windows up high (at the level of the reading room) determined the narrow verticality of the vestibule's elevation and proportions. Much taller than it is wide, the vestibule gives the impression of a vertically compressed, shaft-like space. Anyone schooled exclusively in the classical architecture of Bramante and the High Renaissance would have been appalled by Michelangelo's indifference here to classical norms in proportion and in the application of the rules of the classical orders. For example, he used columns in pairs and sank them into the walls, where they perform no supporting function. Michelangelo also split columns in halves around corners. Elsewhere, he placed scroll *corbels* on the walls beneath columns. They seem to hang from the moldings, holding up nothing. He arbitrarily broke through pediments as well as through cornices and stringcourses. He sculpted pilasters that taper downward instead of upward. In short, the High Renaissance master, working in a Mannerist mode, disposed willfully and abruptly of classical architecture. Moreover, in the vast, flowing stairway (the latest element of the vestibule) that protrudes tonguelike into the room from the "mouth" of the doorway to the library, Michelangelo foreshadowed the dramatic movement of Baroque architecture (see page 702). With his customary trailblazing independence of spirit, Michelangelo created an interior space that conveyed all the strains and tensions found in his statuary and in his painted figures.

Michelangelo's art began in the style of the Quattrocento, became emblematic of High Renaissance art, and, at the end, moved toward Mannerism. He was 89 when he died in 1564, still hard at work on Saint Peter's and other projects. Few artists, then or since, could escape his influence.

IL GESÙ Probably the most influential building of the later Cinquecento was the mother church of the Jesuit order, Il Gesù, or Church of Jesus (FIGS. 22-57 and 22-58) in Rome. The activity of the Society of Jesus, known as the Jesuits, was an important component of the Counter-Reformation (see page 641). Ignatius of Loyola (1491–1556), a Spanish nobleman who dedicated his life to the service of God, founded the Jesuits in 1534 with preaching and missionary work as the key components of their spiritual assignment. In 1540, Pope Paul III formally recognized his group as a religious order. The Jesuits were the papacy's invaluable allies in its quest to reassert the supremacy of the Catholic Church. Particularly

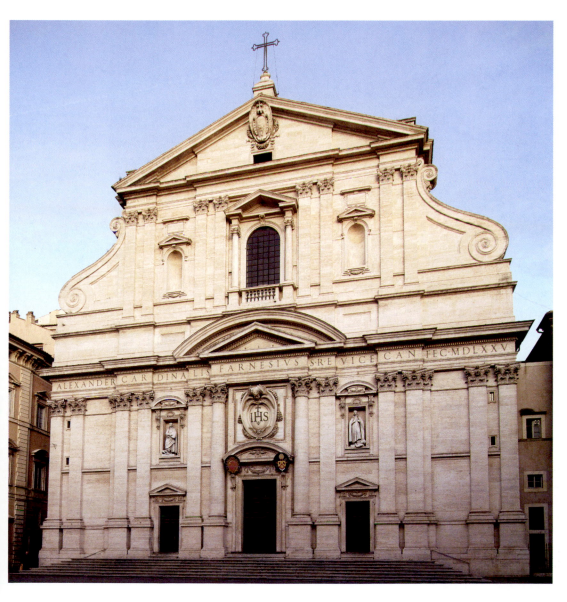

22-57 GIACOMO DELLA PORTA, west facade of Il Gesù, Rome, Italy, begun 1568.

In Giacomo della Porta's innovative design, the march of pilasters and columns builds to a climax at the central bay. Many Roman Baroque church facades are architectural variations of Il Gesù.

PROBLEMS AND SOLUTIONS
Rethinking the Basilican Church

As a major participant in the Counter-Reformation, the Jesuit order needed a church appropriate to its new prominence. In 1568, with the financial backing of Cardinal Alessandro Farnese (1520–1589), the order turned to GIACOMO DA VIGNOLA (1507–1573), who designed Il Gesù's plan (FIG. **22-58**), and GIACOMO DELLA PORTA (ca. 1533–1602), who was responsible for the facade (FIG. 22-57)—and who later designed the dome of Saint Peter's (FIG. 22-25).

The plan of the Church of Jesus in Rome is a monumental expansion of Alberti's scheme for Sant'Andrea (FIGS. 21-46 and 21-47) in Mantua. In Il Gesù, the nave (FIG. 22-57) takes over the main volume of space, making the structure a great hall with side chapels. The transept is no wider than the nave and chapels, and Vignola also eliminated the normal deep choir in front of the altar. Consequently, all worshipers have a clear view of the celebration of the Eucharist. The wide acceptance of Vignola's plan in the Catholic world, even in modern times, speaks to its suitability for the performance of Catholic rituals.

The opening of the church building into a single great hall provides an almost theatrical setting for large promenades and processions (which combined social with priestly functions). Above all, the ample space could accommodate the great crowds that gathered to hear the eloquent preaching of the Jesuits.

The facade of Il Gesù (FIG. 22-57) was also not entirely original, but it too had an enormous influence on later church design. The union of the lower and upper stories, achieved by scroll buttresses, harks back to Alberti's Santa Maria Novella (FIG. 21-36A). Its classical pediment is familiar in Alberti's work (FIG. 21-45), as well as in Palladio's (FIGS. 22-28 and 22-30). The paired pilasters appear in Michelangelo's design for Saint Peter's (FIG. 22-25). Della Porta skillfully synthesized these existing motifs and unified the two stories. The horizontal march of the pilasters and columns builds to a dramatic climax at the central bay, and the bays of the facade snugly fit the nave-chapel system behind them. Many Roman church facades of the 17th century are architectural variations on della Porta's design. Chronologically and stylistically, Il Gesù belongs to the Late Renaissance, but its enormous influence on later basilican churches marks it as one of the most significant monuments for the development of Italian Baroque ecclesiastical architecture.

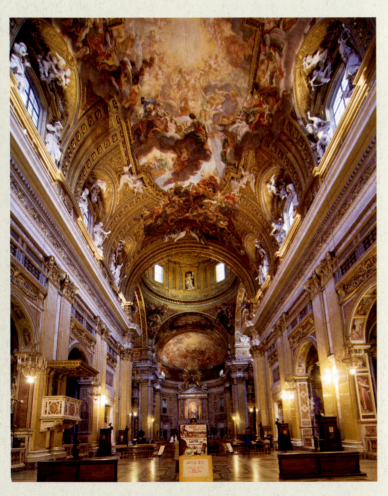

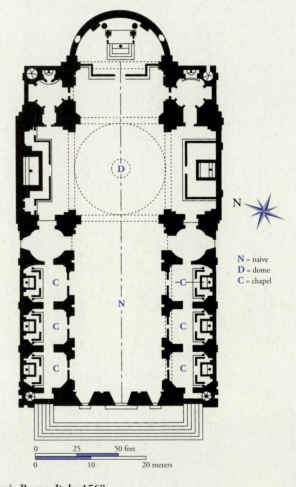

N = naive
D = dome
C = chapel

22-58 GIACOMO DA VIGNOLA, interior looking east (*left*) and plan (*right*) of Il Gesù, Rome, Italy, 1568.

Giacomo da Vignola's plan for Il Gesù, with its exceptionally wide nave with side chapels instead of aisles—ideal for grand processions—won wide acceptance in the Catholic world.

successful in the field of education, the order established numerous schools. In addition, its members were effective missionaries and carried the message of Catholicism to the Americas, Asia, and Africa.

The Jesuits also made their mark in the history of architecture with the construction of Il Gesù (see "Rethinking the Basilican Church," above), which had an enormous influence on church design in the Baroque era, discussed in detail in the next chapter.

RENAISSANCE AND MANNERISM IN CINQUECENTO ITALY

High and Late Renaissance 1495–1600

- During the High (1500–1520) and Late (1520–1600) Renaissance periods in Italy, artists, often in the employ of the papacy, further developed the interest in classical cultures, perspective, proportion, and human anatomy that had characterized Quattrocento Italian art.

- Leonardo da Vinci, the quintessential "Renaissance man," won renown as a painter for his sfumato (misty haziness) and for his psychological insight in depicting biblical narrative (*Last Supper*) and contemporary personalities (*Mona Lisa*).

- Raphael favored lighter tonalities than Leonardo and clarity over obscurity. His sculpturesque figures appear in landscapes under blue skies (*Madonna of the Meadows*) or in grandiose architectural settings rendered in perfect perspective (*School of Athens*).

- Michelangelo was a pioneer in several media, including architecture, but his first love was sculpture. He carved (*David, Moses*) and painted (Sistine Chapel ceiling) emotionally charged figures with heroic physiques, preferring pent-up energy to Raphael's calm, ideal beauty.

- Whereas most Florentine and Roman artists emphasized careful design preparation based on preliminary drawing (disegno), Venetian artists, such as Giovanni Bellini and Giorgione, focused on color and the process of paint application (colorito), landscape, and a poetic approach to painting (poesia).

- The greatest master of the Venetian painting school was Titian, famed for his rich surface textures and dazzling display of color in all its nuances. In paintings such as *Venus of Urbino,* he established oil color on canvas as the standard medium of the Western pictorial tradition.

- The leading architect of the early 16th century was Bramante, who championed the classical style of the ancients. He based his design for the Tempietto—the first High Renaissance building—on antique models, but the combination of parts was new and original.

- Andrea Palladio, an important theorist as well as architect, carried on Bramante's classical style during the Late Renaissance. Famed for his villa designs, he had a lasting influence on later European and American architecture.

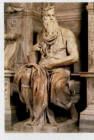

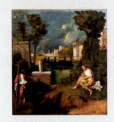

Michelangelo, *Moses*, ca. 1513–1515

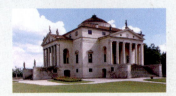

Giorgione, *The Tempest*, ca. 1509–1510

Palladio, *Villa Rotonda*, ca. 1550–1570

Mannerism 1520–1600

- Mannerism emerged in the 1520s as an alternative to the High Renaissance style. A prime feature of Mannerist art is artifice. Renaissance artists generally strove to create art that appeared natural, whereas Mannerist artists were less inclined to disguise the contrived nature of art production. Ambiguous space, departures from expected conventions, and unusual presentations of traditional themes are hallmarks of Mannerist painting.

- Parmigianino's *Madonna with the Long Neck* exemplifies the elegant stylishness of Mannerist painting. The elongated proportions of the figures, the enigmatic line of columns without capitals, and the ambiguous position of the figure with a scroll are the antithesis of High Renaissance classical proportions, clarity of meaning, and rational perspective.

- Mannerism was also a sculptural style. Benvenuto Cellini created a costly saltcellar for the table of the French king Francis I. The figures, based on antique statuary, have the slim waists and long limbs that appealed to Mannerist taste.

- The leading Mannerist architect was Giulio Romano, who rejected the balance, order, and stability of the High Renaissance style. In the Palazzo del Tè in Mantua, the divergences from architectural convention parody Bramante's classical style and include triglyphs that slip out of the Doric frieze.

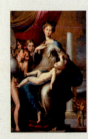

Parmigianino, *Madonna with the Long Neck,* 1534–1540

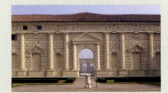

Giulio Romano, *Palazzo del Tè,* 1525–1535

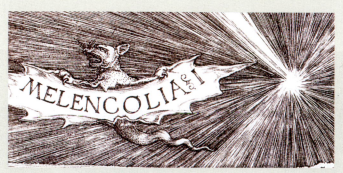

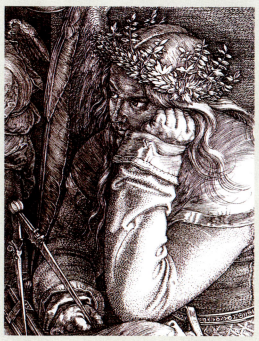

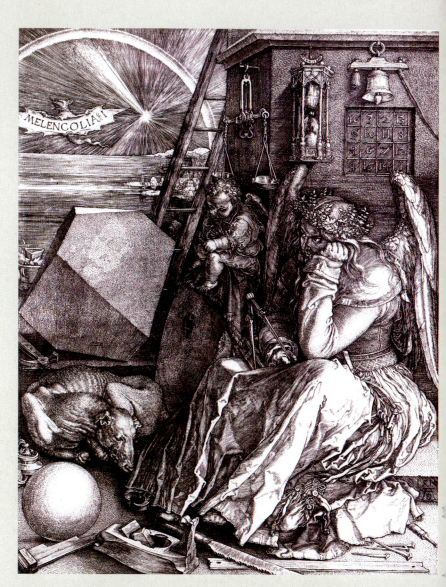

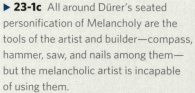
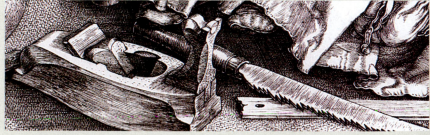

◄ **23-1a** The Roman numeral on the bat's banner refers to the first level of melancholy: artistic melancholy. However, the burst of light suggests that artists can overcome depression and produce great art.

▲ **23-1b** In this "self-portrait" of his artistic personality, Dürer represented Melancholy as a brooding winged woman. Melancholy's face is obscured by shadow, underscoring her state of mind.

23-1 **ALBRECHT DÜRER**, *Melencolia I*, 1514. Engraving, $9\frac{3}{8}'' \times 7\frac{1}{2}''$. Victoria & Albert Museum, London.

▶ **23-1c** All around Dürer's seated personification of Melancholy are the tools of the artist and builder—compass, hammer, saw, and nails among them—but the melancholic artist is incapable of using them.

High Renaissance and Mannerism in Northern Europe and Spain

ALBRECHT DÜRER, MELANCHOLIC GENIUS

In northern Europe, as in Italy, one by-product of the Renaissance was the celebration of artistic genius, accompanied in many cases by probing introspection (literally "looking inside") on the part of individual artists. One German artist who looked within was ALBRECHT DÜRER (1471–1528) of Nuremberg, the first artist outside Italy to become an international celebrity. Dürer was a highly skilled painter, but his reputation today as in his own time rests primarily on his graphic art, which he promoted with an astute businessman's skill. With the aid of his wife, his mother, and an agent, Dürer aggressively marketed his engravings and woodcuts and became a wealthy man. Moreover, in 1506, to protect his financial interests, Dürer filed the first lawsuit in history over artistic copyright, accusing an Italian artist of copying his prints.

One of Dürer's most famous works, *Melencolia I* (FIG. 23-1), reveals not only his unsurpassed skill with the engraver's burin but also a great deal about his psyche as a Renaissance artist. In *Melencolia I,* Dürer took up the theme of melancholy, one of the temperaments associated with the "four humors"— the fluids that were the basis of the theories about body functions developed by the ancient Greek physician Hippocrates and practiced in medieval physiology. The Italian humanist Marsilio Ficino (1433–1499) had written an influential treatise (*De vita triplici,* 1482–1489) in which he asserted that artists were distinct from the population at large because they were born under the sign of the planet Saturn, named for the ancient Roman god. They shared that deity's melancholic temperament because they had an excess of black bile (one of the four humors) in their systems. Artists therefore were "saturnine"—eccentric and capable both of inspired artistic frenzy and melancholic depression. Raphael had depicted Michelangelo in the guise of the brooding Heraclitus in his *School of Athens* (FIG. 22-9), and Dürer used a similarly posed female figure for his winged personification of Melancholy.

In 1510, in *De occulta philosophia,* Heinrich Cornelius Agrippa (1486–1535) of Nettesheim identified three levels of melancholy. The first was artistic melancholy, which explains the Roman numeral on the banner carried by the bat—a creature of the dark—in Dürer's engraving. Above the brooding figure of Melancholy is an hourglass with the sands of time running out. All around her are the tools of the artist and builder (compare FIG. 13-32)—compass, hammer, nails, and saw among them. However, those tools are useless to the frustrated artist while suffering from melancholy. Melancholy's face is obscured by shadow, underscoring her state of mind. But Dürer also included a burst of light on the far horizon behind the bat, an optimistic note suggesting that artists can overcome their depression and produce works of genius—such as this engraving.

NORTHERN EUROPE IN THE 16TH CENTURY

The dissolution of the Burgundian Netherlands in 1477 led in the early 16th century to a realignment in the European geopolitical landscape (MAP 23-1, page 678). France and the Holy Roman Empire absorbed the former Burgundian territories and increased their power. But by the end of the century, through calculated marriages, military exploits, and ambitious territorial expansion, Spain was the dominant European state. Throughout the Continent, monarchs increasingly used art and architecture to glorify their reigns and to promote a stronger sense of cultural and political unity among their subjects, thereby laying the foundation for today's European nations. Wealthy merchants also cultivated art as a status symbol, and the commissioning and collecting of artworks became less and less the exclusive province of the aristocracy.

These important societal changes occurred against the backdrop of a momentous religious crisis. Concerted attempts to reform Church practices led to the Reformation and the establishment of Protestantism (as distinct from Catholicism), which in turn prompted the Church of Rome's response, the Counter-Reformation (see page 641). Ultimately, the Reformation split Christendom in half and produced a hundred years of civil war between Protestants and Catholics.

NORTHERN HUMANISM The tumultuous religious conflict engulfing 16th-century Europe did not, however, prevent—and may even have accelerated—the exchange of intellectual and artistic ideas, because artists frequently moved from one area to another in search of religious freedom and lucrative commissions. Catholic Italy and the (mostly) Protestant Holy Roman Empire shared in a lively commerce—economic and cultural—and 16th-century art throughout Europe was a major beneficiary of that exchange. Humanism filtered up from Italy and spread throughout northern Europe. Humanists north of the Alps, like their southern counterparts, cultivated knowledge of classical cultures and literature, but they focused more on reconciling humanism with Christianity.

Among the most influential of these "Christian humanists" were the Dutchman Desiderius Erasmus (1466–1536) of Rotterdam and the Englishman Sir Thomas More (1478–1535). Erasmus demonstrated his interest in both Italian humanism and religion with his "philosophy of Christ," emphasizing education and scriptural knowledge. Both an ordained priest and an avid scholar, Erasmus wrote (in Latin) his most famous essay, *In Praise of Folly*, in 1509, which he published two years later. In this widely read work, Erasmus satirized not just the Church of Rome but various social classes as well. His ideas were to play an important role in the development of the Reformation, but he consistently declined to join any of the Reformation sects. Equally well educated was Thomas More, who served King Henry VIII (r. 1509–1547; FIG. 23-11A). Henry eventually ordered More's execution because of More's opposition to England's break with the Catholic Church. In France, François Rabelais (ca. 1494–1553), a former monk who advocated rejecting stagnant religious dogmatism, disseminated the humanist spirit.

The turmoil emerging during the 16th century lasted well into the 17th century and permanently affected the face of Europe. The concerted challenges to established authority and the persistent philosophical inquiry eventually led to the rise of new political systems (for example, the nation-state) and new economic systems (such as capitalism).

GERMANY

Although at the opening of the 16th century many Christians in the Holy Roman Empire expressed dissatisfaction with the Church of Rome, Martin Luther had not yet posted his *Ninety-five Theses* which launched the Protestant Reformation. The Catholic clergy in Germany still offered artists important commissions.

MATTHIAS GRÜNEWALD Matthias Neithardt, known conventionally as MATTHIAS GRÜNEWALD (ca. 1480–1528), worked for the archbishops of Mainz in several capacities, from court painter and decorator to architect, hydraulic engineer, and superintendent of works. Grünewald eventually moved to northern Germany, where he settled at Halle in Saxony. Around 1512, he began work on the *Isenheim Altarpiece* (FIG. 23-2), a complex and fascinating polyptych reflecting Catholic beliefs and incorporating several references to Catholic doctrines, such as the lamb (symbol of the son of God), whose wound spurts blood into a chalice in the *Crucifixion* (FIG. 23-2, *top*) on the exterior of the altarpiece.

Created for the monastic hospital order of Saint Anthony of Isenheim, the *Isenheim Altarpiece* takes the form of a carved wood shrine by NIKOLAUS HAGENAUER (active 1493–1538) featuring large painted and gilded statues of Saints Anthony Abbot, Augustine, and Jerome in the main zone, and smaller statues of Christ and the 12 apostles in the predella (FIG. 23-2, *bottom*). To Hagenauer's centerpiece, carved around 1505, Grünewald added between 1512 and 1515 two pairs of painted moveable wings that open at the center. Hinged at the sides, one pair stands directly behind the other. The exterior panels of the first pair (visible when the altarpiece is closed, FIG. 23-2, *top*) are *Crucifixion* in the center, *Saint Sebastian* on the left, *Saint Anthony Abbot* on the right, and *Lamentation* in the predella. When these exterior wings are open, four additional scenes (not illustrated)—*Annunciation, Angelic Concert, Madonna and Child*, and *Resurrection*—appear. Opening this second pair of wings exposes Hagenauer's interior shrine, flanked by Grünewald's *Meeting of Saints Anthony and Paul* and *Temptation of Saint Anthony* panels (FIG. 23-2, *bottom*).

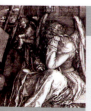

HIGH RENAISSANCE AND MANNERISM IN NORTHERN EUROPE AND SPAIN

1500–1530
- In Catholic countries, commissions for religious works, such as the *Isenheim Altarpiece*, continue, but, consistent with Reformation values, Protestant patrons prefer secular themes, such as portraiture, classical mythology, and the macabre, including death and witchcraft
- Albrecht Dürer achieves international fame (and wealth) as a master printmaker

1530–1560
- Netherlandish painters inject moralizing religious messages into seemingly secular genre paintings
- Hans Holbein, Caterina van Hemessen, and Levina Teerlinc achieve renown as portrait painters
- In France under Henry II (r. 1547–1559), architectural designs are a mix of Italian and Northern Renaissance elements

1560–1600
- Pieter Bruegel the Elder, the greatest Netherlandish artist of the mid-16th century, produces masterful landscapes that nonetheless focus on human activities
- Greek-born El Greco settles in Toledo and creates paintings that are a uniquely personal mix of Byzantine and Italian Mannerist elements. His hybrid style captured the fervor of Spanish Catholicism

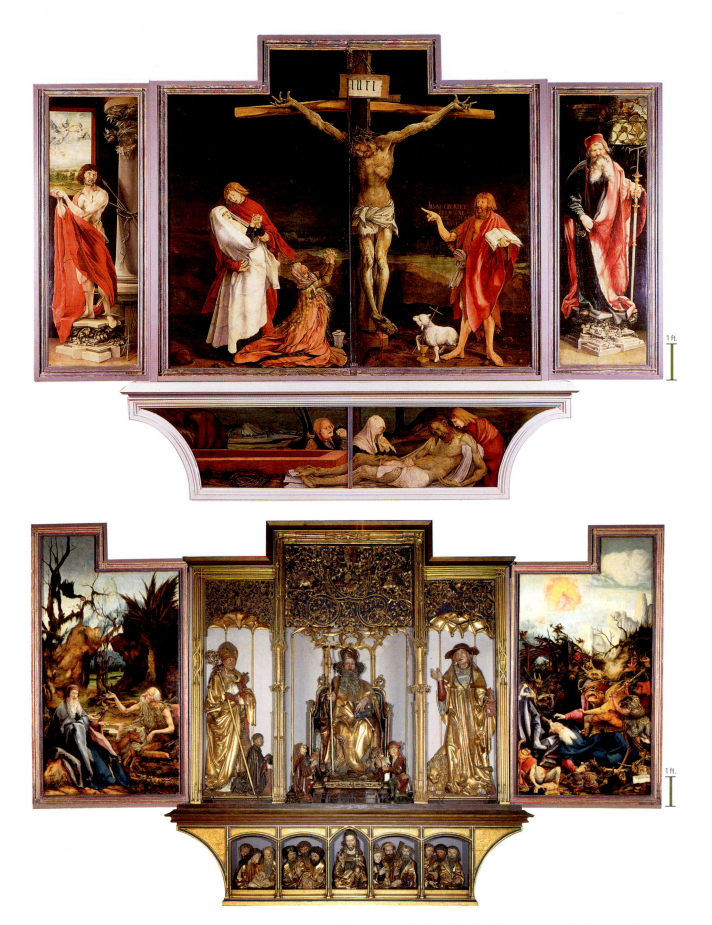

23-2 Matthias Grünewald, *Isenheim Altarpiece* (*top*: closed; *bottom*: open), from the chapel of the Hospital of Saint Anthony, Isenheim, France, ca. 1512–1515. Oil on wood, center panel 9' 9$\frac{1}{2}$" × 10' 9", each wing 8' 2$\frac{1}{2}$" × 3' $\frac{1}{2}$", predella 2' 5$\frac{1}{2}$" × 11' 2". Shrine carved by Nikolaus Hagenauer, ca. 1505. Painted and gilt limewood, 9' 9$\frac{1}{2}$" × 10' 9". Musée d'Unterlinden, Colmar.

Befitting its setting in a monastic hospital, Matthias Grünewald's *Isenheim Altarpiece* includes painted panels depicting suffering and disease but also miraculous healing, hope, and salvation.

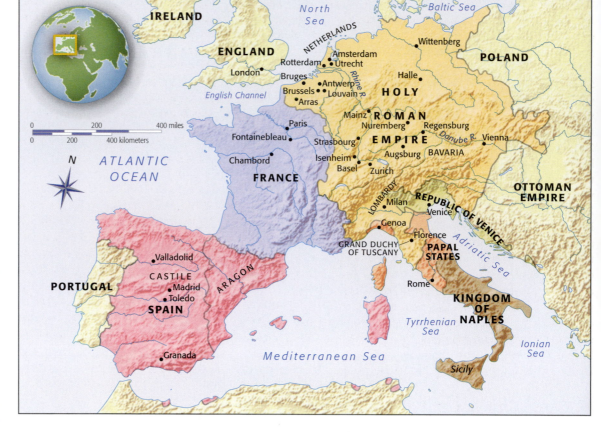

MAP 23-1 Europe in the early 16th century.

The placement of this altarpiece in the choir of a church adjacent to the monastery's hospital dictated much of the imagery. Saints associated with the plague and other diseases and with miraculous cures, such as Saints Anthony and Sebastian, appear prominently in the *Isenheim Altarpiece*. Grünewald's panels specifically address the themes of dire illness and miraculous healing and accordingly emphasize the suffering of the order's patron saint, Anthony Abbot (see "Early Christian Saints," page 237). The painted images served as warnings, encouraging increased devotion from monks and hospital patients. They also functioned therapeutically by offering some hope to the afflicted. Indeed, Saint Anthony's legend emphasized his dual role as vengeful dispenser of justice (by inflicting disease) and benevolent healer.

One of the most memorable scenes is *Temptation of Saint Anthony* (FIG. 23-2, *bottom right*). It is a terrifying image of the five temptations (lack of faith, despair, impatience, spiritual pride, and avarice), depicted as an assortment of ghoulish and bestial creatures in a dark landscape, attacking the saint. In the foreground, Grünewald painted a grotesque image of a man, whose oozing boils, withered arm, and distended stomach all suggest a horrible disease. Medical experts have connected these symptoms with ergotism (a disease caused by ergot, a fungus that grows especially on rye). Doctors did not discover the cause of this disease until about 1600. People lived in fear of its recognizable symptoms (convulsions and gangrene) and called the illness "Saint Anthony's Fire." Ergotism was one of the major diseases treated at the Isenheim hospital. Indeed, Grünewald depicted Christ's skin covered with sores. Furthermore, ergotism often compelled amputation, and viewers of the *Isenheim Altarpiece* have noted that the two moveable halves of the altarpiece's predella (FIG. 23-2, *top*), if slid apart, make it appear as if Christ's legs have been amputated. The same observation applies to the two main exterior panels. Due to the off-center placement of the cross, opening the left panel "severs" one arm from the crucified figure.

Thus Grünewald carefully selected and presented his altarpiece's iconography to be particularly meaningful for patients at this hospital. In the interior shrine, the artist balanced the horrors of the disease and the punishments awaiting those who did not repent with scenes such as *Meeting of Saints Anthony and Paul*, depicting the two saints, healthy and aged, conversing peacefully. Even the exterior panels (the closed altarpiece; FIG. 23-2, *top*) convey these same concerns. *Crucifixion* emphasizes Christ's pain and suffering, but the knowledge that this act redeemed humanity tempers the misery. In addition, Saint Anthony appears in the right wing as a devout follower of Christ who, like Christ, endured intense suffering for his faith. Saint Anthony's appearance on the exterior thus reinforces the themes that Grünewald intertwined throughout this entire work—themes of pain, illness, and death, as well as those of hope, comfort, and salvation. Grünewald also brilliantly used color to enhance the effect of the painted scenes of the altarpiece. He intensified the contrast of horror and hope by playing subtle tones and soft harmonies against shocking dissonances of color.

ALBRECHT DÜRER A slightly older contemporary of Grünewald was Albrecht Dürer (FIG. 23-1), who put the younger artist in charge of his studio during one of his trips to Italy. Dürer was the most famous northern European artist of his generation and one of the greatest printmakers of any era. Unlike Grünewald, Dürer traveled extensively, visiting and studying in Colmar, Basel, Strasbourg, Venice, Antwerp, and Brussels, among other locales. As a result, Dürer met many of the leading humanists and artists of his time, including Erasmus of Rotterdam and the Venetian master Giovanni Bellini (FIGS. 21-40, 22-32, and 22-33). Fascinated with the classical ideas of the Italian Renaissance, Dürer was among the first Northern Renaissance artists to travel to Italy expressly to study Italian art and its underlying theories at their source. After his first journey in 1494–1495 (the second was in 1505–1506), he incorporated many Italian developments into his prints and paintings. Art historians have acclaimed Dürer as the first artist north of the Alps to understand fully the basic aims of the Renaissance in Italy. Like Leonardo da Vinci, Dürer wrote theoretical treatises on a variety of subjects, including perspective, fortification, and the ideal in human proportions. Unlike Leonardo, he both finished and published his writings. Dürer also was the first northern European artist to leave a record of his life and career through his correspondence, a detailed diary, and a series of self-portraits.

SELF-PORTRAITS Dürer's earliest preserved self-portrait—a silverpoint drawing now in the Albertina in Vienna—dates to 1484, when he was only 13, two years before he began his formal education as an apprentice in the workshop of Michael Wolgemut (FIG. 20-22). In 1498, a few years after his first visit to Italy, he painted a likeness of himself in the Italian mode—a seated half-length portrait in three-quarter view in front of a window through which the viewer sees a landscape. The *Self-Portrait* reproduced here (FIG. 23-3), painted just two years later, is markedly different in character. Inscribed with his monogram and the date (*left*) and four lines (*right*) stating that the painting depicts him at age 28, the panel portrays the artist in a fur-trimmed coat in a rigid frontal posture against a dark background. Dürer has a short beard and shoulder-length hair, and the portrait intentionally evokes medieval devotional images of Christ. The position of Dürer's right hand resembles but does not duplicate (which would have been blasphemous) Christ's standard gesture of blessing in Byzantine icons (FIG. 9-34). The focus on the hand is also a reference to the artist's hand as a creative instrument. Doubtless deeply affected by the new humanistic view that had

emerged in Renaissance Italy of the artist as a divinely inspired genius (see "Albrecht Dürer, Melancholic Genius," page 675), Dürer responded by painting himself as a Christlike figure. He also embraced Italian artists' interest in science, as is evident in his botanically accurate 1503 watercolor study *Great Piece of Turf* (FIG. 23-3A).

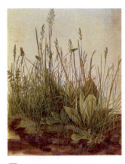

🡵 **23-3A** DÜRER, *Great Piece of Turf*, 1503.

FALL OF MAN Trained as a goldsmith by his father before he took up painting and printmaking, Dürer developed an extraordinary proficiency in handling the burin. This technical ability, combined with his extraordinary skill in drawing, enabled Dürer to produce a body of graphic work that few artists have rivaled for quality and number. Many of his prints were book illustrations, and Dürer also sold prints in single sheets, which people of ordinary means could buy, expanding his audience considerably and, as noted, making him a wealthy man. Erasmus praised Dürer as "the Apelles [the most renowned ancient Greek painter] of black lines,"[1] and the German artist's mastery of all aspects of printmaking is evident also in his woodcuts (FIG. I-9).

One of Dürer's early masterpieces, *Fall of Man* (*Adam and Eve*; FIG. 23-4), represents the first distillation of his studies of the Vitruvian theory of human proportions (compare FIG. 22-5A),

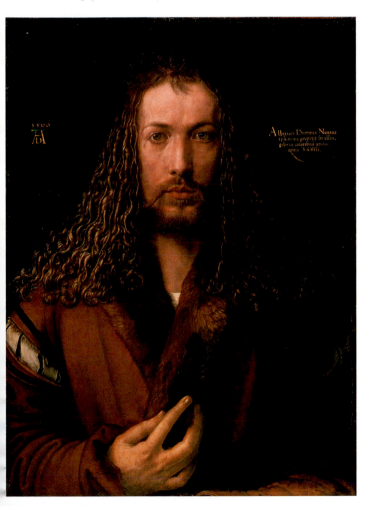

23-3 ALBRECHT DÜRER, *Self-Portrait,* 1500. Oil on wood, 2' 2¼" × 1' 7¼". Alte Pinakothek, Munich.

Dürer here presents himself as a frontal Christlike figure reminiscent of medieval icons. It is an image of the artist as a divinely inspired genius, a concept inconceivable before the Renaissance.

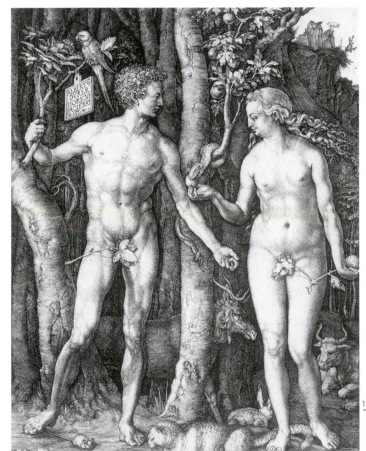

23-4 ALBRECHT DÜRER, *Fall of Man* (*Adam and Eve*), 1504. Engraving, 9⅞" × 7⅝". Museum of Fine Arts, Boston (centennial gift of Landon T. Clay).

Dürer was the first Northern Renaissance artist to achieve international celebrity. *Fall of Man,* with two figures based on ancient statues, reflects his studies of the Vitruvian theory of human proportions.

a theory based on arithmetic ratios. Clearly outlined against the dark background of a northern European forest, the two idealized figures of Adam and Eve stand in poses reminiscent of specific classical statues of Apollo and Venus. Preceded by numerous geometric drawings in which the artist attempted to systematize sets of ideal human proportions in balanced contrapposto poses, the final print presents Dürer's concept of the "perfect" male and female figures. Yet he tempered this idealization with naturalism, demonstrating his well-honed observational skills in his rendering of the background foliage and animals (compare FIGS. 23-3A and **23-4A**). The gnarled bark of the trees and the feathery leaves authenticate the scene, as do the various creatures skulking underfoot. The animals populating the print are symbolic. The choleric cat, the melancholic elk, the sanguine rabbit, and the phlegmatic ox represent humanity's temperaments based on the four humors (see page 675), which, prior to the fall of man, are in balance. Nonetheless, the tension between the cat and the mouse in the foreground symbolizes the relation between Adam and Eve at the crucial moment before they commit the original sin.

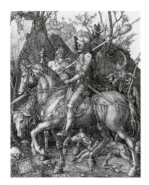

⬧ 23-4A DÜRER, *Knight, Death, and the Devil*, 1513.

FOUR APOSTLES Dürer's major work in the oil medium is *Four Apostles* (FIG. **23-5**), a two-panel painting he produced without commission and presented to the city fathers of Nuremberg in 1526 to be hung in the city hall. Saints John and Peter appear on the left panel, Mark and Paul on the right (see "Early Christian Saints," pages 236–237). In addition to showcasing Dürer's mastery of the oil technique, his brilliant use of color and light and shade, and his ability to imbue the four saints with individual personalities and portraitlike features, *Four Apostles* documents Dürer's support for the German theologian Martin Luther (1483–1546), who sparked the Protestant Reformation. Dürer conveyed his Lutheran sympathies by his positioning of the figures. He relegated Saint Peter (as representative of the pope in Rome) to a secondary role by placing him behind John the Evangelist (compare Konrad Witz's earlier treatment of Peter in *Miraculous Draft of Fish* [FIG. 20-19], widely interpreted as a commentary on the limited powers of the pope). John assumed particular prominence for Luther because of the evangelist's focus on Jesus as a person in his Gospel. In addition, Peter and John both read from the Bible, the single authoritative source of religious truth, according to Luther. Dürer emphasized the Bible's centrality by depicting it open to the passage "In the beginning was the Word, and the Word was with God, and the Word was God" (John 1:1). At the bottom of the panels, Dürer included quotations from the four apostles' books, using Luther's German translation of the New Testament. The excerpts warn against the coming of perilous times and the preaching of false prophets who will distort God's word.

LUTHER AND THE REFORMATION The Protestant Reformation, which came to fruition in the early 16th century, had its roots in long-term, growing dissatisfaction with the Catholic Church's leadership. The deteriorating relationship between the faithful and the Church of Rome's hierarchy stood as an obstacle for the millions who sought a meaningful religious experience. Particularly damaging was the perception that the Roman popes concerned themselves more with temporal power and material wealth than

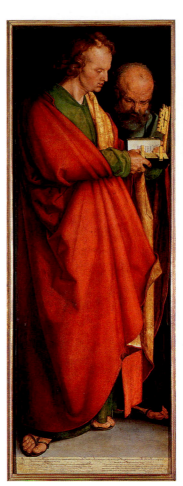
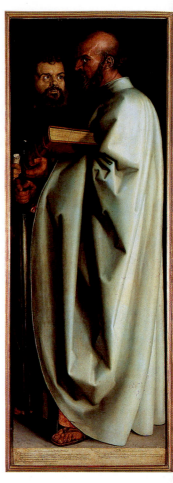

23-5 ALBRECHT DÜRER, *Four Apostles,* from the city hall, Nuremberg, Germany, 1526. Oil on wood, each panel 7' 1" × 2' 6". Alte Pinakothek, Munich.

Dürer's support for Lutheranism surfaces in his portraitlike depictions of four saints on two painted panels. Peter, representative of the pope in Rome, plays a secondary role behind John the Evangelist.

with the salvation of their Christian flock. The fact that many 15th-century popes and cardinals came from wealthy families, such as the Medici, intensified this perception. It was not only those at the highest levels who seemed to ignore their spiritual duties. Archbishops, bishops, and abbots began to accumulate numerous offices, thereby increasing their revenues but making it more difficult for them to fulfill all of their responsibilities. By 1517, dissatisfaction with the Roman Church had grown so widespread that Luther felt free to openly challenge papal authority by posting on October 31 in Wittenberg his *Ninety-five Theses,* in which he enumerated his objections to Catholic practices, especially the sale of indulgences. *Indulgences* were Church-sanctioned remittances (or reductions) of time Catholics had to spend in Purgatory for confessed sins. The increasing frequency of their sale suggested that those who could afford to purchase indulgences were buying their way into Heaven.

Luther's goal was significant reform and clarification of major spiritual issues, but his ideas ultimately led to splitting Western Christendom apart. According to Luther, the Catholic Church's extensive ecclesiastical structure needed casting out, for it had no basis in scripture. The Bible and nothing else could serve as the foundation for Christianity. Luther called the pope the Antichrist (for which Pope Leo X excommunicated him in 1520) and the Church of Rome the "whore of Babylon." He denounced ordained

RELIGION AND MYTHOLOGY

Catholic versus Protestant Views of Salvation

A central concern of the Protestant reformers was the question of how Christians achieve salvation. Rather than perceive salvation as something for which weak and sinful humans must constantly strive through good deeds performed under the watchful eye of a punitive God, Martin Luther argued that faithful individuals attained redemption solely by God's bestowal of his grace. Therefore, people cannot earn salvation. Further, no ecclesiastical machinery with all its miraculous rites and Church-sanctioned indulgences could save sinners face-to-face with God. Only absolute faith in Christ could redeem sinners and ensure salvation. Redemption by faith alone, with the guidance of holy scripture, was the fundamental doctrine of Protestantism.

In *Law and Gospel* (FIG. 23-6), a woodcut dated about a dozen years after Luther set the Reformation in motion with his *Ninety-five Theses,* Lucas Cranach the Elder gave visual expression to the doctrinal differences between Protestantism and Catholicism. Cranach contrasted Catholicism (based on Old Testament law, according to Luther) and Protestantism (based on the Gospel belief in God's grace) in two images separated by a centrally placed tree that has leafy branches only on the Protestant side. On the left half, judgment day has arrived, as represented by Christ's appearance at the top of the scene, hovering amid a cloud halo and accompanied by angels and saints. Christ raises his left hand in the traditional gesture of damnation, and, below, a skeleton drives off a terrified person to burn for eternity in Hell. This person tried to live a good and honorable life, but despite his efforts, he fell short. Moses stands to the side, holding the tablets of the law—the Ten Commandments, which Catholics follow in their attempt to attain salvation.

In contrast to this Catholic reliance on good works and clean living, Protestant doctrine emphasized God's grace as the source of redemption. Accordingly, God showers the sinner in the right half of the print with grace, as streams of blood flow from the crucified Christ. At the far left are Adam and Eve, whose original sin necessitated Christ's sacrifice. In the lower right corner of the woodcut, Christ emerges from the tomb and promises salvation to all who believe in him.

23-6 LUCAS CRANACH THE ELDER, *Law and Gospel,* ca. 1530. Woodcut, $10\frac{5}{8}$" × $1'\frac{3}{4}$". British Museum, London.

Lucas Cranach was a close friend of Martin Luther, whose *Ninety-five Theses* launched the Protestant Reformation in 1517. This woodcut contrasts Catholic and Protestant views of how to achieve salvation.

---

priests and also rejected most of Catholicism's sacraments other than baptism and communion, decrying them as obstacles to salvation (see "Catholic versus Protestant Views of Salvation," above, and FIG. 23-6). Luther maintained that for Christianity to be restored to its original purity, the Catholic Church needed cleansing of all the doctrinal impurities that had collected through the ages. Luther advocated the Bible as the source of all religious truth. The Bible—the sole scriptural authority—was the word of God, which did not exist in the Church's councils, law, and rituals. Luther facilitated the lay public's access to biblical truths by publishing the first translation of the Bible in a vernacular language.

ART AND THE REFORMATION In addition to doctrinal differences, Catholics and Protestants took divergent stances on the role of visual imagery in religion. Catholics embraced church decoration as an aid to communicating with God (see "The Council of Trent,"

page 642). In contrast, Protestants believed that images of Christ, the Virgin, and saints could lead to idolatry and distracted viewers from focusing on the real reason for their presence in church—to communicate directly with God. Because of this belief, Protestant churches were relatively bare, and the extensive church pictorial programs found especially in Italy but also in northern Europe (FIGS. 20-18, 20-19, and 23-2) were not as prominent in Protestant churches.

The Protestant concern over the role of religious imagery escalated at times to outright *iconoclasm*—the objection to and destruction of religious imagery, a revival of an attitude that, centuries before, led to an outright ban on religious art in the Byzantine Empire (see "Icons and Iconoclasm," page 271). In encouraging a more personal relationship with God, Protestant leaders spoke out against much of the religious art being produced. In his 1525 tract *Against the Heavenly Prophets in the Matter of Images and*

Sacraments, Martin Luther explained his attitude toward religious imagery:

> I approached the task of destroying images by first tearing them out of the heart through God's Word and making them worthless and despised. . . . For when they are no longer in the heart, they can do no harm when seen with the eyes. . . . I have allowed and not forbidden the outward removal of images. . . . And I say at the outset that according to the law of Moses no other images are forbidden than an image of God which one worships. A crucifix, on the other hand, or any other holy image is not forbidden.[2]

In fact, Luther approved the inclusion of illustrations in his translations of the Bible as well as painted altarpieces in churches, which he believed served a didactic purpose. However, two influential Protestant theologians based in Switzerland—Huldrych (Ulrich) Zwingli (1484–1531) and French-born John Calvin (Jean Cauvin, 1509–1564)—were more vociferous in cautioning their followers about the potentially dangerous nature of all religious imagery. Zwingli and Calvin's condemnation of religious imagery often led to eruptions of iconoclasm. Particularly violent waves of iconoclastic fervor swept Basel, Zurich, Strasbourg, and Wittenberg in the 1520s. In an episode known as the Great Iconoclasm, bands of Calvinists visited Catholic churches in the Netherlands in 1566, shattering stained-glass windows, smashing statues, and destroying paintings and other artworks that they perceived as idolatrous. These strong reactions to art, which reflected the religious fervor of the time, also serve as dramatic demonstrations of the power of art—and of how much art matters in society.

LUCAS CRANACH THE ELDER The artist most closely associated with the Protestant Reformation and with Martin Luther in particular was Lucas Cranach the Elder (1472–1553), who provided the illustrations for Luther's vernacular Bible. Cranach and Luther were godfathers to each other's children, and many scholars have dubbed Cranach "the painter of the Reformation." Cranach was also an accomplished graphic artist who used the new, inexpensive medium of prints on paper to promote Lutheran ideology (FIG. 23-6). Cranach's work encompasses a wide range of themes, however. For example, for aristocratic Saxon patrons he produced a large number of paintings of classical myths featuring female nudes in suggestive poses.

One classical theme that Cranach depicted several times was *Judgment of Paris,* of which the small panel (FIG. 23-7) now in Karlsruhe is the best example. Homer recorded the story in the eighth century BCE, but Cranach's source was probably the elaboration of the Greek tale in Roman times by Lucian (ca. 120–ca. 180). Mercury chose a handsome young shepherd named Paris to be the judge of a beauty contest among three goddesses—Juno, wife of Jupiter; Minerva, Jupiter's virgin daughter and goddess of wisdom and war; and Venus, the goddess of love (see "The Gods and Goddesses of Mount Olympus," page 105). According to Lucian, each goddess attempted to bribe Paris with rich rewards if he chose her. Venus won by offering Paris the most beautiful woman in the world, Helen of Troy, and thus set in motion the epic war between the Greeks and Trojans recounted in Homer's *Iliad* (see page 84).

No one, however, could confuse Cranach's painting with an ancient depiction of the myth. The setting is a German landscape with a Saxon castle in the background, and the seated shepherd is a knight in full armor wearing a fashionable hat. Mercury, an aged man (as he never is in ancient art), also wearing armor, bends over to draw Paris's attention to the three goddesses. They are nude save

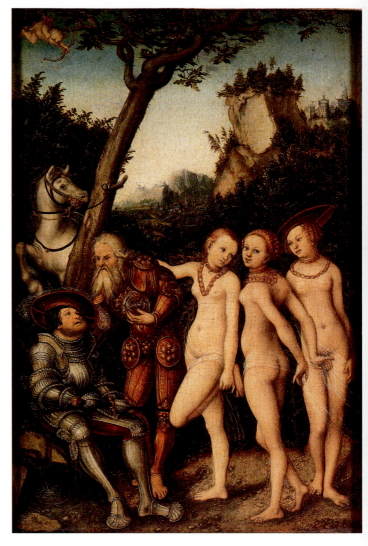

23-7 Lucas Cranach the Elder, *Judgment of Paris,* 1530. Oil on wood, $1' 1\frac{1}{2}'' \times 9\frac{1}{2}''$. Staatliche Kunsthalle, Karlsruhe.

For aristocratic German patrons, Cranach painted many classical myths featuring seductive female nudes. In his *Judgment of Paris,* the Greek shepherd is a knight in armor in a Saxon landscape.

for their transparent veils, their fine jewelry, and, in the case of Juno, an elegant hat. Cranach's goddesses are loosely based on classical representations of the Three Graces (compare FIG. 21-28), although ancient artists never depicted Juno or Minerva undressed. The German painter's figures also do not have the proportions (or modesty) of Praxiteles's *Aphrodite of Knidos* (FIG. 5-62) or Botticelli's *Venus* (FIG. 21-1). Slender, with small heads and breasts and long legs, they pose seductively before the judge. Venus performs a dance for Paris, but he seems indifferent to all three goddesses. Only the rearing horse appears to be excited by the spectacle—a touch of humor characteristic of Cranach.

HANS BALDUNG GRIEN When Albrecht Dürer undertook his second trip to Italy in 1505, he placed his most gifted assistant, Hans Baldung Grien (ca. 1484–1545), in charge of his studio. The son of a prosperous attorney and the brother of a university professor, Baldung chose to pursue printmaking (FIG. 23-8) and painting (FIG. 23-9) as a profession rather than the law or letters. He eventually settled in Strasbourg, a center of humanistic learning, where he enjoyed a long and successful career. Baldung produced some religious works, although none on the scale of Grünewald's

ART AND SOCIETY

Witchcraft, Disease, Plague, and Death

In an age when the normal life span was only about 40 years and disease, plague, and superstitious fear were commonplace, it is natural that these themes would figure prominently in some artworks, such as Matthias Grünewald's *Isenheim Altarpiece* (FIG. 23-2), painted for the Hospital of Saint Anthony in Isenheim. Death figures prominently too in the work of Grünewald's contemporary, Hans Baldung Grien, who also explored exotic and erotic subjects, including witchcraft.

Witchcraft was a counter-religion in the 15th and 16th centuries involving magical rituals, secret potions, and Devil worship. Witches prepared brews that they inhaled or rubbed into their skin, sending them into hallucinogenic trances in which they allegedly flew through the night sky on broomsticks or goats. The popes condemned all witches, and Church inquisitors vigorously pursued these demonic heretics and subjected them to torture to wrest confessions from them. People also feared witches because they thought that they could create storms and hailstorms that ruined crops and caused famines. Witchcraft fascinated Baldung, and he turned to the subject repeatedly. For him and his contemporaries, witches were evil forces in the world, threats to man—as was Eve herself, whom Baldung also frequently depicted as a temptress responsible for original sin.

In *Witches' Sabbath* (FIG. 23-8), Baldung depicted a night scene in a forest featuring a coven of nude witches, although 16th-century witches performed their rites clothed. Female nudity and macabre scenes were popular with men, who avidly purchased the relatively inexpensive prints that Baldung created in large numbers. The coven in the *Witches' Sabbath* woodcut includes both young seductresses and old hags. They gather around a covered jar from which a fuming concoction escapes into the air. One young witch rides through the night sky on a goat. She sits backward—Baldung's way of suggesting that witchcraft is the inversion of the true religion, Christianity.

Witches' Sabbath does not address death and illness directly, but the inevitability of old age and death, which, with a strong dose of eroticism, are the central elements in Baldung's *Three Ages of Woman and Death* (FIG. 23-9), a subject he returned to repeatedly during his career. Albrecht Dürer—in whose workshop Baldung trained—had portrayed Death and Famine (FIG. I-9) in his woodcuts, and the emaciated figure of Death in Baldung's painting owes a debt to his master's work, as does the beautiful nude young woman Death approaches from behind. She is a variation on Dürer's Eve in *Fall of Man* (FIG. 23-4), an engraving Dürer produced while Baldung was his apprentice. Baldung's oil painting is a commentary on *vanitas* (Latin, "vanity," especially with regard to the transience of life), another popular subject.

The voluptuous, fair-skinned young woman gazes at her reflection in a mirror as she combs her long hair, oblivious that Death pursues her. The maiden appears two more times in the same painting at two different ages—as an infant who plays with one end of the young woman's transparent mantle and as a wrinkled, dark-skinned old woman who rushes in from the left to try to push Death away. Baldung tells the viewer that the old woman will not succeed in warding off Death. Indeed, the sand in the hourglass that Death holds mockingly over the maiden's head will run out too soon. (An hourglass also looms over Dürer's personified Melancholy in *Melencolia I*, FIG. 23-1.)

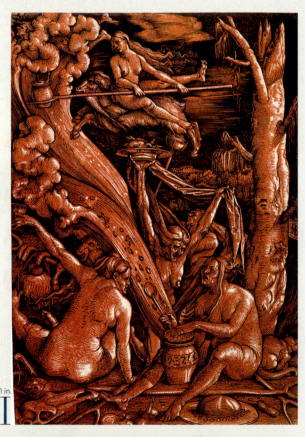

23-8 HANS BALDUNG GRIEN, *Witches' Sabbath*, 1510. Chiaroscuro woodcut, 1' 2$\frac{7}{8}$" × 10$\frac{1}{4}$". British Museum, London.

Baldung's woodcut depicts witches gathered around a cauldron containing a secret potion. One witch flies mounted backward on a goat, suggesting that witchcraft is the inversion of Christianity.

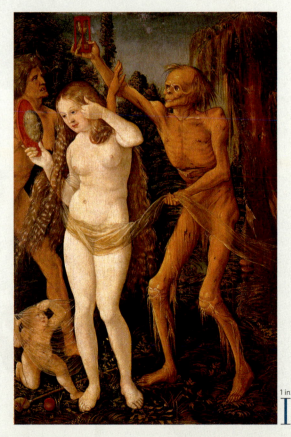

23-9 HANS BALDUNG GRIEN, *Three Ages of Woman and Death*, 1510. Oil on wood, 1' 3$\frac{3}{4}$" × 1' 3$\frac{3}{4}$". Kunsthistorisches Museum, Vienna.

Baldung often explored macabre themes featuring female nudity. Here, Death approaches a maiden as she admires her reflection. Beside her are an old woman and an infant—the maiden at different ages.

Isenheim Altarpiece (FIG. 23-2). His reputation rested primarily on his exploration of nontraditional subjects, such as witchcraft (see "Witchcraft, Disease, Plague, and Death," page 683).

Witches' Sabbath (FIG. 23-8) is a *chiaroscuro woodcut,* a recent innovation usually attributed to the Flemish woodcutter Jost de Negker (ca. 1485–ca. 1544). The technique requires the use of two blocks of wood instead of one. The printmaker carves and inks one block (the *key block*) in the usual way in order to produce a traditional black-and-white print (see "Printed Books," page 577). Then the artist cuts a second block (the *tone block*) consisting of broad highlights to be inked in grays or colors and printed over the first

block's impression. Chiaroscuro woodcuts therefore incorporate some of the qualities of painting and feature tonal subtleties absent in traditional woodcuts.

ALBRECHT ALTDORFER Although Dürer, Cranach, and Baldung sold their artworks primarily to private patrons, other artists in 16th-century Germany, as elsewhere in Europe, earned their income in the employ of rulers, and their work promoted the political agendas of their patrons. In 1529, for example, the duke of Bavaria, Wilhelm IV (r. 1508–1550), commissioned ALBRECHT ALTDORFER (ca. 1480–1538) of Regensburg to paint *Battle of Issus* (FIG. 23-10)

23-10 ALBRECHT ALTDORFER, *Battle of Issus,* 1529. Oil on wood, 5' 2¼" × 3' 11¼". Alte Pinakothek, Munich.

Interweaving landscape, history, and 16th-century politics, Altdorfer painted Alexander the Great's defeat of the Persians for a patron who had just embarked on a military campaign against the Ottoman Turks.

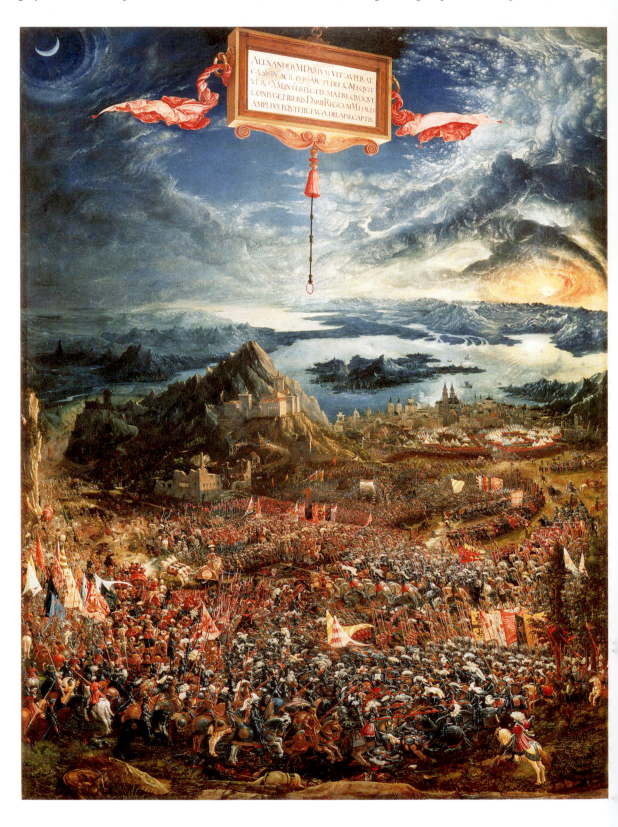

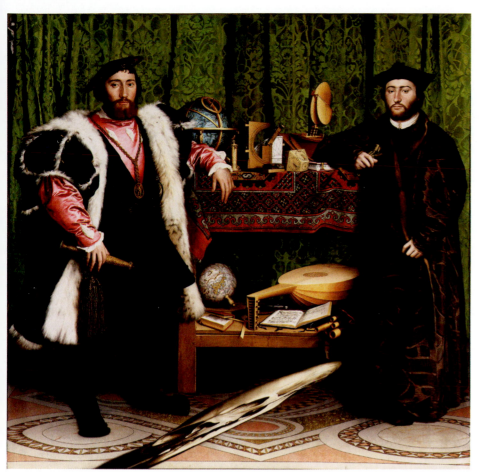

23-11 Hans Holbein the Younger, *The French Ambassadors*, 1533. Oil and tempera on wood, 6' 8" × 6' 9½". National Gallery, London.

In this double portrait, Holbein depicted two humanists with a collection of objects reflective of their worldliness and learning, but he also included an anamorphic skull, a reminder of death.

HANS HOLBEIN Also in the employ of the rich and powerful for much of his career was Hans Holbein the Younger (ca. 1497–1543), who excelled as a portraitist. Born in Augsburg, Germany, and trained by his father, Holbein produced many of his best portraits in England. The surfaces of Holbein's paintings are as lustrous as enamel, and the details are exact and exquisitely drawn, consistent with the tradition of 15th-century Flemish art. Yet he also incorporated Italian ideas about monumental composition and sculpturesque form. Holbein is a leading example of the increasingly international outlook of 16th-century European artists.

Holbein began his artistic career in Basel, where he became a master in the painter's guild in 1519 and met Erasmus of Rotterdam, whose portrait he painted several times. Because of the immediate threat of a religious civil war in Basel, Erasmus suggested that Holbein leave for England and gave him a recommendation to Thomas More, chancellor of England under Henry VIII. Holbein arrived in England in 1526 and quickly obtained important commissions—for example, to paint More's portrait. Holbein returned to Basel in 1528 but went back to England in 1532 and remained there until his death in 1543. In 1533, he painted one of his most ambitious works, a double portrait (FIG. **23-11**) of the French ambassadors to England, Jean de Dinteville (1504–1557) and Georges de Selve (1509–1542). A few years later (1536), Holbein became the King's Painter and produced numerous portraits of Henry VIII (FIG. **23-11A**).

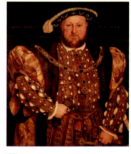

23-11A Holbein the Younger, *Henry VIII*, 1540.

The French Ambassadors (FIG. 23-11) exhibits Holbein's considerable talents—his strong sense of composition, his subtle linear patterning, his gift for recording likenesses, his marvelous sensitivity to color, and his faultless technique. The two men, both ardent humanists, stand at opposite ends of a side table covered with an oriental rug and a collection of objects reflective of their worldliness and their interest in learning and the arts. These include mathematical and astronomical models and implements (compare FIG. 26-24), a lute with a broken string, compasses, a sundial, flutes, globes, and an open hymnbook with Luther's translation of *Veni, Creator Spiritus* and of the Ten Commandments.

Of particular interest is the long gray shape that slashes diagonally across the picture plane and interrupts the stable, balanced, and serene composition. This form is an *anamorphic image*, a distorted image recognizable only when viewed with a special device, such as a cylindrical mirror, or by looking at the painting at an

at the commencement of his military campaign against the invading Ottoman Turks (see page 300). The panel depicts Alexander the Great's defeat of King Darius III of Persia in 333 BCE near a town called Issus on the Pinarus River. Altdorfer announced the subject—which the Greek painter Philoxenos of Eretria (FIG. 5-70) had represented two millennia before—in the Latin inscription suspended in the sky. The parallels between the historical and contemporary conflicts were no doubt significant to the duke. Both involved Western societies engaged in battles against Eastern foes with different values—the Persians in antiquity and the Ottomans in 1528. Altdorfer reinforced this connection by attiring the figures in 16th-century armor (many of the "Persian" soldiers wear Turkish turbans) and depicting them battling in 16th-century military formations.

Altdorfer was one of the first to draw and paint landscapes as subjects in their own right, and *Battle of Issus* reveals his interest in recording natural locales. The battle takes place in an almost cosmological setting. From a bird's-eye view, the clashing armies swarm in the foreground. In the distance, craggy mountain peaks rise next to still bodies of water. Amid swirling clouds, a blazing sun descends. Although the spectacular topography may appear invented, Altdorfer derived his depiction of the landscape from a map of the Mediterranean world published in 1493 in the *Nuremberg Chronicle* (see page 577). Specifically, the viewer sees the terrain and sea from the mountains of Greece to the Nile Valley in Egypt. In addition, Altdorfer may have acquired his information about this battle from the German scholar Johannes Aventinus (1477–1534), whose account of Alexander's victory describes the bloody daylong battle. Appropriately, given Alexander's designation as the "sun god," the sun sets over the victorious Greeks on the right, while a small crescent moon (a symbol of ancient Persia) hovers in the upper left corner over the retreating enemy forces.

acute angle. In this case, if the viewer stands off to the right, the distorted image becomes a skull. Although scholars disagree on the skull's precise meaning, it certainly refers to death. Artists commonly incorporated skulls into paintings as reminders of mortality. Indeed, Holbein depicted a skull on the metal medallion on Jean de Dinteville's hat. Holbein may have intended the skulls, in conjunction with the crucifix that appears half hidden behind the curtain in the upper left corner, to encourage viewers to ponder death and resurrection. (A faint image of a skull appears on the polygonal block at the left in Dürer's *Melencolia I* [FIG. 23-1].)

Holbein's portrait of the two ambassadors may also allude to the growing tension between secular and religious authorities. Jean de Dinteville was a titled landowner, Georges de Selve a bishop. The inclusion of Luther's translations next to the lute with the broken string (a symbol of discord) may subtly refer to this religious strife. In any case, *The French Ambassadors* is a painting of supreme artistic achievement. Holbein rendered the still-life objects with the same meticulous care as he did the men themselves, the woven design of the deep emerald curtain behind them, and the Italian marble-inlay floor, drawn in perfect perspective.

THE NETHERLANDS

With the demise of the duchy of Burgundy in 1477 and the division of that territory between France and the Holy Roman Empire (MAP 23-1), the Netherlands at the beginning of the 16th century consisted of 17 provinces (corresponding to modern Holland, Belgium, and Luxembourg). The Netherlands was among the most commercially advanced and prosperous countries in Europe. Its extensive network of rivers and easy access to the Atlantic Ocean provided a

setting that encouraged overseas trade, and shipbuilding was one of the Netherlands' most profitable enterprises. The region's commercial center shifted toward the end of the 15th century, partly because of the buildup of silt in the Bruges estuary. Traffic relocated to Antwerp, which became the hub of economic activity in the Netherlands after 1510. As many as 500 ships a day passed through Antwerp's harbor, and large trading companies from Germany, Italy, Spain, Portugal, and England established themselves in the city.

During the second half of the 16th century, Philip II of Spain (r. 1556–1598) controlled the Netherlands. Philip had inherited the region from his father, Charles V (r. 1516–1556), and he sought to force the entire population to become Catholic. His heavy-handed tactics and repressive measures led in 1579 to revolt and the formation of two federations: the Union of Arras, a Catholic union of southern Netherlandish provinces, which remained under Spanish dominion, and the Union of Utrecht, a Protestant union of northern provinces, which became the Dutch Republic (MAP 25-1).

As in Germany (FIG. 23-2) at the opening of the 16th century, Netherlandish artists continued to receive commissions from Catholic churches for large-scale altarpieces and other religious works. But with the rise of Protestantism, most artists in the Netherlands focused on secular subjects. Netherlandish art of this period provides a wonderful glimpse into the lives of various levels of society, from nobility to peasantry, capturing their activities, environment, and values.

HIERONYMUS BOSCH The leading Netherlandish painter of the early 16th century was HIERONYMUS BOSCH (ca. 1450–1516), one of the most fascinating artistic personalities in history. Bosch's most famous painting, the *Garden of Earthly Delights* (FIG. 23-12), is also

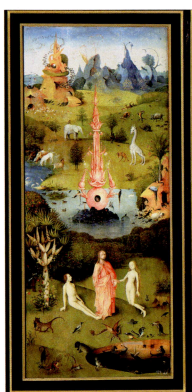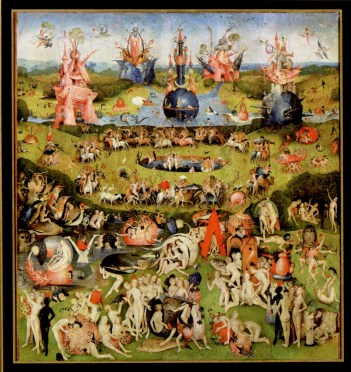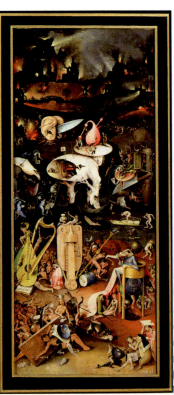

23-12 HIERONYMUS BOSCH, *Garden of Earthly Delights,* 1505–1510. Oil on wood, center panel 7' 2 5/8" × 6' 4 3/4", each wing 7' 2 5/8" × 3' 2 1/4". Museo del Prado, Madrid.

In the fantastic sunlit landscape that is Bosch's Paradise, scores of nude people in the prime of life blithely cavort. The horrors of Hell include sinners enduring tortures tailored to their conduct while alive.

his most puzzling, and no interpretation has ever won universal acceptance. Although the work is a large triptych, which would suggest a religious function as an altarpiece, *Garden of Earthly Delights* was on display in the palace of Count Henry III of Nassau-Breda (r. 1516–1538) no later than seven years after its completion. This suggests that the triptych was a secular commission, and some scholars have proposed that given the work's central themes of sex and procreation, the painting may commemorate a wedding. Marriage was a familiar theme in Netherlandish painting. Fifteenth-century examples include *Giovanni Arnolfini and His Wife* (FIG. 20-7) and *A Goldsmith in His Shop* (FIG. 20-10). Any similarity to those earlier paintings ends there, however. Whereas Jan van Eyck and Petrus Christus grounded their depictions of betrothed couples in contemporary Netherlandish life and custom, Bosch's image portrays a visionary world of fantasy and intrigue—a painted world without close parallel until the advent of Surrealism more than 400 years later (see page 921).

In the left panel, God (in the form of Christ) presents Eve to Adam in a landscape, presumably the Garden of Eden. Bosch's wildly imaginative setting includes an odd pink fountainlike structure in a body of water and an array of fanciful and unusual animals, including a giraffe, an elephant, and winged fish.

The central panel is a continuation of Paradise, a sunlit landscape filled with nude people, including exotic figures of African descent, who frequently appear in Renaissance paintings (for example, FIG. 21-49), both north and south of the Alps. All those in Paradise are in the prime of youth. They blithely cavort amid bizarre creatures and unidentifiable objects. Some of the youths exuberantly stand on their hands or turn somersaults. The numerous fruits and birds in the scene are fertility symbols and suggest procreation. Indeed, many of the figures pair off as couples.

In contrast to the orgiastic overtones of the central panel is the terrifying image of Hell in the right wing, where viewers must search through the inky darkness to find all of the fascinating though repulsive details that Bosch recorded. Beastly creatures devour people, while other condemned souls endure tortures tailored to their conduct while alive. A glutton must vomit eternally. A miser squeezes gold coins from his bowels. A spidery monster fondles a promiscuous woman while toads bite her.

Scholars have traditionally interpreted Bosch's triptych as a warning to viewers of the fate awaiting the sinful, decadent, and immoral, but as a secular work, *Garden of Earthly Delights* may have been intended for a learned audience fascinated by *alchemy*—the medieval study of seemingly magical chemical changes. (Witchcraft also involved alchemy; see page 683.) Details throughout the triptych are based on chemical apparatus of the day, which Bosch knew well because his in-laws were pharmacists.

QUINTEN MASSYS Antwerp's growth and prosperity, along with its wealthy merchants' propensity for collecting and purchasing art, attracted artists to the city. Among them was QUINTEN MASSYS (ca. 1466–1530), who became Antwerp's leading master after 1510. The son of a Louvain blacksmith, Massys demonstrated a willingness to explore the styles and modes of a variety of models, from Jan van Eyck and Rogier van der Weyden to Albrecht Dürer, Hieronymus Bosch, and Leonardo da Vinci. Yet his eclecticism was subtle and discriminating, enriched by an inventiveness that gave a personal stamp to his paintings.

In *Money-Changer and His Wife* (FIG. 23-13), Massys presented a professional man transacting business. He holds scales, checking the weight of coins on the table. The artist's detailed rendering of the figures, setting, and objects suggests a fidelity to observable fact, and provides insight into developing commercial practices. But *Money-Changer and His Wife* is also a commentary on Netherlandish values and mores. The painting highlights the financial transactions that were an increasingly prominent part of 16th-century secular life in the Netherlands and that distracted Christians from their religious duties. The banker's wife, for example, shows more interest in watching her husband weigh money than in reading her prayer book. Massys incorporated into his painting numerous references to the importance of a moral, righteous, and spiritual life, including a carafe with water and a candlestick, traditional religious symbols. The couple

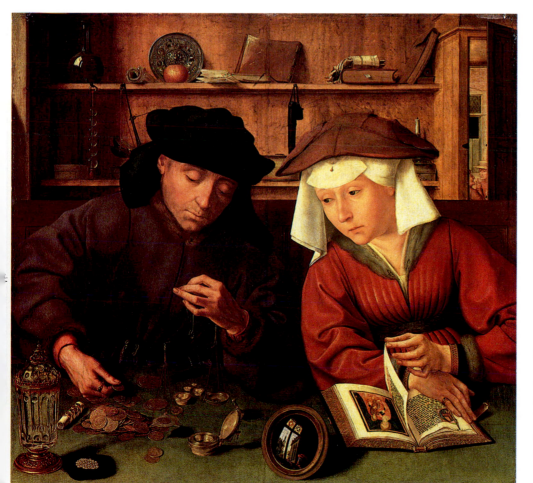

23-13 QUINTEN MASSYS, *Money-Changer and His Wife*, 1514. Oil on wood, 2' 3¾" × 2' 2⅜". Musée du Louvre, Paris.

Massys's depiction of a secular financial transaction is also a commentary on Netherlandish values. The banker's wife shows more interest in the money-weighing than in her prayer book.

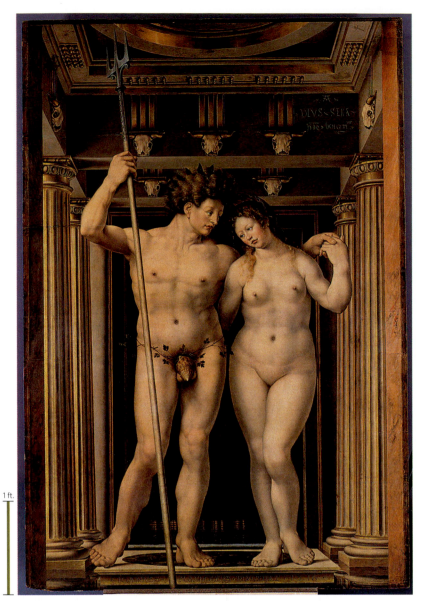

23-14 Jan Gossaert, *Neptune and Amphitrite*, 1516. Oil on wood, 6′ 2″ × 4′ $\frac{3}{4}$″. Gemäldegalerie, Staatliche Museen zu Berlin, Berlin.

Dürer's *Fall of Man* (FIG. 23-4) inspired the poses of Gossaert's classical deities, but the architectural setting is probably based on the sketches that Gossaert made of ancient buildings during his trip to Rome.

writing about 15 years after Gossaert's death, claimed that "Giovanni di Mabuse [Jan Gossaert] was almost the first to bring from Italy into Flanders the true method of making scenes full of nude figures."[3]

In fact, Gossaert derived much of his classicism from Albrecht Dürer, whose *Fall of Man* (FIG. 23-4) inspired the composition and poses in Gossaert's *Neptune and Amphitrite* (FIG. 23-14). However, in contrast to Dürer's exquisitely small engraving, Gossaert's painting is more than 6 feet tall and 4 feet wide. The artist executed the painting with characteristic Netherlandish polish, skillfully drawing and carefully modeling the life-size figures. Gossaert depicted the sea god with his traditional attribute, the *trident* (see "The Gods and Goddesses of Mount Olympus," page 105), and wearing a laurel wreath and an ornate conch shell in place of Dürer's fig leaf. Amphitrite is fleshy and, like Neptune, stands in a contrapposto stance. The architectural frame, which resembles the *cella* of a classical temple (FIG. 5-46), is an unusual mix of Doric and Ionic elements and *bucrania* (ox skull decorations), a common motif in ancient architectural ornamentation. Gossaert likely based the classical setting on sketches he had made of ancient buildings while in Rome. (Several of his drawings of ancient statues and of the Colosseum are preserved.)

Gossaert had traveled to Italy as part of an official delegation to Pope Julius II led by Philip, Admiral of Burgundy (1498–1517) and Bishop of Utrecht (1517–1524), who commissioned Gossaert to paint *Neptune and Amphitrite*. The subject must have held special appeal for the admiral, but Philip did not display the work publicly. He kept the representation of the nude god and goddess in the innermost room of his castle.

PIETER AERTSEN Gossaert's *Neptune and Amphitrite* is exceptional in treating a Greco-Roman subject. More typical, and another example of the Netherlandish tendency to inject reminders about spiritual well-being into paintings of everyday life, is *Butcher's Stall* (FIG. 23-15) by Pieter Aertsen (ca. 1507–1575) of Amsterdam, who became a master in Antwerp's Guild of Saint Luke in 1535 and a citizen of his adopted city in 1542. He returned to Amsterdam in 1557 and worked there until his death two decades later.

Butcher's Stall is one of the *genre* scenes (paintings of daily life) for which Aertsen achieved fame. On display is an array of meat products—a side of a hog, chickens, sausages, a stuffed intestine, pig's feet, meat pies, a cow's head, a hog's head, and hanging entrails. Also visible are fish, pretzels, cheese, and butter. But, like Massys, Aertsen embedded strategically placed religious images in his painting. In the background (FIG. 23-15, *center left*), Joseph leads a donkey carrying Mary and the Christ Child. The holy family stops to offer alms to a beggar and his son, while the people behind the holy family wend their way toward a church. Furthermore, the crossed fishes on the platter and the pretzels and wine in the rafters on the upper left all refer to "spiritual food" (pretzels were often served as

ignores them, focusing solely on money. On the right, through a window, an old man talks with another man, a reference to idleness and gossip. The reflected image in the convex mirror on the counter offsets this image of sloth and foolish chatter. There, a man reads what is most likely a Bible or prayer book. Behind him is a church steeple. An inscription on the original frame (now lost) read, "Let the balance be just and the weights equal" (Lev. 19:36), an admonition that applies both to the money-changer's professional conduct and eventually to judgment day. Nonetheless, the couple in this painting has tipped the balance in favor of the pursuit of wealth.

JAN GOSSAERT Bosch and Massys spent their entire careers in the Netherlands, but many of their contemporaries succumbed to the lure of Italy. Jan Gossaert (ca. 1478–1535), known to his contemporaries as "the Apelles of our age," was one of those who traveled to Italy (in 1508–1509) and became fascinated with classical antiquity and mythology (FIG. 23-14), although he also painted traditional Christian themes (FIG. 23-14A). Giorgio Vasari (see "Vasari's *Lives*," page 636),

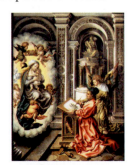

23-14A Gossaert, *Saint Luke Drawing the Virgin*, ca. 1520–1525.

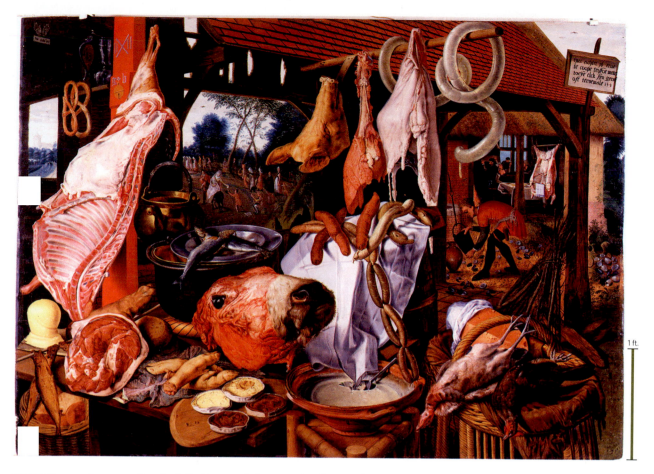

23-15 PIETER AERTSEN, *Butcher's Stall*, 1551. Oil on wood, 4' $\frac{3}{8}$" × 6' 5$\frac{3}{4}$". Uppsala University Art Collection, Uppsala.

Butcher's Stall appears to be a genre painting, but in the background, Joseph leads a donkey carrying Mary and the Christ Child. Aertsen balanced images of gluttony with allusions to salvation.

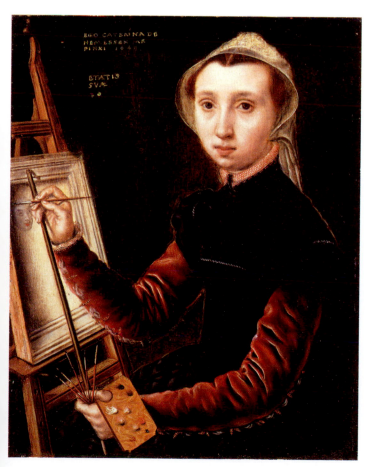

bread during Lent). Aertsen accentuated these allusions to salvation through Christ by contrasting them to their opposite—a life of gluttony, lust, and sloth. He represented this degeneracy with the oyster and mussel shells (which Netherlanders believed possessed aphrodisiacal properties) scattered on the ground on the painting's right side, along with the people seen eating and carousing nearby under the roof. Underscoring the general theme is the placard at the right advertising land for sale—Aertsen's moralistic reference to a recent scandal involving the transfer of land from an Antwerp charitable institution to a land speculator.

CATERINA VAN HEMESSEN With the accumulation of wealth in the Netherlands, private portraits increased in popularity. The example illustrated here (FIG. **23-16**), by CATERINA VAN HEMESSEN (1528–1587), is the first known northern European self-portrait by a woman. The artist signed the work "Caterina van Hemessen painted me / 1548 / her age 20" and confidently presented herself as a painter who interrupts her work at her easel to look toward the viewer. She holds brushes, a palette, and a *maulstick* (a stick used to steady the hand while painting) in her left hand, and delicately applies pigment to the panel with her right hand. Professional women artists remained unusual in the 16th century in

23-16 CATERINA VAN HEMESSEN, *Self-Portrait*, 1548. Oil on wood, 1' $\frac{3}{4}$" × 9$\frac{7}{8}$". Kunstmuseum Basel, Basel.

In this first known northern European self-portrait by a woman, Caterina van Hemessen represented herself as a confident artist momentarily interrupting her work to look out at the viewer.

The Netherlands **689**

23-17 Attributed to Levina Teerlinc, *Elizabeth I as a Princess*, ca. 1559. Oil on wood, 3' 6¾" × 2' 8¼". Royal Collection, Windsor Castle, Windsor.

Teerlinc received greater compensation for her work for the British court than did her male contemporaries. Her considerable skill is evident in this life-size portrait of Elizabeth I as a young princess.

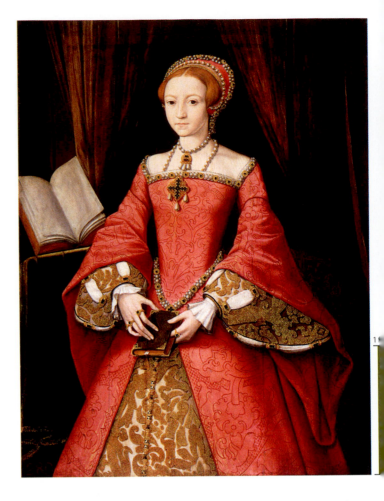

large part because of the difficulty in obtaining formal training (see "The Artist's Profession in Flanders," page 566). Caterina was typical in having been taught by her father, Jan Sanders van Hemessen (ca. 1500–1556), a well-known painter in Antwerp who had traveled in Italy in the 1520s. She acquired an enviable reputation for her portraits of women and enjoyed the patronage of Mary, queen consort of Hungary (1505–1558).

LEVINA TEERLINC Another Netherlandish woman painter was Levina Teerlinc (ca. 1515–1576) of Bruges. She established such a high reputation that Henry VIII (FIG. 23-11A) invited her to England and appointed her royal *paintrix* in 1546, three years after the death of Hans Holbein the Younger. Teerlinc became a formidable rival of her male contemporaries at the court and received greater compensation for her work than they did for theirs. Teerlinc's considerable skill is evident in a life-size portrait (FIG. **23-17**) attributed to her, which depicts Elizabeth I as a composed, youthful princess. Daughter of Henry VIII and Anne Boleyn, Elizabeth was probably in her late 20s when she posed for this portrait. Appropriate to her station in life, Elizabeth wears an elegant brocaded gown, extravagant jewelry, and a headdress based on a style popularized by her mother.

23-18 Joachim Patinir, *Landscape with Saint Jerome*, ca. 1520–1524. Oil on wood, 2' 5⅛" × 2' 11⅞". Museo del Prado, Madrid.

Joachim Patinir, a renowned Netherlandish landscape painter, subordinated the story of Saint Jerome to the depiction of craggy rock formations, verdant rolling fields, and expansive bodies of water.

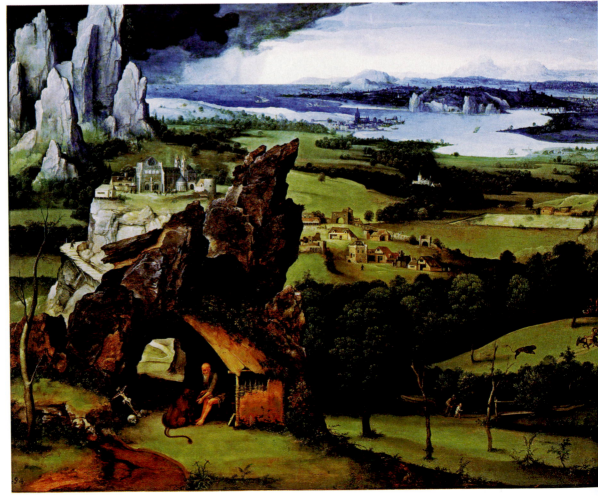

That Teerlinc enjoyed such success is a testament to her determination and skill, given the difficulties that women faced in a profession dominated by men. Women also played an important role as patrons in 16th-century northern Europe. Politically powerful women such as Mary of Hungary, van Hemessen's patron, and Margaret of Austria (1480–1530), regent of the Netherlands during the early 16th century, were active collectors and patrons, and contributed significantly to the thriving state of the arts. As did other art patrons, these women collected and commissioned art not only for the aesthetic pleasure it provided but also for the status it bestowed on them and the cultural sophistication it represented.

JOACHIM PATINIR In addition to portrait and genre painting, landscape painting flourished in the 16th-century Netherlands. Particularly well known for his landscapes was JOACHIM PATINIR (ca. 1480–1524), who became a master in Antwerp's painters' guild in 1515. In fact, the word *Landschaft* (landscape) first emerged in German literature as a characterization of an artistic category when Dürer described Patinir as a "good landscape painter." In *Landscape with Saint Jerome* (FIG. 23-18), Patinir subordinated the saint, who removes a thorn from a lion's paw in the foreground, to the exotic and detailed landscape populated by other figures and animals. As is typical of his work, in this painting Patinir depicted the countryside from a high vantage point in order to achieve a broad and distant panorama. Craggy rock formations, verdant rolling fields, villages with church steeples, expansive bodies of water, and a dramatic sky fill most of the panel. Although nature figures more prominently in his religious paintings than do the biblical protagonists, Patinir had little interest in exploring Italian linear perspective. In fact, his bird's-eye views are inconsistent: the terrain is represented from above, but individual features, such as trees and rocky outcroppings, are seen head-on. He did, however, use different blues, making them paler with increasing distance to suggest recession.

PIETER BRUEGEL THE ELDER The greatest Netherlandish painter of the mid-16th century was PIETER BRUEGEL THE ELDER (ca. 1528–1569). Trained in Antwerp and influenced by Patinir, although he was an apprentice in a different studio, Bruegel was also a landscape painter. In Brueghel's paintings, however, no matter how huge a slice of the world the artist depicted, human activities remain the dominant theme. Like many of his contemporaries, Bruegel traveled to Italy, where between 1551 and 1554 he went as far south as Sicily, and was in Rome in 1553. Unlike other artists, however, Bruegel chose not to incorporate classical elements into his paintings. He settled in Brussels in 1563.

Bruegel's *Netherlandish Proverbs* (FIG. 23-19), painted several years after the artist returned to Antwerp from Italy, depicts a Netherlandish village populated by a wide range of people, encompassing nobility, peasants, and clerics. Seen from the kind of bird's-eye view that Patinir favored is a mesmerizing array of activities reminiscent of the topsy-turvy scenes of Bosch (FIG. 23-12). In fact, contemporaries referred to Bruegel as "a second Bosch." Nonetheless, *Netherlandish Proverbs* is unlike anything Bosch ever painted, and the purpose and meaning of Bruegel's anecdotal details are clear, whereas Bosch's are difficult to interpret, at least for modern viewers. By illustrating more than a hundred proverbs in this one painting, the artist indulged his Netherlandish audience's obsession with proverbs, passion for detailed and clever imagery, and interest in human folly—the subject of Erasmus's most famous work, *In Praise of Folly*.

As the viewer scrutinizes the myriad vignettes within the painting, Bruegel's close observation and deep understanding of human nature become apparent. The proverbs depicted include, on the far left, a man in blue gnawing on a pillar. "He who bites a church pillar" is a religious zealot engaged in folly. To his right, a man "beats his head against a wall" (a frustrated idiot who has attempted something impossible). On the roof a man "shoots one arrow after the

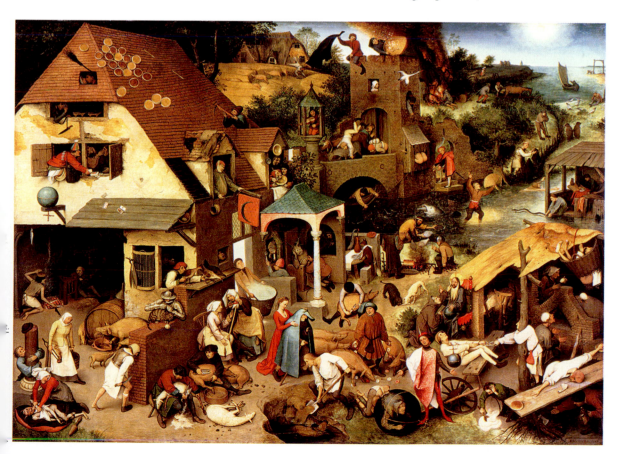

23-19 PIETER BRUEGEL THE ELDER, *Netherlandish Proverbs,* 1559. Oil on wood, 3' 10" × 5' 4$\frac{1}{8}$". Gemäldegalerie, Staatliche Museen zu Berlin, Berlin.

In this painting of a Netherlandish village, Bruegel indulged his audience's obsession with proverbs and passion for clever imagery, and demonstrated his deep understanding of human nature.

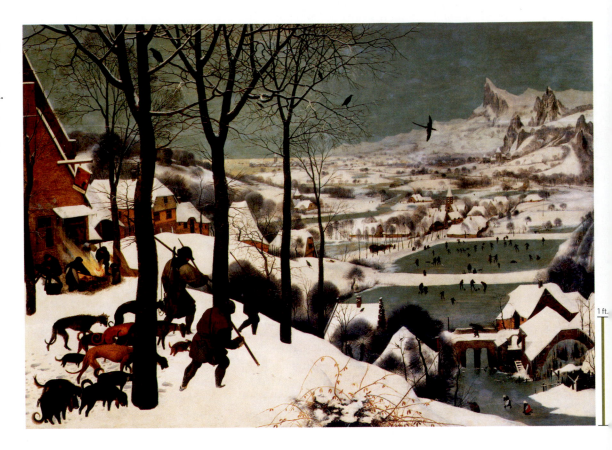

23-20 PIETER BRUEGEL THE ELDER, *Hunters in the Snow*, 1565. Oil on wood, 3' 10$\frac{1}{8}$" × 5' 3$\frac{3}{4}$". Kunsthistorisches Museum, Vienna.

In *Hunters in the Snow,* one of a series of paintings illustrating different seasons, Bruegel draws the viewer diagonally into the expansive winter landscape by his mastery of line, shape, and composition.

1 ft.

other, but hits nothing" (a fool who throws good money after bad). In the far distance, near the burst of sunlight, the "blind lead the blind"—a subject to which Bruegel returned several years later in one of his most famous paintings.

In contrast to Patinir's Saint Jerome, lost in the landscape, the vast cast of often comical characters in Bruegel's *Netherlandish Proverbs* fills the panel, so much so that the artist almost shut out the sky. *Hunters in the Snow* (FIG. **23-20**) and *Fall of Icarus* (FIG. **23-20A**) are very different in character and illustrate the dynamic variety of Bruegel's work. *Hunters* is one of a series of six paintings he produced in Brussels illustrating sea-

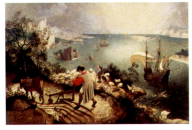

23-20A BRUEGEL THE ELDER, *Fall of Icarus*, ca. 1555–1556.

sonal changes, with each painting representing not a season but a pair of months. The paintings were a private commission and hung in the home of Nicolaes Jongelinck, a wealthy Antwerp merchant. The series, which Bruegel completed in a single year, grew out of the tradition of depicting months and peasants in Books of Hours (FIGS. 20-15 and 20-16). The painting, which must represent December/January, shows human figures and landscape locked in winter cold, reflecting the particularly severe winter of 1565. The weary hunters return with their hounds, women build fires, skaters skim the frozen pond, and the town and its church huddle in their mantle of snow. Bruegel rendered the landscape in an optically accurate manner. It develops smoothly from foreground to background and draws the viewer diagonally into its depths, starting with the row of bare trees in the left foreground. The painter's supreme skill in using line and shape and his subtlety in tonal harmony make this one of the great landscape paintings in Western art.

FRANCE

As Holbein's *French Ambassadors* (FIG. 23-11) illustrates, France in the early 16th century continued its efforts to secure widespread recognition as a political power and cultural force. Under Francis I (r. 1515–1547), the French established a firm foothold in Milan and its environs, and waged a campaign (known as the Habsburg-Valois Wars) against Charles V, King of Spain and Holy Roman Emperor. These wars, which occupied Francis for most of his reign, involved disputed territories—southern France, the Netherlands, the Rhineland, northern Spain, and Italy—and reflect France's central role in the shifting geopolitical landscape (MAP 23-1).

The French king also took a strong position in the religious controversies of his day. By the mid-16th century, the split between Catholics and Protestants had become so pronounced that subjects often felt compelled either to accept the religion of their sovereign or emigrate to a territory where the sovereign's religion corresponded with their own. France was predominantly Catholic, and in 1534, Francis declared Protestantism illegal. The state persecuted its Protestants—the Huguenots, a Calvinist sect—and drove them underground. Calvin himself fled from France to Switzerland two years later. The Huguenots' commitment to Protestant Calvinism eventually led to one of the bloodiest religious massacres in European history when the Huguenots and Catholics clashed in Paris in August 1572. The violence quickly spread throughout France with the support of many nobles, which presented a serious threat to the king's authority.

JEAN CLOUET As the rulers of antiquity and other Renaissance monarchs had done, Francis commissioned portraits of himself to assert his authority. The finest is the portrait that JEAN CLOUET (ca. 1485–1541) painted about a decade after Francis became king. Clouet probably came from the Netherlands to France during the

THE PATRON'S VOICE
Francis I, Royal Art Patron and Collector

With the coming of age of Francis I, the Catholic Church, the primary patron of art and architecture in medieval France, yielded that position to the French monarchy. The patronage of Francis I, extensively chronicled in a rich trove of contemporary documents, is an illuminating case study of what can result from the confluence of vast wealth, absolute power, and sophisticated taste.

Francis expended especially large sums on building projects, including a royal hunting lodge at Chambord (FIG. 23-22). After his decision in 1528 to relocate to Paris from the Loire valley, he undertook the remodeling of the Louvre, then a medieval fortress (FIG. 20-16), and constructed new palaces in the Bois du Boulogne forest outside Paris, at Saint-Germain-en-Laye, and most significantly at Fontainebleau.

Francis favored art that was at once elegant, erotic, and unorthodox. Appropriately, Mannerism held great appeal for him, and he hired three prominent Italian Mannerists to create artworks for his pleasure and to decorate the new palace at Fontainebleau: Benvenuto Cellini (FIGS. 22-52 and 22-52A), Rosso Fiorentino (1494–1540), and Francesco Primaticcio (1504–1570). Francis had earlier enticed Leonardo da Vinci to come to France after the king won control of Milan in 1516 (see page 629). Leonardo was given a generous pension and an elegant home at Cloux, where he died three years later (without having produced any important works for the king).

Anecdotes abound attesting to Francis's deep personal interest in the artists in his employ. The king was capable of both extravagant praise and harsh criticism. On one occasion he rebuked Cellini for not living up to his promises and warned the artist about the consequences if he did not change his ways:

> I gave you express orders to make me twelve silver statues. . . . You have chosen to execute a saltcellar [FIG. 22-52], and vases and busts and doors, and a heap of other things. . . . You have neglected my wishes and worked for the fulfillment of your own. . . . I tell you, therefore, plainly: do your utmost to obey my commands; for if you stick to your own fancies you will run your head against a wall.*

Francis probably made his greatest mark, however, as a collector. Through diplomatic gifts that he received and the artworks that his agents commissioned or acquired on his behalf in Italy, Francis formed a magnificent collection. With some horror, Giorgio Vasari, the great chronicler of Renaissance artists' lives (see "Giorgio Vasari's *Lives*," page 636), took note in his biography of Andrea del Sarto (FIG. 22-8A) of the king's ravenous appetite for Italian art and of how the artistic patrimony of Vasari's beloved Florence was being exported to France:

> In Florence . . . Giovanbattista della Palla . . . was not only having executed all the sculptures and pictures he could, to send to France for King Francis I, but was also buying antiques of all sorts and pictures of every kind, provided only that they were by the hands of good masters; and every day he was packing them up and sending them off.†

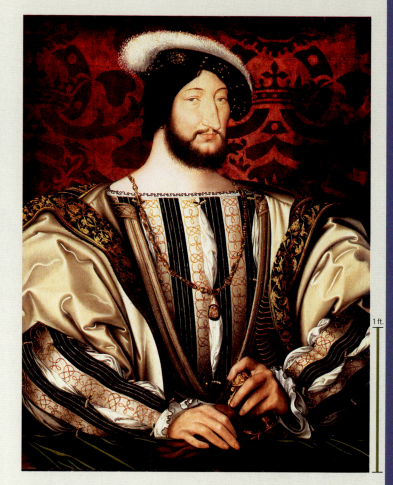

23-21 JEAN CLOUET, *Francis I*, ca. 1525–1530. Tempera and oil on wood, 3' 2" × 2' 5". Musée du Louvre, Paris.

Clouet's portrait of the elegantly dressed Francis I reveals the artist's skill, but the flattening of the king's features and disproportion between his head and body give the painting a formalized quality.

Francis's art treasures became the core of one of the world's greatest museums, the Musée du Louvre. A brief list just of the works in *Art through the Ages* that Francis once owned will suffice to indicate the quality of his collection: Leonardo da Vinci's *Madonna of the Rocks* (FIG. 22-2) and *Mona Lisa* (FIG. 22-5); Bronzino's *Venus, Cupid, Folly, and Time* (FIG. 22-45); Michelangelo's *Bound Slave* (FIG. 22-15); and Cellini's saltcellar (FIG. 22-52) and *Genius of Fontainebleau* (FIG. 22-52A). In addition, Francis's collection boasted works by Perugino, Raphael, Andrea del Sarto, Titian, Giulio Romano, and Rosso Fiorentino, as well as tapestries and ancient statues.

*Quoted by Robert J. Knecht, *Renaissance Warrior and Patron: The Reign of Francis I*. (New York: Cambridge University Press, 1994), 456.
†Translated by Janet Cox-Rearick, *The Collection of Francis I: Royal Treasures* (New York: Abrams, 1996), 87.

reign of Louis XII (r. 1498–1515). He soon established a studio specializing in portraiture and received royal commissions. In *Francis I* (FIG. 23-21), Clouet presented the French monarch as a worldly ruler magnificently bedecked in silks and brocades, wearing a gold chain with a medallion of the Order of Saint Michael, a French order

founded by Louis XI in 1469. Francis appears suave and confident, with his hand resting on the pommel of a dagger. Despite the careful detail, the portrait also exhibits an elegantly formalized quality, the result of Clouet's suppression of modeling, which flattens features, seen particularly in Francis's neck. The disproportion between the

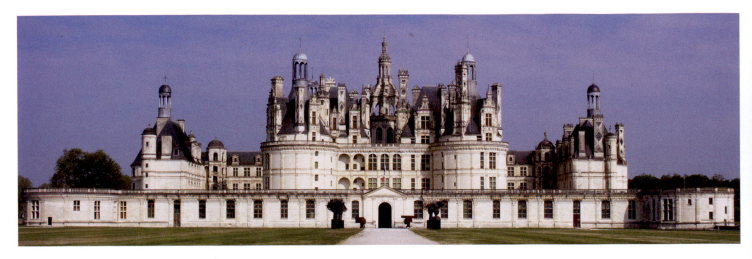

23-22 Château de Chambord (looking northwest), Chambord, France, begun 1519.

French Renaissance châteaux, which developed from medieval castles, served as country houses for royalty. King Francis I's Château de Chambord reflects Italian palazzo design, but it has a Gothic roof.

king's small head and his broad body, swathed in heavy layers of fabric, adds to the formalized nature.

Portraiture was, however, a relatively minor interest of Francis's. He was a great patron of sculpture and the decorative arts; a passionate collector of paintings, especially those of Italian masters; and a builder on a grand scale (see "Francis I, Royal Art Patron and Collector," page 693).

CHÂTEAU DE CHAMBORD Among Francis's architectural commissions is the grandiose Château de Chambord (FIG. **23-22**). As a building type, the *château* developed from medieval castles, but, reflecting more peaceful times, Renaissance châteaux served as country houses for royalty, who usually built them near forests for use as hunting lodges. Many, including Chambord, still featured protective surrounding moats, however. Construction of the Château de Chambord began in 1519, but Francis I never saw its completion. Chambord's plan, originally drawn by a pupil of Giuliano da Sangallo (FIGS. 22-26 and 22-27), includes a central square block with four corridors in the shape of a cross, and a broad central stair-

case that gives access to groups of rooms—ancestors of the modern suite of rooms or apartments. At each of the four corners, a round tower punctuates the square plan. From the exterior, Chambord presents a carefully contrived horizontal accent on three levels, with continuous moldings separating its floors. Windows align precisely, one exactly over another. The Italian Renaissance palazzo served as the model for this matching of horizontal and vertical features, but above the third level, the structure's lines break chaotically into a jumble of high *dormers* (projecting gable-capped windows), chimneys, and turrets that are the heritage of French Gothic residential architecture—for example, the Louvre palace (FIG. 20-16) in Paris.

LOUVRE, PARIS Chambord, despite its Italian elements, is essentially a French building. During the reign of Francis's successor, Henry II (r. 1547–1559), however, translations of Italian architectural treatises appeared, and Italian architects themselves came to work in France. Moreover, the French turned to Italy for study and travel. These exchanges caused a more extensive revolution in style than had transpired earlier, although certain French elements derived from

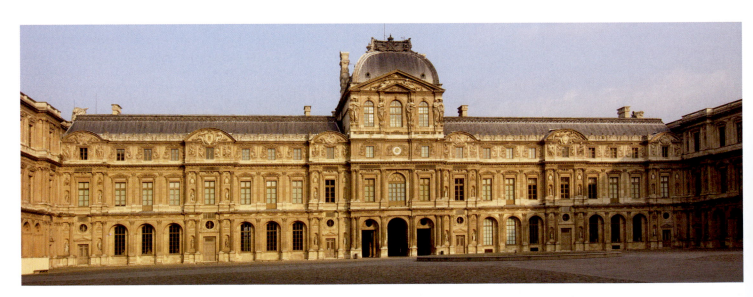

23-23 PIERRE LESCOT, west wing of the Cour Carrée (Square Court; looking west) of the Louvre, Paris, France, begun 1546.

Pierre Lescot's design for the Louvre palace reflects Italian Renaissance architectural models, but the decreasing height of the stories, large windows, and steep roof are northern European features.

the Gothic tradition persisted. This incorporation of Italian architectural ideas characterizes the redesigned Louvre in Paris, originally a medieval palace and fortress (FIG. 20-16). Since Charles V's renovation of the Louvre in the mid-14th century, the castle had fallen into a state of disrepair. Francis I initiated the project to renovate the royal palace (see "Francis I," page 693) when he decided in 1528 to move his court to Paris from the Loire valley. It was not until 1546, however, that Francis commissioned PIERRE LESCOT (1510–1578) to build a new palace. Francis died the following year, but work continued under Henry II, who greatly enlarged the project, enabling Lescot to design a palace that has become synonymous with the classical style of 16th-century French architecture.

Lescot and his associates were familiar with the architectural style of Bramante and his school. In the west wing of the Cour Carrée (Square Court; FIG. 23-23) of the Louvre, each of the stories forms a complete order, and the cornices project enough to furnish a strong horizontal accent. The arcading on the ground story reflects the ancient Roman use of arches and produces more shadow than in the upper stories due to its recessed placement, thereby strengthening the design's visual base. On the second story, the pilasters rising from bases and the alternating curved and angular pediments have direct antecedents in several High Renaissance palaces—for example, the Palazzo Farnese (FIG. 22-26) in Rome. Yet the decreasing height of the stories, the scale of the windows (proportionally much larger than in Italian Renaissance buildings), and the steep roof are northern European elements. Especially French are the pavilions jutting from the wall. A motif that the French long favored—double columns framing a niche—punctuates the pavilions. The richly articulated wall surfaces feature relief sculptures by JEAN GOUJON (ca. 1510–1565), who had previously collaborated with Lescot on the Fountain of the Innocents (FIG. 23-23A) in Paris.

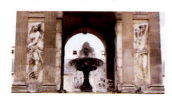
⬈ 23-23A GOUJON, Fountain of the Innocents, 1547-1549.

Other northern European countries imitated this French classical manner—its double-columned pavilions, tall and wide windows, profuse statuary, and steep roofs—although with local variations. The modified classicism that the French embraced became the model for building projects north of the Alps through most of the 16th century.

SPAIN

Spain's ascent to power in Europe began in the mid-15th century with the marriage of Isabella of Castile (1451–1504) and Ferdinand of Aragon (1452–1516) in 1469. By the end of the 16th century, Spain had emerged as the dominant European power. Under the Habsburg rulers Charles V and Philip II, the Spanish Empire controlled a territory greater in extent than any ever known—a large part of Europe, the western Mediterranean, a strip of North Africa, and vast expanses in the New World. Spain acquired many of its New World colonies through aggressive overseas exploration. Among the most notable conquistadors sailing under the Spanish flag were Christopher Columbus (1451–1506), Vasco Núñez de Balboa (ca. 1475–1517), Ferdinand Magellan (1480–1521), Hernán Cortés (1485–1547), and Francisco Pizarro (ca. 1470–1541). The Habsburg Empire, enriched by New World plunder, supported the most powerful military force in Europe. Spain defended and then promoted the interests of the Catholic Church in its battle against the inroads of the Protestant Reformation. Indeed, Philip II earned

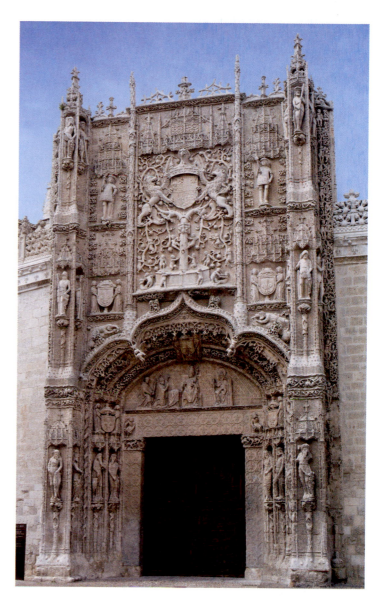

23-24 Portal, Colegio de San Gregorio, Valladolid, Spain, ca. 1498.

The Plateresque architectural style takes its name from *platero* (Spanish, "silversmith"). At the center of this portal's Late Gothic tracery is the coat of arms of King Ferdinand and Queen Isabella.

the title "Most Catholic King." Spain's crusading spirit, nourished by centuries of war with Islam (see page 298), prepared the country to assume the role of the most Catholic civilization of Europe and the Americas. In the 16th century, for good or for ill, Spain left the mark of its power, religion, language, and culture on two hemispheres.

COLEGIO DE SAN GREGORIO During the 15th century and well into the 16th, a Late Gothic style of architecture, the Plateresque, prevailed in Spain. *Plateresque* derives from the Spanish word *platero* ("silversmith"), and delicately executed ornamentation resembling metalwork is the defining characteristic of the Plateresque style. The Colegio de San Gregorio (Seminary of Saint Gregory; FIG. 23-24) in the Castilian city of Valladolid handsomely exemplifies the Plateresque manner, which Spanish expansion into the Western Hemisphere also brought to New Spain (FIG. 23-24A). Great

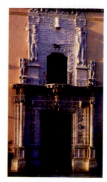
⬈ 23-24A Casa de Montejo, Mérida, 1549.

carved retables, like the German altarpieces that influenced them (FIGS. 20-20, 20-21, and 23-2, *bottom*), appealed to church patrons and architects in Spain, and the portals of Plateresque facades often resemble elegantly carved retables set into an otherwise blank wall.

The Plateresque entrance of San Gregorio is a lofty sculptured stone screen bearing no functional relation to the architecture behind it. On the entrance level, lacelike tracery reminiscent of Moorish design hems the flamboyant ogival arches. (Spanish hatred of the Moors did not discourage Spanish architects from adapting Moorish motifs—a habit that dates to the Visigothic age; see page 320.) A great screen, paneled into sculptured compartments, rises above the tracery. In the center, the branches of a huge pomegranate tree (symbolizing Granada, the Moorish capital of Spain, which the Habsburgs captured in 1492) wreathe the coat of arms of King Ferdinand and Queen Isabella. Cupids play among the tree branches, and, flanking the central panel, niches frame armed pages of the court, heraldic wild men symbolizing aggression, and armored soldiers, attesting to Spain's proud new militancy. In typical Plateresque and Late Gothic fashion, the activity of a thousand intertwined motifs unifies the whole design, which, in sum, creates an exquisitely carved panel greatly expanded in scale from the retables that inspired it.

EL ESCORIAL Under Philip II, the Plateresque style gave way to an Italian-derived classicism that also characterized 16th-century French architecture (FIG. 23-23). The Italian style is on display in the expansive complex called El Escorial (FIG. **23-25**), which JUAN BAUTISTA DE TOLEDO (d. 1567) and JUAN DE HERRERA (ca. 1530–1597), principally the latter, constructed for Philip II. In his will, Charles V stipulated that a "dynastic pantheon" be built to house the remains of past and future monarchs of Spain. Philip II, obedient to

his father's wishes, chose a site some 30 miles northwest of Madrid in rugged terrain with barren mountains. Here, he built El Escorial, not only a royal mausoleum but also a church, a monastery, and a palace. Legend has it that the gridlike plan for the enormous complex, 625 feet wide and 520 feet deep, symbolized the gridiron on which Saint Lawrence, El Escorial's patron saint, suffered his martyrdom (see "Early Christian Saints," page 237).

The vast structure is in keeping with Philip's austere character, his passionate Catholicism, his proud reverence for his dynasty, and his stern determination to impose his will worldwide. He insisted that in designing El Escorial, the architects should focus on simplicity of form, severity in the whole, nobility without arrogance, and majesty without ostentation. The result is a classicism of Doric severity, ultimately derived from Italian architecture and with the grandeur of Saint Peter's (FIGS. 24-3 and 24-4) implicit in the scheme, but without close parallel in European architecture.

Only the three entrances, with the dominant central portal framed by *superimposed orders* and topped by a pediment in the Italian fashion, break the long sweep of the structure's severely plain walls. Massive square towers punctuate the four corners. The stress is on the central axis, echoed in the two flanking portals. The construction material for the entire complex (including the church)—granite, a difficult stone to work—conveys a feeling of starkness and gravity. The church's imposing facade and the austere geometry of the interior complex, with its blocky walls and ponderous arches, produce an effect of overwhelming strength and weight. The entire complex is a monument to the collaboration of a great king and remarkably understanding architects. El Escorial stands as the overpowering architectural expression of Spain's spirit in its heroic epoch and of the character of Philip II, the extraordinary ruler who directed it.

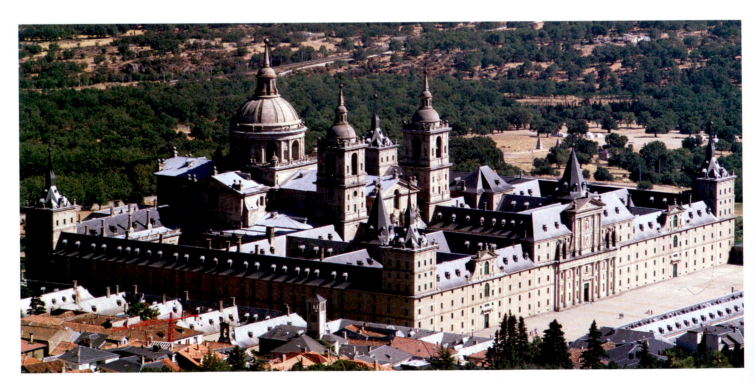

23-25 JUAN DE HERRERA and JUAN BAUTISTA DE TOLEDO, aerial view (looking southeast) of El Escorial, near Madrid, Spain, 1563–1584.

Conceived by Charles V and built by Philip II, El Escorial is a royal mausoleum, church, monastery, and palace in one. The complex is classical in style, with severely plain walls and massive towers.

EL GRECO Reflecting the increasingly international character of European art as well as the mobility of artists, the greatest Spanish painter of the era was not a Spaniard. Born on Crete, Domenikos Theotokopoulos, called EL GRECO (ca. 1547–1614), emigrated to Italy as a young man. In his youth, he absorbed the traditions of Late Byzantine frescoes and mosaics. While still young, El Greco went to Venice, where he worked in Titian's studio, although Tintoretto's paintings (FIG. 22-48) seem to have made a stronger impression on him. A brief trip to Rome explains the influences of Roman and Florentine Mannerism on his work. By 1577, he had left for Spain to spend the rest of his life in Toledo.

El Greco's art is a strong personal blending of Byzantine and Mannerist elements. The intense emotionalism of his paintings, which naturally appealed to Spanish piety, and a great reliance on and mastery of color bound him to 16th-century Venetian art and to Mannerism. El Greco's art was not strictly Spanish, for it had no Spanish antecedents and little effect on later Spanish painters. Nevertheless, El Greco's hybrid style captured the fervor of Spanish Catholicism.

VIEW OF TOLEDO El Greco's singular vision is evident in *View of Toledo* (FIG. 23-26), the only pure landscape he ever painted. As does so much of El Greco's work, this painting breaks sharply with tradition. The Greek-born artist depicted the Spanish city from a nearby hilltop and drew attention to the great spire of Toledo's cathedral by leading the viewer's eye along the diagonal line of the bridge crossing the Tajo River and continuing with the city's walls. El Greco knew Toledo intimately, and every building is recognizable, although he rearranged some of their positions. For example, he moved the Alcazar palace to the right of the cathedral. Yet El Greco rendered no structure in meticulous detail, as most Renaissance painters would have done, and the color palette is not true to nature but limited to greens and grays. The atmosphere is eerie. Dramatic bursts of light in the stormy sky cast a ghostly pall over the city. The artist applied oil pigment to canvas in broad brushstrokes typical of his late, increasingly abstract painting style, with the result that the buildings and trees do not have sharp contours and almost seem to shake.

Art historians have compared *View of Toledo* to Giorgione da Castelfranco's *Tempest* (FIG. 22-34) and the dramatic lighting to works by Tintoretto (FIG. 22-48), and indeed, El Greco's Venetian training is evident. Still, the closest parallels lie not in the past but in the future—in paintings such as Vincent van Gogh's *Starry Night* (FIG. 28-19) and in 20th-century Expressionism and Surrealism (see pages 885 and 921).

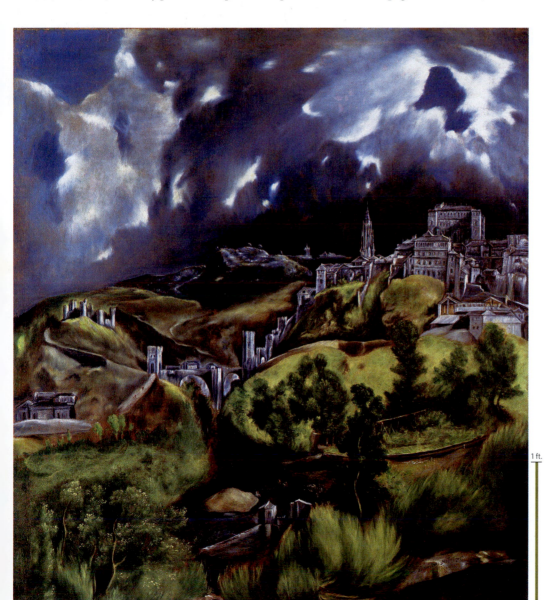

23-26 EL GRECO, *View of Toledo,* ca. 1610. Oil on canvas, 3' 11 ¾" × 3' 6 ¾". Metropolitan Museum of Art, New York (H. O. Havemeyer Collection. Bequest of Mrs. H. O. Havemeyer, 1929).

View of Toledo is the only pure landscape El Greco ever painted. The dark, stormy sky casts a ghostly pall over the Spanish city. The painted exemplifies the artist's late, increasingly abstract, style.

1 ft.

El Greco's art is a blend of Byzantine and Italian Mannerist elements. His intense emotional content captured the fervor of Spanish Catholicism, and his dramatic use of light foreshadowed the Baroque style.

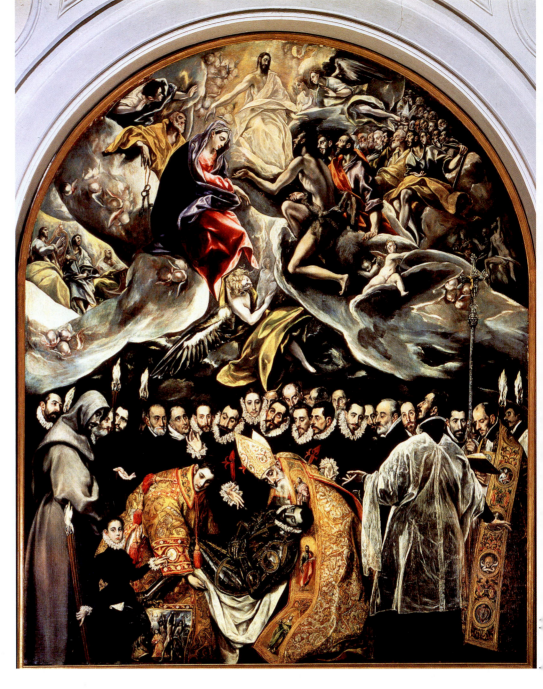

BURIAL OF COUNT ORGAZ More typical of El Greco's work is *Burial of Count Orgaz* (FIG. 23-27), painted in 1586 for the church of Santo Tomé in Toledo. El Greco based the painting on the legend of the count of Orgaz, who had died some three centuries before and who had been a great benefactor of Santo Tomé. According to the legend, Saints Stephen and Augustine miraculously descended from Heaven to lower the count's body into its sepulcher in the church. In the painting, El Greco carefully distinguished the terrestrial and celestial spheres. The brilliant Heaven above irradiates the earthly burial scene below. The painter represented the terrestrial realm with a firm realism, whereas he depicted the celestial, in his quite personal manner, with elongated undulating figures, fluttering draperies, and a visionary swirling cloud. Below, the two saints lovingly lower the count's armor-clad body, the armor and heavy draperies painted with all the rich sensuousness of the Venetian school. A solemn chorus of personages dressed in black fills the background. Among the witnesses to the miracle are El Greco himself; his young son, Jorge Manuel; the priest who commissioned the painting; and the Spanish king Philip II. In the carefully individualized features of these figures, El Greco demonstrated that he was also a great portraitist.

The upward glances of some of the figures below and the flight of an angel above link the painting's lower and upper spheres. The action of the angel, who carries the count's soul in his arms as Saint John and the Virgin intercede for it before the throne of Christ, reinforces this connection. El Greco's deliberate change in style to distinguish between the two levels of reality gives the viewer an opportunity to see the artist's early and late manners in the same work, one below the other. His relatively sumptuous and realistic presentation of the earthly sphere is still strongly rooted in Venetian art, but the abstractions and distortions that El Greco used to show the immaterial nature of the heavenly realm characterize his later style. His elongated figures existing in undefined spaces, bathed in a cool light of uncertain origin, explain El Greco's usual classification as a Mannerist, but his art is impossible to classify using conventional labels. Although El Greco used Mannerist formal devices, his primary concerns were conveying emotion and religious fervor and arousing those feelings in viewers. The forcefulness of his paintings is the result of his unique, highly developed expressive style, which foreshadowed developments of the Baroque era in Spain and Italy, examined in the next chapter.

HIGH RENAISSANCE AND MANNERISM IN NORTHERN EUROPE AND SPAIN

Germany

- Widespread dissatisfaction with the Church in Rome led to the Protestant Reformation, splitting Christendom in half. Protestants, led by Martin Luther, objected to the sale of indulgences and rejected most of the sacraments of the Catholic Church. They also condemned ostentatious church decoration as a form of idolatry that distracted the faithful from communication with God.

- As a result, Protestant churches were relatively bare, but art, especially prints, still played a role in Protestantism. Lucas Cranach the Elder, for example, effectively used visual imagery to contrast Catholic and Protestant views of salvation in his woodcut *Law and Gospel*.

- The greatest German printmaker of the 16th century was Albrecht Dürer, who was also a painter. His works range from biblical to botanical subjects and reflect his studies of classical statuary and of the Vitruvian theory of human proportions. Dürer's engravings rival painting in tonal quality.

- Other German artists, such as Matthias Grünewald and Hans Baldung Grien, explored disease, death, witchcraft, and eroticism in their art. Hans Holbein was a renowned portraitist who became court painter in England.

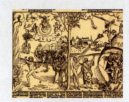

Cranach, *Law and Gospel*, ca. 1530

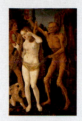

Baldung Grien, *Three Ages of Woman and Death*, 1510

The Netherlands

- The Netherlands was one of the most commercially advanced and prosperous countries in 16th-century Europe. Much of Netherlandish art of this period provides a picture of contemporary life and values. Quentin Massys's *Money-Changer and His Wife*, for example, is a commentary on a couple's obsession with wealth. Pieter Aertsen's *Butcher's Stall* seems to be a straightforward genre scene, but includes the holy family offering alms to a beggar in the background, providing a stark contrast between gluttony and religious piety.

- Landscapes were the specialty of Joachim Patinir. Pieter Bruegel's repertoire also included landscape painting. His *Hunters in the Snow* is one of a series of paintings depicting seasonal changes and the activities associated with them, as in traditional Books of Hours.

- Women artists of the period include Caterina van Hemessen, who painted the earliest northern European self-portrait of a woman, and Levina Teerlinc, who produced portraits for the English court.

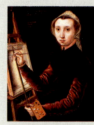

Van Hemessen, *Self-Portrait*, 1548

France

- King Francis I fought against Holy Roman Emperor Charles V and declared Protestantism illegal in France. An admirer of Italian art, he invited several prominent Mannerists to work at his court and decorate his palace at Fontainebleau. His art collection formed the core of the Musée du Louvre.

- French architecture of the 16th century mixes Italian and Northern Renaissance elements, as in Pierre Lescot's design of the renovated Louvre palace and Francis's château at Chambord, which combines classical motifs derived from Italian palazzi with a Gothic roof silhouette.

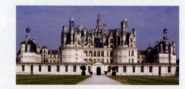

Château de Chambord, begun 1519

Spain

- At the end of the 16th century, Spain was the dominant power in Europe, with an empire greater in extent than any ever known, including vast territories in the New World. The Spanish Plateresque style of architecture, which spread to New Spain, takes its name from *platero* ("silversmith") and features delicate ornamentation resembling metalwork.

- Under Philip II, the Plateresque style gave way to an Italian-derived classicism, seen at its best in El Escorial, a royal mausoleum, monastery, and palace complex near Madrid.

- The leading painter of 16th-century Spain was the Greek-born El Greco, who combined Byzantine style, Italian Mannerism, and the religious fervor of Catholic Spain in such works as *Burial of Count Orgaz*.

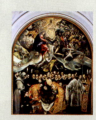

El Greco, *Burial of Count Orgaz*, 1586

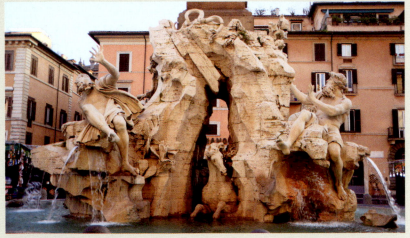

▲ **24-1a** As water flows from a travertine grotto supporting an ancient Egyptian obelisk, Bernini's marble personifications of major rivers of four continents twist and gesticulate emphatically.

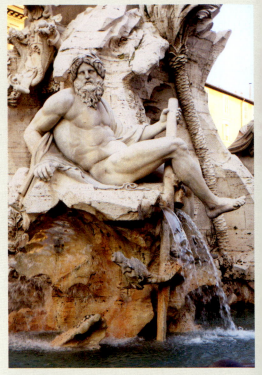

▲ **24-1b** Each of the four rivers has an identifying attribute. The Ganges (Asia) most closely resembles a Greco-Roman river god. Bernini's personification of the easily navigable Ganges holds an oar.

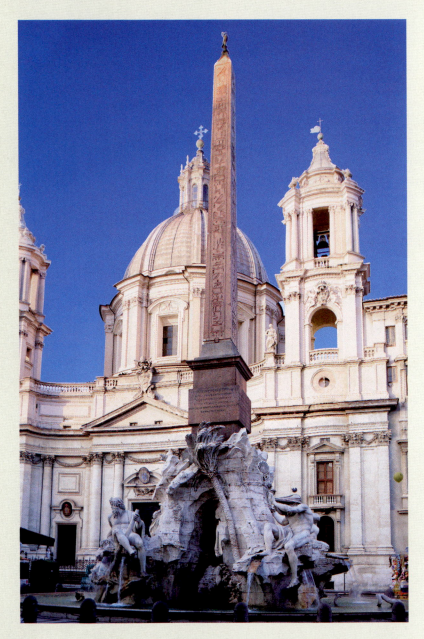

| 24-1 | **GIANLORENZO BERNINI, Fountain of the Four Rivers (looking southwest with Sant'Agnese in Agone in the background), Piazza Navona, Rome, Italy, 1648–1651.** |

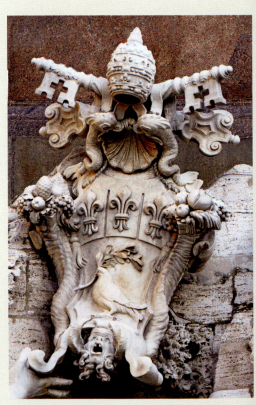

▲ **24-1c** Crowning the grotto is Pope Innocent X's coat of arms, with the Pamphili family's dove symbolizing the Holy Spirit and the triumph of the Church in all parts of the then-known world.

The Baroque in Italy and Spain

BAROQUE ART AND SPECTACLE

One of the most popular tourist attractions in Rome is the Fountain of the Four Rivers (FIG. **24-1**) in Piazza Navona, by GIANLORENZO BERNINI (1598–1680). Architect, painter, sculptor, playwright, and stage designer, Bernini was one of the most important and imaginative artists of the Baroque era in Italy and its most characteristic and sustaining spirit. Nonetheless, the fountain's patron, Pope Innocent X (r. 1644–1655), did not want Bernini to win this commission. Bernini had been the favorite sculptor of the Pamphili pope's predecessor, Urban VIII (r. 1623–1644), who spent so extravagantly on art and himself and his family that he nearly bankrupted the Vatican treasury. Innocent emphatically opposed the excesses of the Barberini pope and shunned Bernini, awarding new papal commissions to other sculptors and architects. Bernini was also in disgrace at the time because of his failed attempt to erect bell towers for the new facade (FIG. 24-3) of Saint Peter's. When Innocent announced a competition for a fountain in Piazza Navona (MAP 22-1), site of the Pamphili family's palace and parish church, Sant'Agnese in Agone (FIG. 24-1, *rear*), he pointedly did not invite Bernini to submit a design. However, the renowned sculptor succeeded in having a model of his proposed fountain placed where the pope would see it. When Innocent examined it, he was so captivated that he declared that the only way anyone could avoid employing Bernini was not to look at his work.

Bernini's bold design, executed in large part by his assistants, called for a sculptured travertine grotto supporting an ancient *obelisk* that Innocent had transferred to Piazza Navona from the *circus* (chariot racecourse) of the Roman emperor Maxentius (r. 305–312) on the Via Appia. The piazza was once the site of the *stadium* of Domitian (r. 81–96), a long and narrow theater-like structure for footraces and other athletic contests, which explains the piazza's unusual shape and the church's name (*agone* means "foot race" in Italian). Water rushes from the artificial grotto into a basin filled with marble statues personifying major rivers of four continents—the Danube (Europe), Nile (Africa), Ganges (Asia), and Plata (Americas). The reclining figures twist and gesticulate, consistent with the Italian Baroque taste for artworks incorporating movement and drama. The Nile covers his face—Bernini's way of acknowledging that the Nile's source was unknown at the time. The Rio de la Plata has a hoard of coins, signifying the wealth of the New World. The Ganges, easily navigable, holds an oar. The Danube, awestruck, reaches up to the papal coat of arms. A second reference to Innocent X is at the apex of the obelisk, where the Pamphili dove also symbolizes the Holy Spirit and the triumph of Christianity in all parts of the then-known world. The scenic effect of the cascading water would have been heightened whenever Piazza Navona was flooded for festival pageants. Bernini's fountain epitomizes the Baroque era's love for uniting art and spectacle.

"BAROQUE" ART AND ARCHITECTURE

Art historians traditionally describe 17th-century European art as *Baroque*, but the term is problematic because the period encompasses a broad range of styles and genres. Although its origin is unclear, "Baroque" may have come from the Portuguese word *barroco*, meaning an irregularly shaped pearl. Use of the term can be traced to the late 18th century, when critics disparaged the Baroque period's artistic production, in large part because of perceived deficiencies in comparison to the art of the Italian Renaissance. Over time, this negative connotation faded, but the term stuck. "Baroque" remains useful to describe the distinctive new style that emerged during the early 1600s—a style of complexity and drama seen especially in Italian art of this period. Whereas Renaissance artists reveled in the precise, orderly rationality of classical models, Baroque artists embraced dynamism, theatricality, and elaborate ornamentation, all used to spectacular effect, often on a grandiose scale, as in Bernini's Four Rivers Fountain (FIG. 24-1).

ITALY

Although in the 16th century the Roman Catholic Church launched the Counter-Reformation in response to—and as a challenge to—the Protestant Reformation, the considerable appeal of Protestantism continued to preoccupy the popes throughout the 17th century. The Treaty of Westphalia (see page 732) in 1648 formally recognized the principle of religious freedom, serving to validate Protestantism, predominantly in the German states. With the Catholic Church as the leading art patron in 17th-century Italy, the aim of much of Italian Baroque art was to restore Roman Catholicism's predominance and centrality. The Council of Trent, one 16th-century Counter-Reformation initiative, firmly resisted Protestant objections to using images in religious worship, insisting on their necessity for teaching the laity (see "The Council of Trent," page 642). Baroque art and architecture in Italy, especially in Rome, embodied the renewed energy of the Counter-Reformation and the papacy's zeal to communicate the Catholic message to the populace.

Architecture and Sculpture

At the end of the 16th century, Pope Sixtus V (r. 1585–1590) had played a key role in the Catholic Church's lengthy campaign to reestablish its preeminence. He augmented the papal treasury and intended to rebuild Rome as an even more magnificent showcase of Church power. Between 1606 and 1667, several strong and ambitious popes—Paul V, Urban VIII, Innocent X, and Alexander VII—made many of Sixtus V's dreams a reality. Rome still bears the marks of their patronage everywhere.

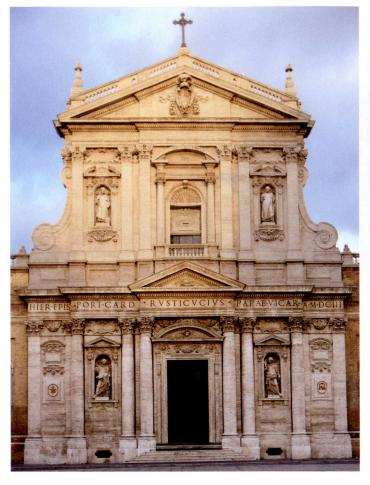

24-2 CARLO MADERNO, facade of Santa Susanna (looking north), Rome, Italy, 1597–1603.

Santa Susanna's facade is one of the earliest manifestations of the Baroque spirit. The rhythm of the columns and pilasters mounts dramatically toward the emphatically stressed vertical axis.

SANTA SUSANNA The facade (FIG. 24-2) that CARLO MADERNO (1556–1629) designed at the turn of the century for the Roman church of Santa Susanna stands as one of the earliest manifestations of the Baroque artistic spirit. In its general appearance, Maderno's facade resembles Giacomo della Porta's immensely influential design for Il Gesù (FIG. 22-57), the church of the Jesuits in Rome. But the later facade has a greater verticality that concentrates and dramatizes the major features of its model. The tall central section projects forward from the horizontal lower story, and the scroll buttresses connecting the two levels are narrower and set at a sharper angle. The elimination of an arch framing the pediment over the doorway further enhances the design's vertical thrust. The rhythm

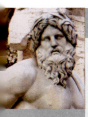

THE BAROQUE IN ITALY AND SPAIN

1600-1625
- Paul V commissions Maderno to complete Saint Peter's
- Carracci introduces quadro riportato fresco painting in the Palazzo Farnese
- Caravaggio pioneers tenebrism in Baroque painting
- Bernini creates *David* and *Apollo and Daphne* for Cardinal Scipione Borghese

1625-1650
- Borromini designs San Carlo alle Quattro Fontane and the Chapel of Sant'Ivo in Rome
- Gentileschi, the leading woman artist of the 17th century, achieves international renown
- Ribera and Zurbarán paint scenes of martyrdom in Catholic Spain
- Philip IV of Spain appoints Velázquez court painter

1650-1675
- Bernini designs the colonnaded oval piazza in front of Saint Peter's
- Murillo creates the canonical image of the Immaculate Virgin
- Velázquez paints *Las Meninas*
- Catholic churches in New Spain emulate but do not copy European models

1675-1700
- Gaulli and Pozzo paint illusionistic ceiling frescoes in Il Gesù and Sant'Ignazio in Rome
- Guarini brings the Baroque architectural style of Rome to Turin

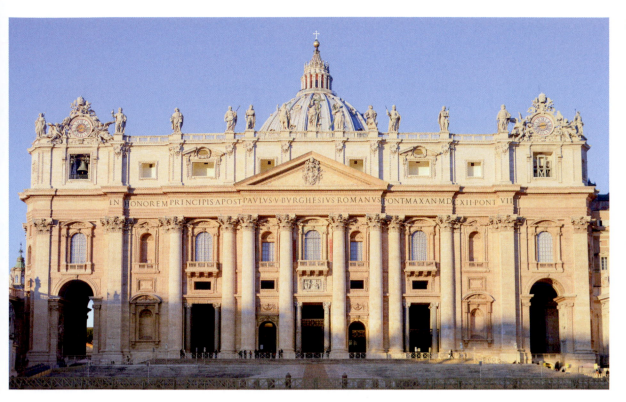

For the facade of Saint Peter's, Maderno elaborated on his design for Santa Susanna (FIG. 24-2). The two outer bays with bell towers were not part of his plan and detract from the verticality he sought.

of Santa Susanna's vigorously projecting columns and pilasters mounts dramatically toward the emphatically stressed central axis. The recessed niches, which contain statues and create pockets of shadow, heighten the sculptural effect.

MADERNO AND SAINT PETER'S The drama inherent in Santa Susanna's facade appealed to Pope Paul V (r. 1605–1621), who commissioned Maderno in 1606 to complete Saint Peter's in Rome. As the symbolic seat of the papacy, the church that Constantine originally built over the first pope's tomb (see page 243) was the very emblem of Western Christendom. In light of Counter-Reformation concerns, the Baroque popes wanted to conclude the already century-long rebuilding project and reap the prestige embodied in the mammoth new church. In many ways, Maderno's facade (FIG. **24-3**) is a gigantic expansion of the elements of Santa Susanna's first level. But the compactness and verticality of the smaller church's facade are not as prominent because Saint Peter's enormous breadth counterbalances them. Special circumstances must be taken into consideration when assessing Maderno's design, however. Because he had to match the preexisting core of an incomplete building, Maderno did not have the luxury of formulating a totally new concept for Saint Peter's. Moreover, the facade's two outer bays with bell towers were not part of the architect's original design. Hence, had the facade been constructed according to Maderno's initial concept, it would have exhibited greater verticality and visual coherence.

Maderno's plan (MAP **24-1**) also departed from the Renaissance central plans for Saint Peter's designed by Bramante (FIG. 22-22) and, later, by Michelangelo (FIG. 22-24). Paul V asked Maderno to add three nave bays to the earlier nucleus because Church officials had decided that the central plan was too closely associated with ancient temples, such as the Pantheon (FIG. 7-49). Further, the spatial organization of the longitudinal basilican plan of the original fourth-century church (FIG. 8-9) reinforced the symbolic distinction between clergy and laity and also was much better suited for religious processions. Lengthening the nave, however, pushed the dome farther back from the

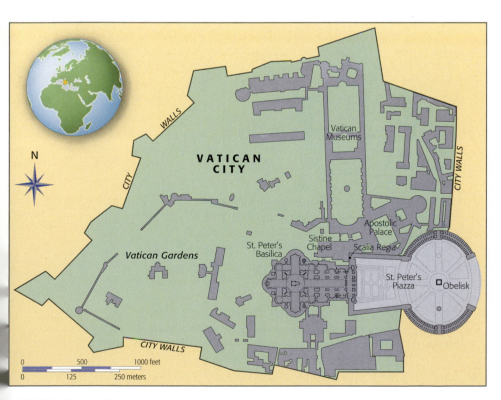

MAP 24-1 Vatican City.

PROBLEMS AND SOLUTIONS
Completing Saint Peter's

Old Saint Peter's had a large forecourt, or *atrium* (FIG. 8-10, no. 6), in front of the church proper, and in the mid-17th century, Gianlorenzo Bernini, who had long before established his reputation as a supremely gifted architect and sculptor (see page 701), received the prestigious commission to construct a monumental colonnade-framed piazza (FIG. 24-4) in front of Maderno's facade. Bernini's design had to incorporate two preexisting structures on the site—an obelisk that the ancient Romans had brought from Egypt (which Pope Sixtus V had moved to its present location in 1585 as part of his vision of Christian triumph in Rome) and a fountain that Maderno constructed in front of the church. Bernini's solution was to co-opt these features to define the long axis of a vast oval embraced by two colonnades joined to Maderno's facade.

Four rows of huge *Tuscan columns* make up the two colonnades, which terminate in classical temple fronts. The colonnades extend a dramatic gesture of embrace to all who enter the piazza, symbolizing the welcome that the Roman Catholic Church gave its members during the Counter-Reformation. Bernini himself referred to his colonnades as the welcoming arms of Saint Peter's.

Beyond their symbolic resonance, the colonnades served visually to counteract the natural perspective and bring the facade closer to the viewer. Emphasizing the facade's height in this manner, Bernini subtly and effectively compensated for its extensive width. Thus a Baroque transformation expanded the compact central designs of Bramante and Michelangelo into a dynamic complex of axially ordered elements that reach out and enclose spaces of vast dimension. By its sheer scale and theatricality, the completed Saint Peter's fulfilled the desire of the Counter-Reformation Church to present an awe-inspiring and authoritative vision of itself.

24-4 Aerial view of Saint Peter's (looking northwest), Vatican City, Rome, Italy. Piazza designed by **GIANLORENZO BERNINI**, 1656–1667.

The dramatic gesture of embrace that Bernini's colonnade makes as worshipers enter Saint Peter's piazza symbolizes the welcome the Catholic Church wished to extend during the Counter-Reformation.

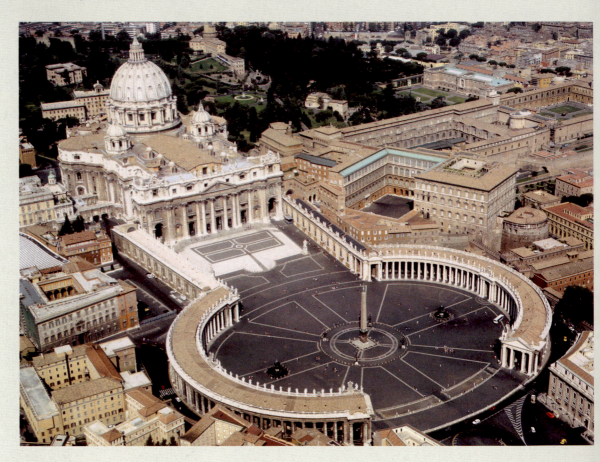

facade, and all but destroyed the effect Michelangelo had planned—a structure pulled together and dominated by its dome. When viewed at close range (FIG. 24-3), the dome barely emerges above the facade's soaring frontal plane. Seen from farther back, standing in the great piazza (FIG. 24-4) erected later by Bernini (see "Completing Saint Peter's," above), Maderno's dome appears to have no drum. Visitors must move back quite a distance from the front (or fly over the church, FIG. 24-4) to see the dome and drum together. Today, visitors to the Vatican can appreciate the effect Michelangelo intended only by viewing Saint Peter's from the back (FIG. 22-25).

BALDACCHINO Bernini's colonnaded piazza in front of Saint Peter's was neither his first nor his last project for the Vatican. For Pope Alexander VII (r. 1665–1667) he tackled the difficult problem of designing a stairway in the papal palace, the Scala Regia (FIG. **24-4A**). Within the great basilica itself, he erected a gigantic bronze *baldacchino* (FIG. **24-5**) directly beneath Giacomo della Porta's dome (FIG. 22-25). Completed between 1624 and 1633, the canopy-like structure (*baldacco* is Italian for "silk from Baghdad," such as for a cloth canopy) stands almost 100 feet high (the height of an average eight-story building) and serves both functional and symbolic purposes. It marks the high altar in the nave and the tomb of Saint Peter beneath the basilica,

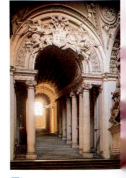

24-4A BERNINI, Scala Regia, Vatican, 1663-1666.

Every thumbnail illustration has a corresponding full-size Bonus Image and accompanying Bonus Essay online.

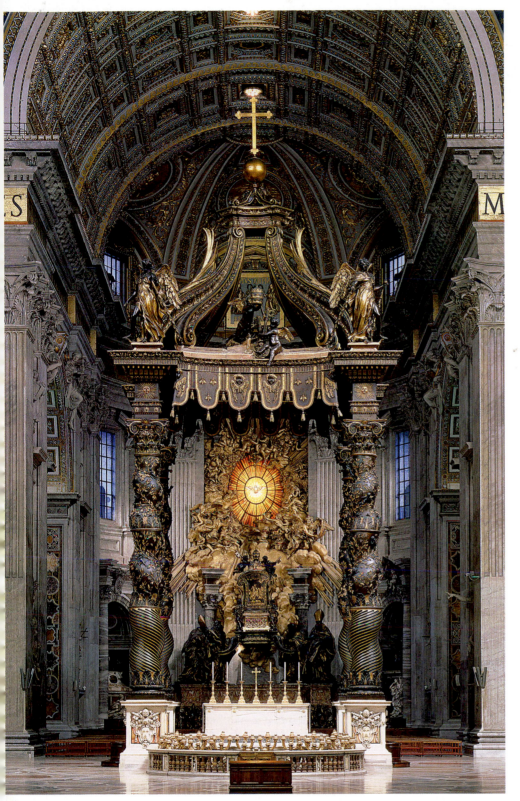

Bernini's baldacchino serves both functional and symbolic purposes. It marks Saint Peter's tomb and the high altar, and it visually bridges the marble floor and the lofty vaults and dome above.

thereby invoking the past to reinforce the primacy of the Church of Rome in the 17th century. At the top of the vine-entwined columns, four colossal angels stand guard at the upper corners of the canopy. Forming the canopy's apex are four serpentine brackets that elevate the orb and the cross. Since the time of Constantine (FIG. 7-79, *right*; compare FIG. 9-2), the orb and the cross had served as symbols of the Church's triumph. The baldacchino also features numerous bees, symbols of Urban VIII's family, the Barberini. Bernini's design thus effectively gives visual form to the triumph of Christianity and to the papal claim to supremacy in formulating Church doctrine.

The construction of the baldacchino was itself a remarkable feat. Each of the bronze columns consists of five sections cast from wood models using the *lost-wax process* (see "Hollow-Casting," page 127). Although Bernini did some of the work himself, including cleaning and repairing the wax molds and doing the final cleaning and *chasing* (engraving and embossing) of the bronze casts, he contracted out much of the project to experienced bronze-casters and sculptors. The superstructure is predominantly cast bronze, although some of the sculptural elements are brass or wood. The enormous scale of the baldacchino required a considerable amount of bronze. On Urban VIII's orders, workmen dismantled the portico of the ancient Roman temple

and provides a dramatic, compelling presence at the crossing, visually bridging the marble floor and the lofty vaults and dome above. Its columns also serve as a frame for the elaborate sculpture representing the throne of Saint Peter (the Cathedra Petri) at the far end of the nave (FIG. 24-5, *rear*).

On a symbolic level, the baldacchino's decorative elements speak to the power of the Catholic Church and of Pope Urban VIII. Partially fluted and wreathed with vines, the structure's four spiral columns are Baroque versions of the comparable columns of the ancient baldacchino over the same spot in Old Saint Peter's,

of all gods, the Pantheon (FIG. 7-49), to acquire the bronze for the baldacchino—an ideologically appropriate act, given the Church's rejection of polytheism.

The concepts of triumph and grandeur permeate every aspect of the 17th-century design of Saint Peter's. Suggesting a great and solemn procession, the main axis of the complex traverses the piazza (marked by the central obelisk; FIG. 24-4) and enters Maderno's nave. It comes to a temporary halt at the altar beneath Bernini's baldacchino (FIG. 24-5), but it continues on toward its climactic destination at another great altar in the apse.

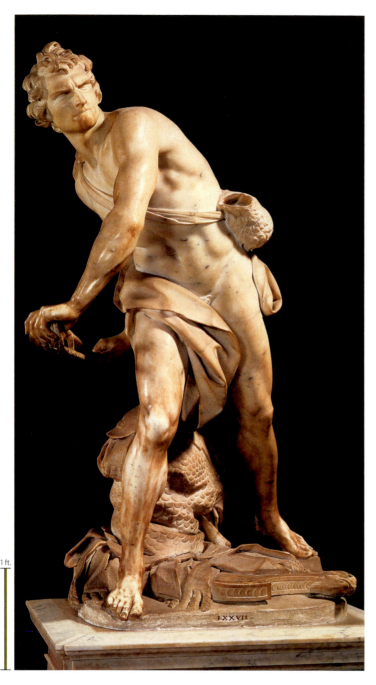

24-6 Gianlorenzo Bernini, *David,* from the Villa Borghese, Rome, Italy, 1623. Marble, 5' 7" high. Galleria Borghese, Rome.

Bernini's sculptures are expansive and theatrical, and the element of time plays an important role in them. His emotion-packed *David* seems to be moving through both time and space.

DAVID Bernini's baldacchino is, like his Four Rivers Fountain (FIG. 24-1), a masterpiece of the sculptor's craft even more than the architect's. In fact, although Bernini achieved an international reputation as an architect, his fame rests primarily on his sculpture. The biographer Filippo Baldinucci (1625–1696) observed: "[T]here was perhaps never anyone who manipulated marble with more facility and boldness. He gave his works a marvelous softness . . . making the marble, so to say, flexible."[1] Bernini's sculpture is expansive and theatrical, and the element of time usually plays an important role in it, as in the pronounced movement of the personified rivers—and the cascading water—in his Piazza Navona fountain.

A sculpture that predates both the Four Rivers Fountain and the baldacchino in Saint Peter's is Bernini's *David* (FIG. 24-6). The Baroque master surely knew the Renaissance statues of the biblical hero fashioned by Donatello (FIG. 21-11), Verrocchio (FIG. 21-12), and Michelangelo (FIG. 22-13). Bernini's *David* differs fundamentally from those earlier masterpieces, however. Michelangelo portrayed David before his encounter with his larger-than-life adversary, and Donatello and Verrocchio depicted David after his triumph over Goliath. Bernini chose to represent the combat itself and aimed to capture the split-second of maximum action. Bernini's *David* has his muscular legs firmly planted, straddling his lyre (David is here psalmist as well as hero). The body armor at David's feet is the protection King Saul offered him but that David rejected because he placed his faith in the Lord.

In Bernini's statue, David begins the violent, pivoting motion that will launch the stone from his sling. (A bag full of stones is at David's left hip, suggesting that he thought the fight would be tough and long.) Unlike Myron, the fifth-century BCE Greek sculptor who froze his *Discus Thrower* (FIG. 5-40) at a fleeting moment of inaction, Bernini selected the most dramatic of an implied sequence of poses, requiring the viewer to think simultaneously of the continuum and of this tiny fraction of it. The suggested continuum imparts a dynamic quality to the statue. The energy that is confined in Michelangelo's figures (FIGS. 22-14 and 22-15) bursts forth in Bernini's *David.* The Baroque statue seems to be moving through time and through space. This kind of sculpture cannot be inscribed in a cylinder or confined in a niche. Its unrestrained action demands space around it. Nor is it self-sufficient in the Renaissance sense, as its pose and attitude direct attention beyond it to the unseen Goliath. Bernini's *David* moves out into the space surrounding it, as do Apollo and Daphne in the marble group (FIG. 24-6A) that he carved for the same patron, Cardinal Scipione Borghese (1576–1633). Further, the expression of intense concentration on David's face contrasts vividly with the classically placid visages of Donatello's and Verrocchio's versions and is more emotionally charged even than Michelangelo's. The tension in David's face augments the dramatic impact of Bernini's sculpture.

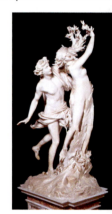

24-6A Bernini, *Apollo and Daphne,* 1623–1624.

ECSTASY OF SAINT TERESA Another work displaying the motion and emotion that are hallmarks of Italian Baroque art is Bernini's *Ecstasy of Saint Teresa* in the Cornaro chapel (FIG. 24-7) of the Roman church of Santa Maria della Vittoria (Saint Mary of Victory, so named because of the Virgin's aid in a 1620 Catholic victory near Prague during the Thirty Years' War). The work exemplifies the Baroque master's refusal to limit his statues to firmly defined spatial settings. For this commission, Bernini marshaled the full capabilities of architecture, sculpture, and painting to charge the entire chapel with palpable tension. In the Cornaro chapel, Bernini drew on the considerable knowledge of the theater that he derived from writing plays and producing stage designs.

The marble sculpture (FIG. 24-8) that serves as the chapel's focus depicts Saint Teresa of Avila (1515–1582), a nun of the Carmelite order and one of the great mystical saints of the Spanish Counter-Reformation, who only recently had been canonized by the Catholic Church. Teresa's conversion occurred after the death

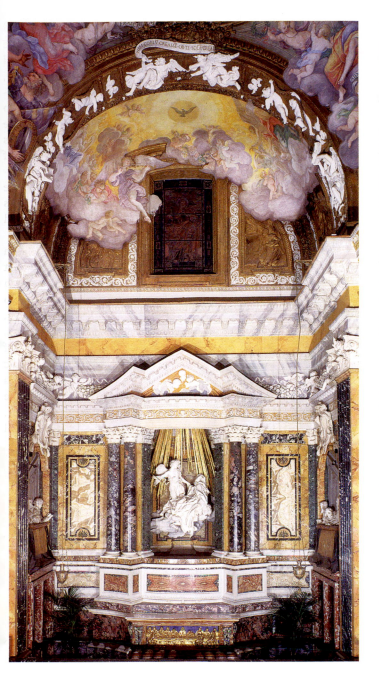

24-7 GIANLORENZO BERNINI, *Cornaro chapel, Santa Maria della Vittoria, Rome, Italy, 1645–1652.*

In the Cornaro chapel, Bernini, the quintessential Baroque artist, marshaled the full capabilities of architecture, sculpture, and painting to create an intensely emotional experience for worshipers.

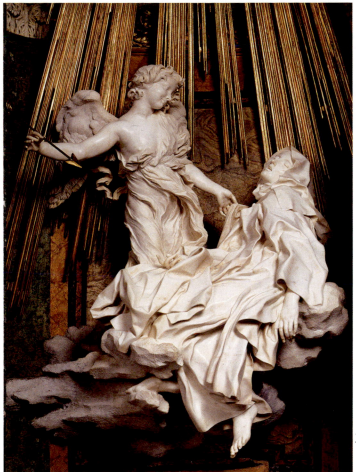

24-8 GIANLORENZO BERNINI, *Ecstasy of Saint Teresa,* Cornaro chapel, Santa Maria della Vittoria, Rome, Italy, 1645–1652. Marble, height of group 11' 6".

The passionate drama of Bernini's depiction of Saint Teresa correlated with the ideas of Ignatius Loyola, who argued that the re-creation of spiritual experience would encourage devotion and piety.

of her father, when she fell into a series of trances, saw visions, and heard voices. Feeling a persistent pain, she attributed it to the fire-tipped arrow of divine love that an angel had thrust repeatedly into her heart. In her writings, Saint Teresa described this experience as making her swoon in delightful anguish.

In Bernini's hands, the entire Cornaro chapel became a theater for the production of this mystical drama. The niche in which it takes place appears as a shallow *proscenium* (the part of the stage in front of the curtain) crowned with a broken Baroque pediment and ornamented with polychrome marble. On either side of the chapel, sculpted portraits of members of the family of Cardinal Federico Cornaro (1579–1673) watch the heavenly drama unfold

from choice balcony seats. Bernini depicted the saint in ecstasy, unmistakably a mingling of spiritual and physical passion, swooning back on a cloud, while the smiling angel aims his arrow. The sculptor's supreme technical virtuosity is evident in the visual differentiation in texture among clouds, rough cloth and gauzy material, smooth flesh, and feathery wings—all carved from the same white marble. Light from a hidden window of yellow glass pours down in golden rays suggesting the radiance of Heaven, whose painted representation covers the vault.

The passionate drama of Bernini's *Ecstasy of Saint Teresa* correlated with the ideas disseminated earlier by Ignatius Loyola (1491–1556), who founded the Jesuit order in 1534 (see page 671) and whom the Catholic Church canonized as Saint Ignatius in 1622. In his book *Spiritual Exercises,* Ignatius argued that the re-creation of spiritual experiences in artworks would do much to increase devotion and piety. Thus theatricality and sensory impact were useful vehicles for achieving Counter-Reformation goals (see "The Council of Trent," page 642). Bernini was a devout Catholic, which undoubtedly contributed to his understanding of those goals. His inventiveness, technical skill, sensitivity to his patrons' needs, and energy made him the quintessential Italian Baroque artist.

PROBLEMS AND SOLUTIONS
Rethinking the Church Facade

Although Carlo Maderno incorporated sculptural elements in his designs for the facades of Santa Susanna (FIG. 24-2) and Saint Peter's (FIG. 24-3), those church fronts still develop along relatively lateral planes, the traditional approach to facade design. In contrast, Francesco Borromini rethought the very nature of a church facade. In his design for San Carlo alle Quattro Fontane (FIG. 24-9) in Rome, he set the building's front in undulating motion, creating a dynamic counterpoint of concave and convex elements on two levels (for example, the sway of the cornices). He enhanced the three-dimensional effect with deeply recessed niches. Borromini's facade therefore stands in sharp opposition to the idea, which has its roots in antiquity, that a facade should be a flat frontispiece that defines a building's outer limits. In Borromini's hands, the church facade became a pulsating, engaging screen inserted between interior and exterior space, designed not to separate but to provide a fluid transition between the two.

In fact, San Carlo has not one but two facades, underscoring the functional interrelation of the building and its environment. The second facade (FIG. 24-9, *left*), a narrow bay crowned with its own small tower, turns away from the main facade (FIG. 24-9, *right*) and, following the curve of the street, faces an intersection.

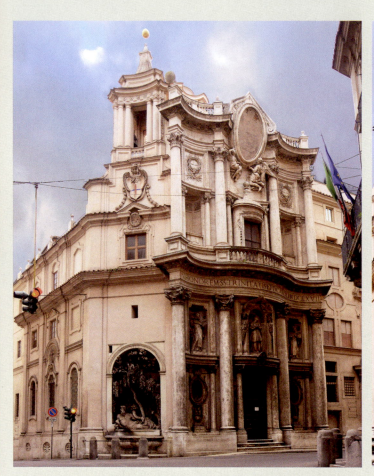
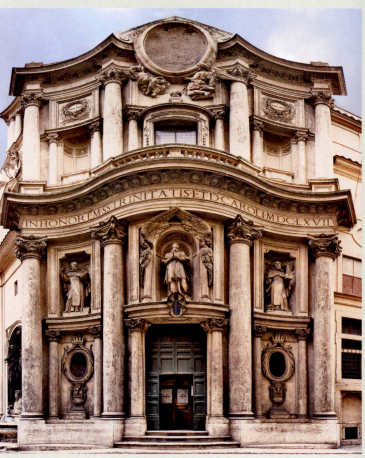

24-9 FRANCESCO BORROMINI, two views of the facade of San Carlo alle Quattro Fontane (*left:* looking south; *right:* looking southeast), Rome, Italy, 1638–1641.

Borromini rejected the notion that a church should have a flat frontispiece. He set San Carlo's facade in undulating motion, creating a dynamic counterpoint of concave and convex elements.

SAN CARLO ALLE QUATTRO FONTANE As gifted as Bernini was as an architect, FRANCESCO BORROMINI (1599–1667) took Italian Baroque architecture to even greater dramatic heights. In the little church of San Carlo alle Quattro Fontane (Saint Charles at the Four Fountains; FIG. 24-9), Borromini went much further than any of his predecessors or contemporaries in emphasizing a building's sculptural qualities, both inside and out (see "Rethinking the Church Facade," above). His innovative style had an enormous influence on later Baroque architects throughout Italy and beyond. The Palazzo Carignano (FIG. 24-9A) in Turin, for example, designed by GUARINO GUARINI (1624–1683), depends heavily on Borromini's work in Rome.

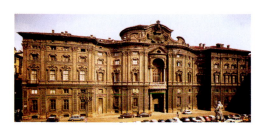

⬀ 24-9A GUARINI, Palazzo Carignano, Turin, 1679–1692.

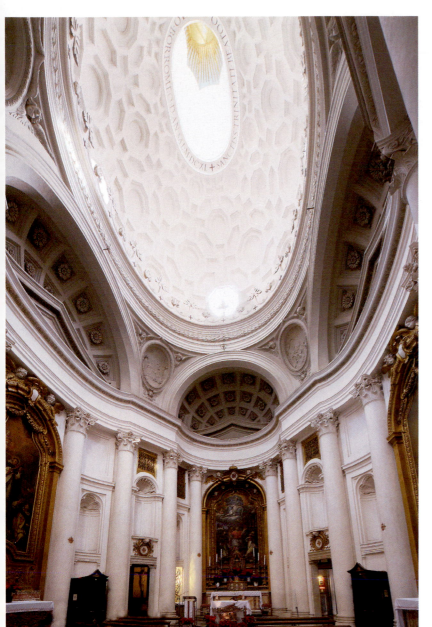

24-10 Francesco Borromini, interior of San Carlo alle Quattro Fontane (looking northwest and up into the dome), Rome, Italy, 1638–1641.

The plan of San Carlo is a hybrid of a Greek cross and an oval. The walls pulsate in a way that reverses the facade's movement. The molded, dramatically lit space flows from entrance to altar.

The interior (FIG. 24-10) of San Carlo alle Quattro Fontane is as remarkable as its exterior. The radical design is in part Borromini's ingenious response to an awkward site, but it is also a provocative variation on the theme of the centrally planned church. In plan (FIG. 24-11, *left*), San Carlo is a hybrid of a *Greek cross* (a cross with four arms of equal length) and an oval, with a long axis between entrance and apse. The side walls move in an undulating flow that reverses the facade's motion. Vigorously projecting columns define the space into which they protrude just as much as they accent the walls to which they are attached. Capping this molded interior space is a deeply coffered oval dome (FIG. 24-11, *right*) that seems to float on the light entering through windows hidden in its base. Rich variations on the basic theme of the oval—dynamic curves relative to the static circle—create an interior that flows from entrance to altar, unimpeded by the segmentation so characteristic of Renaissance buildings.

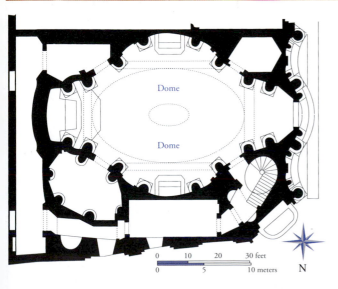

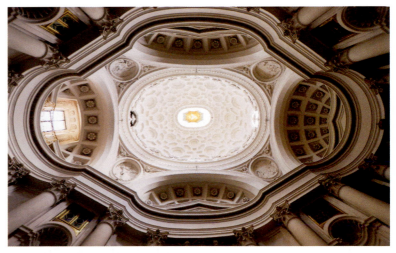

24-11 Francesco Borromini, plan (*left*) and view of dome from below (*right*), San Carlo alle Quattro Fontane, Rome, Italy, 1638–1641.

Instead of using a traditional round dome, Borromini capped the interior of San Carlo with a deeply coffered oval dome that seems to float on the light entering through windows hidden in its base.

Italy **709**

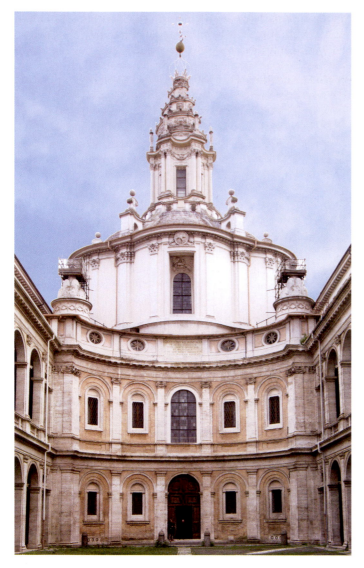

24-12 FRANCESCO BORROMINI, facade of Sant'Ivo alla Sapienza (looking east), Rome, Italy, begun 1642.

In characteristic fashion, Borromini played concave against convex forms on the upper level of the Chapel of Saint Ives. Pilasters restrain the forces that seem to push the bulging forms outward.

CHAPEL OF SAINT IVO Borromini carried the unification of interior space even further in Sant'Ivo alla Sapienza (FIG. 24-12), the chapel dedicated to Saint Ives, the patron saint of jurists, at the east end of the courtyard of the "Sapienza," the 17th-century seat of the University of Rome (*sapienza* means "wisdom" or "learning"). In his characteristic manner, Borromini played concave against convex forms on the upper level of the chapel's exterior. The arcaded courtyard, which frames the lower levels of the chapel's facade, had already been constructed when Borromini began work, and he adjusted his design to achieve a harmonious merging of the new and older parts of the college. Above the inward-curving lower two stories of the Saint Ives chapel rises a convex drumlike structure that supports

24-14 FRANCESCO BORROMINI, view of dome from below, Sant'Ivo alla Sapienza, Rome, Italy, begun 1642.

Unlike Renaissance domes, Borromini's Baroque dome is an organic form that evolves out of and shares the qualities of the supporting walls, and it cannot be separated from them.

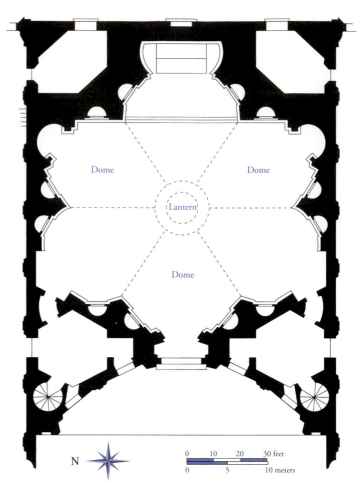

24-13 FRANCESCO BORROMINI, plan of Sant'Ivo alla Sapienza, Rome, Italy, begun 1642.

The interior elevation of Borromini's Saint Ives chapel fully reflects all the elements of its highly complex plan, which is star-shaped with rounded points and apses on all sides.

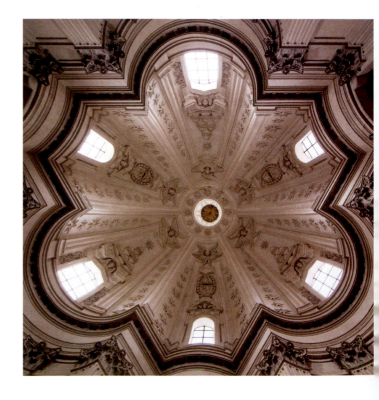

the dome's lower parts. Clusters of pilasters restrain the forces that seem to push the bulging forms outward. Buttresses above the pilasters curve upward to brace a tall, ornate *lantern* topped by a spiral that, screwlike, seems to fasten the structure to the sky.

The centralized plan (FIG. 24-13) of the interior of the Sant'Ivo chapel is that of a hexagonal star with rounded points and apses on all sides. Indentations and projections along the angled, curving walls create a highly complex plan, with all the elements fully reflected in the interior elevation. From floor to lantern, the wall panels rise in a continuously tapering sweep halted only momentarily by a single horizontal cornice (FIG. 24-14). Thus the dome is not a separate unit placed on a supporting block, as in Renaissance buildings. It is an organic part that evolves out of and shares the qualities of the supporting walls, and it cannot be separated from them. This carefully designed progression up through the lantern creates a dynamic and cohesive shell that encloses and energetically molds a scalloped fragment of space. Few architects have matched Borromini's ability to translate extremely complicated designs into masterfully unified structures, but some later architects, including Guarini, an accomplished mathematician as well as architect, designed even more complex domes (FIG. 24-14A).

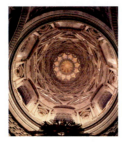

24-14A GUARINI, Chapel of the Holy Shroud, Turin, 1667–1694.

Painting

Although architecture and sculpture provided the most obvious vehicles for manipulating space and creating theatrical effects, painting continued to be an important art form in 17th-century Italy.

Among the most noted Italian Baroque painters were Annibale Carracci and Caravaggio, whose styles, although quite different, were both thoroughly in accord with the period.

ANNIBALE CARRACCI A native of Bologna, ANNIBALE CARRACCI (1560–1609) received much of his training at an art academy founded there by several members of his family, among them his cousin Ludovico Carracci (1555–1619) and brother Agostino Carracci (1557–1602). The Bolognese academy was the first significant institution of its kind in the history of Western art. The Carracci established it on the premises that art can be taught—the basis of any academic philosophy of art—and that art instruction must include the classical and Renaissance traditions in addition to the study of anatomy and life drawing.

In *Flight into Egypt* (FIG. 24-15), based on the biblical narrative from Matt. 2:13–14, Annibale Carracci created the "ideal" or "classical" landscape, in which nature appears ordered by divine law and human reason. Tranquil hills and fields, quietly gliding streams, serene skies, unruffled foliage, shepherds with their flocks—all the props of the pastoral scene and mood familiar in Venetian Renaissance paintings (FIG. 22-35)—expand to fill the picture space in *Flight into Egypt* and similar paintings. Carracci regularly included screens of trees in the foreground, dark against the sky's even light. In contrast to many Renaissance artists, he did not create the sense of deep space through linear perspective but rather by varying light and shadow to suggest expansive atmosphere. In *Flight into Egypt*, streams or terraces, carefully placed one above the other and narrowed, zigzag through the terrain, leading the viewer's eyes back to the middle ground. As in many Venetian Renaissance paintings, the background of Carracci's *Flight into Egypt* is filled with walled towns or citadels, towers, temples, monumental tombs, and villas.

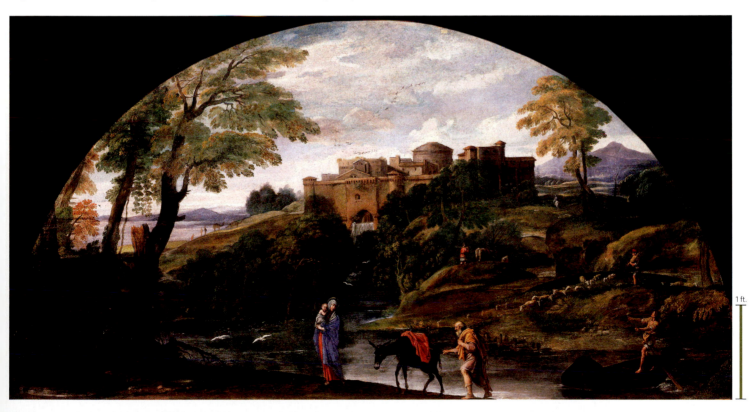

1 ft.

24-15 ANNIBALE CARRACCI, *Flight into Egypt*, 1603–1604. Oil on canvas, 4' × 7' 6". Galleria Doria Pamphili, Rome.

Carracci's landscapes idealize antiquity and the idyllic life. Here, the pastoral setting takes precedence over the narrative of Mary, the Christ Child, and Saint Joseph wending their way slowly to Egypt.

24-16 Annibale Carracci, *Loves of the Gods,* ceiling frescoes in the gallery, Palazzo Farnese (FIG. 22-26), Rome, Italy, 1597–1601.

On the shallow curved vault of this gallery in the Palazzo Farnese, Annibale Carracci arranged the mythological scenes in a quadro riportato format resembling easel paintings on a wall.

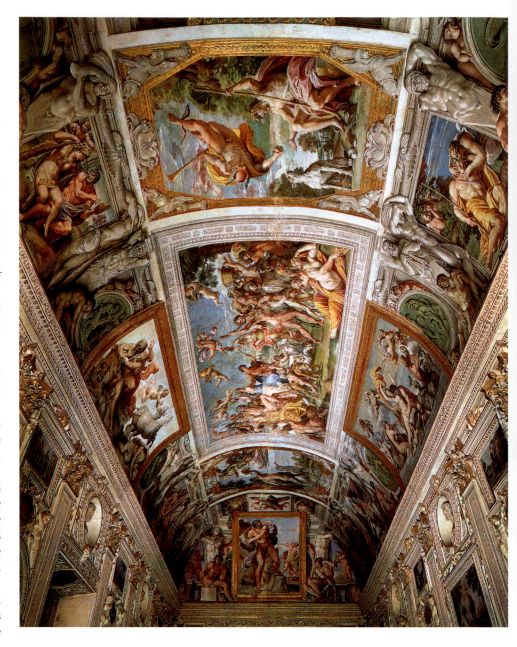

These constructed environments captured idealized antiquity and the idyllic life. Although the artists often took the subjects for these classically rendered scenes from religious or heroic stories, they favored pastoral landscapes over narratives. Here, Annibale greatly diminished the size of Mary, the Christ Child, and Saint Joseph, who simply become part of the landscape as they wend their way slowly to Egypt after having been ferried across a stream.

LOVES OF THE GODS Carracci's most notable works are his frescoes (FIG. **24-16**) in the Palazzo Farnese in Rome. Cardinal Odoardo Farnese (1573–1626)—a wealthy descendant of Pope Paul III, who built the palace (FIGS. 22-26 and 22-27) in the 16th century—commissioned Annibale to decorate the ceiling of the palace's gallery to celebrate the wedding of the cardinal's brother. Appropriately, the title of the fresco's iconographic program is *Loves of the Gods*—interpretations of the varieties of earthly and divine love, based on Ovid's *Metamorphoses.*

Carracci arranged the scenes in a format resembling framed easel paintings on a wall, but in the Farnese gallery, the paintings cover a shallow curved vault. The term for this type of simulation of easel painting for ceiling design is *quadro riportato* ("transferred framed panel"). By adapting the northern European and Venetian tradition of easel painting to the Florentine and Roman fresco tradition, Carracci reoriented the direction of painting in central Italy. He made the quadro riportato format fashionable for more than a century.

Flanking the framed pictures are polychrome seated nude youths, who turn their heads to gaze at the scenes around them, and standing Atlas figures painted to resemble marble statues. Carracci derived these motifs from the Sistine Chapel ceiling (FIG. 22-17), but he did not copy Michelangelo's figures. Notably, the chiaroscuro of the Farnese gallery frescoes differs for the pictures and the figures surrounding them. Carracci modeled the figures inside the panels in an even light. In contrast, light from beneath illuminates the outside figures, as if they were tangible three-dimensional beings or statues lit by torches in the gallery below. This interest in illusion, already manifest in the Renaissance, continued in the grand ceiling compositions (FIGS. 24-21 to 24-24) of the mature Baroque. In the crown of the vault, the long panel, *Triumph of Bacchus,* is an ingenious mixture of Raphael's drawing style and lighting and Titian's more sensuous and animated figures. Carracci succeeded in adjusting their authoritative styles to create something of his own—no easy achievement.

CARAVAGGIO Michelangelo Merisi, known as CARAVAGGIO (1573–1610) after his northern Italian birthplace, developed a distinctive personal style that had tremendous influence throughout Europe. His outspoken disdain for the classical masters (probably more rhetorical than real) drew bitter criticism from many painters, one of whom denounced him as the "anti-Christ of painting." Giovanni Pietro Bellori, the most influential critic of the age and an admirer of Annibale Carracci, believed that Caravaggio's refusal to emulate the models of his distinguished predecessors threatened the whole classical tradition of Italian painting that had reached its zenith in Raphael's work (see "Giovanni Pietro Bellori on Annibale Carracci and Caravaggio," page 713). Yet despite this criticism and the problems in Caravaggio's troubled life (police records are an important source of information about the artist), Caravaggio received many commissions, both public and private, and numerous painters paid him the supreme compliment of borrowing from his innovations. His influence on later artists, as much outside Italy as within, was immense.

WRITTEN SOURCES
Giovanni Pietro Bellori on Annibale Carracci and Caravaggio

The written sources to which art historians turn as aids in understanding the art of the past are invaluable, but they reflect the personal preferences and prejudices of the writers. Pliny the Elder, for example, claimed in the first century CE that "art ceased" after the death of Alexander the Great—a remark usually interpreted as expressing his disapproval of Hellenistic art in contrast to Classical art.* Giorgio Vasari, the biographer and champion of Italian Renaissance artists (see "Giorgio Vasari's *Lives*," page 636), condemned Gothic art as "monstrous and barbarous," and considered medieval art in general a distortion of the noble art of the Greeks and Romans (see page 374).[†] Giovanni Pietro Bellori (1613–1696), the leading biographer of Baroque artists, similarly recorded his admiration for Renaissance classicism as well as his distaste for Mannerism and realism in his opposing evaluations of Annibale Carracci and Caravaggio.

In the opening lines of his *Vita* (*Life*) of Carracci, Bellori praised "the divine Raphael . . . [whose art] raised its beauty to the summit, restoring it to the ancient majesty of . . . the Greeks and the Romans" and lamented that soon after, "artists, abandoning the study of nature, corrupted art with the *maniera*, that is to say, with the fantastic idea based on practice and not on imitation." But fortunately, Bellori observed, just "when painting was drawing to its end," Annibale Carracci rescued "the declining and extinguished art."[‡]

Bellori especially lauded Carracci's Palazzo Farnese frescoes (FIG. 24-16):

> No one could imagine seeing anywhere else a more noble and magnificent style of ornamentation, obtaining supreme excellence in the compartmentalization and in the figures and executed with the grandest manner in the design with the just proportion and the great strength of chiaroscuro. . . . Among modern works they have no comparison.[§]

In contrast, Bellori characterized Caravaggio as talented and widely imitated but misguided in his rejection of classicism in favor of realism.

> [Caravaggio] began to paint according to his own inclinations; not only ignoring but even despising the superb statuary of antiquity and the famous paintings of Raphael, he considered nature to be the only subject fit for his brush. As a result, when he was shown the most famous statues of [the ancient sculptors] Phidias [FIG. 5-46] and Glykon [FIG. 5-66] in order that he might use them as models, his only answer was to point toward a crowd of people, saying that nature had given him an abundance of masters. . . . [W]hen he came upon someone in town who pleased him he made no attempt to improve on the creations of nature.**

> [Caravaggio] claimed that he imitated his models so closely that he never made a single brushstroke that he called his own, but said rather that it was nature's. Repudiating all other rules, he considered the highest achievement not to be bound to art. For this innovation he was greatly acclaimed, and many talented and educated artists seemed compelled to follow him . . . Nevertheless he lacked *invenzione*, decorum, *disegno*, or any knowledge of the science of painting. The moment the model was taken from him, his hand and his mind became empty. . . . Thus, as Caravaggio suppressed the dignity of art, everybody did as he pleased, and what followed was contempt for beautiful things, the authority of antiquity and Raphael destroyed. . . . Now began the imitation of common and vulgar things, seeking out filth and deformity.[††]

*Pliny, *Natural History*, 25.52.
[†]Giorgio Vasari, *Introduzione alle tre arti del disegno* (1550), ch. 3.
[‡]Giovanni Pietro Bellori, *Le vite de' pittori, scultori e architetti moderni* (Rome, 1672). Translated by Catherine Enggass, *The Lives of Annibale and Agostino Carracci by Giovanni Pietro Bellori* (University Park: Pennsylvania University Press, 1968), 5–6.
[§]Ibid., 33.
**Translated by Howard Hibbard, *Caravaggio* (New York: Harper & Row, 1983), 362.
[††]Ibid., 371–372.

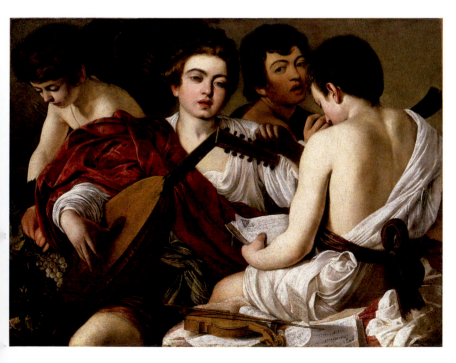

MUSICIANS One of Caravaggio's earliest major works is *Musicians* (FIG. **24-17**), which portrays four figures, including three musicians. The promising artist painted the canvas around 1595 when he was living in the household of Francesco Maria Bourbon Del Monte (1549–1627), whom Sixtus V appointed cardinal in 1588. Del Monte was a lover of art and music who headed a papal committee to study the reform of liturgical music and who oversaw the Sistine Choir, at that time an all-male ensemble of castrated singers. Caravaggio moved into Del

24-17 CARAVAGGIO, *Musicians*, from the Palazzo Madama, Rome, Italy, ca. 1595. Oil on canvas, $3' \frac{1}{4}" \times 3' 10\frac{5}{8}"$. Metropolitan Museum of Art, New York (Rogers Fund, 1952).

While Caravaggio lived in the home of Cardinal Del Monte, a lover of the good life and a patron of art and music, he painted this canvas depicting three androgynous musicians and Cupid plucking grapes.

24-18 CARAVAGGIO, *Calling of Saint Matthew,* ca. 1597–1601. Oil on canvas, 11' 1" × 11' 5". Contarelli chapel, San Luigi dei Francesi, Rome.

The stark contrast of light and dark is a key feature of Caravaggio's style. Here, Christ, cloaked in mysterious shadow, summons Levi the tax collector (Saint Matthew) to a higher calling.

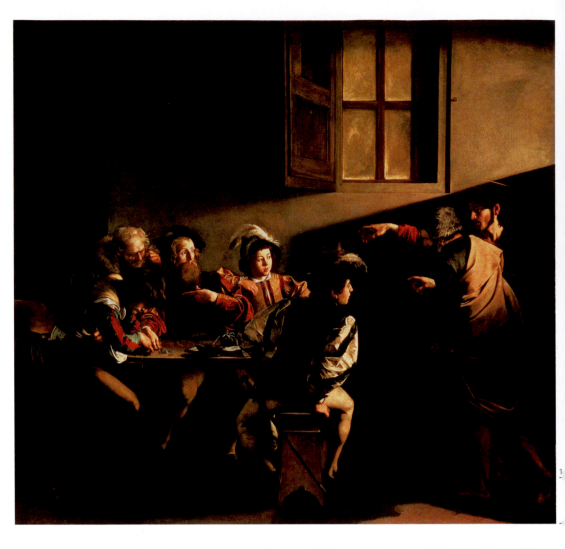

Monte's home in the Palazzo Madama and drew a salary from the cardinal in return for producing an unspecified number of paintings while in his employ. This arrangement assured the gifted young painter a steady income for the first time and permitted him to hire a servant, who also lived in the cardinal's palace. Contemporaneous accounts describe Caravaggio at that time as a frequenter of taverns who always carried a sword, an illegal act for which he was arrested at least twice. (The police dropped the charges each time upon learning of his relationship to Del Monte.)

In *Musicians,* Caravaggio presented a tableau of four tightly cropped life-size half-length figures. The central figure is a young lute player who looks seductively directly at the viewer—that is, at Cardinal Del Monte, because this was a private commission for his personal collection. The horn player in the background is a self-portrait of Caravaggio. With his mostly bare back to the viewer, a third musician (his violin is in the foreground next to his left leg) studies a musical score. The fourth figure, in the upper left corner of the canvas, has wings and a quiver of arrows. He is Cupid, the adolescent god of love, who picks grapes, a reference to Bacchus, wine, and feasting—all themes that Caravaggio addressed repeatedly in his paintings of the 1590s. Caravaggio even painted a portrait of himself in the guise of Bacchus. Art historians have frequently cited the markedly homoerotic nature of this portrayal of sensual, partially undraped, androgynous young men with full lips as evidence of the cardinal's alleged homosexuality and of the artist's bisexuality, but secure evidence is lacking. Nonetheless, the painting's subject and Caravaggio's rendition of it undoubtedly appealed to the cardinal's well-documented

interest in "the good life" alongside his ecclesiastical duties.

CALLING OF SAINT MATTHEW Del Monte's home in Rome was next to the church of San Luigi dei Francesi (Saint Louis of the French), and the cardinal was instrumental in obtaining for Caravaggio the commission to provide paintings honoring Saint Matthew for the Contarelli chapel in the left aisle near the apse of the church. *Calling of Saint Matthew* (FIG. **24-18**) is one of them. The painting is characteristic of Caravaggio's mature style and displays all the qualities for which he became famous—and for which he received scathing criticism (see "Giovanni Pietro Bellori," page 713).

In *Calling of Saint Matthew* and his other religious paintings—for example *Conversion of Saint Paul* (FIG. **24-18A**) and *Entombment* (FIG. **24-18B**)—Caravaggio injected naturalism into the representation of sacred subjects, reducing them to human dramas played out in the harsh and dingy settings of his time

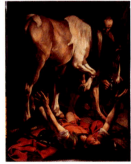

24-18A CARAVAGGIO, *Conversion of Saint Paul,* ca. 1601.

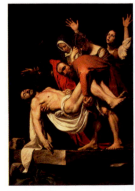

24-18B CARAVAGGIO, *Entombment,* ca. 1603.

and place. The unidealized figures that he selected from the fields and the streets of Italy, however, were effective precisely because of their familiarity. The commonplace setting of *Calling of Saint Matthew*—a tavern with unadorned walls—is typical of Caravaggio's mature canvases. Into this mundane environment, cloaked in mysterious shadow and almost unseen, Christ, identifiable initially only by his indistinct halo, enters from the right. With a commanding gesture, he summons Levi, the Roman tax collector, to a higher calling (see "Early Christian Saints," page 237). The astonished Levi—his face highlighted for the viewer by the beam of light emanating from an unspecified source above Christ's head and outside the picture—points to himself in disbelief. Although Christ's extended arm is reminiscent of the Lord's in Michelangelo's *Creation of Adam* (FIG. 22-18), the position of his hand and wrist is similar to Adam's. This reference was highly appropriate, because the Church considered Christ to be the second Adam. Whereas Adam was responsible for the fall of humankind, Christ is the vehicle of its redemption. The conversion of Levi (who became Matthew) brought his salvation.

In Caravaggio's many paintings of religious scenes, the figures are still heroic, with powerful bodies and clearly delineated contours in the Renaissance tradition (see especially FIGS. 24-18A and 24-18B), but the stark and dramatic contrast of light and dark, which at first shocked and then fascinated his contemporaries, obscures the more traditional aspects of his style. Art historians call Caravaggio's use of dark settings that envelop their occupants—which profoundly influenced European art, especially in Spain and the Netherlands—*tenebrism,* from the Italian word *tenebroso,* or "shadowy" manner. In Caravaggio's work, tenebrism also contributed greatly to the essential meaning of his pictures. In *Calling of Saint Matthew,* the beam of light directing the viewer's attention to the seated tax collector is the divine light beckoning him to join the Son of God in his earthly mission.

ARTEMISIA GENTILESCHI Caravaggio's combination of naturalism and drama appealed both to patrons and to artists, and he had many followers. Among them was the most celebrated woman artist of the era, ARTEMISIA GENTILESCHI (ca. 1593–1653), whose father, Orazio (1563–1639), her teacher, was himself strongly influenced by Caravaggio. The daughter's successful career, pursued in Florence, Venice, Naples, and Rome, helped disseminate Caravaggio's style throughout the peninsula.

In *Judith Slaying Holofernes* (FIG. 24-19), Gentileschi adopted the tenebrism and what might be called the "dark" subject matter Caravaggio favored. Significantly, she chose a narrative involving a

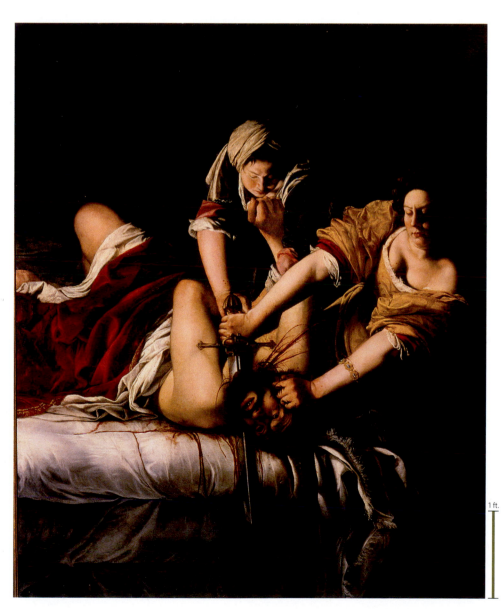

24-19 ARTEMISIA GENTILESCHI, *Judith Slaying Holofernes,* ca. 1614–1620. Oil on canvas, 6' 6⅓" × 5' 4". Galleria degli Uffizi, Florence.

Narratives involving heroic women were a favorite theme of Gentileschi. In *Judith Slaying Holofernes,* the dramatic lighting of the action in the foreground emulates Caravaggio's tenebrism.

1 ft.

ARTISTS ON ART
The Letters of Artemisia Gentileschi

Artemisia Gentileschi (FIG. 24-20) was the most renowned—although by no means the only—woman painter in 17th-century Europe (see "Women in the Renaissance Art World," page 656). Among the others who had highly successful careers was perhaps most notably Gentileschi's younger contemporary Elisabetta Sirani (1638–1665) of Bologna. Famed for the speed with which she completed paintings, Sirani produced some 200 canvases and prints during her short-lived career and took over the direction of her father's workshop when he became ill.

Gentileschi was the first woman ever admitted to membership in Florence's Accademia del Disegno (Academy of Design). Like Sirani and other women who could not become apprentices in all-male studios (see "The Artist's Profession," page 566), she learned her craft from her father. Never forgotten in subsequent centuries, Artemisia owes her modern fame to the seminal 1976 exhibition catalogue *Women Artists: 1550–1950,*[*] which brought to the fore many other notable artists and opened a new chapter in feminist art history.

In addition to scores of paintings created for wealthy patrons, among them the king of England and the grand duke of Tuscany, Gentileschi left behind 28 letters, some of which reveal that she believed that patrons treated her differently because of her gender. Three 1649 letters written in Naples to Don Antonio Ruffo (1610–1678) in Messina make her feelings explicit.

> I fear that before you saw the painting you must have thought me arrogant and presumptuous. . . . [I]f it were not for Your Most Illustrious Lordship . . . I would not have been induced to give it for one hundred and sixty, because everywhere else I have been I was paid one hundred *scudi* per figure. . . . You think me pitiful, because a woman's name raises doubts until her work is seen.[†]

> I was mortified to hear that you want to deduct one third from the already very low price that I had asked. . . . It must be that in your heart Your Most Illustrious Lordship finds little merit in me.[‡]

> As for my doing a drawing and sending it, [tell the gentleman who wishes to know the price for a painting that] I have made a solemn vow never to send my drawings because people have cheated me. In particular, just today I found myself [in the situation] that, having done a drawing of souls in Purgatory for the Bishop of St. Gata, he, in order to spend less, commissioned another painter to do the painting using my work. If I were a man, I can't imagine it would have turned out this way, because when the concept has been realized and defined with lights and darks, and established by means of planes, the rest is a trifle.[§]

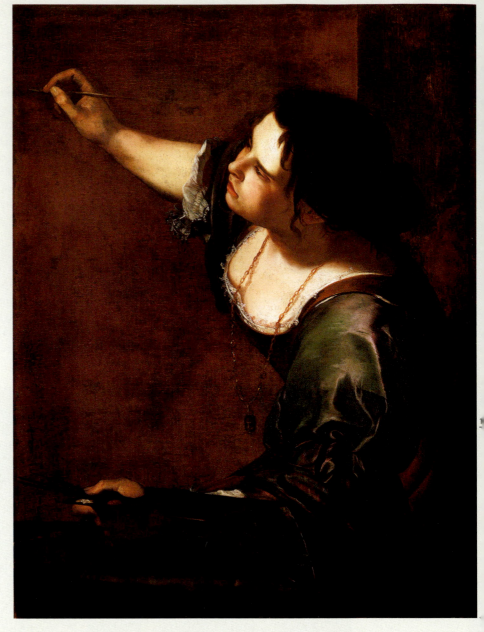

24-20 ARTEMISIA GENTILESCHI, *Self-Portrait as the Allegory of Painting*, ca. 1638–1639. Oil on canvas, 3' $2\frac{7}{8}$" × 2' $5\frac{5}{8}$". Royal Collection, Kensington Palace, London.

Gentileschi here portrayed herself in the guise of La Pittura (Painting) with brush and palette. To paint a self-portrait from the side, Gentileschi had to set up a pair of mirrors to record her features.

[*]Ann Sutherland Harris and Linda Nochlin, *Women Artists: 1550–1950* (Los Angeles: Los Angeles County Museum of Art, 1976), 118–124.
[†]Letter dated January 30, 1649. Translated by Mary D. Garrard, *Artemisia Gentileschi: The Image of the Female Hero in Italian Baroque Art* (Princeton, N.J.: Princeton University Press, 1989), 390.
[‡]Letter dated October 23, 1649. Ibid., 395–396.
[§]Letter dated November 13, 1649. Ibid., 397–398.

heroic woman, a favorite theme of hers. The story, from the book of Judith, relates the delivery of Israel from the Assyrians. Having succumbed to Judith's charms, the Assyrian general Holofernes invited her to his tent for the night. When he fell asleep, Judith cut off his head. In this version of the scene (Gentileschi produced more than one painting of the subject), Judith and her maidservant behead Holofernes. Blood spurts everywhere as the two women summon all their strength to wield the heavy sword. The tension and strain are palpable. The controlled highlights on the action in the foreground recall Caravaggio's work and heighten the drama here as well.

LA PITTURA During the brief period that Orazio Gentileschi was the official painter of the English king Charles I (r. 1625–1649), Artemisia painted perhaps her most unusual work, an allegory of Painting (*La Pittura;* FIG. **24-20**). Most art historians believe that the painting, which was in the collection of the king at the time of his execution in 1649, is a self-portrait.

Gentileschi's personified image of Painting as a woman closely follows the prescription for representing La Pittura set forth by Cesare Ripa (d. 1622) in his widely circulated handbook called *Iconologia,* published in 1593. Until the 16th century, only Poetry and Music had a fixed iconography. The inclusion of Painting in *Iconologia* reflects the newly elevated status that painters held during the Renaissance. Ripa described La Pittura as a beautiful woman with disheveled hair painting with her brush in one hand and holding her palette in the other. She wears a gold chain with a pendant in the form of a mask, because masks imitate faces and painting is the art of imitation. The chain symbolizes the continuous linkage of master to pupil from generation to generation. Gentileschi incorporated all of these traits into her painting, but instead of representing La Pittura as a frontal, emblematic figure, she portrayed her as actively engaged in her craft, seen from her left side. The viewer's eye follows the line of her left arm through the curve of her shoulders and

right arm to her right hand, the instrument of artistic genius. It is noteworthy that the canvas in this painting is blank. This is not a self-portrait of the artist at work on a specific painting (compare FIGS. 23-16, 25-11, 26-16, and 26-17) but a portrait of Gentileschi as Painting herself.

In almost all Renaissance and Baroque self-portraits, the artist gazes at the viewer. The frontal view not only provides the fullest view of the artist's features, but it is also the easiest to paint because the artist needs only to look in a mirror in order to record his or her features (FIG. 22-43). To create this self-portrait, however, Gentileschi had to set up two mirrors to paint her likeness from an angle, a highly original break from tradition and an assertion of her supreme skill in a field dominated by men (see "The Letters of Artemisia Gentileschi," page 716).

GUIDO RENI Caravaggio was not the only early-17th-century painter to win a devoted following. GUIDO RENI (1575–1642), known to his many admirers as "the divine Guido," trained in the Bolognese art academy founded by the Carracci family. The influence of Annibale Carracci and Raphael is evident in *Aurora* (FIG. **24-21**), a ceiling fresco in the Casino Rospigliosi in Rome. Aurora (Dawn) leads Apollo's chariot, while the Hours dance about it. Guido conceived *Aurora* as a quadro riportato, following the format of the paintings in Annibale's *Loves of the Gods* (FIG. 24-16), and provided the quadro with a complex and convincing illusionistic frame. The fresco exhibits a fluid motion, soft modeling, and sure composition, although without Raphael's sculpturesque strength. It is an intelligent interpretation of the Renaissance master's style. Consistent with the precepts of the Bolognese academy, the painter also looked to antiquity for models. The ultimate sources for the *Aurora* composition were Roman reliefs (FIG. 7-42) and coins depicting emperors in triumphal chariots accompanied by flying Victories and other personifications.

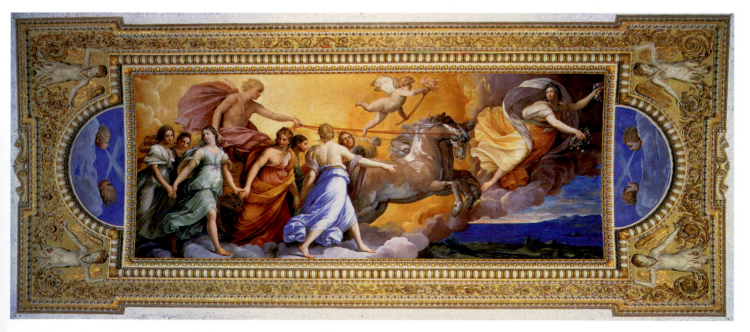

24-21 GUIDO RENI, *Aurora,* ceiling fresco in the Casino Rospigliosi, Rome, Italy, 1613–1614.

The "divine Guido" conceived *Aurora* as a quadro riportato, reflecting his training in the Bolognese art academy. The scene of Dawn leading Apollo's chariot derives from ancient Roman reliefs.

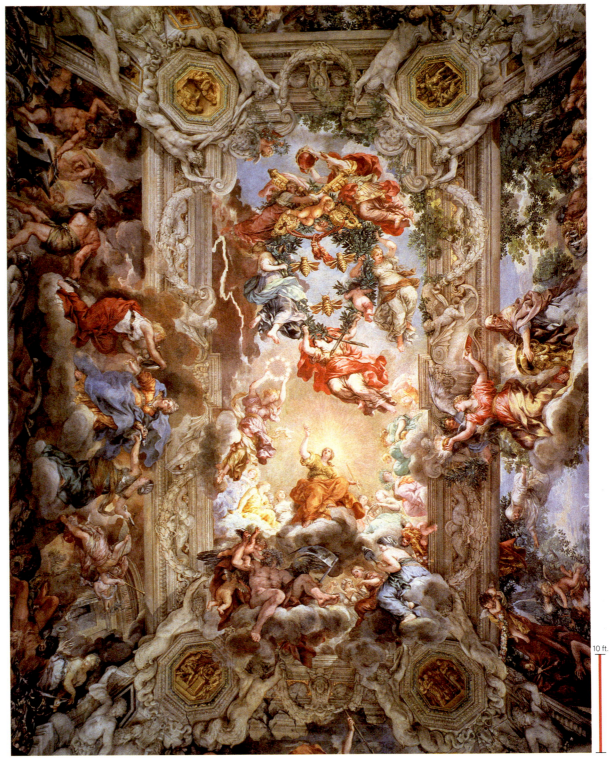

10 ft.

24-22 PIETRO DA CORTONA, *Triumph of the Barberini,* ceiling of the Gran Salone, Palazzo Barberini, Rome, Italy, 1633–1639. Fresco, 78' × 46'.

In this dramatic ceiling fresco, Divine Providence appears in a halo of radiant light directing Immortality, holding a crown of stars, to bestow eternal life on the family of Pope Urban VIII.

PIETRO DA CORTONA Looking up at a painting is different from viewing a painting hanging on a wall, even in the case of quadro riportato ceiling designs. The considerable height and expansive scale of most ceiling frescoes induce a feeling of awe. Patrons who wanted to burnish their public image or control their legacy found grandiose ceiling frescoes to be perfect vehicles. In 1633, Pope Urban VIII commissioned a ceiling fresco for the Gran Salone (the main reception hall) of the Palazzo Barberini in Rome. The most important decorative commission of the 1630s, the lucrative assignment went to PIETRO DA CORTONA (1596–1669), a Tuscan architect and painter who had moved to Rome two decades before. The immense (78-by-46-foot) *Triumph of the Barberini* (FIG. **24-22**) overwhelms spectators with the glory of the Barberini family (and Urban VIII in particular). The iconographic program for this fresco, designed

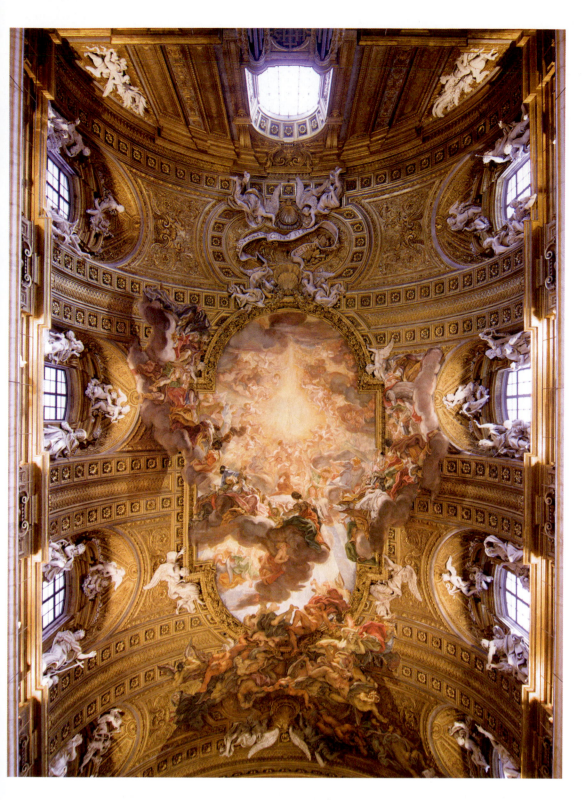

24-23 GIOVANNI BATTISTA GAULLI, *Triumph of the Name of Jesus,* ceiling fresco with stucco figures on the nave vault of Il Gesù (FIG. 22-58, *right*), Rome, Italy, 1676–1679.

In the nave of Il Gesù, gilded architecture opens up to offer the faithful a glimpse of Heaven. To heighten the illusion, Gaulli painted figures on stucco extensions that project outside the painting's frame.

by the poet Francesco Bracciolini (1566–1645), centered on the accomplishments of the Barberini. Divine Providence appears in a halo of radiant light directing Immortality, holding a crown of stars, to bestow eternal life on the family. The virtues Faith, Hope, and Charity hold aloft a gigantic laurel wreath (also a symbol of immortality), which frames three bees (the Barberini family's symbols, which also appeared in Bernini's baldacchino, FIG. 24-5). Also present are the papal tiara and keys announcing the personal triumphs of Urban VIII.

GIOVANNI BATTISTA GAULLI *Triumph of the Name of Jesus* (FIG. 24-23) in the nave of Il Gesù (FIG. 22-58) vividly demonstrates

the dramatic impact that Baroque ceiling frescoes could have in ecclesiastical contexts. As the mother church of the Jesuit order, Il Gesù played a prominent role in Counter-Reformation efforts. In this monumental fresco by GIOVANNI BATTISTA GAULLI (1639–1709), gilded architecture opens up in the center of the ceiling to offer the faithful a stunning glimpse of Heaven. Gaulli represented Jesus as a barely visible monogram (IHS) floating heavenward in a blinding radiant light. In contrast, sinners experience a violent descent back to Earth. The painter glazed the gilded architecture to suggest shadows, thereby enhancing the scene's illusionistic quality. To further heighten the illusion, Gaulli painted many of the sinners on three-dimensional stucco extensions projecting outside the painting's frame.

PROBLEMS AND SOLUTIONS

How to Make a Ceiling Disappear

The effectiveness of Italian Baroque religious art depended on the drama and theatricality of individual images, as well as on the interaction and fusion of architecture, sculpture, and painting. Sound enhanced this experience. Architects designed churches with acoustical effects in mind, and in an Italian Baroque church filled with music, the power of both image and sound must have been very moving. Through simultaneous stimulation of the senses of both sight and hearing, the faithful might well have been transported into a trancelike state that would, indeed, as the great English poet John Milton (1608–1674) eloquently stated in *Il Penseroso* (1631), "bring all Heaven before [their] eyes."*

Seventeenth-century ecclesiastical officials keenly realized that spectacular paintings high above the ground offered perfect opportunities to impress on worshipers the glory and power of the Catholic Church. In conjunction with the theatricality of Italian Baroque architecture and sculpture, grandiose frescoes on church ceilings contributed to creating transcendent spiritual environments well suited to the needs of the Catholic Church in Counter-Reformation Rome.

As Giovanni Battista Gaulli did in his *Triumph of the Name of Jesus* (FIG. 24-23) for Il Gesù, in his fresco (FIG. 24-24) for the ceiling of the nave of the Roman church honoring Saint Ignatius, Fra Andrea Pozzo created the illusion of Heaven opening up above the congregation. To accomplish this, the artist painted an extension of the church's architecture into the vault so that the roof seems to be lifted off. As Heaven and earth commingle, Christ receives Saint Ignatius in the presence of figures personifying the four corners of the world. A disk in the nave floor marks the spot where the viewer should stand to gain the whole perspective illusion. For worshipers looking up from this point, the vision is complete. They find themselves in the presence of the heavenly and spiritual, the ultimate goal of Italian Baroque ecclesiastical art and architecture.

*John Milton, *Il Penseroso* (1631, published 1645), 166.

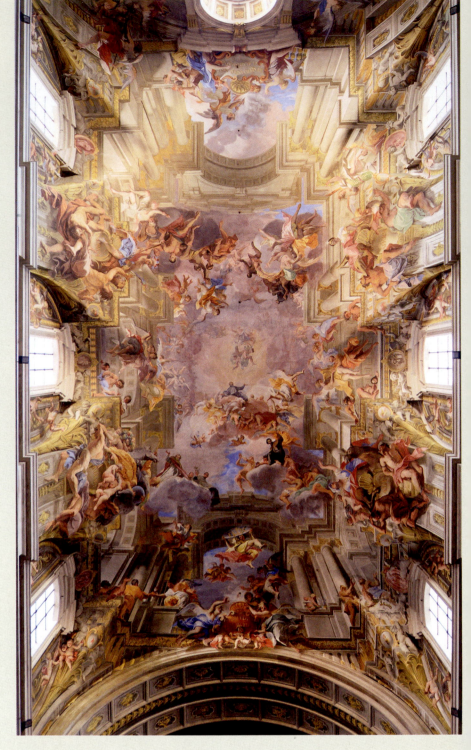

24-24 Fra Andrea Pozzo, *Glorification of Saint Ignatius,* ceiling fresco in the nave of Sant'Ignazio, Rome, Italy, 1691–1694.

By merging real and painted architecture, Pozzo created the illusion that the vaulted ceiling of Sant'Ignazio has been lifted off and that the nave opens to Heaven above the worshipers' heads.

FRA ANDREA POZZO Another master of ceiling decoration was Fra Andrea Pozzo (1642–1709), a lay brother of the Jesuit order and a master of perspective, on which he wrote an influential treatise. Pozzo designed and executed the vast ceiling fresco *Glorification of Saint Ignatius* (FIG. **24-24**) for the church of Sant'Ignazio in Rome (see "How to Make a Ceiling Disappear," above). Like Il Gesù, Sant'Ignazio was a prominent Counter-Reformation church because of its dedication to the founder of the Jesuit order. The Jesuits played a major role in Catholic education and sent legions of missionaries to the New World and Asia.

SPAIN AND NEW SPAIN

During the 16th century, Spain had established itself as an international power. The Habsburg kings had built a dynastic state encompassing Portugal, part of Italy, the Netherlands, and extensive areas of the New World (see pages 695 and 1084). By the beginning of the 17th century, however, the Habsburg Empire was in decline, and although Spain mounted an aggressive effort during the Thirty Years' War (see page 732), by 1660 the imperial age of the Spanish Habsburgs was over. In part, the demise of the Habsburg Empire was due to economic woes. The military campaigns that Philip III (r. 1598–1621) and his son Philip IV (r. 1621–1665) waged during the Thirty Years' War were costly and led to the imposition of higher taxes. The increasing tax burden placed on Spanish subjects in turn incited revolts and civil war in Catalonia and Portugal in the 1640s, further straining an already fragile economy.

Painting and Sculpture

Although the dawn of the Baroque period found the Spanish kings struggling to maintain control of their dwindling empire, both Philip III and Philip IV understood the prestige that great artworks brought and the value of visual imagery in communicating effectively with a wide audience. Thus both kings continued to spend lavishly on art.

JUAN SÁNCHEZ COTÁN One painter who made a major contribution to the development of Spanish art, although he did not receive any royal commissions, was JUAN SÁNCHEZ COTÁN (1560–1627). Born in Orgaz, outside Toledo, Sánchez Cotán moved to Granada and became a Carthusian monk in 1603. Although he painted religious subjects, his greatest works are the *still lifes* (paintings of artfully arranged inanimate objects) that he produced before

entering monastic life (and never thereafter). Few in number, they nonetheless established still-life painting as an important genre in 17th-century Spain.

Still Life with Game Fowl (FIG. 24-25) is one of Sánchez Cotán's most ambitious compositions, but it conforms to the pattern he adopted for all his still lifes. A niche or a window—the artist clearly wished the setting to be indeterminate—fills the entire surface of the canvas. At the bottom, fruits and vegetables, including a melon—cut open with a slice removed—rest on a ledge. Above, suspended on strings from a nail or hook outside the frame, are a quince and four game fowl. All are meticulously rendered and brightly illuminated, enhancing the viewer's sense of each texture, color, and shape, yet the background is impenetrable shadow. The sharp and unnatural contrast between light and dark imbues the still life with a sense of mystery that is absent, for example, in Dutch still-life paintings (FIGS. 23-15, 25-21, 25-22, and 25-23). There may, in fact, be a religious reference. Sánchez Cotán once described his 11 paintings of fruits, vegetables, and birds as "offerings to the Virgin"—probably a reference to the Virgin as the *fenestra coeli* ("window to Heaven") and the source of spiritual food for the faithful.

JOSÉ DE RIBERA In the 17th century, Spain maintained its passionate commitment to Catholic orthodoxy, and, as in Counter-Reformation Italy, Spanish Baroque artists sought ways to move viewers and encourage greater devotion and piety. Scenes of death and martyrdom had great appeal in Spain. They provided artists with opportunities both to depict extreme emotion and to elicit passionate feelings. Spain prided itself on its saints—Saint Teresa of Avila (FIG. 24-8) and Saint Ignatius Loyola (FIG. 24-24) were both Spanish-born—and martyrdom scenes appear frequently in Spanish Baroque art.

As a young man, JOSÉ (JUSEPE) DE RIBERA (ca. 1588–1652) emigrated to Naples and fell under the spell of Caravaggio, whose

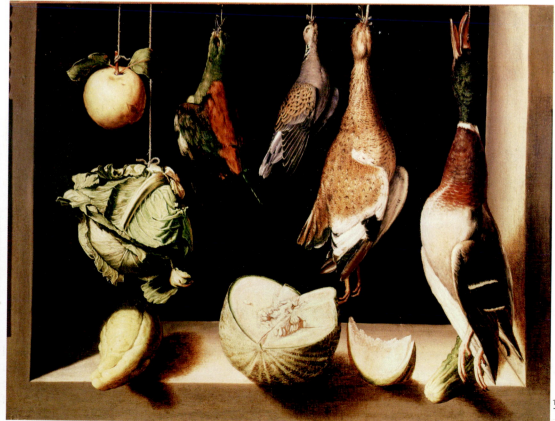

24-25 JUAN SÁNCHEZ COTÁN, *Still Life with Game Fowl*, ca. 1600–1603. Oil on canvas, 2' 2¾" × 2' 10⅞". Art Institute of Chicago, Chicago (gift of Mr. and Mrs. Leigh B. Block).

Sánchez Cotán established still life as an important genre in Spain. His compositions feature brightly illuminated fruits, vegetables, and birds, hanging or on a ledge, against a dark background.

1 in.

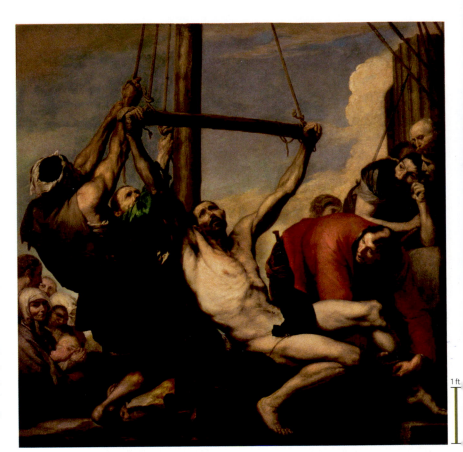

24-26 José de Ribera, *Martyrdom of Saint Philip,* ca. 1639. Oil on canvas, 7' 8" × 7' 8". Museo del Prado, Madrid.

Martyrdom scenes were popular in Counter-Reformation Spain. Scorning idealization of any kind, Ribera represented Philip's executioners hoisting him into position to die on a cross.

innovative style he introduced to Spain. Emulating Caravaggio, Ribera made naturalism and compelling drama primary ingredients of his paintings, which often embraced brutal themes, reflecting the harsh times of the Counter-Reformation and the Spanish taste for stories showcasing courage and devotion. Ribera's *Martyrdom of Saint Philip* (FIG. **24-26**) is grim and dark in both subject and form. Scorning idealization of any kind, Ribera represented Philip's executioners hoisting him into position after tying him to a cross, the instrument of Christ's own martyrdom. The saint's rough, heavy body and swarthy, plebeian features express a kinship between him and his tormentors, who are similar to the types of figures found in Caravaggio's paintings. The patron of this painting is unknown, but it is possible that Philip IV commissioned the work, because Saint Philip was the king's patron saint.

FRANCISCO DE ZURBARÁN Another prominent Spanish painter of dramatic works was FRANCISCO DE ZURBARÁN (1598–1664), whose primary patrons throughout his career were rich Spanish monastic orders. Many of his paintings are quiet and contemplative, appropriate for prayer and devotional purposes. Zurbarán painted *Saint Serapion* (FIG. **24-27**) as a devotional image for the funerary chapel of the monastic Order of Mercy in Seville, which was founded to aid Christians who had been taken prisoner by the Moors. The saint, who participated in the Third Crusade of 1196, suffered martyrdom while preaching the Gospel to Muslims. According to one account, the monk's captors tied him to a tree and then tortured and decapitated him. The Order of Mercy dedicated itself to self-sacrifice, and Serapion's membership in this order amplified the resonance of Zurbarán's painting. In *Saint Serapion,* the monk emerges from a dark background and fills the foreground. The bright light shining on him calls attention to the saint's tragic death and increases the dramatic impact of the image. In the background are two barely visible tree branches. A small note next to the saint identifies him for viewers. The coarse features of the Spanish monk label him as common (Serapion had not yet been declared a saint at the time Zurbarán portrayed him), no doubt evoking empathy from a wide audience.

JUAN MARTÍNEZ MONTAÑÉS The drama and fervor of Spanish Baroque religious painting have parallels in 17th-century Spanish sculpture. Especially noteworthy is the work of JUAN MARTÍNEZ MONTAÑÉS (1568–1649), the leading sculptor of Seville. Variously called by his contemporaries "the Sevillian Phidias" and "the Andalusian Lysippos," references to two of the most famous ancient Greek sculptors, Montañés was primarily known as "the god of wood" because of his mastery of the art of *polychrome* (painted) and gilded wood sculptures.

One of the major commissions that Montañés received during his long career (he died at age 81 in the 1649 plague in Seville) was to

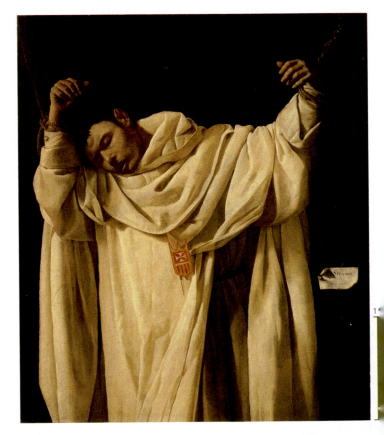

24-27 Francisco de Zurbarán, *Saint Serapion,* 1628. Oil on canvas, 3' 11½" × 3' 4¾". Wadsworth Atheneum Museum of Art, Hartford (The Ella Gallup Sumner and Mary Catlin Sumner Collection Fund).

The light shining on Serapion calls attention to his tragic death and increases the painting's dramatic impact. The monk's coarse features label him as common, evoking empathy from a wide audience.

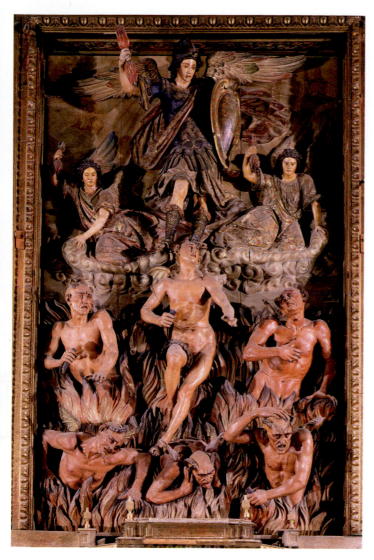

24-28 Juan Martínez Montañés, *Battle of Demons and Angels,* main panel of the retablo in the apse of San Miguel, Jerez de la Frontera, Spain, ca. 1609–1613. Painted and gilded wood.

Montañés was the leading Spanish Baroque sculptor. This polychrome and gilded wood retablo panel of the archangel Michael defeating the rebel angels may be an allegory of Catholicism's triumph over Protestantism.

provide relief sculptures for the enormous multistory *retablo* (Spanish, "altarpiece") that fills the apse of the church of San Miguel (Saint Michael) at Jerez de la Frontera in southern Spain (MAP 25-1). The retablo is the work of several sculptors and took decades to complete. The main panel (FIG. 24-28), by Montañés, celebrates the victory of the archangel Michael, the church's namesake, over the rebel angels. Contemporaries viewed the biblical story as an allegory of the triumph of Catholicism over Protestantism. In the Spanish sculptor's conception of the theme (compare Domenico Beccafiumi's *Fall of the Rebel Angels,* FIG. 22-42A), Michael and his angels are handsome and beautifully proportioned, classically inspired figures who attack from above (that is, from Heaven) the ugly, writhing agents of the Devil. The arrangement of the demons from Hell owes a debt to the famous Hellenistic-style *Laocoön* (FIG. 5-89) statuary group discovered in Rome in 1506. Although stylistically related to Baroque sculpture in Italy, Spanish Baroque sculpture is a distinct regional variation. Compared to the pure white marble statues of Bernini and his Italian contemporaries, the lifelike polychrome wood statues and reliefs of 17th-century Spain elicit a very different reaction from the viewer.

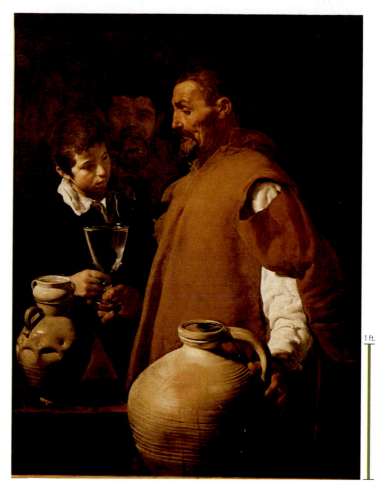

24-29 Diego Velázquez, *Water Carrier of Seville,* ca. 1619. Oil on canvas, 3' 5½" × 2' 7¾". Victoria & Albert Museum, London.

In this early work—a genre scene that seems to convey a deeper significance—the contrast of darks and lights, and the plebeian nature of the figures, reveal Velázquez's debt to Caravaggio.

DIEGO VELÁZQUEZ The foremost Spanish painter of the Baroque age—and the greatest beneficiary of royal patronage—was Diego Velázquez (1599–1660). An early work, *Water Carrier of Seville* (FIG. 24-29), reveals Velázquez's impressive command of the painter's craft when he was only about 20 years old. In this genre scene that seems to convey a deeper significance, Velázquez rendered the figures with clarity and dignity, and his careful and convincing depiction of the water jugs in the foreground, complete with droplets of water, adds to the scene's credibility. The plebeian nature of the figures and the contrast of darks and lights again reveal the influence of Caravaggio, whose work Velázquez had studied.

Like many other Spanish artists, Velázquez produced religious pictures—for example, *Christ on the Cross* (FIG. 24-29A)—as well as genre scenes, but his renown in his day rested primarily on the works he painted for King Philip IV (see "Velázquez and Philip IV," page 724). After the king appointed Velázquez court painter, the artist largely abandoned both religious and genre subjects in favor of royal portraits (FIG. 24-30A) and canvases recording historical events.

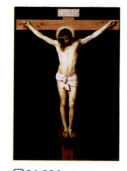

24-29A Velázquez, *Christ on the Cross,* ca. 1631–1632.

THE PATRON'S VOICE
Velázquez and Philip IV

Trained in Seville, Diego Velázquez was quite young when he came to the attention of Philip IV. The painter's immense talent impressed the king, and Philip named him chief court artist and palace chamberlain, a position that also involved overseeing the rapidly growing royal art collection and advising the king on acquisitions and display. Among the works in Philip IV's possession were paintings by Titian, Annibale Carracci, Guido Reni, Albrecht Dürer, and Velázquez's famous Flemish contemporary, Peter Paul Rubens (see page 732).

With the exception of two extended trips to Italy and a few excursions, Velázquez remained in Madrid for the rest of his life. His close relationship with Philip IV and his high office as chamberlain gave him prestige and a rare guaranteed income. But, like most artists before the modern era, Velázquez above all had to please his patron and consequently had little opportunity to choose his own subjects. One sign of Velázquez's fertile imagination as well as mastery of the brush is that he, like Michelangelo (see "Michelangelo in the Service of Julius II," page 623), was able to create timeless artworks from the assignments he received.

A case in point is the painting Velázquez produced on the king's orders to commemorate the Spanish victory over the Dutch in 1625. Painted in 1635, *Surrender of Breda* (FIG. 24-30) was part of an extensive program of decoration for the Hall of Realms in Philip IV's new secondary pleasure palace in Madrid, the Palacio del Buen Retiro. The huge canvas (more than 12 feet long and almost as tall) was one of 10 paintings celebrating recent Spanish military successes, not only in Europe but in the New World as well. Among the most troublesome situations for Spain was the conflict in the Netherlands. Determined to escape Spanish control, the northern Netherlands broke from the Habsburg Empire in the late 16th century. Skirmishes continued to flare up along the border between the northern (Dutch) and southern (Spanish) Netherlands, and in 1625, Philip IV sent General Ambrogio di Spínola to Breda to reclaim the town for Spain.

Velázquez depicted the victorious Spanish troops, organized and well armed, on the right side of the painting. In sharp contrast, the defeated Dutch on the left appear bedraggled and disorganized. In the

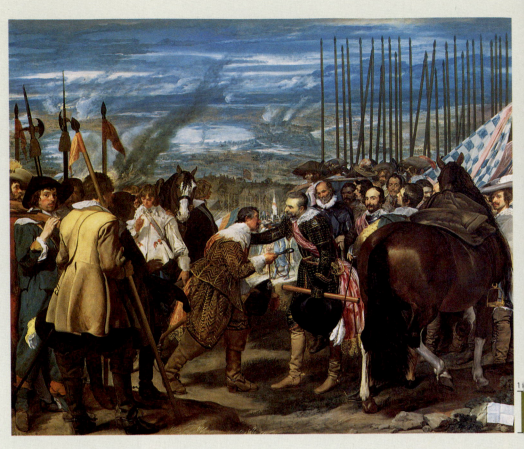

24-30 DIEGO VELÁZQUEZ, *Surrender of Breda*, 1634–1635. Oil on canvas, 10' 1" × 12' $\frac{1}{2}$". Museo del Prado, Madrid.

As Philip IV's court artist, Velázquez produced many history paintings, including fictional representations such as this one depicting the Dutch mayor of Breda surrendering to a Spanish general.

center foreground, the mayor of Breda, Justinus of Nassau, hands the city's keys to the Spanish general—although no encounter of this kind ever occurred. Velázquez's fictional record of the event glorifies not only the strength of the Spanish military but also the benevolence of Spínola. Velázquez did not portray the Spanish general astride his horse, lording over the vanquished Dutch mayor, but rather painted him standing and magnanimously stopping Justinus from kneeling. Indeed, the terms of surrender were notably lenient, and Spínola allowed the Dutch to retain their arms—which they used to recapture the city in 1637.

Velázquez also painted dozens of portraits of Philip IV (FIG. 24-30A) and his family and retinue, including *Las Meninas* (FIG. 24-31), one of the greatest paintings in the history of Western art, a work that Philip admired so much that he displayed it in his personal office.

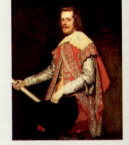

⬈ 24-30A VELÁZQUEZ, *Philip IV*, 1644.

LAS MENINAS After an extended visit to Rome from 1648 to 1651, Velázquez returned to Spain. In 1656, he painted his greatest work, *Las Meninas* (*The Maids of Honor*; FIG. 24-31). The setting is the artist's studio in the palace of the Alcázar, the official royal residence in Madrid. After the death of Prince Baltasar Carlos in 1646, Philip IV ordered part of the prince's chambers converted into a studio for Velázquez. The painter represented himself standing before a large canvas. The young Infanta (Princess) Margarita appears in the foreground with her two maids-in-waiting, her favorite dwarfs, and a large dog. In the middle ground are a woman in widow's attire and

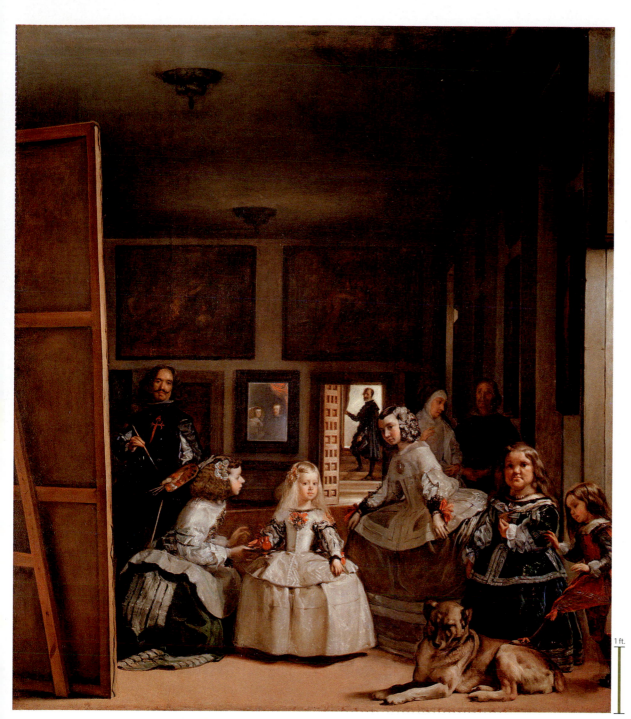

24-31 DIEGO VELÁZQUEZ, *Las Meninas* (*The Maids of Honor*), 1656. Oil on canvas, 10' 5" × 9'. Museo del Prado, Madrid.

Velázquez intended this huge and complex work, with its cunning contrasts of real, mirrored, and picture spaces, to elevate both himself and the profession of painting in the eyes of Philip IV.

1 ft.

a male escort. In the background, a chamberlain stands in a brightly lit open doorway. Scholars have been able to identify everyone in the room, including the two meninas and the dwarfs.

Las Meninas is noteworthy for its visual and narrative complexity. Indeed, art historians have yet to agree on any particular reading or interpretation. A central issue preoccupying scholars has been what, exactly, is taking place in *Las Meninas*. What is Velázquez depicting on the huge canvas in front of him? He may be painting this very picture—an informal image of the infanta and her entourage. Alternately, Velázquez may be painting a portrait of King Philip IV and Queen Mariana, whose reflections appear in the mirror on the far wall. If so, that would suggest the presence of the king and queen in the viewer's space, outside the confines of the picture. Other scholars have proposed that the mirror image is not a reflection of the royal couple standing in Velázquez's studio but a

reflection of the portrait the artist is in the process of painting on the canvas before him. This question will probably never be definitively resolved.

More generally, *Las Meninas* is Velázquez's attempt to elevate both himself and his profession. As first painter to the king and as chamberlain of the palace, Velázquez was conscious not only of the importance of his court office but also of the honor and dignity belonging to his profession as a painter. Throughout his career, Velázquez hoped to be ennobled by royal appointment to membership in the ancient and illustrious Order of Santiago (Saint James). Because he lacked a sufficiently noble lineage, he gained entrance only with difficulty at the very end of his life, and then only through the pope's dispensation. In the painting, Velázquez wears the order's red cross on his doublet, painted there, legend says, by Philip IV. In all likelihood, Velázquez painted it. In the artist's mind, *Las Meninas* might have embodied the idea of the great king visiting his studio, as Alexander the Great visited the studio of the painter Apelles in ancient times. The figures in the painting all appear to acknowledge the royal presence. Placed among them in equal dignity is Velázquez, face-to-face with his sovereign.

The location of the completed painting reinforced this act of looking—of seeing and being seen. *Las Meninas* hung in Philip IV's personal office in another part of the palace. Thus, although occasional visitors admitted to the king's private quarters may have seen this painting, Philip was the primary audience. Each time he stood before the canvas, he again participated in the work as the probable subject of Velázquez's painting within the painting and as the object of the figures' gazes. In *Las Meninas*, Velázquez elevated the art of painting, in the person of the painter, to the highest status. The king's presence enhanced this status—either in person as the viewer of *Las Meninas* or as a reflected image in the painting itself. The paintings that appear in *Las Meninas* further reinforced this celebration of the painter's craft. On the wall above the doorway and the mirror, two faintly recognizable pictures are copies made by Velázquez's son-in-law, Juan del Mazo (ca. 1612–1667), of paintings by Peter Paul Rubens. The paintings depict the immortal gods as the source of art. Ultimately, Velázquez sought ennoblement not for himself alone but for his art as well.

Las Meninas is extraordinarily complex visually. Velázquez's optical report of the event, authentic in every detail, pictorially summarizes the various kinds of images in their different levels and degrees of reality. He portrayed the realities of image on canvas, of mirror image, of optical image, and of the two painted images. This work—with its cunning contrasts of real spaces, mirrored spaces, picture spaces, and pictures within pictures—itself appears to have been taken from a large mirror reflecting the entire scene. This would mean that the artist did not paint the princess and her suite as the main subjects of *Las Meninas* but himself in the process of painting them. *Las Meninas* is a pictorial summary and a commentary on the essential mystery of the visual world, as well as on the ambiguity that results when different states or levels interact or are juxtaposed.

Velázquez employed several devices in order to achieve this visual complexity. For example, the extension of the composition's pictorial depth in both directions is noteworthy. The open doorway and its ascending staircase lead the eye beyond the artist's studio, and the mirror and the outward glances of several of the figures incorporate the viewer's space into the picture as well. (Compare how the mirror in Jan van Eyck's *Giovanni Arnolfini and His Wife* [FIG. 20-7] similarly incorporates the area in front of the canvas into the picture, although less obviously and without a comparable extension of space beyond the rear wall of the room.) Velázquez also masterfully observed and represented form and shadow. Instead of putting lights abruptly beside darks, following Caravaggio, Velázquez allowed a great number of intermediate values of gray to come between the two extremes. His matching of

tonal gradations approached effects later discovered in the age of photography.

BARTOLOMÉ ESTEBAN MURILLO No Spanish painter of the second half of the 17th century could challenge Velázquez in stature or quality, but one painter, BARTOLOMÉ ESTEBAN MURILLO (1617–1682), had an influence on later painters that was in some ways more pervasive than Velázquez's. Murillo was born in Seville, where in 1645 he received his first important commission—a series of paintings of the life of Saint Francis for the cloister of San Francisco el Grande. His most famous works, however, depict the Immaculate Virgin (for example, *Immaculate Conception of the Escorial*, FIG. 24-32), an immensely popular theme in fervently Catholic Spain. For centuries, the Spanish Church had lobbied the popes in Rome to certify that the Virgin, like Christ, had been conceived

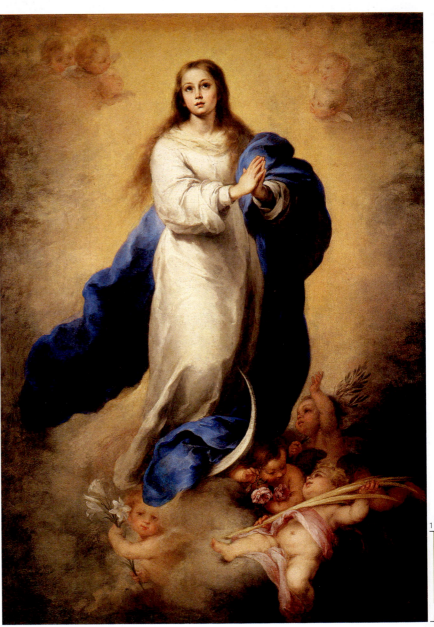

24-32 BARTOLOMÉ ESTEBAN MURILLO, *Immaculate Conception of the Escorial*, ca. 1661–1670. Oil on canvas, 6' 9 $\frac{1}{8}$" × 4' 8 $\frac{5}{8}$". Museo del Prado, Madrid.

Murillo established the canonical image of the Immaculate Virgin—a beautiful young praying woman ascending to Heaven on clouds, accompanied by angels bearing symbols of her purity.

without sin, a position supported by the Franciscan order. The Dominicans, in contrast, insisted that the Virgin had not been miraculously conceived but was purified while in her mother's womb. Many Spanish painters received commissions to paint Mary's immaculate conception in accord with the standard Counter-Reformation iconography. In Murillo's painting, the Virgin, wearing a white gown and a blue cloak, rises heavenward on clouds, riding on a crescent moon (as described in the Apocalypse) and accompanied by angels carrying attributes referring to her purity (roses, lilies, a mirror) and her suffering (palm fronds).

Murillo's many *Virgin of the Immaculate Conception* paintings set the standard for representations of this subject. The *Immaculate Conception of the Escorial* (FIG. 24-32) is probably his best. In 1661, Pope Alexander VII officially decreed that Mary was free of original sin, causing great celebration in Spain and putting an end to the controversy. The Escorial *Immaculate Conception* has fewer angels and attributes than Murillo's earlier versions. The Spanish master represented Mary as a beautiful, humble young woman, her hands clasped in prayer, slowly ascending to Heaven. By using light colors and making the angels in the upper half of the canvas almost disappear in the clouds, Murillo imbued the scene with a sense of weightlessness. His formulation of the theme became canonical, not only in Spain but in the Spanish colonies in the New World.

Architecture

The Baroque architecture of Spain and its colonies in the Western Hemisphere has closer affinities to the lavish surface decoration of the Plateresque style of the late 15th and 16th centuries (FIGS. 23-24 and 23-24A) than to the more severe style of El Escorial (FIG. 23-25). The important Romanesque church of Saint James at Santiago de Compostela (FIG. 12-7A), for example, received a new Baroque-style facade in the 17th century, and Baroque taste also determined the look of the churches that the Spanish conquerors erected in the New World. As in Rome at the same time, the richest and most influential architectural patron in Latin America was the Catholic Church.

MEXICO CITY The largest building constructed anywhere in New Spain during the colonial period was Metropolitan Cathedral of the Assumption of Mary (FIG. **24-33**) in Mexico City. The project began shortly after the victory of Hernàn Cortès over the Aztec Empire (see page 1084) on the site of the Templo Mayor (FIG. 35-3), the ceremonial and religious center of the Aztec capital city of Tenochtitlán (see MAP 35-1). The cathedral building campaign lasted nearly three centuries, completed only in 1817. Most of the present enormous (360-foot-long and 179-foot-wide) structure dates to the 17th century

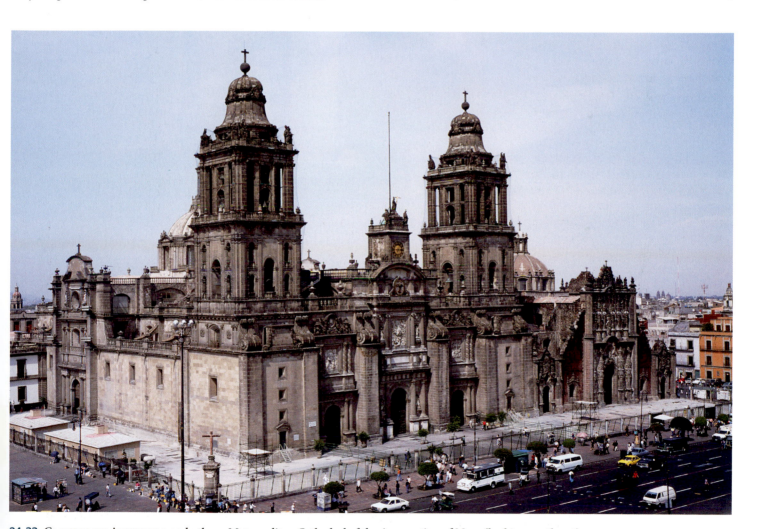

24-33 CLAUDIO DE ARCINIEGA and others, Metropolitan Cathedral of the Assumption of Mary (looking northeast), Mexico City, Mexico, 1573–1817.

The largest building in colonial Latin America is Mexico City's Metropolitan Cathedral, built on the site of the religious center of the conquered Aztec capital. The design reflects Roman Baroque church exteriors.

24-34 Jean-Baptiste Gilles or Martinez de Oviedo, west facade of the Iglesia La Compañía de Jesús (Church of the Society of Jesus), Cuzco, Peru, 1650–1668.

The Baroque facade of the Jesuits' church in the former capital of the Inka Empire is a distinctive colonial variation without close parallels in Europe. The design resembles a grandiose Spanish retablo.

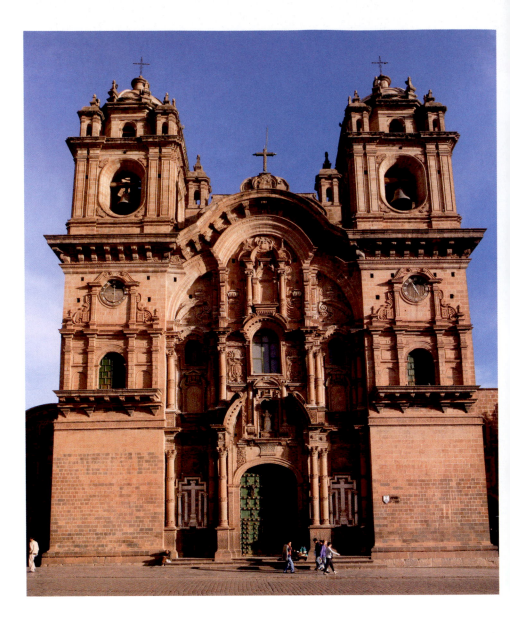

and follows the plan drawn by Claudio de Arciniega (ca. 1520–1593) in 1569. Construction commenced in 1573, using stones from the Aztec pyramid-temple of Huitzilopochtl. Dominating the wide facade are twin cupola-capped towers that date to the 18th century. The articulation of the lower facade, erected during the second half of the 17th century, reflects the style of the churches of Baroque Rome.

CUZCO A purer example of Baroque style in New Spain is the Church of the Society of Jesus (FIG. **24-34**) in Cuzco, Peru (see MAP 35-2), erected during a concentrated period of 18 years after an earthquake in 1650 destroyed an earlier church at the heart of the former Inka capital (see page 1091). Designed either by the Flemish Jesuit architect-priest Jean-Baptiste Gilles (1596–1675) or the Spanish retablo master Martinez de Oviedo (d. 1670), the church's facade, which resembles a grandiose retablo framed by comparatively plain twin bell towers, is a distinctive colonial variation of Baroque architecture without close parallels in Europe. The design captures the dynamic projecting and receding elements of the facades of contemporaneous Roman churches without copying any of them. The predominantly curvilinear motifs rise in waves to a crescendo in the richly carved upper cornice, which also unites the towers with the center of the facade.

The churches of New Spain are eloquent symbols of the triumph of Christianity, and specifically of the Catholic Church, in the Western Hemisphere, and, more generally, of the subjugation of the native populations and their cultural values by the kings of Spain and their armies, priests, and artists.

THE BAROQUE IN ITALY AND SPAIN

Italy

- Art historians call the art of 17th-century Italy and Spain "Baroque," a term that probably derives from the Portuguese word for an irregularly shaped pearl. Baroque art is dynamic and theatrical, in vivid contrast to the precision and orderly rationality of Renaissance classicism.

- Baroque architects emphatically rejected the classical style. Gianlorenzo Bernini's colonnade framing the piazza in front of Saint Peter's is not a traditional rectangular atrium but two curving arms welcoming worshipers.

- Francesco Borromini emphasized the sculptural qualities of buildings. The facades of his churches—for example, San Carlo alle Quattro Fontane—are not flat frontispieces but undulating surfaces that provide a fluid transition from exterior to interior space. The interiors of his buildings pulsate with energy and feature complex domes that grow organically from curving walls.

- Bernini achieved even greater renown as a sculptor. His *David* represents the biblical hero in action, hurling stones at Goliath. In *Ecstasy of Saint Teresa,* Bernini marshaled the full capabilities of architecture, sculpture, and painting to create an intensely emotional experience for worshipers, consistent with the Counter-Reformation principle of using artworks to inspire devotion and piety.

- In painting, Caravaggio broke new ground by employing stark and dramatic contrasts of light and dark (tenebrism) and by setting religious scenes in everyday locales filled with rough-looking common people. Caravaggio's combination of drama and realism attracted both admiring followers—including Artemisia Gentileschi, the leading woman painter of the 17th century—and harsh critics. The biographer Giovanni Pietro Bellori, for example, deplored Caravaggio's abandonment of the noble style of Raphael and the ancients and his "suppression of the dignity of art." Bellori preferred the more classical style of Annibale Carracci and the Bolognese art academy.

- Illusionistic ceiling paintings were very popular in Baroque Italy. The major ceiling painters were Pietro da Cortona, Giovanni Battista Gaulli, and Fra Andrea Pozzo. In Sant'Ignazio in Rome, by merging the church's architecture with the painted nave vault, Pozzo created the illusion that Heaven is opening up above worshipers' heads.

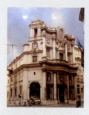

Borromini, San Carlo alle Quattro Fontane, Rome, 1638–1641

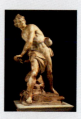

Bernini, *David,* 1623

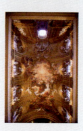

Gaulli, *Triumph of the Name of Jesus,* 1676–1679

Spain and New Spain

- Although the power of the Habsburg kings declined during the 17th century, the royal family, which was devoutly Catholic, continued to spend lavishly on art.

- Spanish artists eagerly embraced the drama and emotionalism of Italian Baroque art. Scenes of death and martyrdom were popular in Counter-Reformation Spain. Painters such as José de Ribera and Francisco de Zurbarán adopted Caravaggio's lighting and realism to produce moving images of martyred saints.

- The greatest Spanish Baroque artist was Diego Velázquez, court painter to Philip IV. Velázquez depicted themes ranging from genre and religious subjects to royal portraits and historical events, such as *Surrender of Breda.* His masterwork, *Las Meninas,* is extraordinarily complex and mixes real spaces, mirrored spaces, picture spaces, and pictures within pictures. It is a celebration of the art of painting itself.

- The paintings, sculptures, and buildings of 17th-century Spain profoundly influenced the art and architecture of the Spanish colonies in the Western Hemisphere, but the buildings of New Spain—for example, the Church of the Jesuits in Cuzco—have no close parallels in Europe.

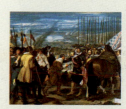

Velázquez, *Surrender of Breda,* 1634–1635

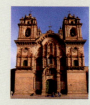

Church of the Jesuits, Cuzco, 1650–1668

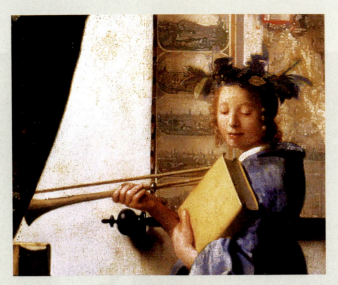

25-1a Vermeer's model wears a laurel wreath and holds a trumpet and book, traditional attributes of Clio, the muse of history. The light illuminating her may allude to the light of artistic inspiration.

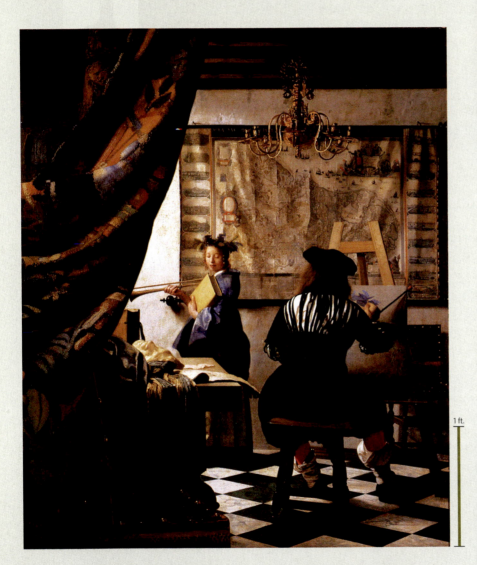

1 ft.

25-1   Jan Vermeer, *Allegory of the Art of Painting*, 1670–1675. Oil on canvas, 4' 4" × 3' 8". Kunsthistorisches Museum, Vienna.

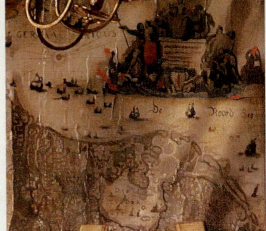

25-1b Proud Dutch patrons adorned their homes with worldly goods, including maps of the newly independent United Provinces of the Netherlands, and domestic scenes became a popular painting genre.

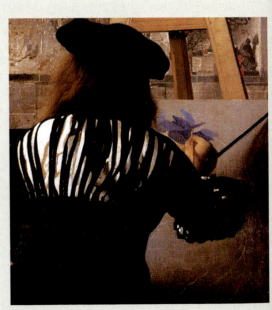

25-1c Usually interpreted as an allegory of the art of painting inspired by history, this canvas shows Vermeer at work with his back to the viewer, dressed in clothing reminiscent of historical Burgundian attire.

The Baroque in Northern Europe

THE ART OF PAINTING IN A DUTCH HOME

In 1648, after decades of continuous border skirmishes with the Spaniards, the northern Netherlands achieved official recognition as the United Provinces of the Netherlands (the Dutch Republic; MAP 25-1, page 737). The new independent republic owed its ascendance largely to its success in international trade. Dutch ships laden with goods roamed the world, sailing as far as North and South America, western Africa, China, Japan, and the Pacific islands, spreading prosperity to a greatly expanded middle class.

Although steeped in the morality and propriety central to the Calvinist ethic, members of the Dutch middle class sought ways to announce their success and newly acquired status. House furnishings, paintings, tapestries, and porcelain were among the items they collected and displayed in their homes. Those homes also became a popular subject for artworks. Many Dutch patrons collected small paintings depicting intimate domestic scenes of family members engaged in the activities of daily life. Dutch taste thus presents a sharp contrast with the Italian Baroque penchant for dazzling, large-scale ceiling frescoes and opulent room decoration (see Chapter 24). Indeed, the stylistic, as opposed to the chronological, designation "Baroque" is ill suited to these 17th-century northern European artworks.

The leading Dutch painter of interior scenes was JAN VERMEER (1632–1675), whose most complex and intriguing painting is *Allegory of the Art of Painting* (FIG. 25-1). The artist himself appears in the painting, with his back to the viewer and dressed in clothing reminiscent of historical Burgundian attire. He is hard at work on a painting of the model standing before him. She wears a laurel wreath and holds a trumpet and book, traditional attributes of Clio, the muse of history. The map of the provinces (an increasingly common wall adornment in Dutch homes) on the back wall serves as yet another reference to history.

As in many of Vermeer's domestic scenes, the viewer is outside the space of the action, looking in through the drawn curtain, which also separates the artist in his studio from the rest of the house. Some art historians have suggested that the light radiating from an unseen window on the left, illuminating both the model and the canvas being painted, alludes to the light of artistic inspiration. Accordingly, many scholars have interpreted this painting as an allegory—a reference to painting inspired by history. Vermeer's mother-in-law confirmed this allegorical reading in 1677 when, after Vermeer's death, 26 of his works were scheduled for sale to pay his widow's debts. In her written claim to retain the painting for herself, she described the painting as "the piece . . . wherein the Art of Painting is portrayed."[1]

WAR AND TRADE IN NORTHERN EUROPE

During the 17th and early 18th centuries, numerous geopolitical shifts occurred in Europe as the fortunes of individual countries rose and fell. Pronounced political and religious friction resulted in widespread unrest and warfare. Indeed, between 1562 and 1721, all of Europe was at peace for a mere four years. The major conflict of this period was the Thirty Years' War (1618–1648), which ensnared Spain, France, Sweden, Denmark, the Netherlands, Germany, Austria, Poland, the Ottoman Empire, and the Holy Roman Empire. Although the outbreak of the war had its roots in the conflict between militant Catholics and militant Protestants, the driving force quickly shifted to secular, dynastic, and nationalistic concerns. Among the major political entities vying for expanded power and authority in Europe were the Bourbon dynasty of France and the Habsburg dynasties of Spain and the Holy Roman Empire. The war, which concluded with the Treaty of Westphalia in 1648, was largely responsible for the political restructuring of Europe (MAP 25-1, page 737). As a result, the United Provinces of the Netherlands (the Dutch Republic), Sweden, and France expanded their authority. Spanish and Danish power diminished. In addition to reconfiguring territorial boundaries, the Treaty of Westphalia in essence granted freedom of religious choice throughout Europe. This treaty thus marked the abandonment of the idea of a united Christian Europe, and accepted the practical realities of secular political systems. The building of today's nation-states was emphatically under way.

The 17th century also brought heightened economic competition to Europe. Much of the foundation for worldwide mercantilism—extensive voyaging and geographic exploration, improved mapmaking, and advances in shipbuilding—had been laid in the previous century. In the 17th century, however, changes in financial systems, lifestyles, and trading patterns, along with expanding colonialism, fueled the creation of a worldwide marketplace. The Dutch founded the Bank of Amsterdam in 1609, which eventually became the center of European transfer banking. By establishing a system in which merchant firms held money on account, the bank relieved traders of having to transport precious metals as payment. Trading practices became more complex. Rather than simple reciprocal trading, triangular trade (trade among three parties) facilitated access to a larger pool of desirable goods. Exposure to an ever-growing array of goods affected European diets and lifestyles. Tea (from China) and, later, coffee (from island colonies) became popular beverages over the course of the 17th century. Equally explosive was the growth of sugar use. Sugar, tobacco, and rice were slave crops, and the slave trade expanded to meet the demand for these goods. Traders captured and enslaved Africans and shipped them to European colonies and the Americas to provide the requisite labor force for producing these commodities.

The resulting worldwide mercantile system permanently changed the face of Europe. The prosperity that international trade generated affected social and political relationships, necessitating new rules of etiquette and careful diplomacy. With increased disposable income, more of the newly wealthy spent money on art, significantly expanding the market for artworks, especially small-scale paintings for private homes, the specialty of Jan Vermeer (FIG. 25-1), among other leading artists of the era.

FLANDERS

In the 16th century, the Netherlands had come under the crown of Habsburg Spain when Emperor Charles V retired, leaving the Spanish kingdoms, their Italian and American possessions, and the Netherlandish provinces to his only legitimate son, Philip II (r. 1556–1598). (Charles bestowed his imperial title and German lands on his brother.) Philip's repressive measures against the Protestants led the northern provinces to break from Spain and establish the Dutch Republic. The southern provinces remained under Spanish control and retained Catholicism as their official religion. The political distinction between modern Holland and Belgium more or less reflects this original separation, which in the 17th century signaled not only religious but also artistic differences.

Painting

The major artistic medium of 17th-century Flanders (the Spanish Netherlands) was oil painting, as during the Renaissance (see "Oil Painting," page 559). Flemish Baroque painters retained close connections to the Baroque art of Catholic Europe. In contrast, the Dutch schools of painting developed their own subjects and styles, consistent with their reformed religion and the new political, social, and economic structure of the Dutch Republic.

PETER PAUL RUBENS The greatest 17th-century Flemish painter was PETER PAUL RUBENS (1577–1640), a towering figure in the history of Western art. Rubens built on the innovations of the Italian Renaissance and Baroque masters to formulate the first truly pan-European painting style. Rubens's art is an original and powerful synthesis of the manners of many masters, especially Michelangelo, Titian, Carracci, and Caravaggio. His style had wide appeal, and his influence was international. Among the most learned individuals of his time, Rubens possessed an aristocratic education and a courtier's manner, diplomacy, and tact, which, with his facility for language, made him the associate of princes and scholars. He became court painter to the dukes of Mantua (descended from Mantegna's patrons), friend of King Philip IV (r. 1621–1665) of Spain and his adviser on collecting art, painter to Charles I (r. 1625–1649) of England and Marie de' Medici (1573–1642) of France, and permanent court

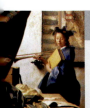

THE BAROQUE IN NORTHERN EUROPE

1600–1625
- Peter Paul Rubens is the leading painter in Catholic Flanders
- The founding of the Bank of Amsterdam in 1609 initiates an era of Dutch preeminence in international trade
- In the northern Netherlands, Calvinist patrons favor genre scenes, portraits, and still lifes

1625–1650
- Frans Hals achieves renown for his group portraits of Dutch burghers
- Rembrandt, the foremost Dutch Baroque painter, is also a master of etching
- The Treaty of Westphalia concludes the Thirty Years' War in 1648

1650–1675
- Jacob van Ruisdael and other Dutch artists specialize in landscape painting
- Jan Vermeer uses a camera obscura as an aid in painting domestic interiors
- Nicolas Poussin champions classical "grand manner" painting in Rome

1675–1700
- Louis XIV, the Sun King, builds a grandiose palace and garden complex at Versailles
- Sir Christopher Wren designs Saint Paul's Cathedral in London

painter to the Spanish governors of Flanders. Rubens also won the confidence of his royal patrons in matters of state, and they often entrusted him with diplomatic missions of the highest importance.

To produce a steady stream of paintings for a rich and powerful international clientele, Rubens employed scores of assistants. He also became a highly successful art dealer, buying and selling contemporary artworks and classical antiquities for royal and aristocratic clients throughout Europe, who competed with one another in amassing vast collections of paintings and sculptures. One of those collections became the subject of a painting (FIG. **25-1A**) by Rubens and JAN BRUEGEL THE ELDER (1568–1625). Rubens's many enterprises made him a rich man, able to afford a magnificent townhouse in Antwerp and a castle in the countryside. Rubens, like Raphael, was a successful and renowned artist, a consort of kings, a shrewd man of the world, and a learned philosopher.

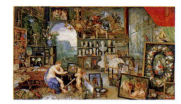
⬈ **25-1A** BRUEGHEL and RUBENS, *Allegory of Sight*, ca. 1617–1618.

ELEVATION OF THE CROSS When he was 23 years old, Rubens departed Flanders for Italy and remained there from 1600 until 1608. During these years, he studied the works of Italian Renaissance and Baroque masters and laid the foundations of his mature style. Shortly after returning home, he painted *Elevation of the Cross* (FIG. **25-2**) for the church of Saint Walburga in Antwerp. Later moved to the city's cathedral, the altarpiece in the form of a triptych is one of numerous commissions for religious works that Rubens received at this time. By investing in sacred art, Flemish churches sought to affirm their allegiance to Catholicism and Spanish Habsburg rule after a period of Protestant iconoclastic fervor in the region.

Rubens's interest in Italian art, especially the works of Michelangelo and Caravaggio, is evident in the Saint Walburga triptych. The choice of this episode from the passion cycle provided Rubens with the opportunity to depict heavily muscled men in unusual poses straining to lift the heavy cross with Christ's body nailed to it. Here, as in his *Lion Hunt* (FIG. I-13), Rubens, deeply impressed by Michelangelo's heroic twisting sculpted and painted nude male figures, showed his prowess in representing foreshortened anatomy and the contortions of violent action. Rubens placed the body of Christ on the cross as a diagonal that cuts dynamically across the picture while inclining back into it. The whole composition seethes with a power that comes from strenuous exertion, from elastic human sinew taut with effort. The tension is emotional as well as physical, as reflected not only in Christ's face but also in the features

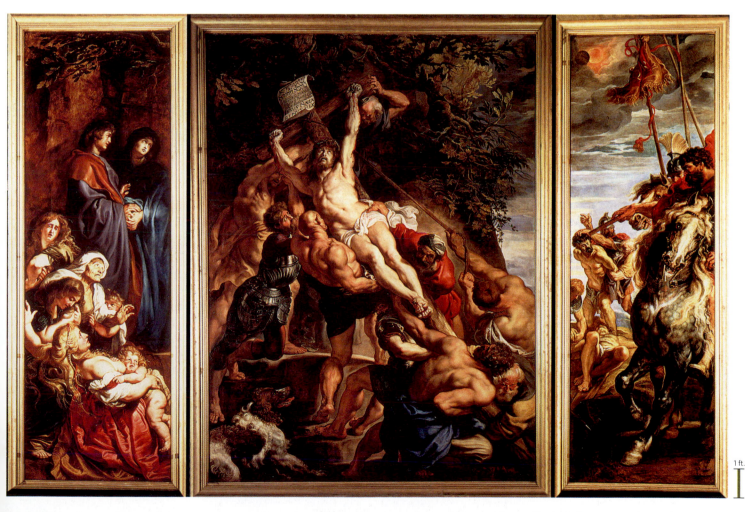

1 ft.

25-2 PETER PAUL RUBENS, *Elevation of the Cross,* from Saint Walburga, Antwerp, 1610. Oil on wood, 15' 1⅞" × 11' 1½" (center panel), 15' 1⅞" × 4' 11" (each wing). Antwerp Cathedral, Antwerp.

In this triptych, Rubens explored foreshortened anatomy and violent action. The whole composition seethes with a power that comes from heroic exertion. The tension is emotional as well as physical.

of his followers. Bright high-lights and areas of deep shadow inspired by Caravaggio's tene-brism (see page 715), hallmarks of Rubens's work at this stage of his career, enhance the drama.

Although Rubens later developed a much subtler col-oristic style in paintings such as *Garden of Love* (FIG. 25-2A),

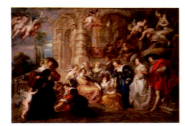

⏺ **25-2A** RUBENS, *Garden of Love*, 1630-1632.

the human body in action, draped or undraped, male or female, remained the focus of his art. This interest, combined with his vora-cious intellect, led Rubens to copy the works of classical antiquity and of the Italian masters. During his last two years in Rome, Rubens made many black-chalk drawings of great artworks, including figures in Michelangelo's Sistine Chapel frescoes (FIG. 22-17) and the ancient marble group (FIG. 5-89) of Laocoön and his two sons. In a Latin treatise he wrote titled *De imitatione statuarum* (*On the Imitation of Statues*), Rubens stated: "I am convinced that in order to achieve the highest perfection one needs a full understanding

ARTISTS ON ART
Rubens on *Consequences of War*

In the ancient and medieval worlds, artists rarely wrote commentaries on the works they produced. (The Greek sculptor Polykleitos is a nota-ble exception; see "Polykleitos's Prescription for the Perfect Statue," page 129.) Beginning with the Renaissance, however, the increased celebrity that artists enjoyed and the ready availability of paper encour-aged artists to record their intentions in letters to friends and patrons.

In March 1638, Peter Paul Rubens wrote a letter to Justus Suster-mans (1597–1681), court painter of Grand Duke Ferdinando II de' Medici of Tuscany, explaining his *Consequences of War* (FIG. 25-3) and his attitude toward the European military conflicts of his day.

> The principal figure is Mars, who has left the open temple of Janus (which in time of peace, according to Roman custom, remained closed) and rushes forth with shield and blood-stained sword, threatening the people with great disaster. He pays little heed to Venus, his mistress, who, accompanied by Amors and Cupids, strives with caresses and embraces to hold him. From the other side, Mars is dragged forward by the Fury Alekto, with a torch in her hand. Near by are monsters personifying Pestilence and Famine, those inseparable partners of War. On the ground, turning her back, lies a woman with a broken lute, representing Harmony, which is incom-

patible with the discord of War. There is also a mother with her child in her arms, indicating that fecundity, procreation and charity are thwarted by War, which corrupts and destroys everything. In addi-tion, one sees an architect thrown on his back, with his instruments in his hand, to show that which in time of peace is constructed for the use and ornamentation of the City, is hurled to the ground by the force of arms and falls to ruin. I believe, if I remember rightly, that you will find on the ground, under the feet of Mars a book and a drawing on paper, to imply that he treads underfoot all the arts and letters. There ought also to be a bundle of darts or arrows, with the band which held them together undone; these when bound form the symbol of Concord. Beside them is the caduceus and an olive branch, attribute of Peace; these are also cast aside. That grief-stricken woman clothed in black, with torn veil, robbed of all her jewels and other ornaments, is the unfortunate Europe who, for so many years now, has suffered plunder, outrage, and misery, which are so injurious to everyone that it is unnecessary to go into detail. Europe's attribute is the globe, borne by a small angel or genius, and surmounted by the cross, to symbolize the Christian world.*

Given the allegorical complexity of *Consequences of War*, the com-positional unity and unbridled energy of the personified figures in the painting are all the more remarkable.

*Translated by Kristin Lohse Belkin, *Rubens* (London: Phaidon, 1998), 288-289.

25-3 PETER PAUL RUBENS, *Consequences of War*, 1638–1639. Oil on canvas, 6' 9" × 11' 3$\frac{7}{8}$". Galleria Palatina, Palazzo Pitti, Florence.

Since the Renaissance, artists have left behind many letters shedding light on their lives and work. In a 1638 letter, Rubens explained the meaning of each figure in this allegorical painting.

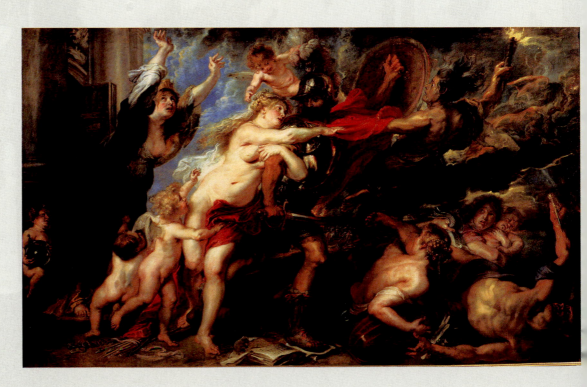

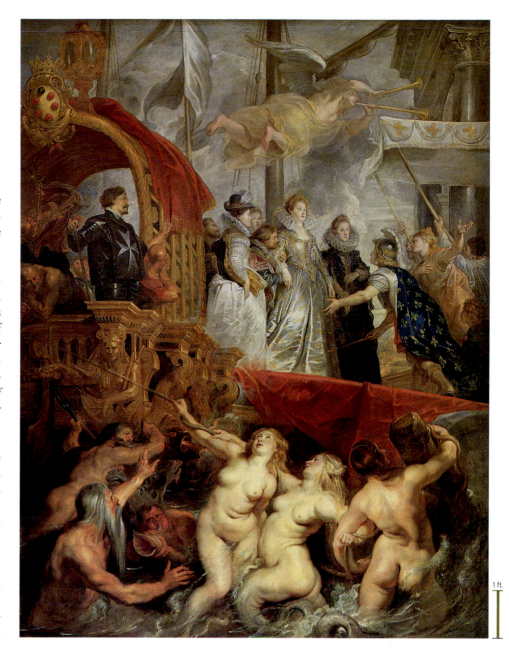

25-4 PETER PAUL RUBENS, *Arrival of Marie de' Medici at Marseilles,* from the Luxembourg Palace, Paris, France, 1622–1625. Oil on 21 canvases, 12' 11½" × 9' 7". Musée du Louvre, Paris.

Rubens painted 24 large canvases glorifying Marie de' Medici's career. In this historical-allegorical picture of robust figures in an opulent setting, the sea and sky rejoice at the queen's arrival in France.

1 ft.

of the [ancient] statues, indeed a complete absorption in them; but one must make judicious use of them and before all avoid the effect of stone."[2]

CONSEQUENCES OF WAR Once Rubens established his reputation, commissions from kings, queens, dukes, and other elite patrons throughout Europe soon followed. One of these commissions was *Consequences of War* (FIG. **25-3**), which Rubens painted in 1638 for Ferdinando II de' Medici, the grand duke of Tuscany (r. 1621–1670). Like *Elevation of the Cross* (FIG. 25-2), *Consequences of War* is a chaotic scene filled with twisting, straining, foreshortened male and female bodies, but Rubens used the commission from the Medici duke as an opportunity to express his desire for peace in an age when war was constant. *Consequences of War* is a commentary on the Thirty Years' War (see "Rubens on *Consequences of War*," page 734).

MARIE DE' MEDICI Rubens's interaction with royalty and aristocracy provided the Flemish master with an understanding of the ostentation and spectacle of Baroque (particularly Italian) art that appealed to the wealthy and privileged. Rubens, the born courtier, reveled in the pomp and majesty of royalty. Likewise, those in power embraced the lavish spectacle that served the Catholic Church so well in Italy. The magnificence and splendor of Baroque imagery reinforced the authority and right to rule of the highborn. Among Rubens's royal patrons was Marie de' Medici, a member of the famous Florentine banking family and widow of Henry IV (r. 1589–1610), the first Bourbon king of France. She commissioned Rubens to paint a series of huge canvases memorializing and glorifying her career. Between 1622 and 1626, Rubens, working with amazing creative energy, produced with the aid of his many assistants 21 historical-allegorical pictures and three portraits designed to hang in the queen's new palace, the Luxembourg, in Paris. (Today, they are on display in a huge exhibition hall in the Louvre, the former palace of the kings of France.) Remarkably, each of the paintings, although conceived as an instrument of royal propaganda to flatter the queen and impress her subjects and foreign envoys, is also a great work of art—a supreme testimony to Rubens's skill and the talents of his small army of assistants.

In *Arrival of Marie de' Medici at Marseilles* (FIG. **25-4**), a 13-foot-tall tableau that may be the best of the series, Marie disembarks at that southern French port after her sea voyage from Italy. An allegorical personification of France, draped in a cloak decorated with the *fleur-de-lis* (the floral symbol of French royalty; compare FIG. 25-24), welcomes her. The sea and sky rejoice at the queen's safe arrival. Neptune and the Nereids (daughters of the sea god Nereus) salute her, and the winged and trumpeting personified Fame swoops overhead. Conspicuous in the galley's opulently carved stern-castle, under the Medici coat of arms, stands the imperious commander of the vessel, the only immobile figure in the composition. In black and silver, this figure makes a sharp accent amid the swirling ivory, gold, and red brushstrokes. Rubens enriched the surfaces with a decorative splendor that pulls the whole composition together. The audacious vigor that customarily enlivens the painter's figures, beginning with the muscle-bound twisting sea creatures, vibrates through the entire design.

ANTHONY VAN DYCK Most of the leading painters of the next generation in Flanders were at one time trained or employed in Rubens's studio. The master's most famous pupil was ANTHONY VAN DYCK (1599–1641). Early on, the younger man, unwilling to be overshadowed by Rubens's undisputed stature, left his native

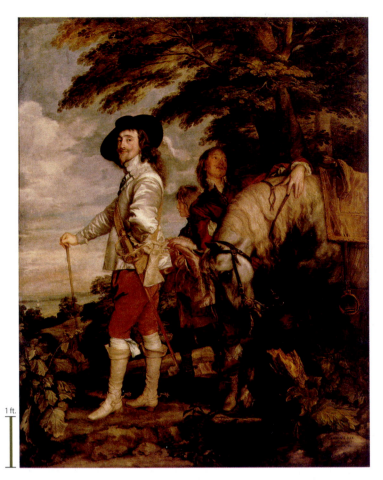

25-5 ANTHONY VAN DYCK, *Charles I at the Hunt,* ca. 1635. Oil on canvas, 8' 11" × 6' 11½". Musée du Louvre, Paris.

Van Dyck specialized in court portraiture. In this painting, he depicted the absolutist monarch Charles I at a sharp angle so that the king, a short man, appears to be looking down at the viewer.

Antwerp for Genoa and then London, where he became court portraitist to Charles I and was awarded a knighthood. Although Van Dyck created dramatic compositions of high quality, his specialty became the portrait. He developed a courtly manner of great elegance that influenced many artists throughout Europe and resounded in English portrait painting well into the 19th century.

In one of his finest works, *Charles I at the Hunt* (FIG. 25-5), the ill-fated English king stands on a hillock with the Thames River in the background. An equerry and a page attend him. The portrait is a stylish image of relaxed authority, as if the king is out for a casual ride in his park, but no one can mistake the regal poise and the air of

25-6 CLARA PEETERS, *Still Life with Flowers, Goblet, Dried Fruit, and Pretzels,* 1611. Oil on panel, 1' 7¾" × 2' 1¼". Museo del Prado, Madrid.

Peeters was a pioneer of still-life painting. In this breakfast piece, she reveals her virtuosity in depicting a variety of objects. She laid the groundwork for many Dutch still-life painters.

absolute authority that Charles's Parliament resented and was soon to rise against. Here, the king turns his back on his attendants as he surveys his domain. Van Dyck's placement of the monarch is exceedingly artful. He stands off center, but as the sole figure seen against the sky and with the branches of the trees pointing to him, he is the immediate focus of the viewer's attention, whose gaze the king returns. In this masterful composition, Van Dyck also managed to make Charles I, who was of short stature, seem taller than his attendants and even his horse. The painter also portrayed the king looking down on the observer, befitting his exalted position.

CLARA PEETERS Some 17th-century Flemish artists specialized in still-life painting, as did Sánchez Cotán (FIG. 24-25) in Spain. A pioneer of this genre was CLARA PEETERS (1594–ca. 1657), a native of Antwerp who spent time in Holland and laid the groundwork for Pieter Claesz (FIG. 25-21), Willem Kalf (FIG. 25-22), Rachel Ruysch (FIG. 25-23), and other Dutch masters of still-life painting. Peeters won renown for her depictions of food and flowers together, and for still lifes featuring bread and fruit, known as *breakfast pieces*. In *Still Life with Flowers, Goblet, Dried Fruit, and Pretzels* (FIG. **25-6**), Peeters's considerable skills are evident. One of a series of four paintings, each of which depicts a typical early-17th-century meal, this breakfast piece reveals Peeters's virtuosity in depicting a wide variety of objects convincingly, from the smooth, reflective surfaces of the glass and silver goblets to the soft petals of the blooms in the vase. Peeters often painted the objects in her still lifes against a dark background, thereby negating any sense of deep space (compare FIG. 24-25). In this breakfast piece, she enhanced the sense of depth in the foreground by placing the leaves of the flower on the stone ledge as though they were encroaching into the viewer's space.

DUTCH REPUBLIC

With the founding of the Bank of Amsterdam in 1609, Amsterdam emerged as the financial center of the Continent. In the 17th century, the city had the highest per capita income in Europe. The Dutch economy also benefited enormously from the country's expertise on the open seas, which facilitated establishing lucrative

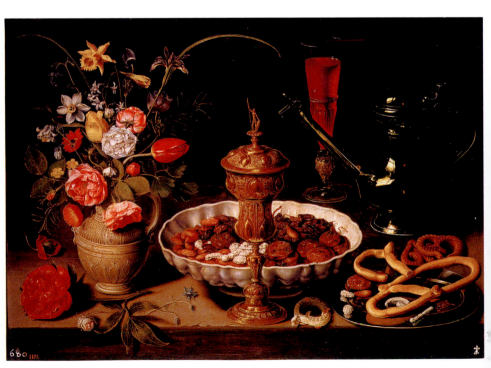

MAP 25-1 Europe in 1648 after the Treaty of Westphalia.

trade routes to ports as far away as Japan, Africa, and South America (see page 748). Due to this prosperity and in the absence of an absolute ruler, political power increasingly passed into the hands of a wealthy class of merchants and manufacturers, especially in cities such as Amsterdam, Haarlem, and Delft (MAP 25-1). All of these bustling cities were located in Holland (the largest of the seven United Provinces), which explains why many historians informally use the name "Holland" to refer to the entire country.

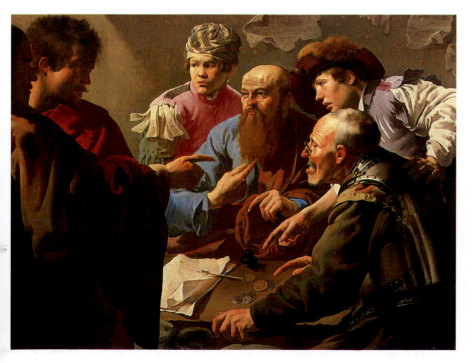

25-7 HENDRICK TER BRUGGHEN, *Calling of Saint Matthew*, 1621. Oil on canvas, 3′ 4″ × 4′ 6″. Centraal Museum, Utrecht.

Although middle-class patrons in the Protestant Dutch Republic preferred genre scenes, still lifes, and portraits, some artists, including Hendrick ter Brugghen, also painted religious scenes.

Ter Brugghen and van Honthorst

Religious differences were a major consideration during the northern Netherlands' insistent quest for independence in the 16th and early 17th centuries. Whereas Spain and the southern Netherlands were Catholic, the people of the northern Netherlands were predominantly Protestant. The prevailing Calvinism demanded a puritanical rejection of art in churches, and thus artists produced relatively little religious art in the Dutch Republic at this time (especially compared with the volume of commissions created in the wake of the Counter-Reformation in areas dominated by Catholicism; see "The Council of Trent," page 642, and "Middle-Class Patronage," page 738).

HENDRICK TER BRUGGHEN Some artists in the Dutch Republic did produce religious art, however. HENDRICK TER BRUGGHEN (1588–1629) of Utrecht, for example, painted *Calling of Saint Matthew* (FIG. 25-7) in 1621 after returning from a trip to Italy, selecting as his subject a theme Caravaggio had painted (FIG. 24-18) for the church of San

ART AND SOCIETY

Middle-Class Patronage and the Art Market in the Dutch Republic

Throughout history, the wealthy have been the most avid art collectors. Indeed, the money necessary to commission major artworks from leading artists can be considerable. During the 17th century in the Dutch Republic, however, the prosperity that a large proportion of the population enjoyed expanded the range of art patrons significantly. As a result, one distinguishing hallmark of Dutch art production during this period was how it catered to the tastes of a middle-class audience, broadly defined. An aristocracy and an upper class of shipowners, rich businesspeople, high-ranking officers, and directors of large companies still existed, and these groups continued to be major patrons of the arts. But as the Dutch economy expanded, new patrons—traders, craftspeople, bureaucrats, and soldiers—also commissioned and collected art.

Although the financial success that the middle class increasingly enjoyed resulted in sharply higher investment in home furnishings and art (see "The Art of Painting in a Dutch Home," page 731), the Calvinist disdain for excessive ostentation led these new Dutch collectors to favor small, low-key works—portraits of bourgeois men and women (FIGS. 25-9, 25-10, 25-12, and 25-13), still lifes (FIGS. 25-21, 25-22, and 25-23), genre scenes (FIGS. 25-8, 25-19, and 25-20), and landscapes (FIGS. 25-17, 25-18, 25-18A, and 25-18B). This focus contrasted with the Italian Baroque penchant for gigantic ceiling frescoes and oil paintings with religious subjects (see Chapter 24). Stylistically, the art of northern Europe, although also called "Baroque" by art historians, differs markedly from Italian Baroque art.

It is risky to generalize about the spending and collecting habits of the Dutch middle class, but probate records, contracts, and archived inventories reveal some interesting facts. These records suggest that an individual earning between 1,500 and 3,000 guilders a year could live quite comfortably. A house could be purchased for 1,000 guilders.

Another 1,000 guilders could buy all the necessary furnishings for a middle-class home, including a significant amount of art, particularly paintings. Although there was, of course, considerable variation in prices, many artworks were very affordable. Prints, for example, were extremely cheap because of the high number of copies artists produced of each picture. Paintings of interior and genre scenes were relatively inexpensive in 17th-century Holland, perhaps costing one or two guilders each. Small landscapes fetched between three and four guilders. Commissioned portraits were the most costly. The size of the work and quality of the frame (see "Framed Paintings," page 564), as well as the reputation of the artist, were other factors in determining the price of a painting, regardless of the subject.

With the exception of portraits, Dutch artists produced most of their paintings for an anonymous market, hoping to appeal to a wide audience. To ensure success, artists in the United Provinces adapted to the changed conditions of art production and sales. They marketed their paintings in many ways, selling their works directly to buyers who visited their studios and through art dealers, exhibitions, fairs, auctions, and even lotteries. Because of the uncertainty of these sales mechanisms (as opposed to the certainty of an ironclad contract for a commission from a church, king, or duke), artists became more responsive to market demands. Specialization became common among Dutch artists. For example, painters might limit their practice to portraits, still lifes, or landscapes—the most popular genres among middle-class patrons.

Artists did not always sell their paintings. Frequently, they used their work to pay off loans or debts. Tavern debts, in particular, could be settled with paintings, which may explain why many art dealers, including Jan Vermeer (FIG. 25-1) and his father before him, were also innkeepers. This connection between art dealing and other businesses eventually solidified, and innkeepers, for example, often would have art exhibitions in their taverns hoping to make a sale. The institutions of today's open art market—dealers, galleries, auctions, and estate sales—owe their establishment to the emergence in the 17th century of a prosperous middle class in the Dutch Republic.

25-8 GERRIT VAN HONTHORST, *Supper Party*, 1620. Oil on canvas, 4' 8" × 7'. Galleria degli Uffizi, Florence.

Genre scenes were popular subjects among middle-class Dutch patrons. Gerrit van Honthorst's *Supper Party* may also have served as a Calvinist warning against the sins of gluttony and lust.

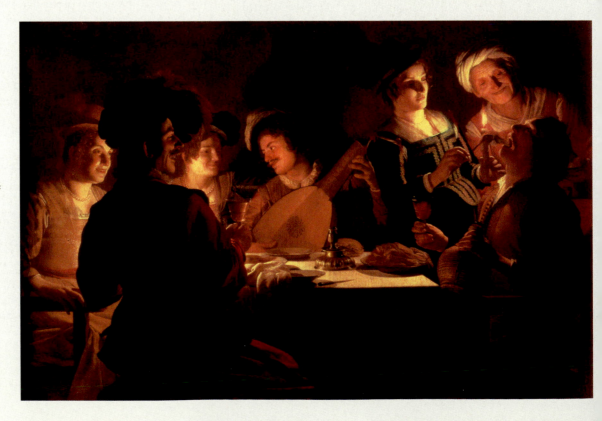

Luigi dei Francesi in Rome. The moment of the narrative chosen and the naturalistic depiction of the figures echo Caravaggio's work. But although ter Brugghen was an admirer of the Italian master, he dispensed with Caravaggio's stark contrasts of dark and light and instead presented the viewer with a more colorful palette of soft tints. Further, the Dutch painter compressed the figures into a small but well-lit space, creating an intimate effect compared with Caravaggio's more spacious setting.

MERCANTILIST PATRONAGE Given the absence of an authoritative ruler and the Calvinist concern for the potential misuse of religious art, commissions from royalty or the Catholic Church, prominent in the art of other European countries, were uncommon in the United Provinces. With the new prosperity, however, an expanding class of merchants with different tastes emerged as art patrons. In contrast to Italian, Spanish, and Flemish Baroque art, 17th-century Dutch art centered on genre scenes, landscapes, portraits of middle-class men and women, and still lifes, all of which appealed to the newly prosperous Dutch merchants (see "Middle-Class Patronage and the Art Market in the Dutch Republic," page 738).

GERRIT VAN HONTHORST Typical of 17th-century Dutch genre scenes is *Supper Party* (FIG. 25-8) by GERRIT VAN HONTHORST (1590–1656). In this painting, van Honthorst presented an informal gathering of unidealized figures. While a musician serenades the group, his companions delight in watching a young woman feeding a piece of chicken to a man whose hands are both occupied—one holds a jug and the other a glass. Van Honthorst spent several years in Italy, and while there he carefully studied Caravag-

gio's work, as did fellow Utrecht painter Hendrick ter Brugghen. The Italian artist's influence surfaces in the mundane tavern setting and the nocturnal lighting of *Supper Party*. Fascinated by nighttime effects, van Honthorst frequently placed a hidden light source in his pictures and used it as a pretext to work with dramatic and starkly contrasting dark and light effects.

Seemingly lighthearted genre scenes were popular in Baroque Holland, but Dutch viewers could also interpret them moralistically. For example, *Supper Party* can be read as a warning against the sins of gluttony (represented by the man on the right) and lust (the woman feeding the glutton is, in all likelihood, a prostitute with her aged procuress at her side). Or perhaps the painting represents the loose companions of the Prodigal Son (Luke 15:13; see FIG. 25-14)—panderers and prostitutes drinking, singing, strumming, and laughing. Strict Dutch Calvinists no doubt approved of such interpretations. Others simply took delight in the immediacy of the scenes or the skill of artists such as van Honthorst.

Hals and Leyster

Many Dutch artists excelled in painting portraits, which were in high demand. Two of the most important portrait specialists were FRANS HALS (ca. 1581–1666), the leading painter in Haarlem, and Judith Leyster.

FRANS HALS In addition to individual patrons, groups of Dutch citizens often asked Hals to paint portraits of them. Representing the members of a group, such as the Haarlem regents of an old men's home (FIG. 25-9) or the Saint Hadrian militia (FIG. 25-10),

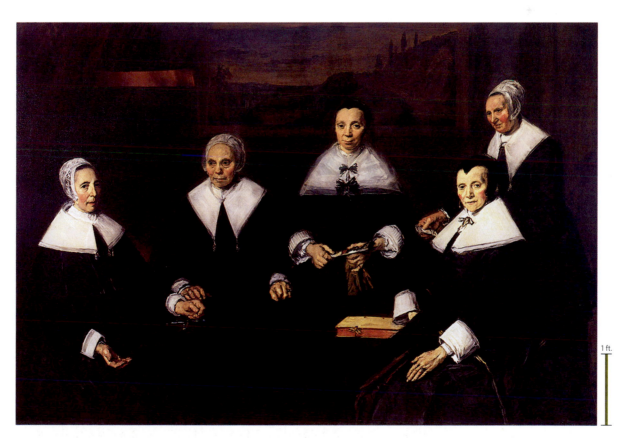

25-9 FRANS HALS, *The Women Regents of the Old Men's Home at Haarlem,* 1664. Oil on canvas, 5' 7" × 8' 2". Frans Halsmuseum, Haarlem.

Dutch women played a major role in public life as regents of charitable institutions. A stern puritanical sensibility suffuses Hals's group portrait of the regents of Haarlem's old men's home.

PROBLEMS AND SOLUTIONS
Frans Hals's Group Portraits

Portrait artists traditionally relied heavily on convention—for example, specific poses, settings, attire, and furnishings—to convey a sense of the sitter. Because the subject was usually someone of status or note, such as a pope, king, duchess, condottiere, or wealthy banker, the artist's goal was to produce an image appropriate to the subject's station in life. With the increasing number of Dutch middle-class patrons, portrait painting became more challenging. The Calvinists shunned ostentation, instead wearing subdued and dark clothing with little variation or decoration (FIG. 25-9), and the traditional conventions became inappropriate and thus unusable. Despite these difficulties, or perhaps because of them, Frans Hals produced lively portraits that seem far more relaxed than traditional formulaic portraiture. He injected an engaging spontaneity into his images and conveyed the individuality of his sitters as well. His manner of execution, using light and rapid brushstrokes, intensified the casualness, immediacy, and intimacy in his paintings. The poses of his figures, the highlights on their clothing, and their facial expression all seem instantaneously created.

Hals's most ambitious portraits reflect the widespread popularity in the Dutch Republic of very large canvases commemorating the participation of Dutch burghers in civic organizations. These commissions presented greater difficulties to the painter than requests to depict a single sitter. Hals rose to the challenge and achieved great success

with this new portrait genre. His *Archers of Saint Hadrian* (FIG. 25-10) is typical in that the subject is one of the many Dutch civic militia groups that claimed credit for liberating the Dutch Republic from Spain. As did other companies, each year the Archers met in dress uniform for a grand banquet on their saint's feast day. The celebrations sometimes lasted an entire week, prompting an ordinance limiting them to three or four days. These events often included sitting for a group portrait.

In *Archers of Saint Hadrian*, Hals attacked the problem of how to represent each militia member satisfactorily yet retain action and variety in the composition. Whereas earlier group portraits in the Netherlands were rather ordered and regimented images, Hals sought to enliven the depictions. In his portrait of the Saint Hadrian militiamen, each member is both part of the troop and an individual with unique features. The sitters' movements and moods vary markedly. Some engage the viewer directly. Others look away or at a companion. Some are stern, others animated. Each archer is equally visible and clearly recognizable. The uniformity of attire—black military dress, white ruffs, and sashes—did not deter Hals from injecting spontaneity into the work. Indeed, he used those elements to create a lively rhythm extending throughout the composition and energizing the portrait. The impromptu effect—the preservation of every detail and fleeting facial expression—is, of course, the result of careful planning. Yet Hals's vivacious brush appears to have moved instinctively, directed by a plan in his mind but not traceable in any preparatory scheme on the canvas. The result is a portrait that is less a record of "sitters posing for the painter" than it is a snapshot of a social gathering.

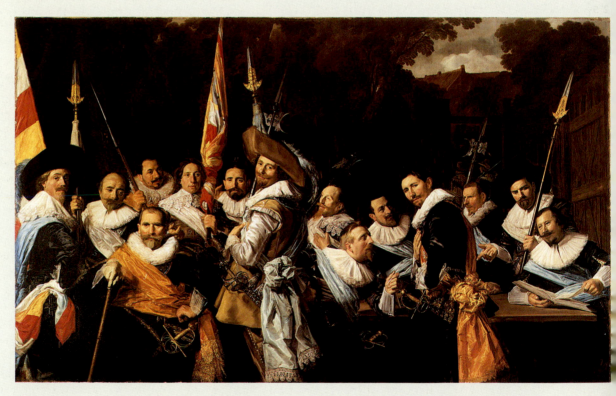

25-10 FRANS HALS, *Archers of Saint Hadrian*, ca. 1633. Oil on canvas, 6' 9" × 11'. Frans Halsmuseum, Haarlem.

In this brilliant composition, Hals succeeded in solving the problem of portraying each individual in a group portrait while retaining action and variety in the painting as a whole.

rather than separate individuals, presented a special problem for the painter, but Hals quickly became a master of the new genre of group portraiture (see "Frans Hals's Group Portraits," above).

Hals's *The Women Regents of the Old Men's Home at Haarlem* (FIG. 25-9) is the finest of his group portraits of Calvinist women engaged in charitable works. Although Dutch women had primary responsibility for the welfare of the family and the orderly opera-

tion of the home, they also populated the labor force in the cities. Among the more prominent roles that educated Dutch women played in public life were as regents of orphanages, hospitals, old age homes, and prisons. In Hals's portrait, the Haarlem regents sit quietly in a manner becoming devout Calvinists. Unlike the more relaxed, seemingly informal character of his other group portraits, a stern, puritanical, and composed sensibility suffuses Hals's accents of the clothing, contributes to the painting's restraint. Both the coloration and the mood of Hals's portrait are appropriate for this commission. Recording the likenesses of the Haarlem regents called for a very different kind of portrait than those Hals made of men at festive militia banquets (FIG. 25-10).

JUDITH LEYSTER Some of Hals's followers developed thriving careers of their own as portraitists. One was JUDITH LEYSTER (1609–1660), who may not have been Hals's pupil, but was a close associate who fully absorbed the master's innovations in technique and composition. In fact, Leyster's *Self-Portrait* (FIG. **25-11**) was once thought to have been painted by Hals himself. The canvas is detailed, precise, and accurate, but also imbued with the spontaneity found in Hals's works. In her self-portrait, Leyster succeeded at communicating a great deal about herself. She depicted herself as an artist, seated in front of a painting on an easel. The palette in her left hand and brush in her right announce the painting as her creation. She thus invites the viewer to evaluate her skill, which both the fiddler on the canvas and the image of herself demonstrate as considerable. Although she produced a wide range of paintings, including still lifes and floral pieces, her specialty was genre scenes such as the comic image seen on the easel. Leyster's quick smile and relaxed pose as she stops her work to meet the viewer's gaze reveal her self-assurance. Although presenting herself as an artist, Leyster did not paint herself wearing the traditional artist's smock, as her more famous contemporary Rembrandt did in his 1659–1660 self-portrait (FIG. 25-15). Her elegant attire distinguishes her socially as a member of a well-to-do family, another important aspect of Leyster's identity.

Rembrandt

REMBRANDT VAN RIJN (1606–1669), Hals's younger contemporary and the leading Dutch painter of his time, was an undisputed genius—an artist of great versatility, a master of light and shadow, and a unique interpreter of the Protestant conception of holy scripture. Born in Leiden, he moved to Amsterdam around 1631, where he could attract a more extensive clientele than possible in his native city.

Rembrandt had trained as a history painter in Leiden, but in Amsterdam he immediately entered the lucrative market for portraiture and soon became renowned for that genre.

ANATOMY LESSON OF DR. TULP In a painting he completed shortly after he arrived in Amsterdam, *Anatomy Lesson of Dr. Nicolaes Tulp* (FIG. **25-12**), Rembrandt deviated even further from the traditional staid group portrait than Hals. Despite Hals's determination to enliven his portraits, he still evenly spread his subjects across the canvas. In contrast, Rembrandt chose to portray the members of the surgeons' guild (who commissioned

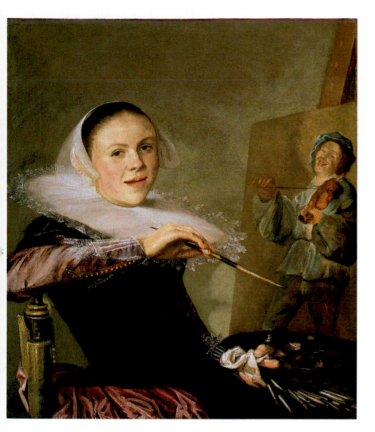

25-11 JUDITH LEYSTER, *Self-Portrait,* ca. 1630. Oil on canvas, 2' 5$\frac{3}{8}$" × 2' 1$\frac{5}{8}$". National Gallery of Art, Washington, D.C. (gift of Mr. and Mrs. Robert Woods Bliss).

Although presenting herself as an artist specializing in genre scenes, Leyster wears elegant attire instead of a painter's smock, placing her socially as a member of a well-to-do family.

portrayal of these regents. The women—all carefully distinguished as individuals—gaze out from the painting with expressions ranging from dour disinterest to kindly concern. The somber and virtually *monochromatic* (one-color) palette, punctuated only by the white

25-12 REMBRANDT VAN RIJN, *Anatomy Lesson of Dr. Nicolaes Tulp,* 1632. Oil on canvas, 5' 3$\frac{3}{4}$" × 7' 1$\frac{1}{4}$". Mauritshuis, The Hague.

In this early work, Rembrandt used an unusual composition, arranging members of Amsterdam's surgeons' guild clustered on one side of the painting as they watch Dr. Tulp dissect a corpse.

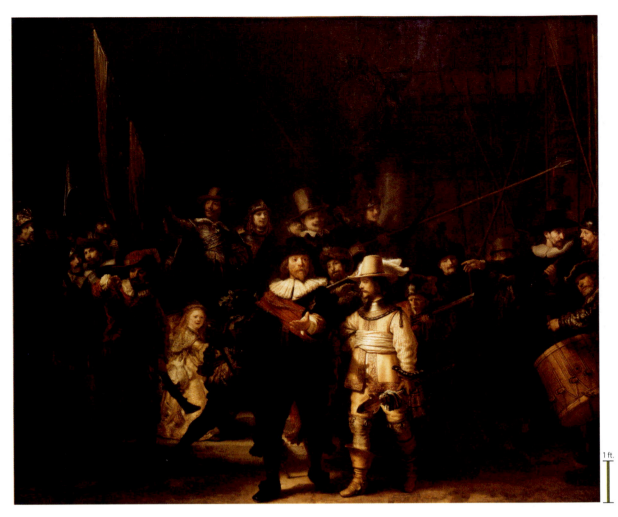

1 ft.

25-13 REMBRANDT VAN RIJN, *The Company of Captain Frans Banning Cocq* (*Night Watch*), from the Musketeers Hall, Amsterdam, Netherlands, 1642. Oil on canvas, 11′ 11″ × 14′ 4″ (trimmed from original size). Rijksmuseum, Amsterdam.

Rembrandt's dramatic use of light contributes to the animation of this militia group portrait in which the artist showed the company members rushing to organize themselves for a parade.

this group portrait) clustered on the painting's left side. In the foreground appears the corpse that Dr. Tulp, a noted physician, is in the act of dissecting. Rembrandt diagonally placed and foreshortened the corpse, activating the space by disrupting the strict horizontal, planar orientation typical of traditional portraiture. He depicted each of the "students" specifically, and although they wear virtually identical attire, their poses and facial expressions suggest the varying degrees of intensity with which they watch Dr. Tulp's demonstration—or ignore it. One, at the apex of Rembrandt's triangular composition of bodies, gazes at the viewer instead of at the operating table. Another directs his attention to the open book (an anatomy manual) at the cadaver's feet. Rembrandt produced this painting when he was 26 and just beginning his career. His innovative approach to group portraiture is therefore all the more noteworthy.

NIGHT WATCH Rembrandt amplified the complexity and energy of the group portrait in *The Company of Captain Frans Banning Cocq* (FIG. **25-13**), better known as *Night Watch*. This more commonly used title is a misnomer, however. The painting is not a nocturnal scene, nor are the figures portrayed posted on a watch in defense of their city. It features dramatic lighting, but the painting's darkness (which explains in part the commonly used title) is the result of the varnish the artist used, which darkened considerably over time.

It was not the painter's intention to portray his subjects moving about at night.

Night Watch was one of six paintings by different artists commissioned by various groups around 1640 for the assembly and banquet room of Amsterdam's new Musketeers Hall, the largest and most prestigious interior space in the city. From the limited information available about the commission, it appears that two officers, Captain Frans Banning Cocq and Lieutenant Willem van Ruytenburch, along with 16 members of their militia, contributed to Rembrandt's fee. The canvas also includes 16 additional figures, among them a girl just to the left of center, whom scholars have never been able to identify, despite her prominence in the composition.

Unfortunately, in 1715, when city officials moved Rembrandt's painting to Amsterdam's town hall, they trimmed it on all sides (by as much as 2 feet). Even in its truncated form, *The Company of Captain Frans Banning Cocq* is still a huge canvas (nearly 15 feet wide), but it is an incomplete record of the artist's resolution of the challenge of portraying 18 patrons at once. Rembrandt's apparent goal was to capture the excitement and frenetic activity of men preparing for a parade, and he succeeded brilliantly. Comparing this militia group portrait to Hals's *Archers of Saint Hadrian* (FIG. 25-10) reveals Rembrandt's inventiveness in enlivening what was, by then, becoming a conventional format for Dutch group portraits. Rather than present assembled men posed in orderly fashion, the younger artist chose to portray the company members rushing about in the act of organizing themselves, thereby animating the image considerably. At the same time, he managed to record the three most important stages of using a musket—loading, firing, and readying the weapon for reloading—details that must have pleased his patrons.

RETURN OF THE PRODIGAL SON The Calvinist injunction against religious art did not prevent Rembrandt from making a series of religious paintings and prints. In the Dutch Republic, paintings depicting biblical themes were not objects of devotion, but they still brought great prestige, and Rembrandt and other artists vied to demonstrate their ability to represent in dramatic new ways the stories narrated in holy scripture. One of Rembrandt's earliest biblical paintings, *Blinding of Samson* (FIG. 25-13A), reveals the young artist's debt to Rubens and Caravaggio. His mature works, however, differ markedly from the religious art of Baroque Italy and Flanders. Rembrandt had a

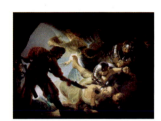

⤢ **25-13A** Rembrandt, *Blinding of Samson*, 1636.

special interest in probing the states of the human soul. The spiritual stillness of his later religious paintings is that of inward-turning contemplation, far from the choirs and trumpets and the heavenly tumult of Bernini (FIG. 24-7) or Pozzo (FIG. 24-24).

The Dutch artist's psychological insight and his profound sympathy for human affliction produced, at the end of his life, one of the most moving pictures in the history of biblical art, *Return of the Prodigal Son* (FIG. 25-14). In this Old Testament parable, the younger of two sons leaves his home and squanders his wealth on a life of sin. When he becomes poor and hungry and sees the error of his ways, he returns home. In Rembrandt's painting, the forgiving father tenderly embraces his lost son, who crouches before him in weeping contrition, while three figures, immersed to varying degrees in the soft shadows, note the lesson of mercy. The light, everywhere mingled with shadow, directs the viewer's attention by illuminating the father and son and largely veiling the witnesses (see "Rembrandt's Use of Light and Shade," below). Its focus is the beautiful, spiritual face of the old man. Secondarily, the light touches the contrasting stern face of the foremost witness. The painting demonstrates the degree to which Rembrandt developed a personal style completely in tune with the simple eloquence of the biblical passage.

MATERIALS AND TECHNIQUES
Rembrandt's Use of Light and Shade

Among the hallmarks of the style of Rembrandt van Rijn, the leading painter in the 17th-century Dutch Republic, is his masterful use of light and shade. Rembrandt's pictorial method involved refining light and shade into finer and finer nuances until they blended with one another. Earlier painters' use of abrupt lights and darks gave way, in the work of artists such as Rembrandt and Velázquez (FIGS. 24-29 to 24-31), to gradation. Although these later artists sacrificed some of the dramatic effects of sharp chiaroscuro, a greater fidelity to appearances more than offsets those sacrifices. In fact, the recording of light in small gradations is closer to reality because the eye perceives light and dark not as static but as always subtly changing.

In general, Renaissance artists represented forms and faces in a flat, neutral modeling light (even Leonardo's shading is of a standard kind). They represented the *idea* of light, rather than showed how humans perceive light. Artists such as Rembrandt discovered gradations of light and dark as well as degrees of differences in pose, in the movements of facial features, and in psychic states. They arrived at these differences optically, not conceptually or in terms of some ideal. Rembrandt found that by manipulating the direction, intensity, and distance of light and shadow, and by varying the surface texture with tactile brushstrokes, he could render subtle nuances of character and mood, both in individuals and whole scenes, as in his touching portrayal of the prodigal son's return (FIG. 25-14). He discovered for the modern world that variations of light and shade, subtly modulated, can be read as emotional differences. In the visible world, light, dark, and the wide spectrum of values between the two are charged with meanings and feelings that sometimes are independent of the shapes and figures they modify. The theater and the photographic arts have used these discoveries to great dramatic effect.

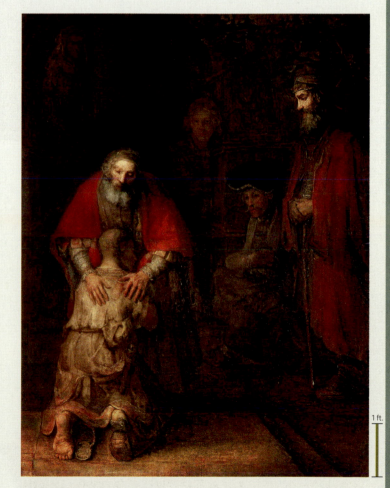

1 ft.

25-14 Rembrandt van Rijn, *Return of the Prodigal Son*, ca. 1665. Oil on canvas, 8' 8" × 6' 9". State Hermitage Museum, Saint Petersburg.

In Rembrandt's moving representation of this biblical parable, light mingled with shadow directs the viewer's attention by illuminating the father and son while largely veiling the witnesses.

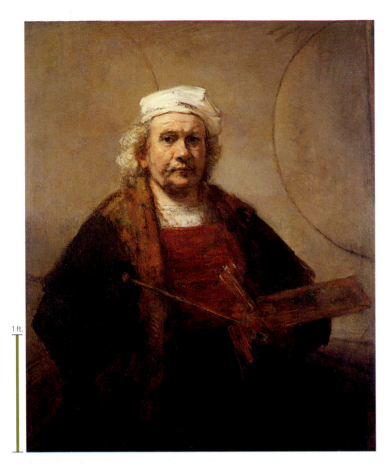

25-15 REMBRANDT VAN RIJN, *Self-Portrait,* ca. 1659–1660. Oil on canvas, 3' 8¾" × 3' 1". Kenwood House, London (Iveagh Bequest).

In this late self-portrait, Rembrandt's interest in revealing the soul is evident in the attention given to his expressive face. The controlled use of light and the nonspecific setting contribute to this focus.

SELF-PORTRAITS Rembrandt carried over the spiritual quality of his religious works into his later portraits (FIGS. 25-15 and 25-15A) by the same means—what could be called the "psychology of light." Light and dark are not in conflict in his portraits. They are reconciled, merging softly and subtly to produce the visual equivalent of quietness. Their prevailing mood is one of tranquil meditation, of philosophical resignation, of musing recollection—indeed, a whole cluster of emotional tones heard only in silence.

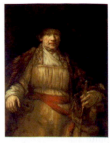

⚓ **25-15A** REMBRANDT, *Self-Portrait,* 1658.

In his self-portrait now in Kenwood House (FIG. 25-15), the light source outside the upper left of the painting bathes the painter's face in soft highlights, leaving the lower part of his body in shadow. The artist depicted himself as possessing dignity and strength, and the portrait serves as a summary of the many stylistic and professional concerns that occupied him throughout his career. Rembrandt's distinctive use of light is evident, as is the assertive brushwork suggesting his confidence and self-assurance. He presented himself as a working artist holding his brushes, palette, and maulstick (compare FIG. 23-16) and wearing his studio garb—a smock and painter's turban. The circles on the wall behind him (the subject of much scholarly debate) may allude to a legendary sign of artistic virtuosity—the ability to draw a perfect circle freehand. Rembrandt's abiding interest in revealing the human soul emerges here in his careful focus on his expressive visage. His controlled use of light and the nonspecific setting contribute to this focus.

X-rays of the painting have revealed that Rembrandt originally depicted himself in the act of painting. His final resolution, with the viewer's attention drawn to his face, produced a portrait not just of the artist but of the man as well. Indeed, Rembrandt's nearly 70 self-

25-16 REMBRANDT VAN RIJN, *Christ with the Sick around Him, Receiving the Children (Hundred-Guilder Print),* ca. 1649. Etching and engraving, 11" × 1' 3¼". Pierpont Morgan Library, New York.

Rembrandt's mastery of the newly perfected medium of etching is evident in his expert use of light and dark to draw attention to Christ as he preaches compassionately to the blind and lame.

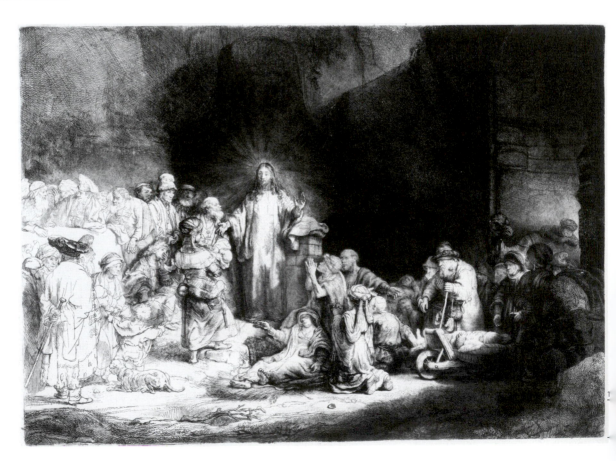

portraits in various media have no parallel in sheer quantity. They reflect the artist's deeply personal connection to his craft.

ETCHINGS Rembrandt's virtuosity also extended to the graphic media, especially etching (see "Engraving and Etching," page 578). Many printmakers adopted etching after its perfection early in the 17th century, because the technique afforded greater freedom in drawing the design than engraving did. The etcher covers a copper plate with a layer of wax or varnish, and then incises the design into this surface with a pointed tool, exposing the metal below but not cutting into its surface. Next, the artist immerses the plate in acid, which etches, or eats away, the exposed parts of the metal, acting in the same way the burin does in engraving. The wax's softness gives etchers greater carving freedom than woodcutters and engravers have working directly in more resistant wood and metal. If Rembrandt had never painted, he still would be acclaimed, as he principally was in his lifetime, for his prints. Prints were a major source of income for Rembrandt, as they were for Albrecht Dürer (see page 675), and he often reworked the plates so that they could be used to produce a new issue or edition. This constant reworking was unusual within the context of 17th-century printmaking practices.

HUNDRED-GUILDER PRINT One of Rembrandt's most celebrated graphic works is *Christ with the Sick around Him, Receiving the Children* (FIG. 25-16). Indeed, the title by which this print has been known since the early 18th century—the *Hundred-Guilder Print*— refers to the high sale price it brought during Rembrandt's lifetime. (As noted, a comfortable house could be purchased for 1,000 guilders.) *Christ with the Sick* demonstrates the artist's mastery of all aspects of the printmaker's craft, for Rembrandt used both engraving and etching to depict the figures and the setting. As in his other religious works, Rembrandt suffused this print with a deep and abiding piety, presenting the viewer not the celestial triumph of the Catholic Church but the humanity and humility of Jesus.

Christ appears in the center preaching compassionately to, and simultaneously blessing, the blind, the lame, and the young, who are spread throughout the composition in a dazzling array of standing, kneeling, and lying positions. Also present is a young man in elegant garments with his head in his hand, lamenting Christ's insistence that the wealthy need to give their possessions to the poor in order to gain entrance to Heaven. The tonal range of the print is remarkable. At the right, the figures near the city gate are in deep shadow. At the left, the figures, some rendered almost exclusively in outline, are in bright light—not the light of day but the illumination radiating from Christ himself. A second, unseen source of light comes from the right and casts the shadow of the praying man's arms and head onto Christ's tunic. Technically and in terms of its humanity, Rembrandt's *Hundred-Guilder Print* is his supreme achievement as a printmaker.

Cuyp and Ruisdael

After gaining independence from Spain, the Dutch undertook an extensive land reclamation project lasting almost a century. Dikes and drainage systems cropped up across the countryside, affecting Dutch social and economic life. The marshy and swampy nature of much of the terrain made it less desirable for large-scale exploitation, so the extensive feudal landowning system elsewhere in Europe never developed in the United Provinces. Most Dutch families owned and worked their own farms, cultivating a feeling of closeness to the land. Consequently, landscape scenes abound in 17th-century Dutch art.

AELBERT CUYP One Dutch artist who established his reputation as a specialist in landscape painting was AELBERT CUYP (ca. 1620–1691). His works were the products of careful observation and a deep respect for and understanding of Dutch topography. *Distant View of Dordrecht, with a Milkmaid and Four Cows, and Other Figures* (FIG. 25-17) reveals Cuyp's skillful use of the oil medium to record nature, but as was the norm at the time, Cuyp painted his canvases in his studio, not outdoors. Unlike the idealized classical landscapes in many Italian Renaissance paintings, Cuyp's Dordrecht landscape is particularized. The church in the background, for example, is a faithful representation of the city's Grote Kerk (Great Church). The dairy cows, shepherds, and milkmaid in the foreground refer to a cornerstone of the Dutch economy—dairy products such as butter and cheese, the demand for which increased with the development of urban centers. The credibility of this and similar paintings rests on Cuyp's pristine rendering of each detail.

25-17 AELBERT CUYP, *Distant View of Dordrecht, with a Milkmaid and Four Cows, and Other Figures (The "Large Dort")*, late 1640s. Oil on canvas, 5' 1" × 6' 4⅞". National Gallery, London.

Unlike idealized Italian Renaissance landscapes, Cuyp's painting portrays a particular locale. The cows, shepherds, and milkmaid refer to the Dutch Republic's important dairy industry.

25-18 Jacob van Ruisdael, *View of Haarlem from the Dunes at Overveen*, ca. 1670. Oil on canvas, 1' 10" × 2' 1". Mauritshuis, The Hague.

In this painting, Ruisdael succeeded in capturing a specific, realistic view of Haarlem, its windmills, and Saint Bavo church, but he also imbued the landscape with a quiet serenity approaching the spiritual.

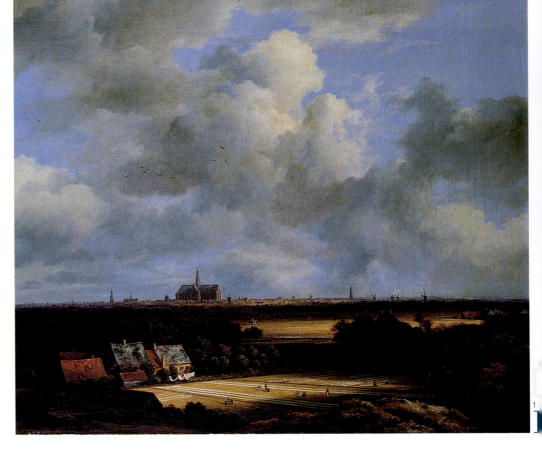

JACOB VAN RUISDAEL Depicting the Dutch landscape with precision and sensitivity was also a specialty of JACOB VAN RUISDAEL (ca. 1628–1682). In *View of Haarlem from the Dunes at Overveen* (FIG. **25-18**), Ruisdael provided an overarching view of this major Dutch city. The specificity of the artist's image—the Saint Bavo church in the background, the numerous windmills that refer to the land reclamation efforts, and the figures in the foreground stretching linen to be bleached (a major industry in Haarlem)—reflects the pride Dutch painters took in recording their homeland and the activities of their fellow citizens. Nonetheless, in this painting the inhabitants and dwellings are so small that they blend into the land itself, unlike the figures in Cuyp's view of Dordrecht. Moreover, the horizon line is low, so the sky fills almost three-quarters of the canvas surface, and the sun illuminates the landscape only in patches, where it has broken through the clouds above. In *View of Haarlem,* Ruisdael not only captured the appearance of a specific locale but also succeeded in imbuing the work with a quiet serenity that is almost spiritual. Less typical of his work, but also one of the great landscape paintings of the 17th century, is Ruisdael's allegorical *Jewish Cemetery* (FIG. **25-18A**).

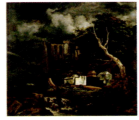

⬈ **25-18A** RUISDAEL, *Jewish Cemetery,* ca. 1655–1660.

Vermeer

Although he also painted landscapes, such as *View of Delft* (FIG. **25-18B**), Jan Vermeer made his reputation as a painter of interior scenes, another popular subject among middle-class patrons (see "The Art of Painting in a Dutch Home," page 731). These paintings offer the viewer glimpses into the private lives of prosperous, responsible, and cultured citizens of the United

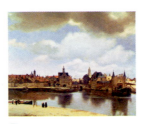

⬈ **25-18B** VERMEER, *View of Delft,* ca. 1661.

Provinces. Despite his fame as a painter today, Vermeer derived much of his income from his work as an innkeeper and art dealer in Delft (see "Middle-Class Patronage and the Art Market," page 738), and he completed no more than 35 paintings that can be definitively attributed to him. He began his career as a painter of biblical and historical themes, but soon abandoned those traditional subjects in favor of domestic scenes. Flemish artists of the 15th century also had painted domestic interiors, but sacred personages often occupied those scenes (for example, FIG. 20-4). In contrast, Vermeer and his contemporaries composed neat, quietly opulent interiors of Dutch middle-class dwellings featuring women especially but also men and occasionally children engaging in household tasks or at leisure.

WOMAN HOLDING A BALANCE In two of Vermeer's finest paintings—*The Letter* (FIG. **25-18C**) and *Woman Holding a Balance* (FIG. **25-19**)—women are the primary occupants of the Dutch homes. Both paintings are highly idealized depictions of the social values of the burghers of his day. In *Woman Holding a Balance,* a beautiful young woman wearing a veil and a fur-trimmed jacket stands in a room in her home. Light coming from a window illuminates the scene, as in many of the artist's paintings (compare FIG. 25-1). The woman stands before a table on which are spread her most precious possessions—

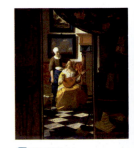

⬈ **25-18C** VERMEER, *The Letter,* 1666.

pearl necklaces, gold chains, and gold coins, which reflect the sunlight that also shines on the woman's face and the fingers of her right hand. In fact, the perspective orthogonals direct the viewer's

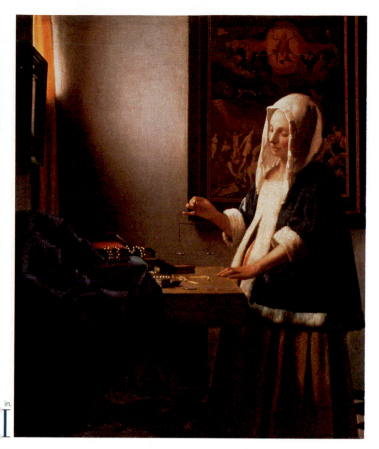

results that he reworked compositionally, enabling him to achieve, for example, a beautiful stability of rectilinear shapes by carefully positioning the figures and furniture in a room. Vermeer's compositions evoke a matchless classical serenity.

Enhancing this quality are colors so true to the optical facts and so subtly modulated that they suggest that Vermeer was far ahead of his time in color science. For example, Vermeer realized that shadows are not colorless and dark, that adjoining colors affect each other, and that light is composed of colors. Thus he painted reflections off of surfaces in colors modified by others nearby. Some scholars have suggested that Vermeer also perceived the phenomenon that modern photographers call "circles of confusion," which appear on out-of-focus negatives. Vermeer could have seen them in images projected by the camera obscura's primitive lenses. He approximated these effects with light dabs that, in close view, give the impression of an image slightly "out of focus." When the observer draws back a step, however, as if adjusting the lens, the color spots cohere, giving an astonishingly accurate illusion of the third dimension.

Steen

Whereas Vermeer's paintings reveal the charm and beauty of Dutch domesticity, the works of JAN STEEN (ca. 1625–1679) provide a counterpoint. In *Feast of Saint Nicholas* (FIG. 25-20), instead of depicting a tidy, calm Dutch household, Steen opted for a scene of chaos and disruption. Saint Nicholas has just visited this residence, and the children are in an uproar as they search their shoes

25-19 JAN VERMEER, *Woman Holding a Balance,* ca. 1664. Oil on canvas, 1' 3$\frac{7}{8}$" × 1' 2". National Gallery of Art, Washington, D.C. (Widener Collection).

Vermeer's woman holding empty scales in perfect balance, ignoring pearls and gold on the table, is probably an allegory of the temperate life. On the wall behind her is a depiction of the Last Judgment.

attention neither to the woman's head nor to her treasures but to the hand in which she holds a balance for weighing gold. The scales, however, are empty—in perfect balance, the way Ignatius of Loyola advised Catholics (Vermeer was a Catholic convert in the Protestant Dutch Republic) to lead a temperate, self-aware life and to balance one's sins with virtuous behavior. The mirror on the wall may refer to self-knowledge, but it may also symbolize, as do the pearls and gold, the sin of vanity. Bolstering that interpretation is the large framed *Last Judgment* painting on the back wall in which Christ, weigher of souls, appears in a golden aureole directly above the young woman's head. Therefore, this serene domestic scene is pregnant with hidden meaning. The woman holds the scales in balance and contemplates the kind of life (one free from the temptations of worldly riches) that she must lead in order to be judged favorably on judgment day.

Vermeer, like Rembrandt (see page 743), was a master of pictorial light and used it with immense virtuosity. He could render space so convincingly through his depiction of light that in his works, the picture surface functions as an invisible glass pane through which the viewer looks into the constructed illusion. Art historians believe that Vermeer used as tools both mirrors and the *camera obscura,* an ancestor of the modern camera based on passing light through a tiny pinhole or lens to project an image on a screen or the wall of a room. (In later versions, artists projected the image on a ground-glass wall of a box whose opposite wall contained the pinhole or lens.) Vermeer did not simply copy the camera's image, however. Instead, the camera obscura and the mirrors helped him obtain

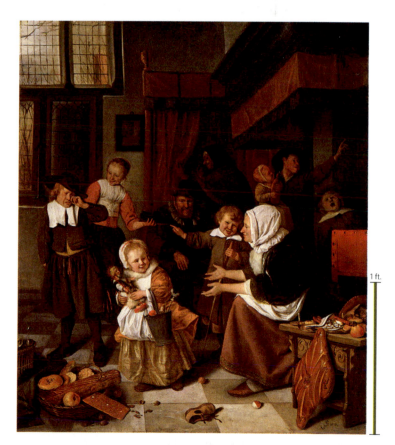

25-20 JAN STEEN, *Feast of Saint Nicholas,* ca. 1660–1665. Oil on canvas, 2' 8$\frac{1}{4}$" × 2' 3$\frac{3}{4}$". Rijksmuseum, Amsterdam.

Steen's lively scene of Dutch children discovering their Christmas gifts may also have an allegorical dimension. *Feast of Saint Nicholas* probably alludes to selfishness, pettiness, and jealousy.

ART AND SOCIETY
Dutch *Vanitas* Still-Life Paintings

Peter Mundy, a widely traveled Englishman, commented in 1640 on the irony that the Dutch Republic produced almost nothing on its own land, yet because of its success in international trade, Dutch citizens enjoyed great wealth and could afford rare commodities from around the world:

> For although the land (and that with much labor) is brought only to pasture . . . yet by means of their shipping they are plentifully supplied with what the earth affords for the use of man . . . from any part of the world . . . Europe, Asia, Africa or America . . . with the most precious and rich commodities of those parts.*

The prosperous Dutch were justifiably proud of their accomplishments, and the popularity of still-life paintings—particularly images of accumulated goods, such as *Still Life with a Late Ming Ginger Jar* (FIG. 25-22)—reflected this pride. These paintings of worldly possessions marked the emergence of an important new class of art patrons—wealthy merchants—who had tastes distinctly different from those of the leading patrons elsewhere in Baroque Europe, namely royalty and the Catholic Church. Dutch still lifes, which were well suited to the Protestant ethic rejecting most religious art, are among the finest

ever painted. They are meticulously crafted images both scientific in their optical accuracy and poetic in their beauty and lyricism.

One of the best Dutch paintings of this genre is *Vanitas Still Life* (FIG. 25-21) by Pieter Claesz, in which the painter presented the material possessions of a prosperous household strewn across a tabletop or dresser. The ever-present morality and humility central to the Calvinist faith tempered Dutch pride in worldly goods, however. Thus, although Claesz fostered the appreciation and enjoyment of the beauty and value of the objects he depicted, he also reminded the viewer of life's transience by incorporating references to death. Art historians call works of this type *vanitas* ("vanity") paintings, and each features a *memento mori* ("reminder of death"). In *Vanitas Still Life,* references to mortality include the skull, timepiece, tipped glass, and cracked walnut. All suggest the passage of time or someone or something that was here but now is gone. Claesz emphasized this element of time (and demonstrated his technical virtuosity) by including a self-portrait reflected in the glass ball on the left side of the table. He appears to be painting this still life. But in an apparent challenge to the message of inevitable mortality that vanitas paintings convey, the portrait serves to immortalize the artist.

*Quoted in Julie Berger Hochstrasser, *Still Life and Trade in the Dutch Golden Age* (New Haven, Conn.: Yale University Press, 2007), 16.

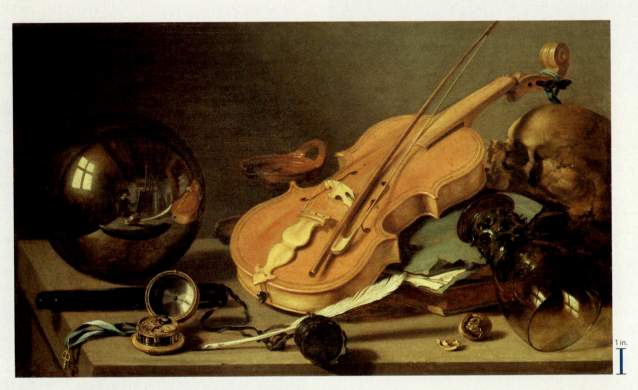

25-21 PIETER CLAESZ, *Vanitas Still Life,* 1630s. Oil on panel, 1' 2" × 1' 11½". Germanisches Nationalmuseum, Nuremberg.

In the 17th century, an important new class of patrons emerged in the Dutch Republic—successful merchants who took pride in their material possessions, the fruit of worldwide trade.

---

for the Christmas gifts he has left. Steen masterfully recorded the children's personalities. Some of them are delighted. The little girl in the center clutches her gifts, clearly unwilling to share with the other children despite her mother's pleas. Others are disappointed. The boy on the left is in tears because he received only a birch rod. An appropriately festive atmosphere reigns, which contrasts sharply

with the decorum prevailing in Vermeer's works. Like the paintings of other Dutch artists, Steen's lively scenes often take on an allegorical dimension and moralistic tone. Steen frequently used children's activities as satirical comments on foolish adult behavior. *Feast of Saint Nicholas* is not his only allusion to selfishness, pettiness, and jealousy.

Claesz, Kalf, and Ruysch

As already discussed (see "Middle-Class Patronage," page 738), the rise of a new class of art patrons in the Dutch Republic prompted artists to focus on a new range of subjects. Still-life painting was one of the most popular. The leading Dutch practitioners of this genre were PIETER CLAESZ (1597–1660; FIG. **25-21**), Willem Kalf (FIG. 25-22), and Rachel Ruysch (FIG. 25-23). Often, these still-life paintings had a double appeal to Dutch patrons as celebrations of their prosperity and as reminders of the transience of life (see "Dutch *Vanitas* Still-Life Paintings," page 748).

WILLEM KALF As Dutch prosperity increased, precious objects and luxury items made their way into still-life paintings. *Still Life with a Late Ming Ginger Jar* (FIG. **25-22**) by WILLEM KALF (1619–1693) reflects both the wealth that Dutch citizens had accrued and the painter's exquisite skills, both technical and aesthetic. Kalf highlighted the breadth of Dutch maritime trade through his depiction of the Persian floral carpet, the Chinese jar used to store ginger (a luxury item), and the Mediterranean orange and peeled lemon. He delighted in recording the lustrous sheen of fabric and the light glinting off reflective surfaces. As is evident in this image, Kalf's works present an array of ornamental objects, such as the Venetian and Dutch glassware and the silver plate. The inclusion of the watch suggests that this work, like Claesz's *Vanitas Still Life* (FIG. 25-21), may also be a vanitas painting, if less obviously so.

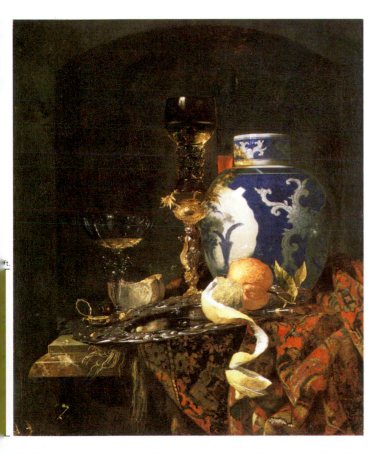

25-22 WILLEM KALF, *Still Life with a Late Ming Ginger Jar*, 1669. Oil on canvas, 2' 6" × 2' 1¾". Indianapolis Museum of Art, Indianapolis (gift in commemoration of the 60th anniversary of the Art Association of Indianapolis, in memory of Daniel W. and Elizabeth C. Marmon).

The opulent objects, especially the Persian carpet and Chinese jar, attest to the prosperous Dutch maritime trade. Kalf's inclusion of a watch suggests that this painting may be a vanitas still life.

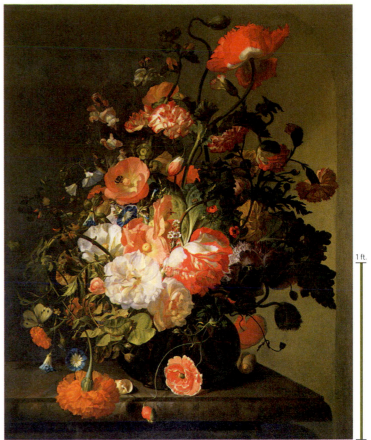

1 ft.

25-23 RACHEL RUYSCH, *Flower Still Life*, after 1700. Oil on canvas, 2' 5¾" × 1' 11⅞". Toledo Museum of Art, Toledo (purchased with funds from the Libbey Endowment, gift of Edward Drummond Libbey).

Flower paintings were very popular in the Dutch Republic. Ruysch achieved international renown for her lush paintings of floral arrangements, noted also for their careful compositions.

RACHEL RUYSCH As living objects that soon die, flowers, particularly cut blossoms, appeared frequently in vanitas paintings. However, floral painting as a distinct genre also enjoyed great popularity in the Dutch Republic because the Dutch were the leading growers and exporters of flowers in 17th-century Europe. One of the major practitioners of flower painting was RACHEL RUYSCH (1664–1750), who from 1708 to 1716 served as court painter to the elector Palatine (the ruler of the Palatinate, a former division of Bavaria) in Düsseldorf, Germany. Ruysch's father was a professor of botany and anatomy, which may account for her interest in and knowledge of plants and insects. She acquired an international reputation for her lush paintings and was able to charge very high prices for her work. *Flower Still Life* (FIG. **25-23**) is one of her finest paintings. In this canvas, the lavish floral arrangement is so full, many of the blossoms seem to be spilling out of the vase. However, Ruysch's floral still lifes are not pictures of real floral arrangements, but idealized groupings of individually studied flowers, often combining perfect specimens of flowers that bloomed at different times of the year and could never be placed on a table at the same time. Her careful composition of the individual elements in the illustrated example is evident in her arrangement of the flowers to create a diagonal running from the lower left to the upper right corner of the canvas, offsetting the opposing diagonal of the table edge.

FRANCE

In France, monarchical authority had been increasing for centuries, culminating in the reign of Louis XIV (r. 1661–1715), who sought to determine the direction of French society and culture. Although its economy was not as expansive as the Dutch Republic's, France became Europe's largest and most powerful nation in the 17th century. Against this backdrop, the arts flourished.

Louis XIV

The preeminent French art patron of the 17th century was King Louis XIV himself. Determined to consolidate and expand his power, Louis was a master of political strategy and propaganda. He established a carefully crafted and nuanced relationship with the nobility, granting them sufficient benefits to keep them pacified but simultaneously maintaining rigorous control to avoid insurrection or rebellion. He also ensured subservience by anchoring his rule in *divine right* (belief in a king's absolute power as God's will), rendering Louis's authority incontestable. So convinced was Louis of his importance and centrality to the French kingdom that he eagerly adopted the title "le Roi Soleil" ("the Sun King"). Like the planets and the sun, all of France revolved around Louis XIV.

The Sun King's desire for control extended to all realms of French life, including art. Louis and his principal adviser, Jean-Baptiste Colbert (1619–1683), strove to organize art and architecture in the service of the state. They fully appreciated the power of art as propaganda and the value of visual imagery for cultivating a public persona, and they spared no expense to raise great monuments celebrating the king's absolute power. Louis and Colbert sought to regularize taste and establish the classical style as the preferred French manner. The founding of the Royal Academy of Painting and Sculpture in 1648 served to advance this goal.

PORTRAITURE Louis XIV maintained a workshop of artists, each with a specialization—for example, faces, fabric, architecture, landscapes, armor, or fur. Thus many of the king's portraits were a group effort. *Louis XIV* (FIG. **25-24**) by HYACINTHE RIGAUD (1659–1743) is probably largely the work of his assistants, but he designed the composition and painted the king's face himself—on paper, affixed to the canvas after the rest of the painting was complete. Rigaud's portrait successfully conveys the image of an absolute monarch. The king, age 63 when he commissioned this portrait, stands with his left hand on his hip and gazes directly at the viewer. His elegant ermine-lined fleur-de-lis coronation robes (compare FIG. 25-4) hang loosely from his left shoulder, suggesting an air of haughtiness. Louis also draws his garment back to expose his legs. (The king was a ballet dancer in his youth and was proud of his well-toned legs.) The portrait's majesty derives in large part from the composition. The Sun King is the unmistakable focal point of the image, and Rigaud placed him so that he seems to look down on the viewer. (Louis XIV was only 5 feet, 4 inches tall—a fact that drove him to design the red-heeled shoes he wears in this painting.) The carefully detailed environment in which the king stands also contributes to the portrait's stateliness and grandiosity, as does the painting's sheer size (more than 9 feet tall).

Rigaud's portrait was originally intended as a gift to Louis's grandson, Philip V of Spain, but the Sun King was so pleased with it that he kept it for his own collection. Only three years later did Louis commission Rigaud to produce a copy for Philip. The image soon became iconic, and Rigaud's studio produced more copies for various European aristocrats.

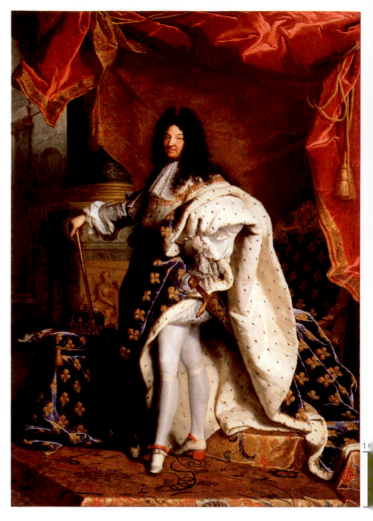

25-24 HYACINTHE RIGAUD, *Louis XIV*, 1701. Oil on canvas, 9′ 2″ × 6′ 3″. Musée du Louvre, Paris.

In this portrait set against a stately backdrop, Rigaud portrayed the 5′ 4″ Sun King wearing red high-heeled shoes and with his ermine-lined coronation robes thrown over his left shoulder.

THE LOUVRE The first great architectural project that Louis XIV and his adviser Colbert undertook was the closing of the east side of the Louvre's Cour Carré (FIG. 23-23), left incomplete by Pierre Lescot in the 16th century. The king summoned the renowned architect and sculptor Gianlorenzo Bernini (see page 701) from Rome to submit plans, but Bernini envisioned an Italian palace on a monumental scale, which would have involved the demolition of all previous work. His plan rejected, Bernini indignantly returned home. Louis then turned to three French architects—CLAUDE PERRAULT (1613–1688), LOUIS LE VAU (1612–1670), and CHARLES LE BRUN (1619–1690)—for the Louvre's east facade (FIG. **25-25**). The design is a brilliant synthesis of French and Italian classical elements, culminating in a new and definitive formula. The facade has a central and two corner projecting columnar pavilions resting on a stately podium. The central pavilion is in the form of a classical temple front. To either side is a giant colonnade of paired columns, resembling the columned flanks of a temple folded out like wings. The designers favored an even roofline, balustraded and broken only by the central pediment, over the traditional French pyramidal roof of the Louvre's west wing (FIG. 23-23). The emphatically horizontal sweep of the 17th-century facade brushed aside all memory of Gothic verticality. The stately proportions and monumentality

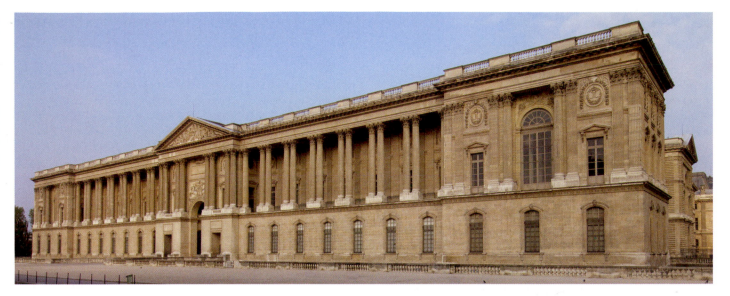

25-25 CLAUDE PERRAULT, LOUIS LE VAU, and CHARLES LE BRUN, east facade of the Louvre (looking southwest), Paris, France, 1667–1670.

The design of the Louvre's east facade is a brilliant synthesis of French and Italian classical elements, including a central pavilion resembling an ancient temple front with a pediment.

of the Baroque design were both an expression of the new official French taste and a symbol of centrally organized authority.

VERSAILLES Work on the Louvre had barely begun when Louis XIV decided to convert a royal hunting lodge at Versailles, south of Paris, into a great palace (see "The Sun King's Palace at Versailles," page 752, and FIG. **25-26**). The enormous palace might appear unbearably ostentatious were it not for its extraordinary setting in a vast park, which makes the palace seem almost an adjunct. The park of Versailles must rank among the world's greatest artworks in both

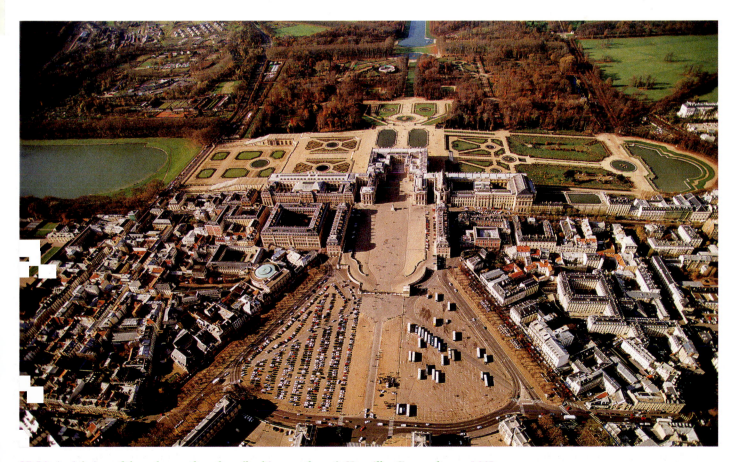

25-26 Aerial view of the palace and gardens (looking northwest), Versailles, France, begun 1669.

Louis XIV ordered his architects to convert a royal hunting lodge at Versailles into a gigantic palace and vast park with a satellite city with three radial avenues whose axes intersect in the king's bedroom.

The Sun King's Palace at Versailles

To realize his vision of a grandiose palace worthy of a "Sun King," Louis XIV assembled a veritable army of architects, decorators, sculptors, painters, and landscape designers under the general management of Charles Le Brun to design and construct his new royal residence at Versailles (FIG. 25-26). At the king's direction, Le Brun and his team converted the remodeling of a simple hunting lodge into the greatest architectural project of the age—a defining statement of French Baroque style and a grandiose symbol of Louis XIV's power and ambition.

Planned on a gigantic scale, the project called not only for a large palace flanking a vast park but also for the construction of a satellite city to house court and government officials, military and guard detachments, courtiers, and servants (thereby keeping them all under the king's close supervision). Le Brun laid out this town to the east of the palace along three radial avenues that converge on the palace. Their axes, in a symbolic assertion of the ruler's absolute power over his domains, intersected in the king's spacious bedroom, which served as an official audience chamber. The palace itself, more than a quarter-mile long, is perpendicular to the dominant east-west axis running through the associated city and park.

Every detail of the extremely rich decoration of the palace's interior received careful attention. The architects and decorators designed everything from wall paintings to doorknobs in order to reinforce the splendor of Versailles and to exhibit the very finest sense of artisanship. Of the literally hundreds of rooms within the palace, the most famous is the Galerie des Glaces, or Hall of Mirrors (FIG. **25-27**), designed by JULES HARDOUIN-MANSART (1646–1708) and Le Brun. This hall overlooks Le Nôtre's

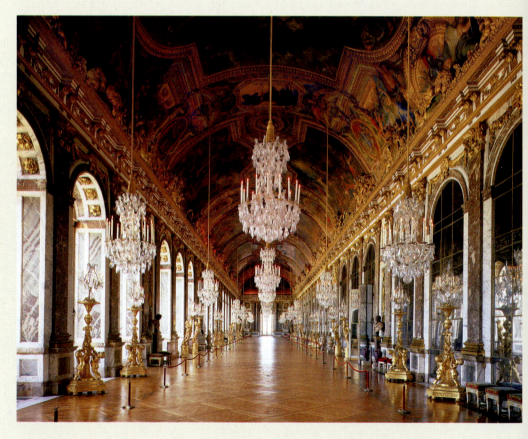

25-27 JULES HARDOUIN-MANSART and CHARLES LE BRUN, Galerie des Glaces (Hall of Mirrors), palace of Versailles, Versailles, France, ca. 1680.

In this grandiose hall overlooking the park of the Sun King's palace at Versailles, hundreds of mirrors illusionistically extend the room's width and once reflected its gilded and jeweled furnishings.

park (FIG. 25-26) from the second floor and extends along most of the width of the central block. Although deprived of its original sumptuous furniture, which included gold and silver chairs and bejeweled trees, the 240-foot-long Galerie des Glaces retains much of its splendor today. Hundreds of mirrors, set into the wall opposite the windows, alleviate the hall's tunnel-like quality and illusionistically extend the width of the room. The mirror, that ultimate source of illusion, was a favorite element of Baroque interior design. Here, it also enhanced the dazzling extravagance of the great festivals that Louis XIV was so fond of hosting. From the Galerie des Glaces, the king and his guests could enjoy a sweeping vista down the tree-lined central axis of the Versailles park and across terraces, lawns, pools, and lakes toward the horizon.

As a symbol of absolute power, Versailles has no equal. It also expresses, in the most monumental terms of its age, the rationalistic creed—based on scientific advances, such as the physics of Sir Isaac Newton (1642–1727) and the mathematical philosophy of René Descartes (1596–1650)—that all knowledge must be systematic and all science must be the consequence of the intellect imposed on matter. The majestic and rational design of Versailles proudly proclaims the mastery of human intelligence (and the mastery of Louis XIV) over the disorderliness of nature.

---

size and concept. Here, ANDRÉ LE NÔTRE (1613–1700) transformed an entire forest into a park. Although its geometric plan may appear stiff and formal, the park in fact offers an almost unlimited assortment of vistas, as the French architect used not only the multiplicity of natural forms but also the terrain's slightly rolling contours with stunning effectiveness.

The formal gardens near the palace provide a transition from the frozen architectural forms to the natural living ones. Here, the elegant shapes of trimmed shrubs and hedges define the tightly designed geometric units. Each unit is different from its neighbor and has a focal point in the form of a sculptured group, a pavilion, a reflecting pool, or a fountain. Farther away from the palace, the design loosens as trees, in shadowy masses, screen or frame views of open countryside. Le Nôtre carefully composed all vistas for maximum effect. Light and shadow, formal and informal, dense growth and open meadows—all play against one another in unending combinations and variations. No photograph or series of photographs can reveal the design's full richness. The park unfolds itself only to

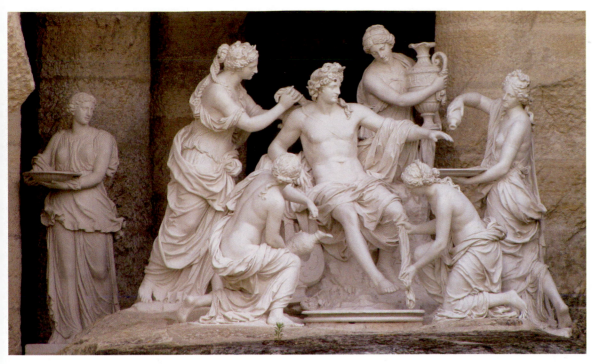

25-28 François Girardon and Thomas Regnaudin, *Apollo Attended by the Nymphs of Thetis*, Grotto of Thetis, park of Versailles, Versailles, France, 1664–1670. Marble, life-size.

Girardon's study of ancient sculpture and Poussin's figural compositions influenced the design of this mythological group. Apollo, often equated with the sun, alludes to Louis XIV, the Sun King.

those walking through it. In this respect, it is a temporal artwork. Its aspects change with the time of day, the seasons, and the relative position of the observer.

GROTTO OF THETIS Scattered through the vast Versailles park are allegorical references to the Sun King in the form of statues of the Greek god Apollo, who was often identified with the sun (see "The Gods and Goddesses of Mount Olympus," page 105). Perhaps the finest of these is *Apollo Attended by the Nymphs of Thetis* (FIG. 25-28) by François Girardon (1628–1715) with additional statues by Thomas Regnaudin (1622–1706), which in the 18th century were moved by Hubert Robert (1773–1808) to an artificial grotto above a dramatic waterfall (FIG. 25-28A). Both stately and graceful, the nymphs have a compelling charm as they minister to Apollo at the end of the day. Girardon, who also won the commission to make a bronze equestrian statue of the Sun King, had spent time in Rome, and his close study of Greco-Roman sculpture heavily influenced his design of the central group. (Girardon based his Apollo on one of the most famous ancient statues then known, the *Apollo Belvedere* in the Vatican.) The figural compositions of the most renowned French painter of the era, Nicolas Poussin (FIG. 25-31), inspired Girardon's arrangement of the statues as a group. The sculptor's classical style and mythological symbolism well suited France's glorification of royal majesty.

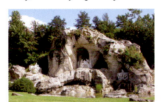

📄 **25-28A** Robert, Baths of Apollo, Versailles, 1777–1781.

ROYAL CHAPEL In 1698, Hardouin-Mansart received the commission to add a Royal Chapel to the Versailles palace complex. The chapel's interior (FIG. 25-29) is essentially rectangular, but because its apse is as high as the nave, the fluid central space takes on a curved, Baroque quality. However, the light entering through the large clerestory windows lacks the directed dramatic effect of the Italian Baroque, instead illuminating the interior's precisely chiseled details brightly and evenly. Pier-supported arcades carry a majestic

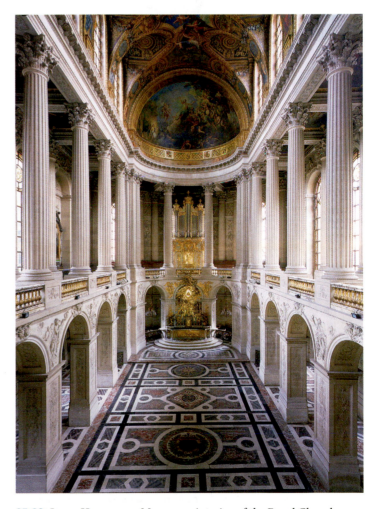

25-29 Jules Hardouin-Mansart, interior of the Royal Chapel, with ceiling decorations by Antoine Coypel, palace of Versailles, Versailles, France, 1698–1710.

Because the apse is as high as the nave, the central space of the Royal Chapel at Versailles has a curved, Baroque quality. Louis XIV could reach the royal pew directly from his apartments.

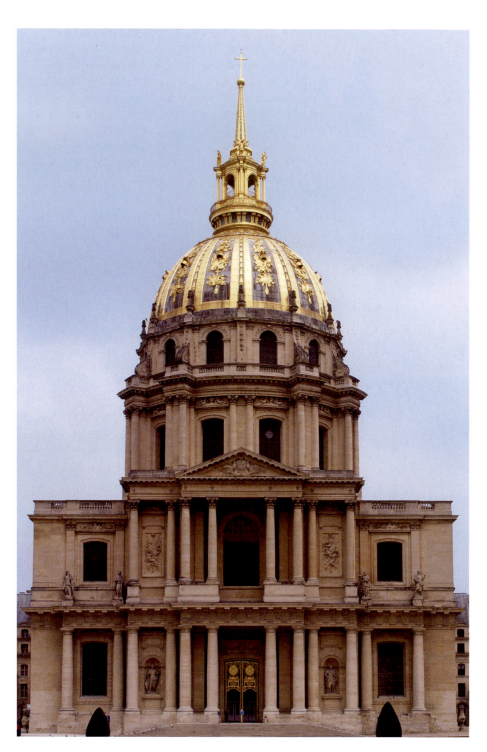

25-30 JULES HARDOUIN-MANSART, Église du Dôme (looking north), Church of the Invalides, Paris, France, 1676–1706.

Hardouin-Mansart's church marries the Italian and French architectural styles. The grouping of the orders is similar to the Italian Baroque manner but without the dramatic play of curved surfaces.

frame is not unlike that in Italian Baroque architecture but without the dramatic play of curved surfaces characteristic of many 17th-century Italian churches—for example, Borromini's San Carlo (FIG. 24-9) in Rome. The compact facade is low and narrow in relation to the vast drum and dome, seeming to serve simply as a base for them. The overpowering dome, conspicuous on the Parisian skyline, is itself expressive of the Baroque love for dramatic magnitude, as is the way its designer aimed for theatrical effects of light and space. The dome consists of three shells, the lowest cut off so that a visitor to the interior looks up through it to the one above, which is filled with light from hidden windows in the third, outermost dome. CHARLES DE LA FOSSE (1636–1716) painted the second dome in 1705 with an Italian-inspired representation of the heavens opening up to receive Saint Louis, patron of France (see page 390).

Poussin and Claude Lorrain

Louis XIV's embrace of classicism enticed many French artists to study Rome's ancient and Renaissance monuments. But even before the Sun King ascended to the throne in 1661, NICOLAS POUSSIN (1594–1665) of Normandy had spent most of his life in Rome, where he produced grandly severe paintings modeled on those of Titian and Raphael. He also carefully formulated a theoretical explanation of his method and was ultimately responsible for establishing classical painting as an important ingredient of 17th-century French art (see "Poussin's Notes for a Treatise on Painting," page 755). His classical style presents a striking contrast to the contemporaneous Baroque style of his Italian counterparts in Rome, underscoring the multifaceted character of the art of 17th-century Europe.

row of Corinthian columns defining the royal gallery. The royal pew is at the rear, accessible directly from the king's apartments. Amid the restrained decoration, only the illusionistic ceiling paintings, added in 1708 and 1709 by ANTOINE COYPEL (1661–1722), suggest the drama and complexity of Italian Baroque art.

ÉGLISE DU DÔME, PARIS Another of Hardouin-Mansart's masterworks, the Église du Dôme (FIG. **25-30**), or Church of the Invalides, in Paris, also marries the Italian Baroque and French classical architectural styles. An intricately composed domed square of great scale, the church adjoins the veterans hospital that Louis XIV established for the disabled soldiers of his many wars. Two firmly separated levels, the upper one capped by a pediment, compose the frontispiece. The grouping of the orders and of the bays they

ET IN ARCADIA EGO Poussin's *Et in Arcadia Ego* (*Even in Arcadia, I* [am present]; FIG. **25-31**) exemplifies the "grand manner" of painting that the artist advocated. It features a lofty subject rooted in the classical world and figures based on antique statuary. Rather than depicting dynamic movement and intense emotions, as his Italian contemporaries in Rome did, Poussin emulated the rational order and stability of Raphael's paintings. Dominating the foreground are three shepherds living in the idyllic land of Arcadia. They study an

ARTISTS ON ART
Poussin's Notes for a Treatise on Painting

As the leading proponent of classical painting in 17th-century Rome, Nicolas Poussin outlined the principles of classicism in notes for an intended treatise on painting, left incomplete at his death. In those notes, Poussin described the essential ingredients necessary to produce a beautiful painting in "the grand manner":

> The grand manner consists of four things: subject-matter or theme, thought, structure, and style. The first thing that, as the foundation of all others, is required, is that the subject-matter shall be grand, as are battles, heroic actions, and divine things. But assuming that the subject on which the painter is laboring is grand, his next consideration is to keep away from minutiae . . . [and paint only] things magnificent and grand . . . Those who elect mean subjects take refuge in them because of the weakness of their talents.*

The idea of beauty does not descend into matter unless this is prepared as carefully as possible. This preparation consists of three things: arrangement, measure, and aspect or form. Arrangement means the relative position of the parts; measure refers to their size; and form consists of lines and colors. Arrangement and relative position of the parts and making every limb of the body hold its natural place are not sufficient unless measure is added, which gives to each limb its correct size, proportionate to that of the whole body [compare "Polykleitos's Prescription for the Perfect Statue," page 129], and unless form joins in, so that the lines will be drawn with grace and with a harmonious juxtaposition of light and shadow.†

Poussin applied these principles in paintings such as *Et in Arcadia Ego* (FIG. 25-31), a work peopled with perfectly proportioned statuesque figures attired in antique garb.

*Translated by Robert Goldwater and Marco Treves, eds., *Artists on Art,* 3d ed. (New York: Pantheon Books, 1958), 155.
†Ibid., 156.

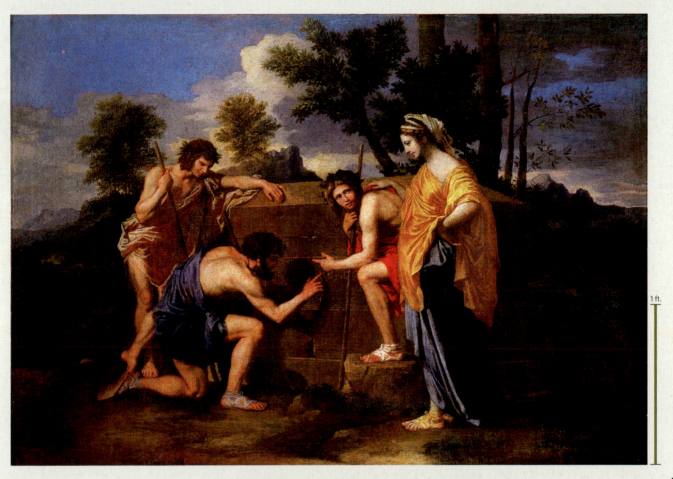

1 ft.

25-31 NICOLAS POUSSIN, *Et in Arcadia Ego,* ca. 1655. Oil on canvas, 2' 10" × 4'. Musée du Louvre, Paris.

Poussin was the leading proponent of classicism in 17th-century Rome. His "grand manner" paintings are models of "arrangement and measure" and incorporate figures inspired by ancient statuary.

inscription on a tomb as a statuesque female figure quietly places her hand on the shoulder of one of them. She may be the spirit of death, reminding these mortals, as does the inscription, that death is found even in Arcadia, supposedly a spot of paradisiacal bliss. The countless draped female statues surviving in Italy from Roman times supplied the models for this figure, and the posture of the youth with one foot resting on a boulder derives from Greco-Roman statues of Neptune, the sea god, leaning on his trident. The classically compact and balanced grouping of the figures, the even light, and the thoughtful and reserved mood complement Poussin's classical figure types.

France   755

25-32 NICOLAS POUSSIN, *Landscape with Saint John on Patmos,* 1640. Oil on canvas, 3' 3½" × 4' 5⅝". Art Institute of Chicago, Chicago (A. A. Munger Collection).

Poussin placed Saint John in a classical landscape amid broken columns, an obelisk, and a ruined temple, suggesting the decay of great civilizations and the coming of the new Christian era.

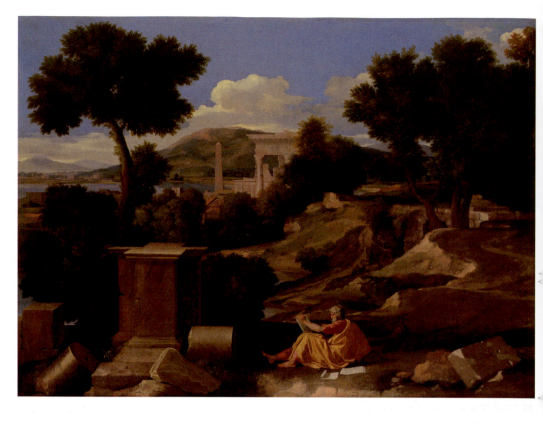

SAINT JOHN ON PATMOS In *Et in Arcadia Ego,* monumental figures dominate the landscape setting, but the natural world looms large in many of Poussin's paintings. *Landscape with Saint John on Patmos* (FIG. **25-32**) is one of a pair of canvases Poussin painted for Gian Maria Roscioli (d. 1644), secretary to Pope Urban VIII. The second landscape represents Saint Matthew, reclining in right profile, who faced Saint John when the two canvases, now in different museums on different continents, hung side by side in Rome. An eagle stands behind John, just as an angel, Matthew's attribute, stands beside him (see "The Four Evangelists," page 318). John, near the end of his life on the Greek island of Patmos, composed the book of Revelation, his account of the end of the world and the second coming of Christ, a prophetic vision of violent destruction and the Last Judgment (see "Early Christian Saints," page 237).

Poussin's setting, however, is a serene classical landscape beneath a sunny sky. (He created a similar setting in *Burial of Phocion* [FIG. **25-32A**], which he painted later in the decade.) Saint John reclines in the foreground, posed like a Greco-Roman river god, amid shattered columns and a pedestal for a statue that disappeared long ago. In the middle ground, two oak trees frame the ruins of a classical temple and an Egyptian obelisk, many of which the

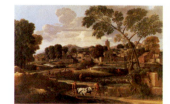

25-32A POUSSIN, *Burial of Phocion,* 1648.

25-33 CLAUDE LORRAIN, *Landscape with Cattle and Peasants,* 1629. Oil on canvas, 3' 6" × 4' 10½". Philadelphia Museum of Art, Philadelphia (George W. Elkins Collection).

Claude used atmospheric and linear perspective to transform the rustic Roman countryside filled with peasants and animals into an ideal classical landscape bathed in sunlight in infinite space.

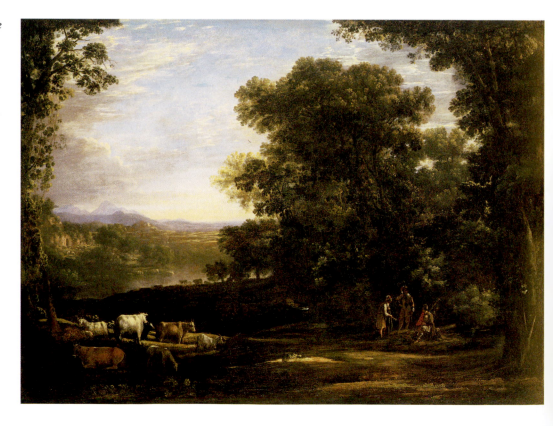

Romans brought to their capital from the Nile and the popes reused in their building projects—for example, in the piazza in front of Saint Peter's (FIG. 24-4) and in Bernini's Fountain of the Four Rivers (FIG. 24-1). The decaying buildings suggest the decline of great empires—to be replaced by Christianity in a new era. In the distance are hills, sky, and clouds, all of which Poussin represented with pristine clarity, ignoring the rules of atmospheric perspective. His landscapes are not portraits of specific places, as are the Dutch landscapes of Ruisdael (FIG. 25-18) and Vermeer (FIG. 25-18B). Rather, they are imaginary settings constructed according to classical rules of design. Poussin's clouds, for example, echo the contours of his hills.

CLAUDE LORRAIN Claude Gellée, called CLAUDE LORRAIN (1600–1682) after his birthplace in the duchy of Lorraine, which was technically independent from the French monarchy during this period, rivaled Poussin in fame. Claude modulated in a softer style Poussin's disciplined rational art, with its sophisticated revelation of the geometry of landscape. Unlike the figures in Poussin's pictures, those in Claude's landscapes tell no dramatic story, point out no moral, praise no hero, and celebrate no saint. Indeed, the figures in Claude's paintings often appear to be added as mere excuses for the radiant landscape itself. For the French artist, painting involved essentially one theme—the beauty of a broad sky suffused with the golden light of dawn or sunset glowing through a hazy atmosphere and reflecting brilliantly off rippling water.

In *Landscape with Cattle and Peasants* (FIG. 25-33), the figures in the right foreground chat in animated fashion. In the left foreground, cattle relax contentedly. In the middle ground, cattle amble slowly away. The well-defined foreground, distinct middle ground, and dim background recede in serene orderliness, until all form dissolves in a luminous mist. Atmospheric and linear perspective reinforce each other to turn a vista into a typical Claudian vision, an ideal classical world bathed in sunlight in infinite space (compare FIG. I-1).

Claude's formalizing of nature with balanced groups of architectural masses, screens of trees, and sheets of water followed the great tradition of classical landscape. It began with the backgrounds of Venetian paintings (FIGS. 22-33 to 22-35) and continued in the art of Annibale Carracci (FIG. 24-15) and Poussin (FIGS. 25-32 and 25-32A). Yet Claude, like the Dutch painters, studied the light and the atmospheric nuances of nature, making an important contribution. He recorded carefully in hundreds of sketches the look of the Roman countryside, its gentle terrain accented by stone-pines, cypresses, and poplars and by the ever-present ruins of ancient aqueducts, tombs, and towers. He made these the fundamental elements of his compositions. Claude's landscapes owe their timeless appeal to the distinctive combination of the natural beauty of the outskirts of Rome and the mystique of the past.

Claude achieved his marvelous effects of light by painstakingly placing on his canvas tiny brushstrokes representing small value gradations, which imitated, though on a very small scale, the range of values of outdoor light and shade. Avoiding the problem of high-noon sunlight overhead, Claude preferred, and convincingly rendered, the sun's rays as they gradually illuminated the morning sky or, with their dying glow, set the pensive mood of evening. Thus he matched the moods of nature with those of human subjects. Claude's infusion of nature with human feeling and his recomposition of nature in a calm equilibrium greatly appealed to many landscape painters of the 18th and early 19th centuries.

Le Nain, Callot, La Tour

Although classicism was an important element of French art during the 17th and early 18th centuries, not all artists embraced the "grand manner." The works of LOUIS LE NAIN (ca. 1593–1648) have more in common with contemporaneous Dutch art than Renaissance or ancient art. Nevertheless, subjects that in Dutch painting were opportunities for boisterous good humor (FIG. 25-20), Le Nain treated with somber stillness. *Family of Country People* (FIG. 25-34) reflects the thinking of 17th-century French social theorists who celebrated the natural virtue of peasants who worked

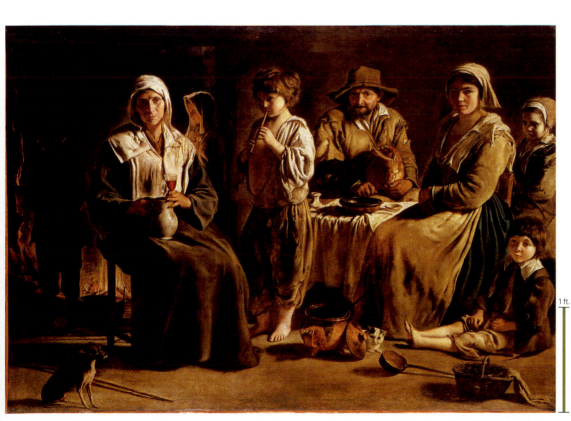

25-34 LOUIS LE NAIN, *Family of Country People*, ca. 1640. Oil on canvas, 3' 8" × 5' 2". Musée du Louvre, Paris.

Le Nain's painting expresses the grave dignity of a peasant family made stoic by hardship. It reflects 17th-century French social theory, which celebrated the natural virtue of those who worked the soil.

1 ft.

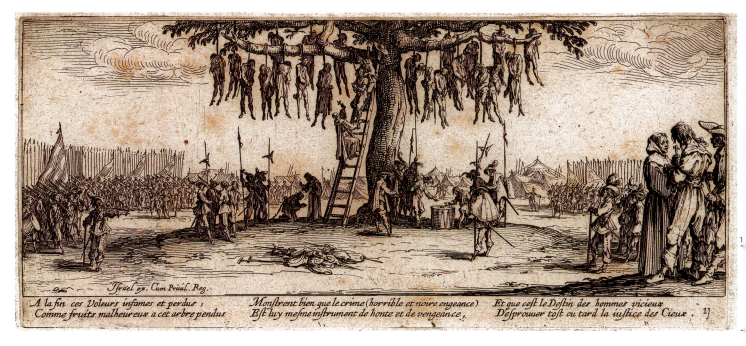

25-35 JACQUES CALLOT, *Hanging Tree,* from the *Miseries of War* series, 1629–1633. Etching, 3¾″ × 7¼″. Bibliothèque Nationale, Paris.

Callot's *Miseries of War* etchings were among the first realistic pictorial records of the human disaster of military conflict. *Hanging Tree* depicts a mass execution of thieves in the presence of an army.

the soil. Le Nain's painting expresses the grave dignity of one peasant family made stoic and resigned by hardship. These drab country folk surely had little reason for merriment. The peasant's lot, never easy, was miserable during the Thirty Years' War. The anguish and frustration of the peasantry, suffering from the cruel depredations of unruly armies living off the countryside, often erupted in violent revolts that the same armies savagely suppressed. This family, however, is pious, docile, and calm. Because Le Nain depicted peasants with dignity and quiet resignation, despite their harsh living conditions, some scholars have suggested that he intended his paintings to please wealthy urban patrons.

JACQUES CALLOT Two other prominent artists from Lorraine were Jacques Callot and Georges de La Tour. JACQUES CALLOT (ca. 1592–1635) conveyed a sense of military life during these troubled times in a series of prints called *Miseries of War.* Callot confined himself almost exclusively to the art of etching and was widely influential. Rembrandt was among those who knew and learned from his work. Callot developed a very hard surface for the copper plate to enable fine and precise delineation with the needle. His

quick, vivid touch and faultless drawing produced panoramas sparkling with sharp details of life—and death—despite their small size (roughly 4 by 7 inches). In the *Miseries of War* series, he observed these details coolly, presenting without comment images based on events he must have witnessed in the wars in Lorraine.

In *Hanging Tree* (FIG. 25-35), Callot depicted a mass execution of thieves (identified in the text at the bottom of the etching). The event takes place in the presence of a disciplined army, drawn up on parade with banners, muskets, and lances, their tents in the

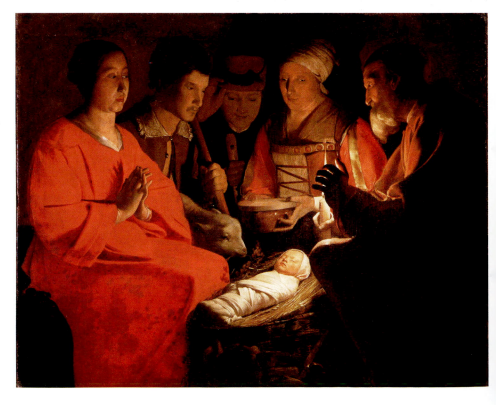

25-36 GEORGES DE LA TOUR, *Adoration of the Shepherds,* 1645–1650. Oil on canvas, 3′ 6″ × 4′ 6″. Musée du Louvre, Paris.

Without the aid of the title, this candlelit nighttime scene could be a genre painting instead of a biblical narrative. La Tour did not even paint halos around the heads of the holy personages.

background. Hanged men sway in clusters from the branches of a huge cross-shaped tree. A monk climbs a ladder, holding up a crucifix to a man while the executioner adjusts the noose around the man's neck. At the foot of the ladder, another victim kneels to receive absolution. Under the crucifix-tree, men roll dice on a drumhead, hoping to win the belongings of the executed. (This may be an allusion to the soldiers who cast lots for the garments of the crucified Christ.) In the right foreground, a hooded priest consoles a bound man. Callot's *Miseries of War* etchings are among the first realistic pictorial records of the human disaster of armed conflict.

GEORGES DE LA TOUR France, unlike the Dutch Republic, was a Catholic country, and religious themes, although not as common as in Italian and Spanish Baroque art, occupied some 17th-century French painters. Among the French artists who painted biblical subjects was GEORGES DE LA TOUR (1593–1652). His work, particularly his use of light, suggests a familiarity with Caravaggio's art (see page 715), which he may have learned about from painters in Utrecht, such as ter Brugghen and van Honthorst (FIGS. 25-7 and 25-8). Although La Tour used the devices of Caravaggio's Dutch followers, his effects are strikingly different from theirs. His *Adoration of the Shepherds* (FIG. 25-36) makes use of the night setting favored by the Utrecht school, much as van Honthorst portrayed it. But here, the light, its source shaded by an old man's hand, falls upon a very different company in a very different mood. A group of humble men and women, coarsely clad, gather in prayerful vigil around a luminous baby Jesus. Without the aid of the title, this work might be construed as a genre piece, a narrative of some event from peasant life. Nothing in the environment, placement, poses, dress, or attributes of the figures distinguishes them as the Virgin Mary, Joseph, Christ Child, or shepherds. The artist did not even give the religious personages halos. The light is not spiritual but material: it comes from a candle.

La Tour's scientific scrutiny of the effects of light, as it throws precise shadows on surfaces intercepting it, nevertheless had religious intention and consequence. The light illuminates a group of ordinary people held in a mystic trance induced by their witnessing the miracle of the incarnation. In this timeless tableau of simple people, La Tour eliminated the dogmatic significance and traditional iconography of the birth of the Savior. Still, these people reverently contemplate something they regard as holy. The devout of any religious persuasion can read this painting, regardless of their familiarity with the biblical account.

The supernatural calm pervading *Adoration of the Shepherds* is characteristic of the mood of Georges de La Tour's art. He achieved this by eliminating motion and emotive gesture (only the light is dramatic), by suppressing surface detail, and by simplifying body volumes. These stylistic traits are among those associated with classical and Renaissance art. Thus several apparently contradictory elements meet in the work of La Tour: classical composure, fervent spirituality, and genre realism.

ENGLAND

In England, in sharp distinction to France, the common law and the Parliament kept royal power in check. England also differed from France (and Europe in general) in other significant ways. Although an important part of English life, religion was not the contentious issue it was on the Continent. The religious affiliations of the English included Catholicism, Anglicanism, Protestantism, and Puritanism (the English version of Calvinism). In the economic realm, England was the one country (other than the Dutch Republic) to take advantage of the opportunities that overseas trade offered. As an island, Britain (which after 1603 consisted of England, Wales, and Scotland), like the Dutch Republic, possessed a large and powerful navy, as well as excellent maritime capabilities.

Jones and Wren

In the realm of art, the most significant English achievements were in the field of architecture, much of it, as in France, incorporating classical elements.

INIGO JONES The most important English architect of the first half of the 17th century was INIGO JONES (1573–1652), architect to Kings James I (r. 1603–1625) and Charles I (FIG. 25-5). Jones spent considerable time in Italy. He greatly admired the classical authority and restraint of Andrea Palladio's buildings and studied with great care his treatise on architecture (see page 647). Jones took many motifs from Palladio's villas and palaces, and he adopted Palladio's basic design principles for his own architecture, which transformed the medieval city of London. The nature of Jones's achievement is evident in the buildings he designed for his royal patrons, among them the Banqueting House (FIG. 25-37) at Whitehall, used, as its name reveals, for royal banquets and other festive occasions.

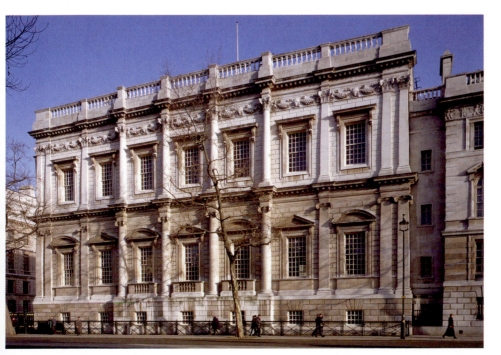

25-37 INIGO JONES, **Banqueting House (looking northeast), Whitehall, London, England, 1619–1622.**

Jones was a great admirer of the classical architecture of Palladio, and he adopted motifs from the Italian architect's villas and palaces for the buildings he designed for his royal patrons.

(Adorning the ceiling of the grand interior hall is a 1634–1636 painting by Rubens depicting the apotheosis of James I.) For this structure, a symmetrical block of great clarity and dignity, Jones superimposed two orders (Ionic below, Corinthian above), using columns in the center and pilasters near the ends. The balustraded roofline, uninterrupted in its horizontal sweep, predates the Louvre's east facade (FIG. 25-25) by more than 40 years. Palladio would have recognized and approved all of the design elements, but the building as a whole is not a copy of his work. Although relying on the revered Italian's architectural vocabulary and syntax, Jones retained his independence as a designer. For two centuries, his influence in English architecture was almost as authoritative as Palladio's.

CHRISTOPHER WREN London's majestic Saint Paul's Cathedral (FIG. **25-38**) is the work of England's most renowned architect, CHRISTOPHER WREN (1632–1723). A mathematical genius and skilled engineer whose work won Isaac Newton's praise, Wren became professor of astronomy at Gresham College in London at age 25. Mathematics led to architecture, and Charles II (r. 1649–1685) asked Wren to prepare a plan for restoring the old Gothic church dedicated to Saint Paul. Wren proposed to remodel the building based on Roman structures. Within a few months, the Great Fire of London, which destroyed the old structure and many other churches in the city in 1666, gave Wren his opportunity. Although Jones's work strongly influenced him, Wren also traveled in France, where the splendid palaces and state buildings being created in and around Paris at the time of

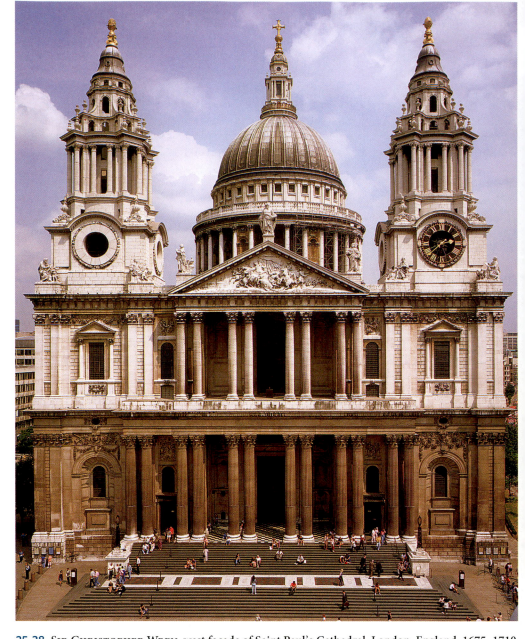

25-38 SIR CHRISTOPHER WREN, west facade of Saint Paul's Cathedral, London, England, 1675–1710.

Wren's cathedral replaced an old Gothic church. The facade design owes much to Palladio (FIG. 22-30) and Borromini (FIG. 24-12). The great dome recalls Saint Peter's in Rome (FIGS. 22-25 and 24-4).

the expansion of the Louvre palace (FIG. 25-25) must have impressed him. Wren also closely studied prints illustrating Baroque architecture in Italy. In Saint Paul's, he harmonized Palladian, French, and Italian Baroque features.

In view of its size, Saint Paul's Cathedral was built with remarkable speed—in little more than 30 years—and Wren lived to see it completed. The building's form underwent constant refinement during construction, and Wren did not determine the final appearance of the towers until after 1700. In the splendid skyline composition, two foreground towers act effectively as foils to the great dome. Wren must have known similar schemes that Italian architects had devised for Saint Peter's (FIG. 24-4) in Rome to solve

the problem of the relationship between the facade and dome. Certainly, the influence of Borromini (FIGS. 24-1, rear, and 24-12) is evident in the upper levels and lanterns of the towers. The lower levels owe a debt to Palladio (FIG. 22-30), and the superposed paired columnar porticos recall the Louvre's east facade (FIG. 25-25). Wren's skillful eclecticism brought all these foreign features into a monumental unity.

Wren designed many other London churches after the Great Fire. Even today, Wren's towers and domes punctuate the skyline of London. Saint Paul's dome is the tallest of all. Wren's legacy was significant and long-lasting, both in England and in colonial America, as examined in the next chapter.

THE BAROQUE IN NORTHERN EUROPE

Flanders

- In the 17th century, Flanders remained Catholic and under Spanish control. Flemish Baroque art was more closely tied to the Baroque art of Italy than was the art of much of the rest of northern Europe.

- The leading Flemish painter of this era was Peter Paul Rubens, whose work and influence were international in scope. A diplomat as well as an artist, he counted kings and queens among his patrons and friends. His paintings, for example, the series of huge canvases he painted for Marie de'Medici to glorify her career, exhibit Baroque splendor in color and ornament, and feature robust and foreshortened figures in swirling motion.

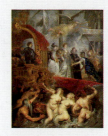

Rubens, *Marie de' Medici at Marseilles*, 1622–1625

Dutch Republic

- The Dutch Republic received official recognition of its independence from Spain in the Treaty of Westphalia of 1648. Worldwide trade and banking brought prosperity to its predominantly Protestant citizenry, which largely rejected church art in favor of private commissions of portraits, genre scenes, landscapes, and still lifes.

- Frans Hals produced innovative portraits of middle-class patrons in which a lively informality replaced the formulaic patterns of traditional portraiture. Aelbert Cuyp and Jacob van Ruisdael specialized in landscapes depicting specific places, not idealized Renaissance settings. Pieter Claesz, Willem Kalf, and others specialized in still lifes featuring meticulous depictions of worldly goods, sometimes amid reminders of death.

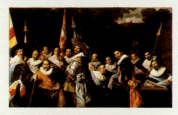

Hals, *Archers of Saint Hadrian*, ca. 1633

- Rembrandt van Rijn, the greatest Dutch artist of the age, treated a broad range of subjects, including religious themes and portraits. His oil paintings are notable for their dramatic impact and subtle gradations of light and shade as well as the artist's ability to convey human emotions. Rembrandt was also a master printmaker.

- Jan Vermeer specialized in painting the occupants of serene, comfortable Dutch homes. His convincing representation of interior spaces depended in part on his employment of a camera obscura. Vermeer was also a master of light and color and understood that shadows are not colorless.

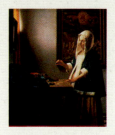

Vermeer, *Woman Holding a Balance*, ca. 1664

France and England

- The major art patron in 17th-century France was the Sun King, the absolutist monarch Louis XIV, who expanded the Louvre in Paris and built a vast palace and garden complex at nearby Versailles featuring sumptuous furnishings and sweeping vistas. Among the architects that Louis employed were Charles Le Brun and Jules Hardouin-Mansart, who succeeded in marrying Italian Baroque and French classical styles.

- The leading French proponent of classical painting was Nicolas Poussin, who spent most of his life in Rome and championed the "grand manner" of painting. This style called for heroic or divine subjects and classical compositions with figures often modeled on ancient statues.

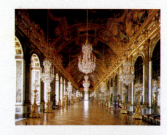

Galerie des Glaces, Versailles, ca. 1680

- Claude Lorrain, whose fame rivaled Poussin's, specialized in classical landscapes rendered in linear and atmospheric perspective. His compositions often incorporated ancient ruins.

- In 17th-century England, architecture was the most important art form. Two architects who achieved international fame were Inigo Jones and Christopher Wren. They harmonized the architectural principles of Andrea Palladio with the Italian Baroque and French classical styles in buildings such as the Banqueting House (Jones) and Saint Paul's Cathedral (Wren) in London.

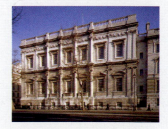

Jones, Banqueting House, London, 1619–1622

Notes

INTRODUCTION

1. Quoted in George Heard Hamilton, *Painting and Sculpture in Europe, 1880–1940*, 6th ed. (New Haven, Conn.: Yale University Press, 1993), 345.
2. Quoted in *Josef Albers: Homage to the Square* (New York: Museum of Modern Art, 1964), n.p.

CHAPTER 20

1. Francisco de Hollanda, *De pintura antigua* (1548), quoted in Robert Klein and Henri Zerner, *Italian Art, 1500–1600: Sources and Documents* (Englewood Cliffs, N.J.: Prentice Hall, 1966), 33.

CHAPTER 21

1. Translated by Catherine Enggass, in Howard Saalman, ed., *Antonio Manetti, Life of Brunelleschi* (University Park: Pennsylvania State University Press, 1970), 42.
2. Giorgio Vasari, "Life of Lorenzo Ghiberti." Translated by Gaston du C. de Vere, ed., *Giorgio Vasari, Lives of the Painters, Sculptors and Architects* (New York: Knopf, 1996), 1:304.
3. Ghiberti, *Commentarii*, 2.22. Quoted in Elizabeth Gilmore Holt, ed., *A Documentary History of Art, I: The Middle Ages and the Renaissance* (Princeton, N.J.: Princeton University Press, 1981), 161.
4. Stephen J. Campbell and Michael W. Cole, *Italian Renaissance Art* (New York: Thames & Hudson, 2011), 151.
5. Quoted in H. W. Janson, *The Sculpture of Donatello* (Princeton, N.J.: Princeton University Press, 1965), 154.
6. Vasari, "Life of Masaccio." Translated by Gaston du C. de Vere, 1:318.
7. Martial, *Epigrams*, 10.32.

CHAPTER 22

1. Plato, *Ion*, 534. Translated by Benjamin Jowett, *The Dialogues of Plato*, 4th ed. (Oxford: Clarendon Press, 1953), 1:107–108.
2. Leonardo da Vinci to Ludovico Sforza, ca. 1480–1481. Elizabeth Gilmore Holt, ed., *A Documentary History of Art* (Princeton: Princeton University Press, 1981), 1:274–275.

3. Quoted in Anthony Blunt, *Artistic Theory in Italy, 1450–1600* (London: Oxford University Press, 1964), 34.
4. James M. Saslow, *The Poetry of Michelangelo: An Annotated Translation* (New Haven, Conn.: Yale University Press, 1991), 407.
5. Giorgio Vasari, *Lives of the Painters, Sculptors and Architects*. Translated by Gaston du C. de Vere (New York: Knopf, 1996), 2:736.
6. Quoted in A. Richard Turner, *Renaissance Florence: The Invention of a New Art* (New York: Abrams, 1997), 163.
7. Quoted in Bruce Boucher, *Andrea Palladio: The Architect in His Time* (New York: Abbeville Press, 1998), 229.
8. Quoted in Robert J. Clements, *Michelangelo's Theory of Art* (New York: New York University Press, 1961), 320.
9. Giorgio Vasari, *The Lives of the Artists*. Translated by Julia Conaway Bondanella and Peter Bondanella (New York: Oxford University Press, 1991), 489.

CHAPTER 23

1. Translated by Erwin Panofsky, in Wolfgang Stechow, *Northern Renaissance Art 1400–1600: Sources and Documents* (Evanston, Ill.: Northwestern University Press, 1989), 123.
2. Translated by Bernhard Erling, in Stechow, 129–130.
3. Translated by Fred S. Kleiner. Giorgio Vasari, *De' più eccelenti pittori scultori ed architettori* (Gaetano Milanesi, ed.; Florence: Sansoni, 1881), 7:584.

CHAPTER 24

1. Filippo Baldinucci, *Vita del Cavaliere Giovanni Lorenzo Bernini* (1681). Translated by Robert Enggass, in Enggass and Jonathan Brown, *Italian and Spanish Art 1600–1750: Sources and Documents* (Evanston, Ill.: Northwestern University Press, 1992), 116.

CHAPTER 25

1. Albert Blankert, *Johannes Vermeer van Delft 1632–1675* (Utrecht: Spectrum, 1975), 133, no. 51. Translated by Bob Haak, *The Golden Age: Dutch Painters of the Seventeenth Century* (New York: Abrams, 1984), 450.
2. Translated by Kristin Lohse Belkin, *Rubens* (London: Phaidon, 1998), 47.

Glossary

NOTE: *Text page references are in parentheses. References to bonus image online essays are in* blue.

a secco—Italian, "dry." See *fresco.* (627)

abstract—Nonrepresentational; forms and colors arranged without reference to the depiction of an object. (5)

additive light—Natural light, or sunlight, the sum of all the wavelengths of the visible *spectrum.* See also *subtractive light.* (7)

additive sculpture—A kind of sculpture *technique* in which materials (for example, clay) are built up or "added" to create form. (11)

aerial perspective—See *perspective.* (586)

agone—Italian, "foot race." (701)

aisle—The portion of a *basilica* flanking the *nave* and separated from it by a row of *columns* or *piers.* (12)

alchemy—The study of seemingly magical changes, especially chemical changes. (687)

altarpiece—A panel, painted or sculpted, situated above and behind an altar. See also *retable.* (415, 558)

amphitheater—Greek, "double theater." A Roman building type resembling two Greek theaters put together. The Roman amphitheater featured a continuous elliptical cavea around a central arena. (411)

anamorphic image—A distorted image that must be viewed by some special means (such as a mirror) to be recognized. (685)

aphros—Greek, "foam." (581)

apostle—Greek, "messenger." One of the 12 disciples of Jesus. (417)

apse—A recess, usually semicircular, in the wall of a building, commonly found at the east end of a *church.* (424)

arcade—A series of *arches* supported by *piers* or *columns.* (424)

Arcadian (adj.)—In Renaissance and later art, depictions of an idyllic place of rural peace and simplicity. Derived from Arcadia, an ancient district of the central Peloponnesos in southern Greece. (650)

arch—A curved structural member that spans an opening and is generally composed of wedge-shaped blocks (*voussoirs*) that transmit the downward pressure laterally. See also *thrust.* (412)

architrave—The *lintel* or lowest division of the *entablature;* also called the epistyle. (669)

arcuated—*Arch*-shaped. (14-9A, 20-6A)

armature—The crossed, or diagonal, *arches* that form the skeletal framework of a *Gothic rib vault.* In sculpture, the framework for a clay form. (11)

arriccio—In *fresco* painting, the first layer of rough lime plaster applied to the wall. (419)

ashlar masonry—Carefully cut and regularly shaped blocks of stone used in construction, fitted together without mortar. (607)

atmospheric perspective—See *perspective.* (586, 20-11A, 20-11B)

atrium (pl. **atria**)—The central reception room of a Roman domus that is partly open to the sky. Also, the open, *colonnaded* court in front of and attached to a Christian *basilica.* (704)

attribute—(n.) The distinctive identifying aspect of a person—for example, an object held, an associated animal, or a mark on the body. (v.) To make an *attribution.* (5)

attribution—Assignment of a work to a maker or makers. (6)

bacchanal—An orgiastic revel in which the followers of the Greco-Roman god Bacchus take part. (654)

baldacchino—A canopy on *columns,* frequently built over an altar. The term derives from *baldacco.* (704)

baldacco—Italian, "silk from Baghdad." See *baldacchino.* (704)

baldric—A sashlike belt worn over one shoulder and across the chest to support a sword. (24-30A)

Baroque/baroque—The traditional blanket designation for European art from 1600 to 1750. Uppercase *Baroque* refers to the art of this period, which features dramatic theatricality and elaborate ornamentation in contrast to the simplicity and orderly rationality of *Renaissance* art, and is most appropriately applied to Italian art. Lowercase *baroque* describes similar stylistic features found in the art of other periods—for example, the Hellenistic period in ancient Greece. The term derives from *barroco.* (702)

barrel vault—See *vault.* (606)

barroco—Portuguese, "irregularly shaped pearl." See *Baroque.* (702)

basilica (adj. **basilican**)—In Roman architecture, a public building for legal and other civic proceedings, rectangular in plan, with an entrance usually on a long side. In Christian architecture, a *church* somewhat resembling the Roman basilica, usually entered from one end and with an *apse* at the other. (424, 604)

bas-relief—See *relief.* (12)

battlement—A low parapet at the top of a circuit wall in a fortification. (427)

bay—The space between two *columns,* or one unit in the *nave arcade* of a *church;* also, the passageway in an *arcuated* gate. (424)

belvedere—Italian, "beautiful view." A building or other structure with a view of a *landscape* or seascape. (648)

Bharat Mata—Mother India; the female personification of India. (1043)

bibliophile—Lover of books. (572)

Book of Hours—A Christian religious book for private devotion containing prayers to be read at specified times of the day. (571)

bosquet—French, "grove." One of the subdivisions within the gardens of the palace at Versailles. (25-28A)

bottega—An artist's studio-shop. (590)

braccia—Italian, "arm." A unit of measurement; 1 braccia equals 23 inches. (604)

breakfast piece—A Dutch *still life* that includes bread and fruit. (736)

breviary—A Christian religious book of selected daily prayers and Psalms. (571)

bucranium (pl. **bucrania**)—Latin, "bovine skull." A common motif in classical architectural ornament. (688)

buon fresco—See *fresco.* (419, 627)

burgomeister—Chief magistrate (mayor) of a Flemish city. (561)

burin—A pointed tool used for *engraving* or *incising.* (578)

bust—A freestanding sculpture of the head, shoulders, and chest of a person. (11)

buttress—An exterior masonry structure that opposes the lateral *thrust* of an *arch* or a *vault.* A pier buttress is a solid mass of masonry. A flying buttress consists typically of an inclined member carried on an arch or a series of arches and a solid buttress to which it transmits lateral thrust. (21-29A, 21-29B)

Byzantine—The art, territory, history, and culture of the Eastern Christian Empire and its capital of Constantinople (ancient Byzantium). (411)

caduceus—See *kerykeion*. (602)

camera obscura—Latin, "dark room." An ancestor of the modern camera in which a tiny pinhole, acting as a lens, projects an image on a screen, the wall of a room, or the ground-glass wall of a box; used by artists in the 17th, 18th, and early 19th centuries as an aid in drawing from nature. (747)

campanile—A bell tower of a *church*, usually, but not always, free-standing. (427)

campo—Italian, "field." (421)

canon—A rule (for example, of proportion). The ancient Greeks considered beauty to be a matter of "correct" proportion and sought a canon of proportion, for the human figure and for buildings. The fifth-century BCE sculptor Polykleitos wrote the *Canon,* a treatise incorporating his formula for the perfectly proportioned *statue.* Also, a *church* official who preaches, teaches, administers sacraments, and tends to pilgrims and the sick. (10)

canonization (adj. **canonized**)—The declaration by the Catholic Church of a person as a *saint* after his or her death, often as a *martyr.* (14-5A)

capital—The uppermost member of a *column,* serving as a transition from the shaft to the *lintel.* In *classical* architecture, the form of the capital varies with the *order.* (412)

capriccio—Italian, "originality." One of several terms used in Italian *Renaissance* literature to praise the originality and talent of artists. (628)

cartoon—In painting, a full-size preliminary drawing from which a painting is made. (419, 626)

carving—A sculptural *technique* in which the artist cuts away material (for example, from a stone block) in order to create a *statue* or a *relief.* (11)

cassone (pl. **cassoni**)—A carved chest, often painted or gilded, popular in *Renaissance* Italy for the storing of household clothing. (655)

casting—A sculptural *technique* in which the artist pours liquid metal, plaster, clay, or another material into a *mold.* When the material dries, the sculptor removes the cast piece from the mold. (11)

cathedral—A bishop's *church.* The word derives from *cathedra,* referring to the bishop's chair. (423)

cella—The chamber at the center of an ancient temple; in a *classical* temple, the room (Greek, *naos*) in which a diety statue usually stood. (643, 688)

central plan—See *plan.* (606)

chancel arch—The arch separating the chancel (the *apse* or *choir*) or the *transept* from the *nave* of a basilica or *church.* (424)

chapter house—The meeting hall in a *monastery.* (605)

chartreuse—A Carthusian *monastery.* (557)

chasing—The engraving or embossing of metal. (705)

château (pl. **châteaux**)—French, "castle." A luxurious country residence for French royalty, developed from medieval castles. (694)

cherub—A chubby winged child angel. (573)

chiaroscuro—In drawing or painting, the treatment and use of light and dark, especially the gradations of light that produce the effect of modeling. (420, 626)

chiaroscuro woodcut—A *woodcut technique* using two blocks of wood instead of one. The printmaker carves and inks one block in the usual way in order to produce a traditional black-and-white print. Then the artist cuts a second block consisting of broad highlights that can be inked in gray or color and printed over the first block's impression. (684)

choir—The space reserved for the clergy and singers in the *church,* usually east of the *transept* but, in some instances, extending into the *nave.* (12)

Christophoros—Greek, "he who carries Christ"—that is, Saint Christopher. (20-21A)

chronology—In art history, the dating of art objects and buildings. (2)

church—Christian house of worship.

Cinquecento—Italian, "500"—that is, the 16th century (the 1500s) in Italy. (623)

circus—An ancient Roman chariot racecourse. (701)

city-state—An independent, self-governing city. (417)

Classical/classical—The art and culture of ancient Greece between 480 and 323 BCE. Lowercase *classical* refers more generally to Greco-Roman art and culture. (412)

clerestory—The windowed (fenestrated) part of a building that rises above the roofs of the other parts. The oldest known clerestories are Egyptian. In Roman *basilicas* and medieval *churches,* clerestories are the windows that form the *nave's* uppermost level below the timber ceiling or the *vaults.* (424, 20-6A)

cloister—A *monastery* courtyard, usually with covered walks or ambulatories along its sides. (597)

collage—A composition made by combining on a flat surface various materials, such as newspaper, wallpaper, printed text and illustrations, photographs, and cloth. (8)

colonnade—A series or row of *columns,* usually spanned by *lintels.*

color—The value, or tonality, of a color is the degree of its lightness or darkness. The intensity, or saturation, of a color is its purity, its brightness or dullness. See also *primary colors, secondary colors,* and *complementary colors.* (7)

colorito—Italian, "colored" or "painted." A term used to describe the application of paint. Characteristic of the work of 16th-century Venetian artists who emphasized the application of paint as an important element of the creative process. Central Italian artists, in contrast, largely emphasized *disegno*—careful design preparation based on preliminary drawing. (651)

colossal order—An architectural design in which the *columns* or *pilasters* are two or more stories tall. Also called a giant order. (618)

column—A vertical, weight-carrying architectural member, circular in cross-*section* and consisting of a base (sometimes omitted), a shaft, and a *capital.* (10, 412, 609)

complementary colors—Those pairs of *colors,* such as red and green, that together embrace the entire *spectrum.* The complement of one of the three *primary colors* is a mixture of the other two. (7)

compline—The last prayer of the day in a *Book of Hours.* (571)

compose—See *composition.* (7)

Composite capital—A capital combining *Ionic* volutes and *Corinthian* acanthus leaves, first used by the ancient Romans. (21-34A)

composition—The way in which an artist organizes *forms* in an artwork, either by placing shapes on a flat surface or arranging forms in space. (7)

compound pier—A *pier* with a group, or cluster, of attached shafts, or responds, especially characteristic of *Gothic* architecture. (14-13A)

condottiere (pl. **condottieri**)—An Italian mercenary general. (582)

confraternity—In Late Antiquity, an association of Christian families pooling funds to purchase property for burial. In late medieval Europe, an organization founded by laypersons who dedicated themselves to strict religious observances. (415)

connoisseur—An expert in *attributing* artworks to one artist rather than another. More generally, an expert on artistic *style.* (6)

continuous narration—The depiction of the same figure more than once in the same space at different stages of a story. (20-11A)

contour line—In art, a continuous *line* defining the outer shape of an object. (7)

contrapposto—The disposition of the human figure in which one part is turned in opposition to another part (usually hips and legs one way, shoulders and chest another), creating a counterpositioning of the body about its central axis. Sometimes called "weight shift" because the weight of the body tends to be thrown to one foot, creating tension on one side and relaxation on the other. (586)

corbel—A projecting wall member used as a support for some element in the superstructure. Also, horizontal rows of stone (courses) or brick in which each course projects beyond the one beneath it. Two such walls, meeting at the topmost course, create a *corbeled arch* or *corbeled vault.* (427, 671)

Corinthian capital—A more ornate form than *Doric* or *Ionic*; it consists of a double row of acanthus leaves from which tendrils and flowers grow, wrapped around a bell-shaped echinus. Although this *capital* is often cited as the distinguishing feature of the Corinthian *order*, in strict terms no such order exists. The Corinthian capital is a substitute for the standard capital used in the Ionic order. (412, 600)

cornice—The projecting, crowning member of the *entablature* framing the *pediment*; also, any crowning projection. (607)

corona civica—Latin, "civic crown." A Roman honorary wreath worn on the head. (7)

cross-hatching—See *hatching*. (578)

crossing—The space in a *cruciform church* formed by the intersection of the *nave* and the *transept*. (14-19A)

crossing square—The area in a *church* formed by the intersection (*crossing*) of a *nave* and a *transept* of equal width, often used as a standard *module* of interior proportion. (21-31A)

cruciform—Cross-shaped. (21-31B)

crypt—A *vaulted* space under part of a building, wholly or partly underground; in *churches*, normally the portion under an *apse*. (14-5A)

cupola—An exterior architectural feature composed of a drum with a shallow cap; a *dome*. (665)

cura animarum—Latin, "care of souls," the duty of a Catholic priest. (642)

Curia—The papal court in the Vatican. (644)

cutaway—An architectural drawing that combines an exterior view with an interior view of part of a building. (12, 629)

di sotto in sù—Italian, "from below upward." A *perspective* view seen from below. (619, 664)

dictator perpetuo—In the Roman Republic, the supreme magistrate with extraordinary powers, appointed during a crisis for a specified period. Julius Caesar eventually became dictator perpetuo, dictator for life. (184–185)

diptych—A two-paneled painting or *altarpiece*; also, an ancient Roman, Early Christian, or Byzantine hinged writing tablet, often of ivory and carved on the external sides. (562)

disegno—Italian, "drawing" and "design." *Renaissance* artists considered drawing to be the external physical manifestation (*disegno esterno*) of an internal intellectual idea of design (*disegno interno*). (628, 651, 713)

divine right—The belief in a king's absolute power as God's will. (750)

documentary evidence—In art history, the examination of written sources in order to determine the date of an artwork, the circumstances of its creation, or the identity of the artist(s) who made it. (2)

doge—Italian (Venetian dialect), "duke." (432, 609)

dome—A hemispherical *vault*; theoretically, an *arch* rotated on its vertical axis. In Mycenaean architecture, domes are beehive-shaped. (14-19A)

donor portrait—A portrait of the individual(s) who commissioned (donated) a religious work (for example, an *altarpiece*) as evidence of devotion. (561)

Doric—One of the two systems (or *orders*) invented in ancient Greece for articulating the three units of the *elevation* of a *classical* building—the platform, the *colonnade*, and the superstructure (*entablature*). The Doric order is characterized by, among other features, *capitals* with funnel-shaped echinuses, *columns* without bases, and a *frieze* of *triglyphs* and metopes. See also *Ionic*. (609, 669)

dormer—A projecting gable-capped window. (694)

dressed masonry—Stone blocks shaped to the exact dimensions required, with smooth faces for a perfect fit. (607)

drypoint—An *engraving* in which the design, instead of being cut into the plate with a *burin*, is scratched into the surface with a hard steel "pencil." See also *etching, intaglio*. (578)

Duecento—Italian, "200"—that is, the 13th century (the 1200s) in Italy. (412)

duomo—Italian, "cathedral." (428)

edition—A set of impressions taken from a single *incised* metal plate or carved woodblock. (577)

elevation—In architecture, a head-on view of an external or internal wall, showing its features and often other elements that would be visible beyond or before the wall. (12, 424)

enamel—A decorative coating, usually colored, fused onto the surface of metal, glass, or ceramics. (666)

engaged column—A half-round *column* attached to a wall. See also *pilaster*. (609)

engraving—The process of *incising* a design in hard material, often a metal plate (usually copper); also, the *print* or impression made from such a plate. (576, 578)

entablature—The part of a building above the *columns* and below the roof. The entablature has three parts: *architrave, frieze,* and *pediment*.

escutcheon—An emblem bearing a coat of arms. (654)

etching—A kind of *engraving* in which the design is *incised* in a layer of wax or varnish on a metal plate. The parts of the plate left exposed are then etched (slightly eaten away) by the acid in which the plate is immersed after incising. See also *drypoint, intaglio*. (578)

Eucharist—In Christianity, the partaking of the bread and wine, which believers hold to be either Christ himself or symbolic of him. (558)

facade—Usually, the front of a building; also, the other sides when they are emphasized architecturally. (424)

fantasia—Italian, "imagination." One of several terms used in Italian *Renaissance* literature to praise the originality and talent of artists. (628)

fenestra coeli—Latin, "window to Heaven." (721)

feudalism—The medieval political, social, and economic system held together by the relationship between landholding liege lords and the vassals who were granted tenure of a portion of their land and in turn swore allegiance to the liege lord. (556)

fidere—Latin, "to trust." (562)

finial—A crowning ornament. (562)

fleur-de-lis—A three-petaled iris flower; the royal flower of France. (735)

florin—The denomination of gold coin of *Renaissance* Florence that became an international currency for trade. (428)

flying buttress—See *buttress*. (12, 20-6A)

fons vitae—Latin, "fountain of life." A symbolic fountain of everlasting life. (558)

foreshortening (adj. **foreshortened**)—The use of *perspective* to represent in art the apparent visual contraction of an object that extends back in space at an angle to the perpendicular plane of sight. (9, 411)

form—In art, an object's shape and structure, either in two dimensions (for example, a figure painted on a surface) or in three dimensions (such as a *statue*). (7)

formal analysis—The visual analysis of artistic *form*. (7)

freestanding sculpture—See *sculpture in the round*. (11)

fresco—Painting on lime plaster, either dry (dry fresco, or fresco secco) or wet (true, or buon, fresco). In the latter method, the pigments are mixed with water and become chemically bound to the freshly laid lime plaster. Also, a painting executed in either method. (419)

fresco secco—See *fresco*. (419, 627)

frieze—The part of the *entablature* between the *architrave* and the *cornice*; also, any sculptured or painted band. (669)

genius—Latin, "spirit." In art, the personified spirit of a person or place. (22-52A)

genre—A *style* or category of art; also, a kind of painting that realistically depicts scenes from everyday life. (5, 572, 688)

gesso—Plaster mixed with a binding material, used as the base coat for paintings on wood panels. (566, 21-28A)

giant order—See *colossal order*. (618)

gigantomachy—In ancient Greek mythology, the battle between gods and giants. (670)

giornata (pl. **giornate**)—Italian, "day." The section of plaster that a *fresco* painter expects to complete in one session. (419)

glaze—A vitreous coating applied to pottery to seal and decorate the surface; it may be colored, transparent, or opaque, and glossy or *matte*. In *oil painting*, a thin, transparent, or semitransparent layer applied over a *color* to alter it slightly. (559, 606)

glazing—The application of successive layers of *glaze* in *oil painting*. (559)

gold leaf—Gold beaten into tissue-paper-thin sheets that then can be applied to surfaces. (416)

Gothic—Originally a derogatory term named after the Goths, used to describe the history, culture, and art of western Europe in the 12th to 14th centuries. Typically divided into periods designated Early (1140–1194), High (1194–1300), and Late (1300–1500). (412, 558)

Greek cross—A cross with four arms of equal length. (646, 709)

grisaille—A *monochrome* painting done mainly in neutral grays to simulate sculpture. (420, 640, 20-9A)

groin vault—See *vault*. (14-13A)

guild—An association of merchants, craftspersons, or scholars in medieval and *Renaissance* Europe. (422, 555)

halo—An aureole appearing around the head of a holy figure to signify divinity. (416)

harpies—Mythological creatures of the underworld. (22-8A)

hatching—A series of closely spaced drawn or *engraved* parallel *lines*. Cross-hatching employs sets of lines placed at right angles. (578, 20-21A)

hierarchy of scale—An artistic convention in which greater size indicates greater importance. (11, 14-16A)

high relief—See *relief*. (12)

horizon line—See *perspective*. (567, 587)

hue—The name of a *color*. See also *primary colors, secondary colors,* and *complementary colors*. (7)

humanism—In the *Renaissance,* an emphasis on education and on expanding knowledge (especially of *classical* antiquity), the exploration of individual potential and a desire to excel, and a commitment to civic responsibility and moral duty. (418)

icon—A portrait or image; especially in *Byzantine churches,* a panel with a painting of sacred personages that are objects of veneration. In the visual arts, a painting, a piece of sculpture, or even a building regarded as an object of veneration. (416)

iconoclasm—The destruction of religious or sacred images. In Byzantium, the period from 726 to 843 when there was an imperial ban on such images. The destroyers of images were known as iconoclasts. Those who opposed such a ban were known as iconophiles. (564, 681)

iconography—Greek, the "writing of images." The term refers both to the content, or subject, of an artwork and to the study of content in art. It also includes the study of the symbolic, often religious, meaning of objects, persons, or events depicted in works of art. (5)

ikegobo—A Benin royal shrine. (10)

Il Magnifico—Italian, "the magnificent one," the epithet of Lorenzo de' Medici. (581)

illuminated manuscript—A luxurious handmade book with painted illustrations and decorations. (416)

illusionism (adj. **illusionistic**)—The representation of the three-dimensional world on a two-dimensional surface in a manner that creates the illusion that the person, object, or place represented is three-dimensional. See also *perspective*. (8, 419)

impasto—A layer of thickly applied pigment. (658)

impost block—The uppermost block of a wall or *pier* beneath the *springing* of an *arch*. (605)

incise—To cut into a surface with a sharp instrument, especially to decorate metal and pottery. (578)

indulgence—A religious pardon for a sin committed. (641, 680)

ingegno—Italian, "innate talent." One of several terms used in Italian *Renaissance* literature to praise the originality and talent of artists. (628)

intaglio—A graphic *technique* in which the design is *incised,* or scratched, on a metal plate, either manually (*engraving, drypoint*) or chemically (*etching*). The incised lines of the design take the ink, making this the reverse of the *woodcut technique*. (578)

intensity—See *color*. (7)

internal evidence—In art history, the examination of what an artwork represents (people, clothing, hairstyles, and so on) in order to determine its date. Also, the examination of the *style* of an artwork to identify the artist who created it. (3)

International Gothic—A *style* of 14th- and 15th-century painting begun by Simone Martini, who fused the French *Gothic* manner with Sienese art. This style appealed to the aristocracy because of its brilliant *color,* lavish costumes, intricate ornamentation, and themes involving splendid processions of knights and ladies. (424, 593)

intonaco—In *fresco* painting, the last layer of smooth lime plaster applied to the wall; the painting layer. (419)

invenzione—Italian, "invention." One of several terms used in Italian *Renaissance* literature to praise the originality and talent of artists. (628, 713)

Ionic—One of the two systems (or orders) invented in ancient Greece for articulating the three units of the elevation of a classical building: the platform, the colonnade, and the superstructure (*entablature*). The Ionic order is characterized by, among other features, volutes, *capitals, columns* with bases, and an uninterrupted *frieze*.

kerykeion—In ancient Greek mythology, a serpent-entwined herald's rod (Latin, *caduceus*), the attribute of Hermes (Roman Mercury), the messenger of the gods. (602)

key block—In the production of *chiaroscuro woodcuts,* the block that carries the linear design. (684)

keystone—See *voussoir*. (669)

king's gallery—The band of *statues* running the full width of the *facade* of a *Gothic cathedral* directly above the *rose window*. (424)

lancet—In *Gothic* architecture, a tall narrow window ending in a *pointed arch*. (558, 14-5A)

landscape—A picture showing natural scenery, without narrative content. (5, 428)

Landschaft—German, "landscape." (691)

lantern—A small towerlike structure, usually with windows, capping the top of a *dome* to stabilize the dome and admit light to the interior. (711, 21-29A, 21-29B)

lateral section—See *section*. (12)

laudatio—Latin, "essay of praise." (591)

line—The extension of a point along a path, made concrete in art by drawing on or chiseling into a *plane*. (7)

linear perspective—See *perspective*. (567, 587, 588)

lintel—A horizontal beam used to span an opening.

loggia—A gallery with an open *arcade* or a *colonnade* on one or both sides. (597, 14-20A)

longitudinal plan—See *plan*. (606)

longitudinal section—See *section*. (12)

lost-wax process—A bronze-*casting* method in which a figure is modeled in wax and covered with clay; the whole is fired, melting away the wax (French, *cire perdue*) and hardening the clay, which then becomes a *mold* for molten metal. Also called the cire perdue process. (705)

low relief—See *relief*. (12)

lunette—A semicircular area (with the flat side down) in a wall over a door, niche, or window; also, a painting or *relief* with a semicircular frame. (571)

machicolated gallery—A gallery in a defensive tower with holes in the floor to allow stones or hot liquids to be dumped on enemies below. (427)

magus (pl. **magi**)—One of the three wise men from the East who presented gifts to the infant Jesus. (594)

maniera—Italian, "style" or "manner." See *Mannerism*. (659, 713)

maniera greca—Italian, "Greek manner." The Italo-*Byzantine* painting *style* of the 13th century. (415, 636)

Mannerism—A *style* of later *Renaissance* art that emphasized "artifice," often involving contrived imagery not derived directly from nature. Such artworks showed a self-conscious stylization involving complexity, caprice, fantasy, and polish. Mannerist architecture tended to flout the *classical* rules of order, stability, and symmetry, sometimes to the point of parody. (624, 658)

mano—Italian, "hand." (658)

martyr—A person who chooses to die rather than deny his or her religious belief. See also *saint*.

martyrium (pl. **martyria**)—A shrine to a Christian *martyr*. (645)

mass—The bulk, density, and weight of matter in *space*. (8)

Mass—The Catholic and Orthodox ritual in which believers understand that Christ's redeeming sacrifice on the cross is repeated when the priest consecrates the bread and wine in the *Eucharist*. (558)

matins—In Christianity, early morning prayers. (571)

matte—In painting, pottery, and photography, a dull finish. (558)

maulstick—A stick used to steady the hand while painting. (689)

mausoleum (pl. **mausolea**)—A monumental tomb. The name derives from the mid-fourth-century BCE tomb of Mausolos at Halikarnassos, one of the Seven Wonders of the ancient world. (557)

medium (pl. **media**)—The material (for example, marble, bronze, clay, *fresco*) in which an artist works; also, in painting, the vehicle (usually liquid) that carries the pigment. (7)

mela medica—Italian, "medicinal apples" (oranges). The emblem of the Medici family of *Renaissance* Florence. (601)

memento mori—Latin, "reminder of death." In painting, a reminder of human mortality, usually represented by a skull. (748)

mendicants—In medieval Europe, friars belonging to the Franciscan and Dominican orders, who renounced all worldly goods, lived by contributions of laypersons (the word *mendicant* means "beggar"), and devoted themselves to preaching, teaching, and doing good works. (415)

module (adj. **modular**)—A basic unit of which the dimensions of the major parts of a work are multiples. The principle is used in sculpture and other art forms, but it is most often employed in architecture, where the module may be the dimensions of an important part of a building, such as the diameter of a *column*. (10, 604)

mold—A hollow form for *casting*. (11)

monastery—A group of buildings in which monks live together, set apart from the secular community of a town.

monastic order—An organization of monks living according to the same rules. For example, the Benedictine, Franciscan, and Dominican orders. (415)

monochrome (adj. **monochromatic**)—One *color*. (741)

mosque—The Islamic building for collective worship. From the Arabic word *masjid*, meaning a "place for bowing down."

mural—A wall painting. (418)

mystery play—A dramatic enactment of the holy mysteries of the Christian faith, performed at *church* portals and in city squares. (420, 558)

mystic marriage—A spiritual marriage of a woman with Christ. (569)

naturalism (adj. **naturalistic**)—The *style* of painted or sculpted representation based on close observation of the natural world that was at the core of the *classical* tradition. (411)

nave—The central area of an ancient Roman *basilica* or of a *church*, demarcated from *aisles* by *piers* or *columns*. (424)

nave arcade—In *basilica* architecture, the series of *arches* supported by *piers* or *columns* separating the *nave* from the *aisles*. (20-6A)

Neo-Platonism—An ancient school of philosophy based on the ideas of Plato, revived during the *Renaissance* and modified by the teachings of Christianity. (581)

nipote—Italian, "nephew." (21-40A)

nymphs—In *classical* mythology, female divinities of springs, caves, and woods. (581)

obelisk—A tall four-sided monolithic pillar with a pyramidal top—symbolic of the Egyptian sun god Re. (701)

oculus (pl. **oculi**)—Latin, "eye." The round central opening of a *dome*. Also, a small round window in a *Gothic cathedral*. (605, 619, 14-5B)

ogee arch—An *arch* composed of two double-curving lines meeting at a point. (432)

ogive (adj. **ogival**)—The diagonal *rib* of a *Gothic vault*; a pointed, or Gothic, *arch*. (413, 21-29A, 21-29B)

oil painting—A painting *technique* using oil-based pigments that rose to prominence in northern Europe in the 15th century and is now the standard medium for painting on canvas. (558)

order—In *classical* architecture, a *style* represented by a characteristic design of the *columns* and *entablature*. See also *superimposed orders*.

orthogonal—A line imagined to be behind and perpendicular to the picture *plane*; the orthogonals in a painting appear to recede toward a *vanishing point* on the horizon. (567, 587)

paintrix—Latin, "woman painter." (690)

palazzo (pl. **palazzi**)—Italian, "palace." (606)

palazzo pubblico—Italian, "public palace." City hall. (426)

palmette—A *classical* decorative motif in the form of stylized palm leaves. (609)

parallel hatching—See *hatching*. (578)

parapet—A low, protective wall along the edge of a balcony, roof, or bastion. (427)

parchment—Lambskin prepared as a surface for painting or writing. (628)

pastel—A powdery paste of pigment and gum used for making crayons; also, the pastel crayons themselves.

pediment—In *classical* architecture, the triangular space (gable) at the end of a building, formed by the ends of the sloping roof above the *colonnade*; also, an ornamental feature having this shape. (604)

pendentive—A concave, triangular section of a hemisphere, four of which provide the transition from a square area to the circular base of a covering *dome*. Although pendentives appear to be hanging (pendant) from the dome, they in fact support it. (606)

period style—See *style*. (3)

personal style—See *style*. (4)

personification—An *abstract* idea represented in bodily form. (5, 428)

perspective—A method of presenting an illusion of the three-dimensional world on a two-dimensional surface. In linear perspective, the most common type, all parallel lines or surface edges converge on one, two, or three vanishing points located with reference to the eye level of the viewer (the horizon line of the picture), and associated objects are rendered smaller the farther from the viewer they are intended to seem. Atmospheric, or aerial, perspective creates the illusion of distance by the greater diminution of *color* intensity, the shift in color toward an almost neutral blue, and the blurring of contours as the intended distance between eye and object increases. (8, 417, 587)

physical evidence—In art history, the examination of the materials used to produce an artwork in order to determine its date. (2)

piano nobile—Italian, "noble floor." The main (second) floor of a building. (610)

piazza—Italian, "plaza." (421)

picturesque garden—An "unordered" garden designed in accord with the Enlightenment taste for the natural. (25-28A)

pier—A vertical, freestanding masonry support. (12)

Pietà—A painted or sculpted representation of the Virgin Mary mourning over the body of the dead Christ. (565)

pilaster—A flat, rectangular, vertical member projecting from a wall of which it forms a part. It usually has a base and a *capital* and is often fluted. (564, 592)

pinnacle—In *Gothic churches*, a sharply pointed ornament capping the *piers* or flying *buttresses*; also used on *church facades*. (421, 424)

pittura—Italian, "painting. (717)

plan—The horizontal arrangement of the parts of a building or of the buildings and streets of a city or town, or a drawing or diagram showing such an arrangement. In an axial plan, the parts of a building are organized longitudinally, or along a given axis; in a central plan, the parts of the structure are of equal or almost equal dimensions around the center. (12)

plane—A flat surface. (7)

Plateresque—A *style* of Spanish architecture characterized by elaborate decoration based on *Gothic*, Italian *Renaissance*, and Islamic sources; derived from the Spanish word *platero*, meaning "silversmith." (695)

platero—See *Plateresque*. (695)

poesia—A term describing "poetic" art, notably Venetian *Renaissance* painting, which emphasizes the lyrical and sensual. (652)

pointed arch—A narrow *arch* of pointed profile, in contrast to a semicircular arch. (3, 432)

polychrome—Multicolored. (722)

polyptych—An *altarpiece* composed of more than three sections. (558)

portico—A roofed *colonnade*; also an entrance porch. (597)

predella—The narrow ledge on which an *altarpiece* rests on an altar. (421)

prefiguration—In Early Christian art, the depiction of Old Testament persons and events as prophetic forerunners of Christ and New Testament events. (569, 583)

primary colors—Red, yellow, and blue—the *colors* from which all other colors may be derived. (7)

print—An artwork on paper, usually produced in multiple impressions. (577)

proportion—The relationship in size of the parts of persons, buildings, or objects, often based on a *module*. (10)

proscenium—The part of a theatrical stage in front of the curtain. (707)

provenance—Origin or source; findspot. (3)

psalter—A book containing the Psalms. (571)

pulpit—A raised platform in a *church* or *mosque* on which a priest or imam stands while leading the religious service. (412)

punchwork—Tooled decorative work in *gold leaf*. (423)

putto (pl. **putti**)—A cherubic young boy. (592)

quadrifrons—Latin, "four-fronted." An *arch* with four equal *facades* and four *arcuated bays*. (23-23A)

quadro riportato—A ceiling design in which painted scenes are arranged in panels that resemble framed pictures transferred to the surface of a shallow, curved *vault*. (712)

quatrefoil—A shape or *plan* in which the parts assume the form of a cloverleaf. (430)

Quattrocento—Italian, "400"—that is, the 15th century (the 1400s) in Italy. (581)

quoins—The large, sometimes *rusticated*, usually slightly projecting stones that often form the corners of the exterior walls of masonry buildings. (646)

refectory—The dining hall of a Christian *monastery*. (597)

regional style—See *style*. (3)

relief—In sculpture, figures projecting from a background of which they are part. The degree of relief is designated high, low (bas), or sunken. In the last, the artist cuts the design into the surface so that the highest projecting parts of the image are no higher than the surface itself. (12, 577)

relief sculpture—See *relief*. (11)

Renaissance—French, "rebirth." The term used to describe the history, culture, and art of 14th- through 16th-century western Europe during which artists consciously revived the *classical* style. (411, 418)

renovatio—Latin, "renewal." During the Carolingian period, Charlemagne sought to revive the culture of ancient Rome (*renovatio imperii Romani*). (412)

renovatio imperii Romani—See *renovatio*. (412)

retable—An architectural screen or wall above and behind an altar, usually containing painting, sculpture, or other decorations. See also *altarpiece*. (558)

retablo—Spanish, "altarpiece." (723)

revetment—In architecture, a wall covering or facing. (420)

rib—A relatively slender, molded masonry arch that projects from a surface. In *Gothic* architecture, the ribs form the framework of the *vaulting*. A diagonal rib is one of the ribs that form the X of a *groin vault*. A transverse rib crosses the *nave* or *aisle* at a 90-degree angle.

rib vault—A *vault* in which the diagonal and transverse *ribs* compose a structural skeleton that partially supports the masonry web between them. (14-5A)

Romanesque—"Roman-like." A term used to describe the history, culture, and art of medieval western Europe from ca. 1050 to ca. 1200. (424, 558, 21-36A)

rose window—A circular *stained-glass* window. (424)

rotunda—The circular area under a *dome*; also, a domed round building. (558)

roundel—See *tondo*. (606)

rustication (adj. **rusticated**)—To give a rustic appearance by roughening the surfaces and beveling the edges of stone blocks to emphasize the joints between them. Rustication is a *technique* employed in ancient Roman architecture, and was also popular during the *Renaissance*, especially for stone courses at the ground-floor level. (607, 14-9B)

sacra conversazione—Italian, "holy conversation." A style of *altarpiece* painting popular after the middle of the 15th century, in which *saints* from different epochs are joined in a unified space and seem to be conversing either with one another or with the audience. (650)

sacra rappresentazione (pl. **sacre rappresentazioni**)—Italian, "holy representation." A more elaborate version of a *mystery play* performed for a lay audience by a *confraternity*. (420)

saint—From the Latin word *sanctus*, meaning "made holy by God." Applied to persons who suffered and died for their Christian faith or who merited reverence for their Christian devotion while alive. In the Roman Catholic Church, a worthy deceased Catholic who is canonized by the pope. (412)

sapienza—Italian, "knowledge" or "wisdom." (710)

sarcophagus (pl. **sarcophagi**)—Greek, "consumer of flesh." A coffin, usually of stone. (413)

saturation—See *color*. (7)

satyr—A Greek mythological follower of Dionysos having a man's upper body, a goat's hindquarters and horns, and a horse's ears and tail. (28-32A)

school—A chronological and stylistic classification of works of art with a stipulation of place. (6)

scriptorium (pl. **scriptoria**)—The writing studio of a *monastery*. (577, 20-21A)

scudo (pl. **scudi**)—Italian, "shield." A coin denomination in 17th-century Italy. (716)

sculpture in the round—Freestanding figures, *carved* or modeled in three dimensions. (11)

secco—Italian, "dry." See also *fresco*. (419, 627)

secondary colors—Orange, green, and purple, obtained by mixing pairs of *primary colors* (red, yellow, blue). (7)

section—In architecture, a diagram or representation of a part of a structure or building along an imaginary *plane* that passes through it vertically. Drawings showing a theoretical slice across a structure's width are lateral sections. Those cutting through a building's length are longitudinal sections. See also *elevation* and *cutaway*. (12)

segmental pediment—A *pediment* with a curved instead of a triangular *cornice*. (646)

sfumato—Italian, "smoky." A smokelike haziness that subtly softens outlines in painting; particularly applied to the paintings of Leonardo da Vinci and Correggio. (559, 629)

sibyl—A Greco-Roman mythological prophetess. (562, 639, 22-18A)

signoria—Italian, "lordship." The governing body of medieval and *Renaissance* Florence. (14-9B)

silverpoint—A *stylus* made of silver, used in drawing in the 14th and 15th centuries because of the fine *line* it produced and the sharp point it maintained. (555)

sinopia—A burnt-orange pigment used in *fresco* painting to transfer a *cartoon* to the *arriccio* before the artist paints the plaster. (419)

space—In art history, both the actual area that an object occupies or a building encloses and the *illusionistic* representation of space in painting and sculpture. (8)

spectrum—The range or band of visible *colors* in natural light. (7)

stadium—An ancient Roman long and narrow theater-like structure for footraces and other athletic contests. (701)

stained glass—In *Gothic* architecture, the colored glass used for windows. (12, 14-5A, 20-6A)

stanza (pl. **stanze**)—Italian, "room." (630)

statue—A three-dimensional sculpture. (11)

stigmata—In Christian art, the wounds Christ received at his crucifixion that miraculously appear on the body of a *saint*. (416, 612)

still life—A picture depicting an arrangement of inanimate objects. (5, 721)

stretcher bar—One of a set of wood bars used to stretch canvas to provide a taut surface for painting. (564)

stringcourse—A raised horizontal *molding,* or band, in masonry. Its principal use is ornamental, but it usually reflects interior structure. (607)

style—A distinctive artistic manner. Period style is the characteristic style of a specific time. Regional style is the style of a particular geographical area. Personal style is an individual artist's unique manner. (3, 658)

stylistic evidence—In art history, the examination of the *style* of an artwork in order to determine its date or the identity of the artist. (3)

stylobate—The uppermost course of the platform of a *classical* Greek temple, which supports the *columns.* (643)

stylus—A needlelike tool used in *engraving* and *incising*; also, an ancient writing instrument used to inscribe clay or wax tablets. (555, 578)

subtractive light—The painter's light in art; the light reflected from pigments and objects. See also *additive light.* (7)

subtractive sculpture—A kind of sculpture *technique* in which materials are taken away from the original mass; *carving.* (11)

superimposed orders—*Orders* of architecture that are placed one above another in an *arcaded* or *colonnaded* building, usually in the following sequence: *Doric* or *Tuscan* (the first story), *Ionic,* and *Corinthian.* Superimposed orders are found in later Greek architecture and were used widely by Roman and *Renaissance* builders. (696)

symbol—An image that stands for another image or encapsulates an idea. (5)

technique—The processes artists employ to create *form,* as well as the distinctive, personal ways in which they handle their materials and tools. (7)

tempera—A *technique* of painting using pigment mixed with egg yolk, glue, or casein; also, the *medium* itself. (415, 558, 559)

tenebrism—Painting in the "shadowy manner," using violent contrasts of light and dark, as in the work of Caravaggio. The term derives from *tenebroso.* (715)

tenebroso—Italian, "shadowy." See *tenebrism.* (715)

terminus ante quem—Latin, "point [date] before which." (2)

terminus post quem—Latin, "point [date] after which." (2)

terracotta—Hard-baked clay, used for sculpture and as a building material. It may be *glazed* or painted. (426, 606)

terribilità—Italian, "the sublime shadowed by the fearful." A term used to describe Michelangelo Buonarroti. (623)

texture—The quality of a surface (rough, smooth, hard, soft, shiny, dull) as revealed by light. In represented texture, a painter depicts an object as having a certain texture even though the *pigment* is the real texture. (8)

tholos (pl. **tholoi**)—A temple with a circular plan. Also, the burial chamber of a tholos tomb. (643)

thrust—The outward force exerted by an *arch* or a *vault* that must be counterbalanced by a *buttress.* (21-29A, 21-29B)

tonality—See *color.* (7)

tondo (pl. **tondi**)—A circular painting or *relief* sculpture. (592)

tone block—In the production of *chiaroscuro woodcuts,* the block that carries the coloring. (684)

tracery—Ornamental stonework for holding *stained glass* in place, characteristic of *Gothic cathedrals.* In plate tracery, the glass fills only the "punched holes" in the heavy ornamental stonework.

In bar tracery, the stained-glass windows fill almost the entire opening, and the stonework is unobtrusive. (425, 558)

tramezzo—A screen placed across the *nave* of a *church* to separate the clergy from the lay audience. (14-5B)

transept—The part of a *church* with an axis that crosses the *nave* at a right angle. (586, 14-5A)

transubstantiation—The transformation of the Eucharistic bread and wine into the body and blood of Christ. (24-18B)

Trecento—Italian, "300"—that is, the 14th century (the 1300s) in Italy. (417)

trefoil arch—A triple-lobed arch. (412)

trident—The three-pronged pitchfork associated with the ancient Greek sea god Poseidon (Roman Neptune). (688)

triforium—In a *Gothic cathedral,* the blind arcaded gallery below the *clerestory*; occasionally, the *arcades* are filled with *stained glass.* (20-6A)

triglyph—A triple projecting, grooved member of a *Doric frieze* that alternates with metopes. (669)

triptych—A three-paneled painting, ivory plaque, or *altarpiece.* Also, a small, portable shrine with hinged wings used for private devotion. (425)

triumphal arch—In Roman architecture, a freestanding *arch* commemorating an important event, such as a military victory or the opening of a new road. (596)

trompe l'oeil—French, "fools the eye." A form of *illusionistic* painting that aims to deceive viewers into believing that they are seeing real objects rather than a representation of those objects. (619, 669, 24-14A)

true fresco—See *fresco.* (419)

trumeau—In *church* architecture, the pillar or center post supporting the lintel in the middle of the doorway. (20-2A)

Tuscan column—The standard type of Etruscan *column.* It resembles ancient Greek *Doric* columns but is made of wood, is unfluted, and has a base. Also a popular motif in *Renaissance* and *Baroque* architecture. (609, 643, 704)

tympanum (pl. **tympana**)—The space enclosed by a lintel and an *arch* over a doorway. (614, 14-13A, 22-52A)

value—See *color.* (7)

vanishing point—See *perspective.* (567, 587)

vanitas—Latin, "vanity." A term describing paintings (particularly 17th-century Dutch *still lifes*) that include references to death. (683, 748)

vault (adj. **vaulted**)—A masonry roof or ceiling constructed on the *arch* principle, or a concrete roof of the same shape. A barrel (or tunnel) vault, semicylindrical in cross-*section,* is in effect a deep arch or an uninterrupted series of arches, one behind the other, over an oblong space. A quadrant vault is a half-barrel vault. A groin (or cross) vault is formed at the point at which two barrel vaults intersect at right angles. In a ribbed vault, there is a framework of *ribs* or arches under the intersections of the vaulting sections. A sexpartite vault is one whose ribs divide the vault into six compartments. A fan vault is a vault characteristic of English Perpendicular *Gothic* architecture, in which radiating ribs form a fanlike pattern. (12)

vellum—Calfskin prepared as a surface for writing or painting. (628)

vita—Italian, "life." Also, the title of a biography. (713)

volume—The *space* that *mass* organizes, divides, or encloses. (8)

voussoir—A wedge-shaped stone block used in the construction of a true *arch.* The central voussoir, which sets the arch, is called the *keystone.* (669)

weld—To join metal parts by heating, as in assembling the separate parts of a *statue* made by *casting.* (11)

woodcut—A wood block on the surface of which those parts not intended to *print* are cut away to a slight depth, leaving the design raised; also, the printed impression made with such a block. (576, 577)

Bibliography

This list of books is very selective, but comprehensive enough to satisfy the reading interests of the beginning art history student and general reader. Significantly expanded from the previous edition, the 15th edition bibliography can also serve as the basis for undergraduate research papers. The resources listed range from works that are valuable primarily for their reproductions to those that are scholarly surveys of schools and periods or monographs on individual artists. The emphasis is on recent in-print books and on books likely to be found in college and municipal libraries. No entries for periodical articles appear, but the bibliography begins with a list of some of the major journals that publish art historical scholarship in English.

Selected Periodicals

African Arts
American Art
American Indian Art
American Journal of Archaeology
Antiquity
Archaeology
Archives of American Art
Archives of Asian Art
Ars Orientalis
Art Bulletin
Art History
Art in America
Art Journal
Artforum International
Artnews
Burlington Magazine
Gesta
History of Photography
Journal of Egyptian Archaeology
Journal of Roman Archaeology
Journal of the Society of Architectural Historians
Journal of the Warburg and Courtauld Institutes
Latin American Antiquity
October
Oxford Art Journal
Women's Art Journal

General Studies

Baxandall, Michael. *Patterns of Intention: On the Historical Explanation of Pictures.* New Haven, Conn.: Yale University Press, 1985.

Bindman, David, ed. *The Thames & Hudson Encyclopedia of British Art.* London: Thames & Hudson, 1988.

Boström, Antonia. *The Encyclopedia of Sculpture.* 3 vols. London: Routledge, 2003.

Broude, Norma, and Mary D. Garrard, eds. *The Expanding Discourse: Feminism and Art History.* New York: Harper Collins, 1992.

Bryson, Norman. *Vision and Painting: The Logic of the Gaze.* New Haven, Conn.: Yale University Press, 1983.

Bryson, Norman, Michael Ann Holly, and Keith Moxey. *Visual Theory: Painting and Interpretation.* New York: Cambridge University Press, 1991.

Burden, Ernest. *Illustrated Dictionary of Architecture.* 2d ed. New York: McGraw-Hill, 2002.

Büttner, Nils. *Landscape Painting: A History.* New York: Abbeville, 2006.

Carrier, David. *A World Art History and Its Objects.* University Park: Pennsylvania State University Press, 2012.

Chadwick, Whitney. *Women, Art, and Society.* 5th ed. New York: Thames & Hudson, 2012.

Cheetham, Mark A., Michael Ann Holly, and Keith Moxey, eds. *The Subjects of Art History: Historical Objects in Contemporary Perspective.* New York: Cambridge University Press, 1998.

Chilvers, Ian, and Harold Osborne, eds. *The Oxford Dictionary of Art.* 3d ed. New York: Oxford University Press, 2004.

Ching, Francis D. K., Mark Jarzombek, and Vikramaditya Prakash. *A Global History of Architecture.* 2d ed. Hoboken, NJ: Wiely, 2010.

Corbin, George A. *Native Arts of North America, Africa, and the South Pacific: An Introduction.* New York: Harper Collins, 1988.

Crouch, Dora P., and June G. Johnson. *Traditions in Architecture: Africa, America, Asia, and Oceania.* New York: Oxford University Press, 2000.

Curl, James Stevens. *Oxford Dictionary of Architecture and Landscape Architecture.* 2d ed. New York: Oxford University Press, 2006.

Davis, Whitney. *A General Theory of Visual Culture.* Princeton, N.J.: Princeton University Press, 2011.

Duby, Georges, ed. *Sculpture: From Antiquity to the Present.* 2 vols. Cologne: Taschen, 1999.

Encyclopedia of World Art. 17 vols. New York: McGraw-Hill, 1959–1987.

Evers, Bernd, and Christof Thoenes. *Architectural Theory from the Renaissance to the Present.* Cologne: Taschen, 2011.

Fielding, Mantle. *Dictionary of American Painters, Sculptors, and Engravers.* 2d ed. Poughkeepsie, N.Y.: Apollo, 1986.

Fine, Sylvia Honig. *Women and Art: A History of Women Painters and Sculptors from the Renaissance to the 20th Century.* Rev. ed. Montclair, N.J.: Alanheld & Schram, 1978.

Fleming, John, Hugh Honour, and Nikolaus Pevsner. *The Penguin Dictionary of Architecture and Landscape Architecture.* 5th ed. New York: Penguin, 2000.

Frazier, Nancy. *The Penguin Concise Dictionary of Art History.* New York: Penguin, 2000.

Freedberg, David. *The Power of Images: Studies in the History and Theory of Response.* Chicago: University of Chicago Press, 1989.

Gaze, Delia, ed. *Dictionary of Women Artists.* 2 vols. London: Routledge, 1997.

Hall, James. *Dictionary of Subjects and Symbols in Art.* 2d ed. Boulder, Colo.: Westview, 2008.

Harris, Anne Sutherland, and Linda Nochlin. *Women Artists: 1550–1950.* Los Angeles: Los Angeles County Museum of Art; New York: Knopf, 1977.

Hauser, Arnold. *The Sociology of Art.* Chicago: University of Chicago Press, 1982.

Hults, Linda C. *The Print in the Western World: An Introductory History.* Madison: University of Wisconsin Press, 1996.

Ingersoll, Richard, and Spiro Kostof. *World Architecture: A Cross-Cultural History.* New York: Oxford University Press, 2012.

Kemp, Martin. *The Science of Art: Optical Themes in Western Art from Brunelleschi to Seurat.* New Haven, Conn.: Yale University Press, 1990.

Kirkham, Pat, and Susan Weber, eds. *History of Design: Decorative Arts and Material Culture, 1400–2000.* New Haven, Conn.: Yale University Press, 2013.

Kostof, Spiro, and Gregory Castillo. *A History of Architecture: Settings and Rituals.* 2d ed. Oxford: Oxford University Press, 1995.

Kultermann, Udo. *The History of Art History.* New York: Abaris, 1993.

Le Fur, Yves, ed. *Musée du Quai Branly: The Collection. Art from Africa, Asia, Oceania, and the Americas.* Paris: Flammarion, 2009.

Lucie-Smith, Edward. *The Thames & Hudson Dictionary of Art Terms.* 2d ed. New York: Thames & Hudson, 2004.

Moffett, Marian, Michael Fazio, and Lawrence Wadehouse. 3d ed. *A World History of Architecture.* London: Laurence King, 2013.

Morgan, Anne Lee. *Oxford Dictionary of American Art and Artists.* New York: Oxford University Press, 2008.

Murray, Peter, and Linda Murray. *The Penguin Dictionary of Art and Artists.* 7th ed. New York: Penguin, 1998.

Nelson, Robert S., and Richard Shiff, eds. *Critical Terms for Art History*. Chicago: University of Chicago Press, 1996.

Pazanelli, Roberta, ed. *The Color of Life: Polychromy in Sculpture from Antiquity to the Present*. Los Angeles: J. Paul Getty Museum, 2008.

Penny, Nicholas. *The Materials of Sculpture*. New Haven, Conn.: Yale University Press, 1993.

Pevsner, Nikolaus. *A History of Building Types*. London: Thames & Hudson, 1987. Reprint of 1979 ed.

———. *An Outline of European Architecture*. 8th ed. Baltimore: Penguin, 1974.

Pierce, James Smith. *From Abacus to Zeus: A Handbook of Art History*. 7th ed. Upper Saddle River, N.J.: Pearson Prentice Hall, 1998.

Placzek, Adolf K., ed. *Macmillan Encyclopedia of Architects*. 4 vols. New York: Macmillan, 1982.

Podro, Michael. *The Critical Historians of Art*. New Haven, Conn.: Yale University Press, 1982.

Pollock, Griselda. *Vision and Difference: Femininity, Feminism, and Histories of Art*. London: Routledge, 1988.

Pregill, Philip, and Nancy Volkman. *Landscapes in History Design and Planning in the Eastern and Western Traditions*. 2d ed. Hoboken, N.J.: Wiley, 1999.

Preziosi, Donald, ed. *The Art of Art History: A Critical Anthology*. New York: Oxford University Press, 1998.

Read, Herbert. *The Thames & Hudson Dictionary of Art and Artists*. Rev. ed. New York: Thames & Hudson, 1994.

Reid, Jane D. *The Oxford Guide to Classical Mythology in the Arts 1300–1990s*. 2 vols. New York: Oxford University Press, 1993.

Rogers, Elizabeth Barlow. *Landscape Design: A Cultural and Architectural History*. New York: Abrams, 2001.

Roth, Leland M. *Understanding Architecture: Its Elements, History, and Meaning*. 2d ed. Boulder, Colo.: Westview, 2006.

Schama, Simon. *The Power of Art*. New York: Ecco, 2006.

Slatkin, Wendy. *Women Artists in History: From Antiquity to the 20th Century*. 4th ed. Upper Saddle River, N.J.: Prentice Hall, 2000.

Squire, Michael. *The Art of the Body: Antiquity and Its Legacy*. New York: Oxford University Press, 2011.

Steer, John, and Antony White. *Atlas of Western Art History: Artists, Sites, and Monuments from Ancient Greece to the Modern Age*. New York: Facts on File, 1994.

Stratton, Arthur. *The Orders of Architecture: Greek, Roman, and Renaissance*. London: Studio, 1986.

Summers, David. *Real Spaces: World Art History and the Rise of Western Modernism*. London: Phaidon, 2003.

Sutcliffe, Antony. *Paris: An Architectural History*. New Haven, Conn.: Yale University Press, 1996.

Sutton, Ian. *Western Architecture: From Ancient Greece to the Present*. New York: Thames & Hudson, 1999.

Trachtenberg, Marvin, and Isabelle Hyman. *Architecture, from Prehistory to Post-Modernism*. 2d ed. Upper Saddle River, N.J.: Prentice Hall, 2003.

Turner, Jane, ed. *The Dictionary of Art*. 34 vols. New ed. New York: Oxford University Press, 2003.

Watkin, David. *A History of Western Architecture*. 5th ed. London: Laurence King, 2011.

Wescoat, Bonna D., and Robert G. Ousterhout, eds. *Architecture of the Sacred: Space, Ritual, and Experience from Classical Greece to Byzantium*. New York: Cambridge University Press, 2012.

West, Shearer. *Portraiture*. New York: Oxford University Press, 2004.

Wittkower, Rudolf. *Sculpture Processes and Principles*. New York: Harper & Row, 1977.

Wren, Linnea H., and Janine M. Carter, eds. *Perspectives on Western Art: Source Documents and Readings from the Ancient Near East through the Middle Ages*. New York: Harper & Row, 1987.

Zijlmans, Kitty, and Wilfried van Damme, eds. *World Art Studies: Exploring Concepts and Approaches*. Amsterdam: Valiz, 2008.

Medieval Art, General

Alexander, Jonathan J. G. *Medieval Illuminators and Their Methods of Work*. New Haven, Conn.: Yale University Press, 1992.

The Art of Medieval Spain, AD 500–1200. New York: Metropolitan Museum of Art, 1993.

Benton, Janetta Rebold. *Art of the Middle Ages*. New York: Thames & Hudson, 2002.

Binski, Paul. *Painters (Medieval Craftsmen)*. Toronto: University of Toronto Press, 1991.

Calkins, Robert G. *Illuminated Books of the Middle Ages*. Ithaca, N.Y.: Cornell University Press, 1983.

———. *Medieval Architecture in Western Europe: From AD 300 to 1500*. New York: Oxford University Press, 1998.

Coldstream, Nicola. *Masons and Sculptors (Medieval Craftsmen)*. Toronto: University of Toronto Press, 1991.

———. *Medieval Architecture*. New York: Oxford University Press, 2002.

Cross, Frank L., and Livingstone, Elizabeth A., eds. *The Oxford Dictionary of the Christian Church*. 3d ed. New York: Oxford University Press, 1997.

De Hamel, Christopher. *A History of Illuminated Manuscripts*. Oxford: Phaidon, 1986.

———. *Scribes and Illuminators (Medieval Craftsmen)*. Toronto: University of Toronto Press, 1992.

Doig, Allan. *Liturgy and Architecture: From the Early Church to the Middle Ages*. New York: Ashgate, 2008.

Heller, Ena Giurescu, and Patricia C. Pongracz. *Perspectives on Medieval Art: Learning through Looking*. New York: Museum of Biblical Art, 2010.

Holcomb, Melanie, ed. *Pen and Parchment: Drawing in the Middle Ages*. New York: Metropolitan Museum of Art, 2009.

Hourihane, Colum, ed. *The Grove Encyclopedia of Medieval Art and Architecture*. New York: Oxford University Press, 2012.

Kessler, Herbert L. *Seeing Medieval Art*. Toronto: Broadview, 2004.

———. *Spiritual Seeing: Picturing God's Invisibility in Medieval Art*. Philadelphia: University of Pennsylvania Press, 2000.

Lasko, Peter. *Ars Sacra, 800–1200*. 2d ed. New Haven, Conn.: Yale University Press, 1994.

Murray, Peter, and Linda Murray. *The Oxford Companion to Christian Art and Architecture*. New York: Oxford University Press, 1996.

Pelikan, Jaroslav. *Mary through the Centuries: Her Place in the History of Culture*. New Haven, Conn.: Yale University Press, 1996.

Prache, Anne. *Cathedrals of Europe*. Ithaca, N.Y.: Cornell University Press, 1999.

Raguin, Virginia Chieffo. *Stained Glass from Its Origins to the Present*. New York: Abrams, 2003.

Ross, Leslie. *Medieval Art: A Topical Dictionary*. Westport, Conn.: Greenwood, 1996.

Schütz, Bernard. *Great Cathedrals*. New York: Abrams, 2002.

Sekules, Veronica. *Medieval Art*. New York: Oxford University Press, 2001.

Snyder, James, Henry Luttikhuizen, and Dorothy Verkerk. *Art of the Middle Ages*. 2d ed. Upper Saddle River, N.J.: Prentice Hall, 2006.

Stokstad, Marilyn. *Medieval Art*. 2d ed. Boulder, Colo.: Westview, 2004.

Tasker, Edward G. *Encyclopedia of Medieval Church Art*. London: Batsford, 1993.

CHAPTER 14
Late Medieval Italy

Bomford, David. *Art in the Making: Italian Painting before 1400*. London: National Gallery, 1989.

Borsook, Eve, and Fiorelli Superbi Gioffredi. *Italian Altarpieces 1250–1550: Function and Design*. Oxford: Clarendon, 1994.

Bourdua, Louise. *The Franciscans and Art Patronage in Late Medieval Italy*. New York: Cambridge University Press, 2004.

Cole, Bruce. *Sienese Painting: From Its Origins to the Fifteenth Century*. New York: Harper Collins, 1987.

Derbes, Anne. *Picturing the Passion in Late Medieval Italy: Narrative Painting, Franciscan Ideologies, and the Levant*. New York: Cambridge University Press, 1996.

Derbes, Anne, and Mark Sandona, eds. *The Cambridge Companion to Giotto*. New York: Cambridge University Press, 2004.

Flores d'Arcais, Francesca. *Giotto*. 2d ed. New York: Abbeville, 2012.

Hills, Paul. *The Light of Early Italian Painting*. New Haven, Conn.: Yale University Press, 1987.

Maginnis, Hayden B. J. *Painting in the Age of Giotto: A Historical Reevaluation*. University Park: Pennsylvania State University Press, 1997.

———. *The World of the Early Sienese Painter*. University Park: Pennsylvania State University Press, 2001.

Meiss, Millard. *Painting in Florence and Siena after the Black Death*. Princeton, N.J.: Princeton University Press, 1976.

Moskowitz, Anita Fiderer. *Italian Gothic Sculpture, c. 1250–c. 1400*. New York: Cambridge University Press, 2001.

———. *Nicola & Giovanni Pisano: The Pulpits: Pious Devotion, Pious Diversion*. London: Harvey Miller, 2005.

Norman, Diana, ed. *Siena, Florence, and Padua: Art, Society, and Religion 1280–1400*. New Haven, Conn.: Yale University Press, 1995.

Poeschke, Joachim. *Italian Frescoes: The Age of Giotto, 1280–1400*. New York: Abbeville, 2005.

Pope-Hennessy, John. *Italian Gothic Sculpture*. 3d ed. Oxford: Phaidon, 1986.

Stubblebine, James H. *Duccio di Buoninsegna and His School*. Princeton, N.J.: Princeton University Press, 1979.

White, John. *Art and Architecture in Italy: 1250–1400.* 3d ed. New Haven, Conn.: Yale University Press, 1993.

———. *Duccio: Tuscan Art and the Medieval Workshop.* London: Thames & Hudson, 1979.

Renaissance Art, General

Adams, Laurie Schneider. *Italian Renaissance Art.* Boulder, Colo.: Westview, 2001.

Ames-Lewis, Francis, ed. *Florence.* Artistic Centers of the Italian Renaissance. New York: Cambridge University Press, 2011.

Anderson, Christy. *Renaissance Architecture.* New York: Oxford University Press, 2013.

Andrés, Glenn M., John M. Hunisak, and Richard Turner. *The Art of Florence.* 2 vols. New York: Abbeville, 1988.

Campbell, Gordon. *The Grove Encyclopedia of Northern Renaissance Art.* New York: Oxford University Press, 2009.

———. *Renaissance Art and Architecture.* New York: Oxford University Press, 2005.

Campbell, Lorne. *Renaissance Portraits: European Portrait-Painting in the Fourteenth, Fifteenth, and Sixteenth Centuries.* New Haven, Conn.: Yale University Press, 1990.

Campbell, Stephen J., and Michael W. Cole. *Italian Renaissance Art.* New York: Thames & Hudson, 2011.

Christian, Kathleen, and David J. Drogin, eds. *Patronage and Italian Renaissance Sculpture.* Burlington, Vt.: Ashgate, 2010.

Christiansen, Keith, and Stefan Weppelmann, eds. *The Renaissance Portrait from Donatello to Bellini.* New York: Metropolitan Museum of Art, 2011.

Cole, Bruce. *Italian Art, 1250–1550: The Relation of Renaissance Art to Life and Society.* New York: Harper & Row, 1987.

———. *The Renaissance Artist at Work: From Pisano to Titian.* New York: Harper Collins, 1983.

Cranston, Jodi. *The Poetics of Portraiture in the Italian Renaissance.* New York: Cambridge University Press, 2000.

Freedman, Luba. *The Revival of the Olympian Gods in Renaissance Art.* New York: Cambridge University Press, 2003.

Frommel, Christoph Luitpold. *The Architecture of the Italian Renaissance.* London: Thames & Hudson, 2007.

Furlotti, Barbara, and Guido Rebecchini. *The Art of Mantua: Power and Patronage in the Renaissance.* Los Angeles: J. Paul Getty Museum, 2008.

Hall, Marcia B. *Color and Meaning: Practice and Theory in Renaissance Painting.* Cambridge: Cambridge University Press, 1992.

———, ed. *Rome.* Artistic Centers of the Italian Renaissance. New York: Cambridge University Press, 2005.

Hartt, Frederick, and David G. Wilkins. *History of Italian Renaissance Art.* 7th ed. Upper Saddle River, N.J.: Prentice Hall, 2010.

Haskell, Francis, and Nicholas Penny. *Taste and the Antique: The Lure of Classical Sculpture 1500–1900.* New Haven, Conn.: Yale University Press, 1981.

Humfrey, Peter, ed. *Venice and the Veneto.* Artistic Centers of the Italian Renaissance. New York: Cambridge University Press, 2008.

Joost-Gaugier, Christiane L. *Italian Renaissance Art: Understanding Its Meaning.* Malden, Mass.: Wiley-Blackwell, 2013.

Kent, F. W., and Patricia Simons, eds. *Patronage, Art, and Society in Renaissance Italy.* Canberra: Humanities Research Centre and Clarendon Press, 1987.

King, Catherine E. *Renaissance Women Patrons: Wives and Widows in Italy, c. 1300–1550.* Manchester: Manchester University Press, 1998.

Landau, David, and Peter Parshall. *The Renaissance Print, 1470–1550.* New Haven, Conn.: Yale University Press, 1996.

Levey, Michael. *Florence: A Portrait.* Cambridge, Mass.: Harvard University Press, 1998.

Lubbock, Jules. *Storytelling in Christian Art from Giotto to Donatello.* New Haven, Conn.: Yale University Press, 2006.

Paoletti, John T., and Gary M. Radke. *Art, Power, and Patronage in Renaissance Italy.* Upper Saddle River, N.J.: Prentice Hall, 2005.

Partridge, Loren. *Art of Renaissance Florence, 1400–1600.* Berkeley and Los Angeles: University of California Press, 2009.

Pope-Hennessy, John. *Introduction to Italian Sculpture.* 3d ed. 3 vols. New York: Phaidon, 1986.

Richardson, Carol M., Kim W. Woods, and Michael W. Franklin, eds. *Renaissance Art Reconsidered: An Anthology of Primary Sources.* Malden, Mass.: Blackwell, 2007.

Romanelli, Giandomencio, ed., *Venice: Art & Architecture.* Cologne: Könemann, 2005.

Rosenberg, Charles M., ed. *The Court Cities of Northern Italy: Milan, Parma, Piacenza, Mantua, Ferrara, Bologna, Urbino, Pesaro, and Rimini.* Artistic Centers of the Italian Renaissance. New York: Cambridge University Press, 2010.

Servida, Sonia. *The Story of Renaissance Architecture.* New York: Prestel, 2011.

Smith, Jeffrey Chipps. *The Northern Renaissance.* New York: Phaidon, 2004.

Snyder, James, Larry Silver, and Henry Luttikhuizen. *Northern Renaissance Art: Painting, Sculpture, the Graphic Arts from 1350 to 1575.* 2d ed. Upper Saddle River, N.J.: Prentice Hall, 2005.

Strinati, Claudio, and Pomeroy, Jordana. *Italian Women Artists from Renaissance to Baroque.* Milan: Skira, 2007.

Thomson, David. *Renaissance Architecture: Critics, Patrons, and Luxury.* Manchester: Manchester University Press, 1993.

Tinagli, Paola. *Women in Italian Renaissance Art: Gender, Representation, Identity.* Manchester: Manchester University Press, 1997.

Wittkower, Rudolf. *Architectural Principles in the Age of Humanism.* 4th ed. London: Academy, 1988.

Woods, Kim W. *Making Renaissance Art.* New Haven, Conn.: Yale University Press, 2007.

———. *Viewing Renaissance Art.* New Haven, Conn.: Yale University Press, 2007.

Woods-Marsden, Joanna. *Renaissance Self-Portraiture: The Visual Construction of Identity and the Social Status of the Artist.* New Haven, Conn.: Yale University Press, 1998.

CHAPTER 20
Late Medieval and Early Renaissance Northern Europe

Ainsworth, Maryan W., and Maximiliaan P. J. Martens. *Petrus Christus, Renaissance Master of Bruges.* New York: Metropolitan Museum of Art, 1994.

Art from the Court of Burgundy: The Patronage of Philip the Bold and John the Fearless 1364–1419. Cleveland: Cleveland Museum of Art, 2004.

Baxandall, Michael. *The Limewood Sculptors of Renaissance Germany.* New Haven, Conn.: Yale University Press, 1980.

Borchert, Till-Holger. *Age of Van Eyck: The Mediterranean World and Early Netherlandish Painting, 1430–1530.* New York: Thames & Hudson, 2002.

Brinkmann, Bodo. *Konrad Witz.* Ostfildern: Hatje Cantz, 2011.

Campbell, Lorne. *The Fifteenth-Century Netherlandish Schools.* London: National Gallery Publications, 1998.

———. *Van der Weyden.* London: Chaucer, 2004.

Chapuis, Julien. *Stefan Lochner: Image Making in Fifteenth-Century Cologne.* Turnhout, Belgium: Brepols, 2004.

———, ed. *Tilman Riemenschneider, c. 1460–1531.* Washington, D.C.: National Gallery of Art, 2004.

Châtelet, Albert. *Early Dutch Painting.* New York: Konecky, 1988.

Friedlander, Max J. *Early Netherlandish Painting.* 14 vols. New York: Praeger/Phaidon, 1967–1976.

———. *From Van Eyck to Bruegel.* 3d ed. Ithaca, N.Y.: Cornell University Press, 1981.

Harbison, Craig. *The Mirror of the Artist: Northern Renaissance Art in Its Historical Context.* New York: Abrams, 1995.

Jacobs, Lynn F. *Early Netherlandish Carved Altarpieces, 1380–1550: Medieval Tastes and Mass Marketing.* Cambridge: Cambridge University Press, 1998.

Kemperdick, Stephan. *Rogier van der Weyden.* Cologne: H. F. Ullmann, 2007.

Kemperdick, Stephan, and Jocen Sander, eds. *The Master of Flémalle and Rogier van der Weyden.* Ostfildern: Hatje Cantz, 2009.

Lane, Barbara G. *The Altar and the Altarpiece: Sacramental Themes in Early Netherlandish Painting.* New York: Harper & Row, 1984.

Lehrs, Max, Joram Meron, and Anja Eichelberg. *Martin Schongauer: The Complete Engravings: A Catalogue Raisonné.* San Francisco: Alan Wofsy, 2005.

Meiss, Millard. *French Painting in the Time of Jean de Berry: The Limbourgs and Their Contemporaries.* New York: Braziller, 1974.

Michiels, Alfred. *Hans Memling.* London: Parkstone, 2008.

Morand, Kathleen. *Claus Sluter: Artist at the Court of Burgundy.* Austin: University of Texas Press, 1991.

Müller, Theodor. *Sculpture in the Netherlands, Germany, France, and Spain: 1400–1500.* New Haven, Conn.: Yale University Press, 1986.

Nash, Susie. *Northern Renaissance Art.* New York: Oxford University Press, 2008.

Os, Henk van. *The Art of Devotion in the Late Middle Ages in Europe, 1300–1500.* Princeton, N.J.: Princeton University Press, 1995.

Pächt, Otto. *Early Netherlandish Painting from Rogier van der Wayden to Gerard David.* New York: Harvey Miller, 1997.

Panofsky, Erwin. *Early Netherlandish Painting: Its Origins and Character.* 2 vols. Cambridge, Mass.: Harvard University Press, 1966.

Parshall, Peter, ed. *The Woodcut in Fifteenth-Century Europe.* New Haven, Conn.: Yale University Press, 2009.

Parshall, Peter, and Rainer Schoch. *Origins of European Printmaking: Fifteenth-Century Woodcuts and Their Public.* New Haven, Conn.: Yale University Press, 2005.

Périer-d'Ieteren, Catherine. *Dieric Bouts: The Complete Works.* London: Thames & Hudson, 2006.

Prevenier, Walter, and Wim Blockmans. *The Burgundian Netherlands.* Cambridge: Cambridge University Press, 1986.

Tomlinson, Amanda. *Van Eyck.* London: Chaucer, 2007.

Wilson, Jean C. *Painting in Bruges at the Close of the Middle Ages: Studies in Society and Visual Culture.* University Park: Pennsylvania State University Press, 1998.

Wolfthal, Diane. *The Beginnings of Netherlandish Canvas Painting, 1400–1530.* New York: Cambridge University Press, 1989.

CHAPTER 21
The Renaissance in Quattrocento Italy

Ahl, Diane Cole. *Fra Angelico.* New York: Phaidon, 2008.

———, ed. *The Cambridge Companion to Masaccio.* New York: Cambridge University Press, 2002.

Ames-Lewis, Francis. *Drawing in Early Renaissance Italy.* 2d ed. New Haven, Conn.: Yale University Press, 2000.

———. *The Intellectual Life of the Early Renaissance Artist.* New Haven, Conn.: Yale University Press, 2000.

Baxandall, Michael. *Painting and Experience in Fifteenth-Century Italy: A Primer in the Social History of Pictorial Style.* 2d ed. New York: Oxford University Press, 1988.

Bober, Phyllis Pray, and Ruth Rubinstein. *Renaissance Artists and Antique Sculpture: A Handbook of Sources.* Oxford: Oxford University Press, 1986.

Borsook, Eve. *The Mural Painters of Tuscany.* New York: Oxford University Press, 1981.

Cole, Alison. *Virtue and Magnificence: Art of the Italian Renaissance Courts.* New York: Abrams, 1995.

Cole, Bruce. *Masaccio and the Art of Early Renaissance Florence.* Bloomington: Indiana University Press, 1980.

Dempsey, Charles. *The Portrayal of Love: Botticelli's* Primavera *and Humanist Culture at the Time of Lorenzo the Magnificent.* Princeton, N.J.: Princeton University Press, 1992.

Edgerton, Samuel Y., Jr. *The Heritage of Giotto's Geometry: Art and Science on the Eve of the Scientific Revolution.* Ithaca, N.Y.: Cornell University Press, 1991.

———. *The Renaissance Rediscovery of Linear Perspective.* New York: Harper & Row, 1976.

Gilbert, Creighton, ed. *Italian Art 1400–1500: Sources and Documents.* Evanston, Ill.: Northwestern University Press, 1992.

Goldthwaite, Richard A. *The Building of Renaissance Florence: An Economic and Social History.* Baltimore: Johns Hopkins University Press, 1980.

Goy, Richard J. *Building Renaissance Venice: Patrons, Architects, and Builders c. 1430–1500.* New Haven, Conn.: Yale University Press, 2006.

Grafton, Anthony. *Leon Battista Alberti: Master Builder of the Italian Renaissance.* Cambridge, Mass.: Harvard University Press, 2002.

Henry, Tom. *The Life and Art of Luca Signorelli.* New Haven, Conn.: Yale University Press, 2012.

Heydenreich, Ludwig H. *Architecture in Italy, 1400–1500.* 2d ed. New Haven, Conn.: Yale University Press, 1996.

Hollingsworth, Mary. *Patronage in Renaissance Italy: From 1400 to the Early Sixteenth Century.* Baltimore: Johns Hopkins University Press, 1994.

Holmes, Megan. *Fra Filippo Lippi: The Carmelite Painter.* New Haven, Conn.: Yale University Press, 1999.

Kemp, Martin. *Behind the Picture: Art and Evidence in the Italian Renaissance.* New Haven, Conn.: Yale University Press, 1997.

Kempers, Bram. *Painting, Power, and Patronage: The Rise of the Professional Artist in the Italian Renaissance.* London: Penguin, 1992.

Kent, Dale. *Cosimo de' Medici and the Florentine Renaissance: The Patron's Oeuvre.* New Haven, Conn.: Yale University Press, 2000.

Lieberman, Ralph. *Renaissance Architecture in Venice.* New York: Abbeville, 1982.

Lindow, James R. *The Renaissance Palace in Florence: Magnificence and Splendour in Fifteenth-Century Italy.* Burlington Vt.: Ashgate, 2007.

Manca, Joseph. *Andrea Mantegna and the Italian Renaissance.* New York: Parkstone, 2006.

McAndrew, John. *Venetian Architecture of the Early Renaissance.* Cambridge, Mass.: MIT Press, 1980.

Murray, Peter. *Renaissance Architecture.* New York: Electa/Rizzoli, 1985.

Musacchio, Jacqueline Marie. *Art, Marriage, and Family in the Florentine Renaissance Palace.* New Haven, Conn.: Yale University Press, 2009.

Olson, Roberta J. M. *Italian Renaissance Sculpture.* London: Thames & Hudson, 1992.

Osborne, June. *Urbino: The Story of a Renaissance City.* Chicago: University of Chicago Press, 2003.

Payne, Alina A. *The Architectural Treatise in the Italian Renaissance: Architectural Invention, Ornament and Literary Culture.* New York: Cambridge University Press, 1999.

Poeschke, Joachim. *Donatello and His World: Sculpture of the Italian Renaissance.* New York: Abrams, 1993.

Radke, Gary M., ed. *The Gates of Paradise: Lorenzo Ghiberti's Renaissance Masterpiece.* New Haven, Conn.: Yale University Press, 2007.

Seymour, Charles. *Sculpture in Italy: 1400–1500.* New Haven, Conn.: Yale University Press, 1992.

Tavernor, Robert. *On Alberti and the Art of Building.* New Haven, Conn.: Yale University Press, 1999.

Turner, A. Richard. *Renaissance Florence: The Invention of a New Art.* New York: Abrams, 1997.

Wackernagel, Martin. *The World of the Florentine Renaissance Artist: Projects and Patrons, Workshops and Art Market.* Princeton, N.J.: Princeton University Press, 1981.

Welch, Evelyn. *Art and Society in Italy 1350–1500.* Oxford: Oxford University Press, 1997.

White, John. *The Birth and Rebirth of Pictorial Space.* 3d ed. Boston: Faber & Faber, 1987.

Wright, Alison. *The Pollaiuolo Brothers: The Arts of Florence and Rome.* New Haven, Conn.: Yale University Press, 2005.

Zöllner, Frank. *Sandro Botticelli.* New ed. New York: Prestel, 2009.

CHAPTER 22
Renaissance and Mannerism in Cinquecento Italy

Bazzotti, Ugo. *Palazzo Te: Giulio Romano's Masterwork.* London: Thames & Hudson, 2012.

Beltramini, Guido, and Howard Burns. *Palladio.* London: Royal Academy, 2008.

Blunt, Anthony. *Artistic Theory in Italy, 1450–1600.* London: Oxford University Press, 1975.

Brambilla Barcilon, Pinnin. *Leonardo: The Last Supper.* Chicago: University of Chicago Press, 2001.

Brock, Maurice. *Bronzino.* Paris: Flammarion, 2002.

Brown, David Alan, and Sylvia Ferino-Pagden, eds. *Bellini, Giorgione, Titian, and the Renaissance of Venetian Painting.* New Haven, Conn.: Yale University Press, 2006.

Brown, Patricia Fortini. *Art and Life in Renaissance Venice.* New York: Abrams, 1997.

Cole, Bruce. *Titian and Venetian Painting, 1450–1590.* Boulder, Colo.: Westview, 2000.

Cooper, Tracy E. *Palladio's Venice: Architecture and Society in a Renaissance Republic.* New Haven, Conn.: Yale University Press, 2005.

Cranston, Jodi. *The Muddled Mirror: Materiality and Figuration in Titian's Later Paintings.* University Park, Pa.: Pennsylvania State University Press, 2010.

Dal Pozzolo, Enrico. *Giorgione.* Milan: Motta, 2010.

De Vecchi, Pierluigi. *Raphael.* New York: Abbeville, 2002.

Ekserdjian, David. *Correggio.* New Haven, Conn.: Yale University Press, 1997.

———. *Parmigianino.* New Haven, Conn.: Yale University Press, 2006.

Falomir, Miguel, ed. *Tintoretto.* Madrid: Museo Nacional del Prado, 2007.

Ferino-Pagden, Sylvia, and Giovanna Nepi Scirè. *Giorgione: Myth and Enigma.* Milan: Skira, 2004.

Franklin, David. *Painting in Renaissance Florence, 1500–1550.* New Haven, Conn.: Yale University Press, 2001.

Freedberg, Sydney J. *Painting in Italy: 1500–1600.* 3d ed. New Haven, Conn.: Yale University Press, 1993.

Goffen, Rona. *Piety and Patronage in Renaissance Venice: Bellini, Titian, and the Franciscans.* New Haven, Conn.: Yale University Press, 1986.

———. *Renaissance Rivals: Michelangelo, Leonardo, Raphael, Titian.* New Haven, Conn.: Yale University Press, 2002.

Hall, Marcia B. *After Raphael: Painting in Central Italy in the Sixteenth Century.* New York: Cambridge University Press, 1999.

———. *The Sacred Image in the Age of Art: Titian, Tintoretto, Barocci, El Greco, Caravaggio.* New Haven, Conn.: Yale University Press, 2011.

———, ed. *The Cambridge Companion to Raphael.* New York: Cambridge University Press, 2005.

Hollingsworth, Mary. *Patronage in Sixteenth Century Italy.* London: John Murray, 1996.

Holt, Elizabeth Gilmore, ed. *A Documentary History of Art. Vol. 2, Michelangelo and the Mannerists.* Rev. ed. Princeton, N.J.: Princeton University Press, 1982.

Humfrey, Peter. *Painting in Renaissance Venice.* New Haven, Conn.: Yale University Press, 1995.

———. *Titian.* London: Phaidon, 2007.

Huse, Norbert, and Wolfgang Wolters. *The Art of Renaissance Venice: Architecture, Sculpture, and Painting.* Chicago: University of Chicago Press, 1990.

Ilchman, Frederick, ed. *Titian, Tintoretto, Veronese: Rivals in Renaissance Venice*. Boston: Museum of Fine Arts, 2009.

Kliemann, Julian-Matthias, and Michael Rohlmann. *Italian Frescoes: High Renaissance and Mannerism, 1510–1600*. New York: Abbeville, 2004.

Levey, Michael. *High Renaissance*. New York: Viking Penguin, 1978.

Lotz, Wolfgang. *Architecture in Italy, 1500–1600*. 2d ed. New Haven, Conn.: Yale University Press, 1995.

Meilman, Patricia, ed. *The Cambridge Companion to Titian*. New York: Cambridge University Press, 2004.

Natali, Antonio. *Andrea del Sarto*. New York: Abbeville, 1999.

Nichols, Tom. *Tintoretto: Tradition and Identity*. London: Reaktion, 2004.

Partridge, Loren. *The Art of Renaissance Rome*. New York: Abrams, 1996.

Pietrangeli, Carlo, André Chastel, John Shearman, John O'Malley, S.J., Pierluigi de Vecchi, Michael Hirst, Fabrizio Mancinelli, Gianluigi Colalucci, and Franco Bernbei. *The Sistine Chapel: The Art, the History, and the Restoration*. New York: Harmony, 1986.

Pilliod, Elizabeth. *Pontormo, Bronzino, Allori: A Genealogy of Florentine Art*. New Haven, Conn.: Yale University Press, 2001.

Pope-Hennessy, John. *Italian High Renaissance and Baroque Sculpture*. 3d ed. 3 vols. Oxford: Phaidon, 1986.

Rosand, David. *Painting in Cinquecento Venice: Titian, Veronese, Tintoretto*. New Haven, Conn.: Yale University Press, 1982.

Rowe, Colin, and Leon Satkowski. *Italian Architecture of the 16th Century*. New York: Princeton Architectural Press, 2002.

Rubin, Patricia Lee. *Giorgio Vasari: Art and History*. New Haven, Conn.: Yale University Press, 1995.

Shearman, John K. G. *Mannerism*. Baltimore: Penguin, 1978.

———. *Only Connect . . . Art and the Spectator in the Italian Renaissance*. Princeton, N.J.: Princeton University Press, 1990.

Summers, David. *Michelangelo and the Language of Art*. Princeton, N.J.: Princeton University Press, 1981.

Talvacchia, Bette. *Raphael*. London: Phaidon, 2007.

Tronzo, William, ed. *St. Peter's in the Vatican*. New York: Cambridge University Press, 2005.

Wallace, William. *Michelangelo: The Artist, the Man, and His Times*. New York: Cambridge University Press, 2009.

Wilde, Johannes. *Venetian Art from Bellini to Titian*. Oxford: Clarendon, 1981.

Williams, Robert. *Art, Theory, and Culture in Sixteenth-Century Italy: From Techne to Metatechne*. New York: Cambridge University Press, 1997.

Zöllner, Frank. *Leonardo da Vinci: The Complete Paintings and Drawings*. Cologne: Taschen, 2007.

CHAPTER 23
High Renaissance and Mannerism in Northern Europe and Spain

Ainsworth, Maryan W. *Man, Myth, and Sensual Pleasures: Jan Gossart's Renaissance. The Complete Works*. New York: Metropolitan Museum of Art, 2010.

Bartrum, Giulia, ed. *Albrecht Dürer and His Legacy: The Graphic Work of a Renaissance Artist*. Princeton, N. J.: Princeton University Press, 2003.

Bätschmann, Oskar, and Pascal Griener. *Hans Holbein*. Princeton, N. J.: Princeton University Press, 1997.

Blunt, Anthony. *Art and Architecture in France, 1500–1700*. Rev. ed. New Haven, Conn.: Yale University Press, 1999.

Brinkmann, Bodo, ed. *Cranach*. London: Royal Academy of Arts, 2008.

Buck, Stephanie, and Jochen Sander. *Hans Holbein the Younger: Painter at the Court of Henry VIII*. New York: Thames & Hudson, 2004.

Chapius, Julien. *Tilman Riemenschneider: Master Sculptor of the Late Middle Ages*. Washington, D.C.: National Gallery of Art, 1999.

Chastel, André. *French Art: The Renaissance, 1430–1620*. Paris: Flammarion, 1995.

Cox-Rearick, Janet. *The Collection of Francis I: Royal Treasures*. New York: Abrams, 1996.

Davies, David, and John H. Elliott. *El Greco*. London: National Gallery, 2003.

Dixon, Laurinda. *Bosch*. New York: Phaidon, 2003.

Farago, Claire, ed. *Reframing the Renaissance: Visual Culture in Europe and Latin America, 1450–1650*. New Haven, Conn.: Yale University Press, 1995.

Foister, Susan. *Holbein and England*. New Haven, Conn.: Paul Mellon Centre for British Art, 2005.

Gibson, W. S. *"Mirror of the Earth": The World Landscape in Sixteenth-Century Flemish Painting*. Princeton, N.J.: Princeton University Press, 1989.

Harbison, Craig. *The Mirror of the Artist: Northern Renaissance Art in Its Historical Context*. New York: Abrams, 1995.

Jollet, Etienne. *Jean and François Clouet*. London: Thames & Hudson, 1997.

Knecht, Robert J. *Renaissance Warrior and Patron: The Reign of Francis I*. New York: Cambridge University Press, 1994.

Koerner, Joseph Leo. *The Reformation of the Image*. Chicago: University of Chicago Press, 2004.

Landau, David, and Peter Parshall. *The Renaissance Print: 1470–1550*. New Haven, Conn.: Yale University Press, 1994.

Marías, Fernando. *El Greco: Life and Work—A New History*. London: Thames & Hudson, 2013.

Price, David Hotchkiss. *Albrecht Dürer's Renaissance: Humanism, Reformation, and the Art of Faith*. Ann Arbor: University of Michigan Press, 2003.

Roberts-Jones, Philippe, and Françoise Roberts-Jones. *Pieter Bruegel*. New York: Abrams, 2002.

Silver, Larry. *Hieronymous Bosch*. New York: Abbeville, 2006.

———. *Pieter Bruegel*. New York: Abbeville, 2011.

Smith, Jeffrey Chipps. *Dürer*. London: Phaidon: 2012.

———. *German Sculpture of the Later Renaissance, c. 1520–1580: Art in an Age of Uncertainty*. Princeton, N.J.: Princeton University Press, 1993.

Stechow, Wolfgang. *Northern Renaissance Art, 1400–1600: Sources and Documents*. Evanston, Ill.: Northwestern University Press, 1989.

Thomson, David. *Renaissance Paris: Architecture and Growth, 1475–1600*. Los Angeles and Berkeley: University of California Press, 1984.

Wood, Christopher S. *Albrecht Altdorfer and the Origins of Landscape*. Chicago: University of Chicago Press, 1993.

Zerner, Henri. *Renaissance Art in France: The Invention of Classicism*. Paris: Flammarion, 2003.

Baroque Art, General

Blunt, Anthony, ed. *Baroque and Rococo: Architecture and Decoration*. Cambridge: Harper & Row, 1982.

Harris, Ann Sutherland. *Seventeenth-Century Art & Architecture*. 2d ed. Upper Saddle River, N.J.: Prentice Hall, 2008.

Harrison, Charles, Paul Wood, and Jason Gaiger, eds. *Art in Theory, 1648–1815: An Anthology of Changing Ideas*. Oxford: Blackwell, 2000.

Held, Julius, and Donald Posner. *17th- and 18th-Century Art: Baroque Painting, Sculpture, Architecture*. New York: Abrams, 1971.

Lagerlöf, Margaretha R. *Ideal Landscape: Annibale Carracci, Nicolas Poussin, and Claude Lorrain*. New Haven, Conn.: Yale University Press, 1990.

Lawrence, Cynthia, ed. *Women and Art in Early Modern Europe: Patrons, Collectors, and Connoisseurs*. University Park: Pennsylvania State University Press, 1997.

Lemerle, Frédérique, and Yves Pauwels. *Baroque Architecture, 1600–1750*. Paris: Flammarion, 2008.

Minor, Vernon Hyde. *Baroque & Rococo: Art & Culture*. New York, Abrams, 1999.

Norberg-Schulz, Christian. *Baroque Architecture*. New York: Rizzoli, 1986.

———. *Late Baroque and Rococo Architecture*. New York: Electa/Rizzoli, 1985.

Tarabra, Daniela, and Claudia Zanlungo. *The Story of Baroque Architecture*. New York: Prestel, 2012.

Toman, Rolf. *Baroque: Architecture, Sculpture, Painting*. Cologne: Könemann, 1998.

CHAPTER 24
The Baroque in Italy and Spain

Bailey, Gauvin Alexander. *Baroque & Rococo*. London: Phaidon, 2012.

Bissel, R. Ward. *Artemisia Gentileschi and the Authority of Art*. University Park: Pennsylvania State University Press, 1999.

Brown, Jonathan. *The Golden Age of Painting in Spain*. New Haven, Conn.: Yale University Press, 1991.

———. *Velázquez: Painter and Courtier*. New Haven, Conn.: Yale University Press, 1988.

Christiansen, Keith, and Judith W. Mann. *Orazio and Artemisia Gentileschi*. New York: Metropolitan Museum of Art, 2001.

Contini, Roberto, and Francesco Solinas. *Artemisia Gentileschi: The Story of a Passion*. Milan: 24 Ore Cultura, 2011.

Enggass, Robert, and Jonathan Brown. *Italy and Spain, 1600–1750: Sources and Documents*. Upper Saddle River, N.J.: Prentice Hall, 1970.

Freedberg, Sydney J. *Circa 1600: A Revolution of Style in Italian Painting*. Cambridge, Mass.: Harvard University Press, 1983.

Fried, Michael. *The Moment of Caravaggio*. Princeton, N.J.: Princeton University Press, 2010.

Haskell, Francis. *Patrons and Painters: A Study in the Relations between Italian Art and Society in the Age of the Baroque*. Rev. ed. New Haven, Conn.: Yale University Press, 1980.

Krautheimer, Richard. *The Rome of Alexander VII, 1655–1677*. Princeton, N.J.: Princeton University Press, 1985.

Montagu, Jennifer. *Roman Baroque Sculpture: The Industry of Art*. New Haven, Conn.: Yale University Press, 1989.

O'Malley, John W., and Gauvin Alexander Bailey. *The Jesuits and the Arts, 1540–1773*. Philadelphia: Saint Joseph's University Press, 2005.

Puglisi, Catherine. *Caravaggio*. London: Phaidon, 2000.

Schroth, Sarah, and Ronni Baer. *El Greco to Velazquez: Art during the Reign of Philip III*. Boston: Museum of Fine Arts, 2008.

Spear, Richard E., and Philip Sohm, eds. *Painting for Profit: The Economic Lives of Seventeenth-Century Italian Painters*. New Haven, Conn.: Yale University Press, 2010.

Strinati, Claudio, and Pomeroy, Jordana. *Italian Women Artists from Renaissance to Baroque*. Milan: Skira, 2007.

Tomlinson, Janis. *From El Greco to Goya: Painting in Spain 1561–1828*. Upper Saddle Ridge, N.J.: Prentice Hall, 1997.

Tronzo, William, ed. *St. Peter's in the Vatican*. New York: Cambridge University Press, 2005.

Trusted, Marjorie. *The Arts of Spain: Iberia and Latin America 1450–1700*. University Park: Pennsylvania State University Press, 2007.

Varriano, John. *Caravaggio: The Art of Realism*. University Park: Pennsylvania University Press, 2006.

———. *Italian Baroque and Rococo Architecture*. New York: Oxford University Press, 1986.

Wittkower, Rudolf. *Art and Architecture in Italy 1600–1750*. 6th ed. 3 vols. Revised by Joseph Connors and Jennifer Montagu. New Haven, Conn.: Yale University Press, 1999.

CHAPTER 25
The Baroque in Northern Europe

Alpers, Svetlana. *The Art of Describing: Dutch Art in the Seventeenth Century*. Chicago: University of Chicago Press, 1984.

———. *The Making of Rubens*. New Haven, Conn.: Yale University Press, 1995.

———. *Rembrandt's Enterprise: The Studio and the Market*. Chicago: University of Chicago Press, 1988.

Bajou, Valérie. *Versailles*. New York: Abrams, 2012.

Belkin, Kristin Lohse. *Rubens*. London: Phaidon, 1998.

Biesboer, Pieter, Martina Brunner-Bulst, Henry D. Gregory, and Christian Klemm. *Pieter Claesz: Master of Haarlem Still Life*. Zwolle: Waanders, 2005.

Blunt, Anthony. *Art and Architecture in France, 1500–1700*. Rev. ed. New Haven, Conn.: Yale University Press, 1999.

Brown, Christopher. *Scenes of Everyday Life: Dutch Genre Painting of the Seventeenth Century*. London: Faber & Faber, 1984.

Bryson, Norman. *Word and Image: French Painting of the Ancien Régime*. Cambridge: Cambridge University Press, 1981.

Carr, Dawson W., ed. *Velázquez*. London: National Gallery, 2006.

Chapman, Perry. *Rembrandt's Self-Portraits: A Study in 17th-Century Identity*. Princeton, N.J.: Princeton University Press, 1990.

Chastel, André. *French Art: The Ancien Régime, 1620–1775*. New York: Flammarion, 1996.

Chong, Alan, and Wouter Kloek. *Still-Life Paintings from the Netherlands, 1550–1720*. Zwolle: Waanders, 1999.

Franits, Wayne. *Dutch Seventeenth-Century Genre Painting: Its Stylistic and Thematic Evolution*. New Haven, Conn.: Yale University Press, 2008.

———. *Looking at Seventeenth-Century Dutch Art: Realism Reconsidered*. Cambridge: Cambridge University Press, 1997.

———, ed. *The Cambridge Companion to Vermeer*. New York: Cambridge University Press, 2001.

Haak, Bob. *The Golden Age: Dutch Painters of the Seventeenth Century*. New York: Abrams, 1984.

Hochstrasser, Julie Berger. *Still Life and Trade in the Dutch Golden Age*. New Haven, Conn.: Yale University Press, 2007.

Keazor, Henry. *Nicholas Poussin, 1594–1665*. Cologne: Taschen, 2007.

Kiers, Judikje, and Fieke Tissink. *Golden Age of Dutch Art: Painting, Sculpture, Decorative Art*. New York: Thames & Hudson, 2000.

Liedtke, Walter. *Vermeer: The Complete Paintings*. Antwerp: Ludion, 2008.

———. *A View of Delft: Vermeer and His Contemporaries*. Zwolle: Wanders, 2000.

Mérot, Alain. *French Painting in the Seventeenth Century*. New Haven, Conn.: Yale University Press, 1995.

Muller, Sheila D., ed. *Dutch Art: An Encyclopedia*. New York: Garland, 1997.

North, Michael. *Art and Commerce in the Dutch Golden Age*. New Haven, Conn.: Yale University Press, 1997.

Olson, Todd P. *Poussin and France*. New Haven, Conn.: Yale University Press, 2000.

Rosenberg, Jakob, Seymour Slive, and E. H. ter Kuile. *Dutch Art and Architecture, 1600–1800*. New Haven, Conn.: Yale University Press, 1979.

Schama, Simon. *The Embarrassment of Riches: An Interpretation of Dutch Culture in the Golden Age*. Berkeley: University of California Press, 1988.

Schroth, Sarah, and Ronni Baer, eds. *El Greco to Velázquez: Art during the Reign of Philip III*. Boston: Museum of Fine Arts, 2008.

Slatkes, Leonard J., and Wayne Franits. *The Paintings of Hendrick ter Brugghen 1588–1629: Catalogue Raisonné*. Philadelphia: John Benjamins, 2007.

Stechow, Wolfgang. *Dutch Landscape Painting of the 17th Century*. 3d ed. Oxford: Phaidon, 1981.

Summerson, John. *Inigo Jones*. New Haven, Conn.: Yale University Press, 2000.

Sutton, Peter C. *Masters of 17th Century Dutch Landscape Painting*. Boston: Museum of Fine Arts, 1988.

Thompson, Ian. *The Sun King's Garden: Louis XIV, André Le Nôtre and the Creation of the Gardens of Versailles*. London: Bloomsbury, 2006.

Vlieghe, Hans. *Flemish Art and Architecture, 1585–1700*. New Haven, Conn.: Yale University Press, 1998.

Westermann, Mariët. *Rembrandt*. London: Phaidon, 2000.

———. *A Worldly Art: The Dutch Republic 1585–1718*. New Haven, Conn.: Yale University Press, 1996.

Zega, Andres, and Bernd H. Dams. *Palaces of the Sun King: Versailles, Trianon, Marly: The Châteaux of Louis XIV*. New York: Rizzoli, 2002.

Zell, Michael. *Reframing Rembrandt: Jews and the Christian Image in Seventeenth-Century Amsterdam*. Berkeley: University of California Press, 2002.

Credits

The author and publisher are grateful to the proprietors and custodians of various works of art for photographs of these works and permission to reproduce them in this book. Sources not included in the captions are listed here.

NOTE: *All references in the following credits are to figure numbers unless otherwise indicated.*

Before 1300—p. xxi: John Burge/Cengage Learning; **p. xxiii:** (t) © 2008 Fred S. Kleiner, (bl) © 2013 Fred S. Kleiner, (br) © 2011 Fred S. Kleiner; **p. xxiv:** John Burge/Cengage Learning; **p. xxv:** (tl) Jonathan Poore/Cengage Learning, (tr) Scala/Art Resource, NY, (bl) Jonathan Poore/Cengage Learning, (br) Copyright Photo Henri Stierlin, Geneve; **p. xxvi:** (l) John Burge/Cengage Learning, (r) Jonathan Poore/Cengage Learning; **p. xxvii:** (tl) John Burge/Cengage Learning, (tr) Jonathan Poore/Cengage Learning, (bl) John Burge/Cengage Learning, (br) Jonathan Poore/Cengage Learning; **p. xxviii:** (tl) David Pearson/Alamy, (tr) Alinari/Art Resource, (b) John Burge/Cengage Learning; **p. xxix:** (l) Royal Ontario Museum, (cl) The Art Archive/Olympia Museum Greece/Gianni Dagli Orti/Picture Desk, (cr) Scala/Art Resource, NY, (r) Scala/Art Resource, NY; **p. xxx:** (l) The Metropolitan Museum of Art, The Cloisters Collection, 1954 (54.1.2). Image © The Metropolitan Museum (r) Scala/Art Resource, NY; **p. xxxi:** (l) The Trustees of The British Museum/Art Resource, NY, (r) Firenze, Biblioteca Medicea Laurenziana, Ms. Laur. Plut. 1.56, c. 13v; **p. xxxii:** (l) akg-images/Bildarchiv Monheim (r) Scala/Art Resource, NY; **p. xxxiii:** (l) Giraudon/Art Resource, NY, (r) Scala/Art Resource, NY; **p. xxxiv:** Freer Gallery of Art, Smithsonian Institution, Washington, DC. Purchase, F1949.9a-d; **p. xxxv:** (l) © Dinodia/AGE Fotostock.com, (r) Saskia Ltd.

Introduction—Opener: National Gallery, London/Art Resource, NY; **I-2:** Hirshhorn Museum and Culture Garden, Smithsonian Institution, Washington, DC, Joseph H. Hirshhorn Purchase Fund, 1992 © City and county of Denver, courtesy the Clyfford Still Museum. Photo: akg images; **I-3:** Interior view of the choir, begun after 1284 (photo), French School, (13th century)/Beauvais Cathedral, Beauvais, France/© Paul Maeyaert/The Bridgeman Art Library; **I-4:** akg-images/Rabatti-Dominigie; **I-5:** National Gallery of Art, Alfred Stieglitz Collection, Bequest of Georgia O'Keeffe 1987.58.3; **I-6:** Art © Estate of Ben Shahn/Licensed by VAGA, New York, NY. Photo: Whitney Museum of American Art, New York (gift of Edith and Milton Lowenthal in memory of Juliana Force); **I-7:** © Jonathan Poore/Cengage Learning; **I-8:** akg-images; **I-9:** The Metropolitan Museum of Art/Art Resource, NY; **I-10:** Courtesy Saskia Ltd., © Dr. Ron Wiedenhoeft; **I-11:** © 2011 The Josef and Anni Albers Foundation/Artists Rights Society (ARS), New York. Photo: © Whitney Museum of American Art; **I-12:** Photograph © 2011 Museum of Fine Arts, Boston. 11.4584; **I-13:** bpk, Berlin/Staatsgemaeldesammlungen, Munich, Germany/Art Resource, NY; **I-14:** Jürgen Liepe, Berlin; **I-15:** The Trustees of the British Museum/Art Resource, NY; **I-16:** Nimatallah/Art Resource, NY; **I-17:** Scala/Art Resource, NY; **I-18:** Cengage Learning; **I-19 left:** Portrait of Te Pehi Kupe wearing European clothes, c.1826 (w/c), Sylvester, John (fl.1826)/© National Library of Australia, Canberra, Australia/The Bridgeman Art Library; **I-19 right:** Public Domain.

Chapter 14—Opener: Scala/Art Resource, NY; **14-2:** © Jonathan Poore/Cengage Learning; **14-3:** © Jonathan Poore/Cengage Learning; **14-4:** © Jonathan Poore/Cengage Learning; **14-5:** Scala/Art Resource, NY; **14-5A:** Alinari/Art Resource, NY; **14-5B:** Photo by Ralph Lieberman; **14-5C:** Erich Lessing/Art Resource, NY; **14-6:** Scala/Ministero per i Beni e le Attività culturali/Art Resource, NY; **14-7:** Art Resource/The Art Archive; **14-8:** Summerfield Press/Corbis Art/Corbis; **14-9:** Scala/Art Resource, NY; **14-9A:** akg images; **14-9B:** Alinari/Art Resource, NY; **14-10:** Scala/Art Resource, NY; **14-11:** Scala/Art Resource, NY; **14-11A:** Scala/Art Resource, NY; **14-12:** Scala/Art Resource, NY; **14-13:** © Jonathan Poore/Cengage Learning; **14-13A:** © Jonathan Poore/Cengage Learning; **14-14:** Canali Photobank; **14-15:** Scala/Art Resource, NY; **14-16:** © Jonathan Poore/Cengage Learning; **14-16A:** Scala/Art Resource, NY; **14-17:** Scala/Art Resource, NY; **14-18:** Scala/Art Resource, NY; **14-19:** Alinari/Art Resource, NY; **14-19A:** Scala/Art Resource, NY; **14-19B:** © Jonathan Poore/Cengage Learning; **14-20:** South Door of the Baptistry of San Giovanni, 1336 (bronze), Pisano, Andrea (1270–1349)/Baptistery, Florence, Italy/The Bridgeman Art Library; **14-2A:** Scala/Art Resource, NY; **14-21:** © Jonathan Poore/Cengage Learning; **14-22:** © Jonathan Poore/Cengage Learning; **14-23:** © Fred S. Kleiner, 2012.

Chapter 20—Opener: Photograph © 2011 Museum of Fine Arts, Boston. 93.153; **20-1a:** Photograph © 2011 Museum of Fine Arts, Boston. 93.153; **20-1b:** Photograph © 2011 Museum of Fine Arts, Boston. 93.153; **20-1c:** Photograph © 2011 Museum of Fine Arts, Boston. 93.153; **20-2:** Erich Lessing/Art Resource, NY; **20-2A:** © Jonathan Poore/Cengage Learning; **20-3:** Erich Lessing/Art Resource, NY; **20-4:** Image copyright © The Metropolitan Museum of Art. Image source: Art Resource, NY; **20-5:** Scala/Art Resource, NY; **20-6:** Erich Lessing/Art Resource, NY; **20-6A:** Bildarchiv Preussischer Kulturbesitz/Art Resource, NY; **20-7:** Erich Lessing/Art Resource, NY; **20-8:** © National Gallery, London/Art Resource, NY; **20-8A:** Copyright © 1999 Board of Trustees, National Gallery of Art, Washington, DC; **20-9:** Erich Lessing/Art Resource, NY; **20-9A:** © Jonathan Poore/Cengage Learning; **20-10:** Image copyright © The Metropolitan Museum of Art. Image source: Art Resource, NY; **20-11:** The Art Archive/St Peters Church Louvain/Picture Desk; **20-11A:** Giraudon/Art Resource, NY; **20-11B:** Scala/Art Resource, NY; **20-12:** Scala/Art Resource, NY; **20-13:** Erich Lessing/Art Resource, NY; **20-14:** Erich Lessing/Art Resource, NY; **20-14A:** Image copyright © The Metropolitan Museum of Art/Art Resource, NY; **20-15:** Musée Condé/Grand Palais/Art Resource, NY; **20-16:** Musée Condé/Grand Palais/Art Resource, NY; **20-17:** The Art Archive/Osterreichisches National Bibliothek Vienna/Eileen Tweedy/Picture Desk; **20-18:** bpk, Berlin/Gemaeldegalerie, Staatliche Museen/Art Resource, NY; **20-19:** Musée d'Art et d'Histoire, Geneva; **20-19A:** Erich Lessing/Art Resource, NY; **20-20:** Erich Lessing/Art Resource, NY; **20-21:** AKG Images; **20-21A:** Buxheim Saint Christopher, 1423. Hand-colored woodcut, 11 3/8" × 8 1/8". John Rylands University Library, University of Manchester, Manchester; **20-22:** Historical Picture Archive/CORBIS; **20-23:** Scala/Art Resource, NY.

Chapter 21—Opener: Summerfield Press Ltd.; **21-2:** Erich Lessing/Art Resource, NY; **21-3:** Erich Lessing/Art Resource, NY; **21-4:** © Jonathan Poore/Cengage Learning; **21-5:** © Jonathan Poore/Cengage Learning; **21-6:** © Jonathan Poore/Cengage Learning; **21-7:** © Jonathan Poore/Cengage Learning; **21-8:** © Jonathan Poore/Cengage Learning; **21-9:** © Jonathan Poore/Cengage Learning; **21-10:** Scala/Art Resource, NY; **21-11:** Erich Lessing/Art Resource; **21-11A:** akg-images/Rabatti-Dominigie; **21-12:** Erich Lessing/Art Resource; **21-13:** Scala/Art Resource, NY; **21-14:** © Jonathan Poore/Cengage Learning; **21-15:** © 2013 Fred S. Kleiner; **21-16:** © 2010 Fred Kleiner; **21-17:** Erich Lessing/Art Resource, NY; **21-18:** Scala/Art Resource, NY; **21-19:** Canali Photobank, Italy; **21-20:** Erich Lessing/Art Resource, NY; **21-21:** Canali Photobank, Italy; **21-22:** Scala/Art Resource, NY; **21-23:** National Gallery, London/Art Resource, NY; **21-24:** Canali Photobank, Italy; **21-25:** Scala/Art Resource, NY; **21-25A:** Nicolo Orsi Battaglini/Art Resource, NY; **21-26:** Scala/Art Resource; **21-27:** Giovanna Tornabuoni, nee Albizzi, 1488, detail (oil on panel), Ghirlandaio, Domenico (Domenico Bigordi) (1449–94)/Thyssen-Bornemisza Collection, Madrid, Spain/The Bridgeman Art Library; **21-28:** Scala/Art Resource, NY; **21-28A:** Rabatti-Dominigie/Galleria degli Uffizi/akg-images; **21-29:** Image copyright © The Metropolitan Museum of Art/Art Resource, NY; **21-29A:** © Jonathan Poore/Cengage Learning; **21-29B:** Cengage Learning; **21-30:** © Jonathan Poore/Cengage Learning; **21-31:** View of the Nave, 1425–46 (photo), Brunelleschi, Filippo (1377–1446)/San Lorenzo, Florence, Italy/The Bridgeman Art Library; **21-31A:** Alinari/Art Resource, NY; **21-31B:** Cengage Learning; **21-32:** © Jonathan Poore/Cengage Learning; **21-33:** Cengage Learning; **21-34:** © Jonathan Poore/Cengage Learning; **21-34A:** © Jonathan Poore/Cengage Learning; **21-35:** © Jonathan Poore/Cengage Learning; **21-36:** © Jonathan Poore/Cengage Learning; **21-36A:** © Jonathan Poore/Cengage Learning; **21-37:** © Jonathan Poore/Cengage Learning; **21-38:** © 2010 Fred Kleiner; **21-39:** Cameraphoto Arte, Venice/Art Resource, NY; **21-40:** © The Frick Collection. 1915.1.03; **21-4A:** Scala/Art Resource, Inc.; **21-41:** Scala/Art Resource, Inc.; **21-42:** Scala/Art Resource, NY; **21-43:** Scala/Ministero per i Beni e le Attività culturali/Art Resource, NY; **21-44:** Scala/Art Resource, NY; **21-44A:** Scala/Ministero per i Beni e le Attività culturali/Art Resource, NY; **21-45:** Alinari/Art Resource, NY; **21-46:** Cengage Learning; **21-47:** Canali Photobank, Italy; **21-48:** Scala/Art Resource, NY; **21-49:** Scala/Art Resource, NY; **21-49A bottom:** © Jonathan Poore/Cengage Learning; **21-49A top:** St. James the Great on his Way to Execution (fresco) (b/w photo) (detail), Mantegna, Andrea (1431–1506)/Ovetari Chapel, Eremitani Church, Padua, Italy/Alinari/The Bridgeman Art Library; **21-50:** Erich Lessing/Art Resource, NY.

Chapter 22—Opener: Canali Photobank; **22-1a:** © Bracchietti-Zigrosi/Vatican Museums; **22-1b:** Vatican Museums and Galleries, Vatican City, Italy/The Bridgeman Art Library International; **22-1c:** akg-images/Electa; **22-2:** Erich Lessing/Art Resource, NY; **22-3:** The Art Archive/National Gallery London/Eileen Tweedy/Picture Desk; **22-4:** Alinari/Art Resource, NY; **22-5:** RMN-Grand Palais/Art

Resource, NY; **22-5A:** Scala/Art Resource, NY; **22-6:** The Royal Collection © 2011 Her Majesty Queen Elizabeth II; **22-6A:** Réunion des Musées Nationaux/Art Resource, NY; **22-7:** Erich Lessing/Art Resource, NY; **22-8:** Erich Lessing/Art Resource, NY; **22-8A:** Scala/Art Resource, NY; **22-9:** © M. Sarri 1983/Photo Vatican Museums; **22-10:** Scala/Ministero per i Beni e le Attività culturali/Art Resource, NY; **22-10A:** Erich Lessing/Art Resource, NY; **22-11:** Scala/Art Resource, NY; **22-12:** Araldo de Luca/CORBIS; **22-13:** Arte & Immagini srl/CORBIS; **22-14:** Scala/Art Resource, NY; **22-15:** Scala/Art Resource, NY; **22-16:** Scala/Art Resource, NY; **22-17:** Photo Vatican Museums; **22-18:** © Bracchietti-Zigrosi/Vatican Museums; **22-18A:** Vatican Museums and Galleries, Vatican City, Italy/The Bridgeman Art Library International; **22-18B:** Sistine Chapel Ceiling: Libyan Sibyl, c. 1508–10 (fresco), Buonarroti, Michelangelo (1475–1564)/Vatican Museums and Galleries, Vatican City/Alinari/Bridgeman Images; **22-19:** akg-images/Electa; **22-20:** Erich Lessing/Art Resource, NY; **22-21:** © Jonathan Poore/Cengage Learning; **22-22:** Cengage Learning; **22-23:** © The Trustees of the British Museum/Art Resource, NY; **22-23A:** Tips Images/SuperStock; **22-24:** Cengage Learning; **22-25:** Tips Images/SuperStock; **22-26:** © Jonathan Poore/Cengage Learning; **22-27:** Alinari Archives/CORBIS; **22-28:** Marka/SuperStock; **22-29:** Cengage Learning; **22-30:** © 2010 Fred S. Kleiner; **22-31:** L.Hammel/A.van der Voort/akg-images; **22-31A:** Scala/Art Resource, NY; **22-32:** Scala/Art Resource, NY; **22-33:** © 1999 Board of Trustees, National Gallery of Art, Washington, DC; **22-34:** Cameraphoto Arte, Venice/Art Resource, NY; **22-35:** Erich Lessing/Art Resource, NY; **22-36:** Scala/Art Resource, NY; **22-37:** Scala/Art Resource, NY; **22-38:** Erich Lessing/Art Resource, NY; **22-39:** Scala/Ministero per i Beni e le Attività culturali/Art Resource, NY; **22-40:** Erich Lessing/Art Resource, NY; **22-4A:** Lavinia Fontana (Italian, 1552–1614) Portrait of a Noblewoman ca. 1580 Oil on canvas, 45 1/4 × 35 1/4 in. Gift of Wallace and Wilhelmina Holladay. National Museum of Women in the Arts; **22-41:** Scala/Art Resource, NY; **22-42:** Scala/Art Resource, NY; **22-42A:** The Art Archive/Pinacoteca Nazionale di Siena/Alfredo Dagli Orti/Picture Desk; **22-43:** Erich Lessing/Art Resource, NY; **22-44:** Scala/Ministero per i Beni e le Attività culturali/Art Resource, NY; **22-45:** National Gallery, London/Art Resource, NY; **22-46:** Portrait of Eleanor of Toledo and her Son, Giovanni de Medici, c. 1544–45 (tempera on panel), Bronzino, Agnolo (1503–72)/Galleria degli Uffizi, Florence, Italy/The Bridgeman Art Library; **22-46A:** Image copyright © The Metropolitan Museum of Art/Art Resource, NY; **22-47:** The Bridgeman Art Library International; **22-48:** Scala/Art Resource, NY; **22-49:** Scala/Art Resource, NY; **22-50:** Canali Photobank, Italy; **22-51:** Alinari/Art Resource, NY; **22-52:** Erich Lessing/Art Resource, NY; **22-52A:** The Nymph of Fontainebleau, 1542 (bronze), Cellini, Benvenuto (1500–71)/Louvre, Paris, France/Lauros/Giraudon/The Bridgeman Art Library; **22-53:** © 2006 Fred S. Kleiner; **22-54:** SuperStock/SuperStock; **22-55:** Scala/Art Resource, NY; **22-56:** © Jonathan Poore/Cengage Learning; **22-57:** © Jonathan Poore/Cengage Learning; **22-58:** Cengage Learning.

Chapter 23—Opener: V&A Images, London/Art Resource, NY; **23-1a:** The Metropolitan Museum of Art. Image source: Art Resource, NY; **23-1b:** The Metropolitan Museum of Art. Image source: Art Resource, NY; **23-1c:** Foto Marburg/Art Resource, NY; **23-2a and b:** O. Zimmermann/Musée d'Unterlinden, Colmar; **23-3:** akg-images; **23-3A:** The Great Piece of Turf, 1503 (bodycolours, heightened with opaque white on vellum), Dürer or Duerer, Albrecht (1471–1528)/Graphische Sammlung Albertina, Vienna, Austria/Giraudon/The Bridgeman Art Library; **23-4:** Photograph © 2011 Museum of Fine Arts, Boston. 68.187; **23-4A:** The Trustees of the British Museum/Art Resource, NY; **23-5:** Bildarchiv Preussischer Kulturbesitz/Art Resource, NY; **23-6:** The British Museum; **23-7:** LUCAS CRANACH THE ELDER, Judgment of Paris, 1530. Oil on wood, 1' 1-1/2" × 9-1/2". Staatliche Kunsthalle, Karlsruhe. **23-8:** The Trustees of the British Museum/Art Resource, NY; **23-9:** Erich Lessing/Art Resource, NY; **23-10:** Bildarchiv Preussischer Kulturbesitz/Art Resource, NY; **23-11:** Heritage Image Partnership Ltd/Alamy; **23-11A:** Scala/Art Resource, NY; **23-12:** The Garden of Earthly Delights, c. 1500 (oil on panel), Bosch, Hieronymus (c. 1450–1516)/Prado, Madrid, Spain/The Bridgeman Art Library; **23-13:** RMN-Grand Palais/Art Resource, NY; **23-14:** Bildarchiv Preussischer Kulturbesitz/Art Resource, NY; **23-14A:** Erich Lessing/Art Resource, NY; **23-15:** Uppsala University Art Collection; **23-16:** Oeffentliche Kunstsammlung Basel, photo Martin Bühler; **23-17:** The Royal Collection © 2011 Her Majesty Queen Elizabeth II; **23-18:** Erich Lessing/Art Resource, NY; **23-19:** bpk, Berlin/Gemaeldegalerie, Staatliche Museen/Joerg P. Anders/Art Resource, NY; **23-20:** Kunsthistorisches Museum, Vienna; **23-2A:** Scala/Art Resource, NY; **23-21:** RMN-Grand Palais/Art Resource, NY; **23-22:** © Jonathan

Poore/Cengage Learning; **23-23:** © Jonathan Poore/Cengage Learning; **23-23A:** © 2009 Fred S. Kleiner; **23-24A:** John Elk III; **23-25:** Adam Woolfitt/Robert Harding/Getty Images; **23-26:** Image copyright © The Metropolitan Museum of Art/Art Resource, NY; **23-27:** Scala/Art Resource, NY.

Chapter 24—Opener, 24-1a, 24-1b, 24-1c: Jonathan Poore/Cengage Learning; **24-2:** © Jonathan Poore/Cengage Learning; **24-3:** © Jonathan Poore/Cengage Learning; **24-4:** Alinari Archives/Corbis; **24-4A:** Canali Photobank, Italy; **24-5:** akg-images/Joseph Martin; **24-6:** Scala/Art Resource, NY; **24-6A:** Araldo de Luca/Corbis; **24-7:** akg-images/Pirozzi; **24-8:** Araldo de Luca; **24-9A:** Scala/Art Resource, NY; **24-9 left:** © Jonathan Poore/Cengage Learning; **24-9 right:** Vladimir Khirman/Alamy; **24-10:** © Jonathan Poore/Cengage Learning; **24-12:** © Jonathan Poore/Cengage Learning; **24-13:** Cengage Learning 2016; **24-14:** © Jonathan Poore/Cengage Learning; **24-14A:** Dome of the Chapel of the Holy Shroud, 1668–94 (photo), Guarini, Guarino (1624–83)/Turin Cathedral, Turin, Italy/Alinari/The Bridgeman Art Library; **24-15:** Alinari/Art Resource, NY; **24-16:** Scala/Art Resource, NY; **24-17:** Image copyright © The Metropolitan Museum of Art/Art Resource, NY; **24-18:** Scala/Art Resource, NY; **24-18A:** Scala/Art Resource, NY; **24-18B:** Scala/Art Resource, NY; **24-19:** Alinari/Art Resource, NY; **24-20:** The Royal Collection © 2011 Her Majesty Queen Elizabeth II; **24-21:** Nimatallah/Art Resource, NY; **24-22:** Glorification of the Reign of Pope Urban VIII (1568–1644) ceiling painting in the Great Hall, 1633–39 (fresco), Cortona, Pietro da (Berrettini) (1596–1669)/Palazzo Barberini, Rome, Italy/The Bridgeman Art Library; **24-23:** © Jonathan Poore/Cengage Learning; **24-24:** © Jonathan Poore/Cengage Learning; **24-25:** Erich Lessing/Art Resource, NY; **24-26:** Erich Lessing/Art Resource, NY; **24-27:** Wadsworth Atheneum Museum of Art/Art Resource, NY; **24-28:** Album/Art Resource, NY; **24-29:** Erich Lessing/Art Resource, NY; **24-29A:** Scala/Art Resource, NY; **24-30:** Scala/Art Resource, NY; **24-3A:** The Frick Collection, NY; **24-31:** Erich Lessing/Art Resource, NY; **24-32:** Erich Lessing/Art Resource, NY; **24-33:** Angelo Hornak/Alamy; **24-34:** © Beren Patterson/Alamy.

Chapter 25—Opener: Erich Lessing/Art Resource, NY; **25-1A:** Erich Lessing/Art Resource, NY; **25-2:** IRPA-KIK, Brussels, www.kikirpa.be; **25-2A:** Erich Lessing/Art Resource, NY; **25-3:** Scala/Art Resource, NY; **25-4:** Erich Lessing/Art Resource, NY; **25-5:** RMN-Grand Palais/Art Resource, NY; **25-6:** Scala/Art Resource, NY; **25-7:** Centraal Museum, Utrecht, photo Ernst Moritz, The Hague; **25-8:** Supper with the Minstrel and his Lute, c. 1617 (oil on canvas), Honthorst, Gerrit van (1590–1656)/Galleria degli Uffizi, Florence, Italy/Alinari/The Bridgeman Art Library; **25-9:** Universal Images Group/SuperStock; **25-10:** age fotostock/Alamy; **25-11:** National Gallery of Art; **25-12:** Erich Lessing/Art Resource, NY; **25-13:** The Nightwatch, c. 1642 (oil on canvas), Rembrandt Harmenszoon van Rijn (1606–69)/Rijksmuseum, Amsterdam, The Netherlands/Artothek/The Bridgeman Art Library; **25-13A:** akg-images; **25-14:** Return of the Prodigal Son, c. 1668–69 (oil on canvas) by Rembrandt Harmensz. van Rijn (1606–69) Hermitage, St. Petersburg, Russia/The Bridgeman Art Library; **25-15:** © English Heritage Photo Library/The Bridgeman Art Library International; **25-15A:** Rembrandt Harmensz van Rijn (1606–1669) Self-Portrait, 1658. oil on canvas. 52-5/8 in. × 40-7/8 in. (133.67 cm × 103.82 cm) Henry Clay Frick Bequest. Accession number: 1906.1.97; **25-16:** The Pierpont Morgan Library/Art Resource, NY; **25-17:** National Gallery, London/Art Resource, NY; **25-18:** Mauritshuis, The Hague; **25-18A:** Erich Lessing/Art Resource, NY; **25-18B:** View of Delft, c. 1660–61 (oil on canvas), Vermeer, Jan (1632–75)/Mauritshuis, The Hague, The Netherlands/Giraudon/The Bridgeman Art Library; **25-18C:** akg-images; **25-19:** National Gallery of Art; **25-20:** Rijksmuseum, Amsterdam; **25-21:** akg-images; **25-22:** The Bridgeman Art Library International; **25-23:** The Toledo Museum of Art, OH. Purchased with funds from the Libbey Endowment, Gift of Edward Drummond Libbey, 1956.57; **25-24:** © RMN-Grand Palais/Art Resource, NY; **25-25:** © Jonathan Poore/Cengage Learning; **25-26:** © Yann Arthus-Bertrand/Altitude; **25-27:** Massimo Listri/Corbis; **25-28:** © Fred S. Kleiner 2012; **25-28A:** © Fred S. Kleiner 2012; **25-29:** akg-images/Paul M. R. Maeyaert; **25-30:** © Jonathan Poore/Cengage Learning; **25-31:** Erich Lessing/Art Resource, NY; **25-32:** Nicolas Poussin, French, 1594–1665, Landscape with Saint John on Patmos, 1640, oil on canvas, 100.3 × 136.4 cm, A. A. Munger Collection, 1930.500 post-treatment. Reproduction, The Art Institute of Chicago. **25-32A:** Scala/Art Resource, NY; **25-33:** Photo copyright © Philadelphia Museum of Art, E1950-2-1; **25-34:** Réunion des Musées Nationaux/Art Resource, NY; **25-35:** Erich Lessing/Art Resource, NY; **25-36:** Erich Lessing/Art Resource, NY; **25-37:** Angelo Hornak/Corbis; **25-38:** Angelo Hornak/Corbis.

Index